ATM
FOUNDATION
FOR BROADBAND
NETWORKS

VOLUME 1, SECOND EDITION

ISBN 0-13-083218-9

9 780130 832184

90000

Prentice Hall Series In
Advanced Communications Technologies

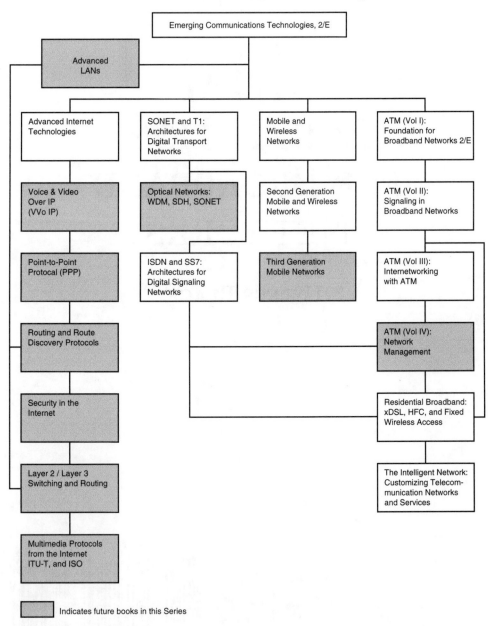

Emerging Communications Technologies, 2/E

Advanced LANs

Advanced Internet Technologies

SONET and T1: Architectures for Digital Transport Networks

Mobile and Wireless Networks

ATM (Vol I): Foundation for Broadband Networks 2/E

Voice & Video Over IP (VVo IP)

Optical Networks: WDM, SDH, SONET

Second Generation Mobile and Wireless Networks

ATM (Vol II): Signaling in Broadband Networks

Point-to-Point Protocol (PPP)

ISDN and SS7: Architectures for Digital Signaling Networks

Third Generation Mobile Networks

ATM (Vol III): Internetworking with ATM

Routing and Route Discovery Protocols

ATM (Vol IV): Network Management

Security in the Internet

Residential Broadband: xDSL, HFC, and Fixed Wireless Access

Layer 2 / Layer 3 Switching and Routing

The Intelligent Network: Customizing Telecommunication Networks and Services

Multimedia Protocols from the Internet ITU-T, and ISO

Indicates future books in this Series

ATM
FOUNDATION
FOR BROADBAND
NETWORKS

Volume I, Second Edition

UYLESS BLACK

Prentice Hall PTR
Upper Saddle River, New Jersey 07458
http://www.phptr.com

Library of Congress Cataloging-in-Publication Data

Black, Uyless D.
    ATM—foundation for broadband networks, 2/E / Uyless Black.
        p. cm.
    Includes bibliographical references and index.
    ISBN 0–13–083218–9
    1. Asynchronous transfer mode. 2. Broadband communication
systems. I. Title.
    TK5105.35.B53   1995
    621.382—dc20   95–5961
                                                              CIP

Acquisitions editor: Mary Franz
Cover designer: Talar Agasyan
Cover design director: Jerry Votta
Manufacturing manager: Alexis R. Heydt
Marketing manager: Miles Williams
Compositor/Production services: Pine Tree Composition, Inc.

© 1999 by Uyless Black
Published by Prentice Hall PTR
Prentice-Hall, Inc.
A Simon & Schuster Company
Upper Saddle River, New Jersey 07458

Prentice Hall books are widely used by corporations and government agencies for training, marketing, and resale.

The publisher offers discounts on this book when ordered in bulk quantities. For more information contact:

>   Corporate Sales Department
>   Phone: 800–382–3419
>   Fax: 201–236–7141
>   E-mail: corpsales@prenhall.com

>   Or write:

>   Prentice Hall PTR
>   Corp. Sales Dept.
>   One Lake Street
>   Upper Saddle River, New Jersey 07458

Printed in the United States of America
10 9 8 7 6 5 4 3 2

ISBN: 0-13-083218-9

Prentice-Hall International (UK) Limited, *London*
Prentice-Hall of Australia Pty. Limited, *Sydney*
Prentice-Hall Canada Inc., *Toronto*
Prentice-Hall Hispanoamericana, S.A., *Mexico*
Prentice-Hall of India Private Limited, *New Delhi*
Prentice-Hall of Japan, Inc., *Tokyo*
Simon & Schuster Asia Pte. Ltd., *Singapore*
Editora Prentice-Hall do Brasil, Ltda., *Rio de Janeiro*

I am told by one of my friends that a fictional creature in a novel was discussing the speed of the flight of birds and proclaimed that: perfect speed is being there.

While I do not know about the other thoughts of this creature, I have thought about this one idea many times. Aside from its physical and philosophical implications, it is appropriate to bring to mind that many of the emerging technologies (such as ATM) are attempting to close the gap (the latency) between being in one place, and then another. In this book, the issue is not the flight of birds but the movement of messages of information through a communications network.

Of course, with our current knowledge, we cannot achieve the bird's goal, due to the delay inherent in the physical aspects of travel. So, until we know about (and conquer) other dimensions (if we ever will), we are restricted to interpreting "being there" as the bird's physical flight from one point to another and its quest to make that flight of a shorter duration.

This goal has been an important aspect of communications networks since their inception, and the speed and efficiency of modern networks has surely had a profound effect on our personal and professional lives.

So, this book is dedicated to all of those in our industry who are striving to send the message faster.

At the same time, it is instructive to remember that a faster message does not necessarily make it any better.

Contents

CHAPTER 13   Operations, Administration, and Maintenance (OAM)   363

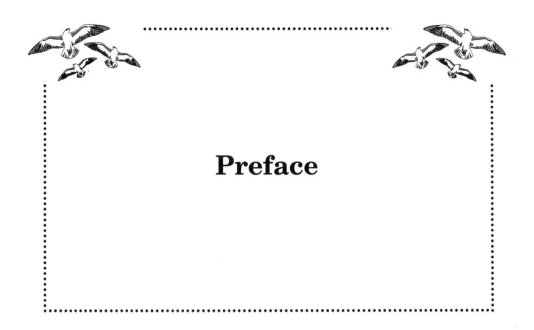

Preface

Some time ago, one of my clients, who is a systems engineer for a large telecommunications firm, told me that one of her major problems is staying abreast of the technologies that are embedded into her company's products. I hear this statement often. Like many others in our industry, this person does not have the time to read the technical specifications published by the standards organizations and the user forums. She must spend her professional time performing the day-to-day tasks of the job, essentially taking care of her clients and her accounts.

The common lament is that many professionals are barely ahead of their customers in their knowledge and ability to field their questions about not just the company products, but how they fit into an overall telecommunications architecture. Increasingly, this systems engineer has been forced to know about many diverse protocols, standards, and architectures. Her clients query her on topics such as the relationship of ATM and Frame Relay, why Novell uses IPX and not IP, why NetBIOS is not routable, etc.

It is to this person that this series is devoted (indeed, most of my books are so focused). It is my hope that I have provided a series that will meet this engineer's needs in the field.

This book is the second book of Prentice Hall's *Advanced Communications Technologies,* which serves as a complement to the flagship book, *Emerging Communications Technologies.*

I have included a chapter on existing technologies, titled "Emerged Technologies". This chapter is a summary of a chapter of the same title from the flagship book for this series. I have added a section in this chapter on why functions and services of several of these technologies (for data networks) have been reduced or eliminated in an ATM network. I suggest the reader review this chapter for two reasons: (a) to make certain the ISDN, X.25, SS7, and T1/E1 systems are understood, and (b) to understand why ATM operations do not include many functions that are an integral part of current data networks.

The ATM story is far from complete. As of this writing, ATM systems are now being deployed, but some of the ATM standards are still being written. One cannot wait to write a book on emerging technologies until they have "emerged," else there would be no book to write. So, this book represents the state of ATM as of the date of submittal of my work to my publisher.

I am happy to say that the first edition of this book has been received very well in the industry. This second edition reflects the changes that have taken place since the publication of the first edition. All chapters have been updated, with emphasis on these new or revised topics:

- Voice over ATM with AAL2
- The Available Bit Rate (ABR) and Unspecified Bit Rate (UBR) procedures
- Updated MIBs and network management
- Internetworking and tunneling with IP
- Inverse multiplexing
- Protection switching

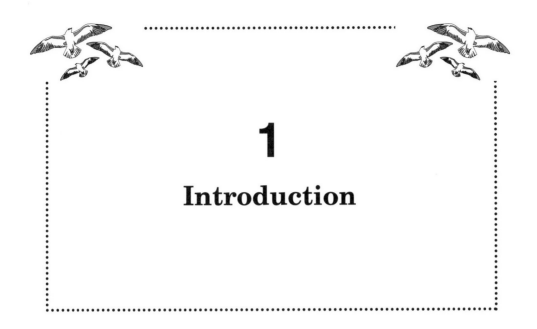

1

Introduction

This chapter discusses the current telecommunications technologies in place today. It explains why the telecommunications industry is implementing new communications technologies to overcome the deficiencies of current systems. An analysis is made of the communications requirements of upcoming user applications.

As a prelude to subsequent chapters, a general overview is provided of the asynchronous transfer mode (ATM) and the synchronous optical network (SONET)/synchronous digital hierarchy (SDH) that are being developed to meet the needs of these applications.

THE PRESENT TELECOMMUNICATIONS INFRASTRUCTURE

Scores of books have been written about the impact of the computer on our society, and the flagship book for this series *(Emerging Communications Technologies)* examines this subject. Studies are cited as well about the role of telecommunications (and the recent growth of cordless telephony, optical fiber, cable television, and video-on-demand technologies) that are having a profound effect on our professional and personal lives. This book shall not reiterate the thoughts cited in these books, but shall concentrate on the technical underpinnings that must be in place for these technologies to flourish.

Present Technologies for Voice, Video, and Data Networks

The present communications infrastructure supporting voice, video, and data networks is founded on technology that is over 25 years old. In spite of their age, these networks have served the industry well, even in recent times, for they have provided a cohesive foundation on which to build the modern telecommunications infrastructure. Yet when we consider that the modern commercial computer is only about 35 years of age and the personal computer came into being in the early 1980s, a 25-year-old technology seems like a technical dinosaur.

In 1962 the U.S. Bell System (as it was known in the pre-divestiture days) installed the first commercial digital voice system in Chicago, Illinois. The system was known as T1, and carried 24 voice channels over copper wire between Bell's telephone offices. The European carriers followed shortly with a similar system, called E1. As technology improved, T1 was deployed in higher capacity systems. Shortly thereafter, T3 became a common carrier system for users who needed greater capacity than the T1 offerings. The T3 system can transport 28 T1 signals, which means one T3 link can support 672 voice calls. And the European carriers followed with the E3 technology.

T1 and T3 have become the foundations for the majority of voice networks systems provided by the North American telephone companies.[1] While these systems were designed originally for voice systems, they now can be configured to support data and video applications as well.

In the early 1970s, another technology was deployed to support data networks. This technology is called *packet switching*. Unlike the T1/E1 and T3/E3 networks, packet switching was designed for data applications, and packet switching networks have become the foundation for the majority of data networks.

At about the same time that packet switching networks were being deployed, the International Telecommunications Union-Telecommunication Standardization Sector (ITU-T, formerly the CCITT) published the X.25 specification. As the reader may know, X.25 defines the procedures for user computers to communicate with network machines (packet switches) and to transport data to another user computer. X.25 has become a widely used industry standard and has facilitated the building of standardized communications interfaces among different vendors' machines.

---

[1]T1 and T3 are often used synonymously with DS1, and DS3. T1 and T3 describe the physical aspects, such as voltages and media specifications, and DS1 and DS3 describe the framing and formatting conventions. This book will use them interchangeably, in deference to common industry practice.

These communications technologies were designed to support fairly modest requirements for voice and data transmissions, at least when compared to modern applications needs. For example, the T1 systems support a transfer rate of 1.544 Mbit/s, and the T3 system operates at approximately 45 Mbit/s. These bit transfer rates may seem high to the reader, but remember that a 45 Mbit/s transport system like T3 only supports 672 voice calls—a lot of T3s have to be in operation to support the public telephone network.

Likewise, X.25 was designed for data systems that operate at only a few bit/s or a few hundred bit/s—typically 600 to 9600 bit/s. Although X.25 can be placed on very high-speed media and can operate quite efficiently at high speeds, a substantial amount of subscriber equipment and software has been designed for modest transfer rates—typically no greater than 19.2 kbit/s.

Once again, sending data at a rate of 19.2 kbit/s may seem fast. After all, this translates to a transfer rate of 2400 characters per second (19,200/8 bits per character), and no one can type in an email message that fast. However, for other applications, this speed is not sufficient. File transfers, database updates, and color graphics (to mention a few) need much greater transfer rates.

Typical Voice Networks.   Table 1–1 provides some examples of typical voice carrier systems. The E1 system (also called CEPT1) is Europe's principal technology for carrier transport systems. Japan's basic technology is also based on T1, but Japan's higher capacity systems are not in alignment with either European or North American systems.

Nonetheless, because telephone networks have historically been highly regulated within a country and controlled by one enterprise (in the United States, AT&T before divestiture, and in other countries, the Postal Telephone and Telegraph Ministries [PTTs]), a national telephone network architecture uses common standards, conventions, and protocols. Thus, interworking different vendors' equipment is relatively simple

Table 1–1   Typical Voice Carrier Systems

Type	Digital Bit Rate	Voice Circuits	Age	Standard or Proprietary
DS1	1.544 Mbit/s	24	32 years	Standard*
E1	2.048 Mbit/s	30	32 years	Standard*
DS3	44.736 Mbit/s	672	31 years	Standard*

*Within national boundaries

(telephones, fax devices, and answering machines are common examples). This situation is not true with the architecture for data networks, as we shall see in the next section.

Typical Data Networks. In contrast to the voice world, data networks and protocols have evolved into an almost bewildering array of disparate and incompatible systems. Table 1–2 provides examples of the more widely known and used standards and vendor products.

Interconnecting some of these systems is almost impossible. When it is possible, the resulting systems are very complex and very expensive, due to the need to provide protocol converters between the systems. Yet these systems form the foundation for our current data networks.

As Table 1–2 shows, some systems are standardized while others are proprietary. Also, they may operate as local area networks (LANs), wide area networks (WANs), or both. Most of them were conceived over ten years ago, although all have been enhanced since their inception.

Why are so many incompatible systems in existence to do one thing: transport data between computers? The answer is simple. The data communications and computer industry, unlike the telephone industry, has had very little regulation imposed upon it. Additionally, this industry is quite young, and many systems and products were developed before standards were written by organizations such as the ITU-T, the ISO, and the Internet task forces.

Table 1–2 Typical Data Networks and Protocols

Vendor or Standard	Sponsor	Age[1]	Standard or Proprietary	WAN or LAN[2]
X.25	ITU-T & ISO	25 years	Standard*	WAN
OSI	ITU-T & ISO	15 years	Standard*	Both
TCP/IP	Internet	13 years	Standard**	Both
SNA	IBM	22 years	Proprietary	Both
DECnet	Digital	22 years	Proprietary	Both
AppleTalk	Apple	12 years	Propriety	LAN
Ethernet	Xerox, Digital, Intel	17 years	Standard***	LAN
Netware	Novell	12 years	Proprietary	LAN

[1]Approximate ages; all have evolved and have been enhanced
[2]WAN is wide area network and LAN is local area network
*Recognized by international standards groups
**A de facto standard by virtue of its wide use
***Revised slightly to become the IEEE 802.3 standard

The current status of the evolution of the data communications industry is both good news and bad news. The good news is that the lack of a dominant player (such as "Ma Bell" in the telephone industry) has lead to much competition and the availability of some extraordinary systems and products at reasonable prices. The bad news is that some customers are saddled with single-vendor systems, because a vendor-specific system cannot operate easily with any other vendor's system.[2]

The industry is realizing that competition can continue but under an umbrella of standards. Frankly, many of the systems and products listed in Table 1–2 do just about the same things, but they do them differently.

PRESENT AND FUTURE REQUIREMENTS

In the past few years, the processing power of an ordinary personal computer (PC) has increased so rapidly that the terms high-speed workstations and mainframe computers are losing their meanings. Small machines are becoming as powerful the once "large machines."

The reader need only take a brief glance at the daily newspaper to grasp the rapid increases in the power and functionality of the computer. The increased capacity of these machines means they can send and receive large amounts of information in a very short time. The end result is the need to upgrade communications systems to support the PC's requirements. Future PCs will necessitate the development of even higher-speed and more powerful communications systems.

The communications infrastructure to support the connection of these computers and new applications must also be upgraded. While individual homes and workstations can continue to use conventional, existing media (the coaxial TV cable and twisted pair on the local loop), the service providers' facilities, media, and networks need more bandwidth.

Downsizing and Outsourcing: Reliance on Telecommunications

In the last few years, several industrialized countries have witnessed a trend known as downsizing. Downsizing entails businesses (mostly large businesses) shedding employees, capital resources, and, in many instances, buildings. With this downsizing comes a new trend—outsourcing. Many of these firms are hiring outside contractors to pro-

---

[2]The situation is changing with the acceptance of the Internet and OSI-based protocols on a worldwide basis.

vide services—such as training, food operations, mailroom operations, and software programming—that were once provided by employees. While these companies must continue their ongoing operations, they are doing it increasingly with distributed computers and communications facilities linking their computers together.

It has long been a cliché that telecommunications is playing one of the most critical roles in our information society and, indeed, in our personal culture. This role will become even more important as more humans learn to interact with the computer and exploit its productivity potential. The trend, of course, will lead toward (this writer hopes) more open societies as the telecommunications infrastructure embeds itself into most people's lives. So, without going into a monologue on the benefits of the telecommunications infrastructure, the next section describes some of the problems faced in current communications architecture.

Present Systems: Too Much or Too Little

Voice.   For today's voice transport systems, the present structure provides adequate capacity for many applications, but as stated earlier and explained in the flagship book for this series, the capacity is insufficient for others. In addition, these transport systems suffer from the asynchronous nature of their design. In this context, asynchronous means that the components of the network are not synchronized with a common clock. Consequently, it is not unusual for errors to occur between transmitting and receiving machines because the machines are using different timing schemes. An analogy would be a person talking too fast to a listener, who misses part of the speech.

Perhaps more serious, it is recognized increasingly that these systems have very limited operations, administration, and maintenance (OAM) capabilities, known by many people as network management capabilities. The supposition (30 years ago) of these simple designs made good sense, because the operations needed to support substantial OAM required more overhead than the limited-capacity network could bear. However, with the increased use of high-speed optical fiber and fast processors, building powerful OAM modules within new systems becomes feasible.

Wide Area Data Networks.   For data communications networks, ironically, it is accepted that the current systems (especially WANs) may be doing too much, in that they are performing a number of redundant functions of marginal benefit. We shall have more to say about this idea in subsequent chapters, but for the present, it can be stated that redundant functions are performed on the majority of user traffic. In X.25, for example, sequencing and flow control, as well as positive acknowledgments (ACKs) and negative acknowledgments (NAKs), are performed at least twice.

With the advent of relatively error-free, high-capacity networks, and with the concomitant implementation of very powerful end-user workstations, the new networks take the view that many of these operations are no longer needed in the network. Indeed, many of the functions are simply removed from the network and placed in the customer premises equipment (CPE), such as user workstations and personal computers.

We return to these important points several times in this book. The reader may refer to Chapter 6 (Errors and Error Rates) and Chapter 7 (Pre-ATM Approach to Traffic Integrity Management, and ATM Approach to Traffic Integrity Management) for immediate follow-up on these ideas.

Local Area Data Networks. It is recognized that the processing power of personal computers and workstations is doubling about every two years. Ten MHz processors were considered state of the art in 1990; 25 MHz processors were in use in 1992, and 350 MHz processors in 1998. The trend will continue and with it an associated need for more bandwidth to support the communications between these machines. A guideline, long accepted in the industry, is that a well-tuned computer system has one bit of I/O (input/output) for every instruction cycle. Workstations have processors that operate with a cycle time of about 1 nanosecond and a performance of 1 billion instructions per second. These workstations create enormous bandwidth demands on communications networks.

LANs have not kept pace with the progress of the CPUs, and with the exception of the fiber distributed data interface (FDDI), the technology has remained in the 4 to 16 Mbit/s range. As a consequence, the last few years have seen a decrease in the number of computers attached to a LAN segment [HERM93]. This trend cannot continue; it is too expensive and complex. Therefore, a new family of LANs is evolving to meet the increased needs of the user stations. The metropolitan area network (MAN) and fast Ethernet are among these solutions. So is ATM, the subject of this book.

Bottleneck at the Local Loop. One of the biggest problems facing the industry is the limited bandwidth of the local loop (the link between the customer premisis equipment (CPE) and the voice, video, or data service providers. While this subject is beyond the scope of this book (but is covered in *Residential Broadband Networks: xDSL, HFC, & Fixed Wireless Access,* a companion book in this series), some new local loop technologies are deploying ATM to help solve the problem.

Costs of Leased Lines

In the past few years, LANs and WANs have been interconnected with bridges, routers, gateways, and packet-switched networks. These internetworking units connect to the LANs and WANs through dedicated communications channels (leased lines). As a general practice, leased lines have been "nailed up" end-to-end through the network to the user's CPE. The user is provided with the leased line on a dedicated basis and the full transmission capacity is available 24 hours a day (with some exceptions). Therefore, the user pays for the circuit regardless of its utilization. Moreover, if a connection is needed to yet another location (say another city in the country), another leased line must be rented from the public telecommunications operators (PTOs), such as AT&T, Sprint, and MCI—once again on a end-to-end, continuous basis.

Even though leased lines are becoming less expensive, the use of these lines to connect internetworking units with LANs and WANs is still a very expensive process. Moreover, reliability problems occur because individual point-to-point leased lines have limited backup capability.

A better approach is to develop a LAN/WAN-carrier network that provides efficient switching technologies for backup purposes as well as high-speed circuits—a network that will allow users to share the expensive leased lines. This concept is called a *virtual network* or a *virtual private network* (VPN).

VIRTUAL COMPANIES AND VIRTUAL NETWORKS

During the past decade, smaller companies increasingly have been competing successfully against their larger rivals. Indeed, some large companies are so unwieldy and so fraught with bureaucracy and overhead that they cannot compete in many arenas with their smaller counterparts. Of course, the value of economy of scale still pertains; for example, my small company is not going to spend the enormous funds needed to develop an ATM switch.

However, the term virtual company is a useful description of a growing industry of small groups or individuals working out of rented business centers or even at home (SOHO: small office/home office). This type of operation gives the illusion of the traditional private enterprise, but it usually has few or no employees, and may not even have a receptionist! Well, the answering service/ answering machine is a virtual receptionist.

A treatise on the reasons for this phenomenon is beyond the scope of this book. Nonetheless, it must be emphasized that the downsizing of companies and the distribution of workloads to remote offices (and homes) cannot occur without the accompanying supporting communications infrastructure. Indeed, the very premise of deconstruction, downsizing, and outsourcing is based on the idea that the smaller companies and their consultants (who act as virtual employees) will have access to each other through high-speed, reliable communications facilities. Increasingly, the facilities are being implemented with a virtual private network (VPN) (an old concept that has been renamed and taken off the shelf for use in today's networks).

The VPN is so named because an individual user or enterprise shares communications channels and facilities with other users. Switches are placed on these channels to allow an end user to have access to multiple end sites. Ideally, users do not perceive that they are sharing a network with each other, thus the term virtual private network—you think you have it, but you don't.

Figures 1–1 and 1–2 illustrate the concepts of VPNs and their advantage over dedicated systems. In Figure 1–1(a), four customer sites from company A are connected to each other through dedicated channels (leased lines). While effective, this approach is very expensive, and it is unlikely that these lines are used on a continuous basis. Company B in Figure 1–1(b) has a separate arrangement connecting its four offices with dedicated lines in the same cities as company A.

In contrast, through the use of a VPN (Figure 1–2), the two companies can share the communications facilities. The VPN provider provides a network for multiple users. This approach allows the traffic to be routed to various endpoints and does not require the end-user devices to "nail up" private leased lines. In some implementations, companies migrating to a VPN have reduced their costs by 30 percent vis-à-vis leased lines.

The difference between fully meshed leased lines and VPNs is even more dramatic when another location is added to a private network. If the user (say company A) wishes full connectivity to all sites, this approach requires the leasing of long-distance lines to all cities. Of course, with a fully meshed VPN, the same number of private lines are required between the switches, but the switches are relaying traffic from multiple users. So, if company A adds an office (say) in Dallas, then it would only require the leasing of one dedicated local loop to the most convenient

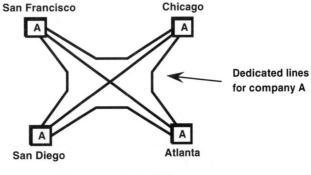

(a) Company A's Facilities

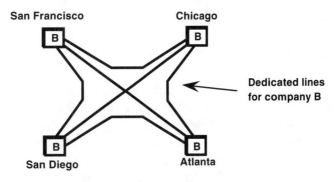

(b) Company B's Facilities

Figure 1–1   Leased lines.

VPN switch. The number of dedicated lines would remain the same as long as additional switches are not added to the network.

VPN is a relatively new term in the computer/communications industry. Yet, this new term describes an old concept; the ideas behind the VPN are not new at all. Public X.25 networks have offered VPN services for years, and switched T1 services also offer VPN-like features. However, we shall see that ATM offers more powerful VPNs than these older technologies.

The first part of this chapter has described some of the problems and challenges that exist in our present climate. The remainder of the chapter describes some solutions, notably ATM and SONET.[3]

---

[3]This book describes SONET. While SDH is quite similar to SONET, the two technologies use different terms and definitions.

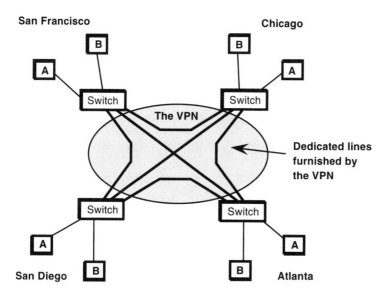

Figure 1–2   Virtual private networks.

FAST RELAY NETWORKS AND ATM

Much of the emerging technology to support modern applications is based on the idea of relaying traffic as quickly as possible. This idea is often called fast packet relay or fast packet switching. These names are considered generic terms in this book and are used in a variety of ways in the industry. Therefore, we will use the term fast relay systems. Currently, fast relay comes in two forms: Frame Relay and cell relay.[4] Figure 1–3 shows the relationships of these two forms of fast relay systems.

Frame Relay uses variable-sized protocol data units (PDUs), which are called *frames*. The technology is based on the link access procedure for the D channel (LAPD) that has long been used in integrated services digital network (ISDN) systems. Most frame-based implementations are using LAPD as the basic frame format for the relaying of the traffic across permanent virtual circuits (PVCs). A modified version of ISDN's Q.931 has been introduced into the industry for control signaling and for setting up connections between the user and the network. Q.931 can

---

[4]I could be called to task for this depiction because I have excluded Fast Ethernet, Gigabit Ethernet, and the emerging residential broadband (RBB) technologies. This depiction is a focus on wide area networks.

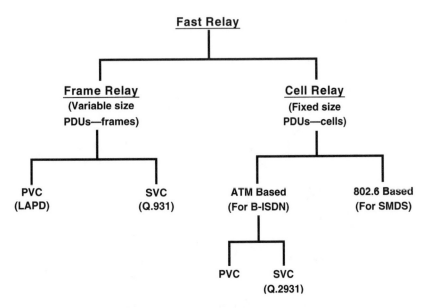

Figure 1–3   Types of relay systems.

form the basis for public switched offerings (switched virtual calls [SVCs]). The reader can refer to Chapter 4 for a tutorial on LAPD and Q.931.

In contrast to Frame Relay, cell relay uses a fixed length PDU, which is called a *cell*. The cell usually consists of a 48-octet payload with a 5-octet header, although some implementations use different cell sizes. This cell (with slight variations) is being used on both the asynchronous transfer mode (ATM) and the IEEE 802.6 standard, more commonly known as the Metropolitan Area Network (MAN) specification. In turn, the 802.6 standard is being used as a basis for the Switched Multimegabit Data Service (SMDS).

The industry is still divided on the advantages and disadvantages of the use of cell relay versus Frame Relay. While there are arguments for both, the trend is toward the use of the cell relay technology. The reasons are many, but before they are explained, a brief summary of cell relay technology is in order.

At the CPE, such as a router or a PBX, a customer's traffic, which could be variable in length, is segmented into a smaller fixed length units called cells. As stated earlier, in most cell relay systems, the cells are only 53 octets in length with 5 octets devoted to a header and the remaining 48 octets consisting of user information (the payload). The term cell is used to distinguish this PDU from variable length PDUs (frames and packets).

The term "asynchronous" in asynchronous transfer mode means the cells can be used without precise timing requirements and not necessarily on a synchronous, periodic basis. The cells may indeed be transported in a synchronous network (such as SONET), but they can be filled based on the needs of the application, which may be in a synchronous or asynchronous fashion. The ATM machines create a continuous stream of cells, and if no traffic is sent, the cells are empty and are called idle cells.

Cell relay is an integrated approach to networking in that it supports the transmission and reception of voice, video, data, and other applications. This capability is of particular interest to large companies that have developed multiple networks to handle different transmission schemes. As examples, common carriers, telephone companies and Postal Telephone and Telegraph Ministries (PTTs) must support many types of applications and historically have implemented a variety of networks to support them.

Why do many people prefer the cell technique over the frame technique? First, the use of fixed length cells provides for more predictable performance in the network than with variable length frames. Transmission delay is more predictable, as is queuing delay inside the switches. In addition, fixed-length buffers (with cell relay technology) are easier to manage than variable-length buffers. In essence, a fixed-length cell relay system is more deterministic than the use of a technology with variable length data units. Cell relay is also easier to implement in hardware than with variable length technology.

Some people have expressed concern about the high overhead of cell relay—because of the ratio of 5 octets of header to every 48 octets of user payload. But many people in the industry believe that the constant concern with efficient utilization of raw bandwidth is not a sound approach for the future. With the capacity of optical fiber and high-speed processors that are entering the marketplace, the approach of cell relay is to concentrate on superior quality-of-service features to the user. The philosophy is straightforward: Let the fast optical channels and the fast computers handle the transmission and processing of the overhead traffic.

Figure 1–3 shows several other aspects of the frame and cell relay technologies. Initial implementations of Frame Relay and cell relay have focused on PVCs (logical connections to the network that are available at any time). Recent enhancements have added SVCs (logical connections that are made available on demand, and not available at any time—similar to a dial-up telephone call).

Table 1–3   Problems that Existing Technologies Cannot Solve [ATM93b]

Problem	1st Place	2nd Place	3rd Place
1. LAN performance above 100 Mbit/s	5	4	2
2. Scalable WAN bandwidth	5	4	1
3. Integration of voice, video, and data	4	3	1
4. Network management and logistics	2	2	4
5. Uniform architecture in LANs, MANs, WANs	2	2	1
6. Bandwidth on demand (pay for use)	1	3	4
7. Network complexity	1	1	0
8. Support for multicast operations	0	1	1
9. Integration of multiple data applications	0	0	3
10. Support for synchronous applications	0	0	2

APPLICATIONS USE OF ATM

In 1993, the ATM Forum conducted a study of 200 companies to determine their plans for the future in relation to the use of ATM and other technologies [ATM93b]. The study entailed the companies' filling in questionnaires, and then consultant John McQuillan followed up with interviews. The study made no claim about its statistical validity, but purported to show accurate indications for the "near" future. The initial usage for ATM focused on data applications, but it was believed that voice and video would become more important in the future. Most respondents viewed that ATM would provide support for voice, video, and data by 1996.[5]

The survey asked the respondents to identify current problems that existing technologies cannot solve. The responses shown in Table 1–3 are similar to those concerns that this writer heard in 1993 (and continues to

---

[5]A few products in 1996 incorporated an integrated ATM switch to support voice, video, and data—but not many. The marketplace did not corroborate this part of the summary.

hear in this second edition) from clients as well. Certainly, the top seven answers in this survey are what I find, so I have left this survey in this new edition because it is still pertinent.

FAST RELAY NETWORKS AND SONET

At the beginning of this chapter, it was stated that for the first time in the history of the computer/communications industry, networks throughout the world are embracing a worldwide set of computer/communications standards. One of these standards deals with multiplexing and signaling hierarchies for digital carrier transport networks. Because of its importance, we shall introduce the subject here, and examine it more closely in later chapters.

During the past 35 years, three different digital multiplexing and signaling hierarchies have evolved throughout the world. These hierarchies were developed in the regions of Europe, Japan, and North America. Fortunately, all are based on the same pulse code modulation (PCM) signaling rate of 8000 samples a second, yielding 125 microsecond sampling slots (1 second/8000 samples = .000125). Therefore, the basic architectures interwork reasonably well.

But the regions vary in how the systems are implemented, which results in extensive and expensive conversion operations if traffic is exchanged between them (Figure 1–4). Moreover, the analog-to-digital conversion schemes also differ between North America and Europe, which further complicates interworking the disparate systems.

Japan and North America base their multiplexing hierarchies on the DS1 rate of 1.544 Mbit/s. Europe uses the E1 2.048 Mbit/s multiplexing scheme. Thereafter, the three approaches multiplex these payloads into larger multiplexed packages at higher bit rates and use different values for the multiplexing integer n.

As depicted in Figure 1–4, the synchronous digital hierarchy (SDH) and the synchronous optical network (SONET, North American term) support the schemes that have been in existence for many years, but specify a different multiplexing hierarchy.

The basic SDH/SONET rate is 155.52 Mbit/s. SDH/SONET then uses an x 155.52 multiplexing scheme, with x as the multiplexing factor (e.g., 155.52 * x, where x is 3, 6, etc.). Rates smaller than 155.52 Mbit/s are available at 51.840 Mbit/s for SONET but not for SDH. We shall have more to say about Figure 1–4 in later chapters, and the other terms in this figure will be explained at that time.

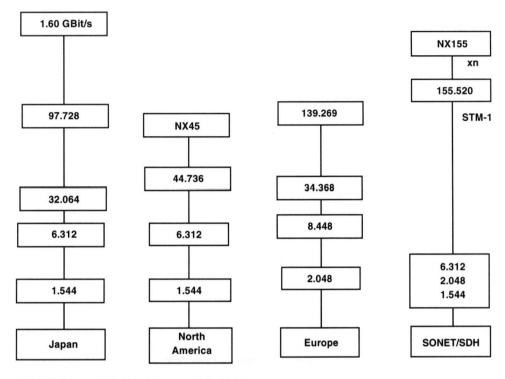

Note: Unless noted otherwise, speeds in Mbit/s

Figure 1–4   SONET and SDH hierarchies.

At long last, worldwide agreement has been reached (with minor exceptions) on a common digital multiplexing transport scheme. This agreement can only foster new technologies and decrease the costs of implementing them.

BROADBAND ISDN

The ITU-T describes the Broadband Integrated Services Digital Network (B-ISDN) as a network built on the concepts of the ISDN model, and a network that is implemented with the ATM and SONET technologies. These two technologies are complementary to each other, as shown in Figure 1–5. In its simplest form, the SONET technology acts as the physical carrier transport system for the user payload. The user payload

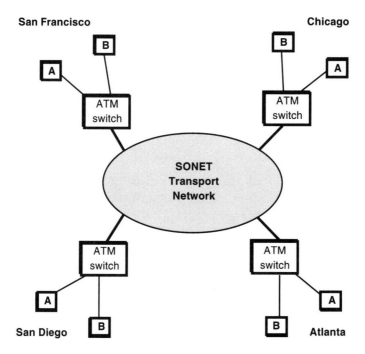

Figure 1–5   ATM and SONET.

is carried in ATM cells. In other words, the SONET network acts as a service provider to the ATM traffic.

Figure 1–5 also shows that the ATM components can act as the user-to-network interface (UNI) with the user's CPE. This approach allows the user to negotiate a wide variety of services at the ATM node. In addition, a SONET system can be terminated at ATM switches. These switches relay the traffic onto outgoing SONET ports or onto local UNIs.

ATM and SONET form the "technical alliance" for B-ISDN. SONET provides extensive operations, administration, and maintenance (OAM) functions and the basic carrier transport services (including backup facilities), and ATM provides services and interfaces to the user machine, as well as switching operations between SONET communications links.

As explained in subsequent chapters, one component of ATM also allows the ATM node to process and support multiapplication systems such as voice, video, data, music, and fax. These application-specific operations remain transparent to SONET.

Table 1–4 summarizes several aspects of ATM and SONET. As explained earlier, both are international standards sponsored by the ITU-T

Table 1–4   Broadband ISDN (B-ISDN)

Vendor or Standard	Sponsor	Age	Standard or Proprietary	WAN or LAN
ATM	ITU-T	2–7 years	Standard	Both
SONET	ITU-T	5–9 years	Standard	Both[1]

[1]Although most SONETs are deployed in WANs

and several other national standards bodies.[6] Although the age columns in Table 1–4 suggest they are rather mature technologies, these numbers reflect the period in which research has been conducted and implementations have been occurring. Indeed, SONET and ATM are still evolving as of this writing, and research on the use of these technologies continues.

Also, SONET and ATM can operate on WANs or LANs, although most implementations of SONET have been in large public wide area carrier transport systems.

The reader might wish to compare Table 1–4 with Tables 1–1 and 1–2, which summarize the emerged technologies. The first thing to note is that ATM and SONET are considered to be single solutions to transport and switching systems in contrast to the multiplicity of standards and proprietary implementations that the industry has fostered in the past. This writer is not suggesting that ATM and SONET are replacements for all the technologies in Tables 1–1 and 1–2. Such is not the case at all. Rather, the design goal of the B-ISDN technologies is to provide for *backbone* transport systems for voice, data, and video applications. Notwithstanding this goal, ATM and SONET, if implemented properly, could result in the paring down or even elimination of some of the technologies listed in Tables 1–1 and 1–2. The rationale for this statement shall be supported in other chapters of this book.

PRINCIPAL SPECIFICATIONS FOR ATM

Figure 1–6 should prove helpful to you as you read the remainder of this book. We will examine each of the depicted operations/functions in this figure, because they provide the basis for the specifications and stan-

---

[6]SONET is not a formal ITU-T Standard. The ITU-T Standard is SDH, which was derived from SONET.

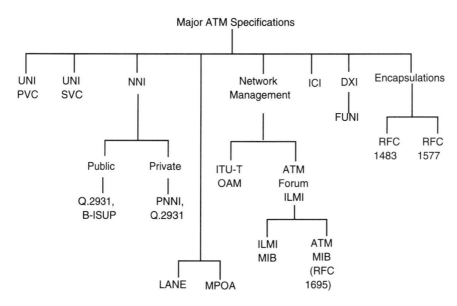

Figure 1–6   Principal standards and specifications for ATM.

Where:

DXI	Data exchange interface
FUNI	Frame UNI
ICI	Intercarrier interface
ILMI	Integrated local management interface
ITU-T	International Telecommunication Union-Telecommunication Standardization Sector
LANE	LAN emulation
MIB	Management information base
MPOA	Multiprotocol over ATM
NNI	Network-to-network interface (also, network-node interface)
OAM	Operations, administration, and maintenance
PNNI	Private network-network interface
PVC	Permanent virtual circuit
RFC	Request for comments
SVC	Switched virtual circuit
UNI	User-network interface

dards from which ATM products are developed and implemented. Specific parts of the book will also give you an update on the status of each of these areas.

As a general statement, the network-node interfaces (network-to-network) (NNI) were completed only last year by the ATM Forum and the ITU-T. The ITU-T operations, administration, and maintenance (OAM) standards are nearing completion. All others have been completed and are at various stages of implementation.

THE ANCHORAGE ACCORD

One of the ongoing complaints about some of the formal standards organizations is the time it takes for them to complete a technical specification. In addition, these specifications (standards) often are incomplete, and issues are left for "further study."

This complaint certainly cannot be levied against the ATM Forum. It has published about 70 specifications. Indeed, there have been complaints that network managers and ATM vendors cannot form a cohesive ATM "outlook," due to the profusion of information emanating from the ATM task forces. I prefer to have this overabundance of information, rather than a sparcity, none at all.

The ATM Forum reached an agreement (the Anchorage Accord) that is designed to address these problems. It contains a set of specifications that are stable and provides guidance on the applicability of the specifications to six specific network environments. These environments are shown Table 1–5 along with the applicable specifications to support each network environment.

In a nutshell, notable progress has been made by the ATM Forum in getting ATM started, and other issues are being addressed, such as voice over ATM.

It is the goal of the ATM Forum to complete the outstanding major specifications as soon as possible in order to facilitate the creation, implementation, and use of standardized ATM products.

SUMMARY

It is recognized that upcoming user applications are demanding greater throughput and lower delay from communications systems. ATM and SONET are designed to provide the capacity to support these applications.

Table 1–5 The Anchorage Accord

ATM Specification	Campus	Legacy LAN	Multimedia Desktop	Extended Campus	Legacy WAN	Multimedia WAN
ATM UNI v3.1	X	X	X	X	X	X
BICI v2.0					X	X
DXI v1.0		X				
ILMI v4.0	X	X	X	X	X	X
LANE over ATM 1.0 Includes LANE Client Management	X	X				
Network Management: Customer Network Management for ATM Public Network Service			X			
Network Management: M4 Interface Requirements & Logical MIB						X
Network Management: CMIP for the M4 Interface						X
Network Management: M4 Public Network View Requirements & Logical MIB						X
Network Management: M4 Logical MIB Addendum						X
Network Management: CES IW Requirements Logical CMIP MIB						X
Network Management: M4 Network View CMIP MIB 1.0						X
Network Management: AAL Management for the M4						X
PNNI v1.0				X	X	X
Frame UNI				X	X	
Circuit Emulation					X	X
Native ATM Services: Semantic Description			X			
Audio Visual Multimedia			X			
ATM Name System 1.0	X		X	X		X
UNI Signaling 4.0	X	X	X	X	X	X

From: *Business Communications Review* (BCR), June 1997, George Dobrowski and Marlis Humphrey.

Optical fiber systems are providing the foundation for the media support of these technologies and high-speed processors are providing the speed to process the traffic.

The movement toward worldwide standards for carrier transport technology, multiplexing techniques, and switching methodologies are at last providing the groundwork for a comprehensive and homogeneous approach to computer/communications networks.

2

The Nature of Analog: and Digital Systems

This chapter provides a general overview of analog and digital transmission systems. It explains how voice and data images are transported over a communications channel and compares analog and digital networks. The concepts of analog modulation are explained, as well as analog-to-digital conversion schemes. The latter part of the chapter deals with network synchronization, timing, and clocks, and contrasts asynchronous, synchronous, plesiochronous, and mesochronous networks.

The reader who has had experience with these subjects need only glance through the first part of this chapter. The latter part of the chapter deals with network synchronization, timing, and clocks. A review of this material is important for all readers (unless the reader works in this field).

ANALOG SYSTEMS

Even though telecommunications systems have evolved from single application networks (voice-only, data-only) to multiapplication networks, the legacy of voice remains in many systems. Consequently, this chapter reviews some of the pertinent characteristics of communications signals and voice transmission as they relate to the subject matter of this book.

Speech is actually a physical disturbance of the air; in effect, it is slight movements of air molecules produced by the human voice. In its essential physical nature, speech is nothing more than a pressure change in the air. Air molecules in close proximity to the mouth push against air molecules in front of them, and, in turn, these molecules push on other molecules further from the mouth. The sound propagates through the air and gradually diminishes in intensity as the disturbance moves further away from the speaking person. The various pressure fluctuations are received by the ear, converted into nerve impulses, and interpreted by the brain as speech.

The speech pattern produces various levels of air pressure. Certain utterances create more air pressure than others. Periods of high-pressure sound signals are called *condensations* (the air is compressed) and periods of low sound levels are called *rarefactions* (the air is less dense). Human speech is a continuous train of these sound waves. The changes in air pressure are gradual (and continuous, if the speech is sustained) from high to low pressure. The shape of the signal resembles a wave and is actually called a *sound wave*. Talking or singing creates a complex set of waveforms that change in pressure several hundred to several thousand times per second.

The telephone handset transforms the physical speech waveform into an electrical waveform. Both waves have very similar characteristics. For example, the various heights of the sound wave are translated by the telephone into signals of continuously variable electrical voltages, or *currents*. The voice waveform spoken into a telephone creates an electrical alternating current: The voltage alternating reverses its polarity, which produces current that reverses its direction.

CYCLES, FREQUENCY, AND PERIOD

The wavelength measures the cycle of the wave; that is, the interval of space or time in which the waveform reaches a successive point. The *cycle* describes a complete oscillation of the wave. The number of oscillations of the acoustical or electrical wave in a given period (usually a second) is called the *frequency* (f). Frequency is expressed in cycles per second, or more commonly *hertz* (Hz). Frequency describes the number of cycles that pass a given point in one second (for example, our ear, a telephone mouthpiece, or a receiver in a computer). The signal travels one wavelength during the time of one cycle.

The time required for the signal to be transmitted over a distance of one wavelength is called the *period* (T). The period describes the duration of the cycle and is a function of the frequency:

$$T = 1/f$$

Also, frequency is the reciprocal of the period:

$$f = 1/T$$

Sound waves (as well as other waveforms such as electrical and light waves) propagate through the air or other media at a certain speed. The *velocity* (V) of a sound wave is about 1090 feet (332 meters) per second, measured at 0° Celsius. The propagation speed of any waveform is calculated as:

$$V = f * (l)$$

Since velocity (V), frequency (f), and wavelength (l) are interrelated, if any two of the values are known, the third can be calculated:

$$V = f * l; \quad l = V/f; \quad f = V/l$$

The transmission medium also determines the propagation velocity. For example, sound travels about four times faster in water than in air and about 15 times faster in metal. Sound propagation velocity also increases with each degree increase in temperature (about 2 feet or 0.6 meters per second).

Voice signals move away from our mouths at about 1090 feet per second in a circular expanding pattern. The train of compressions and rarefactions create the waveform.

BANDWIDTH

The analog voice signal is not made up of one unique frequency. Rather, the voice signal on a communications line consists of waveforms of many different frequencies. The particular mix of these frequencies is what determines the sound of a person's voice. Many phenomena manifest themselves as a combination of different frequencies. The colors in the rainbow, for instance, are combinations of many different lightwave frequencies; musical sounds consist of different acoustic frequencies that are interpreted as higher or lower pitch. These phenomena consist of a range or band of frequencies, called the bandwidth, stated as:

$$BW = f_1 - f_2$$

where: BW = bandwidth; f_1 = highest frequency; f_2 = lowest frequency.

As examples, a piano can produce a wide range of frequencies ranging from about 30 Hz (low notes) to over 4200 Hz (high notes). Its bandwidth is from 30 Hz to 4200 Hz. The human ear can detect sounds over a range of frequencies from around 40 to 18,000 Hz, but the telephone system does not transmit this band of frequencies. The full range is not needed to interpret the voice signal at the receiver, because most of the energy is concentrated between 300 and 3100 Hz. In fact, the vowels in speech occupy mostly the lower portion of the frequency band, and the consonants, which actually contain most of the information in speech, use much less power and generally occupy the higher frequencies. Due to economics, only the frequency band of approximately 200 to 3500 Hz is transmitted across the path.

It is not necessary to reproduce the speech signals with complete accuracy on the channel, because the human ear is not sensitive to precise frequency differences, and the human brain possesses great inferential powers to reconstruct the intelligence of the speech. Even with the frequency cutoffs, 98 percent of the speech energy and 85 percent of the intelligence are still present in a transmission. Nonetheless, the bandlimited channel is one reason why voice conversations sound different on a telephone line.

The so-called voiceband (or voice-grade) channel is defined as a band of 4000 Hz. This means the channel consists of frequencies ranging from 0 to 4000 Hz. The speech signal is bandlimited to between 200 and 3500 Hz. For purposes of convenience and brevity, this book uses the value 3 kHz as the bandwidth for a voiceband channel. The other frequencies on both sides of the speech signal allow for guardbands, which lessen interference among the channels that are placed on the same physical medium, such as a wire or a cable.

We have learned that speech signals on a voiceband channel are made up of many frequencies. This also holds true for other communications circuits such as radio and television channels. The spectrum of the signal describes the range of frequencies of the signal, or its bandwidth.

Bandwidth is a very important concept in communications because the capacity (stated in bits per second) of a communications channel is partially dependent on its bandwidth. If the telephone channel were increased from a bandwidth of 3 kHz to 20 kHz, it could carry all the characteristics of the voice. The same is true for transmitting data; a higher data transmission rate can be achieved with a greater bandwidth.

The greater the bandwidth, the greater the capacity. The frequency spectrum ranges from the relatively limited ranges of the audio frequencies through the radio ranges, the infrared (red light) ranges, the visible light frequencies, and up to the X-ray and cosmic ray bands. The importance of the higher frequencies can readily be seen by an examination of the bandwidth of the audio-frequency spectrum and that of radio. The bandwidth between 10^3 and 10^4 is 9000 Hz (10,000 − 100 = 9000), which is roughly the equivalent to three voice-grade bands. The bandwidth between 10^7 and 10^8 (the HF and VHF spectrum) is 90,000,000 Hz (100,000,000 − 10,000,000 = 90,000,000), which could support several thousand voice band circuits.

BROADBAND AND BASEBAND SIGNALS

Signals are usually categorized as either *broadband* or *baseband*. A broadband signal is identified by the following characteristics (other definitions follow):

- Uses analog waveforms
- Has a large bandwidth (typically in the megahertz to gigahertz range)
- Uses analog modulation
- Often uses frequency division multiplexing for channel sharing

A baseband signal is identified by the following characteristics:

- Uses digital signals (voltage shifts)
- Bandwidth is limited
- Does not use modulation
- May use time division multiplexing for channel sharing

Many people use the term baseband to describe an unmodulated signal. A baseband signal may be used to modulate an analog carrier signal, but the carrier need not be a broadband carrier; it may be a voiceband carrier, which is not considered a broadband signal.

Other Definitions of Broadband

The previous description of broadband is one that had been used in the industry in the past. With some of the emerging technologies, the standards groups have changed this description. Some define a broadband network as any system that operates above the T1/E1 primary rate (1.544 Mbit/s in North America/Japan, and 2.048 Mbit/s elsewhere). Others define broadband as any system that utilizes ISDN architecture with transfer rates above the primary rate. Still others view broadband as any system that uses the ISDN architecture and integrates SONET/SDH and ATM into the architecture.

THE ANALOG-TO-DIGITAL CONVERSION PROCESS

The process of digitization was developed to overcome some of the limitations of analog systems. Several problems arise regarding the analog signal and how it is transmitted across the channel. First, the signal is relayed through amplifiers and other transducers. These devices are designed to perform the relaying function in a linear fashion; that is, the waveform representing the signal maintains its characteristics from one end of the channel to the other. A deviation from this linearity creates a distortion of the waveform. All analog signals exhibit some form of nonlinearity (therefore, a distortion). Unfortunately, the intervening components to strengthen the signal, such as amplifiers, also increase the nonlinearity of the signal.

Second, all signals (digital and analog) are weakened (or attenuated) during transmission through the medium. The decay can make the signal so weak that it is unintelligible at the receiver. A high-quality wire cable with a large diameter certainly mitigates decay, but it cannot be eliminated.

Digital systems overcome these problems by representing the transmitted data with digital and binary images. The analog signal is converted to a series of digital numbers and transmitted through the communications channel as binary data.

Of course, digital signals are subject to the same kinds of imperfections and problems as the analog signal—decay and noise. However, the digital signal is discrete: The binary samples of the analog waveform are represented by specific levels of voltages, in contrast to the nondiscrete levels of an analog signal. Indeed, an analog signal has almost infinite variability. As the digital signal traverses the channel, it is only necessary to sample the absence or presence of a digital binary pulse—not its degree, as in the analog signal.

The mere absence or presence of a signal pulse can be more easily recognized than the magnitude or degree of an analog signal. If the digital signals are sampled at an acceptable rate and at an acceptable voltage level, the signals can then be completely reconstituted before they deteriorate below a minimum threshold. Consequently, noise and attenuation can be completely eliminated from the reconstructed signal. Thus, the digital signal can tolerate the problems of noise and attenuation much better than the analog signal.

The periodic sampling and regeneration process is performed by regenerative repeaters. The repeaters are placed on a channel at defined intervals. The spacing depends on the quality and size of the conductor, the amount of noise on the conductor, its bandwidth, and the bit rate of the transmission. These thoughts are summarized in Figure 2–1.

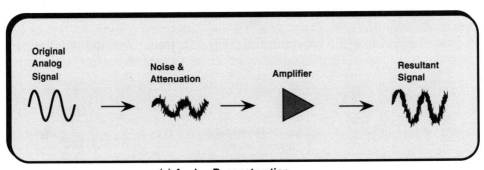

(a) Analog Reconstruction

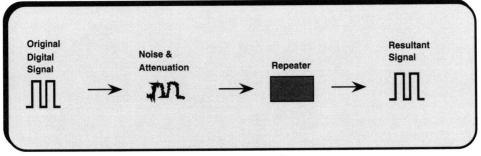

(b) Digital Reconstruction

Figure 2–1   Digital versus analog systems.

Sampling, Quantizing, and Encoding

Several methods are used to change an analog signal into a representative string of digital binary images. Even though these methods entail many processes, they are generally described in three steps: sampling, quantizing, and encoding (Figure 2–2).

The devices performing the digitizing process are called *channel banks* or *primary multiplexers*. They have two basic functions: (1) converting analog signals to digital signals (and vice versa at the other end); and (2) combining (multiplexing) the digital signals into a single time division multiplexed (TDM) data stream (and demultiplexing them at the other end).

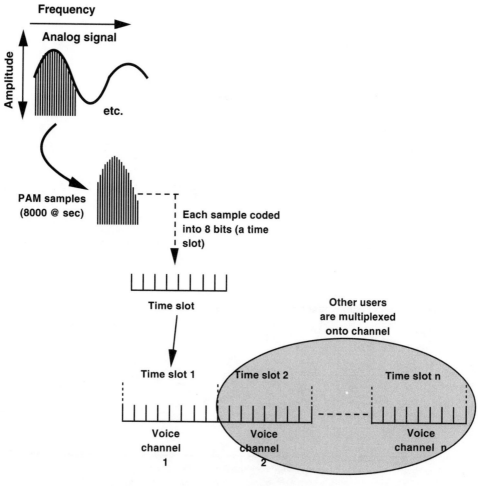

Figure 2–2   Analog-to-digital conversion.

Analog-to-digital conversion is based on Nyquist sampling theory, which states that if a signal is sampled instantaneously at regular intervals and at a rate at least twice the highest frequency in the channel, the samples will contain sufficient information to allow an accurate reconstruction of the signal.

The accepted sampling rate in the industry is 8000 samples per second. Based on Nyquist sampling theory, this rate allows the accurate reproduction of a 4 kHz channel, which is used as the bandwidth for a voice-grade channel. The 8000 samples are more than sufficient to capture the signals in a telephone line if certain techniques (discussed shortly) are used.

With pulse amplitude modulation (PAM), the pulse carrier amplitude is varied with the value of the analog waveform. The pulses are fixed with respect to duration and position. PAM is classified as a modulation technique because each instantaneous sample of the wave is used to modulate the amplitude of the sampling pulse.

The 8 kHz sampling rate results in a sample pulse train of signals with a 125 microseconds (µs) time period between the pulses (1 second/8000 = .000125). Each pulse occupies 5.2 µs of this time period. Consequently, it is possible to interleave sampled pulses from other signals within the 125 µs period. The most common approach in North America utilizes 24 interleaved channels, which effectively fills the 125 µs time period (.0000052 ∗ 24 = .000125). The samples are then multiplexed using TDM and put into a digital TDM frame. TDM provides an efficient and economical means of combining multiple signals for transmission on a common facility and is examined in a later section of this book.

Other Coding Schemes[1]

Differential pulse code modulation (DPCM).   Today's systems have more sophisticated approaches than the conventional PCM technique. One system is differential pulse code modulation (DPCM). This technique encodes the differences between samples of the signal instead of the actual samples. Since an analog waveform's samples are closely correlated with each other (almost sample-to-sample redundant), the range of sample differences requires fewer bits to represent the signal. Studies reveal that the predictability between adjacent 8 kHz samples is 85 per-

---

[1]See companion books to this series for more information on this subject: *T1 and SONET* and *Advanced Internet Technologies.*

cent or higher. This redundancy in the PCM codes can be exploited to reduce the bit rate.

However, DPCM is subject to errors when an input signal changes significantly between samples. The DPCM equipment is not able to code the change accurately, which results in large quantizing errors and signal distortion.

Adaptive DPCM. DPCM can be improved by assigning the 4-bit signals to represent different ranges of the signal. For example, the 4 bits can be coded to represent a change between samples. This technique is called adaptive DPCM, because the systems increase or decrease the volume range covered by each 4-bit sample value.

ADPCM uses a differential quantizer to store the previous sample in a sample-and-hold circuit. The circuit measures the change between the two samples and encodes the change. Differential PCM achieves a smaller voice digitization rate (VDR) than do the conventional PCM techniques (32 kbit/s, for example). These systems have seen extensive use in digital telephony.

Adaptive Predictive DPCM. Some DPCM systems use a feedback signal (based on previous samples) to estimate the input signal. These systems are called adaptive predictive DPCM. The technique is quite useful if the feedback signal varies from the input (due to quantization problems) and the next encoding sample automatically adjusts for the drift. Thus, the quantization errors do not accumulate over a prolonged period.

Many systems store more than one past sample value, with the last three sample values commonly used. The previous samples are then used to produce a more accurate estimate of the next input sample.

Since DPCM and ADPCM do not send the signal but the representation of the change from the previous sample, the receiver must have some method for knowing where the current level is. Due to noise, the level may vary drastically or during periods of speech silence (no talking), several samples may be zero. Periodically, the sender and receiver may be returned (referenced) to the same levels by adjusting them to zero.

TIMING AND SYNCHRONIZATION IN DIGITAL NETWORKS

With the advent of digital networks and the transmission and reception of binary pulses (1s and 0s), it became important to devise some method for sampling these signals accurately at the receiver. In older systems that operate at a relatively low bit rate, the sampling did not have to be very accurate, because the pulse did not change on the line very often. There is an inverse relationship between the number of bits on a channel (in a measured period of time), and the length of time the bit manifests itself at a receiver.

As the networks became faster and more bits per second were transmitted, the time the bits were on the channel decreased significantly. This meant that if there was a slight inaccuracy in the timing of the sampling clock, it might not detect a bit, or, more often, it might not detect several hundred bits in succession. This situation leads to a problem called "slips." Slipping is the loss of timing and the loss of the detection of bits.

PLESIOCHRONOUS NETWORKS

The early systems deployed in the early 1960s were not synchronized to any common frequency source, because they consisted of analog circuits and did not need a precise timing setup. However, as digital networks were employed with the use of T1 technology, timing became an increasing problem. These digital networks were not synchronized to a common frequency, and thus they were called asynchronous networks. (Actually, T1 systems are plesiochronous because the timing is very tightly controlled.)

Each T1 portion of the network is synchronized to a highly accurate primary reference source (PRS) clock. These clocks operate at a stratum 1 clock level and are required to provide a minimum long-term accuracy of $\pm 1.0 * 10^{-11}$. Consequently, at the worst case, the stratum clock will experience one timing error (called a slip) every 20 weeks. Because of this performance and the fact that this technique is fairly inexpensive, PRS clocks are a cost-effective way to improve network performance.

A so-called synchronous network is distinguished by the use of one PRS called the master clock. All components derive their clocking from this master clock. Timing is derived first for the master clock, and then from a slave—for example, a toll office—and then to digital switches, digital cross connects, end offices, and so on. Timing is cascaded down to other equipment such as channel banks and multiplexers.

THE SYNCHRONOUS CLOCK HIERARCHY

Table 2–1 summarizes the synchronous network clock hierarchy and shows long-term accuracy for each stratum level, as well as typical locations of the clocking operations. A more stringent requirement rests with

Table 2–1   Clock Hierarchy for Synchronous Networks

Clock Stratum	Typical Location(s)	Long-Term Accuracy (Minimum)
1	Primary Reference Source (PRS)	$\pm 1.0 \times 10^{-11*}$
2	Class 4 office	$\pm 1.6 \times 10^{-8}$
3	Class 5 office, DCS	$\pm 4.6 \times 10^{-6}$
4	Channel bank, end-user Mux	$\pm 32 \times 10^{-6}$

*Also annotated as .00001 ppm (parts per million)

stratum 1 clocks, which are typically positioned as a PRS. Long-term accuracy for stratum 1 clocks is $\pm 1.0 * 10^{-11}$. The next level of accuracy is the stratum 2 clock, which is usually located in class 4 toll offices. The long-term accuracy for these clocks is $\pm 1.6 * 10^{-8}$. Next in the order of accuracy are the stratum 3 clocks, typically located in the class 5 end office or a digital cross connect (DCS). The long-term accuracy of these clocks is $\pm 4.6 * 10^{-6}$. The last level of the synchronous network clock hierarchy is stratum 4 clock. These clocks are usually located in channel banks or multiplexers at the end-user site. Their accuracy is $\pm 32 * 10^{-6}$.

CLARIFICATION OF TERMS

The terms *asynchronous networks, plesiochronous networks, synchronous networks,* and *mesochronous networks* are used in a variety of ways. To be precise, an asynchronous network is one in which timing between the network elements is not maintained. If the timing is maintained between the components, then it is not very accurate. As an extreme example, asynchronous data communications protocols (such as XModem) have no common clocks, but derive their timing from start and stop bits in the data stream. In contrast, a synchronous network is one in which the network elements are aligned together with precise timing arrangements. The payloads can be traced back to a common reference clock. Some people use yet another term—a mesochronous network. Strictly speaking, a mesochronous network's elements are timed to the same source, and all elements are exactly the same. Mesochronous networks are expensive and hard to achieve. Therefore, another term is used to describe a precisely timed network, or networks—plesiochronous. The term is derived from *plesio,* which is a Greek term meaning "nearly." Today's networks are actually plesiochronous networks in that they do not use synchronous timing, but very precise timing whose variances must fall within a very narrow range. So, in summary, a plesiochronous network is one in which network elements are timed by separate clocks with almost the same timing.

TIMING VARIATIONS

While synchronous networks exhibit very accurate timing, some variation will inevitably exist among the network elements within a network and network elements among networks. This variation, which is generally known as *phase variation,* is usually divided into jitter and wander. *Jitter* is defined as a short-term variation in the phase of a digital signal, which includes all variations above 10 Hz. Causes of jitter include common noise, the bit stuffing processes in multiplexers, or faulty repeaters. In contrast, *wander* is the long-term variation in the phase of a signal and includes all phase variations below 10 Hz. Wander may also include the effects of frequency departure, which is a constant frequency difference between network elements. Wander is almost inevitable in any network, due to the slight variations in clock frequency differences, transmission delay on the path, as well as bit stuffing operations.

Jitter and wander are dealt with in a digital network through the use of *buffers.* These buffers exist at each interface in any machine where the signal is processed (multiplexed, switched, etc.). Buffers act as windows to receive and transmit traffic. Additionally, for digital systems, they can be used to accommodate to frequency departure and phase variations. The buffers are carefully designed to handle the most common variations.

Slips—Controlled and Uncontrolled

Buffers accommodate to problems in frequency departure and phase variation by either "underflowing" or "overflowing." A underflowing buffer will repeat a block of data to compensate for slow timing. In contrast, an overflow buffer will throw away a block of data to accommodate to faster timing. In either condition, underflow or overflow operations are known collectively as *slip.* Obviously, slips result in errors within the network, because the overflowing or underflowing results in either a frame being deleted in the transmission scheme or being repeated.

Slips are either controlled or uncontrolled, the former being desirable and the latter being highly undesirable. As stated, underflow and overflow buffers result in a controlled slip. This term is used because this slip results in the deleting or repeating of a full frame (of 192 bits). This operation is possible because a buffer is actually larger than a frame. The extra buffer allows the most leeway to prevent frequency departure from creating slips on back-to-back frames.

The effect of a controlled slip results in one T1 frame being deleted, which means that 24 DS0 slots are deleted. Fortunately, these control slips do not affect the framing bit and therefore do not propagate to any subsequent back-to-back frames.

The reader may have noticed controlled slip occurring occasionally in a voice circuit, which can usually be detected by a very quick popping or clicking sound. This rare aberration is usually only mildly irritating in a voice signal. For data signals however, it does result in the loss of data. Additionally, if (for example) a network element such as a digital cross connect loses its master clock, it must fall back to its internal clock, which is typically a stratum 3 clock. This type of problem results in a dramatic drop in the quality of the line and an increase in the bit error rate. Evidence has shown that, in the worst case, every 13 seconds a DS0 channel will experience problems.

The next type of slip is the uncontrolled slip, also known as a *change of frame alignment* (COFA). This problem is also known as an unframed buffer slip. This event occurs if only a portion of a frame is either repeated or deleted and is the result of using unframed buffers. Unframed buffers, while having the potential to present more problems, are used because they are less expensive than framed buffers. They are smaller, which decreases latency in the machine, and they are prevalent in asynchronous multiplexers as a matter of course.

COFAs are the result of excessive jitter and wander of the inputs to the asynchronous multiplexers, or any machine that uses unframed buffers. COFA affects multiple frames. The number of affected frames depends on how long it takes the receiving device to perform reframing operations. In many systems, the uncontrolled slip can result in an error of several thousand bits—some 40 to 50 times more serious than a control slip.

Bit or Clock Slips

Another form of slip that exists in digital networks is called a bit slip or clock slip. This problem describes a phase variation of only one clock signal. For example, a T1 that operates at 1/1.544 MHz could experience a bit slip of 0.648 μs.

A one part per million (ppm) frequency departure is equivalent to a one microsecond (μs) phase variation. In a T1 system, frequency departure can result in a control slip every 125 seconds. This value is derived from: 125 μs/1 μs = 125. Consequently, in a day (in which 86,400 seconds exist) a 1 ppm network can experience 691 slips (96400/125 = 691).

SUMMARY

Modern networks use digital techniques for the transport of voice, video, and data traffic. Most voice networks used plesiochronous timing in which the components are timed by separate clocks, but the clocks are almost the same.

Data networks are asynchronous networks, and the network is not synchronized to any clock. Each component runs with its own clock.

The emerging broadband networks are synchronous networks, where network components (and payload) are traced back to a common reference clock, through more than one clock.

3

Layered Protocols
the Model for ATM
and SONET Networks

This chapter introduces the concepts of layered protocols. The focus is on the Open Systems Interconnection (OSI) Model, because the architecture of ATM is based on OSI architecture. For this book, this model is examined in a general manner, with descriptions on the rationale for its use and how it is used in networks. Other books treat the OSI Model in more detail. Of course, in the spirit of the subject matter of this book, the OSI Model is examined in relation to ATM.

The latter part of the chapter also provides an overview of several of the OSI and Internet protocols that operate at the network and transport layers in these two architectures. A knowledge of these systems is important if the reader is to understand how ATM supports the TCP/IP protocol suite.

PROTOCOLS AND THE OSI MODEL

Machines, such as computers and switches, communicate with each other through established conventions called *protocols*. Since computer systems provide many functions to users, more than one protocol is required to support these functions.

A convention is needed to define how the different protocols of the systems interact with each other to support the end user. This convention is referred to by several names: network architecture, communications architecture, or computer-communications architecture. Whatever the term used, most systems are implemented with a set of protocols that are compatible, one hopes, among the communicating machines.

The *Open Systems Interconnection (OSI) Model* was developed in the early 1980s by several standards organizations, principally led by the ITU-T and the ISO. It is now widely used for defining how communications protocols are standardized among different vendors' equipment. This model has provided a blueprint for the design and implementation of computer-based networks.

The ITU-T publishes its OSI Model specifications in the X.200–X.299 Recommendations. The X.200 documents contain slightly over 1100 pages. The ISO publishes its specifications for the OSI Model in several documents, but does not use a numbering scheme that fits the mold of a simple "X.2xx" notation.

The model is organized into seven layers. Each layer contains several to many protocols that are invoked based on the specific needs of the user. However, a protocol entity in a layer need not be invoked, and the model provides a means for two users to negotiate the specific protocols needed for a session that takes place between them.

As suggested in Figure 3–1, each layer is responsible for performing specific functions to support the end-user application. One should not think of a layer as monolithic code; rather each layer is divided into smaller operational entities. These entities are then invoked by the end user to obtain the services defined in the model.

An end user is permitted to negotiate services within layers in its own machine or layers at the remote machine. This capability allows, for example, a relatively low-function machine to indicate to a relatively high-capability machine that it may not support all the operational entities supported by the high-level machine. Consequently, the machines will still be able to communicate with each other, albeit at a lesser mode of service. Conversely, if two large-scale computers, each with the full OSI stack, wish to exchange traffic within a rich functional environment, they may do so by negotiating the desired services.

This concept holds true for networks as well. For example, OSI provides rules on how services can be negotiated between the user and the network. This concept is integral to ATM, because it uses this OSI idea of allowing the user to inform the network about its needs (such as maxi-

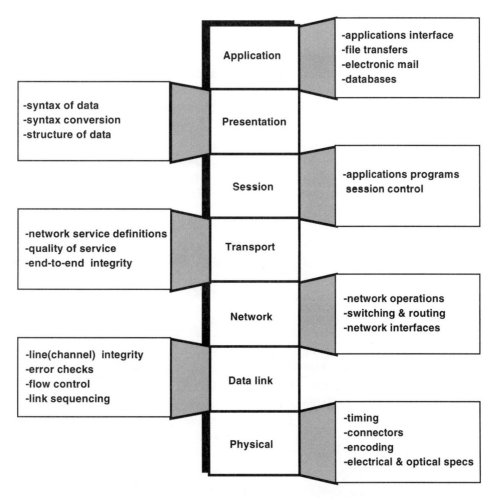

Figure 3–1   Functions of the OSI layers.

mum allowable delay, minimum acceptable throughput, etc.). In turn, it allows the network to inform the user if it can meet these needs, or suggest a lesser quality of service (QOS).

OSI Layer Operations

The layers of the OSI Model and the layers of vendors' models (such as Apple's AppleTalk, IBM's SNA, etc.) contain communications functions at the lower three or four layers. From the OSI perspective, as depicted in Figure 3–2, it is intended that the upper four layers reside in the host computers.

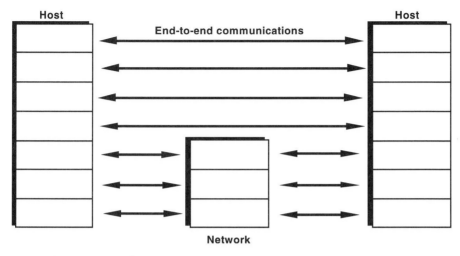

Figure 3–2 Conventional position of host and network layers.

This statement does not mean to imply that the lower three layers reside only in the network. The hardware and software implemented in the lower three layers also exist at the host machine. End-to-end communications, however, occur between the hosts by invoking the upper four layers, and between the hosts and the network by invoking the lower three layers. This concept is shown in Figure 3–2 with arrows drawn between the layers in the hosts and the network. Additionally, the upper four layers also reside in the network, for the network components to communicate with each other and obtain the services of these layers.

The end user application sits on top of the application layer. Therefore, the user obtains all the services of the seven layers of the OSI Model.

CONCEPT OF A SERVICE PROVIDER

In the OSI Model, a layer is considered to be a *service provider* to the layer above it (Figure 3–3). This upper layer is considered to be a service user to its lower layer. The service user avails itself of the functions of the service provider by sending a transaction to the provider. This transaction (called a primitive or service definition) informs the provider as to the nature of the service to be provided (at least, requested). In so far as

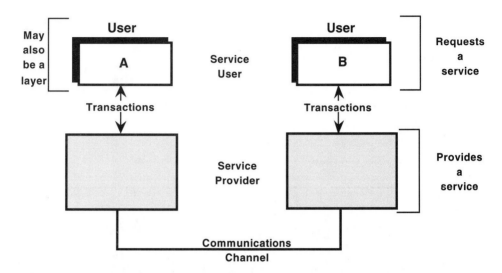

Figure 3–3   The layer as a service provider.

possible, the service provider does provide the service. It may also send a primitive to its user to inform it about what is going on.

At the other machine (B in this figure), the operation at A may manifest itself by service provider B's accepting the traffic from service provider A, providing some type of service, and informing user B about the operation. User B may be allowed to send a primitive back to service provider B, which may then forward traffic back to service provider A. In turn, service provider A may send a transaction to user A about the nature of the operations at site B. The OSI Model provides several variations of this general scenario.

In accordance with the rules of the model, a layer cannot be bypassed. Even if an end user does not wish to use the services of a particular layer, the user must still "pass through" the layer on the way to the next adjacent layer. This pass-through may only entail the invocation of a small set of code, but it still translates to overhead. However, every function in each layer need not be invoked. A minimum subset of functions may be all that is necessary to "conform" to the standard.

Layered network protocols allow interaction between functionally paired layers in different locations without affecting other layers. This concept aids in distributing the functions to the layers. In the majority of layered protocols, the data unit, such as a message or packet, passed from one layer to another is usually not altered, although the data unit contents may be examined and used to append additional data (trailers/headers) to the existing unit.

Each layer contains entities that exchange data and provide functions (horizontal communications) with peer entities at other computers. For example, in Figure 3–4, layer N in machine A communicates logically with layer N in machine B, and the N+1 layers in the two machines follow the same procedure. Entities in adjacent layers in the same computer interact through the common upper and lower boundaries (vertical communications) by passing parameters in the primitives to define the interactions.

Typically, each layer at a transmitting station (except the lowest in most systems) adds "header" information to data. The headers are used to establish peer-to-peer sessions across the layers in the nodes.

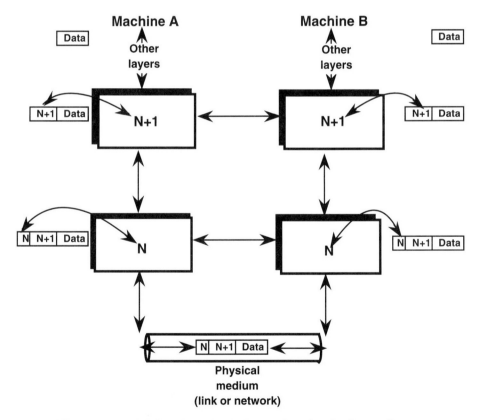

Figure 3–4   Adding header information for horizontal communications.

The important point to understand is that, at the receiving site, the layer entities use the headers created by the peer entity at the transmitting site to implement predefined actions. For example, the ATM cell header created at the ATM layer at the sending machine is used by the receiving ATM layer to determine what actions it is to undertake.

Figure 3–5 shows an example of how machine A sends data to machine B. Data are passed from the upper layers or the user application to layer N+1. This layer adds a header to the data (labeled N+1 in the figure). Layer N+1 also performs actions based on the information in the transaction that accompanied the data from the upper layer.

Layer N+1 then passes the data unit with its N+1 header to layer N. Layer N performs the requested actions, based on the information in the transaction, and adds its header N to the N+1 traffic. This appended traffic is then passed across the communications line (or through a network) to the receiving machine B.

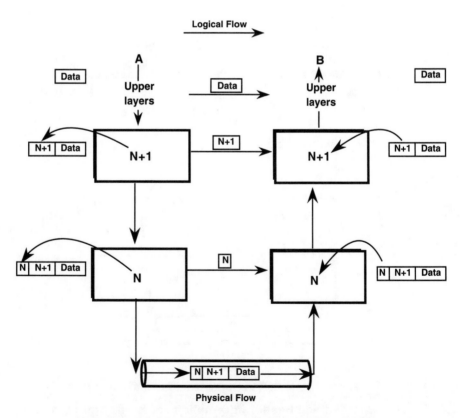

Figure 3–5   Machine A sends data to machine B.

At B, the process is reversed. The headers that were created at A are used by the peer layers at B to determine that actions are to be taken. As the traffic is sent up the layers, the respective layer "removes" its header, performs defined actions, and passes the traffic on up to the next layer.

The user application at site B is presented only with user data—which was created by the sending user application at site A. These user applications are unaware (one hopes) of the many operations in each OSI layer that were invoked to support the end-user data transfer.

The headers created and used at peer layers are not to be altered by any non-peer layer. As a general rule, the headers from one layer are treated as transparent "data" by any other layer.

There are some necessary exceptions to this rule. As examples, data may be altered by a nonpeer layer for the purposes of compression, encryption, or other forms of syntax changing. This type of operation is permissible, as long as the data are restored to the required syntax when presented to the receiving peer layer.

As an exception to the exception, the presentation layer may alter the syntax of the data permanently when the receiving application layer has requested the data in a different syntax (such as ASCII code instead of a string of bits).

Encapsulation/Tunneling

Notwithstanding these exceptions, upper layer traffic and headers are usually sent transparently through a network. This operation is known as encapsulation or tunneling. Another illustration should clarify the matter: Figure 3–6 depicts the relationship of the layers from the standpoint of how data are exchanged between them. Three terms shown in Figure 3–6a are important to this discussion.

- *SDU (service data unit).* User data and control information created at the upper layers that are transferred transparently through a primitive by layer (N+1) to layer (N) and subsequently to (N–1). The SDU identity (and as we just learned, its syntax) is preserved from one end of an (N)-connection to the other.
- *PCI (protocol control information).* Information exchanged by peer (the same) entities at different sites on the network to instruct the peer entity to perform a service function. PCI is also called by the names headers and trailers (which are used in this book).
- *PDU (protocol data unit).* A combination of the SDU and PCI.

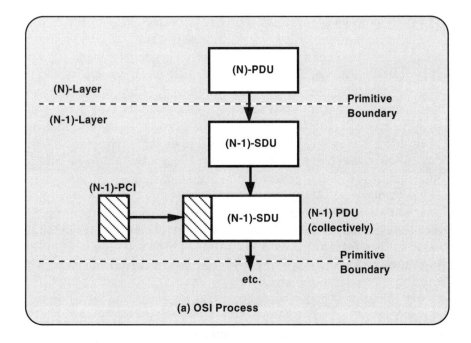

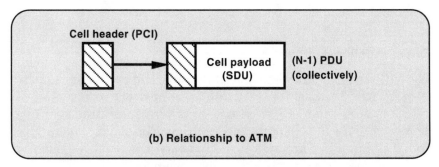

Figure 3–6   Relationship of ATM to the layered operations.

At the transmitting site, the PDU becomes larger as it passes (down) through each layer by adding that layer's header and/or trailer (the encapsulation or tunneling process). At the receiving site, the PDU becomes smaller as it passes (up) through each layer by stripping away that layer's header and/or trailer (the decasulation or detunneling process).

ATM AND THE MODEL

Figure 3–6b shows the relationship of ATM to OSI in regard to PCI, SDU, and PDU. ATM adds PCI to the cell payload. In OSI terms, the ATM cell header is PCI, and the cell payload is an SDU. Taken together, they form the PDU, which is called an ATM cell.

PROTOCOL ENTITIES

As stated earlier, we should not think that an OSI layer is represented by one large monolithic block of software code. While the model does not dictate how the layers are coded, it does establish the architecture whereby a layer's functions can be structured and partitioned into smaller and more manageable modules. These modules are called *entities.*

The idea of the model is for peer entities in peer layers to communicate with each other. Entities may be active or inactive. An entity can be software or hardware. Typically, entities are functions or subroutines in a program. A user is able to tailor the universal OSI services by invoking selected entities through the parameters in the primitives passed to the service provider, although vendors vary on how the entities are actually designed and invoked.

SERVICE ACCESS POINTS (SAPS)

Service access points (SAPs) are OSI addresses and identifiers. The OSI Model states: An (N+1)-entity requests (N)-services via an (N)-service access point (SAP), which permits the (N+1)-entity to interact with an (N)-entity.

Perhaps the best way to think of a SAP is that it is a software port (an identifier) that allows the two adjacent layers in the same machine to communicate with each other, as shown in Figure 3–7. SAPs may also be exchanged across machines in order to identify a process in the machine. In the OSI Model, the SAP can identify a protocol entity that resides in a layer. For example, a SAP value could be reserved for email, while a different SAP value could identify file server software. The reader may know about a UNIX socket—a concept similar to the OSI SAP.

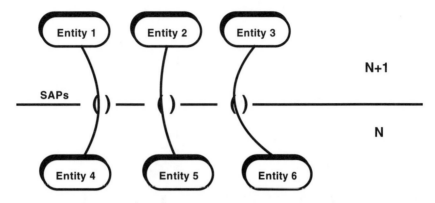

Figure 3–7   OSI service access points (SAPs).

ATM AND OSI LAYERS

Figure 3–8 introduces the ATM layers and compares them to the OSI layered concept. The ATM operations reside in the ATM layer and the ATM adaptation layer (AAL). This chapter explains these layers in a general way. Subsequent chapters provide more detail.

As the figure shows, traffic is passed physically down and up the layers through SAPs. The protocol control information (PCI) is exchanged horizontally between the peer layers of each machine. Starting at the top, the user layer contains the user application and other upper layer protocols. This layer also contains protocols for control signaling, such as network management and protocols to set up an ATM connection between the user and the ATM network.

The AAL is responsible for supporting the different applications in the upper layers. As such, it is quite diverse. Its operations depend upon the nature of the application that it is supporting. For example, it behaves differently when processing voice or data traffic. Among other activities, at the sending machine, it segments the user traffic into 48-byte SDUs and passes them to the ATM layer. At the receiving machine, it accepts 48-byte SDUs from the ATM layer and reassembles them into the original user traffic syntax. The AAL layer is difficult to match to the OSI Model; it has some features of layers 4, 5, and 7.

The ATM layer is responsible for processing the 5-byte cell header. At the sending machine, it adds this header to the 48-byte SDU passed from the AAL. At the receiving machine it processes this header, then passes the 48-byte SDU to the AAL. The ATM layer is also responsible

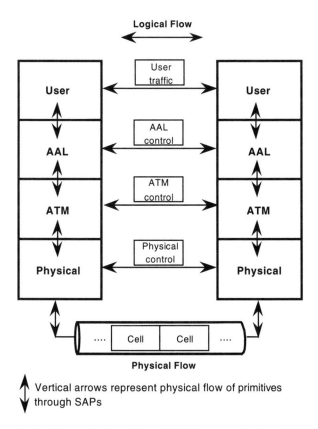

Figure 3–8   The relationship of ATM layers to the OSI Model.

for some flow control operations between machines and for processing the various fields in the cell header. The ATM layer is roughly akin to the OSI layers 2 and 3, with a considerable number of operations removed for the purposes of speed and simplicity.

The physical layer can be implemented with a number of interfaces and protocols. Strictly speaking, ATM does not require any one type of physical layer, although the ITU-T and the ATM Forum have published specifications for ATM running of fiber, twisted pair, and so on.

THE INTERNET PROTOCOLS (TCP/IP)

In the early 1970s, several groups around the world began to address the problem of network and application compatibility in data communications systems. At that time, the term "internetworking," which means the interconnecting of computers and/or networks, was coined. The concepts of internetworking were pioneered by the ITU-T, the ISO, and especially the original designers of the ARPAnet. (The term "ARPA" refers to the Advanced Research Projects Agency, which is a U.S. Department of Defense organization.)

Perhaps one of the most significant developments in these standardization efforts was ARPA's decision to implement the transmission control protocol (TCP) and the internet protocol (IP) around the UNIX operating system. Of equal importance, the University of California at Berkeley was selected to distribute the TCP/IP code. Because the TCP/IP code was nonproprietary, it spread rapidly among universities, private companies, and research centers. Indeed, it has become the *de facto* standard suite of data communications protocols.

In order to grasp the operations of TCP/IP, several terms and concepts must first be understood. The Internet uses the term *gateway* or *router* to describe a machine that performs relaying functions between networks, which are often called *subnetworks*. The term does not mean that they provide fewer functions than a conventional network. Rather, it means that the two networks consist of a full logical network with the subnetworks contributing to the overall operations for internetworking. Stated another way, the subnetworks comprise an *internetwork* or an *internet*.

An internetworking node is designed to remain transparent to the end-user application. Indeed, the end-user application resides in the host machines connected to the networks; rarely are user applications placed in the router node. This approach is attractive from several standpoints. First, the router need not burden itself with application layer protocols. Since they are not invoked at the router, the router can dedicate itself to fewer tasks, such as managing the traffic between networks. It is not concerned with application-level functions such as database access, electronic mail, and file management. Second, this approach allows the router to support any type of application, because the router considers the application message as nothing more than a transparent PDU. This concept is another example of encapsulation/tunneling.

In addition to application layer transparency, most designers attempt to keep the router transparent to the subnetworks and vice versa. That is to say, the router does not care what type of network is attached to it. The principal purpose of the router is to receive a message that contains adequate addressing information that enables the router to route the message to its final destination or to the next router. This feature is also attractive because it makes the router somewhat modular; it can be used on different types of networks.

The Internet Layers

Figure 3–9 shows the relationship of subnetworks and routers to layered protocols. In this figure it is assumed that the user application in host A sends an application PDU, such as a file transfer system, to an application layer protocol in host B. The file transfer software performs a variety of functions and appends a file transfer header to the user data. In many systems, the operations at host B are known as *server operations,* and the operations at host A are known as *client operations.*

As indicated with the arrows going down in the protocol stack at host A, this PDU is passed to the transport layer protocol, TCP. This layer performs a variety of operations and adds a header to the PDU passed to it. The PDU is now called a *segment.* The traffic from the upper layers is considered to be data to the transport layer.

Next, TCP passes the segment to the network layer, also called the IP layer, which again performs specific services and appends a header. This unit (now called a *datagram* in Internet terms) is passed down to the lower layers. Here, a data link layer (or its equivalent) adds its header as well as a trailer, and the data unit (now called a *frame*) is

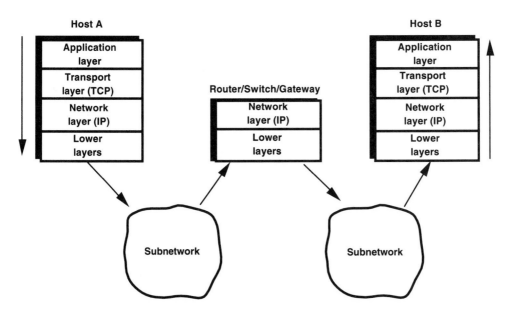

Note: The lower layers may be the traditional data link and physical layers, or the AAL, ATM, and physical layers (see Figure 3–8)

Figure 3–9   Internet layer operations.

launched into the network by the physical layer. Of course, if host B sends data to host A, the process is reversed and the direction of the arrows is changed.

The Internet protocols are unaware of what goes on inside the network. The network manager is free to manipulate and manage the datagram portion of the frame in any manner necessary. However, in most instances the datagram remains unchanged as it is transmitted through the subnet. The frame passes through the subnetwork until its arrival at a router, where it is processed through the lower layers and passed to the IP (network) layer (where it is again called a datagram). Here, routing decisions are made based on the addresses provided by the host computer.

After these routing decisions have been made, the datagram is passed to the communications link that is connected to the appropriate subnetwork (consisting of the lower layers). The datagram is re-encapsulated into the data link layer PDU (usually called a frame) and passed to the next subnetwork. As before, this unit is passed through the subnetwork transparently (usually), where it finally arrives at the host B.

Host B receives the traffic through its lower layers and reverses the process that transpired at host A. That is to say, it decapsulates the headers by stripping them off in the appropriate layer. Each specific header is used by the layer to determine the actions it is to take; the header governs the layer's operations.

IP Functions

IP is an example of a connectionless service. It permits the exchange of traffic between two host computers without any prior call setup. However, these two computers usually share a common connection-oriented transport protocol. Since IP is connectionless, it is possible that the datagrams could be lost between the two end users' stations. For example, an IP router enforces a maximum queue length size, and if this queue length is violated, the buffers will overflow. In this situation, the additional datagrams are discarded. For this reason, a higher level transport layer protocol (such as TCP) is essential to recover from these problems.

IP hides the underlying subnetwork from the end user. In this context, it creates a virtual network to that end user. This aspect of IP is quite attractive because it allows different types of networks to attach to an IP node. As a result, IP is reasonably simple to install and, because of its connectionless design, it is quite robust.

Since IP is a best effort datagram-type protocol, it has no reliability mechanisms. It provides no error recovery for the underlying subnetworks. It has no flow-control mechanisms. The user data may be lost, duplicated, or even arrive out of order. It is not the job of IP to deal with these problems. As we shall see later, most of the problems are passed to the next higher layer, TCP.

IP supports fragmentation operations. The term *fragmentation* refers to an operation where a PDU is divided or segmented into smaller units. This feature can be quite useful, because all networks do not use the same size PDU.

For example, X.25-based WANs typically employ a PDU (called a packet in X.25) with a data field of 128 octets. Some networks allow negotiations to a smaller or larger PDU size. The Ethernet standard limits the size of a PDU to 1500 octets.

Without the use of fragmentation, a gateway would be tasked with trying to resolve incompatible PDU sizes between networks. IP solves the problem by establishing the rules for fragmentation at the gateway and reassembly at the receiving host.

IP is designed to rest on top of the underlying subnetwork (such as an Ethernet LAN or an ATM network)—insofar as possible in a transparent manner. This means that IP assumes little about the characteristics of the underlying network or networks. As stated earlier, from the design standpoint this is quite attractive to engineers because it keeps the subnetworks relatively independent of IP.

As the reader might expect, the transparency is achieved by encapsulation. The data sent by the host computer are encapsulated into an IP datagram. The IP header identifies the address of the receiving host computer. The IP datagram and header are further encapsulated into the specific protocol of the transit network. For example, a transit network could be an X.25 network or Ethernet.

After the transit network has delivered the traffic to an IP node, its control information is stripped away. The node then uses the destination address in the datagram header to determine where to route the traffic. Typically, it then passes the datagram to a subnetwork by invoking a subnetwork access protocol (for example, Ethernet on a LAN, or X.25 on a WAN). This protocol is used to encapsulate the datagram header and user data into the headers and trailers used by the subnetwork. This process is repeated at each router, and eventually the datagram arrives at the final destination, where it is delivered to the receiving station.

IP Addresses. TCP/IP networks use a 32-bit address to identify a host computer and the network to which the host is attached. The structure of the IP address is:

IP Address = Network Address + Host Address

IP addresses are classified by their formats (Figure 3–10). Four formats are permitted: class A, class B, class C, or class D. The first bits of the address specify the format of the remainder of the address field in relation to the network and host subfields. The host address is also called the local address (also called the host field).

Class A addresses provide for networks that have a large number of hosts. The host ID field (local address) is 24 bits. Therefore, 2^{24} hosts can be identified. Seven bits are devoted to the network ID, which supports an identification scheme for as many as 127 networks (bit values of 1 to 127).

Class B addresses are used for networks of intermediate size. Fourteen bits are assigned for the network ID, and 16 bits are assigned for the host ID. Class C networks contain fewer than 256 hosts (2^8). Twenty-one bits are assigned to the network ID. Finally, class D addresses are reserved for multicasting, which is a form of broadcasting but within a limited area.

Classless Addresses.   The use of class-based addresses has created problems in the Internet. In a nutshell, they are too restrictive. This subject is beyond the scope of this book. I refer you to a companion book in this series, *Advanced Internet Technologies.*

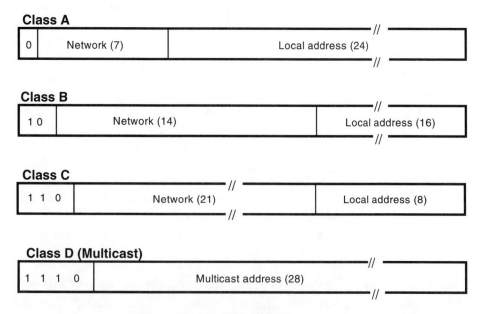

Figure 3–10   IP address formats.

TCP Operations

IP is not designed to recover from certain problems, nor does it guarantee the delivery of traffic. IP is designed to discard datagrams that are in error or have exceeded the number of permissible transit hops in an internet.

However, certain user applications require assurance that all traffic has been delivered safely to the destination. Furthermore, the transmitting user may need to know that the traffic has been delivered at the receiving host. The mechanisms to achieve these important services reside in TCP. The job of TCP may be quite complex. It must be able to satisfy a wide range of applications requirements, and equally important, it must be able to accommodate to a dynamic environment within an internet.

TCP establishes and manages sessions between its local users and these users' remote communicating partners. This means that TCP must maintain an awareness of the users' activities in order to support the users' data transfer through the Internet.

TCP resides in the transport layer of the conventional seven-layer model. It is situated above IP and below the upper layers. Figure 3–9 also illustrates that TCP is not invoked at the router for the support of end user traffic. It is designed to reside in the host computer or in a machine that is tasked with end-to-end integrity of the transfer of user data. In practice, TCP is usually placed in the user host machine.[1]

TCP is designed to run over the IP. Since IP is a connectionless protocol with very few functions, the tasks of reliability, flow control, sequencing, and application session management are given to TCP. Although TCP and IP are tied together so closely that they are used in the same context (TCP/IP), TCP can also support other network layer protocols.

Many of the TCP functions (such as flow control, reliability, and sequencing) could be handled within an application program. But it makes little sense to code these functions into each application. Moreover, applications programmers are usually not versed in error-detection and flow control operations. The preferred approach is to develop generalized software that provides community functions suitable for a wide range of applications and then invoke these programs from the application software. This allows the application programmer to concentrate on solving application problems, and it isolates the programmer from the nuances and problems of network operations.

---

[1]In certain situations, TCP is invoked at the router to support the transfer of user traffic. But these situations are the exceptions and not the general rule.

TCP is a connection-oriented protocol. TCP maintains status information about each user data stream flowing into and out of the TCP module. TCP is responsible for the reliable transfer of each of the octets passed to it from an upper layer. A sequence number is assigned to each byte transmitted. The receiving TCP module uses a checksum routine to check the data for damage that may have occurred during the transmission process. If the data are acceptable, TCP returns a positive acknowledgment (ACK) to the sending TCP module. TCP also checks for duplicate data. In the event the sending TCP transmits duplicate data, the receiving TCP discards the redundant data.

TCP uses an inclusive acknowledgment scheme, which means the acknowledgment number acknowledges all bytes up to and including the acknowledgment number less one. The receiver's TCP module is also able to flow control the sender's data, which is a very useful tool to prevent buffer overrun and a possible saturation of the receiving machine.

TCP provides a graceful close to a connection between the two users. A graceful close ensures that all traffic has been acknowledged before the connection is removed.

TCP Ports.   A TCP upper layer user in a host machine is identified by a port identifier. The port identifier is concatenated with the IP address to form a socket. This address must be unique throughout the Internet and a pair of sockets uniquely identifies each endpoint connection. As examples:

Sending socket = Source IP address + source port number

Receiving socket = Destination IP address + destination port number

Although the mapping of ports to higher layer processes can be handled as an internal matter in a host, the Internet publishes numbers for frequently used applications such as email and file transfer routines.

THE OSI NETWORK AND TRANSPORT LAYER

OSI includes protocols at the network and transport layer that perform functions similar to TCP and IP. They have not yet seen extensive use in the industry, but their use is growing.

The OSI connectionless network protocol (CLNP) is quite similar to IP. Indeed, it was derived from IP. The OSI Transport Layer Protocol, class 4 (TP4) performs functions similar to TCP, but is considerably more powerful and complex. Since the basic functions of the OSI and Internet layers 3 and 4 are about the same, I shall not expend any more time on these systems.

SUMMARY

The OSI Model uses the concepts of layered protocols. Key aspects of the model are service definitions for vertical communications and protocol specifications for horizontal communications. OSI is organized around the concepts of encapsulation and decapsulation (tunneling and detunneling), while service access points (SAPs) form the basis for OSI "ports." B-ISDN, ATM, and SONET make extensive use of the OSI Model.

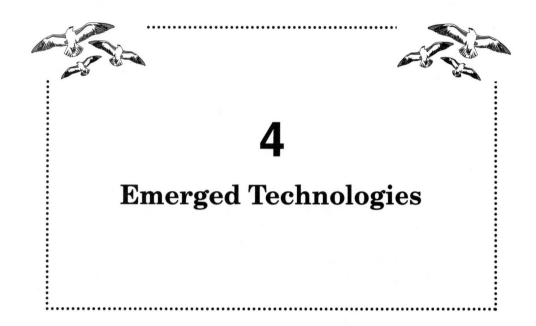

4

Emerged Technologies

This chapter provides an overview of the communications technologies that have been in use in the industry for the past two to three decades, thus the term, emerged technologies. These technologies are covered:

- T1 and E1 carrier systems
- X.25
- Integrated Services Digital Network (ISDN)
- Signaling System Number 7 (SS7)

COMPARISON OF SWITCHING SYSTEMS

Figure 4–1 summarizes the progress made in switching technologies since the 1960s. The methods of switching are compared in terms of relay technology, typical media employed with the switch, the size of the PDU (packet, message, etc.), and the delay encountered with the switching operation.

The relay techniques for earlier switching systems used a direct connection between the input and output lines, such as a crossbar switch. Later systems used buffering techniques to store the traffic on disk (a

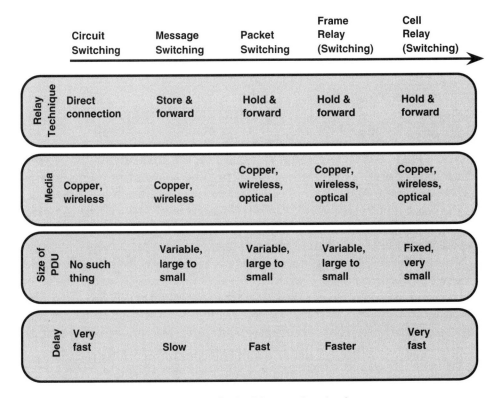

	Circuit Switching	Message Switching	Packet Switching	Frame Relay (Switching)	Cell Relay (Switching)
Relay Technique	Direct connection	Store & forward	Hold & forward	Hold & forward	Hold & forward
Media	Copper, wireless	Copper, wireless	Copper, wireless, optical	Copper, wireless, optical	Copper, wireless, optical
Size of PDU	No such thing	Variable, large to small	Variable, large to small	Variable, large to small	Fixed, very small
Delay	Very fast	Slow	Fast	Faster	Very fast

Figure 4–1   Switching technologies.

store-and-forward technology), while newer systems hold the traffic directly in memory, which is called a *hold-and-forward technology.*

Earlier switching systems used copper as the media for the input and output ports of the switch. With the advent of the optical fiber technology, high-capacity systems make use of optical fiber for the transmission media.

The size of the PDU has varied from nonexistent, in technologies such as circuit switching, to systems that employ a variable length PDU—ranging from a few octets to several thousand octets. Cell relay takes a different approach by using fixed small PDUs to increase the efficiency of the operations at the switch.

Finally, older systems, with the exception of circuit switching, were somewhat slow in the delay encountered at the switch due to the processing of very large data units and to the cumbersome nature of how the CPU operated and how the software was written. These emerged technologies are being replaced by very fast switches with efficient software (and with many of the switching elements residing in silicon).

THE T1/E1 SYSTEMS

Purpose of T1 and E1

The T1/E1 systems are high-capacity networks designed for the digital transmission of voice, video, and data. The original implementations of T1/E1 digitized voice signals to take advantage of the superior aspects of digital technology. Shortly after the inception of T1 in North America, the ITU-T published the E1 standards, which were implemented in Europe. E1 is similar to (but not compatible with) T1.

The earlier T1/E1 systems used asynchronous techniques; devices in the network did not operate with common clocks, and therefore were not synchronized closely together (more on this subject later). Today these components operate within a specified error tolerance range, and so are more accurately called plesiochronous networks. In most parts of the world, the present system is called the plesiochronous digital hierarchy, or PDH.

T1 is based on multiplexing 24 users onto one physical TDM circuit. T1 operates at 1,544,000 bit/s, which was (in the 1960s) about the highest rate that could be supported across twisted-wire pair for a distance of approximately one mile. Interestingly, the distance of one mile (actually about 6000 feet) represented the spacing between manholes in large cities. They were so spaced to permit maintenance work such as splicing cables and the placing of amplifiers. This physical layout provided a convenient means to replace the analog amplifiers with digital repeaters.

The term T1 was devised by the U.S. telephone industry to describe a specific type of carrier equipment. Today, it is used to describe a general carrier system, a data rate, and various multiplexing and framing conventions. A more concise term is DS1, which describes a multiplexed digital signal carried by the T carrier. To keep matters simple, this book uses the term T1 synonymously with the term DS1, and the term T3 synonymously with DS3. Just be aware that the T designator stipulates the carrier system, but the digital transmission hierarchy schemes are designated as DS-n, where n represents a multiplexing level and framing convention of DS1. Table 4–1 lists the more common digital multiplexing schemes used in Europe, North America, and Japan.

Today, the majority of T1/E1 offerings digitize the voice signal through pulse code modulation (PCM) or adaptive differential pulse code

Table 4–1 Carrier Systems Multiplexing Hierarchy

North America	Japan	Europe
64 kbit/s	64 kbit/s	64 kbit/s
1.544 Mbit/s 24 voice channels	1.544 Mbit/s 24 voice channels	2.048 Mbit/s 30 voice channels
6.312 Mbit/s 96 voice channels	6.312 Mbit/s 96 voice channels	8.448 Mbit/s 120 voice channels
44.736 Mbit/s 672 voice channels	32.064 Mbit/s 480 voice channels	34.368 Mbit/s 480 voice channel
274.176 Mbit/s 4032 voice channels	97.728 Mbit/s 1440 voice channels	139.264 Mbit/s 1920 voice channels

modulation (ADPCM). Whatever the encoding technique, once the analog images are translated to digital bit streams, then many T1 systems are able to time division multiplex voice and data together in 24 user slots within each frame.

Typical Topology

Figure 4–2 shows a T1 topology (the same type of topology is permitted with the E1 technology). Actually, there is no typical topology for these systems. Examples can range from a simple point-to-point topology shown here, where two T1 multiplexers operate on one 1.544 Mbit/s link, to those that can employ digital cross connect systems (DCS) that add, drop, and/or switch payload as necessary across multiple links.

Voice, data, and video images can use one digital "pipe." Data transmissions are terminated through a statistical time division multiplexer (STDM), which then uses the TDM to groom the traffic across the transmission line through a T1 channel service unit (CSU), or other equipment, such as a data service unit (DSU). A DSU and a CSU may be combined as well. The purpose of the CSU is to convert signals at the user device to signals acceptable to the digital line and, vice versa, at the receiver. The CSU performs clocking and signal regeneration on the channels. It also performs functions such as line conditioning (equalization), which keeps the signal's performance consistent across the channel bandwidth; signal reshaping, which reconstitutes the binary pulse stream; and loop-back testing, which entails the transmission of test signals between the DSU and the network carrier's equipment.

The bandwidth of a line can be divided into various T1 subrates. For example, a video system could utilize a 768 kbit/s band, the STDM in

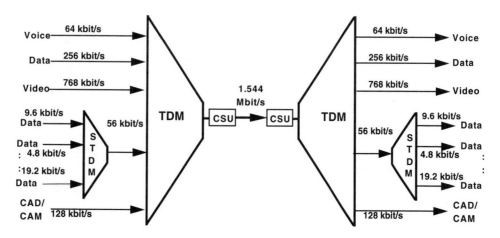

Figure 4–2   A typical T1 topology.

turn could multiplex various data rates up to a 56 kbit/s rate, and per-haps a CAD/CAM operation could utilize 128 kbit/s of the bandwidth.

T1 and E1 Layers

In relation to the OSI model, the T1 and E1 layers reside in only one layer—the physical layer (Figure 4–3). This layer defines the connectors, signaling conventions, framing formats, and the like that are found in most physical layers.

T1/E1 PDUs

The T1 frame (or the OSI term, PDU) consists of 24 8-bit slots and a framing bit (Figure 4–4). To decode the incoming data stream, a receiver must be able to associate each sample with the proper TDM channel. At a minimum, the beginning and ending of the frame must be recognized. The function of the framing bit is to provide this delineation. The fram-ing bit is in the 193rd bit of each frame. It is not part of the user's infor-

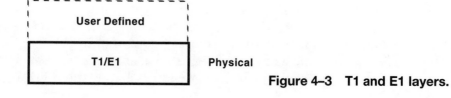

Figure 4–3   T1 and E1 layers.

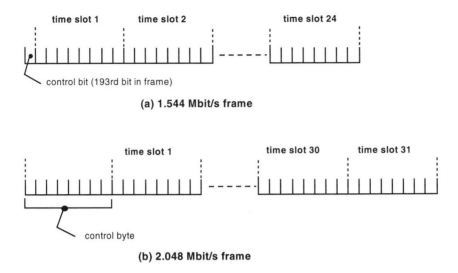

(a) 1.544 Mbit/s frame

(b) 2.048 Mbit/s frame

Figure 4–4   T1 and E1 frames.

mation, but added by the system for framing. The use of this bit varies, depending on the type of the T1 system and the age of the technology.

Some T1 channel banks use the eighth bit in every 8-bit slot for control signaling. Examples of control signaling are off-hook, on-hook, ringing, busy signals, and battery reversal. During the development of the later T1 equipment, the designers recognized that every eighth bit was not needed for signaling. Consequently, later equipment, known as D2 channel banks, uses the eighth bit of every sixth and twelfth frame to provide signaling information. The least significant bit in these frames is overwritten with a signaling bit. This concept is called *bit robbing,* and the respective sixth and twelfth robbed frame bits are called the A and B bits.

For the transmission of data, the eighth bit is unreliable, so most vendors have chosen to ignore this bit for data signaling. As a result, the majority of T1 and related systems use a 56 kbit/s transmission rate (8000 slots/second * 7 bits per slot = 56000) instead of the 64 kbit/s rate (8000 slots/second * 8 bits per slot = 64000).

The rate for the 2.048 Mbit rate is similar to its counterpart T1 in that they both use a 125 µs time frame (Figure 4–4). However, the E1 frame is divided into 31 TDM slots and preceded by an 8-bit time slot that is used for control purposes. E1 reserves this slot in the frame for its *out-of-band signaling,* and thereby obviates the cumbersome bit robbing scheme found in T1. Robbing is not a good idea—nor is bit robbing—and therefore, the emerging technologies discussed in this book (with some minor exceptions like T1) use out-of-band signaling instead. That is to say, bandwidth is reserved for control signaling rather than robbing bits to perform the function.

Conclusions on T1/E1

The T1/E1 systems have served the industry well. However, they are quite limited in their management operations and they provide very little support for end-user control for the provisioning of services. In the old days, the use of bandwidth (control headers) for network management was not encouraged due to the limited transmission capacity of the facilities to accommodate this overhead traffic. Today, the prevailing idea is to exploit the high capacity of optical fibers and the processors and to allocate a greater amount of bandwidth (larger control headers) to support more network management services.

These older technologies also use awkward multiplexing schemes. Due to their history of using an asynchronous timing structure, timing differences between machines are accommodated by stuffing extra bits (bit stuffing) periodically in the traffic streams. These bits cannot be un-stuffed when the traffic is demultiplexed from the higher rates (see Table 4–1) to the lower rates. Indeed, the traffic must be completely demultiplexed at the multiplexers and/or switches to make the payload accessible for further processing.

One should be careful about criticizing a technology that was conceived and implemented over thirty-five years ago. In retrospect, T1 and E1 were significant steps forward in the progress of the telecommunications industry. But like most everything else in this industry (thankfully, not life), things do not improve with age and must be replaced. As we shall see, SONET/SDH are those replacements. But, T1/E1 will be with us for a long time.

X.25

Purpose of X.25

X.25 was designed to perform a function similar to that of the ISDN (discussed later): to provide for an interface between an end-user device and a network (known as a user-network interface, or UNI). However, for X.25, the end-user device is a data terminal and the network is a packet-switched data network; for ISDN, the end-user device was (originally) a voice terminal (telephone) and the network was (originally) a circuit-switched voice network. The comparison is apt, because both protocols have similar architectures, as will be explained in this section.

The idea of the X.25 interface, as conceived by the ITU-T study groups in the early 1970s, was to define unambiguous rules about how a public packet data network would handle a user's payload and accommodate to various QOS features (called X.25 facilities) that were requested by the user. X.25 was also designed to provide strict flow control on user payloads and to provide substantial management services for the user payload, such as the sequencing and acknowledgment of traffic.

The ITU-T issued the X.25 Recommendation in 1974. It was revised in 1976, 1978, 1980, 1984, 1988, and the last revision was made in 1992. Since 1974, the standard has been expanded to include many options, services, and facilities, and several of the newer OSI protocols and service definitions operate with X.25. X.25 is a popular interface standard for wide area packet networks. Unlike, T1/E1, X.25 uses STDM techniques and is designed as a transport system for data—not voice.

Typical Topology

The placement of X.25 in packet networks is widely misunderstood. X.25 is not a packet switching specification. It is a packet network interface specification (Figure 4–5). X.25 says nothing about operations within the network. Hence, from the perspective of X.25, the internal network operations are not known. For example, X.25 is not aware if the network uses adaptive or fixed directory routing, or if the internal operations of the network are connection-oriented or connectionless. The reader may have heard of the term "network cloud." Its origin is derived from these concepts.

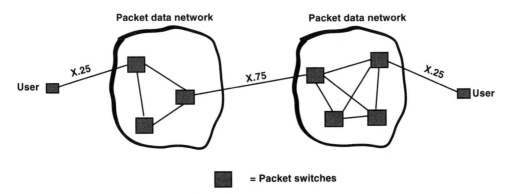

Figure 4–5   Typical X.25 topology.

It is obvious from an examination of Figure 4–5 that X.25 is classified as a user network interface (UNI). It defines the procedures for the exchange of data between a user device (DTE) and the network (DCE). Its formal title is "Interface between Data Terminal Equipment and Data Circuit Terminating Equipment for Terminals Operating in the Packet Node on Public Data Networks." In X.25, the DCE is the "agent" for the packet network to the DTE.

X.25 establishes the procedures for two packet-mode DTEs to communicate with each other through a network. It defines the two DTE sessions with their respective DCEs. The idea of X.25 is to provide common procedures between a user station and a packet network (DCE) for establishing a session and exchanging data. The procedures include functions such as identifying the packets of specific user terminals or computers, acknowledging packets, rejecting packets, initiating error recovery, flow control, and other services. X.25 also provides for a number of QOS functions, such as reverse charge, call redirect, and transit delay selection, which are called X.25 facilities.

X.75 is a complementary protocol to X.25. X.75 is a internetworking interface (a network-to-network interface, or NNI), although it is used often today for other configurations such as amplifying and enhancing an interface on ISDN systems to support X.25-based applications, and even satellite systems.

X.25 Layers

The X.25 Recommendation encompasses the lower three layers of the OSI model. Like ISDN, the lower two layers exist to support the third layer. Figure 4–6 shows the relationships of the X.25 layers. The physical layer (first layer) is the physical interface between the DTE and DCE, and is either a V-Series, X.21, or X.21 bis interface. Of course, X.25 networks can operate with other physical layer interfaces (as examples, V.35, the EIA 422 standard from the Electronic Industries Association, and even high-speed 2.048 Mbit/s interfaces). X.25 assumes the data link layer (second layer) to be Link Access Procedure, Balanced (LAPB). The LAPB protocol is a subset of HDLC (High Level Data Link Control).

X.25 PDUs

The X.25 packet is carried within the LAPB frame as the I (information) field (Figure 4–7). LAPB ensures that the X.25 packets are transmitted correctly across the link, after which the frame fields are discarded (stripped), and the packet is presented to the network layer. The

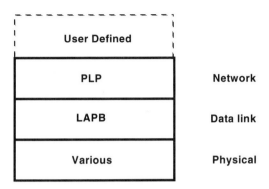

Various: V Series, X.21, X.21*bis,* etc.

LAPB: Link access procedure, balanced

Figure 4–6   The X.25 layers.   PLP: Packet layer procedures

principal function of the link layer is to deliver the packet error-free despite the error-prone nature of the communications link. In this regard, it is quite similar to LAPD in ISDN. In X.25, a packet is created at the network layer and inserted into a frame that is created at the data link layer.

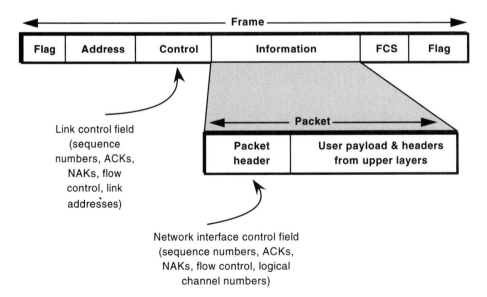

Figure 4–7   X.25 PDUs (packet and frame).

The network layer, also called packet layer procedures or PLP, is responsible for establishing, managing, and tearing down the connections between the user and the network.

Figure 4–7 illustrates that sequence numbers, ACKs, NAKs, and flow control techniques are implemented in two different fields residing in the X.25 PDU. First, the control field in the link header is used at layer 2 (LAPB) to control operations on the link between the user device and network node. Second, the packet header is used at layer 3 (PLP) and contains sequence numbers, ACKs, and so on to control each user session running on the link between the user device and network node. As we shall see in this book, some of the emerging technologies take the stand that these operations are either redundant or unnecessary, and so they are either eliminated or decreased substantially.

Other Noteworthy Aspects of X.25

X.25 uses logical channel numbers (LCNs) to identify the DTE connections to the network. An LCN is really nothing more than a virtual circuit identifier (VCI). As many as 4095 logical channels (i.e., user sessions) can be assigned to a physical channel. In practice, however, not all numbers are assigned at one time because of performance considerations. The LCN serves as an identifier (a label) for each user's packets that are transmitted through the physical circuit to and from the network. Typically, the virtual circuit is identified with two different LCNs—one for the user at the local side of the network and one for the user at the remote side of the network.

X.25 defines quite specifically how local-logical channels are established, but it allows the network administration considerable leeway in how the end-to-end virtual circuit is created. Notwithstanding, the network administration must "map" the two LCNs together from each end of the virtual circuit through the network so they can communicate with each other. How this is accomplished is left to the network administration, but it must be done if X.25 is to be used as specified.

The concept of labels, fostered by X.25, is also used by ATM. The reader might make a mental note to return to this section of the book when the subject of ATM labels is discussed.

X.25 Interface Options. X.25 provides two mechanisms to establish and maintain communications between the user devices and the network (and ATM has borrowed these concepts): permanent virtual circuit (PVC) and switched virtual call (SVC).

A sending PVC user is assured of obtaining a connection to the receiving user and of obtaining the required services of the network to support the user-to-user session. X.25 requires that a PVC be established before a session can begin. Consequently, an agreement must be reached by the two users and the network administration before the PVC is allocated. Among other things, agreement must be made about the reservation of LCNs for the PVC session and the establishment of facilities.

A SVC requires that the originating user device must transmit a Call Request packet to the network to start the connection operation. In turn, the network node relays this packet to the remote network node, which sends an Incoming Call packet to the called user device. If this receiving DTE chooses to acknowledge and accept the call, it transmits to the network a Call Accepted packet. The network then transports this packet to the requesting DTE in the form of a Call Connected packet. To terminate the session, a Clear Request packet is sent by either DTE. It is received as a Clear Indication packet, and confirmed by the Clear Confirm packet.

Conclusions on X.25

One could surmise that any data communications technology developed during the 1970s cannot be appropriate to fulfill the requirements of modern applications. Additionally, a substantial segment of the telecommunications industry believes that X.25 is ineffective as an UNI, because of its "overly connection-oriented nature."

It should be remembered that X.25 is old. It was designed to support user traffic on error-prone networks, with the supposition that most user devices were relatively unintelligent. Moreover, X.25 was designed to operate on physical interfaces that are also old (and therefore inherently slow), such as EIA-232-E and V.28.

Nonetheless, X.25 usage continues throughout the world because (1) it is well understood, (2) it is available in off-the-shelf products, (3) extensive conformance tests are available for the product, and (4) it is a cost-effective service for bursty, slow-speed applications, of which there are many.

If one cares for one's data and wishes to maintain some type of control over it, then there must be a connection-oriented data management protocol residing somewhere in the protocol suite—but it need not exist at the network layer. This idea is central to the behavior of ATM. Yes, one needs to take care of the user's data (payload), but the network is not the place to do it. It is more appropriate for the user computer to perform this function. Later chapters will examine the rationale for this premise.

INTEGRATED SERVICES DIGITAL NETWORK (ISDN)

Purpose of ISDN

The initial purpose of the Integrated Services Digital Network (ISDN) was to provide a digital UNI between a user and a network node for the transport of digitized voice and (later) data images. It is now designed to support a wide range of services. In essence, all images (voice, data, television, facsimile, etc.), can be transmitted with ISDN technology.

ISDN has been implemented as an evolutionary technology, and the committees, common carriers, and trade associations who developed the standards wisely recognized that ISDN had to be developed from the long-existing telephone-based integrated digital network (IDN). Consequently, many of the digital techniques developed for T1 and E1 are used in ISDN. This includes signaling rates (32 or 64 kbit/s), transmission codes (bipolar), and even physical plugs (the jacks to the telephone). Thus, the foundations for ISDN have been in development since the mid-1970s.

Typical Topology

The user interface to ISDN is similar to that of X.25. An end-user device connects to an ISDN node through a UNI protocol. Of course, the ISDN and X.25 interfaces are used for two different functions. The X.25 UNI provides a connection to a packet-switched data network, while ISDN provides a connection to an ISDN node (principally for voice), which can then connect to a voice (and perhaps a video or data) network.

Before we begin an analysis of ISDN, two terms must be defined: functional groupings and reference points. *Functional groupings* are sets of capabilities needed in an ISDN user-access interface. Specific functions within a functional grouping may be performed by multiple pieces of equipment or software. *Reference points* are the interfaces dividing the functional groupings. Usually, a reference point corresponds to a physical interface between pieces of equipment. With these thoughts in mind, please examine Figure 4–8, which shows several possibilities for setting up the ISDN components at the SNI (others are permitted).

The reference points labeled R, S, T, and U are logical interfaces between the functional groupings, which can be either a terminal type 1 (TE1), a terminal type 2 (TE2), or a network termination (NT1, NT2) grouping. The purpose of the reference points is to delineate where the responsibility of the network operator ends. If the network operator re-

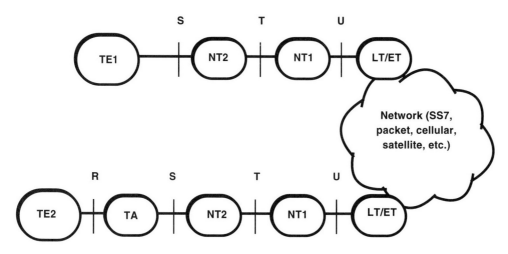

Figure 4–8   Typical ISDN topology.

sponsibility ends at reference point S, the operator is responsible for NT1, NT2, and LT/ET.

The U reference point is the reference point for the 2-wire side of the NT1 equipment. It separates a NT1 from the line termination (LT) equipment. The U interface is a national standard, while interfaces implemented at reference points S and T are international standards. The R reference point represents non-ISDN interfaces, such as EIA-232-D and V.35.

The end-user ISDN terminal is identified by the ISDN term TE1. The TE1 connects to the ISDN through a twisted-pair 4-wire digital link. Figure 4–8 illustrates other ISDN options—one is a user station called a TE2 device, which represents the current equipment in use, such as IBM 3270 terminals, Hewlett-Packard and Sun workstations, and telex devices.

The TE2 connects to a terminal adapter (TA), which is a device that allows non-ISDN terminals to operate over ISDN lines. The user side of the TA typically uses a conventional physical layer interface, such as EIA-232-D or the V-series specifications, and it is not aware that it is connected into an ISDN-based interface. The TA is responsible for the communications between the non-ISDN operations and the ISDN operations.

The TA and TE2 devices are connected to either an ISDN NT1 or NT2 device. The NT1 is a device that connects the 4-wire subscriber wiring to the conventional 2-wire local loop. ISDN allows up to eight terminal devices to be addressed by NT1. The NT1 is responsible for the physical layer functions, such as signaling synchronization and timing. NT1 provides a user with a standardized interface.

The NT2 is a more intelligent piece of equipment. It is typically found in a digital PBX and contains the layer 2 and 3 protocol functions. The NT2 device is capable of performing concentration services in that it multiplexes 23 B+D channels onto the line at a combined rate of 1.544 Mbit/s or 31 B+D channels at a combined rate of 2.048 Mbit/s. The NT1 and NT2 devices may be combined into a single device called NT12. This device handles the physical, data link, and network layer functions. In summary, the TE equipment is responsible for user communications and the NT equipment is responsible for network communications.

As illustrated in Figure 4–9, the TE1 connects to the ISDN through a twisted-pair 4-wire digital link. This link uses TDM to provide three channels, designated as the B, B, and D channels (or 2 B+D). The B channels operate at a speed of 64 kbit/s; the D channel operates at 16 kbit/s. The 2 B+D is designated as the basic rate interface (BRI). ISDN also allows up to eight TE1s to share one 2 B+D link. The purpose of the B channels is to carry the user payload in the form of voice, compressed video, and data. The purpose of the D channel is to act as an out-of-band control channel for setting up, managing, and clearing the B channel sessions.

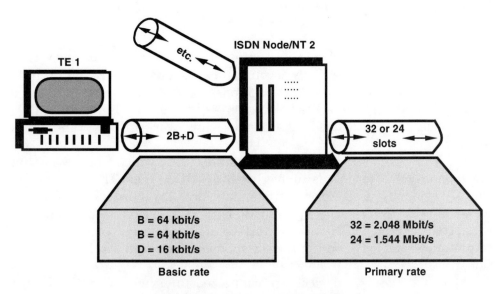

Figure 4–9   ISDN configuration.

In other scenarios, the user DTE is called a TE2 device. As explained earlier, the TE2 device is the current equipment in use, such as IBM 3270 terminals and telex devices. The TE2 connects to a TA, which is a device that allows non-ISDN terminals to operate over ISDN lines. The user side of the TA typically uses a conventional physical layer interface, such as EIA-232-D or the V-series specifications. It is packaged like an external modem or as a board that plugs into an expansion slot on the TE2 devices.

As explained earlier, ISDN supports yet another type of interface called the primary rate interface (PRI). It consists of the multiplexing of multiple B and D channels onto a higher speed interface of either 1.544 Mbit/s (used in North America and Japan) or 2.048 Mbit/s (used in Europe). The 1.544 Mbit/s interface is designated as 23 B+D, and the 2.048 Mbit/s interface is designated as 31 B+D to describe how many B and D channels are carried in the PRI frame.

ISDN Layers

The ISDN approach is to provide an end-user with full support through the seven layers of the OSI model, although ISDN confines itself to defining the operations at layers 1, 2, and 3 of this model. In so doing, ISDN is divided into two kinds of services: the bearer services, responsible for providing support for the lower three layers of the seven-layer standard; and teleservices (e.g., telephone, Teletex, Videotex message handling), responsible for providing support through all seven layers of the model and generally making use of the underlying lower-layer capabilities of the bearer services. The services are referred to as low-layer and high-layer functions, respectively. The ISDN functions are allocated according to the layering principles of the OSI model.

Figure 4–10 shows the ISDN layers. Layer 1 (the physical layer) uses either the basic rate interface (BRI) or 2 primary rate interface (PRI), which is either 23 B+D or 31 B+D. These standards are published in ITU-T's I Series as I.430 and I.431, respectively. Layer 2 (the data link layer) consists of LAPD and is published in the ITU-T Recommendation Q.921. Layer 3 (the network layer) is defined in the ITU-T Recommendation Q.931.

The reader might wish to compare Figure 4–10 with the X.25 layer structure in Figure 4–6. The basic architectures are quite similar in that the data link layer is responsible for the conveyance of the layer 3 (network layer) traffic across the SNI, and the network layer is responsible for establishing and releasing connections. However, with X.25, the net-

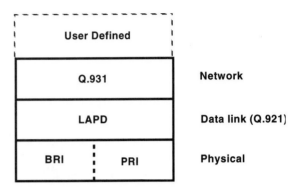

BRI: Basic rate interface (I.430)

PRI: Primary rate interface (I.431)

Figure 4–10   The ISDN layers.   LAPD: Link access procedure for D channel

work layer sessions are virtual circuits used for the transmission and reception of data; with ISDN, the circuits are B channels used for the conveyance of (initially) voice and other types of traffic.

ISDN PDUs

This section provides a more detailed view of the ISDN PDUs than
previous discussions on the PDUs of the other technologies, because the
ISDN layer 3 messages are used (with some modifications) in several of
the emerging communications technologies (i.e., Frame Relay and ATM).

Data link layer frame (LAPD).   The ISDN provides a data link protocol for devices to communicate with each other across the D channel.
This protocol is LAPD, which is a subset of HDLC. The protocol is independent of a transmission bit rate, and it requires a full duplex, bit
transparent, synchronous channel. Figure 4–11 depicts the LAPD frame
and its relationship to the ISDN layer 3, Q.931 specification. The Q.931
message is carried within the LAPD frame in the I (information) field.
LAPD ensures that the Q.931 messages are transmitted across the link,
after which the frame fields are stripped, and the message is presented
to the network layer. The principal function of the link layer is to deliver
the Q.931 message error-free, despite the error-prone nature of the communications link. In this regard, it is quite similar to LAPB in X.25.

LAPD has a frame format similar to HDLC, but LAPD provides for
octets for the address field. This is necessary for multiplexing multiple
sessions and user stations onto the BRI channel. The address field con-

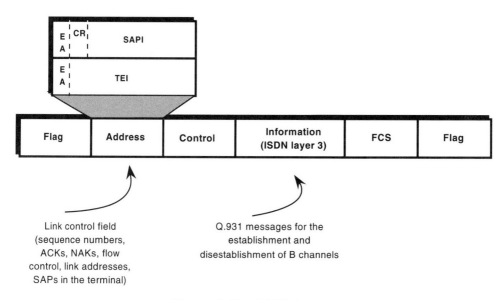

Figure 4–11   LAPD frame.

tains several control bits (which are not relevant to this discussion), a service access point identifier (SAPI), and a terminal endpoint identifier (TEI). The SAPI and TEI fields are known collectively as the data link control identifier (DLCI). These entities are discussed in the following paragraphs.

The SAPI identifies the entity where the data link layer services are provided to the layer above (that is, layer 3). At the present time, these SAPIs are defined in ISDN:

SAPI Value	Frame Carries
0	signaling information
16	user traffic
63	management information

The TEI identifies either a single terminal (TE) or multiple terminals that are operating on the BRI link. The TEI is assigned automatically by a separate assignment procedure. A TEI value of all 1s identifies a broadcast connection.

ISDN layer 3: Q.931.   The ISDN layer 3 messages are used to manage ISDN connections on the B channels. These messages are also used

(with modifications) by Frame Relay and ATM for setting up calls on demand at a UNI and for provisioning services between networks at a NNI.
Table 4–2 lists these messages, and a short explanation is provided later
in this section about the functions of the more significant messages.

The Q.931 messages all use a similar format. Figure 4–12 illustrates
this format. The message contains several parameters to define the circuit connection. It must contain these three parameters:

- *Protocol discriminator:* Distinguishes between user-network call
  control messages and others, such as other layer 3 protocols (X.25,
  for example).
- *Call reference:* Identifies the specific ISDN call at the local UNI. It
  does not have end-to-end significance.

Table 4–2   ISDN Layer 3 Messages

Call Establishment Messages	Call Disestablishment Messages
ALERTING	DETACH
CALL PROCEEDING	DETACH ACKNOWLEDGE
CONNECT	DISCONNECT
CONNECT ACKNOWLEDGE	RELEASE
SETUP	RELEASE COMPLETE
SETUP ACKNOWLEDGE	

Call Information Phase Messages	Miscellaneous Messages
RESUME	CANCEL
RESUME ACKNOWLEDGE	CANCEL ACKNOWLEDGE
RESUME REJECT	CANCEL REJECT
SUSPEND	CONGESTION CONTROL
SUSPEND ACKNOWLEDGE	FACILITY
SUSPEND REJECT	FACILITY ACKNOWLEDGE
USER INFORMATION	FACILITY REJECT
	INFORMATION
	REGISTER
	REGISTER ACKNOWLEDGE
	REGISTER REJECT
	STATUS
	STATUS ENQUIRY

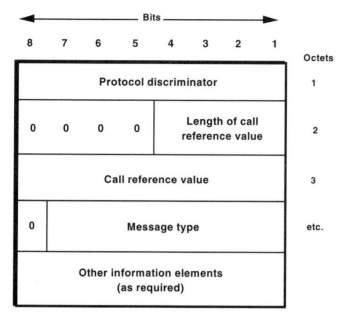

Figure 4–12 The Q.931 message.

- *Message type:* Identifies the message function, such as a SETUP, DISCONNECT, or the like.

The other information elements field may consist of many entries, and its contents depend on the message type.

The SETUP message is sent by the user or the network to indicate a call establishment. In addition to the fields in the message just described, as options, other parameters include the specific ISDN channel identification, originating and destination address, an address for a redirected call, and the designation for a transit network.

The SETUP ACKNOWLEDGE message is sent by the user or the network to indicate the call establishment has been initiated. The parameters for this message are similar to the SETUP message.

The CALL PROCEEDING message is sent by the network or the user to indicate the call is being processed. The message also indicates the network has all the information it needs to process the call.

The CONNECT message and the CONNECT ACKNOWLEDGE messages are exchanged between the network and the network user to indicate the call is accepted between either the network or the user.

These messages contain parameters to identify the session as well as the facilities and services associated with the connection.

To clear a call, the user or the network can send a RELEASE or DISCONNECT message. Typically, the RELEASE COMPLETE is returned, but the network may maintain the call reference for later use, in which case, the network sends a DETACH message to the user.

A call may be temporarily suspended. The SUSPEND message is used to create this action. The network can respond to this message with either a SUSPEND ACKNOWLEDGE or a SUSPEND REJECT.

During an ongoing ISDN connection, the user or network may issue CONGESTION CONTROL messages to flow-control USER INFORMATION messages. The message simply indicates if the receiver is ready to accept messages.

The USER INFORMATION message is sent by the user or the network to transmit information to a (another) user.

If a call is suspended, the RESUME message is sent by the user to request the resumption of the call. This message can invoke a RESUME ACKNOWLEDGE or a RESUME REJECT.

The STATUS message is sent by the user or the network to report on the conditions of the call, or other administrative matters. The STATUS ENQUIRY is sent by the user or the network (but usually the user) to inquire about a state or operation.

ISDN also allows other message formats to accommodate equipment needs and different information elements. This feature provides considerable flexibility in choosing other options and ISDN services.

Conclusions on ISDN

ISDN cannot be considered very successful, based on its performance since its inception in the early 1980s. In North America, the progress of ISDN has been much slower than in Europe because of the lack of a cohesive nationwide implementation policy. This situation has changed in the past few years with the regional Bell Operating Companies (RBOCs) and Bellcore aggressively implementing "National ISDN" throughout the United States. This is leading to extensive central office implementations in both primary and basic rate offerings. Nonetheless, the progress has still been slow.

Notwithstanding, ISDN can be judged successful in another way. It has served the industry well with its specifications of LAPD and the Q.931 messaging protocol. Indeed, these two protocols are found throughout the communications industry. For example, LAPD has been one of the foundation technologies for Frame Relay as well as the link access procedure for modems (LAPM), and Q.931 is used extensively in other signaling systems such as mobile radio, Frame Relay, and ATM.

SIGNALING SYSTEM NUMBER 7 (SS7)

Purpose of SS7

We now turn our attention to Signaling System Number 7 (SS7), a clear channel signaling specification published by the ITU-T. SS7 is the prevalent signaling system for telephone networks for setting up and clearing calls and furnishing services such as 800 operations. It is designed also to operate with the ISDN UNI.

SS7 defines the procedures for the setup, ongoing management, and clearing of a call between telephone users. It performs these functions by exchanging telephone control messages between the SS7 components that support the end-users' connection. Table 4–3 provides a summary of the major functions of SS7.

The SS7 signaling data link is a full duplex, digital transmission channel operating at 64 kbit/s. Optionally, an analog link can be used with either 4 or 3 kHz spacing. The SS7 link operates on both terrestrial and satellite links. The link must be dedicated to SS7. In accordance with the idea of clear channel signaling, no other transmission can be transferred with these signaling messages and extraneous equipment must be disabled or removed from an SS7 link.

Typical Topology

Figure 4–13 depicts a typical SS7 topology. The subscriber lines are connected to the SS7 network through the service switching points (SSPs). The purpose of the SSPs is to receive the signals from the CPE and perform call processing on behalf of the user. SSPs are implemented at end offices or access tandem devices. They serve as the source and destination for SS7 messages. In so doing, SSP initiates SS7 messages either to another SSP or to a signaling transfer point (STP).

The STP is tasked with the translation of the SS7 messages and the routing of those messages between network nodes and databases. The STPs are switches that relay messages between SSPs, STPs, and service

Table 4–3   Examples of SS7 Functions

- Set up and clear down a telephone call
- Provide the called party's number (caller id)
- Indicate that a called party's line is out of service
- Indicate national, international, or other subscriber
- Indicate that called party has cleared
- Identify nature of circuit (satellite/terrestrial)
- Indicate that called party cleared, then went off-hook again
- Use echo-suppression
- Notify to reset a faulty circuit
- Provide status identifiers (calling line identity incomplete, all addresses complete, use of coin station, network congestion, no digital path available, number not in use, blocking signals for certain conditions)
- Check circuit continuity
- Provide call forwarding (and previous routes of the call)
- Provide for an all digital path
- Provide security access calls (called closed user group [CUG])
- Identify malicious calls
- Request to hold the connection
- Provide charging information
- Indicate that a called party's line is free
- Monitor call setup failure
- Provide subscriber busy signal
- Identify: circuits signaling points, called and calling parties, incoming trunks, and transit exchanges

control points (SCPs). The STP principal functions are similar to the layer 3 operations of the OSI model.

The SCPs contain software and databases for the management of the call. For example, 800 services and routing are provided by the SCP. They receive traffic (typically requests for information) from SSPs via STPs and return responses (via STPs) based on the query.

Although Figure 4–13 shows the SS7 components as discrete entities, they are often implemented in an integrated fashion by a vendor's equipment. For example, a central office can be configured with an SSP, an STP, an SCP, or any combination of these elements. These SS7 components are explained in more detail later in this section.

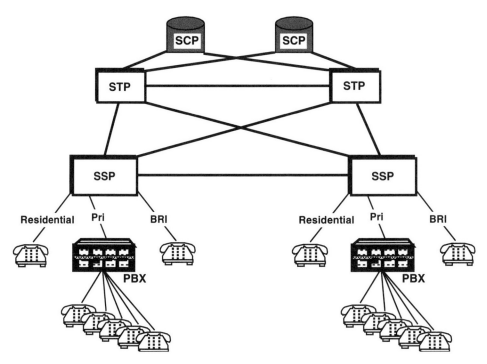

Figure 4–13 Typical SS7 topology.

SS7 Layers

Figure 4–14 shows the layers of SS7. The right part of the figure shows the approximate mapping of these layers to the OSI Model. Beginning from the lowest layers, the message transfer part (MTP) layer 1 defines the procedures for the signaling data link. It specifies the functional characteristics of the signaling links, the electrical attributes, and the connectors. Layer 1 provides for both digital and analog links, although the vast majority of SS7 physical layers are digital. The second layer is labeled MPT layer 2. It is responsible for the transfer of traffic between SS7 components. It is quite similar to an HDLC-type frame and indeed was derived from the HDLC specification. The MPT layer 3 is somewhat related to layers 3 of ISDN and X.25 in the sense that this layer provides the functions for network management and the establishment of message routing, as well as the provisions for passing the traffic to the SS7 components within the SS7 network. Many of the operations at this layer pertain to routing and routing around problem areas in an SS7 network.

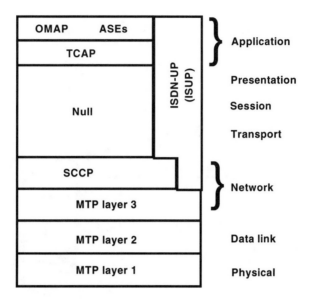

OMAP: Operations, maintenance, administration and provisioning

ASEs: Application service elements

TCAP: Transaction capabilities part

ISDN-UP: ISDN user part

SSCP: Signaling connection part

MTP: Message transfer part

Figure 4–14   The SS7 layers.

Layer 3 of SS7 is organized into functional modules. Their functions are:

- *Message routing:* Selects the link to be used for each message
- *Message distribution:* Selects the user part at the destination point
- *Message discrimination:* Determines at each signaling point if the message is to be forwarded to message routing or to message distribution
- *Signaling traffic management:* Controls the message routing functions of flow control, rerouting, changeover to a less faulty link, and recovery from link failure

- *Signaling link management:* Manages the activity of the layer 2 function and provides a logical interface between layer 2 and layer 3
- *Signaling route management:* Transfers status information about signaling routes to remote signaling points

The Signaling Connection Control Part (SCCP) is also part of the network layer, and provides for both connectionless and connection-oriented services. The main function of SCCP is to provide for translation of addresses, such as ISDN and telephone numbers, to routing identifiers used in the SS7 network.

The ISDN User Part (ISUP) is responsible for transmitting call control information between SS7 network nodes. In essence, ISUP sets up, coordinates, and takes down trunks within the SS7 network. It also provides features such call status checking, trunk management, trunk release, calling party number information, privacy indicators, and detection of application of tones for busy conditions. ISUP inside the network works in conjunction with ISDN Q.931 at the UNI. Thus, ISUP translates Q.931 messages and maps them into appropriate ISUP messages for use in the SS7 network.

The Transaction Capabilities Application Part (TCAP) is an application layer running in layer 7 of the OSI Model. It can be used for a variety of purposes. One use of TCAP is the support of 800 numbers transferred between SCP databases. It is also used to define the syntax between the various communicating components. It uses a standard closely aligned with OSI transfer syntax, called the Basic Encoding Rules (BER), which code each field of traffic with (1) syntax type, (2) length of contents field, and (3) contents field (the information).

Finally, the OMAP and ASEs are used respectively for network management and user-specific services. Both are beyond this general text.

SS7 PDUs

ITU-T Recommendation Q.703 of SS7 describes the procedures for transferring SS7 signaling messages across one link. It performs the operations that are typical of layer two protocols. As shown in Figure 4–15, Q.703 has many similarities to the HDLC protocol. For example, both protocols use flags, error checks, and sending/receiving sequence numbers.

The messages are transferred in variable length signal units (SUs), and the primary task of this layer is to ensure their error-free delivery. The SUs are one of three types:

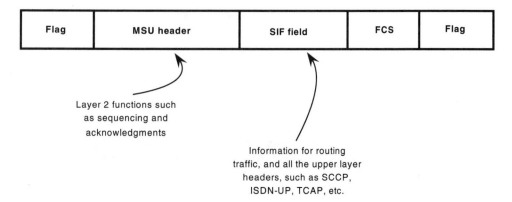

Figure 4–15   SS7 PDUs.

- Message signal unit (MSU)
- Link status signal unit (LSSU)
- Fill-in signal unit (FISU)

The MSU carries the actual signaling message forward to the user part (UP). Q.703 transfers the MSU across the link and determines if the message is uncorrupted. If the message is damaged during the transfer, it is retransmitted. The LSSU and FISU do not transport UP signals; they are used to provide layer 2 control and status signal units between the layer 2 Q.703 protocols at each end of the link.

The SS7 layer 3 functions are called signaling network functions and fall into two categories:

- *Signaling message handling functions:* Directs the message transfer to the proper link or user part
- *Signaling network management functions:* Control the message routing and the configuration of the SS7 network

A message is generated at the originating point and then sent to the destination point. The intermediate nodes are STPs.

The STPs use information in the message to determine its routing. A routing label contains the identification of the originating and destination points. A code is also used to manage load sharing within the network. The routing label is used by the STP in combination with predetermined routing data to make the routing decisions. The route is fixed unless failures occur in the network. In this situation, the routing is modified by layer 3 functions. The load-sharing logic (and code in the label) permit the distribution of the traffic to a particular destination to be distributed to two or more output signaling links.

Conclusions on SS7

SS7 has been a huge success in the industry. It is implemented in public telephone networks by practically all carriers throughout the world. Of course, its success was almost assured because its predecessors were woefully inadequate for supporting control signaling in telephone networks. Additionally, features of SS7 have found their way into other systems such as GSM and even satellite signaling. Work is underway to integrate SS7 and ATM, a subject discussed in Volume II of this ATM series.

ATM AND SONET: REDUCTION OR ENHANCEMENT OF FUNCTIONS IN NETWORKS

From the perspective of the ITU-T, ATM and SONET form the foundation for the Broadband ISDN (B-ISDN). The implementation of these technologies provides for greatly enhanced OAM capabilities from the SONET perspective and greatly reduced responsibility for traffic integrity by the networks' from the ATM perspective. While the ideas behind these two statements may seem contradictory, they in fact are complementary. By employing SONET/ATM components of high reliability and integrity, the loss of payload is rare, and those rare instances or errors can be corrected in a more efficacious manner at the user endpoint. Therefore, from the X.25 perspective, B-ISDN scales down a network, but from the T1 network perspective, B-ISDN enhances a network.

SUMMARY

T1 and E1 were first implemented over 30 years ago, yet remain as the prevalent option for digital carrier systems. Their use will continue, with SONET/SDH eventually replacing them in carriers' backbone networks.

The implementation of the ISDN has been slow, but its components, especially LAPD and Q.931, have been quite successful and are used in a variety of other systems, such as Frame Relay and ATM. However, the long-term viability of a 144 kbit/s 2 B+D offering is gloomy due to the increasing bandwidth needs of user workstations.

X.25, while being an old technology, remains a viable option for many user applications, especially low-speed, asynchronous systems. It is embedded in many systems and products and will remain an option for awhile. Nonetheless, X.25 users will migrate to ATM in the future.

SS7, while an emerged technology, has no competition from any of the emerging communications technologies and will remain as the prevalent out-of-band signaling protocol in the telecommunications industry. Its use will continue to increase, and it is being adapted for use in other technologies, notably ATM.

5

The Broadband Integrated Services Digital Network (B-ISDN) Model

The chapter provides a description of the Broadband Integrated Services Digital Network (B-ISDN), as published by the ITU-T. The B-ISDN user, control, and management planes are described, as well as how an ATM network uses these planes. A summary is provided of possible B-ISDN services as well as a classification scheme for these services. The reader new to the subject of ISDN should read its tutorial in Chapter 4. Also (and once again), be aware that the ITU-T and the B-ISDN Recommendations use the term SDH, and not SONET.

ISDN AND B-ISDN

In the early 1980s when ISDN standards were being established, the former CCITT concentrated on the H1 channel for the primary rate interface (PRI) and the 2 B+D interface for the basic rate interface (BRI). Interest shifted in the mid-1980s to higher-speed channels due to the recognition of the need and the inadequacies of the BRI and PRI technologies. The various standards groups recognized the value of the architecture of ISDN and believed that higher capacity specifications could use the basic concepts of the work performed in the 1980s.

Thus, B-ISDN started out as an extension of ISDN and has many concepts similar to ISDN. For example, functional groupings still consist of TE1, TE2, NT1, NT2, and TA. Reference points are still R, S, and T. As shown in Figure 5–1, these are conveniently tagged with the letter B in front of them to connote the broadband architecture.

It should be emphasized that the similarities between ISDN and B-ISDN are only in concept and work well enough for a general model. In practice, the ISDN and B-ISDN interfaces are not compatible. It is impossible to "upgrade" an ISDN interface by simply supplementing it with B-ISDN functional groups and reference points. Therefore, the reader should consider these terms as abstract conceptions still useful for understanding the overall B-ISDN architecture.

Another point that should be noted is that most of the specifications (Recommendations) developed by the ITU-T are written from the view of the network provider and not the network user. This approach merely reflects the slant of the ITU-T, which historically has been to publish standards for use by public telecommunications operators (PTOs, such as AT&T, British Telecom, MCI, Sprint, etc.).

B-ISDN Configurations

According to the ITU-T I.413 Recommendation, two options exist for configurations at the T_B reference point: a cell-based physical layer, and an SDH-based physical layer. As described in I.413, these configuration options are confusing. The idea of the options is to give the network designer the option of using both ATM and SDH at T_B. Only one interface per B-NT1 is permitted at the T_B reference point. One or more S_B interfaces per B-NT2 are permitted. The ITU-T I.413 Recommendation de-

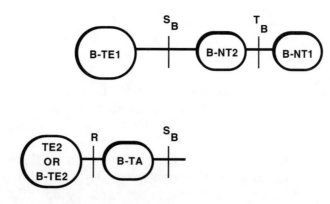

Figure 5–1   B-ISDN functional groups and reference points.

scribes other interface options at the reference points, but as of this writing, several are for further study.

ATM AND THE B-ISDN MODEL

The B-ISDN reference model is based on the OSI reference model and the ISDN standards. Figure 5–2 shows the layers of B-ISDN. The physical layer could consist of different media, even though the ITU-T has encouraged the use of ATM with the SDH/SONET technology.

The B-ISDN model contains three planes. The user plane (U-plane) is responsible for providing user information transfer, flow control, and recovery operations. The control plane (C-plane) is responsible for setting up a network connection and managing the connections. It is also responsible for connection release. The control plane is not needed for permanent virtual circuits (PVCs). The management plane is responsible for operations, administration, and maintenance (OAM).

Plane management has no layered structure. It is responsible for coordination of all the planes. Layer management is responsible for managing the entities in the layers.

The rather abstract view of B-ISDN and ATM in Figure 5–2 can be viewed in a more pragmatic way. The three planes depicted in Figure 5–2

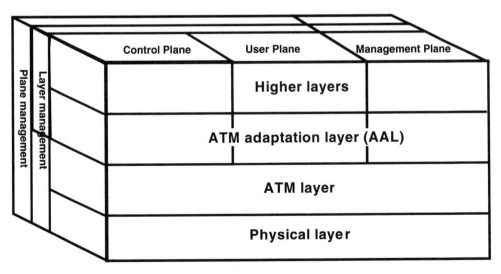

Figure 5–2   ATM and the B-ISDN reference model.

(control, user, and management) are shown in Figure 5–3 with the placements of likely protocols residing in the layers. As stated earlier, the B-ISDN model defines SDH for the physical layer, although Figure 5–3 shows other choices.

The ATM adaptation layer (AAL) is designed to support different types of applications and different types of traffic, such as voice, video, and data. The AAL plays a key role in the ability of an ATM network to support multiapplication operations. It isolates the ATM layer from the myriad operations necessary to support diverse types of traffic. Later chapters reveal that AAL is divided into a convergence sublayer (CS) and a segmentation and reassembly sublayer (SAR). CS operations are tailored, depending on the type of application being supported. SAR operations entail the segmentation of payload into 48-octet SDUs at the originating SAR and reassembling the SDUs into the original payload at the receiver.

The ATM layer's primary responsibility is the management of the sending and receiving of cells between the user node and the network node. It adds and processes the 5-octet cell header.

On the left side of Figure 5–3 is the C-plane. It contains the Q.2931 and B-ISUP signaling protocols, which are used to set up and tear down connections. B-ISUP is designed to operate inside the network (an NNI), whereas Q.2931 is intended to operate at the UNI. B-ISUP is designed to operate in public networks, say those operated by PTOs. PNNI is also

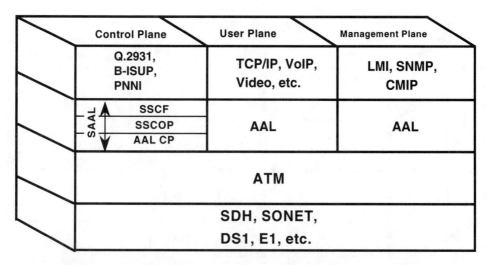

Figure 5–3 Examples of protocol placement in B-ISDN layers.

designed to operate inside the network, but has been designed for private networks. Notwithstanding, PNNI might find its way into public networks because of its powerful methods for route discovery and route aggregation operations. The layer below Q.2931 is the signaling ATM adaptation layer (SAAL). SAAL supports the transport of the signaling messages between any two machines running ATM SVCs. SAAL contains three sublayers. Briefly, they provide the following functions. The AAL common part (AAL CP) detects corrupted traffic transported across any interface using the C-plane procedures. It is usually implemented with AAL type 5, discussed in Chapter 7. The service specific connection-oriented part (SSCOP) supports the transfer of variable length traffic across the interface and recovers from errored or lost service data units. The service specific coordination function (SSCF) provides the interface to the next upper layer, in this case, Q.2931. It is tasked with several coordination functions in the SAAL and interacts with layer management to perform several link management operations. The ATM Vol. II book of this series contains a chapter on SAAL.

In the middle of the figure is the U-plane, which contains user and applications-specific protocols, such as TCP/IP voice over video systems. The invocation of the user plane protocols take place only if (1) the C-plane has set up a connection successfully, or (2) the connection was pre-provisioned.

The M-plane provides the required management services and is implemented with the ATM Integrated Local Management Interface (ILMI, discussed later in this book). The internet Simple Network Management Protocol (SNMP) and/or the OSI Common Management Information Protocol (CMIP) can also reside in the C-plane, but the ITU-T documents do not include them. I include them in this example because the ILMI is not sufficient to handle all management plane requirements (and indeed, ILMI includes the use of SNMP).

Examples of the Operations between Layers in the B-ISDN Planes

Figure 5–4 shows how the layers in the planes in the user machine communicate with the network machine or another user machine. The user device is represented by the stacks of layers on the left side of Figure 5–4, and the network node is represented by the stacks on the right side.

In accordance with conventional OSI concepts described in Chapter 3, each layer in the user machine communicates with its peer layer in the network node, and vice versa. The one exception to this statement is

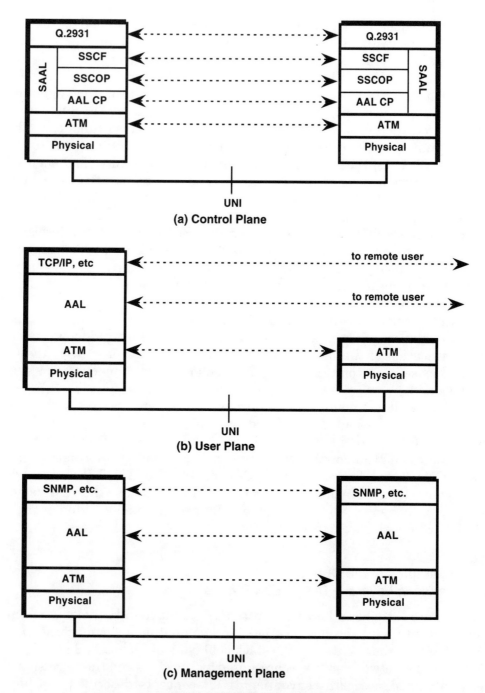

Figure 5–4   Relationships of the B-ISDN peer layers.

at the U-plane. The ATM node (and ATM network) does not process the PDUs of the AAL and the user-specific protocols. This traffic is passed (tunneled) through the network to the corresponding peer layers on the remote side of the network. Once again, this concept is in the spirit of the OSI Model, with its encapsulation/decapsulation techniques and the notion of the transparent aspect of a service data unit (SDU). To the ATM network, AAL and upper layer operations are SDUs. Therefore, for ongoing transfer of user traffic, which should be the bulk of the cells transiting the network, the ATM nodes need only execute the ATM layer, which is the switching element of the node. As we will see, the ATM layer is composed of fast processors and most of the switching operations are performed in hardware. This approach translates into a very fast operation, reducing delay and increasing throughput in comparison to traditional software-based routers. Subsequent chapters explain these three protocol stacks in greater detail.

B-ISDN FUNCTIONS

Figure 5–5 summarizes the ITU-T I.321 view of the major functions of the layers and sublayers of B-ISDN for the user plane, which are also examined in more detail in subsequent chapters. The functions are listed on the left side of the figure, and the layers or sublayers in which the functions operate are shown on the right side of the figure.

The physical layer (PL) contains two sublayers: the physical medium sublayer (PM) and the transmission convergence sublayer (TC). PM functions depend upon the nature of the medium (single mode fiber, microwave, etc.). The physical layer is responsible for typical physical layer functions, such as bit transfer/reception and bit synchronization.

TC is responsible for conventional physical layer operations that are not medium dependent. It is organized into five major functions:

- *Transmission frame generation / recovery* is responsible for the generation and recovery of PDUs (called frames in B-ISDN).
- *Transmission frame adaptation* is responsible for placing and extracting the cell into and out of the physical layer frame. The exact operation depends on the type of frame that is used at the physical layer, such as an SDH envelope or a cell without an SDH envelope.
- *Cell delineation* is responsible for the originating endpoint to de-

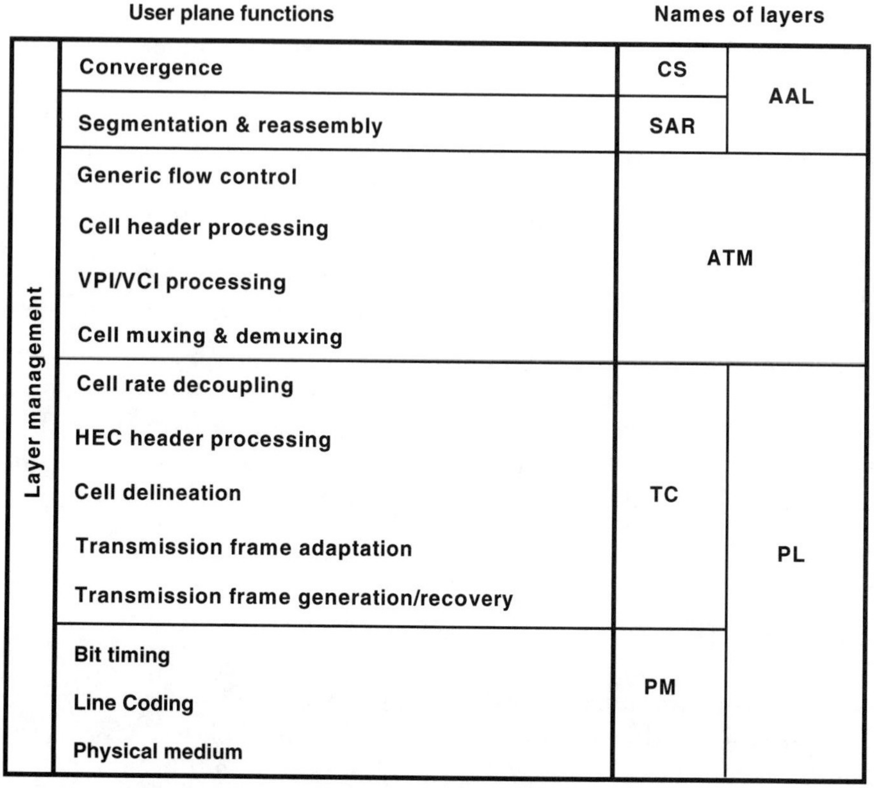

User plane functions   Names of layers

	User plane functions		
Layer management	Convergence	CS	AAL
	Segmentation & reassembly	SAR	
	Generic flow control	ATM	
	Cell header processing		
	VPI/VCI processing		
	Cell muxing & demuxing		
	Cell rate decoupling	TC	PL
	HEC header processing		
	Cell delineation		
	Transmission frame adaptation		
	Transmission frame generation/recovery		
	Bit timing	PM	
	Line Coding		
	Physical medium		

CS   Convergence sublayer
SAR   Segmentation and reassembly sublayer
AAL   ATM adaptation layer
ATM   Asynchronous transfer mode
TC   Transmission convergence sublayer
PM   Physical medium sublayer
PL   Physical layer

Figure 5–5   B-ISDN layer functions.

fine the cell boundaries in order for the receiving endpoint to recover all cells.

- *Cell header processing* is responsible for generating a header error
  control (HEC) field at the originating endpoint and processing it at
  the terminating endpoint in order to determine if the cell header
  has been damaged in transit.

- *Cell rate decoupling* inserts idle cells at the sending end and extracts them at the receiving end in order to adapt to the physical
  layer bit rates.

The ATM layer is independent of the physical layer operations and conceptually does not care if an ATM cell is running on fiber, twisted pair, or other media. However, we shall see that this layer operates best if fiber is the physical medium. At any rate, the ATM layer is organized into four major functions.

- *Cell muxing and demuxing* is responsible for multiplexing (combining) cells from various virtual connections at the originating endpoint and demultiplexing them at the terminating endpoint.
- *VPI/VCI processing* is responsible for processing the labels/identifiers in a cell header at each ATM node. ATM virtual connections are identified by a virtual path identifier (VPI) and a virtual channel identifier (VCI).
- *Cell header processing* creates the cell header (with the exception of the HEC field) at the originating endpoint and interprets/translates it at the terminating endpoint. The VPI/VCI may be translated into a service access point (SAP, see Chapter 3) at this receiver.
- *Generic flow control* is responsible for creating the generic flow control field in the ATM header at the originator and acting upon it at the receiver.

The functions of the AAL, CS, and SAR were described earlier in this chapter.

The AAL acts as the interface to the higher layers. It accommodates to the requirements of different applications (voice, data, etc.) and segments all user traffic PDUs in to 48-octet units for sending to the ATM layer. At the receiving node, it reassembles these units back into the original user PDUs.

B-ISDN SERVICE ASPECTS

The ITU-T Recommendation I.211 describes the services offered by B-ISDN. The services are classified as either interactive services or distribution services. Interactive services, as the name implies, entail an ongoing dialogue between the service user and service provider. The distribution services also entail a dialogue between the service provider and service user, but the dialogue is oriented toward a batch or remote job entry (RJE) basis.

As depicted in Figure 5–6, interactive services are further classified as (1) conversational services, (2) messaging services, and (3) retrieval services. Distribution services are further classified as distribution services without user individual presentation control and distribution services with user individual presentation control.

Conversational services are interactive dialogues with real-time operations. In this context, real time means that there is no store-and-forward operations occurring between the service user and service provider. For example, interactive teleshopping, ongoing message exchanges between two people, LAN-to-LAN communications, and building surveillance fall into the conversational services category.

Messaging services include user-to-user communications, such as video mail service or document mail service, which can be done on a conversational basis, or on demand.

Retrieval services fall into the store-and-forward category where a user can obtain information stored for public use. This information can be retrieved on an individual basis from the service provider to the service user. Archival information is a good example of retrieval services.

Distribution services without user individual presentation control include conventional broadcast services such as television and radio. As the reader might expect, this service provides continuous flows of information where service users can obtain unlimited access to the information.

In contrast, distribution services with user individual presentation control allow the central source to distribute the information to a large or small number of users based on some type of cyclical repetition. Obvi-

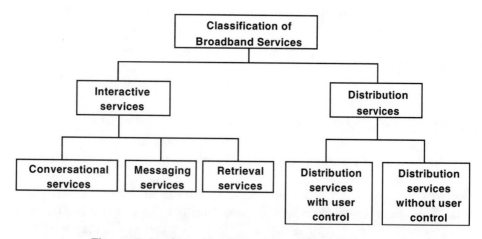

Figure 5–6   Classification of broadband services.

ously, the B-ISDN category of interest here is the emerging video-on-demand market.

SUMMARY

The B-ISDN reference model is organized on the original ISDN recommendations published by the ITU-T. The functional groupings and reference points of ISDN are still pertinent to B-ISDN, except on a broadband basis.

The B-ISDN protocol stacks consist of the C-plane, M-plane, and U-plane. The invocation of these protocol stacks depends on the needs of the user and the network. The ITU-T also defines the major functions of each protocol stack and, in so doing, divides some of the protocol layers into sublayers. The upper layers of the U-plane and M-plane may be user-defined.

The B-ISDN services are classified as interactive services and distribution services, and these services are divided further into specific categories.

6

Asynchronous Transfer Mode (ATM) Basics

This chapter introduces the major functions of ATM. The ATM cells and the user-network interface (UNI) are explained, as well as the ATM multiplexing and routing operations. The rationale for the 53-octet size cell is analyzed, and the issues of delay, error correction/detection, and synchronization are examined. Emphasis is placed on the ATM Forum activities, since this body has assumed the lead role in defining the ATM architecture.

A BRIEF REVIEW

To review briefly the earlier parts of this book, the purpose of ATM is to provide a high-speed, low-delay multiplexing and switching network to support any type of user traffic, such as voice, data, or video applications.

ATM segments and multiplexes user traffic into small, fixed-length units called cells. The cell is 53 octets, with 5 octets reserved for the cell header. Each cell is identified with virtual circuit identifiers contained in the cell header. An ATM network uses these identifiers to relay the traffic through high-speed switches from the sending customer premises equipment (CPE) to the receiving CPE.

ATM provides no error detection operations on the user payload inside the cell. It provides no retransmisson services, and few operations are performed on the small header. The intention of this approach—small cells with minimal services performed—is to implement a network fast enough to support multimegabit transfer rates.[1]

The ITU-T, ANSI, and the ATM Forum have selected ATM to be part of the broadband ISDN (B-ISDN) specification to provide for the multiplexing and switching operations introduced in Chapter 1. ATM resides on top of the physical layer of a conventional layered model, but it does not require the use of a specific physical layer protocol. The physical layer could be implemented with SONET/SDH, DS3, FDDI's physical layer, CEPT4, and others. However, for large public networks, SONET/SDH is the preferred physical layer.

WHY IS ATM CALLED "ASYNCHRONOUS"?

Newcomers to ATM often wonder why ATM has the term "asynchronous" as part of its title, especially since it supports synchronous traffic, such as voice and video applications. The term is used because traffic is not necessarily assigned to fixed slots (cells) on the transmission channel, such as in a conventional time division multiplexing (TDM) system. Therefore, the cells of an application are not always in a fixed, periodic position in the channel. Because of this asynchronous aspect of the scheme, each cell must have a header attached to it that identifies the application's traffic in the cell stream. The scheme permits either synchronous or asynchronous allocation of the cells. Figure 6–1 illustrates these points.

Even synchronous traffic, such as voice, can be placed into an ATM network in an asynchronous (bursty) fashion, as long as the receiving user machine "smooths" the asynchronous, bursty cell flow as a TDM-type presentation to the receiving application.

AN ATM TOPOLOGY

Before an ATM topology is examined, several definitions are in order. As just stated, ATM is part of an B-ISDN that is designed to support public or private networks. Consequently, ATM comes in two forms for the user-to-network interface (UNI):

---

[1]For certain traffic, the ATM adaptation layer (AAL) will perform error checks and retransmissions, a point that is explained in Chapter 7.

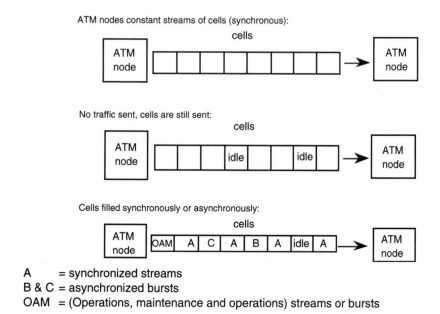

A   = synchronized streams
B & C = asynchronized bursts
OAM   = (Operations, maintenance and operations) streams or bursts

Figure 6–1   ATM support of different traffic types.

- A *public UNI* defines the interface between a public service ATM network and a private ATM switch.
- A *private UNI* defines an ATM interface with an end-user and a private ATM switch.

This distinction may seem somewhat superficial, but it is important because each interface will likely use different physical media and span different geographical distances.

The ATM topology depicted in Figure 6–2 is a conceptual model, as viewed by the standards groups and the ATM Forum. At this embryonic stage in the evolution of ATM, there is no such thing as a typical typology (but Figure 6–3, explained shortly, shows a likely topology).

It is obvious from a brief glance at Figure 6–2 that the ATM interfaces and topology are organized around the ISDN model, introduced in Chapter 5. The UNI can span across public or private S_B, T_B, and U_B interfaces (where $_B$ means broadband). Internal adapters may or may not be involved. If they are involved, a user device (the B-TE1 or B-TE2) is connected through the R reference point to the B-TA. B-NT2s and B-NT1s are also permitted at the interface, with B-NT2 considered to be part of the CPE. For purposes of simplicity, the picture shows only one

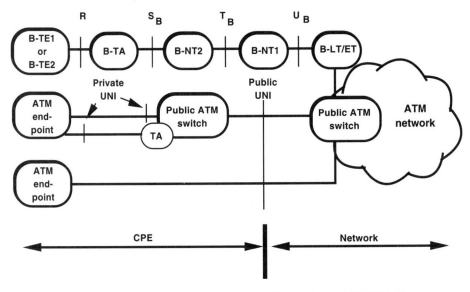

Figure 6–2   An ATM ISDN-based topology. [ATM92a]

side of an ATM network. The other side could be a mirror image of the side shown in Figure 6–2, or it could have variations of the interfaces and components shown in the figure.

Figure 6–3 shows a possible ATM-based topology. As stated briefly in the introduction to this chapter, ATM is designed to support multiapplication service. Its convergence functions permit the relaying of voice, video, and data traffic through the same switching fabric. The interconnection of LANs can also be supported by the ATM technology, because it has convergence and segmentation reassembly (C/SAR or C/S) operations for connectionless data. Convergence services are also provided for fixed bit rate video and variable bit rate video and voice operations.

The WAN in Figure 6–3 could be a public network offered by a public telecommunications operator (PTO, such as AT&T, MCI, or Sprint). The ATM nodes at this interface use a public UNI to the CPE ATM nodes. In turn, the CPE ATM nodes connect with private UNIs to LANs, PBXs, and the like.

ATM allows multiple users to share a line at the UNI by a subscription agreement with each ATM customer (subscriber). This agreement defines the amount of traffic that the network must support, as well as several QOS features, such as delay and throughput. The agreement also restricts how much traffic the subscriber can submit to the network during a measured period.

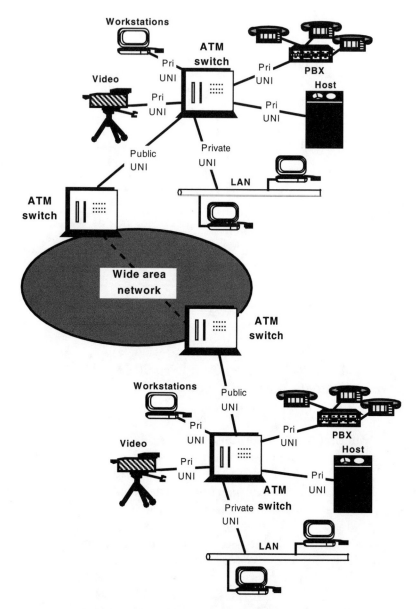

Figure 6–3   A possible ATM topology.

THE ATM INTERFACES

Multiple protocols are required to support full ATM operations. The number of protocols required depends upon where the user traffic is being transported. Figure 6–4 shows the different protocols and proce-

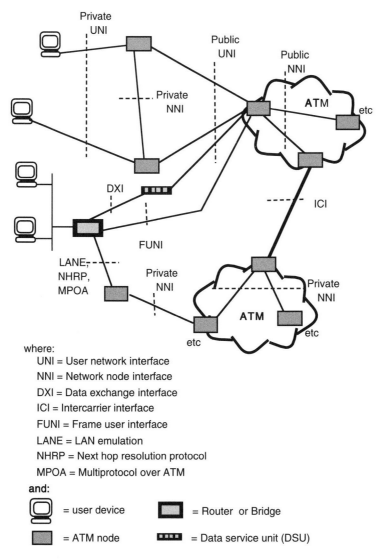

Figure 6–4   The ATM interfaces.

dures may be invoked at several interfaces. I introduce the interfaces here, and describe them in more detail in this and later chapters.

The user network interface (UNI) is the most visible protocol, because it defines the procedures for the interworking between the user equipment and the ATM node. As the figure shows, two forms of UNI are supported, a private UNI and a public UNI. The major difference between these interfaces pertains to the physical communications links between the machines. A private UNI would likely have a link such a private fiber or twisted pair. A public UNI would likely consist of SDH/SONET, DS3, or E3. Also, a private UNI might not have the formal traffic monitoring and policing procedures that exist at the public UNI.

The network node interface (also called in some literature the network-network interface) (NNI) can exist as both a public or private interface as well. It defines the interworking of the ATM network nodes. It has been completed by the ITU-T (for the public NNI) and the ATM Forum (for the private NNI, called PNNI, and PNNI uses the term private network-network interface).

The intercarrier interface (ICI) is an internetworking protocol. As such, it defines the operations and procedures that exist between networks.

The data exchange interface (DXI) has been developed by the ATM Forum to provide a standard procedure for the interfacing of current equipment into an ATM node. The DXI is a very simple protocol and allows an easy migration into ATM. However, it does require the use of a data service unit (DSU). The frame UNI (FUNI) is similar to DXI, but does not require the DSU.

Three other interfaces are now defined by the ATM Forum. They are LAN Emulation (LANE), the Next Hop Resolution Protocol (NHRP), and Multiprotocol over ATM (MPOA). As a whole, these three specifications are designed to internetwork ATM hubs with LANs, and the Internet protocol stacks (IP, for example).

The VPI and VCI Labels

The ITU-T Recommendation requires that an ATM connection be identified with identifiers that are assigned for each user connection in the ATM network. The connection is identified by two values in the cell header: the virtual path identifier (VPI) and the virtual channel identifier (VCI). The VPI and VCI fields constitute a virtual circuit identifier, also called a label. Users are assigned these values when the user enters into a session with a network as a connection-on-demand SVC, or when a user is provisioned to the network as a PVC.

Figure 6–5 shows examples of how the VPI/VCI values can be used. Three applications are connected through the network: a video conference, a data session between a workstation and a host computer, and a telephone call. Each connection is associated with a VPI/VCI value on each side of the network. For example, the video session's connection is associated with VPI 4/VCI 10 at one UNI and VPI 20 and VCI 33 at the other UNI. The manner in which VPI/VCI values are established and

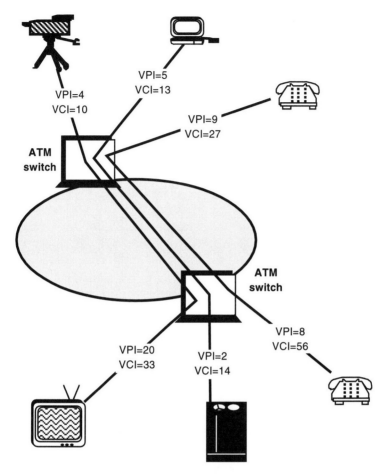

Figure 6–5   Examples of VPI and VCI operations.

managed is left to the network administrator. In this example, VPI/VCI numbers have local significance at each UNI. Of course, the network must assure that these local VPI/VCI values at each UNI are "mapped together" through the network to create an end-to-end virtual circuit.

ATM services can be obtained as a PVC or as an SVC. The term SVC is not used in some of the ATM specifications and is gradually being replaced with the term connection-on-demand, which does convey the idea well. One colleague stated that two terms are needed. The first, "connection-on-demand," is from the user perspective. The other, "connection-on-request," is from the network provider perspective.

In addition, perhaps a better term to describe the ITU-T view of a PVC is that it is a semi-permanent virtual circuit technology. That is, users of two connecting endpoints are preprovisioned in the network, and then given a session (connection) when requested by the user—if the session can be supported by the network; that is, if the network has sufficient bandwidth available to meet the needs of the user session.

The ATM Forum and the ITU-T have published specifications for ATM connections on demand, or SVCs. They are explained in Chapter 10.

The VPIs and VCIs are also used in the ATM network. They are examined by switches in order to determine how to relay the cell through the network. The manner in which the VPI/VCIs are processed in the network is not defined in the ATM standards. As depicted in Figure 6–5, from the perspective of these standards, the VCI/VPI has local significance at the UNI only.

Thus, the VPI/VCI labels are similar to data link connection identifiers (DLCIs) used in Frame Relay networks, and logical channel numbers (LCNs) used in X.25-based networks.

ATM LAYERS

As illustrated in Figure 6–6, the ATM layers are similar to the layers of some other emerging communications technologies (the Metropolitan Area Network [MAN] and the Switched Multimegabit Data Service [SMDS]). ATM provides convergence functions at the ATM adaptation layer (AAL) for connection-oriented and connectionless variable bit rate (VBR) applications. It supports synchronous applications (voice, video) with constant bit rate (CBR) services.

A convenient way to think of the AAL is that it is actually divided into two sublayers, as shown in Figure 6–6. The segmentation and reassembly (SAR) sublayer, as the name implies, is responsible for processing user PDUs that are different in size and format into ATM cells at the sending site and reassembling the cells into the user-formatted PDUs at the receiving site. The other sublayer is called the convergence sublayer (CS), and its functions depend upon the type of traffic being processed by the AAL, such as voice, video, or data.

The SAR entity provides a standardized interface to the ATM layer. The ATM layer is then responsible for relaying and routing the traffic through the ATM switch. The ATM layer is connection-oriented and cells are associated with established virtual connections. Traffic must be seg-

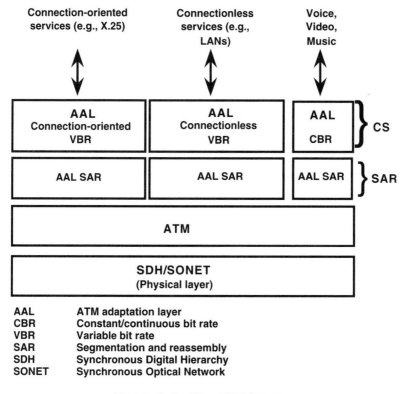

Figure 6–6   The ATM layers.

mented into cells by the AAL before the ATM layer can process the traffic. The switch uses the VPI/VCI label to identify the connection to which the cell is associated.

ATM Layers and OSI Layers

The ATM layers do not map directly with the OSI layers. The ATM layer performs operations typically found in layers 2 and 3 of the OSI Model. The AAL combines features of layers 4, 5, and 7 of the OSI Model. It is not a clean fit, but then, the OSI Model is over 15 years old.

The relationship of the user connections to the AAL and ATM layers is shown in Figure 6–7. The figure also shows that VPI/VCIs can be assigned bidirectionally; that is, bandwidth and QOS need not be the same in both directions of the traffic flow for a connection. For example, consider a client-server application in which the client is obtaining a file transfer from the server. While the initial dialogue between the two end-

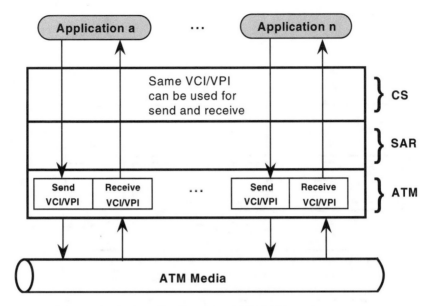

Figure 6–7   Applications and VPI/VCI assignments.

points requires about the same amount of bandwidth in both directions, after the file transfer begins, the server needs more bandwidth than does the client, since most of the traffic (the file) is flowing from the server to the client. ATM provides procedures to set up asymmetrical bandwidth for the virtual connection.

Whatever the implementation of AAL at the user device, the ATM network is not concerned with AAL operations. Indeed, the ATM bearer service is "masked" from these CS and SAR functions. The ATM bearer service includes the ATM and physical layers. The bearer services are application independent, and AAL is tasked with accommodating to the requirements of different applications.

These ideas are amplified in Figure 6–8a. For the transfer of user payload, upper layer protocols (ULP) and AAL operations are not invoked in the ATM network functions. The dotted arrows indicate that logical operations occur between peer layers at the user nodes and the ATM nodes. Therefore, the ULP headers, user payload, and the AAL headers are passed transparently through the ATM network. Of course, as we learned in Chapter 5, AAL must be invoked for the C-plane and M-plane, because AAL must be available to assemble the payload in the cells back to an intelligible ULP PDU. These ideas are shown in Figure 6–8b. The term "maybe" is shown in Figure 6–8b because it may not be

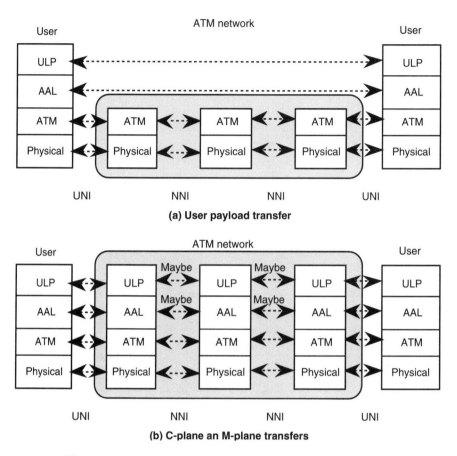

(a) User payload transfer

(b) C-plane an M-plane transfers

Figure 6–8   Relationship of user and network layers.

necessary to invoke AAL or the ULPs at each ATM node. As an example, some OAM messages reside in only one 53-byte cell, so AAL is not needed for SAR functions at these nodes.

RELATIONSHIP OF AAL, ATM, AND THE NETWORK

It is evident that the AAL is responsible for acting as the interface between user applications and the ATM layer. As such, it is expected to enhance the services provided by the ATM layer, based on the specific requirements of the application. As noted earlier, it has the task of supporting different user operations such as voice, video, and data.

To piece together several concepts discussed earlier, Figure 6–9 illustrates several of the major functions of AAL, the ATM layer, and the ATM network. User traffic, digitized images of various payload types (again, voice, video, or data), is segmented by AAL into PDUs of 48 octets. However, these octets do not contain solely user payload. AAL headers (H), and perhaps trailers (T), use part of these 48 octets. The contents and structure of these headers and trailers vary, depending on the type of payload.

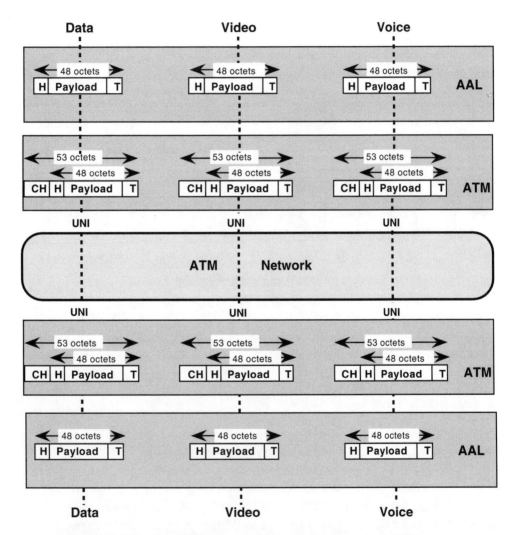

Figure 6–9   Relationships of AAL, ATM layer, and ATM network.

The ATM layer expects to receive and transmit fixed length data units to and from the AAL. Among other tasks, the transmitting ATM layer adds a 5-octet cell header (CH) to the 48-octet AAL PDU and the receiving ATM layer processes this header, then strips it away before passing the 48-octet PDU to the receiving AAL.

The AAL is responsible for operations beyond the SAR functions just described. For example, fixed rate video applications may require the AAL to maintain a concise and fixed time relationship for the transferal of data units between the source and destination applications. As another example, connectionless data applications require that the AAL provide flexible buffering arrangements for these bursty-type transactions.

The ITU-T and other standards groups do not define all the activities and functions that may be invoked at the AAL or between the AAL and the upper layer protocol, because they may already be defined by standards that exist in the upper layer protocols, or they may be left to vendor-specific solutions. Examples not defined in AAL include: (1) the exact manner in which a receiving AAL entity must adjust to delay variations of arriving voice PDUs; (2) how video compression is accomplished; and (3) how different queues are managed. These types of operations are left to either a vendor-specific solution or they are defined in other standards.

The ATM network receives the cells from the ATM and physical layers (physical layer is not shown in Figure 6–9) at the local UNI, and transports these cells to the remote UNI through the use of the ATM cell header. Here, the cells are presented to the user node, where the cell and PDU are processed by the physical, ATM, and AAL layers respectively.

Relationship of Layers to the OSI Layered Architecture

Figure 6–10 shows how the layers of ATM and SONET relate to the OSI model. As discussed in Chapter 3, the layers communicate with each other between two machines through the use of PDUs. At the ATM layer, the PDUs are called cells, and at the physical layer, the PDUs are called frames.

The service definitions define the interactions between adjacent layers in the same machine and use service access points (SAPs) to identify the source and destination communicating parties. The service definitions are known as *primitives* and are actually implemented with computer-specific operations, such as C function calls, UNIX system library calls, and so on.

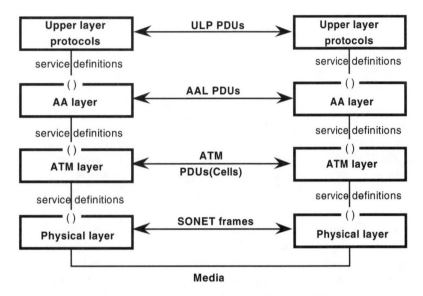

Note: ( ) represents a service access point (SAP)

Figure 6–10   B-ISDN PDUs and service definitions.

Based on the explanations in Chapter 3, it is noted that ATM networks use conventional encapsulation/decapsulation concepts. Therefore, we shall not dwell on the subject further. The interested reader can refer to Chapter 3.

Where to Find Service Definitions and Primitives

In order to simplify the description of the aforementioned topics, the service definitions and primitive calls between (1) the ULP and the AAL and (2) the AAL and the ATM layer are explained in Chapter 7 (see "The AAL/ATM Primitives"). The service definitions and primitive calls between the AAL and the physical layer are described in Chapter 14 (see "The ATM/Physical Layer Primitives"). The service definitions and primitive calls at the M-plane and ATM (not shown in Figure 6–8) are described in Chapter 13 (see "The Layer Management/ATM Primitives").

TYPICAL PROTOCOL STACKS

Figure 6–11 is an example of a typical configuration at the user host machines, routers, and the ATM network nodes. A router is included in this example, because many of the current implementations are using a

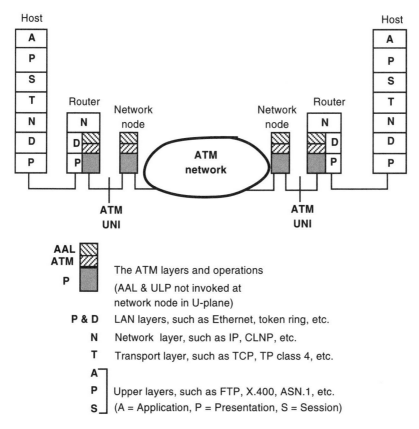

Figure 6–11   Typical protocol stacks (M-plane and C-plane).

router (or something similar to a router) to provide the ATM UNI. The configuration keeps the end-user equipment isolated from the ATM operations and allows the use of a high-speed, cell-based ATM network to transfer traffic between user applications, but does not require the integration of the ATM technology into the architecture of the workstation.

This figure may require some study on the part of the reader, and may require revisiting some material in earlier chapters. As a starter, the tutorial on layered protocols in Chapter 3 is key to understanding this figure. Additionally, as the legend in the figure explains, the AAL and upper layers are not invoked at the ATM node for the transfer of user payload (the U-plane), and these ideas are summarized in this chapter and explained also in Chapter 5.

The protocols and their headers, emanating from the host on the left side of the figure, are received by the router. The data link and physical layer headers (D and P in the figure) used at the local host-router interface are removed by the router. The header of the network layer (N in the figure) is used by the router to determine the destination address of the destination host (for example, this header could be an IP datagram header, and the destination address could be an IP address).

Let us assume a routing table stored at the router reveals that the next node to process the datagram is an ATM node. Therefore, the router must invoke the ATM protocol stack, and create the cells for transport to the ATM network node. The manner in which the cells are created and how the router (or any user machine) interacts with the ATM network is explained further in Chapters 9, 10, and 11.

The cells containing the IP datagram, the headers of the upper layers, and the user payload are transported (tunneled) through the ATM network across the remote UNI to the terminating router. Here, the process is reversed: The cells are reassembled into the original datagram, placed inside the headers and trailers of the physical and data link layers of the remote router-host interface, and sent to the terminating host—up through the layers of the user host machine to the end-user application (A).

ATM PDUS (CELLS)

We have learned that an ATM PDU is called a cell. It is 53 octets in length, with 5 octets devoted to the ATM cell header, and 48 octets used by AAL and the user payload. As shown in Figure 6–12, the ATM cell is configured slightly differently for the UNI than for the NNI. Since various OAM functions operate only at the UNI interface, a flow control field is defined for the traffic traversing this interface, but not at the NNI. The flow control field is called the generic flow control (GFC) field. If GFC is not used, this 4-bit field is set to zeros.

Most of the values in the 5-octet cell header consist of the virtual circuit labels of VPI and VCI. A total of 24 bits are available with 8 bits assigned to VPI and 16 bits assigned to VCI. For the NNI, the VPI field contains 12 bits. A combination of the VPI and VCI field is called the VPCI field.

Use of Two Identifiers

Most of the VPI and VCI overhead values are available for use as the network administrator chooses. Here are some examples of how they

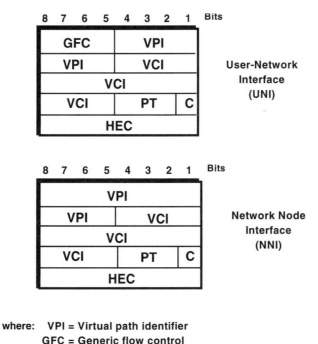

Figure 6–12   The ATM PDU (cell) headers.

can be used. Multiple VCs can be associated with one VP. This approach can be used to assign a certain amount of bandwidth to a VP, and then allocate it among the associated VCs. "Bundling" VCs in VPs allows one OAM message to be transmitted that provides information about multiple VCs, by using the VPI value in the header. Some implementations do not use all the bits of VPI/VCI to avoid processing all the bits in the VP and VC fields. Some implementations examine only the VPI bits at intermediate nodes in the network.

A payload type (PT) identifier field identifies the type of traffic residing in the cell. The cell may contain user traffic or management/control traffic. The ATM Forum has expanded the use of this field to identify other payload types (OAM, control, etc.). One of particular interest is a payload type that indicates that either the cell contains user data and the cell receiver is notified of congestion problems, or the cell contains user data and the cell receiver is notified that congestion has not been experienced. In other words, this field is now used for congestion notification operations. Interestingly, the GFC field does not contain the congestion notification codes, because the name of the field was created before all of its functions were identified. The flow control fields (actually, congestion notification) are contained in the PT identifier field. Chapter 13 describes how the GFC, PT, and the remainder of the first four octets are defined by the ATM Forum to identify OAM and other control signaling at the UNI.

The cell loss priority (C) field is a 1-bit value. If C is set to 1, the cell is subject to being discarded by the network. Whether the cell is discarded depends on network conditions and the policy of the network administrator. Whatever the policy of the administrator may be, the C bit set to 0 indicates a higher priority of the cell to the network. It must be treated with more care than a cell in which the C bit is set to 1.

The header error control (HEC) field is an error check field, which can also correct a 1-bit error. It is calculated on the 5-octet ATM header, and not on the 48-octet user payload. ATM employs an adaptive error detection/correction mechanism with the HEC. The transmitter calculates the HEC value on the first four octets of the header. The 1-octet result becomes the HEC field. The value is the remainder of the division (Modulo 2) by the generator polynomial x^8+x^2+x+1 for the x^8, multiplied by the content of the header. The pattern 01010101 is XORed with the 8-bit remainder, and this result is placed in the last octet of the header. The complementary calculation is performed at the receiver on all five octets.

Metasignaling Cells and Other Cells

The VCI, VPI, and other parts of the first four octets of the cell can be coded in a variety of formats to identify nonuser payload cells. One such convention is called *metasignaling*. It is used to establish a session with the network and negotiate session services. Another convention is called *broadcasting*. With this feature, the VPI and VCI are coded to indicate that the cell is to be broadcast to all stations on the UNI. Other conventions provide for management services, the identification of idle cells (cells that are empty), and unassigned cells. Unassigned cells are sent when the ATM module has no user payload to send, a process called cell decoupling. Thus, the continuous sending of cells at the sender and the continuous reception of cells at the receiver allow the network to operate synchronously, yet support bursty, asynchronous services. Meta-signaling is described in Chapter 13.

RATIONALE FOR THE CELL SIZE

The reader might wonder why a user payload of 48 octets was chosen. Why not 32? Why not 64? The 48-octet size was a result of a compromise between various groups in the standards committees. The compromise resulted in a cell length that is (1) acceptable for voice networks, (2) adaptable to forward error correction operations, (3) able to minimize the number of bits that must be retransmitted from the user device in the event of errors, and (4) able to work with ongoing carrier transport equipment. The small cell also avoids the delay inherent in the processing of long PDUs.

We shall see in Chapter 12 that the SONET/SDH STS-3 payload accommodates the bit rate requirement for high-quality video, even when the video images are carried inside the payload of the ATM cell. In this section of this chapter, the cell size is examined in relation to transmission errors, equipment processing errors, transmission delay, and equipment processing delay.

Ideally, one would like to have a choice of the size of a PDU, based on the quality of the circuits. For error-prone links, it is desirable to have small PDUs for data traffic because the number of bits retransmitted is small. For high-quality links, it is desirable to have larger PDUs in order to increase the ratio of user payload to the cell header. Moreover, it is well known that variable-length PDUs provide greater transmission efficiency than fixed-length PDUs (a demonstration of this fact will follow shortly). However, transmission efficiency is not the only criterion that should be used in making the decision on fixed or variable length PDUs. Equally important is the effect a fixed/variable length PDU has on switching speed and network delay. An analysis of these factors vis-à-vis transmission efficiency led the ITU-T to the decision to use fixed cells.

The transmission efficiency of a protocol can be calculated as:

$$TE = L_i / (L_i + L_o)$$

where TE = transmission efficiency; L_i = length of information field (user traffic); L_o = length of control header. Various studies reveal that the TE is better for variable length PDUs than for fixed length PDUs. It is common sense that the more bits in the information field, the better the TE for a given L_o. However, a large I field entails overhead at a switch, because it takes longer for the cell to be processed and to leave the switch. Indeed, one of the reasons for the migration from message switching systems in the 1970s to packet switching systems was the attractive feature of being able to process a small packet more quickly than a large message. Figure 6–13 shows that for an ATM cell with 10 percent of overhead (the 5 byte header), delay is less than 2 ms for a 64 kbit/s voice transmission [ATM94a].

Therefore, the ITU-T had to balance conflicting factors in choosing a fixed or variable length PDU and the size of the SDU. After a lengthy analysis, with Europe opting for a cell size of 32 octets (and 4-octet header), and the United States and Japan opting for a cell size of 64 octets (with 5-octet header), the difference was split, and the size of 48 octets was selected at the 1989 Group XVIII Geneva meeting.

After extensive deliberations in the standards working groups, it was agreed that a user payload size between 32 and 64 octets would perform satisfactorily because it (1) worked with ongoing equipment (did not require echo cancellers), (2) provided acceptable transmission efficiency, and (3) was not overly complex to implement.

The size of the cell is quite important for speech and video because of the concept of cell length (the duration of the cell on the channel). Cell length is a function of the number of bits in the cell, the compression ratio (if any) reflected in these bits, and the coding rate of the signal (for example, 64 kbit/s). A payload size of anywhere around 32 to 64 octets would be acceptable to an audio listener or video viewer. As examples, consider a digitized voice image with a coding rate of 64 kbit/s:

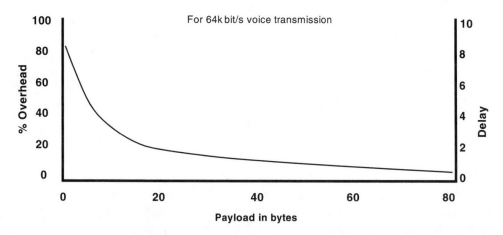

Figure 6–13   Overhead and delay.

- 32 octets * 8 bits per octet = 256 bits
  256/64,000 = .004
- 48 octets * 8 bits per octet = 384 bits
  384/64,000 = .006
- 64 octets * 8 bits per octet = 512 bits
  512/64,000 = .008

Therefore, a cell loss for a 64,000 bit/s signal with 32, 48, or 64 octets in the payload of the cell results in traffic loss of 4 ms, 6 ms, or 8 ms respectively. Eventually, a compromise was reached and the 48-octet size was adapted (less the 5-octet header). Subsequent material describes other factors that contributed to these decisions.

Network Transparency Operations

This section delves into more detail about the ATM cell and its relationship to errors, delay, and the size of the cell. The service data unit (SDU) is a useful OSI term for this discussion. The reader can refer to Chapter 3 if the concept of the SDU is not familiar. Three concepts are examined in this discussion:

Semantic transparency:	Transporting the user's SDUs without error from source to destination
SDU size transparency:	Accommodating the user's variable size SDUs
Time transparency:	Transporting the user's SDUs with a fixed delay between source and destination

Errors and Error Rates

Errors are impossible to eliminate completely in a communications network. As reliable as optical fiber is, noise, signal dispersion, and other impairments will persist. Errors also will occur in equipment due to the malfunctioning of hardware and imperfections in component design, as two examples.

Communications network error rates are measured with a simple formula called the bit error rate (BER). It is calculated as follows:

$$BER = \text{errored bits received / total bits sent}$$

BER is measured over a period of time, which smoothes out the randomness of errors on communications channels. Generally, measurement periods are several orders of magnitude more than the actual BER value.

Another useful statistic is called the block error rate (BLER), which defines the number of blocks sent in relation to the number of blocks received in error. The term block is generic; for this discussion, a block refers to a cell. BLER is calculated as:

BLER = errored blocks received / total blocks sent

Other error statistics are important. One that is pertinent to ATM is called the loss rate, which is the ratio of lost or inserted cells in relation to the total number of cells sent. Lost cells are any cells that are damaged and cannot be corrected, cells that arrive too late to be useful (as in a video application), or cells that are discarded by the network. Inserted cells are cells that are received by a user when they were supposed to go to another user.

These error rate statistics play a key role in the design of the network. As errors increase, user payload (data) must be retransmitted from the user CPE. The end effect is the creation of more traffic in the network. Ideally, one wishes to design a network that is cost effective from the standpoint of its incidence of errors as well as efficient in its treatment of errors. This brings us to the subject of error rates on optical fiber and the size of an ATM cell.

AT&T [ATT89a] conducted a study on the error rates of optical fiber. This study is summarized in Figure 6–14. Under normal operating conditions, most errors occurring on optical fiber are single-bit errors. As this figure illustrates, 99.64 percent of the errors are a single bit. Although not shown in this figure, AT&T also conducted a study on the error rate during maintenance conditions. For example, during switch-over operations on a device, the single bit error probability dropped to 65 percent. Figure 6–14 also reveals that the ATM error handling operations is based on the fact that 6 bits are needed to correct a single bit error for 40 bits of a header, and 8 bits will correct a single bit error and detect 84 percent of multiple bit errors. Therefore, a cell header of 5 bytes, which are the protected bits, is a reasonable compromise in relation to the HEC field of 1 byte, which are the protection bits.

These studies and others paved the way for a more detailed analysis of the effect of using forward error correction (FEC) to correct a one-bit error. Subsequent research has confirmed that small cell headers experiencing a one-bit error can be corrected, which obviates (1) retransmitting data cells and (2) discarding voice/video cells. Since errors are rare on optical fiber, ATM does not execute cumbersome retransmission schemes, and it will correct headers with one-bit errors and discard headers with multiple-bit errors.

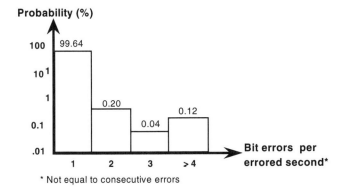

(a) Bit Error Rates on Optical Fiber

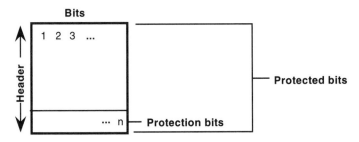

- 6 bits needed to correct a single bit error for 40 bits
- 8 bits will correct a single bit error and detect 84% of multiple bit errors

(b) Header size

Figure 6–14   Bit error rates (BER) on optical fiber. [ATT89a]

However, it is also recognized that errors on optical fiber are actually a mix of single-bit errors and errors that have long bursts. Consequently, some implementations may not invoke the error correction feature, which is ineffective on media exhibiting errors that damage a long string of bits.

Error Correction and Detection

The ATM HEC operations protect the cell header and not the 48-octet payload. The HEC field of 8 bits was selected because it allows the correction of a single-bit error and the detection of multiple bit errors. Figure 6–15 depicts the general logic of the correction and detection functions. Initially, the HEC operation is in the correction mode. If it detects

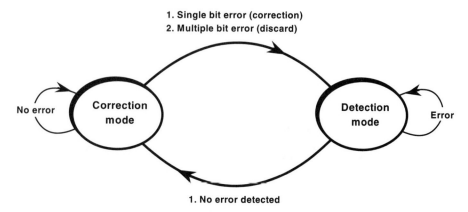

Figure 6–15   Header protection in the HEC field.

either single-bit or multiple-bit errors in the header, it moves to the detection mode. A single-bit error is corrected, and a multiple-bit error results in the discarding of the cell. Once in the correction mode, all cells that have errors are discarded. When a cell with no error is detected, the operation returns to the correction mode. Figure 6–16 shows how a cell is treated if it is either corrupted or uncorrupted, and if the operation is in a correction or detection mode. Refer to the legend in this figure for the explanation.

ATM uses an adaptation of the Hamming code technique known as the Bose-Chadhuri-Hocquenghem (BHC) codes. These codes provide error correction/detection schemes based on the ratio of protection bits in the HEC field (for example) to the protected bits in the cell header (for example). Without delving into error coding theory, which is best left to theoretical texts, it is instructive to note that a 40-bit field (the cell header of 5 octets * 8 bit per octet = 40 bits) needs at least 6 protection bits to correct a single bit. The 6 bits will also detect 36 percent of multiple-bit errors. Improvements to an 84 percent detection rate of multiple-bit errors can be attained if 8 protection bits are used [dePr91]. Of course, this is a good arrangement if optical fiber media are employed, due to optical fiber error characteristics. The HEC field of 8 bits was selected because of these characteristics.

Probability of Discarding Cells

Figure 6–17 illustrates the probability of the ATM network discarding cells in relation to the random bit error rate of a communications

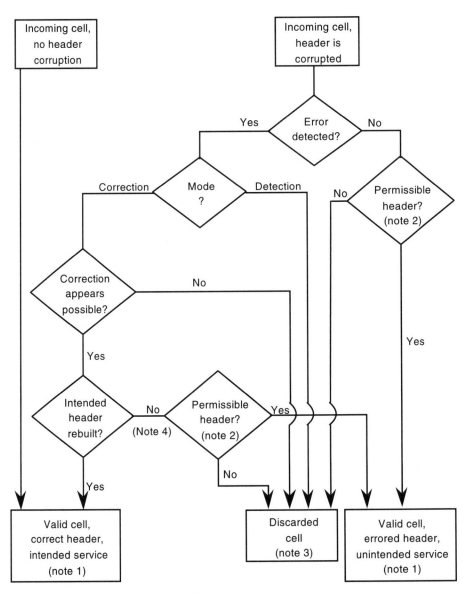

Note 1: Valid cell means cell is free of errors
Note 2: A cell that is not permissible depends on implementation (e.g., invalid VPI/VCI, etc.)
Note 3: Header invalid or not permitted
Note 4: Error correction is not invoked (depends on implementation)

Figure 6–16   ITU-T I.432 view of error handling.

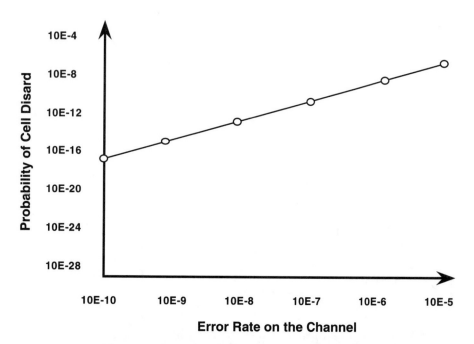

Figure 6–17   Probability of discarding cells.

channel, as published by the ITU-T in I.432. By examining one point on the graph in this figure, even a modest random bit error probability of $10E^{-7}$, the probability of a discarded cell occurring is $10E^{-11}$.

Conclusions.   It can be concluded that the ATM approach of using small cells and small cell headers lends itself to efficient error correction/detection schemes. The next questions are: What size should the full cell be? And, if it is to be small, can it be variable in length or must it be fixed? These two questions are answered in the next two sections.

Overhead of the Cell Approach

The issue of cell overhead is visited in later in Chapter 7. For this discussion, it is noted that the use of small cells (which exhibit a high ratio of overhead to payload) requires an ATM node (switch) to operate at very high speeds, if multiple applications are to be supported simultaneously. Given the same amount of traffic in networks that carry small PDUs (cell networks) versus networks that carry large PDUs (frame networks), the cell networks simply must process more headers and more cells, because, given a steady flow of traffic, there is an inverse ratio between the PDU arrival rate at a node, and the size of the PDU.

For example, consider a Frame Relay network that transports frames. A typical payload is 512 octets, and Frame Relay adds a 2-octet header to this payload. Thus, the ratio of overhead to payload in this Frame Relay example is only .39 percent (16 bits of header / [512 octets × 8 bits per octet] = .0039). In contrast, a typical ATM network carried an overhead ratio of 10.4 percent (40 bits of header / [48 octets × 8 bits per octet] = .1041). Since frames are larger than cells, a node must process more cells than frames, even though the basic link speed into the node is the same for both cell and Frame Relay interfaces.

Actually, the ratio is worse if data transmissions are used as a comparison (which is reasonable, since Frame Relay, at this time, supports only data). The ATM 48-octet payload uses four of these octets for managing and identifying the user traffic at the ATM adaptation layer (AAL). Thus, the ratio of overhead to payload in a typical ATM data network transmission is 70 bits of overhead to 352 bits of data, resulting in an overhead ratio of almost 20 percent.

One must also take into consideration the overhead at the physical layer, and if SONET is used, approximately 4 percent of the channel bandwidth is taken for SONET overhead. Then, one must add in the headers of the upper layer protocols, which are for data transmissions and which can range from 12 to 30 octets for each user PDU.

The overhead cited in the previous paragraph is not an issue in the comparisons of cell and Frame Relay. Notwithstanding, three observations are appropriate:

- ATM must utilize fast processors and high bandwidth channels to compensate for its overhead.
- Even with high bandwidth channels and fast processors, compression operations will still be quite important in ATM networks.
- Comparing the ratio of the overhead bits of *all layers* to the user bits will reveal that, on occasion, actual user traffic is passed though a communications channel.

The "Cell Tax." The criticism of the poor ratio of payload to header bytes is known in some circles as the cell tax. Yet a number of installations that are running ATM state that the cell tax is a small price to pay in relation to the high performance gained in an ATM network. Moreover, some systems are already fraught with overhead, yet their useful features allow their poor use of bandwidth to be overlooked.

Transmission Delay

Previous discussions in this book have explained how certain applications require a predictable and fixed delay of traffic between the source and destination, such as video and voice applications. The task is to design a network that provides time transparency for user payload. This concept means that (for certain applications) the user's payload has a fixed and nonvariable delay between the sender and receiver. In effect, an ATM network must emulate circuit networks, which are designed to provide a fixed delay of voice and video traffic from source to destination.

The ATM layer is not tasked with providing time transparency services to the end-user application. This service is delegated to the AAL and the application running on top of AAL. It entails conditioning the received user payload (typically holding the user payload in a buffer) to achieve a fixed delay from the source to the endpoint(s). For synchronous traffic, the ITU-T requires that transmissions from source to destination shall not incur an overall delay greater than 199 ms. This number is not cast in stone. Many studies reveal a round-trip tolerance, in the absence of echoes, for audio of 600 ms ([EMLI63] and [KITA91]).

As illustrated in Figure 6–18, a number of factors contribute to the delay of a cell. At the sender, delay is incurred when voice and video traffic are translated and segmented into cells by convergence services and segmentation and reassembly (C/SAR) services. At the receiver, delay is incurred for the opposite operations.

Each transmission channel in the end-to-end path incurs a delay in the transport of the cell between the user device or the switch(es). This is shown in Figure 6–18 as propagation delay (PD). While ranges vary on the exact delay in the transmission, it is predictable, because it depends on the distance between the transmitting station and the receiving station. ITU-T provides guidance with ranges running between 4 to 5 µs per km. The IEEE uses a 4.2 µs delay on CSMA/CD networks.

At the switch, two forms of delay are incurred: queuing delay (QD) and switching delay (SD). Because the switches are performing STDM operations, and since traffic arrives asynchronously at the switches, it is necessary to build queues to accommodate peaks in traffic. Obviously, delay varies in relation to the amount of traffic in the network and the time required to process the traffic at the switch.

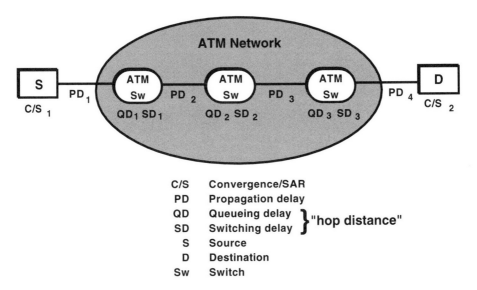

C/S   Convergence/SAR
PD   Propagation delay
QD   Queueing delay ⎫
SD   Switching delay ⎬ "hop distance"
                        ⎭
S   Source
D   Destination
Sw   Switch

Figure 6–18   Factors in delay.

The second factor at the switch is the speed at which traffic is relayed through the switch. SD varies depending on the type of switching operation employed, but it is a fixed delay vis-à-vis the size of the cell. Generally, switches today can process a cell within a broad range of 2 to 30 μs.

Additional delay may be incurred to remove jitter by queuing the traffic slightly longer at the final receiver. Thus, delay through an ATM network entails the summation of the delays incurred at the user devices, the switches, and on the communications links.

It is noted that switching can be performed faster than the line speed. Consequently, switching speed is usually limited by the communications lines (155 Mbit/s, etc.) that are input into the switch (unless excessive queuing occurs).

Given the assumptions and estimates cited above, end-to-end delay of a cell traveling from the sending machine to the receiving machine (in Figure 6–18) is 14.297 ms, well within the ITU-T requirements of 199 ms for digitized voice. This value was derived by the following assumptions:

C/S   12000 μs (6000 μs each at source and destination),
         and variable

PD   2000 μs (assuming a distance of 500 km between
         source and destination)

SD   72 μs (24 μs at each switch, with 3 switches), and variable

QD   225 μs (75 μs at each switch, with 3 switches), and variable

Several conclusions are drawn from this discussion. First, it is obvious that propagation delay (PD) is a factor when compared to some of the other ingredients of delay. In older systems with slow processors, this factor was not considered significant in relation to the relatively large QD, C/S, and SD values. In newer systems, the PD remains the same, of course, but the ratios change. A more important consideration is link speed, discussed shortly.

The second conclusion is the C/S functions may consume considerable overhead if voice and video must be converted to digital signals and then segmented at the transmitter (and have the complementary yet opposite functions performed at the receiver).

The third conclusion is that the C/S functions should be performed only twice: at the source and destination points. If other networks reside between these two machines, additional mapping and convergence functions must be performed to enter and exit the synchronous network. Consequently, the C/S functions play an important role at this additional interface. Finally, be aware that C/S, SD, and QD will vary between machines, and QD is a function of the amount of traffic entering the switch and the size of the queues.

The fourth conclusion is that each hop (switch) on the path adds delay (and variable delay) to the end-to-end transmission. Some vendors call this situation the "hop distance." It is quite important to reduce the hop distance between the sender and receiver if possible, because each hop introduces more delay.

Although not shown in Figure 6–18, another factor is also significant, from which a fifth conclusion can be reached: link speed also determines delay (but not variable delay). For example, a 2.2 Mbyte photograph takes over five minutes to transmit on a 56 kbit/s link and less than 18 seconds on a 1 Mbit/s link [NORT98]. Certainly, fast switches are important, but they need to be connected with fast links if they are to realize their full potential.

The surface has only been touched regarding the design considerations in providing the ATM user semantic, SDU size, and time transparency services. Notwithstanding, we can now move forward to a more detailed examination of the ATM virtual circuits, and the ATM multiplexing and switching operations. Later, the transparency services are revisited in their relation to traffic management in an ATM network.

ATM LABELS

Earlier discussions explained that an ATM connection is identified through two labels called the virtual path identifier (VPI) and virtual channel identifier (VCI). In each direction, at a given interface, different virtual paths are multiplexed by ATM onto a physical circuit. The VPIs and VCIs identify these multiplexed connections.

As shown in Figure 6–19 virtual channel connections can have end-to-end significance between two end users, usually between two AAL entities. The values of these connection identifiers change as the traffic is relayed through the ATM network. For example, in a switched virtual connection, a specific VCI value has no end-to-end significance. It is the responsibility of the ATM network to "keep track" of the different VCI values as they relate to each other on an end-to-end basis. Perhaps a good way to view the relationship of VCIs and VPIs is to think that VCIs are part of VPIs; they exist within the VPIs.

Routing in the ATM network is performed by the ATM switch examining both the VCI and VPI fields in the cell, or only the VPI field. This choice depends on how the switch is designed and if VCIs are terminated within the network–a topic covered in Chapter 8.

The VCI/VPI fields can be used with switched or nonswitched ATM operations. They can be used with point-to-point or point-to-multipoint

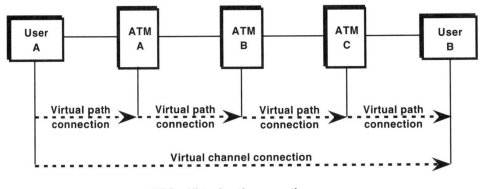

VPC   Virtual path connection
VCC   Virtual channel connection

Figure 6–19   Types of ATM connections.

operations. They can be pre-established (PVCs) or set up on demand, based on signaling procedures, such as Q.2931, derived from the ISDN network layer protocol.

Additionally, the value assigned to the VCI at the user-network interface (UNI) can be assigned by (1) the network, (2) the user, or (3) through a negotiation process between the network and the user.

Multiplexing VCIs and VPIs

So, to review briefly, the ATM layer has two multiplexing hierarchies: the virtual channel and the virtual path. The virtual path identifier (VPI) is a bundle of virtual channels. Each bundle must have the same endpoints. The purpose of the VPI is to identify a group of virtual channel (VC) connections. One approach allows VCIs to be "nailed-up" end-to-end to provide semipermanent connections for the support of a large number of user sessions. VPIs and VCIs can also be established on demand.

The VC is used to identify a unidirectional facility for the transfer of the ATM traffic. The VCI is assigned at the time a VC session is activated in the ATM network. Routing might occur in an ATM network at the VC level. If VCIs are used in the network, the ATM switch must translate the incoming VCI values into outgoing VCI values on the outgoing VC links. The VC links must be concatenated to form a full virtual channel connection (VCC). The VCCs are used for user-to-user, user-to-network, or network transfer of traffic.

The VPI identifies a group of VC links that share the same virtual path connection (VPC). The VPI value is assigned each time the VP is switched in the ATM network. Like the VC, the VP is unidirectional for the transfer of traffic between two contiguous ATM entities.

As shown in Figures 6–20 and 6–21, two different VCs that belong to different VPs at a particular interface are allowed to have the same VCI value (VCI 1, VCI 2). Consequently, the concatenation of VCI and VPI is necessary to uniquely identify a virtual connection.

CELL RELAY BEARER SERVICE (CRBS)

The type of ATM services offered to two communicating users is known as the Cell Relay Bearer Service (CRBS) [MINO93]. In accordance with the OSI term "bearer" service, CRBS offers only basic lower layer services—in this instance, specific services at the ATM layer.

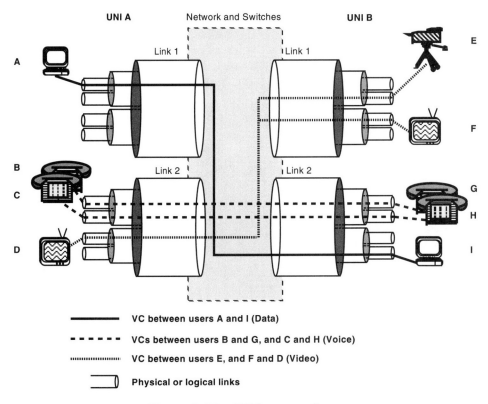

Figure 6–20 ATM connections.

The most valuable aspect to CRBS is the descriptions of how the transfer of cells occur between the ATM users. In this section, we describe these operations:

- Bidirectional symmetric point-to-point (BSPP) service
- Unidirectional point-to-point (UPP) service
- Bidirectional point-to-multipoint (BSPM) service
- Bidirectional asymmetric point-to-multipoint (BAPM) service
- Unidirectional point-to-multipoint (UPM) service
- Bidirectional symmetric multipoint-to-multipoint (BSMM) service
- Bidirectional asymmetric multipoint-to-multipoint (BAMM) service
- Unidirectional multipoint-to-multipoint (UMM) service

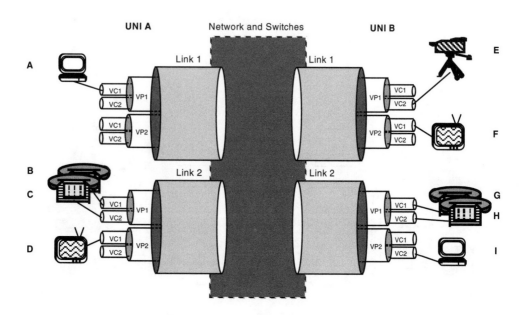

Virtual Circuits:

A to I: UNI A, Link 1, VCI 1, VPI 1 ↔ UNI B, Link 2, VCI 2, VPI 2

B to G: UNI A, Link 2, VCI 1, VPI 1 ↔ UNI B, Link 2, VCI 1, VPI 1

C to H: UNI A, Link 2, VCI 2, VPI 1 ↔ UNI B, Link 2, VCI 2, VPI 1

E to F and D: UNI B, Link 1, VCI 2, VPI1 → UNI A, Link 2, VCI 1, VPI 2,

and → UNI B, Link 1, VCI 1, VPI 2

Figure 6–21   ATM connection identifiers.

The term *bidirectional* means cells are transferred in both directions between the communicating users; unidirectional means cells are transferred in one direction only. The term *symmetric* means the amount of bandwidth, and the QOS (delay, throughput, etc.) are the same in both directions between the users. *Asymmetric* means these operations may be different in each direction of the virtual connection. The term *point-to-point* means cells are transferred from one user to one other user. *Point-to-multipoint* means the cells are transferred from one user to more than one user. Most of these terms and their underlying concepts are self-evident. However, a few comments about point-to-multipoint and multipoint-to-multipoint services should prove useful.

Point-to-Multipoint and Multipoint-to-Multipoint Services

In order to support applications such as telephone conference calls, downline loading of video programs, and video conferencing operations, ATM provides a service called point-to-multipoint connections. From a technical standpoint, a point-to-multipoint connection is nothing more than a collection of associated VC or VP links with their associated endpoints.

In a point-to-multipoint service, the endpoints have a link that serves as the root in a logical tree topology. This approach means that when a root node sends traffic, all of the remaining nodes (which are leaf nodes) receive copies of this traffic. In the present evolution of ATM and the ATM standards, the root node communicates directly with the leaf nodes. The leaf nodes (as of this writing) may not communicate with each other. A multipoint-to-multipoint service assumes a group of users need to be connected to one another, such as in a telephone conference call. Many of the issues surrounding these two services need further study.

SUMMARY

ATM is a high-speed, low-delay multiplexing and switching technology. It supports any type of user traffic, such as voice, data, and video applications.

ATM uses small, fixed-length units called cells. Each cell is identified with VPIs and VCIs that are contained in the cell header. An ATM network uses these identifiers to relay the traffic through high-speed switches.

ATM provides limited error detection operations. It provides no retransmission services for user traffic, and few operations are performed on the small header. The intention of this approach is to implement a network that is fast enough to support multimegabit transfer rates.

ATM also has a layer that operates above it, called the ATM adaptation layer (AAL). This layer performs convergence as well as segmentation and reassembly operations on different types of traffic.

7

The ATM Adaptation Layer (AAL)

This chapter examines the ATM adaptation layer (AAL). The ATM classes of traffic are explained and related to the types of AAL protocol data units (PDUs). The rationale for the size and format of the AAL headers and trailers is analyzed.

Before we begin, a quick review of AAL is in order. The point has been made in earlier discussions that AAL is an essential part of the ATM network because it "converges" (adapts) the user traffic to the cell-based network. It is also important to remember that for transfer of user traffic (the B-ISDN U-plane), the AAL operates at the endpoints of the virtual connection and does not operate within the ATM backbone network. For C-plane and M-plane traffic, AAL may be invoked at the network node of the UNI.

PRINCIPAL TASKS OF THE AAL

The AAL is designed to support different types of applications and different types of traffic, such as voice, video, and data. At first glance, it might appear that the integration of voice, data, and video is a simple matter. After all, once the analog signals have been converted to digital images, all transmissions can be treated as data-bit images. However, if we examine the transmission requirements of voice and data, we find that they are quite different. Be aware the AAL standards do not define completely how to manage and support these requirements. These important functions are either defined in other standards or are vendor-specific.

Voice and video transmissions exhibit a high tolerance for errors. If an occasional cell is distorted, the quality of the voice or video reproduction is not severely affected. In contrast, data transmissions have a low tolerance (more often, no tolerance) for errors. One corrupted bit changes the meaning of the data.

Yet another difference between voice, data, and video transmissions deals with network delay. For the voice or video cell to be translated back to an analog signal in a real-time mode, the network delay for these cells must be constant and generally must be low. Some studies shows that a two-way speech communication can tolerate round-trip delays of up to 600 ms, in the absence of echoes. Other studies show that the perceived quality is better with lower delays—around 200 ms ([EMLI63] and [KITA91]).

For data traffic, the network delay can vary considerably. Indeed, data can be transmitted asynchronously through the network, without regard to precise timing arrangements between the sender and the receiver. To complicate matters further, specific data applications exhibit different delay requirements. For example, LAN-to-LAN traffic is more delay-sensitive than say, email traffic. In contrast, video transmissions must maintain a precise timing relationship between the sender and the receiver.

Since voice and video traffic can afford (on occasion) to be lost or discarded, packets may be discarded in the event of excessive delays and/or congestion in the network. Again, the loss does not severely affect voice fidelity if the lost packets are not detected by a human—who is the ultimate judge of the video and audio quality. As discussed before, data can ill afford to be lost or discarded.

As explained in Chapter 6, the tolerance for cell loss in audio systems is a function of (1) the number of bits in the cell, (2) the compression ratio (if any) reflected in these bits, and (3) the coding rate of the signal (e.g., 32 kbit/s), because the length of a cell loss is the important component in judging the quality of speech and audio. Indeed, a fine line exists in selecting an acceptable length of cell loss. Studies [JAYA81] reveal that losing several samples is disturbing to the listener because it has the effect of impulse noise. Traffic loss of around 32 to 64 ms is quite disruptive, because it means the loss of speech phonemes. On the other hand, cell loss of a duration of some 4 to 16 ms is not very noticeable or disturbing to the listener.

Finally, voice and video transmissions require a short queue length at the network nodes in order to reduce delay, or at least to make the delay more predictable. The short voice packet queue lengths can experience overflow occasionally, with resulting packet loss. However, data packets require the queue lengths to be longer to prevent packet loss in potential overflow conditions.

THE AAL SUBLAYERS

The ATM adaptation layer (AAL) plays a key role in the ability of an ATM network to support multiapplication operations. The type of user payload is identified at the AAL. Therefore, AAL must be able to accommodate to a wide variety of traffic—from connectionless, asynchronous data to connection-oriented, synchronous voice and video applications.

The ATM standards groups decided that the AAL should be divided into two sublayers: the convergence sublayer (CS) and the segmentation and reassembly sublayer (SAR). The rationale for this structure is explained in Chapter 6. This layered architecture is in consonance with the conventional OSI layered architecture approach described in Chapter 3. So, we continue these discussions in the next section of this chapter.

Creating and Processing the AAL PDU

As depicted in Figure 7–1, AAL is responsible for accepting the user traffic, which could range from one octet to several thousand octets, and placing a protocol control information (PCI) (variations of headers and trailers) around it. The length of this initial header and trailer varies depending on the application. It could be as small as 6 octets and can range as high as approximately 40 octets. This initial header and trailer may not be added by all AAL implementations, it will depend on the type of traffic.[1]

The traffic is then segmented into data units ranging in size from 44 to 47 octets. The size varies depending on the type of traffic, such as voice, video, or data.

---

[1]This initial header and trailer is part of the AAL type 3/4 operation and is not used much. I describe it here for continuity.

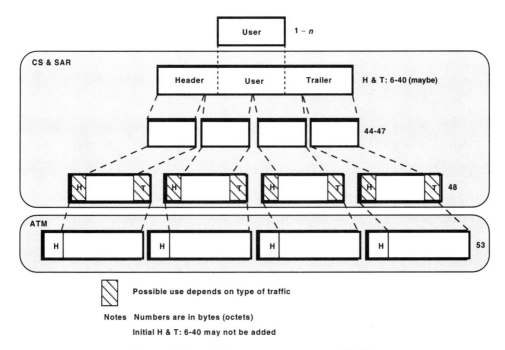

Figure 7–1   AAL convergence and SAR.

The next function entails adding a header and, possibly, a trailer to each data unit. Once again, the nature of the header and the possible use of the trailer will vary depending on the type of payload that is being supported. In any event, the final data unit from this operation is always a 48-octet PDU.

As discussed earlier, the choice of the 48-octet payload was based on several factors. One factor is cell loss for voice transmissions. Given a payload of 384 bits (48 octets * = 384), samples of a digitized voice image (at 64 kbits/s) results in a 1-cell loss of 6 ms—well within the tolerances cited earlier (382 / 64000 = .006).

Moreover, later discussions in this chapter reveal that methods and standards exist to allow the selective shedding of parts of a sample for voice and video, and not an entire sample. This approach results in a very flexible and efficient means to (1) compensate for cell loss, (2) maintain a high-quality signal, and (3) ameliorate potential congestion by reducing the number of bits processed by the network.

The last operation shown in Figure 7–1 is performed by the ATM layer, which adds a 5-octet header to the 48-octet payload, resulting in a 53-octet ATM cell.

In accordance with the ideas of layered protocols, the reverse of these operations takes place at the receiving machine.

CLASSES OF TRAFFIC

AAL is organized around a concept called service classes, which are summarized in Table 7–1. The classes are defined with regards to the following operations:

- Timing between sender and receiver (present or not present)
- Bit rate (variable or constant)
- Connectionless or connection-oriented sessions between sender and receiver
- Sequencing of user payload
- Flow control operations
- Accounting for user traffic
- Segmentation and reassembly (SAR) of user PDUs

Table 7–1   AAL Classes of Traffic

Purpose: Convert and aggregate different traffic into standard formats to support different user applications

- **Class A**
  Constant bit rate (CBR)
  Connection-oriented, e.g., CBR for video
  Timing relationship between source and destination: Required
- **Class B**
  Variable bit rate (VBR)
  Connection-oriented, e.g., VBR video for voice
  Timing relationship between source and destination: Required
- **Class C**
  Variable bit rate (VBR)
  Connection-oriented, e.g., bursty data services
  Timing relationship between source and destination: Not required
- **Class D**
  Variable bit rate (VBR)
  Connectionless, e.g., bursty datagram services
  Timing relationship between source and destination: Not required
- **Class X**
  Traffic type and timing requirements defined by the user (unrestricted)

As of this writing, the ITU-T had approved four classes, A through D. We will now summarize these classes and their major features. Table 7–2 is provided to assist the reader during this discussion.

Classes A and B require timing relationships between the source and destination. Therefore, clocking mechanisms are utilized for this traffic. The synchronization could be performed with a timestamp and/or a synchronous clock. This function can be performed in the application running on top of AAL.

Classes C and D do not require precise timing relationships. A constant bit rate (CBR) is required for class A, and a variable bit rate (VBR) is permitted for classes B, C, and D. Classes A, B, and C are connection-oriented, while class D is connectionless.

It is obvious that these classes are intended to support different types of user applications. For example, class A is designed to support a CBR requirement for high-quality video applications. On the other hand, class B, while connection-oriented, supports VBR applications and is applicable for VBR video and voice applications. Class B service could be used by information retrieval services in which large amounts of video traffic are sent to the user and then delays occur as the user examines the information.

Class C services are the connection-oriented data transfer services such as X.25-type connections. Conventional connectionless services, such as datagram networks, are supported with class D services.

Last, the ATM Forum has specified class X, which is an unrestricted service where the requirements are defined by the user. The Forum has also defined variations of the VBR operations called available bit rate (ABR) and unspecified bit rate (UBR). These categories are explained in Chapter 9.

Table 7–2   Support Operations for AAL Classes

Class	A	B	C	D
Timing	Synchronous		Asynchronous	
Bit transfer	Constant	Variable		
Connection mode		Connection-oriented		Connection-less

RATIONALE FOR AAL TYPES

In order to support different types of user traffic and provide the classes of service just described, AAL employs several protocol types. Each type is implemented to support one or a number of user applications, such as voice, data, and so on. Each type consists of a specific SAR and CS. As a general statement, the type 1 protocol supports class A traffic, type 2 supports class B traffic, and so on, but other combinations are permitted, if appropriate.

The point has been made several times in this book that the very nature of emerging technologies, such as ATM, makes it difficult to write about the subject matter as if the protocols were cast in stone. The AAL is no exception. Initially, the ITU-T published four AAL types to support four classes of traffic. However, as the standards groups became more attuned to the tasks at hand, it was recognized that this approach needed to be modified. Also, little interest was shown (initially) in defining type 2 traffic for class B applications, and it was also acknowledged that a user-specified class of traffic should be included, as well as a provision for interworking frame relay into ATM. So, modifications were made to the specifications to reflect these changes. This chapter includes the latest changes made to AAL, and at the time this book went to press, it is up to date.

One of the major changes is that VBR applications are serviced at the AAL by a common part (CP), and a service specific part (SSP). As the names of these parts imply, the CP is somewhat generic and pertains to a set of VBR applications, and the SSP pertains to a VBR application that requires additional and specific services. With these thoughts in mind, the next part of this chapter provides a review of the AAL protocol types.

DIVIDING CS INTO FURTHER SUBLAYERS

As the AAL has been further defined and refined, the CS has been divided for the support of type 3/4 and 5 traffic. Figure 7–2 shows this change. The two sublayers are the service specific CS (SSCS) and the common part of CS (CPCS). As their names imply, SSCS is designed to support a specific aspect of a data application, and CPCS supports generic functions common to more than one type of data application. Specific examples of these sublayers are provided later in this chapter and in Chapter 10.

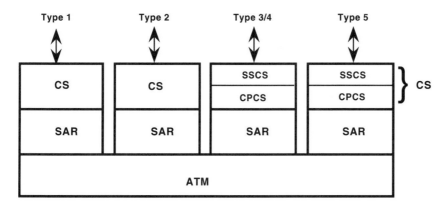

SSCS   Service specific CS

SPCS   Common part CS

Figure 7–2   Dividing the CS into sublayers.

AAL NAMING CONVENTIONS

Before we launch into an examination of the AAL details, a few words are in order about the AAL structure and the naming conventions. Chapter 3 provides the basics for the ensuing discussion. Figure 7–3 shows the conventions for the ATM and AAL layers, as well as the placement of service access points (SAPs), and the naming conventions. Based on the information in Chapter 3, this figure is largely self-explanatory. It can be seen that the naming conventions follow the OSI conventions and use the concepts of service access points (SAPs), service data units (SDUs), protocol data units (PDUs), primitives, encapsulation, decapsulation, and protocol control information (headers and trailers).

AAL TYPE 1 (AAL1)

As we just learned, for class A traffic the bit rate does not vary over time. The term fixed bit rate means that the bit rate is (1) constant and (2) synchronized between sender and receiver (see Figure 7–4). Each sample of the analog image results contains the same number of bits. Traditional 64 kbit/s voice traffic is an example of class A traffic.

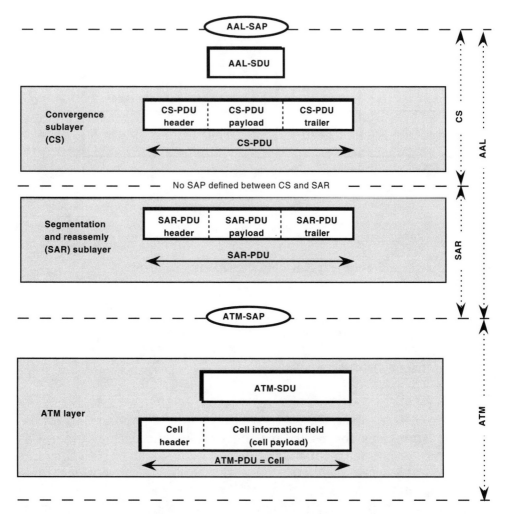

Figure 7–3 AAL general data unit conventions.

THE AAL1 PDU

The AAL uses type 1 PDUs to support applications requiring a CBR transfer to and from the layer above AAL. It is divided into the CS and SAR sublayers. The CS needs a clock for some of its operations. According to I.363, the clock can be derived from the S_B or T_B interface, but in practice, the clock can be derived from other sources (see Chapter 2 for a discussion on clocking). CS is responsible for the following tasks:

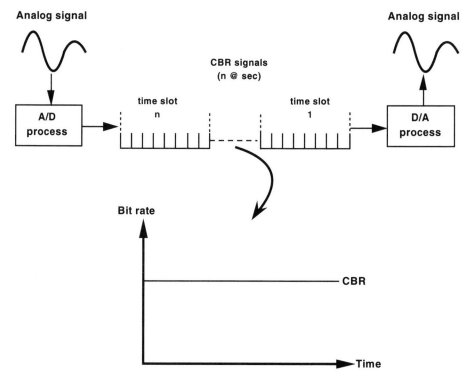

Figure 7–4   Constant bit rate (CBR) applications.

- Accommodating to cell delay variation, and delivering AAL-SDUs to the user at a constant bit rate
- Detecting lost or missequenced cells
- Providing source clock frequency recovery at the receiver (if needed)
- Providing FEC on the AAL1 header

The SAR has the job of receiving a 47-octet PDU from CS and adding a 1-byte header to it at the transmitting side and performing the reverse operation at the receiving side.

As depicted in Figure 7–5, the AAL1 PDU consists of 48 octets with 47 octets available for the application payload. The AAL1 header consists of four bits in the two fields. The first field is a sequence number (SN) and is used for detection of mistakenly inserted cells or lost cells. The SN protection (SNP) field performs error detection on the SN.

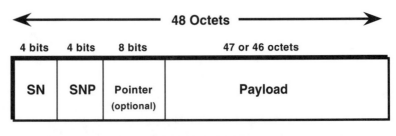

SN   Sequence number (1 bit CSI, 3 bits sequence count)
SNP Sequence number protection
CSI Convergence sublayer indication
      (0 = no pointer; 1 = pointer)

Note: Optional timestamp uses 1 bit of CSI in every other PDU

Figure 7–5   AAL1 PDU.

As mentioned earlier, AAL1 CS is responsible for clock recovery for both audio and video services. This operation can be accomplished through the use of real-time synchronization or through the use of time-stamping.

The SN is not used to request the sender to retransmit the PDU, because of the unacceptable delay this operation would entail. Rather, the detection of traffic loss with the SN can be used as feedback information to the sender to modify its operations (with a knowledge of the nature of the loss [WADA89]).

One bit in the SN field is called the convergence sublayer indication (CSI) and is used to indicate that an 8-bit pointer exists. This pointer capability allows a cell to be partially filled if the user application so requires in order to reduce delay in assembling and processing additional bits or octets.

AAL 1 Modes of Operation

CBR traffic can operate in one of two modes: the unstructured data transfer (UDT) mode or the structured data transfer (SDT) mode. The former is a bit stream operation that has an associated bit clock, and the latter is a byte stream (8 bit octets) operation with a fixed block length that has an associated clock. The intent of the structured mode is to allow the sending of 8-bit samples (or multiple samples in the 8-bit byte for ADPCM coding schemes, etc.).

Synchronization and Clock Recovery

Clock recovery can be provided by a timestamp or an adaptive clock. The first method is called the synchronous residual timestamp (SRTS). The RTS information (4 bits) is carried in a serial bit stream by the CSI bit in successive headers of the AAL PDUs. This value is used at the receiver to determine the frequency difference between a common reference clock (fn) to the local service clock (fs). A derived network clock frequency (fnx) is obtained from the fn. For example, assume an fn for SONET of 155.520 MHz. The fnx for is fn $* 2^{-k}$, where K is a specified integer. For 64 Kbit/s, K = 11, so the fnx is $155.520 * 2^{-11}$, or 75.9375 kHz.

The number of derived clock cycles (mq) is obtained at the sender and conveyed to the receiver in the timestamp field, which allows the receiver to reconstruct the service clock of the sender.

The term "residual" stems from the fact that this method actually sends a value representing the residual part of mq. The residual part is frequency difference information, and can vary. The timestamp represents y, where $y = N * fnx/fs * e$ (N is the period of RTS in cycles of fs, and e is the service clock tolerance m e). This approach is used because it is assumed the nominal part of mq is known at the receiver, so only the residual part mq is conveyed.

The SRTS method assumes the availability of a common synchronous network clock from which sender and receiver can reference. Plesiochronous operations that do not have a common reference clock are not standardized, and vary between vendors and countries.

Other aspects and rules for the SRTS are explained in G.823, G.824, and I.363, if you want to know more about the SRTS method. I.363 also describes the FEC mechanism for unidirectional video services.

For the adaptive clock method, the local CS simply reads the buffer of the incoming traffic with a local clock. The level of the buffer (its fill level) controls the frequency of the clock. The measure of the fill level drives a mechanism to control the local clock.

Running AAL 1 Traffic on a T1 Link

Figure 7–6 shows an example of how AAL1 can be used to support 64 kbit/s voice traffic.[2] The ATM cells are run over a 1.544 Mbit/s T1 link. In

---

[2]This example is an effective, pragmatic way to utilize the T1 plant for ATM traffic. It is not a standard however. To see how the ATM Forum views interworking T1 and ATM, see Chapter 14, and the section titled, "Circuit Emulation Service Interoperability (CES-IS) Specification.

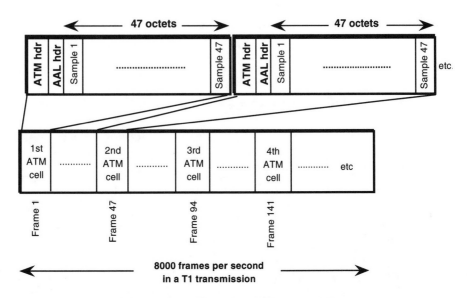

Figure 7–6   Running AAL 1 over T1.

this situation, the T1 line is unchannelized: It is simply providing the raw bandwidth, and the notion of 24 fixed slots per T1 frame does not exist.

Assuming that 47 samples are placed into one cell, an ATM voice call requires 171 cells per second, because 8000 samples per second / 47 samples per cell = 171 (170.212). A system must allocate a cell in every 47th frame on the T1 channel, since 8000 frames a second/171 cells = 47 (46.783). Therefore, a cell is sent in every 47th frame.

This example assumes that the equipment is designed to handle a constant playout at the receiver, and that timing has been provided. The residual timestamp can be used, if necessary. One last point, the 171st cell would not fill the AAL PDU. Therefore, the AAL1 PDU pointer is employed to identify the samples from the remainder of the bytes in the PDU, which are used as padding to achieve a full 48-byte boundary.

AAL TYPE 2 (AAL2)

AAL2 is employed for VBR services where a timing relationship is required between the source and destination sites. Class B traffic, such as VBR audio or video, falls into this category.

The type 2 category of service requires that timing information be maintained between the transmitting and receiving sites. AAL2 is responsible for handling variable cell delay, as well as the detection and handling of lost or missequenced PDUs. Since a cell may be only partially filled because of the bursty aspect of VBR operations, the SAR, in addition to its segmentation and reassembly operations, also maintains a record of how many octets in the user payload area actually contain traffic.

In earlier implementations of digitized voice, all systems used fixed bit-rate schemes. The same statement holds true for earlier video A/D operations. However, shortly after the advent of the analog-to-digital process, research indicated that it would be efficacious to compress the resulting digitized images so that a reduced number of bits would be transmitted through the communications channel.

The manner in which the compression algorithms operate on the data leads to the traffic's exhibiting VBR characteristics. This means that the bit rate varies in time, as depicted in the Figure 7–7. VBR coding is widely employed in video systems to take advantage of visual irrelevancy and variable redundancy. Visual irrelevancy describes the inability of the human eye to comprehend the full details of an image—especially moving images. For example, in television, pictures are actually displayed on the

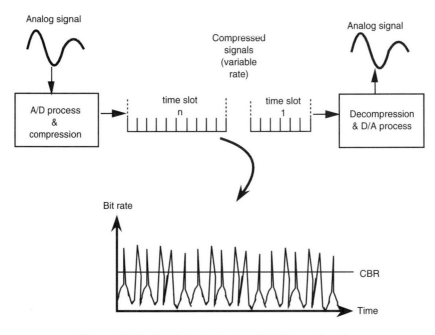

Figure 7–7   Variable bit rate (VBR) applications.

screen between 25 and 30 times a second. However, the human eye is not capable of perceiving these fixed images. Furthermore, due to the analog nature of digital signals, there is a high correlation between adjacent images and, indeed, adjacent pixels within images. So, compression schemes take advantage of variable redundancies.

The AAL 2 PDU

The PDU for AAL type 2 was not defined fully until 1997 (see ITU-T I.136.2, and some issues are still under study). This type is intended to support low bit rate, delay-sensitive applications. An additional idea is the multiplexing of more than one AAL2 stream over one ATM connection, which has been defined in a general manner in earlier ATM specifications, but is defined in considerable detail for AAL2.

The fields in the PDU, depicted in Figure 7–8 are as follows:

OSF	Offset field	Number of octets between start field and packet; acts as a pointer into the payload
SN	Sequence number	Numbers the PDUs
P	Parity	Odd parity check on the start field
CID	Channel ID	Values of 8-255 used to identify user traffic
LI	Length indicator	Number of octets in the payload (default-45)
UUI	User-to-user indication	A user field, transported transparently to users
HEC	Header error control	Error check on the 3-byte packet header
PAD	Padding bytes, if needed	To fill the 48-byte ATM-SDU

The offset field is the first octet in the 48-byte area and always points to the beginning of a user packet (a CPS-SDU). If the payload carries the beginning of a packet, then the offset fields points to the very next byte following it. AAL2 permits a user packet to be split across cells. If this operation is necessary, the offset field points to the beginning of the next packet in the ATM-SDU. The receiver knows how to locate the packet across cells (that is, where the segmented packet ends and where the new packet begins) by the length indicator in the packet header, and the offset field.

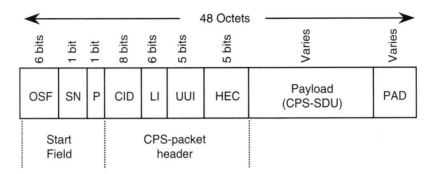

Note: CPS-packet header may exist more than once in ATM-SDU

OSF   Offset field
SN   Sequence number
P   Parity
CID   Channel ID
LI   Length indicator
UUI   User-to-user indication
HEC   Header error control
PAD   Padding bytes, if needed

Figure 7–8   AAL 2 PDU

Example of AAL 2 Support of Voice Traffic. Figure 7–9 provides an example of how AAL2 supports voice traffic. We assume a voice over ATM (VoATM) gateway accepts analog speech at the sender and digitizes it, thus creating G.729.A voice packets, which are presented to AAL2. At the receiving VoATM gateway, this process is reversed.

The G.729.A Recommendation is designed for low-bit rate audio coders and operates at 8 kbit/s. Each G.729.A frame is 10 octets in length. For this example the voice packet is encapsulated with the Real Time Protocol (RTP), thus creating a 14-octet packet (the RTP header is 4 octets in length).[3]

The offset field points to the start of the packet. Recall that this field is placed in the first octet of the 48-octet ATM-SDU. The 14-octet RTP/G.729.A packet is appended with the 3-octet AAL2 packet header, and these 17 octets are placed in the cell payload. The process simply loads the ATM-SDU with contiguous 17 octets until the 48 octets are

---

[3]The subjects of RTP and G.729.A are beyond the scope of this book. See another book in this series titled, *Advanced Internet Technologies* for information on RTP as well as the G.729.A Recommendation.

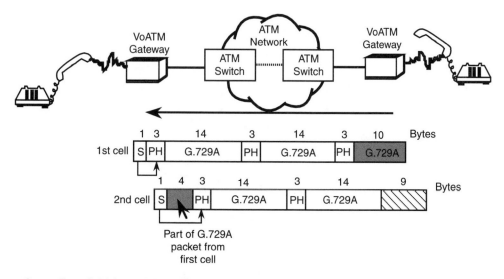

S   Start field (containing offset)
PH   Packet header

Figure 7–9   AAL 2 Support of Voice Traffic.

filled. In this example, the third packet is placed in the last part of the first cell and the first part of the second cell. The offset field in the second cell points to the first CPS packet header, which is the fourth packet in this stream. Recall that the length of the packet is indicated in the packet header. Therefore (and in this example), it is used to determine the remaining octets of the third packet residing in the second cell.

AAL2 Support of Voice and Data Traffic. The previous example showed support of voice only, with fixed-length packets. AAL2 can also support voice and data traffic by multiplexing these applications together, and identifying each traffic stream (fixed-length voice, and variable-length data) with a unique channel identifier (CID). The AAL2 operations to handle these applications are like the example in Figure 7–9: The offset field identifies the packet boundaries, and those packets that cannot fit into one cell, are segmented and the packet's remaining octets are placed in the next cell.

Functional Model for AAL 2

Figures 7–10 and 7–11 show the functional model for AAL2, derived from ITU-T I.363.2. It is a good illustration of the relationships of the

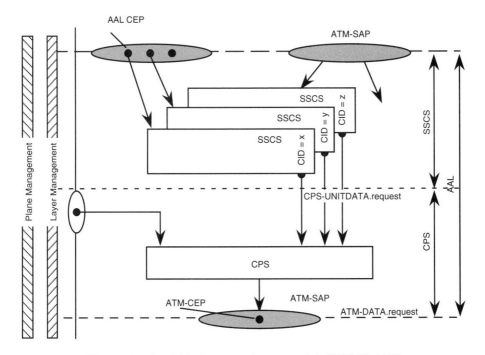

Figure 7–10   AAL 2 transmitter model. [ITN-TI.363]

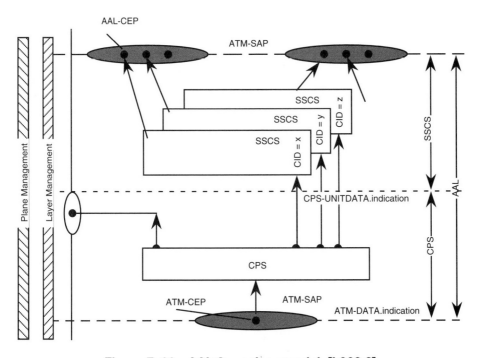

Figure 7–11   AAL 2 receiver model. [I.363.2]

SAPs, the connection end points within the SAPs, the primitives, and the layers. Notice that each AAL-CEP correlates to an SSCS invocation, which is identified with a CID. Also notice in Figure 7–10 that multiple CIDs can be multiplexed into one CPS, and these are conveyed to the ATM layer through the ATM SAP and an associated ATM-CEP. The reverse operations take place at the receiver, as shown in Figure 7–11.

It is evident that there are no primitives defined between SSCS and the layer above SSCS, which is the end-user layer. I find this omission in I.363.2 troublesome, since it does not give the user application programmer guidance about how to construct calls to and from AAL2.

VOICE PACKETIZATION

The AAL does not define the syntax of the payload inside the AAL1 or AAL2 PDUs, and the manner in which the voice or video image is digitized is defined in other standards, or in a vendor's proprietary package. Moreover, AAL2 does not define the timing relationships between the sending and receiving applications and how the receiver adjusts to jitter (variations in the arrival times of the packets) for real-time traffic. In addition, AAL2 does not describe what actions are to take place if traffic is lost (other than to send a diagnostic to layer management), or how to handle silent periods in the speech conversation. RTP provides a timestamp in its header, which is used for timing, but RTP also does not define play-out operations, nor how to handle silent periods.

This section explains how these voice packets can be created and placed in an AAL PDU that supports VBR traffic, based on [CCIT90a] and [SRIR93]. The latter reference is based on the research that led to AT&T's Integrated Access and Cross-Connect System (IACS).[4]

---

[4]This example is based on Recommendation G.764, a relatively old specification, published in 1990. The operations of G.764 to protect the important parts of the speech sample have been assumed by newer G Series specifications dealing with voice coders (vocoders), that implement the interleaving procedures shown in this example, as well as other more elaborate operations, such as bit repetition, convolutional coding, silence/noise playback, and forward error correction (FEC). I have kept G.764 in this second edition because it provides good tutorials on timestamping, support of multiple coding schemes, noise insertion, handling missing voice packets, and play-out procedures at the receiver.

The term "packet" is used in this discussion in deference to industry practice; it defines a group of bits that contain samples of a voice image. Whatever the term used, the voice packet is placed inside the AAL PDU.

Previous discussions in this book have explained that a certain amount of traffic loss (packet discard, misrouting, etc.) for voice is tolerable and acceptable. The amount of loss that can occur is quite variable, ranging from 1 to 10 percent, depending on (1) how the voice images are sampled, (2) how they are coded in the packet, and (3) how they may be discarded. For systems that do not selectively discard traffic, the tolerable loss is low; for systems that selectively discard traffic, the tolerable loss is high. However, for video traffic, the loss of a single cell might cause degradation of the picture if synchronization is lost. Therefore, cell loss must be rare. Studies have shown that a high-quality television signal operating at 155 Mbit/s, in which a cell is not lost for about two hours requires a bit error rate of 10^{-12} and a cell error rate of 10^{-10} [LEE93]. As discussed in Chapter 6, these levels of performance are obtainable with optical fiber.

Grouping Samples into Blocks

To explain the rationale for these suppositions, we will use an example of a digitized voice image of 32 kbit/s. This technique carries 4 bits per sample (4 ∗ 8000 samples per second = 32,000). As shown in Figure 7–12, the voice samples for a 32 kbit/s image are placed into a packet with the 4

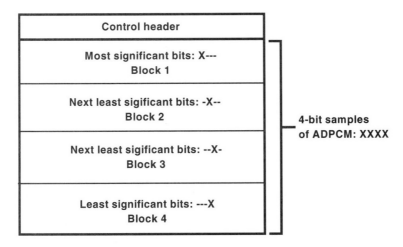

Figure 7–12   Grouping the bits of the samples.

bits of each sample grouped together based on the arithmetic significance of each bit in each sample. That is, the least significant bits (- - -X) are grouped together, followed by the next least significant bits (- -X-), and so on. Since ADPCM (adaptive pulse code modulation) uses 4 bits per sample, the packet contains 4 blocks, one for each bit of the 4-bit sample, and a control header, which is explained shortly.

Assume the following coding for two of the samples in the packet of 4 bits: One sample is 15_{10}, or 1111_2, and the other sample is 7_{10}, or 0111_2. Of course, if a full sample is discarded, all 4 bits of the sample are not available for the digital-to-analog conversion process at the receiver. However, since the bits are not encoded in the packet on a sample-by-sample basis, but rather on the arithmetically significant positions of the bits in the samples, the selective discarding of bits is not so severe.

To see why, consider that an ATM node is measuring congestion, and determines that it must shed traffic. The packet header contains a block-dropping indicator field to track the status of the blocks. (This indicator is explained shortly.) So, the block in the packet containing the least significant bit is dropped. The effect of the samples is (where x is the discarded bit of the samples):

$$15_{10} \text{ or } 1111_2 \text{ is now } 14_{10} \text{ or } 111x_2$$

$$7_{10} \text{ or } 0111_2 \text{ is now } 6_{10} \text{ or } 011x_2$$

This slight change in the sample translates to a different PAM pulse at the receiver, but the distortion is not severe.

The speech stream is coded into the packet (shown in Figure 7–13) in 16 ms time slots. Each packet contains 128 4-bit samples. This coding convention results in a 32 kbit/s transmission stream, based on the following calculations (and depicted graphically in Figure 7–13):

$$1 \text{ second } / 8000 \text{ samples per second} = \text{a } .000125 \text{ sample interval}$$

$$.000125 * .016 = .016 \text{ packet interval}$$

The packet in Figure 7–13 is 64 octets in length (512 bits). Therefore, the 32 kbit/s transmission stream is derived by:

$$1 \text{ second } / .016 = 62.5$$

$$62.5 * 512 \text{ bits} = 32,000$$

The number of blocks in the 16 ms interval depends upon the type of coding used. For example, if 8 bits were carried per sample, then 8 blocks would be needed, and a 64,000 bit rate is required. Table 7–3 shows the

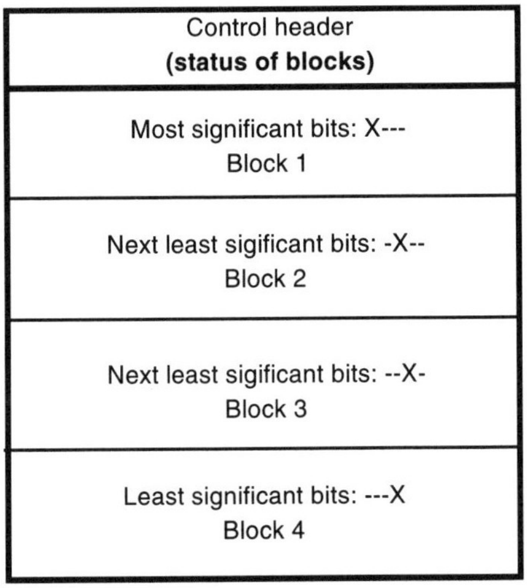

```
┌─────────────────────────────────┐
│         Control header          │
│       (status of blocks)        │
├─────────────────────────────────┤
│   Most significant bits: X---   │
│            Block 1              │
├─────────────────────────────────┤
│  Next least sigificant bits: -X-- │
│            Block 2              │
├─────────────────────────────────┤
│  Next least sigificant bits: --X- │
│            Block 3              │
├─────────────────────────────────┤
│   Least significant bits: ---X   │
│            Block 4              │
└─────────────────────────────────┘
```

Packet interval:

1. 1 sec./8000 = .000125

2. .000125 * 128 = .016

Figure 7–13 Voice packet interval and bit rate.

Bit rate:

1. 1 sec. / .016 * 512 bits (64 byte packet) = 32,000

Table 7–3   Blocks Collected during the Packetization Interval

Coding Type	Number of Blocks
8 bits/sample	8
1 bits/sample	1
2 bits/sample	2
3 bits/sample	3
4 bits/sample	4
5 bits/sample	5
6 bits/sample	6
7 bits/sample	7
8 bit PCM (A-law or m-law)	8
2 bits/sample ADPCM	2
3 bits/sample ADPCM	3
4 bits/sample ADPCM	4
5 bits/sample ADPCM	5
(4,2) embedded ADPCM	4
(5,2) embedded ADPCM	5
(8,6) embedded ADPCM	8

number of blocks collected during the 16 ms interval, based on the coding type used.

A packet size of 64 octets means that the samples are contained in more than one ATM cell. An AAL1 PDU could be used, and the pointer could locate the payload in the payload field. However, using an AAL2 PDU is preferable, because it contains a length field and an offset field, which are essential for proper identification of the related packets of the signal. Nothing precludes the use of an AAL3/4 PDU, since it also contains these fields, as long as the traffic is treated synchronously.

Most voice packet systems also employ digital speech interpolation (DSI), which does not generate packets during periods of silence in a voice conversation. This allows more voice channels to be multiplexed on any given media. Thus, a system such as AT&T's IACS uses a combination of ADPCM and DSI to multiplex 96 voice channels onto a DS1 1.544 Mbits/s channel and 120 voice channels onto a CEPT1 2.048 Mbits/s channel.

Furthermore, block dropping decreases the bursty aspect of digitized voice by smoothing the queues. It has also been demonstrated that this process increases the system capacity by some 20 to 25 percent [SRIR90b].

Combining Voice and Data.   This procedure can transport data as well. For data applications, the block dropping indicator field is coded to show that the data blocks are nondroppable. When data are supported, the node's physical interface must be able to detect modem signals, determine the modem line speed (in bit/s), and assign a coding rate to support the line speed. Furthermore, the node is able to receive and transmit G3 facsimile signals.

The Voice Packet

The format for the ITU-T G.764 voice packet is shown in Figure 7–14. To simplify this discussion, Figure 7–14 does not show octet and bit positions. The packet is encapsulated into an HDLC-type header, which contains an address field, a command/response bit (not used), and a frame type field. The address field is a conventional data link connection identifier (DLCI). The frame type is an HDLC unnumbered information type (UI) and can also be coded to indicate if a cyclic redundancy check (CRC) with the frame check sequence is performed on the frame header and packet header or on the entire frame. The former is called the unnumbered information with header check (UIH).

This option does not protect the voice bits, because the dropping of blocks does not require the recalculation of the CRC, and retransmis-

HDLC-type header
Protocol discriminator
Block dropping indicator
Time stamp

M/P bits	**Coding type**
Sequence number	**Noise**

Nondroppable blocks
Optionally droppable blocks
Frame check sequence

Figure 7–14   Format of G.764 voice packet.

sions in the event of an error are not performed due to the sensitivity of voice traffic to delay.

The protocol discriminator is preset to 01000100. The block dropping indicator contains several fields. One field contains two bits, labeled as C1 and C2. These bits are set to indicate how many blocks are droppable as follows: 00 = no droppable blocks; 01 = one droppable block; 10 = two droppable blocks; 11 = three droppable blocks. C1 and C2 are changed when a block is dropped to indicate how many blocks are still available for dropping.

The timestamp field records the cumulative delay encountered as the packet makes its journey through the network. Its value is not to exceed 200 ms.

The coding type (CT) field indicates the specific analog-to-digital technique used. The coding of this field must adhere to the ITU-T conventions shown in Table 7–4.

The M bit (more data bit) is set to 1 for all packets of a voice burst, except the last packet in the burst. The receiver uses this bit to learn that all samples have arrived. The P bit (poll bit) is not used and is set to zero.

The sequence number (SN) is used at the receiver during the building of the voice burst. It is used to note the first packet in the burst and

Table 7–4   Coding Type (CT) Format

Bit Number					Coding Type
5	4	3	2	1	
0	0	0	0	0	8 bit/sample
0	0	0	0	1	1 bit/sample
0	0	0	1	0	2 bit/sample
0	0	0	1	1	3 bit/sample
0	0	1	0	0	4 bit/sample
0	0	1	0	1	5 bit/sample
0	0	1	1	0	6 bit/sample
0	0	1	1	1	7 bit/sample
0	1	0	0	0	8 bit A-law PCM
0	1	0	0	1	8 bit μ-law PCM
0	1	0	1	0	2 bit/sample ADPCM
0	1	0	1	1	3 bit/sample ADPCM
0	1	1	0	0	4 bit/sample ADPCM
0	1	1	0	1	5 bit/sample ADPCM
0	1	1	1	0	Reserved for future use
0	1	1	1	1	Reserved for future use
1	0	0	0	0	Reserved for future use
1	0	0	0	1	Reserved for future use
1	0	0	1	0	Reserved for future use
1	0	0	1	1	Reserved for future use
1	0	1	0	0	(4,2) embedded ADPCM
1	0	1	0	1	(5,2) embedded ADPCM
1	0	1	1	0	Reserved for future use
1	0	1	1	1	Reserved for future use
1	1	0	0	0	(8,6) embedded ADPCM
1	1	0	0	1	Reserved for future use
		...			
		...			
1	1	1	1	1	Reserved for future use

also to note if a packet has been lost. The value is incremented by 1 for each subsequent packet in the signal. The SN is used with the timestamp to assure that variable delay is removed for the process.

Since this technique uses DSI, a noise field indicates the level of background noise that is to be played in the absence of packets. These bits must be coded in accordance with the ITU-T specifications, shown in Table 7–5.

Finally, the blocks fields contain the samples that were described earlier.

Table 7–5   Noise Field Format

Bit Number	Noise Level
4321	(dBmc0)
0000	Idle code
0001	16.6
0010	19.7
0011	22.6
0100	24.9
0101	26.9
0110	29.0
0111	31.0
1000	32.8
1001	34.6
1010	36.2
1011	37.9
1100	39.7
1101	41.6
1110	43.8
1111	46.6

Packet Buildout at the Receiver

To properly decode voice packets, they must arrive at the receiver (terminating endpoint) experiencing nonvariable delay. However, since variable delay is inevitable due to queuing and switching operations in the network, the receiver masks the variability of the delay through the use of the timestamp (TS) value in the packet header.

For this operation to work correctly, the system must define a maximum allowable delay. This can be defined when a PVC is provisioned, when an SVC is created, or in any manner deemed appropriate by the network administrator. Whatever the value chosen, it must be less than 199 ms, as established by ITU-T G.764. Additionally, the terminating endpoint must check the TS value in the packet as part of this operation and compare it to a predefined constant delay value, and determine if the packet is to be buffered, released to the decoding application, or discarded (buildout operations).

Figure 7–15 shows four possible scenarios that may occur when cells (with voice packets) reach the receiver. After the cell and AAL headers are processed, the terminating endpoint compares the timestamp to the CDV (100 ms in this example). In scenario 1, the packet has arrived with TS = 80 ms, which means it took 80 ms to traverse the network from the originating endpoint to the terminating endpoint. Since 100 – 80 = 20, the packet is held for 20 ms before being given to the decoding application.

In scenario 2, the endpoint has no packets to play out. So, it examines the M bit of the previous packet for this speech signal (which it must

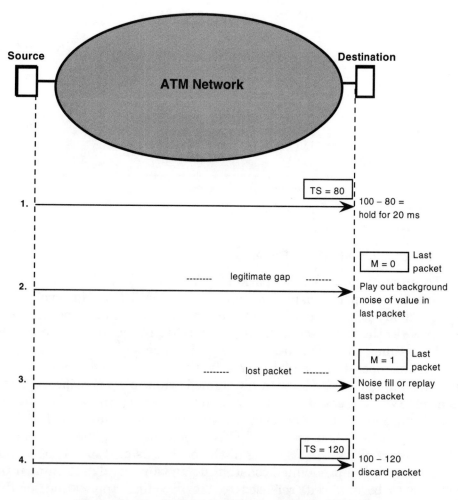

Figure 7–15   Buildout operations at the receiver.

buffer). If M = 0, the gap is legitimate, and the noise field in the previous packet is used to play out appropriate background noise.

Scenario 3 is the same as scenario 2 in that the endpoint has no packets to play out. In this case, the M bit of the previous packet is 1. Therefore, a packet is lost and the terminating endpoint creates a noise fill, replays the previous packet, and so on. This interpolation procedure has not yet been defined in any of the standards, and the ITU-T cites it as for "further study."

In scenario 4, the packet arrives later than the constant delay value (120 ms in the timestamp), and the packet is discarded.

In effect, a buffer at the receiver must eliminate jitter (varying arrival times of the cells, due to variable delay). The application reads out of the receiving buffer based on a local clock. The handling of delay, such as the examples in this section, is usually implemented differently by each network designer. Nonetheless, a scenario such as the one described here is common to some implementations.

AAL TYPES 3, 4, 3/4, AND 5 FOR DATA

Pre-ATM Approach to Traffic Integrity Management

Before an analysis is made of ATM support for data payloads, it will be helpful to pause and reflect on the way (and the reasons why) an ATM network transports data. This section continues the discussions in Chapter 6 on bit error rates and the rationale for the size of the ATM header and payload.

Many of the data communications networks in operation today provide extensive services to the user (which will be called traffic integrity management in this discussion), such as:

- Sequencing the traffic to make certain it arrives in the proper order at the end destination. In the event it arrives out of order, the traffic is stored in a buffer, resequenced, and presented to the end user in the proper order. This operation is quite useful. For example, it ensures that the records of, say, a file transfer, arrive in order.
- Performing error checks on the traffic to make certain the bits in the traffic stream were not distorted due to transmission impairments, such as noise or crosstalk, for example.
- Sending acknowledgments to the sender of the traffic. Based on an

error check operation, the acknowledgment is either positive (ACK) or negative (NAK).

- Retransmitting the traffic in case the originator receives a NAK from the receiver.
- Performing flow control on the user application to prevent the user from saturating the network with too much traffic.

As seen in Figure 7–16, in some networks the operations of sequencing, error checking, acknowledgments (positive and negative), retransmissions, and flow control are performed more than once. These operations are performed at the data link layer (L2), the network layer (L3), the transport layer (L4), and perhaps the application layer (L7) (not shown in this figure), and even again at the network layer inside the network (also not shown in this figure).

Most likely, the reader is wondering why these operations are duplicated. A useful question is, Why should these functions, however useful, be replicated in several layers? Generally, they should not be replicated. Figure 7–17 shows the fields present in the PDU for these three layers. Although the names vary, all layers are performing sequencing with N(S), N(R), P(S), P(R), T(S), and T(R) values, where (S) represents a send SN and

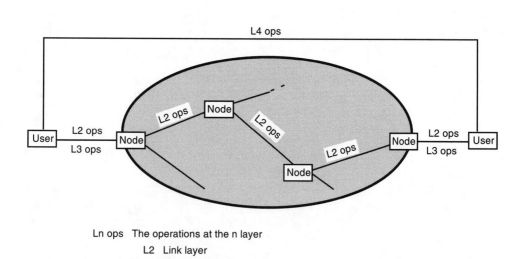

Ln ops   The operations at the n layer

    L2   Link layer

    L3   Network layer

    L4   Transport layer

Figure 7–16   Data integrity operations.

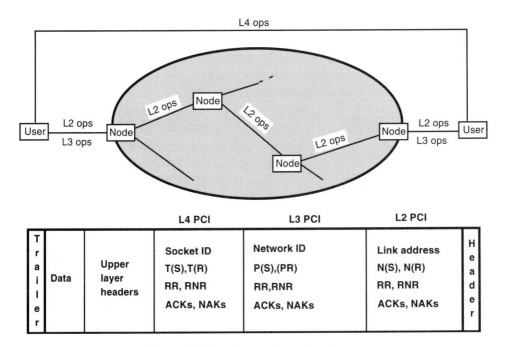

T r a i l e r	Data	Upper layer headers	L4 PCI	L3 PCI	L2 PCI	H e a d e r
			Socket ID	Network ID	Link address	
			T(S),T(R)	P(S),(PR)	N(S), N(R)	
			RR, RNR	RR,RNR	RR, RNR	
			ACKs, NAKs	ACKs, NAKs	ACKs, NAKs	

Figure 7–17 Contents of headers.

(R) represents a receiving SN. All layers are performing ACKs, NAKs, and flow control with receive not ready (RNR) and receive ready (RR).

Notwithstanding, and in deference to past technologies, it has made good sense to perform these operations in several layers, because communications links were (and still are in many systems) quite error-prone, and performing error checks (with ACKs and NAKs) was an effective means to ensure that the traffic on the links was error-free. Thus, layer two (L2) performs a error check on the received data on each link and returns an ACK or NAK to the sender.

Moreover, many data communications protocols are implemented with the well-founded notion that the services provided by other protocols in a network cannot be assumed. For example, the data link layer (L2 in this figure) is usually tasked with performing an error check on the incoming traffic to determine if a transmission impairment (noise, crosstalk, etc.) has distorted the data. However, some data link layer implementations perform these services, and others do not. So, a prudent network layer (L3 in this figure) protocol designer builds error detection and resolution capabilities into the network layer, which operates above the data link layer.

Moreover, the L2 operations affect all users on the link. The layer makes no distinction about what is carried in the L2 frame. Its job is to deliver the frame safely to the destination station on that one link.

On the other hand, the network layer (L3) header identifies each user on the link at the UNI with a network ID, such as a virtual circuit number. Therefore, a finer granularity of control is achieved with this layer. For example, an RNR issued at the link layer affects all users on that link, but an RNR issued at the network layer only affects a selected user—one that is identified by a virtual circuit number.

A transport layer (L4 in this figure) designer can also implement these operations. After all, the L4 operations are not aware of the lower layer operations, and it cannot be assumed that sequencing, flow control, ACKs, and NAKs are performed in an internet in which traffic may be transported across unknown (not preconfigured) networks. However, the transport operations occur between the end-user stations; they do not operate on the link or in the network. In other words, the transport layer provides end-to-end traffic integrity management. The transport header is tunneled through the network and links transparently—these lower layers do not examine the syntax of this header. The transport layer uses socket IDs or OSI service access points (SAPs) to identify each user's traffic between the end-user workstations.

So, the manner in which many data communications systems have evolved during the past 25 years is for each layer to assume that the other layers are not doing any integrity management operations. The end result is that these operations may occur at least once (for certain) and maybe five times: (1) L2; (2) L3 at the UNI; (3) L3 inside the network; (4) L4; (5) L7.

ATM Approach to Traffic Integrity Management

ATM eliminates almost all of these functions at L2 and L3 (see Figure 7–18). In addition, the headers in these layers are combined into the ATM cell header. The reasons for these changes are:

- ATM assumes the transmission media to be relatively error-free. Therefore, the conventional link layer operations of ACKs and NAKs become less necessary.

- Even if L2 ACKs and NAKs are believed to be important, they are not feasible for certain types of traffic that cannot afford the delay in waiting for a retransmission (voice and video traffic). It is inefficient for the ATM network to distinguish between data and

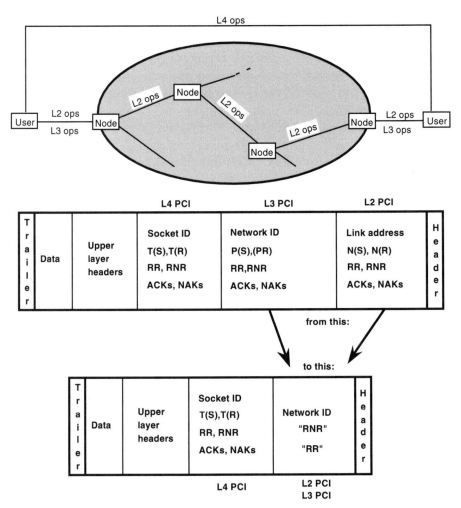

Netword ID   translated to VPI/VCI
"RNR"   translated to congestion notification

Figure 7-18   ATM approach to the use of headers.

voice/video traffic in deciding if NAKs and ACKs should or should not be performed.

- ATM still performs an error check for each cell upon its arrival at each receiving node, but it does not ACK or NAK. In the event of an uncorrectable error, it discards the cell.
- ATM does not eliminate all of the L3 operations. It still uses an ID to identify each user's traffic, which we learned is called the

VPI/VCI in ATM networks. Nonetheless, conventional L3 operations, such as closed user groups, call collects, and call redirects, are eliminated at the ATM UNI.

- Sequencing, ACKs, and NAKs are also eliminated or reduced at L3. One of the reasons for this scaled-down UNI (for data traffic) is that L4 is performing these operations on an end-to-end basis, and the L3 functions become somewhat redundant.

In a nutshell, most of the traffic integrity functions for data applications are removed from the data link and network layers and passed to the transport layer, which resides in the user workstation. This approach allows the user to implement any type or level of integrity function deemed necessary for that application. It also makes for a much faster network, because the network is not spending as much time and overhead in "taking care" of the user payload.

THE ORIGINAL AAL TYPES 3 AND TYPE 4 (AAL3, AAL4)

The original ATM standards established AAL3 for VBR connection-oriented data operations and AAL4 for VBR connectionless data operations. These two types have been combined and are treated as one type. This section of the book describes the initial AAL3 and AAL4, and then explains the revised approach.

AAL3 is used to support connection-oriented VBR services. These bursty-type data services do not require any precise timing relationships to be maintained between the source and destination. Obviously, AAL3 can support class C traffic.

The AAL4 cell is used to support either message-mode service or stream-mode service for data systems (not voice or video). It is designed also to support connectionless services, although the ITU-T also provides for this type to give assured operations in which lost traffic can be retransmitted. With assured operations, flow control is a mandatory feature. In addition, AAL4 operations may also provide nonassured operations in which lost or discarded traffic is not recovered, nor is flow control provided.

AAL3/4

As the AAL standard has matured, it became evident that the original types were inappropriate. Therefore, AAL3 and AAL4 were combined because of their similarities. AAL3/4 is the preferred type for internetworking ATM with the SMDS or a MAN.

Naming Conventions for AAL3/4

Figure 7–19 shows the naming conventions for AAL3/4. The convergence sublayer is divided into the common part convergence sublayer (CPCS) and the service specific convergence sublayer (SSCS). The SSCS

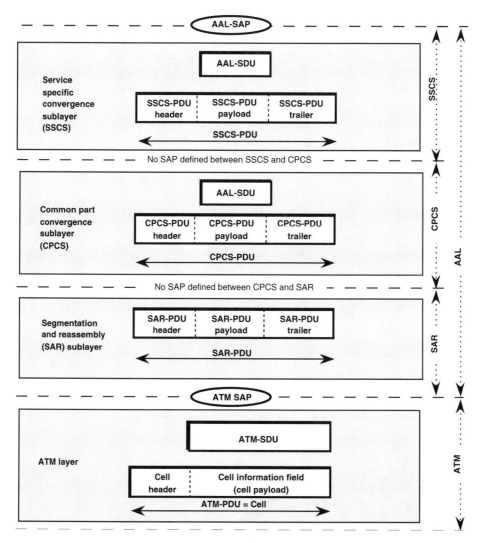

Figure 7–19   AAL3/4 general data unit.

is used to support different user applications, and thus, multiple SSCSs may exist. The SSCS may be null if it is not needed. In this case, it is used only to map primitives of the user upper layer to/from CPCS. The various SDUs, PDUs, headers, and trailers in Figure 7–19 are self-explanatory.

The AAL3/4 PDU

As shown in Figure 7–20, the AAL3/4 PDU carries 44 octets in the payload and 5 fields in the header and trailer. The 2-bit segment type (ST) is used to indicate the beginning of message (BOM = 10), continuation of message (COM = 00), end of message (EOM = 01), or single segment message (SSM = 11). The SN is used for sequencing the traffic. It is incremented by one for each PDU sent, and a state variable at the receiver indicates the next expected PDU. If the received SN is different from the state variable, the PDU is discarded. The message identification (MID) subfield is used to reassemble traffic on a given connection. The length indicator (LI) defines the size of the payload. And, finally, the cyclic redundancy check (CRC) field is a 10-bit field used to determine if an error has occurred in any part of the PDU.

AAL3/4 Headers and Trailers

The AAL3/4 layers and their functions closely resemble their counterparts in MAN and SMDS. As depicted in Figure 7–21, AAL3/4 consists of a CS/SAR. CS is responsible primarily for error checking, and SAR is

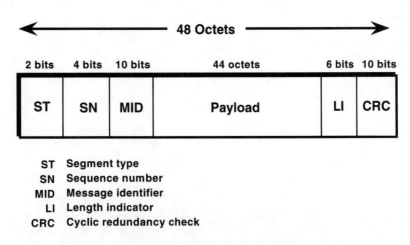

Figure 7–20   AAL3/4 PDU.

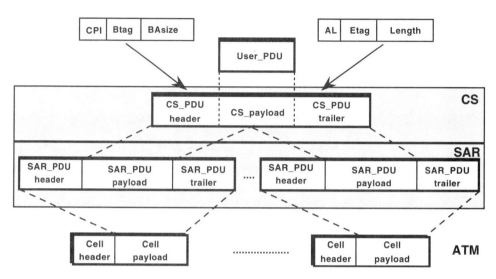

Figure 7–21   AAL3/4 layers and PDUs.

responsible for segmentation and reassembly operations. AAL3/4 can accept and process a user PDU of up to 65,535 octets. Like MAN and SMDS, the traffic is segmented into 53-octet cells for transmission on the media.

As mentioned earlier, AAL3/4 operations support two types of data transfer requirements: a message-mode service and a stream-mode service. The message-mode service allows a single SDU to be segmented into smaller pieces for transmission. In the stream-mode service, one or more fixed size SDUs are transported as one AAL convergence function PDU. The stream-mode will allow a SDU to be as small as one octet.

The CS_PDU headers and trailers are shown in Figure 7–21. The header contains three fields. The common part identifier (CPI) field (one octet) identifies the type of traffic and certain values that are to be implemented in the other fields of the headers and trailers. The Btag field (one octet) is used to identify all CS_PDUs that are associated with a session. The buffer allocation size field (BAsize, two octets) defines the size of the buffer to receive the CS_PDU at the receiver. The trailer also contains three fields. The alignment field (AL) is a filler to align the trailer to a 32-bit boundary. The Etag (one octet) is used with the Btag in the header to correlate all traffic associated with the CS_payload. Finally, the length field specifies the length of the CS_payload (in octets).

AAL3/4 Sequencing and Identification Operations

Figure 7–22 provides an example of how the various fields in the headers and trailers are used to assure all traffic is received and reassembled correctly at the terminating AAL entity. The first PDU always contains the header created by CS at the originating AAL entity: the CPI, Btag, and BAsize. This header is used by the receiving AAL to identify (1) the type of traffic coming in (CPI); (2) the size of the buffer that is to receive all PDUs (BAsize); (3) the tag that will allow the detection of the last PDU (Btag). In this example, the Btag is 44 and the BAsize is 880.

The AAL PDU header contains the segment type field to indicate the BOM, COM, and EOM PDUs. The SN field is incremented by 1 for each successive PDU. In this example, 20 PDUs are sent, so numbers 1 through 15 are placed in the PDUs and a wraparound counter allows the SN values to be reused. The message identification field (MID) is set to 68 in this example to uniquely identify all associated PDUs. The last PDU has its ST set to 01 for EOM. The last PDU has SN = 5, which means the SN wraparound counter started at 1, and wrapped around to 5 for the last PDUs.

During the reassembly process, if any PDU is not received correctly, then all associated PDUs must be dropped. If one PDU is lost, none are retained at the receiver.

If 16 successive PDUs are lost, the 4-bit SN alone will not allow the detection of this type of problem. The BAsize can be used to recover. When the last PDU arrives (EOM set in the segment type field), the re-

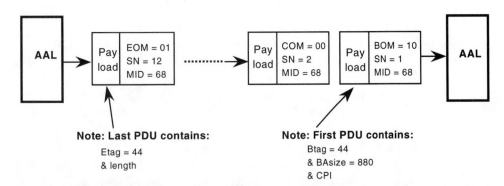

Figure 7–22   Example of AAL3/4 sequencing and identification operations.

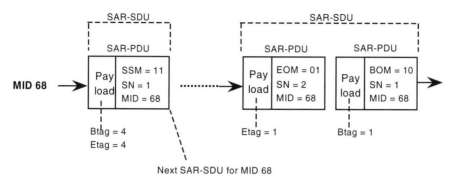

**Figure 7–23   Relationship of sequence numbers and Btag/
Etag values.**

ceiver detects that the buffer is not filled. It knows something is amiss
and discards the buffer.

Figure 7–23 shows other aspects of AAL3/4 operations. Each SAR-
PDU that belongs to one SAR-SDU is sequenced, by incrementing the sequence number by one, with each succeeding SAR-PDU. Successive SAR-
SDUs belonging to one MID are not necessarily sequenced together. The
receiver does not correlate the sequence numbers of successive SAR-
SDU, only the SAR-PDUs within the SAR-SDU. So, send can set the sequence number field to any value (0–15) in the first SAR-PDU on the segmented SAR-SDU. Furthermore, Figure 7–23 also shows that the Btag
and Etag do not have to be continuous sequence numbers for successive
transfers of CPCS-PDUs. For simplicity of implementation, they may indeed be in sequence, but the receiver does not make this check.

A Complete SAR-PDU and CPCS-PDU Example

Figure 7–24 shows the structure and format for the combined SAR
and CPCS PDU for AAL3/4 operations. This figure represents a single-
segment PDU (SSM), which is used for this example because it contains
all the headers and trailers, whereas BOM, COM, and EOM only contain
parts of them. In this example, an original SDU is not long enough to
warrant more than one segmented PDU. Therefore, the SAR header contains the SSM bits of 11 in bits 8, 7 of the first octet of the header. It
must contain the SAR-PDU header and trailer, as well as both the
CPCS-PDU header and CPCS-PDU trailer. The header also contains the
sequence number (SN), which is followed by the message identification
field (MID).

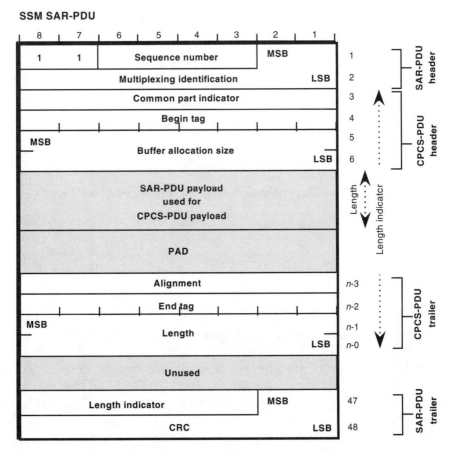

Figure 7–24   Combined SAR and CPCS-PDU: SSM.

The CPCS-PDU header follows with the common part indicator (CPI), the Btag, and the BAsize fields. Next is the user payload, which is followed by CPCS-PDU trailer of the alignment field (AL), the Etag, and the length field. Then follows the SAR-PDU trailer, consisting of the length indicator (LI), and the cyclic redundancy check field (CRC).

Functional Model for AAL3/4

The first release of ITU-T I.363, Annex C described a functional model for AAL3/4. The current release of I.363.2 does not define this model for AAL3/4, but it is included here because it provides a good example of the relationships of the SAPs, layers, and data units. It is similar to the functional model for AAL2, described earlier in this chapter.

Figure 7–25 depicts this model on the send side. The blocks in this figure support a user connection. Each SAR and CPCS pairs represent a segmentation state machine. The interleaver is responsible for allocating the AAL SAR-PDUs from the state machines across the ATM SAP. How this is done is an internal matter.

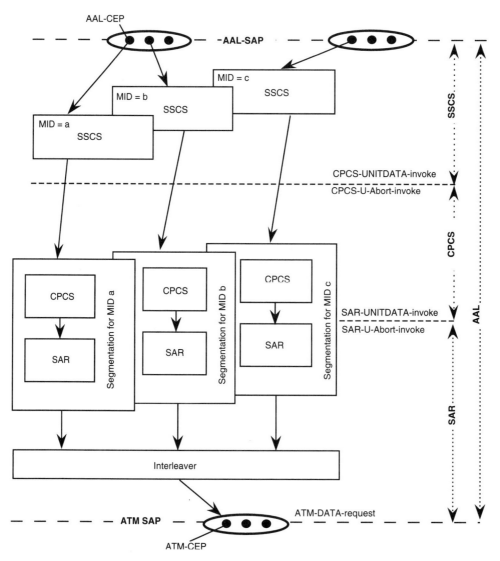

Figure 7–25 AAL3/4 functional model on the send side. [ITUT-TI3.63]

The receiver side model is a mirror image of the send side, as shown
in Figure 7–26. Of course, the operations are reversed. The ATM layer
presents the SDUs to the AAL dispatcher, which uses the MID field to
route the traffic to the proper reassembly state machine.

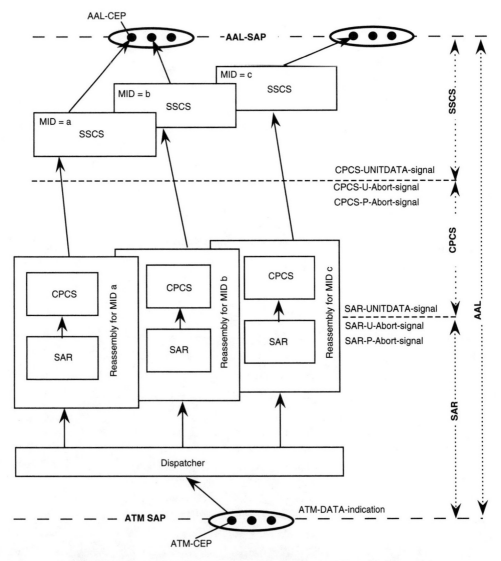

**Figure 7–26   AAL 3/4 functional model on the receive side
type. [ITU-TI.363]**

AAL TYPE 5 (AAL5)

The purpose of AAL5 is to provide guidance for transporting upper layer protocols over ATM. It was conceived because AAL3/4 was considered to contain unnecessary overhead; it was judged that multiplexing could be pushed up to any upper layer, and that the BAsize operations to preallocate buffers at the receiver were not needed.

Structure of AAL 5

As shown in Figure 7–27, the AAL5 structure is similar to the structure for AAL3/4, but is simpler. It contains the convergence sublayer,

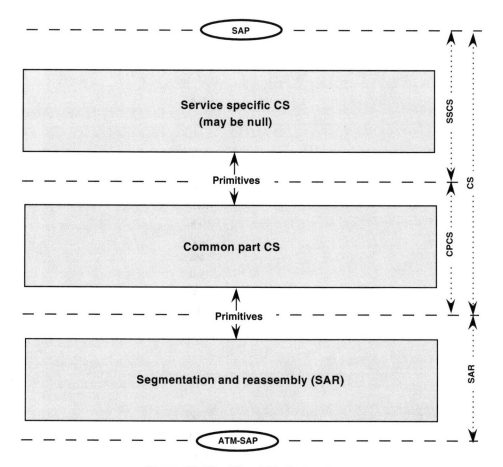

Figure 7–27   The AAL 5 structure.

which is divided into the common part convergence sublayer (CPCS) and the service specific convergence sublayer (SSCS)—obviously, this part is identical to AAL3/4. The SSCS is used to support different user applications, and thus, multiple SSCSs may exist. The SSCS may be null if it is not needed. In this case, it is used only to map primitives of the user upper layer to/from CPCS.

The AAL5 PDU

Figure 7–28 shows the format of the AAL5 PDU. It consists of an 8-octet trailer. The PAD field acts as a filler to fill out the PDU to 48 octets. The CPCS-UU field is used to identify the user payload. The common part indicator (CPI) has not been fully defined in ITU-T I.363. The Length field (L) defines the payload length, and the CRC field is used to detect errors in the SSCS PDU (user data).

AAL5 is a convenient service for frame relay because it supports connection-oriented services. In essence, the frame relay user traffic is given to an ATM backbone network for transport to another frame relay user. Discussion of AAL5 and its relationship to the ATM Forum activities is covered in Chapter 11 (see "Internetworking with ATM Networks").

ANOTHER TYPE—AVAILABLE BIT RATE (ABR)

The ATM Forum has defined another type of service category, called the available bit rate (ABR). Its purpose is to provide a mechanism for con-

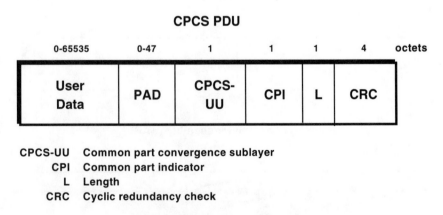

CPCS PDU

| 0-65535 | 0-47 | 1 | 1 | 1 | 4 | octets |

User Data	PAD	CPCS-UU	CPI	L	CRC

CPCS-UU   Common part convergence sublayer
CPI   Common part indicator
L   Length
CRC   Cyclic redundancy check

Figure 7–28   The AAL5 PDU.

trolling traffic flow from LAN-based workstations, and the routers that
service these workstations. Since LAN devices have no "contract" with a
network, no easy method is available to relate the AAL CBR and VBR idea
to a LAN environment. Since this type is concerned principally with traffic
management, I shall defer further discussion on the subject to Chapter 9.

THE AAL/ATM PRIMITIVES

Chapter 3 introduces the concepts of service definitions and primitives. This section continues that discussion, focusing on the operations
between the AAL and ATM layers, the user application and the AAL, as
well as the CS and SAR within the AAL. Remember that primitives specify the type of function call or system library call that is invoked between
two layer entities, as well as the arguments (the primitive parameters)
that are conveyed with the call. This section should be of particular interest to software designers and programmers, but it is presented in a general fashion for all.

Figure 7–29 shows the ATM Forum view of how the primitives are
exchanged between the AAL and ATM layers, as well as their associated
parameters.[5] Two primitives are exchanged, the ATM-DATA.request and
the ATM-DATA.indication. The response and confirm primitives are not
used at this layer boundary.

The ATM-DATA.request transfers an ATM_SDU from AAL to ATM
over an existing connection at the sending machine. The ATM-SDU parameter contains this SDU. Two other parameters are associated with the
request primitive. The SDU-type is used to distinguish between two
types of ATM-SDUs that are associated with the connection. The meaning of this parameter is implementation specific. The submitted loss-
priority parameter indicates the importance of this SDU. It can take on
two values: high priority or low priority. This parameter can be used by
the ATM layer to set the cell loss priority (CLP) bit in the cell header.

The ATM-DATA.indication transfers the ATM_SDU at the receiving
machine's ATM layer to the AAL. It, of course, contains the ATM-SDU
parameter, the SDU-type parameter, and two others. The received loss-
priority parameter reflects value of the CLP bit (it is implementation-

---

[5]These calls will vary somewhat, depending upon the specific AAL type. For rules
on *each* AAL, you should refer to the ITU-T Recommendations.

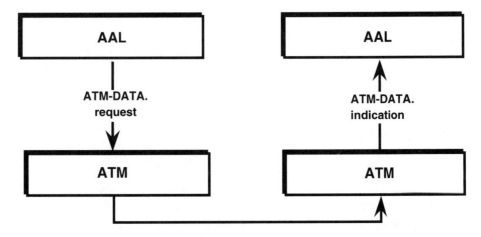

Parameter	Associated Primitives	Meaning	Valid Values
ATM-SDU	ATM-DATA.request ATM-DATA.indication	48-byte pattern for transport	Any 48 byte pattern
SDU-type	ATM-DATA.request ATM-DATA.indication	End-to-end cell type indicator	0 or 1
Submitted Loss-priority	ATM-DATA.request	Requested cell loss-priority	High or low priority
Received Loss-priority	ATM-DATA.indication	Received cell loss priority	High or low priority
Congestion-experienced	ATM-DATA.indication	EFCN indication	True or False

Figure 7–29   The AAL-ATM primitives.

specific) in the cell header. The congestion indication parameter indicates that the ATM-SDU has passed through at least one network node that experienced congestion.

The primitives for class A CBR traffic are shown in Figure 7–30. Two primitives are used, the AAL-DATA.request and the AAL-DATA.indication. The time intervals between the invocations of these primitives must be constant in order to preserve the synchronous nature of the connection and information transfer exchange.

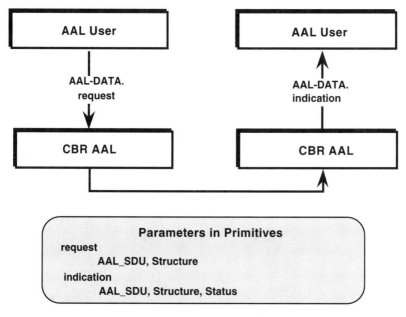

Figure 7–30   The user-AAL CBR primitives.

The parameters in the primitives are also shown in Figure 7–30. The AAL_SDU contains one bit of user payload. The structure parameter is used to support structured information transfer for 8-bit octets. It is set to start to indicate the beginning of a block of traffic; otherwise it is set to continuation. The status parameter is used in the indication primitive to inform the AAL user if AAL judges the AAL_SDU to be errored or not in error. It may also be used to indicate that the AAL_SDU is not relevant (a dummy AAL_SDU, for example).

The CS/SAR primitives for Class A traffic are shown in Figure 7–31. Two primitives are invoked between these two sublayers: the SAR-DATA.invoke and the AAL-DATA.signal. The figure also shows the parameters used in the primitives. The CSDATA parameter contains the 47-octet CS_SDU transferred between the two layers. The SCVAL parameter contains the SN for the CS_SDU. The CSIVAL parameter contains the value for the CSI bit. The SNCK parameter is present in the indication primitive. It is used by SAR to inform CS of the results of the error check performed on the SN.

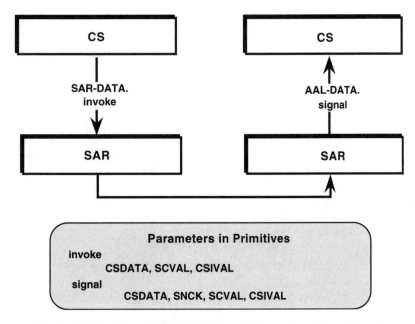

Figure 7–31   The AAL CS/SAR primitives for class A traffic.

SUMMARY

The ATM adaptation layer (AAL) is designed to support different types of applications, and different types of traffic, such as voice, video, or data. The AAL is divided into two sublayers: the convergence sublayer (CS) and the segmentation and reassembly (SAR) sublayer. For some implementations, CS is divided further into the service specific CS (SSCS) and the common part of CS (CPCS). SSCS is designed to support a specific aspect of a data application, and CPCS supports generic functions common to more than one type of data application.

8

ATM Switching Operations

This chapter examines ATM switching operations. It also explains how the VPI and VCI are used by a switch to make routing decisions. Since switching is not part of the ATM standards and vendors use a wide variety of techniques to build their switches, this chapter focuses on the prevalent methods in use today. In most implementations, this part of the ATM node is proprietary; vendors put a large amount of research and development into the switching fabric. In most instances, the author was able to obtain the general architectural descriptions from several vendors. Therefore, this chapter reflects examples of ATM switches as well as a description of current research on cell switching.

Several approaches to cell switching are examined in this chapter. The topic of ATM switching is worthy of an entire book, so the goal of the chapter is more modest and is designed to give the reader a general overview of cell switching architecture and the major components of an ATM switch. Be aware that there is no "best way" to build an ATM switch, and the ATM standards wisely do not address this aspect of the technology.

ATM SWITCHING

One of the most important aspects of ATM is the switch and how fast it relays cells (without cell loss). ATM must accept asynchronous and synchronous traffic, as well as connection-oriented and connectionless traffic. Queuing delay and switching delay must be minimized if the ATM network is to perform satisfactorily in its support of user applications.

One goal of the ATM network is to adapt gracefully to changing network traffic profiles with the ability to adjust to increased or decreased input traffic (within limits, however). Since an ATM network must receive traffic that is somewhat unpredictable, the network must be able to adjust to changing network conditions. All these problems and their solutions are not defined in the ATM standards. Vendors are free to implement the techniques they deem appropriate for their product.

Routing with the Cell Header

As described in earlier chapters, the virtual channels are aggregated through multiplexers and switched (routed) through the network. Two types of switches are used in an ATM network for the multiplexing/demultiplexing and routing of traffic (see Figure 8–1a). Conceptually, a virtual path switch is only required to examine the VPI part of the header for multiplexing/demultiplexing and routing. Virtual channel switches, on the other hand, must examine the whole routing field; that is to say, the VCI and the VPI.

The intent of this approach is to speed up switching and routing at intermediate points. Instead of requiring the switch (in some instances) to examine the entire virtual channel field, the VCI value can be transported transparently through a virtual path connection.

In Figure 8–1b, two virtual path connections exist from user A to ATM B and from ATM B to user B. A node can use the VCI identifier on any virtual path connection (with the use of the VCI). Also, as suggested in Figure 8–1b, virtual path connections exist between the user and the network and within the network itself. This approach could be applied to the North American carrier system in which the VCI 14 could exist in one operator and VCI 23 could exist in another operator. This approach is a "clean" interface and also lends itself to relatively small lookup tables.

The VP and VC switches actually treat virtual path and virtual channel connections the same in the sense that they can be set up on a demand basis or they can be set up on a permanent basis. The network also can use QOS features, such as traffic usage, to associate with either a virtual channel or a virtual path.

Figure 8–2 provides an example of how VPIs and VCIs are translated and mapped at the switch. Figure 8–2a is an example of VPI

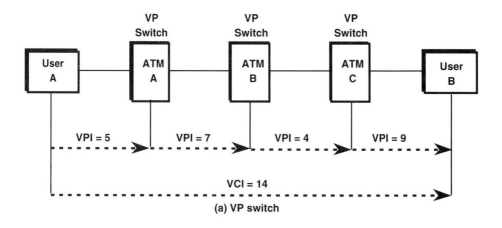

(a) VP switch

OR:

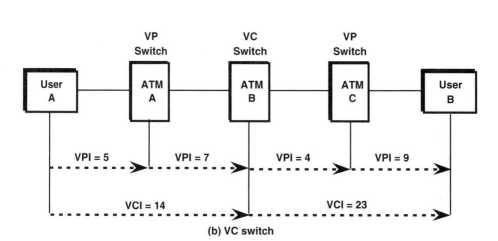

(b) VC switch

Figure 8–1 ATM switches: virtual path and virtual channel switches.

switching. The VCIs are passed unaltered through the switch, and VCIs 14 and 15 remain bundled in a VPI. The incoming VPI 7 is translated to outgoing VPI 4, but the VCI values are not altered.

In contrast, Figure 8–2b shows both VPIs and VCIs being translated and mapped to different values. VCI 14 (in the incoming VPI 7 bundle) is translated and mapped to outgoing VPI 7 with the VCI value changed to 23. The incoming VCI 15 (also bundled into VPI 7) is translated and mapped into VCI 88 and bundled into outgoing VPI 10.

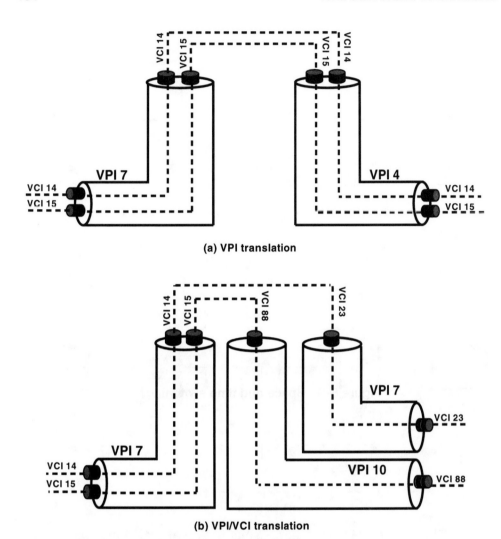

Figure 8–2   VPI/VCI switching.

SPACE AND TIME SWITCHING

Switching has been defined for many years to encompass two realms: space switching and time switching (see Figure 8–3). In either case, the objective of the operation is to transport traffic from an input interface (port) to an output interface (port). The ATM switch functions like classical switching systems in that traffic is physically moved from

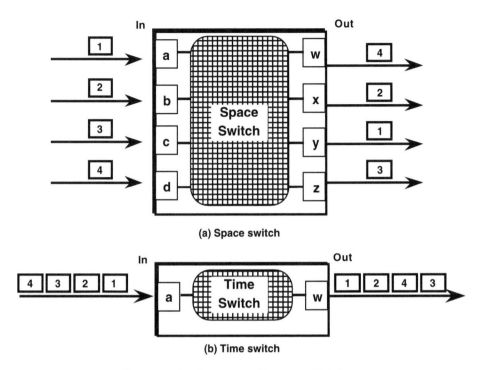

(a) Space switch

(b) Time switch

Figure 8–3   Space and time switching.

input ports to output ports. This concept is called space switching in the sense that different input and output lines are utilized.

The other realm is called time switching (shown in Figure 8–3b), and it has long been used in time slot interchange (TSI) switches. With time switching, the information and time slots are switched to different slots from the input interfaces to the output interfaces. The difference with ATM is that the time slots do not exist for identification purposes such as in a straight TDM switch. The slot is identified by an ATM label (VCI/VPI). Because ATM switches do not use TSI operations, it is possible that the staging switches could contend with each other for the same time slot. Therefore, ATM uses queuing to ameliorate this problem.

DIGITAL CROSS CONNECTS

ATM uses several of the concepts found today in digital cross connect equipment. The switch uses line and trunk identifiers to map incoming connections to outgoing connections. Figure 8–4 shows a line side and

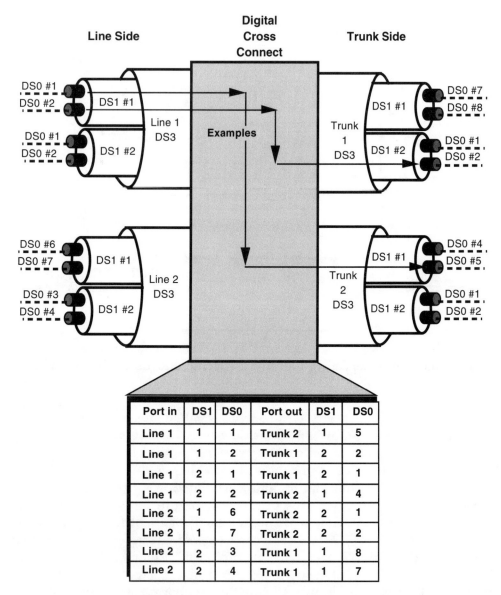

Figure 8–4   A digital cross connect.

a trunk side of a cross connect switch. Each 64 kbit/s DS0 channel is associated with a DS1 number and a physical port (line) number. A mapping table correlates this channel with an outgoing channel. An end-to-end digital circuit is made up of a set of DS1 and DS0 at each physical interface between two end users.

Figure 8–4 shows the mapping table at the bottom of the figure. The top part of the figure shows two examples of how the cross connect table is used. The two sets of arrows should aid you in these two examples. In the first example, DS0 #1 of DS1 #1 on line 1 is mapped to trunk 2, DS1 #1 and DS0 #5. In the second example, DS0 #2 of DS1 #1 on line 1 is mapped to trunk 1, DS1 #2 and DS0 #2. As we shall see in the next section, ATM uses the line and trunk switching concept for its VCI and VPI mapping and switching operations.

THE SWITCHING FABRIC

Before delving into the details of ATM switching, several definitions are needed. First, a switching fabric describes the components of the switch, which include its hardware and software architecture. Second, a network element is a part of the overall switching fabric, such as a software or hardware component.

Figure 8–5 shows a general depiction of ATM switch operation. Later discussions examine specific implementations. The ATM machine receives a cell on an incoming port and reads the VCI/VPI value. This value has been reserved to identify a specific end user for a virtual circuit. It also identifies the outgoing port for the next node that is to receive the traffic. The ATM switch then examines a routing table for the match of the incoming VPI number and corresponding incoming port to that of an outgoing VPI number and corresponding outgoing port. Some implementations do not make use of a routing table, but rely on the switching fabric to be self-routing; these switches are explained later.

The header in the outgoing cell is changed with the new VPI value placed in a field of the cell header. The new VPI value is used by the next ATM switch to perform subsequent routing operations.

POINT-TO-MULTIPOINT OPERATION

Figure 8–6 shows a point-to-multipoint operation, also called a multicast or broadcast. For this example, the switch translates both the VPI and VCI, and the input/output interfaces are not shown. The concept is quite simple. The cross-connect table contains multiple entries. In this example, an incoming cell is sent to two output ports. The table contains the mapping values to change the VPI and VCI values in the cell headers.

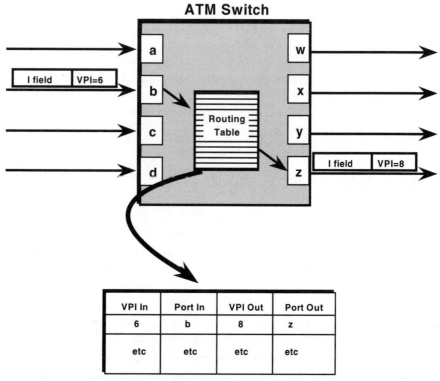

VPI   Virtual path Identifier
Note: VPI *and* VCI may be examined at the VCI/VPI switch

Figure 8–5   ATM routing operations.

Although not shown in the figure, the cross-connect table could have bidirectional significance. That is, either of the cells labeled VPI = 8, VCI = 5 and VPI = 2 and VCI = 9 could be mapped to a cell labeled VPI = 6 and VCI = 4.

MULTIPLEXING, LABEL SWITCHING, AND LABEL MAPPING

An ATM switch also performs multiplexing functions. The information from the input ports are multiplexed onto the output ports. The operations also include switching—the traffic from the input ports is switched to different output ports. While the cells are switched through the switching fabric from input to output ports, their VPI/VCI values, which are called labels, are also translated from one incoming value to

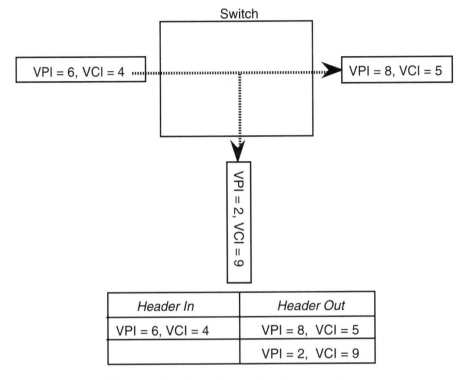

Figure 8–6 Point-to-multipoint operation.

another outgoing value. The headers uniquely identify the users' traffic, although the virtual circuit identifiers can be reused even if they are on different physical ports.

Figure 8–7 shows that an ATM switch is performing space switching by moving traffic from input ports a, b, c, d to output ports w, x, y, z. The switch is also performing header translation, which is sometimes called header mapping. This figure also shows the use of buffers (in this example, these are called output buffers because they exist at the output ports). These buffers are used to assure (most of the time) that cells do not arrive at the same output port at the same time.

The figure also depicts how the VPIs in the cell headers are used to determine the output port for the incoming cell. For example, a cell with VPI 1 arrives at port a. Routing operations reveal that the cell is to be relayed to output x to and its VPI changed to 5. As another example, a cell with VPI 3 arrives at port c. It is relayed to output port z and its label is mapped to VPI 8.

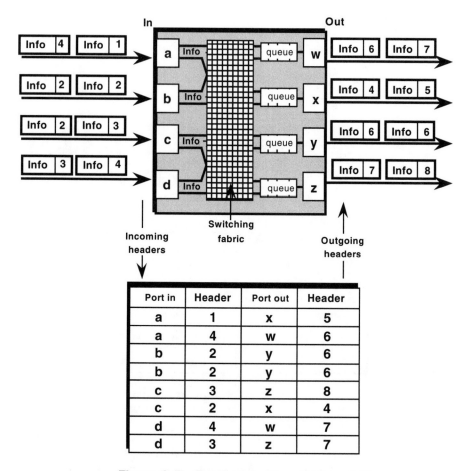

Figure 8–7   Routing and header translation.

Figure 8–7 summarizes the major functions of the ATM switch. It performs space switching, routing, multiplexing, and queuing. It also provides header mapping (header translation) by mapping the VPI values (and usually the VCI values as well).

Figure 8–8 shows how the VPI/VCIs are used at the ATM switches (nodes) to set up a connection and to create the routing table entries. In this example, three connections are created by three originating end users, by sending Q.2931 messages to the network. These messages contain a wide variety of information and are examined in Chapter 10, Call and Connection Control.

Among the fields in the Q.2931 connection request message is a destination address. This address is used by the ATM node to determine the

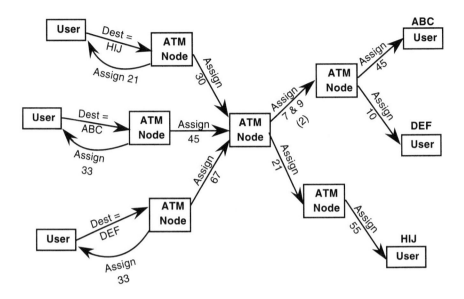

Note: Destination address (Dest = n) is sent to each ATM node to determine the route & is also sent to end-user node at terminating UNI

(2): Two connections are mapped at this node for end points ABC & DEF

Figure 8–8   Setting up the path through the ATM switches.

route that is to be established for the connection. Each node accepts the Q.2931 message, examines the destination address, and then consults a routing table to determine the next node that should receive the message.

A routing table is stored at each node and reflects the state of the network, the available bandwidth at each node, and other such information. It is updated periodically as conditions in the network change. Consequently, when the Q.2931 message is received by an ATM node, it knows the "best route" for this connection—at least to the next neighbor node.

These operations are dependent on how a vendor chooses to perform route discovery and maintain routing tables. The network may search for available bandwidth, and then set up the VPI/VCIs, or it may set them up on a link-by-link basis.

As each node sets up the calls, it reserves a VPI/VCI for each connection. Given an input VPI/VCI value, it selects an unused VPI/VCI value for the output port. The next node receives this value, selects the route, and chooses the VPI/VCI values for its output port, and so on, to the final terminating UNIs. It is the job of the network to select values that are not being used on the same physical interface. This approach allows the VPI/VCI values to be reused.

After the connection is established, only the VPI/VCI values are needed, not the destination address. Figure 8–8 also shows that the originating users do not give the network a VPI/VCI at the originating UNI. The network assigns these values to the user, usually after the connection is completed and verified through the network to the terminating endpoint. This practice varies, but the ATM Forum UNI specification requires that the network take responsibility for assigning VPI/VCIs. The originating end user can be informed of the values it is to use when the network returns a connection confirm message to the user.

PROTECTION SWITCHING

For large ATM networks that must support many users, the issue of network robustness is paramount, and the network provider must devise ways to ensure that the customer's traffic is delivered safely. One method for providing this service is called protection switching, which uses alternate links between ATM nodes to transmit the ATM cells, in case the primary link fails. This concept is depicted in Figure 8–9.

Two links (such as a T3 or SONET link) connect two ATM nodes, node A and node B. One link is the working route (the working link), and the other link is the backup route (the protection link).[1] Let us assume traffic is coming into node A through port a. The cells are switched to port w or x, depending on the conditions of the links attached to node B from node A. In this example, a selector at node B, denoted in the figure by the ✎ , determines which link is to be used for the relaying of traffic from port a onto ports y or z (the traffic on port b is not germane to our discussion at this time).

Two types of protection switching can be implemented in the ATM node: (a) 1+1 protection switching, and (b) 1:n protection switching. With 1+1 protection switching, both links (routes) are used simultaneously to send the same ATM cells; that is, two copies of each cell is sent to node B.

---

[1]The terms working copy and protection copy are also used to identify these concepts. These terms are found in SONET and SDH literature.

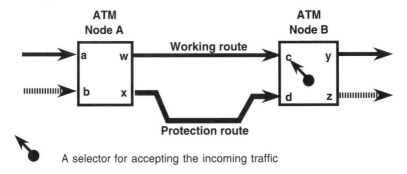

A selector for accepting the incoming traffic

Figure 8–9   Protection switching.

This node uses the selector mechanism to decide which cell copy is to be relayed to ports y or z.

The concepts of 1+1 protection switching are shown in Figure 8–10. The incoming cell on port a has a VPI/VCI value of 1. The cross-connect table at node A is set up to direct this cell to both ports w and x, with the VPI/VCI of 1 mapped to VPI/VCI 7 across port w and VPI/VCI 8 across port x.

In the event of failure of the working link (the link attached to node A's port w and node B's port c), there is another copy of the cell available on the protection link (the link attached to node A's port x and node B's port d). The cross-connect table at node A is configured as shown in Figure 8–10 to achieve the duplicate transfer of the cell to node B, and the

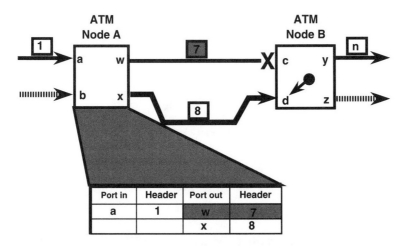

Port in	Header	Port out	Header
a	1	w	7
		x	8

Figure 8–10   1+1 protection switching.

selector at node B selects the cell with VPI/VCI = 8 for further relay. Obviously, the cell with VPI/VCI = 7 did not arrive at node B, and the cross-connect entry of port out = w, header mapping = 7 is superfluous (depicted in the figure by shading).

In contrast to 1+1 protection switching, 1:n protection switching uses a backup (protection) link for 1 to n working links. A common practice is to use the protection link to send traffic, so there are no duplicate cells on this link. In the event of failure of the working route, traffic is diverted to the protection link, and any traffic that was occupying the backup link must be either discarded, or held in a buffer until the working link can be restored. If restoration occurs quickly, the buffered traffic can continue its journey through the network. Otherwise, the traffic will be discarded. Consequently, the traffic on the protection link should be of a lower priority, and not subject to tight timing requirements.

In Figure 8–11, the protection link is transporting asynchronous traffic, such as available bit rate (ABR) or unspecified bit rate (UBR) cells. As long as the working route is operating satisfactorily, the protection link can carry the ABR/UBR traffic.

Also, this example shows the 1:n ratio of 1:1, but installations are free to set the number of working links that are supported by the protection link.

The cross-connect table at node A is configured in a typical manner, as shown at the bottom part of the figure.

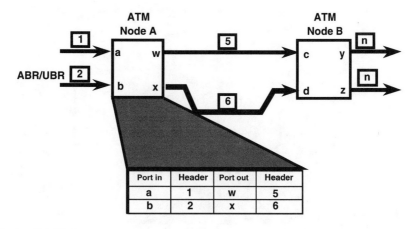

Port in	Header	Port out	Header
a	1	w	5
b	2	x	6

ABR   Available bit rate
UBR   Unspecified bit rate

Figure 8–11   1:n protection switching: Working link operational.

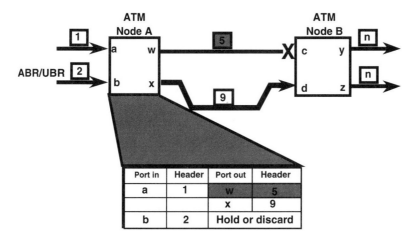

Port in	Header	Port out	Header
a	1	w	5
		x	9
b	2	Hold or discard	

ABR   Available bit rate
UBR   Unspecified bit rate

Figure 8–12   1:n protection switching: Working link is down.

The 1:n protection scheme for recovery operations is shown in Figure 8–12. The working link between nodes A and B is down (the link between node A's port w and node B's port c). The cross-connect table is used to divert the cells to the protection link. The ABR/UBR traffic on the protection link must be held until bandwidth is available for it to be transmitted, or it must be discarded.

The tradeoffs between 1+1 and 1:n protection switching are straightforward. 1+1 provides instantaneous recovery, without loss of traffic, yet requires an expensive redundant link for each working link. On the other hand, 1:n necessitates reconfiguration operations, with the resulting delay and probable loss of traffic, yet the sharing of the backup link translates into a less expensive network topology. The choice of these techniques is a matter for the network operator to decide.

LABEL SWITCHING VERSUS IP ADDRESS ROUTING

With the advent of Internet subnet operations, the routing operations to support diverse topology and addressing needs are greatly enhanced. As an added bonus, the 32-bit IP address space is utilized more effectively.

However, these features translate into a more complex set of operations at the router. Moreover, as the Internet and internets continue to grow, the router may be required to maintain large routing tables. In a conventional routing operation, the processing load to handle many IP addresses in combination with subnet operations can lead to serious utilization problems for the router.

We just learned that label switching uses the VPI/VCI identifier to route the traffic. The VPI/VCI can be used in place of the IP address for routing by encapsulating the IP datagram inside the ATM cell (in the 48-octet payload). The label is examined on a complete value, and not on a bit-by-bit closest match, as done in conventional IP routing. Many of these operations can be performed in hardware, which further speeds-up the process. A companion book in this series, *Advanced Internet Features,* examines this issue in more detail.

SWITCHING TECHNOLOGIES

This section provides an overview of several prominent switching technologies. Vendors often design their switches with a combination of the variety of technologies described here.

Shared Memory Switch

The shared memory switch, as its name implies, provides a common memory for the storage of the cells and the switching fabric (see Figure 8–13). As we learned earlier in this chapter, these cells are organized into separate queues and are routed based on the VPI/VCI values in the

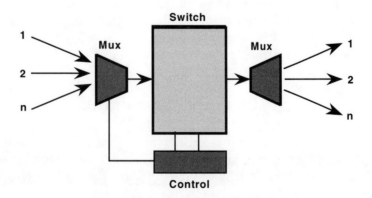

Figure 8–13   Shared memory switch.

header. This illustration shows the use of a multiplexer and demultiplexer at the input ports and output ports, respectively. The cells arriving at the receiving multiplexer are placed onto a single line to the switch, and the switching functions move the traffic from the input queues to the output queues and to the output port(s).

Shared Bus Switch

Figure 8–14 shows a functional view of a shared bus switch architecture. It also shows the switch supporting both frame relay PDUs and ATM PDUs. In most implementations such as shown here, the switch is implemented with two busses for fully redundant operations. The busses actually operate in the cell mode, and traffic is diced into 48-octet pieces with a 5-byte header attached (some implementations are using different size cells). The destination card reassembles the traffic.

Cell traffic is carried through the bus as cells, therefore, both cells or frames can be sent across the bus. As just stated, frames are converted to ATM cells and vice versa, which allows frame and cell relay services to interwork.

Crossbar Switch

Crossbar switching is arranged in one or a combination of three architectures: (1) concentration (more input lines than output lines), (2) expansion (more output lines than input lines), and (3) connection (an

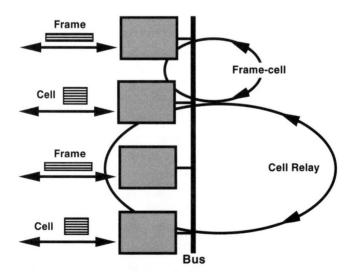

Figure 8–14   Example of a shared bus switch.

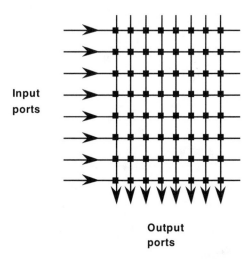

Input
ports

Output
ports

Figure 8–15   Crossbar switching.

equal number of input and output lines). In its simplest form, a circuit switch is a N ¥ M array of lines that connect to each other at crosspoints (see Figure 8–15). In a large switching office, the N lines are input from the subscriber (terminals, computers, etc.) and the M lines are output to other switching offices. The switching fabric of a crossbar switch consists of N^2 crosspoints. Therefore, the size of the switch is limited.

Crossbar Switch with Arbiter (Knockout Switch).   A variation of the crossbar switch is shown in Figure 8–16 [DUBO94]. It is known by several names in the industry—perhaps the best known name is the knockout switch. The switch operates as a conventional crossbar switch in that the horizontal input is connected to a vertical output. Notice that each input line is connected to each output line. In addition, each output port has an arbiter. This component receives cells from the vertical output lines, and places them into a first-in, first-out (FIFO) queue. The queue allows the arbiter to decide which cells gain access to the output port.

Multistage Switching

Crossbar switching is usually performed in more than one array or stage in order to reduce the number of crosspoints. If N lines are to be connected, then N^2 crosspoints are required. Multistage switches are economical for networks when $N > 16^3$ [AMOS79]. Multistage networks are designed with fewer crosspoints, yielding a more economical arrangement.

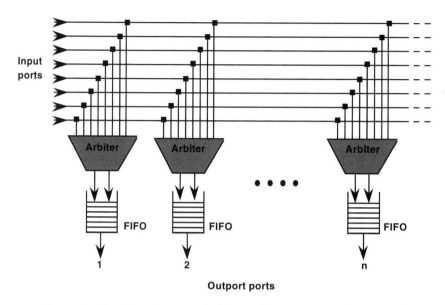

Figure 8–16 Crossbar switching with output arbiter (knock-out switch).

The input and output lines are divided into subgroups of N inputs and N outputs. The input first stage consists of n 3 k matrices. The k output is connected to one of the k center matrices. The third stage consists of k 3 n matrices connected from the center stage to the n outlets. The center stage matrices are all N/n by N/n arrays that permit connections from any first stage to any third stage.

The total number of crosspoints for this three-stage switch is [BELL82]:

$$N_x = 2Nk + k \, (N/n)^2$$

where: N_x = total number of crosspoints; N = number of input and output lines; n = size of each input/output group; k = number of center stage arrays.

Banyan and Delta Switching Networks

A technique that has been employed in the past in high-speed switches is the Banyan network [GOKE73]. As illustrated in Figure 8–17, this switch is characterized by only one path existing between an input to the final output port. With this approach, routing operations are quite simple and straightforward, but cells may be blocked (collide) if more than one arrives at a switching element at the same time.

Input   Output

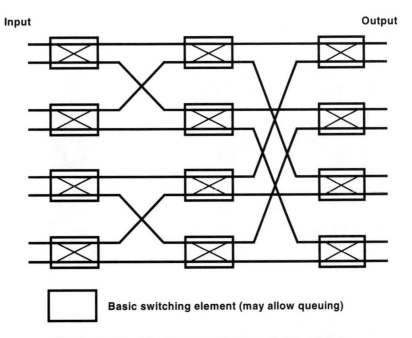

Basic switching element (may allow queuing)

Figure 8–17   The Banyan-Delta switching fabric.

Banyan networks are classified further into subgroups. An (L)-level Banyan network is one in which only the adjacent elements are connected, so each path passes through the same number of L states. A special Banyan implementation is a delta network. It is characterized by having an equal number of inputs lines to outputs lines, with each output identified with a unique value (for example, a destination address). Each digit in an address identifies a next stage of a switching element in the switching fabric.

A number of switching technologies have been proposed for ATM. Some of these proposals and implementations are based on the concept of single-state networks where a single stage of switching element is connected to the inputs and outputs of the switch. Multistage networks (in which several stages of switching elements are connected by various links to form the switching fabric) have also seen use. As of this writing, it is certain that ATM switching will be a melding of several switching techniques, and these techniques will form a switching element that is reproduced and interconnected to form the switching fabric

Figure 8–18 shows a multistage delta network, called a 3-stage folded network. With this approach, traffic that arrives through the input lines (inlets) are examined by (in this example) three decision stages (switching

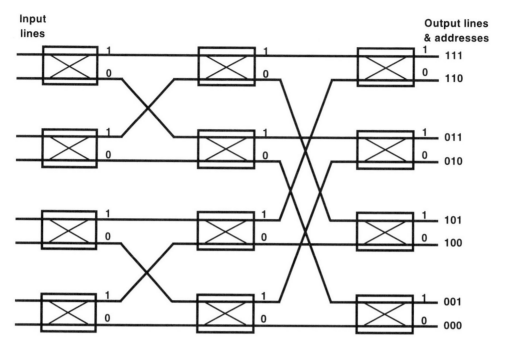

Figure 8–18   A 3-stage folded delta network.

elements). The traffic is passed to subsequent stages on output lines (outlets) based on an analysis of the address (which could be a tag used at the
switch). Each stage is responsible for examining one bit in the address,
typically from the most significant bit (MSB) to the least significant bit
(LSB). In this example, a 3-bit address is used for simplicity.

The resulting address resolution is made one stage at a time in each
bit of the address. As Figure 8–18 shows, the resultant output is based
on the 3-bit address analysis of the three stages.

Figure 8–19 provides an example of an address resolution performed
by the Banyan multistage switch. The bold line indicates the decision
processes performed at the various stages. The destination address (010)
is examined by each of the three stages on a bit-by-bit basis from the
MSB to the LSB. The traffic, with its associated header, and address of
010 is routed to the output line identified as 010.

Collisions may occur in a delta network if cells arrive at a switching
element at the same time. These cells may collide at an intermediate element, even though they are destined for the same output line, or they may
collide at the final element. The probability of collisions occurring can be

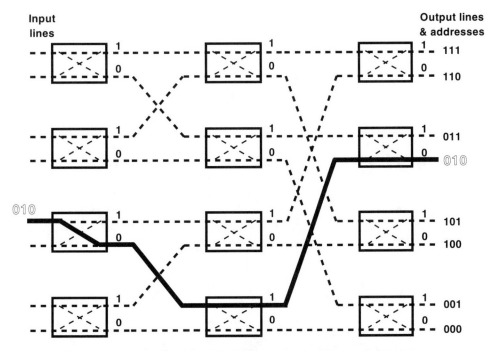

Figure 8–19   Example of address resolution.

reduced by placing buffers in each switching element and allowing the buffers to queue arriving cells, which is an approach that is implemented in a number of high-speed switches. Alternately, the switch can operate at a higher speed than the inlets, thus giving an arrival time at the switching elements with no collision probability. Other mechanisms may be employed, and systems today can operate at a cell loss rate of 10^{-10}.

Figure 8–20 shows three alternatives for the use of buffers and queues within the switching fabric. The first approach places the buffers on the inlet side. Each inlet has a dedicated buffer, which is serviced on a first-in, first-out (FIFO) operation. Logic in the buffer determines when the buffer is to be served and when the cell is to be out-queued to the bus. This approach encounters collisions if two cells at the head of the queue in different buffers are destined for the same switching element. Also, if a queued cell is awaiting the availability of a line to a switching element, subsequent cells in the queue are also blocked even though an inlet may be available.

Output buffers are yet another alternative. This approach requires that a single cell can be served only by an outlet, which also could create

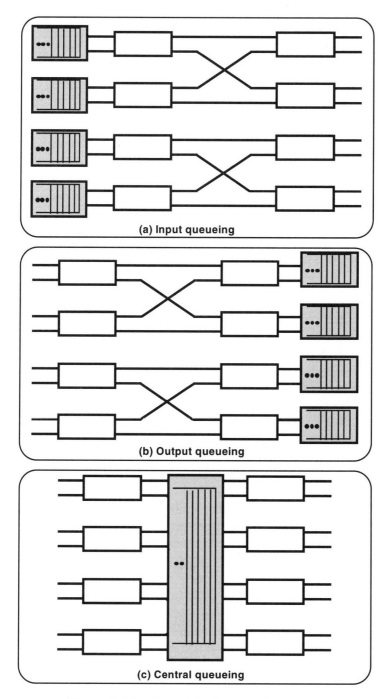

Figure 8–20 Switch buffers and queues.

output collisions and contention. Collisions can occur only if the switching fabric operates at the same speed as the incoming lines to the switching elements. In other words, several cells are contending for the same outlet. As discussed earlier, using different speeds within the switching fabric vis-à-vis the communications lines can reduce this problem. So, if collision is not to occur, cell transfer must be performed at n times the speed of the inlets, where n = the number of possible lines.

The last illustration shows central queuing, which entails nondedicated buffers between the inlets and the outlets; that is to say, a central memory element is used by all inlets to the outlets. This process does not work on the FIFO discipline, because the inlet traffic is placed into a single queue. To service the queues efficiently and fairly, there must be some mechanism to access the entries in the queues and to index the traffic in either sequential or random access operation.

Network switches can be developed that use parallel switching techniques. Figure 8–21 shows a parallel Banyan switch, also called vertical stacking. While switching techniques vary with parallel switching, as a general rule, the ATM cells that belong to the same connection are passed on the same plane of the multidimensioned switch. How this is determined varies among switch designers. During call establishment, decisions are made as to which plane will be used for the connection. The switch contains logic that examines each incoming call, places it on the appropriate plane, and then switches it to the appropriate output line. This approach has proved to be highly efficient, and it provides very high throughput.

VSLI AND ASIC-BASED SWITCHES

In the 1980s, the rise of high-speed and low-cost very large scale integrated (VSLI) circuits, application-specific integrated circuits (ASICs), and random access memory (RAM) chips paved the way for the use of ATM. With ATM, and its use of fixed cells, it was now possible to build very high-speed switches, non-blocking in design (by using RAMs). Much of this recent work has now focused on shared memory switch fabrics. The concept is illustrated in this Figure 8–22.[2]

The idea is for the switch to support different link speeds and interface types—in this example, OC-3, OC-12, and OC-48 rates. Of course, it

---

[2]This idea is found in many ATM switches, and we are highlighting work performed at Lucent (See *Bell Labs Technical Journal,* 2(2), Spring, 1997, "Advances in Shared-Memory Designs for Gigabit ATM Switching," by Kai Y. Eng, and Mark A Pashan.

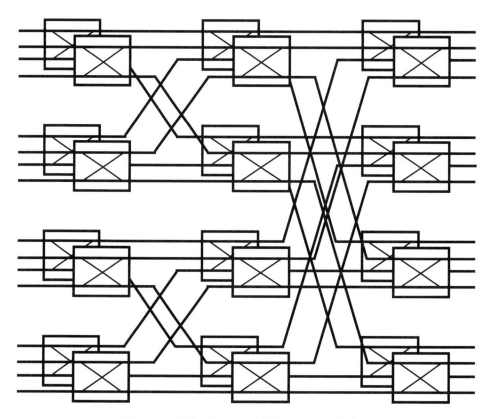

Figure 8–21   A parallel Banyan switch.

is impractical to build one switch for each link type, so the approach is to multiplex the incoming signals to the rate of the highest rate input, a concept called hierarchical multiplexing.

The output demultiplexer may be buffered to handle cells that leave the switch fabric that are destined for the same output link. However, much work has been accomplished in defining buffering operations in the switch fabric that minimize or eliminate the need for output multiplexer buffers. Additionally, while output buffering for each output link is the best approach from the standpoint of performance, it is costly. In contrast, a shared-memory technique reduces costs, and with the use of VLSI chips and RAM, can provide the desired performance.

The ATM switch processes the cells first through a bit-slicing converter, a wide data bus, and a large RAM. During a specific period, the incoming cells are written to RAM and the outgoing cells are read from RAM. The bit-slicing converter accepts cells for the WRITE operation for the input lines and converts the serial stream to a parallel stream (the

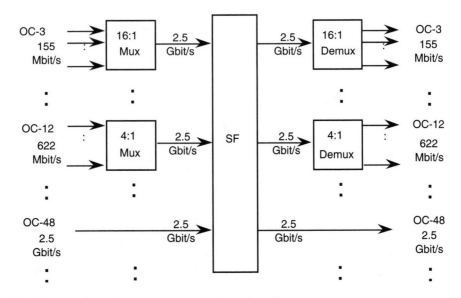

Note: Muxes also perform table look-up for cell routing
SF   Switch fabric

Figure 8–22   ATM hierarchical multiplexing switch.

bit-slicing operation), then multiplexes each cell (one after the other) onto the data bus in such a way that N arriving cells are written into different RAM locations. For the outgoing operations, as many as N cells are read from the RAM through the data bus, and converted back to a serial stream before being sent to the output links.

The fabric interface at the mux is also responsible for a table look-up for cell routing. The VPI or VCI in the cell header is used to determine the output link on the switch, and this information is placed in the cell show so it can be self-routing. With the Lucent approach, the VPI/VCI are replaced in the cell header as part of the conventional mapping/ translation operation.

SUMMARY

The VPI and VCI are used by an ATM switch to make routing decisions. Switching is not part of the ATM standards, so vendors use a wide variety of techniques to build their switches. Several approaches to cell switching are now implemented, but research continues in this area.

9

Traffic Management

This chapter examines several methods for managing user traffic in an ATM network. The emphasis is placed on the operations at the user-network interface (UNI). Ideas on queue management and queue servicing for different applications are explored, as well as how an ATM node must adjust its behavior to varying traffic loads. The chapter includes a description of the work done by the ATM Forum and ITU-T on traffic control and congestion control.

TRAFFIC MANAGEMENT IN AN ATM NETWORK

Digitizing analog images is an easy task with today's technology. These techniques have been around for over 30 years, and are now found in common devices such as personal computers and even children's toys. A more formidable task is the management of the digital images of voice, video, and data applications in a coherent and integrated fashion.

A properly constructed ATM network must manage traffic fairly and provide effective allocation of the network capacity for different sorts of applications, such as voice, video, and data. The ATM network must also provide cost-effective operations relative to the service level (quality of service, QOS) stipulated by the network user, and it must be able to support the different delay requirements of the applications, an important support function known as cell delay variation (CDV) management.

The ATM network must be able to adapt to unforeseen traffic patterns; for example, unusual bursts of traffic from the various end-user devices or applications. Also, the network must be able to shed traffic in certain conditions to prevent or react to congestion. In so doing, it must be able to enforce an allowable peak cell rate for each VPI/VCI connection. This means that when a user's traffic load is presented to the network beyond a maximum peak rate, then it may be discarded.

In addition to these responsibilities, the network must be able to monitor (police) traffic. It must be able to monitor all VPI/VCI connections and verify their correctness (that they are properly mapped into the network and operate effectively). The network must be able to detect problems and emit alarms when certain troubling events are encountered.

An effective ATM network (usually a public network) must be designed with an understanding that both the user and the network assume responsibility for certain QOS operations between them. The user is responsible for agreeing to a service contract with the ATM network that stipulates rules on the use of the network, such as the amount of traffic that can be submitted in a measured time period. In turn, the network assumes the responsibility of supporting the user QOS requirements.

Dealing with High Bandwidth Networks

Any high bandwidth network must deal with links that operate at very high transmission rates. For example, consider the one-way propagation delay of a link across the United States of about 20 ms. A T1 network operating at 1.544 Mbit/s would have 3860 bytes in flight (that is, in the network) during this 20 ms interval, or about 72 cells. This load is not a big problem.[1]

However, with broadband networks operating at higher speeds, the network could have millions of bytes and thousands of cells in flight. For example, in an OC 192 network that carries ATM cell traffic, there could be 24,883,200 bytes and 469,494 cells in flight!

---

[1]These calculations assume the link has no overhead but the ATM cell header. For the OC n links, about 20% of the bandwidth is used for overhead, so the reader can reduce these figures by this amount if SONET is carrying the ATM cells in its envelope.

The figures are based on a simple calculation. Using T1 as the example: 1,544,000 $\times$ .02 (sec.)/ 8 (bits per byte) = *3860* (bytes) / 53 (bytes per cell) = *72.8* ATM cells.

Table 9–1   Data in Flight at High Speeds

Facility	Speed of Line	Bytes*	Cells *
T1	1.5 Mbit/s	3,860	72
OC 3	155 Mbit/s	387,500	7,311
OC 48	2,488 Mbit/s	6,220,800	117,373
OC 192	9,953 Mbit/s	24,883,200	469,494

*Figures assume full bandwidth is available (no T1/OC headers in flight)

Problems, such as link failure or congestion, are intensified in these high-speed networks. Consequently, the network must have the ability to perform preventive measures to avoid congestion and implement mechanisms for rapid dissemination of control information about problems and potential problems. The advanced networks in operation today, do just that—all have preventive congestion control mechanisms and most disseminate control information at propagation speeds.

Table 9–1 shows other examples of "data in flight," based on the type and speed of transmission facility. (This data in flight concept is not my idea, but I have not been able to find its source. I received the example from a person who attended one of my lectures. Any reader who knows this source, please email me and I'll attribute it in the next printing of this text. The same holds true for the next section).

Low Delay Requirements for Processing Cells

Due to the high-speed links that operate in broadband networks, it is imperative that the nodes (switches) in the network exhibit very low delay in their processing of the incoming traffic. In contrast to older networks, these nodes' delay is considerably less than propagation delay.

Most of the cell switching operations discussed in Chapter 8 must be performed in hardware, and the operations at the switch must be simple in order for the switch to be able to keep up with link speeds. Figure 9–1 shows why.[2]

---

[2]These statistics are based on several simple calculations. Using Ethernet as the example: 10,000,000 (Ethernet speed) / 424 (bits in a cell) = 23,584 cells per second to be processed. 1,000,000 (instructions per second) / 23,584 (cells per second) = 42.4 instructions per cell. For an OC 24 link: 1,200,000,000 (link speed) / 424 = 2,830,188 cells per second to be processed. 1,000,000 / 2,830,188 = 0.35 instructions per cell.

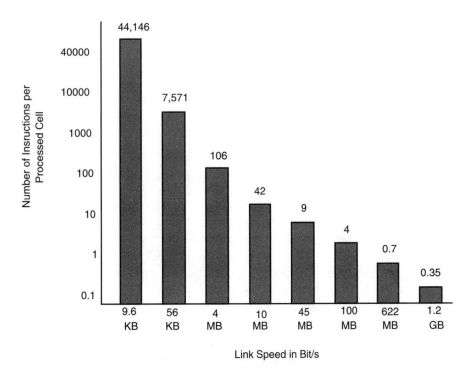

Figure 9–1   Traffic load on the switch.

For purposes of this example, it is assumed that a fictitious node is processing traffic at a rate of 1 MIPS (millions of instructions per second). For slow links, say at 9.6 bit/s, the switch could execute just over 40,000 instructions per cell processed on each cell traversing the switch and still keep the cells in "full flight" through the switch between the input and output links.

But for higher-speed links, the task is more difficult. For example, at Ethernet link speeds of 10 Mbit/s, the switch can execute only 42 instructions per cell. For an OC 24 link, the switch cannot even execute one instruction. In fact, it must process three cells for each executed instruction.

In order for only 35 instructions to be executed per cell, the switch must operate at 100 MIPS. These speeds are certainly possible, and processors are now capable of over 1 GIPs (one billion instructions per second). However, a switch will likely be servicing more than one set of input/output links, and it must devote its instruction execution times to other activities, such as path discovery and network management.

Again, because of these performance requirements, the switching is performed in hardware. What is more, the ATM cell header is very simple, and very little processing time is expended on it. This approach keeps the delay at the switching nodes to a minimum, and reduces latency in the network.

Challenge of Managing a Multiservice Network

Managing a network that supports a mix of traffic is quite different from managing a uni-application network. Additionally, many of the design concepts for traffic management for voice networks do not hold for data networks (see Figure 9–2). In effect, a traditional voice network is a cooperative network. This term means that control and routing decisions for a customer are made with the total network in mind, and individual performance objectives for each call are not a major factor (since, within regulatory requirements and the need to satisfy the customer, all connections are treated the same).

Noncooperative networks are large scale networks that have the individual user (or a user's agent, such as an ISP) making decisions regarding routing and quality of service objectives. In effect, the user is independent with regard to using bandwidth, in contrast to the telephone system, in which the user in not independent. The Internet is such a network, comprised of many systems, very loosely organized, and with nebulous control and quality of service objectives.

In addition, traffic load in a data network is much more variable than in a voice network. And, of course, individual usage of data networks does not follow the same pattern as on a voice network. For example, the holding pattern for a data service is much longer than a voice service.

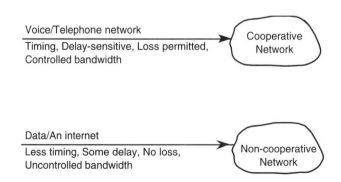

Figure 9–2   Managing a multiservice environment.

Therefore, the multiservice network must be able to accommodate to diverse requirements and must take a new approach for its service model to the customer. At a minimum, it requires the separation of different types of traffic, and providing statistical multiplexing, and quality of service (QOS) features. ATM is designed to support this new model.

CONTROL MECHANISMS

It is obvious that traffic management in an ATM network requires some type of flow control mechanism to prevent the network from becoming congested and discarding cells. Many techniques are available to provide flow control and can be classified as (a) monitoring cell traffic, with cell tagging and possible cell discard actions in the event of problems; and (b) monitoring cell traffic, with feedback mechanisms (a control loop) to the sender to direct the rate of cell emission into the network. Technique (a) is also known as an *open loop* and technique (b) is known as a *closed loop*.

As a general rule, technique (a) assumes the user traffic is fairly predictable and that the user will "behave," and not send traffic beyond an agreed amount. Therefore, under normal operations, there should be no need for a feedback mechanism such as congestion notification, or some other flow control signal.

For technique (b), it is assumed the user traffic load is less predictable, and/or the network has no formal arrangement with the user regarding the amount of traffic the user can send. With this arrangement, some method of feedback is needed to protect the network, and to prevent the user from having to resend traffic that the network discarded because of the network's inability to deliver it.

The Natural Bit Rate

All applications exhibit a natural bit rate [dePr91]—the rate at which the application generates and/or receives a certain number of bits per second (bit/s) based on its "natural requirements." For example, digitized voice using conventional ITU-T standards exhibits a natural bit rate of 32 kbit/s. Large data transfer systems have a fluctuating natural bit rate, depending on the nature of the traffic, but ranging from a few kbit/s to several hundred kbits/s. High definition television (HDTV) has a natural bit rate of approximately 100 to 150 kbit/s, depending on the coding schemes employed on the signals.

The challenge of the ATM network is to support the natural bit rates of all applications being serviced. Because of variable traffic profiles, it may be imperative to discard traffic from certain users if the network experiences congestion problems. This situation is illustrated in Figure 9–3a. For a brief period of time the user exceeds the transfer rate permitted in the network with a burst of traffic. The shadowed portion of the graph is the "burstyness" of the traffic, which exceeds, momentarily, the permitted rate of the network. With ATM networks, this traffic will be tagged for possible discard.

An application's natural bit rate (because of its burstyness) may not use the full rate allocated by the network to this application. The possibility of wasted bandwidth occurring is shown in the striped area of Figure 9–3b. Therefore, some systems (such as an ISDN terminal adapter) can stuff bits into the application's data stream such that it appears to be

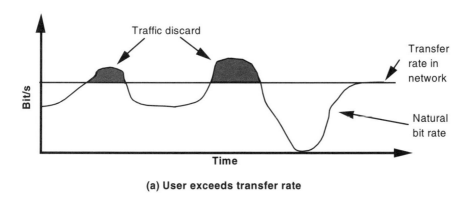

(a) User exceeds transfer rate

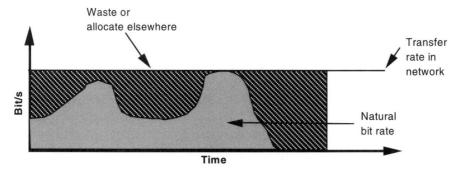

(b) Transfer rate greater than user bit rate

Figure 9–3   Bandwidth allocations. [dePr91]

the same as the transfer rate in the network (or more likely, the transfer rate of the communications link on which the traffic is to be sent). Or, the network can attempt to allocate this bandwidth to other applications.

Potential Congestion Problems

ATM must still deal with the problem of congestion. Most networks provide transmission rules for their users that include agreements on how much traffic can be sent to the network before the traffic flow is regulated (flow-controlled). Flow control is an essential ingredient to prevent congestion in a network. Congestion is a problem that is avoided by network administrators almost at any cost because it results in severe degradation of the network both in throughput and response time.

As the traffic (offered load) in the network reaches a certain point, mild congestion begins to occur with the resulting drop in throughput. If this proceeded in a linear fashion, it would not be so complex a problem. However, at a point at which utilization of the network reaches a certain point, throughput drops exponentially due to serious congestion and the buildup of the servers (queues).

It is being discovered that conventional queuing theory is not always applicable to traffic, especially where there is a mix of traffic types. Therefore, networks must (1) provide some mechanism of informing components in the network when congestion is occurring and (2) provide a flow control mechanism on user devices. With these discussions in mind, the remainder of this chapter examines some approaches to the management of multiapplication traffic.

TRAFFIC CONTROL AND CONGESTION CONTROL

In a B-ISDN, the terms traffic control and congestion control describe different aspects of ATM operations. We concern ourselves with the latter term first. Congestion is defined as a condition that exists at the ATM layer in the network elements (NEs) such as switches, transmission links, or cross connects where the network is not able to meet a stated and negotiated performance objective. In contrast, traffic control defines a set of actions taken by the network to avoid congestion; traffic control takes measures to adapt to unpredictable fluctuations in traffic flows and other problems within the network.

The objectives of both traffic control and congestion control are to protect the network and at the same time provide the user with its stated service contract objectives. For B-ISDN, this includes formally stated QOS objectives. ATM is not designed to rely on AAL to provide any type of traffic control or congestion control measures. While AAL may indeed perform these functions, the design of the ATM network does not assume this service.

Functions to Achieve Traffic Control and Congestion Control

To meet the objectives of traffic control and congestion control, the ATM network must:

- Perform a set of actions called connection admission control (CAC) during a call setup to determine if a user connection will be accepted or rejected. These actions may include acquiring routes for the connection.
- Establish controls to monitor and regulate traffic at the UNI; these actions are called usage parameter control (UPC).
- Accept user input to establish priorities for different types of traffic, through the use of the cell loss priority (CLP) bit.
- Establish traffic shaping mechanisms to obtain a stated goal for managing all traffic (with differing characteristics) at the UNI.

These concepts are described in the following sections.

ALLOCATION OF BANDWIDTH

Since an ATM network is expected to support a wide variety of applications, the network designer must answer the questions of how the natural bit rate of user applications can be accommodated vis-à-vis the transfer rate of the network. Or stated another way, How should the CAC and UPC be established and managed effectively for each user connection? The term "effectively" has two aspects:

1. What is effective for an individual user may not be effective from the network perspective.
2. And, of course the opposite is true—what is effective for the network may not be perceived as effective for the user.

The ATM standards do not stipulate all the specific rules for the CAC and UPC operations. Notwithstanding, this section of the chapter summarizes several approaches that can lead to a fair and effective allocation of the network's bandwidth.

The network exhibits a finite transfer rate, as does each link in the network. Not only must ATM traffic management manage the limited bandwidth within the network, but it also must allocate traffic to each communications link within the network.

To examine the second issue, Figure 9–4 depicts a typical traffic stream that a ATM node might receive (assuming the machine is truly a multiapplication node). Regardless of the capacity of the network, the aggregate transfer rates of all the input lines n must not exceed the transfer rate of the output line m —at least not for a prolonged period (in fractions of milliseconds). Notwithstanding, some buffering of traffic at the multiplexer (ATM node) allows n to exceed m for a short period.

Each queue must be serviced by the multiplexer in a fair and equitable manner. Queue servicing operations should result in appropriate delays and acceptable traffic losses vis-à-vis the application. As examples, (1) CBR video queues should be serviced to depletion; (2) VBR voice queues should not allow the loss of traffic to exceed 1 to 10 percent of the samples (the range depends on how traffic is dropped; see Chapter 7);

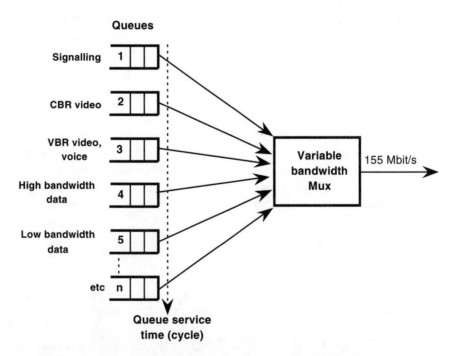

Figure 9–4   Allocating bandwidth using multiple queues.

(3) data queues should allow for no loss of traffic; and (4) the signaling queue contains OAM information and should receive the highest consideration of any of the other queues.

As Figure 9–4 shows, the queues maybe serviced on a cyclical basis (the queue service cycle). Each queue is examined, payload is extracted and transported through the 155 Mbit/s output link. The next queue is examined, payload is extracted, and so on, until the last queue is examined and the process starts over again on the first queue.

The manner in which the queues are set up is not defined in the ATM specifications. Typically, a separate queue is established for each voice and video connection. This approach simplifies queue management.

Let us assume that the queue service cycle assures that delay-sensitive traffic is serviced within 1 to 2 ms. Given this requirement, let us further assume a cycle time of 1.5 ms, which translates to 666.6 service cycles per second (1 second/.0015 = 666.6). Next, assume that the 155.52 output link can accept 353,207 cells per second (155,520,000 [less overhead of the 155.52 Mbit/s frame yields a rate of 149.760 Mbit/s]/424 bits in a 53-octet cell = 353,207). Therefore, this configuration can service 529 cells per service cycle (353,207/666.6 = 529).

Figure 9–5 shows that all queues are serviced during the service cycle. The multiplexer must adjust to the changes in the number of calls

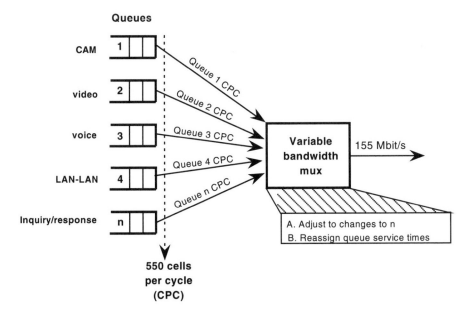

Figure 9–5 Servicing the queues.

and the resultant queues and vary the service times on the queues accordingly. Therefore, it must be able to add/delete queues and adjust its queue extractions accordingly.

The example in Figure 9–5 is based on the use of a SONET STS-3c 155.52 Mbit/s link. Other links with different bit rates obviously affect the value of the cells per service cycle. For example, if the output link were a 44.736 DS3 link, the cells could use 40.704 Mbit/s of this capacity—the other bits are overhead. Therefore, 40,704,000/424 = 86,914 for the number of cells that can be transported per second across the DS3 link. This configuration supports 130 cells per service cycle (86,914/ 666.6 = 130).

The task now is to determine which queues are to have their cells withdrawn during the service cycle and at what rate the cells will be withdrawn from the queues. The general strategy is simple ([SRIR90a] and [SRIR90b]):

- The signaling queue is given the highest priority and should experience little or no delay and experience no loss.
- Delay-sensitive queues are serviced next, if cells are in the queues for T_1 ms, or until these queues are empty.
- Next, delay-insensitive queues are serviced for T_2 ms.
- In some installations, the absence of talkspurts allows data queues to be serviced more frequently.
- When the signaling queue is serviced, either T1 or T2 is suspended and resumed (not restarted) when this queue service is finished.

Thus, all queues are guaranteed an established and minimum bandwidth of (T1/{T1+T2})B for delay sensitive traffic and (T2/{T1+T2})B, delay insensitive traffic, where B is the transfer rate of the output link.

The manner in which the queues are serviced depends on how many cells must be withdrawn per service cycle. Be aware that the number of cells serviced per cycle varies, not only between voice, video, and data, but within those applications as well. For example, a conventional 64 kbit/s voice call operates at about 166 cells per second. In marked contrast, a 32 kbit/s voice call using selective cell discard and compression of silent periods needs only about 38 cells per second. Therefore, the variable bandwidth mux must know how to service each queue in regard to the cell withdrawal rate. Once again, these decisions are vendor-specific.

Computing the Parameters for Queue Servicing

Sriram defines three equations for computing the parameters to be used for servicing the queues [SRIR93]. The first equation assures queue $_i$ that a fraction f_i of the output link bandwidth is available:

$$f_i = \frac{T_i}{\sum\limits_{i=0}^{n} T_i}, \ 0 \leq i \leq n$$

The second equation assures that all the bandwidth assigned to all queues cannot exceed a fraction of $(1 - f_0)$ for the output link capacity:

$$\sum_{i=0}^{n} f_i \leq 1 - f_0$$

The third equation shows that the cycle time for all queues should be from 1 to 2 ms, in order to guarantee consistent service to delay-sensitive traffic.

$$\sum_{i=0}^{n} T_i \leq D_c ms (D_c \approx 1 \text{ to } 2 \text{ ms})$$

where: n is number of queues; f_n is a fraction of the bandwidth of the output link; T_n is the time parameter for servicing the queue n; $D_c = M_c t$ is the service cycle time; M_c is the number of cells withdrawn from the queue during the service cycle time; and t is the cell transmission time on the link.

The reader is encouraged to follow up on this general discussion by pursuing the references and sources cited in this section. Sriram's ongoing work [SRIR93] is especially recommended.

EXAMPLE OF QUEUE MANAGEMENT OPERATIONS

Figure 9–6 shows a common approach to managing time-sensitive and time-insensitive traffic, and builds on the concepts discussed in the previous examples. This specific example is from "Here Comes UBR+," by Houman Modarres, *Telephony*, October 6, 1997 [MODA97].

Two types of queue service algorithms are used in this example. The exhaustive round robin algorithm (ERR) services the highest-priority queue and clears the cells in the queue before proceeding to the next highest priority queue. In addition, it overrides the servicing of any lower-priority queue if cells arrive at a higher-priority queue.

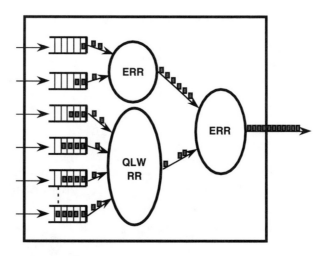

ERR   Exhaustive round robin
QLW RR   Queue length-weighted round robin

Figure 9–6   Queue Service Procedure. [MODA97]

The queue length-weighted round robin algorithm (QLR RR) is used on non-real-time queues. The servicing of these queues is based on the type of traffic and how many cells are stored in the queue. All traffic then is serviced by another ERR algorithm.

Studies show that this approach is quite effective for supporting multiapplication systems (assuming the ATM machine has adequate CPU horsepower and enough buffer space for the queues).

DEALING WITH VARIABLE DELAY

Traffic management operations occur not only at the source UNI but also at the destination node itself. The manner in which traffic management is implemented depends on the type of traffic. Assuming that the traffic has been granted admission at the source UNI into the network, upon its arrival at the end-user device, further traffic management decisions on how to "outplay" the traffic to the user application must be made.

As Figure 9–7 shows, different types of traffic must be handled in different ways. The classes of traffic, 1A, 1B, 2, and 3, represent one method of categorization. The traffic with high bandwidth requirements using isochronous timing is buffered at the receiver if the traffic arrives

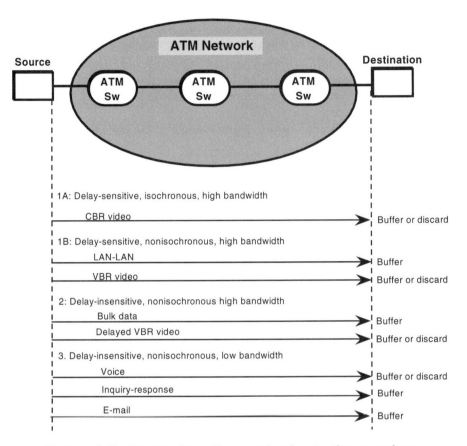

Figure 9–7 Processing the payload at the receiver. [SRIR93]

sooner than a predetermined time. If it arrives after this time, it is discarded. Type 1B traffic, which is delay-sensitive, nonisochronous, high-bandwidth traffic, is handled depending on the specific kind of traffic. For example, LAN-to-LAN traffic would be buffered, whereas variable bit-rate video would be buffered if the traffic arrives early and discarded if the traffic arrives late. Type 2 traffic, which is delay-insensitive, nonisochronous, high-bandwidth traffic, again is handled differently depending of the specific subtype. Data traffic is buffered and delayed VBR video traffic (video that must be delivered at a later time) and is handled like any type of VBR video traffic that, if it is early, is buffered, but if it arrives late, it is discarded.

Finally, class 3 traffic, which is delay insensitive not isochronous, is handled differently for voice than for data. As the reader might now expect, early arriving voice packets are buffered until a payout time is reached, and then late arriving packets are discarded.

In essence, any type of traffic involving data is buffered and held in the buffer for quite some time to prevent discarding it. In contrast, video and voice will be discarded if it arrives too late and it will be buffered (to meet a standard arrival time) if it arrives too early.

The reader may wish to review "Voice Packetization" in Chapter 7 for examples of queue management and outplay operations.

CONNECTION ADMISSION CONTROL (CAC) PROCEDURES

CAC is a set of procedures that operate at the UNI, encompassing actions taken by the network to grant or deny a connection to a user. A connection is granted when the user's traffic contract is examined, revealing that the connection can be supported through the whole network at its required QOS levels (see Figure 9–8).

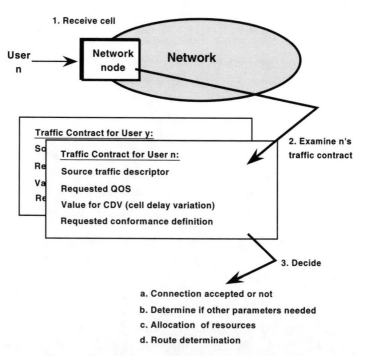

Figure 9–8   Connection admission control (CAC).

The Traffic Contract should contain sufficient information to allow the network to make an intelligent decision about the granting or denial of the connection. This information includes:

- Source traffic descriptor: Values such as the peak cell rate, the sustainable cell rate, and burst tolerance. They may vary with each connection.
- Quality of service for both directions: While several QOS parameters are still under study, parameters such as cell error ratio, cell loss ratio, and cell misinsertion rate have been established.
- Cell delay variation: Amount of end-to-end variation that can occur with the cells of the connection.
- Requested conformance definition: Values describing the conformance of cells for the connection. Values include peak cell rate and sustainable cell rate (SCR) with the cell loss priority (CLP) bit set to either 0 or 1.

USAGE PARAMETER CONTROL (UPC)

After a connection is granted and the network has reserved resources for the connection, each user's session is monitored by the network. This is the UPC operation, which is designed to monitor and control traffic and to check on the validity of the traffic entering the network. UPC maintains the integrity of the network and makes sure that only valid VPIs and VCIs are entering the network (see Figure 9–9).

According to the ATM Forum, several other features are desirable for UPC:

- The ability to detect noncompliant traffic
- The ability to vary the parameters that are checked
- A rapid response to users violating their contracts
- Keeping the operations of noncompliant users transparent to compliant users

TRAFFIC MANAGEMENT AT THE UNI—BASIC CONCEPTS

A wide number of alternatives exist for the management of traffic in an ATM network. This section provides a review of several proposals.

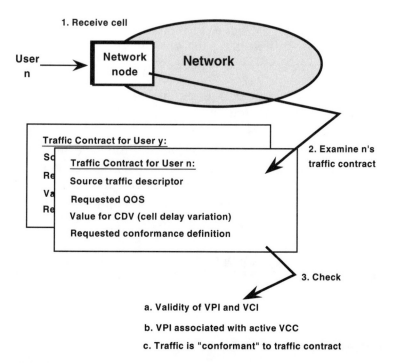

Figure 9–9 Traffic policing with usage parameter control (UPC).

Eckberg Scheme

Figure 9–10 shows one proposal that has met with general approval from the ITU-T. This analysis was provided by Bell Laboratories and its Teletraffic Theory Group, which is supervised by A. E. Eckberg [ECKB92].

The scheme shown in this figure assumes that the user has a service contract with the ATM network wherein certain QOS parameters have been specified. Upon submitting traffic to the network, the user has the option of identifying individual cells with a certain precedence. This decision by the user allows the ATM network service provider to determine how to treat the traffic in the event of congestion problems.

For traffic that is considered to be essential, the network then assumes the responsibility to assure that this traffic is treated fairly vis-à-vis the type of traffic. As an illustration, if the type of traffic is more tolerant to loss, the network then assumes the responsibility of tagging this

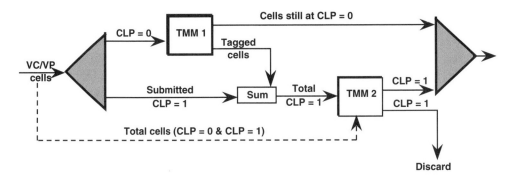

Figure 9–10 Proposed scheme for traffic management (from ITU paper CCITT 371). [ECKB92]

traffic as "possible loss traffic" and perhaps discarding this traffic if network congestion becomes a problem.

The major task of the ATM network is to make certain that the total cells presented to the network are consistent with the total cells processed by the network. This entails balancing the traffic submitted with CLP 0 and CLP 1 to that of the user's service contract.

On the left side of Figure 9–10, the user submits its traffic to the network node with the virtual channel and virtual path identifiers residing in the submitted cell. These identifiers are matched against the user's contract and decisions are made whether to grant the user access to the network.

A transmission monitoring machine (TMM1) is responsible for keeping track of all cells submitted by the user with CLP = 0 (those that should not be lost, such as data). In the event of unusual problems, or (more likely) if the user violates the contract with the network, the TMM1 can change the CLP of 0 to a 1. The cell that is tagged by the TMM1 is called an excessive traffic tag. TMM1 does not tag all cells. It must pass cells that are within the service contract. These cells come from the user with the CLP bit = 0. This value remains at 0 if traffic conditions are acceptable and the user is within its service contract.

The user may submit traffic to the network with CLP bit = 1 (known as externally tagged cells). The ATM network node will sum these tagged cells with the excessive traffic tagged cells and provide a total of frames with a CLP = 1 to TMM2. TMM2 then makes a decision to (1) discard some of the tagged cells or (2) permit these cells to enter the network. Also, ITU-T I.371 permits TMM2 to discard a CLP = 0 cell when necessary. This possibility is not depicted Figure 9–10.

Multiplexing Traffic into the Cells

The manner in which cells are multiplexed onto the communications channel is a proprietary operation, and varies from vendor-to-vendor. The examples in Figure 9–11 show how several applications' bandwidth requirements can be supported by ATM multiplexing cells into an OC-3 frame of 155.52 Mbit/s. I have included tutorial information in the examples of this figure to aid the reader in understanding each example.

The first example is for high-quality video, which requires 135 Mbit/s of bandwidth. This application would use all the cells in an OC-3 frame (allowing for the OC-3 overhead).

The second example is for T1-based video. In this application, every second frame would carry one cell of the application. However, be aware that some vendors will burst multiple cells of an application into the frame, and rely on the receiving machine to smooth the cells back to a synchronous flow vis-à-vis the application.

The third example is for heavily compressed video, which can utilize 511.7 kbit/s (depending upon the compression algorithm). This application would use one cell in every sixth OC-3 frame.

The last example shows that the cells from these applications can be multiplexed into one frame for transport across the communications link.

Traffic Shaping Example

In some commercial ATM systems, the cell shaping output at an ATM node is based on the average cell emission time interval. Table 9–2 shows Nortel's approach in supporting a virtual circuit.[3] The Shape ID is an identifier for each cell shaping operation. Each cell shaping is based on the average cell rate (in cells/sec) and the average cell interval in µseconds (and the inverse of the cell rate). The resulting bandwidth demand (in bit/s) is shown in the last column and is derived from the average cell rate * the cell size. As an example, for Shape ID 1: 665,094 cells/sec * 53 octets per cell (424 bits per cell) = 281,999,856 bit/s.

Token Pools and Leaky Buckets

A number of ATM implementations have adopted the "leaky bucket" approach (see Figure 9–12). The bucket is actually a number of counters

---

[3]The operations in this example are used in several of Nortel's ATM nodes, and Nortel also supports other shaping operations for bursty traffic.

High-quality video can utilize 135.168 Mbit/s

Connection 7 uses almost all cells in an OC-3 frame, because:

155.52. Mbit/s — 5.76 Mbit/s (overhead) = 149.760 Mbit/s available for payload

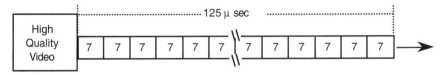

T1-based video can utilize 1.536 Mbit/s

Connection 8 uses one cell in every second OC-3 frame, because:

(1 cell/2 frame) * (8000 frames per sec) * (48 bytes * 8 bits per byte) = 1.536 Mbit/s

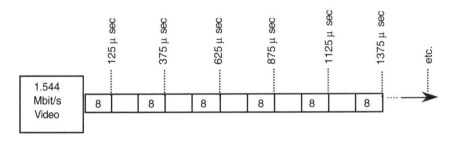

Heavily compressed video can utilize 511.7 kbit/s

Connection 9 uses one cell in every sixth OC-3 frame, because:

(1 cell/6 frame) * (8000 frames per sec) * (48 bytes * 8 bits per byte) = 511.7 Mbit/s

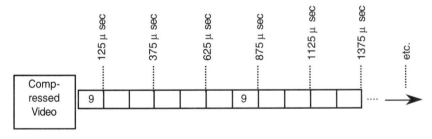

Cells from different connections may be multiplexed into one frame

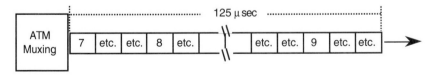

Figure 9–11   Examples of cell loading (calculations assume a 48 byte cell payload). [McCO94]

Table 9–2 Traffic Shaping Example

Shape ID	Average Cell Rate (Cells/sec)	Average Cell Interval (μsec)	Bandwidth Requirement (Bit/s)	
1	665,094	1.50	282	M
2	471,698	2.12	200	M
3	333,333	3.00	141	M
4	235,849	4.24	100	M
5	166,666	6.00	70.7	M
6	117,924	8.48	50	M
7	83,333	12.0	35.3	M
8	58,823	17.0	25	M
9	41,666	24.0	17.7	M
10	29,498	33.9	12.5	M
11	20,833	48.0	8.83	M
12	14,749	67.8	6.25	M
13	10,416	96.0	4.42	M
14	7,407	135	3.12	M
15	5,208	192	2.21	M
16	3,6=0	271	1.56	M
17	2,604	384	1.1	M
18	1,891	543	781	K
19	1,302	768	552	K
20	921	1085	391	K
21	651	1536	276	K
22	460	2171	195	K
23	325	3072	138	K
24	230	4342	97.7	K

that are maintained at the UNI network side for each connection. Periodically, a token generator issues values called tokens, which are placed into a token pool. The token generator can be thought of as a credit accrual timer in that its invocation gives the user credits (rights) to send cells to the network.

When cells are sent to the network, the token pool is reduced for the respective connection by the number of cells that were sent. If the user sends excessive traffic (beyond the service contract), the token pool is exhausted; that is, the user has "used up" its tokens. In such a situation,

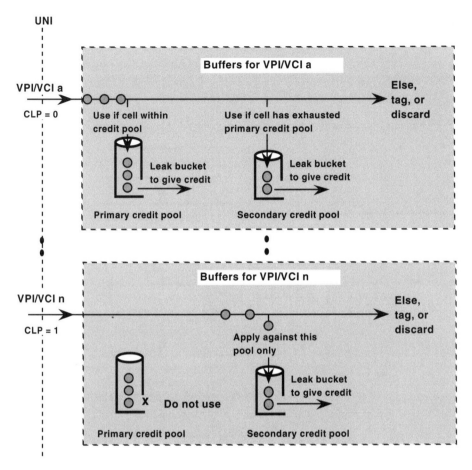

Figure 9–12   The leaky bucket approach.

the cell may have its CLP bit set to 1 by the network and passed into the network, or the cell may be dropped at the UNI without further processing. These decisions depend upon the actual implementation of the specific network.

Some proposals specify two token pools for each connection. One pool is debited for cells in which the CLP bit is set to 0 by the user (a primary pool). Another pool is debited for cells in which the CLP bit is set to 1 by the user (a secondary pool). This approach gives the user some control on which cells may be dropped by the network, because the cells with CLP = 1 are not debited from the primary pool. In later sections of this chapter, I shall return to the subject of token pools and leaky buckets and provide some examples of implementations.

Allocating Resources

Figure 9–13 shows yet another proposed scheme for allocating resources in the network. It is based on the idea of a connection-on-demand, where a user's service request is matched against the current available bandwidth. Thereafter, resources are "gathered" within the

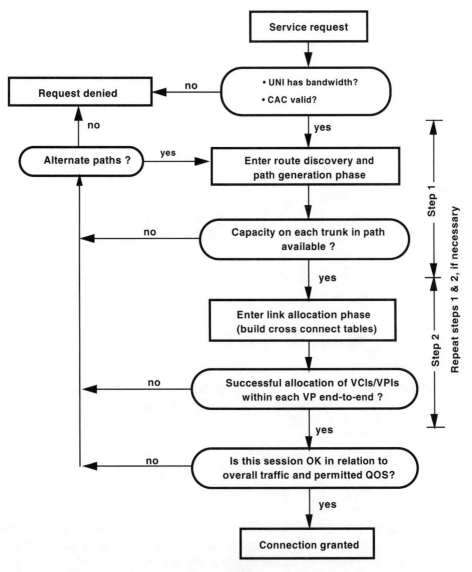

Figure 9–13   Allocation and management scheme.

network to support the user payload. The initial service request is submitted to the ingress node of the network, which makes a determination if sufficient bandwidth is available at the UNI to support the request. If bandwidth is available, the path generation phase is entered, and capacity is reserved for each trunk on the virtual path. During the path generation phase, if capacity is not available on any one trunk, the request is denied. If all goes well, the link allocation phase is entered, and VCIs/VPIs are allocated end-to-end. During the link generation phase, if VCI/VPI allocation is not successful on any one trunk, the request is denied. Finally, an analysis is made of the user request in relation to the overall network traffic and the permitted QOS. If this test is passed, a connection is granted.

ATM BEARER SERVICE ATTRIBUTES AT THE UNI

The ATM Forum defines the bearer service attributes that are made available at the UNI. Table 9–3 lists the attributes for private and public UNIs, some of which pertain to performance and traffic management. Most of the attributes are self-explanatory. A few warrant further explanation in the following sections.

The subjects of point-to-point and multipoint connections as well as PVC and SVCs have been covered in earlier parts of this book.

TRAFFIC CONTROL AND CONGESTION CONTROL

Earlier discussions in this chapter defined traffic control and congestion control. Traffic control specifies the actions taken by the network to avoid congestion. However, if congestion occurs, then congestion control relates to the operations taken by the network to minimize the effects of the congestion. While this distinction may seem somewhat arbitrary, it has important implications for how traffic is monitored and policed at the UNI. Whatever the case may be on the monitoring to achieve traffic control and congestion control, the B-ISDN objectives for these operations are:

- Both traffic control and congestion control must support an ATM QOS consistent with all aspects of the QOS objectives.
- ATM traffic control and congestion control reside at the ATM layer; consequently, the ATM layer should not rely on the ATM

Table 9–3   ATM Bearer Service Attributes at the UNI [ATM94a]

ATM Bearer Service Attribute	Private UNI	Public UNI
Support for point-to-point VPCs	Optional	Optional
Support for point-to-point VCCs	Required	Required*
Support for point-to-multipoint VPCs	Optional	Optional
Support for point-to-multipoint VCCs, SVC	Required	Required*
Support for point-to-multipoint VCCs, PVC	Optional	Optional
Support for permanent virtual connection	Required**	Required**
Support for switched virtual connection	Required**	Required**
Support of specified QOS classes	Optional	Required***
Support of unspecified QOS classes	Optional	Optional
Multiple bandwidth granularities for ATM connections	Optional	Required
Peak rate traffic enforcement via usage parameter control (UPC)	Optional	Required
Sustainable cell rate (SCR) traffic enforcement via UPC	Optional	Optional
Traffic shaping	Optional	Optional
ATM layer fault management	Optional	Required
Interim local management interface	Required	Required

* Public ATM network equipment conforming to this interface specification shall be capable of providing ATM users with a VPC service, a VCC service, or combined VPC/VCC service.
** ATM network equipment conforming to this interface specification shall be capable of providing ATM users with either support for PVC or SVC capability or both.
*** Only one of the specific QOS connection categories is required at the public UNI.

adaptation layer (AAL) to obtain traffic control and congestion control services, nor should the ATM layer rely on any other higher layer protocols residing in the CPE.

- The ATM layer traffic control and congestion control operations should be designed to minimize network complexity.

CELL ARRIVAL RATE AND CELL INTERVAL

In any network that is demand driven, a (somewhat) unpredictable load can be imposed on the network at the UNIs. An ATM network is certainly no exception. We have learned earlier in this chapter that traffic policing and remedial action are required to ensure that traffic load does not jeopardize the performance of the network. Ideally, one would not like to impose restrictions on a user and the user's ability to present payload to the network (after all, payload is so named because it produces revenue). Moreover, in an ideal world, a network is able to accept all user traffic.

Unfortunately, such is not the case in the real world. Because of simple economics, busy signals must be returned to telephone users when the network is busy. It would be somewhat impractical for a network to be designed to accommodate all calls, for example, one that could handle all Mother's Day traffic. Therefore, any network that has an unpredictable (within limits of course) load offered to it must be able to monitor this traffic and take remedial action, if required.

An ATM network provides these important operations by monitoring the cell arrival rate for each connection across the UNI. Of course, if the network were monitoring only one user and its cell arrival profile at each physical interface, the matter would be relatively simple. With the ability to multiplex (potentially) hundreds of sessions on one physical interface, it becomes quite important to monitor each user's traffic pattern and to make adjustments accordingly, which might mean shedding or flow-controlling a specific user's traffic.

Figure 9–14 shows the problem faced by an ATM network. In Figure 9–14a the cell arrival rate to the network node is relatively low. Due to the nature of the user's application and the behavior of the application at

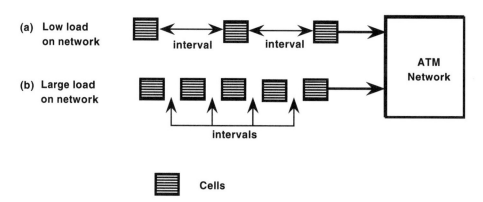

- Cell duration is 2.831 msecs: 53 octets * 8 bits per octet/155.52 Mbit/s - 5.76 Mbit/s
- A 155.52 Mbit/s link transmits 353.207 cells per second: 149.760 Mbit/s/424 bits in a 53-octet cell = 353,207

Figure 9–14   Arrival rate and interval of a user's traffic.

this instance, relatively long intervals are occurring between the arrival of successive cells at the network. Of course, this simplifies greatly the network's ability to handle the traffic.

On the other hand, in Figure 9–14b, the cells are arriving at a much faster rate, which results in the concomitant decrease in the interval between the cells. In a commercially oriented network, Figure 9–14b is preferable to Figure 9–14a, because more payload cells produce more income. However, for the network manager, Figure 9–14b presents a more challenging problem in that the network must adjust and accommodate to the higher traffic loads, a point made earlier in Table 9–1.

Also, the cells depicted in Figure 9–14 may be carrying traffic from different user applications (such as voice, video, and data) and traffic within these applications may require a different level of QOS support from the network. Consequently, a multi-application network must deal with issues other than simple cell arrival rates in accommodating to varying traffic loads. An ATM network must also accommodate to the different QOS emanating from each application. Granted, some applications will have the same QOS profile, which simplifies some of the policing and congestion control operations for that traffic at the UNI. Notwithstanding, the applications presented to this interface will vary significantly in their need for bandwidth-on-demand. Therefore, the network must be able to sustain those traffic bursts, guarantee the cell rate intervals, and provide such services.

With these thoughts in mind, the following sections examine some ideas of how ATM networks accommodate to a widely diverse environment where each application may exhibit different cell intervals and different cell arrival rates.

ATM CELL TRANSFER PERFORMANCE PARAMETERS

The ATM Forum [ATM94c] has defined a set of ATM cell transfer performance parameters to correspond to the ITU-T Recommendation I.350 stipulation for QOS at the UNI. These parameters are summarized in Table 9–4, and the ATM Forum cell rate algorithm is explained in the next section of this chapter. Most of these parameters are self-descriptive. Amplifying information on some of the parameters follows.

The *severely errored cell block ratio (SECBR)* is a sequence of n cells sent consecutively on a given connection. A reasonable way to measure this operation is to assume that a cell block is a sequence of cells trans-

Table 9–4   Cell Transfer Performance Parameters

- Cell error ratio: Errored cells/ Successfully transferred cells + Errored cells
- Severely errored cell block ratio: Severely errored cell blocks/Total transmitted cell blocks
- Cell loss ratio: Lost cells/Total transmitted cells
- Cell misinsertion rate: Misinserted cells/Time interval
- Cell transfer delay: Elapsed time between a cell exit a measurement point its entry at another measurement point
- Mean cell transfer delay: Average of a specified number of cell transfer delays for one or more connections
- Cell delay variation (CDV): Describes the variability of the pattern of cell arrival for a given connection

mitted between OAM cells, although the size of a cell block is not specified in the standards.

The *cell misinsertion rate (CMR)* value is calculated as a rate and not as a ratio, since misinsertion operations are independent of the amount of traffic transmitted.

The *cell delay variation (CDV)* has two performance parameters associated with it: (1) the 1-point CDV, and (2) the 2-point CDV. The 1-point CDV describes the variability in the arrival pattern observed at a measurement point in reference to 1/T. The 2-point CDV describes variability in the arrival pattern observed at an output in relation to the pattern at an input. These concepts are explained in more detail later in this chapter.

The *peak cell rate (PCR)* is coded as cells per second. A further discussion of this parameter is deferred until further related definitions are clarified.

A network operator may or may not provide bearer services to its subscribers. However, some of these services must be implemented if the cell relay network is to operate efficiently. As examples, *peak rate traffic enforcement* and *traffic shaping* must be part of the network's ongoing functions in order to keep congestion under control.

The following definitions for possible cell transfer outcomes between measurement points for transmitted cells are defined based on ITU-T I.356, and [ATM96b]:

- *Successful cell transfer outcome:* The cell is received corresponding to the transmitted cell within a specified time T_{max}. The binary

Table 9–5   Other Useful Definitions

- Multiple bandwidth granularities: The provision for bandwidth on demand for each UNI connection
- Peak cell rate (PCR): The permitted burst profile of traffic associated with each UNI connection (an upper bound)
- Sustainable cell rate (SCR): A permitted upper bound on the average rate for each UNI connection, i.e., an average throughput
- Traffic shaping: Altering the stream of cells emitted into a virtual channel or virtual path connection (cell rate reduction, traffic discarding, etc.)

content of the received cell conforms exactly to the corresponding transmitted cell payload and the cell is received with a valid header field after header error control procedures are completed.

- *Errored cell outcome:* The cell is received corresponding to the transmitted cell within a specified time T_{max}. The binary content of the received cell payload differs from that of the corresponding transmitted cell payload or the cell is received with an invalid header field after header error control procedures are completed.
- *Lost cell outcome:* No cell is received corresponding to the transmitted cell with a specified time T_{max} (examples include "never received" or "late").
- *Misinserted cell outcome:* A cell is received for which there is no corresponding transmitted cell.
- *Severely-errored cell block outcome:* When M or more lost cell outcomes, misinserted cell outcomes, or errored cell outcomes are observed in a received cell block of N cells transmitted consecutively on a given connection.

Table 9–5 defines several other terms and parameters that are used later in this chapter.

ATM LAYER PROVISIONS FOR QUALITY OF SERVICE (QOS)

The performance parameters discussed in the previous section serve as the basis for measuring the QOS provided by the ATM network. The parameters in Table 9–6 are used to assess the QOS in regards to:

Table 9–6   QOS Degradation Factors [ATM94b]

Attribute	CER	SECBR	CLR	CMR	CTD	CDV
Propagation delay					√	
Media errors statistics	√	√	√	√		
Switch architecture			√		√	√
Buffer capacity		√	√		√	√
Number of tandem nodes	√	√	√	√	√	√
Traffic load			√	√	√	√
Failures	√	√	√			
Resource allocation			√		√	√

CER   = Cell error ratio
SECBR   = Severely errored cell block ratio
CLR   = Cell loss ratio
CMR   = Cell misinsertion rate
CTD   = Mean cell transfer delay
CDV   = Cell delay variation

Cell error ratio	accuracy
Severely errored cell block ratio	accuracy
Cell loss ratio	dependability
Cell misinsertion rate	accuracy
Cell transfer delay	speed
Mean cell transfer delay	speed
Cell delay variation	speed

As reliable as an ATM network may be, errors will occur. Software bugs, excessive traffic, uncorrectable errors in the header, and user payload corruption are examples of common problems that will lead to discarded traffic. As a guideline, [ATM94b] summarizes how impairments will affect five critical performance parameters (see Table 9–6).

While the information in Table 9–6 is largely self-evident, a few observations should be made. First, if possible, it is desirable to have as few as possible intermediate nodes (tandem nodes) involved in relaying the cells from the source to the destination, because each node is a potential source for the degradation of all five of the performance parameters shown in the table. The rationale behind this observation is based on well-founded design principles (and common sense). Second, traffic load (that is, excessive traffic load) is to be avoided, because it leads to the degradation of four of the performance parameters shown in the table. It does not affect the cell error ratio. Third, while propagation delay affects only the mean cell transfer delay, its effect on calculating overall delay is quite significant.

ATM FORUM AND ITU-T TRAFFIC CONTROL AND CONGESTION CONTROL

The ATM Forum and ITU-T have defined algorithms for policing the traffic at the UNI for both CBR and VBR traffic. The traffic parameters employed are: (1) PCR for CBR connections and (2) PCR, SCR, and maximum burst size (MBS) for VBR traffic. These parameters are provided by the user during the connection establishment with the SETUP message.

An additional parameter is the burst tolerance (BT), which places a restriction on how much traffic can be sent beyond the SCR before it is tagged as excessive traffic. It is calculated as:

$$BT = (MBS - 1) / (1/SCR - 1/PCR)$$

Generic Cell Rate Algorithm (GCRA)

The generic cell rate algorithm (GCRA) is employed in traffic policing and is part of the user/network service contract. In the ATM Forum specification, the GCRA consists of two parameters: the increment I and the limit L. (As a note, the CCITT I.371 uses the parameters T and t respectively for I and L.) The notation GCRA (I, L) means the generic cell rate algorithm with the increment parameter set to I and the limit parameter set to L. The increment parameter affects the cell rate. The limit parameter affects cell bursts. The GCRA allows, for each cell arrival, a 1-unit leak out of the bucket per unit of time. In its simplest terms, the bucket has finite capacity, and it leaks out at a continuous rate. Its contents can be filled (incremented) by I if L is not exceeded. Otherwise, the incoming cell is defined as nonconforming. This idea is shown in Figure 9–15.

The GCRA is implemented as a continuous-state leaky bucket algorithm or a virtual scheduling algorithm. The two algorithms serve the same purpose: to make certain that cells are conforming (arriving within the bound of an expected arrival time) or nonconforming (arriving sooner than an expected arrival time).

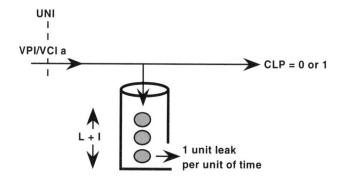

Generic Cell Rate Algorithm, GCRA(I,L):

I   Increment parameter, affects cell rate

L   Limit parameter, affects cell bursts

Leaky bucket:
   • Finite-capacity bucket
   • Contents leak out at a continuous rate of 1 per unit time
   • Contents are incremented by I, if L is not exceeded

Figure 9–15   The I and L parameters.

The virtual scheduling algorithm updates a theoretical arrival time (TAT), which is an expected arrival time of a cell. If the arrival is not too early (later than TAT + L, where L is a network-specified limit parameter), then the cell is conforming. Otherwise, it is nonconforming. If cells arrive after a current value of TAT, then TAT is updated to the current time of the arrival of the cell (expressed as $t_a(k)$, where K cell arrives at time t_a + the increment I). If the cell is nonconforming, then TAT is not changed. Other aspects of the virtual scheduling algorithm are shown in Figure 9–16.

The continuous-state leaky bucket algorithm places a bound on the traffic of L + I. The conceptual bucket has a finite capacity; its contents drain out by one unit for each cell. Its contents are increased by one for each conforming cell. Simply stated, upon the arrival of a cell, if the content of the bucket is less than or equal to the limit L, the cell is conforming. Other aspects of the continuous-state leaky bucket algorithm are also shown in Figure 9–16.

Bandwidth allocation and policing schemes are far from settled, although the ATM Forum and ITU-T approach is supported widely in the

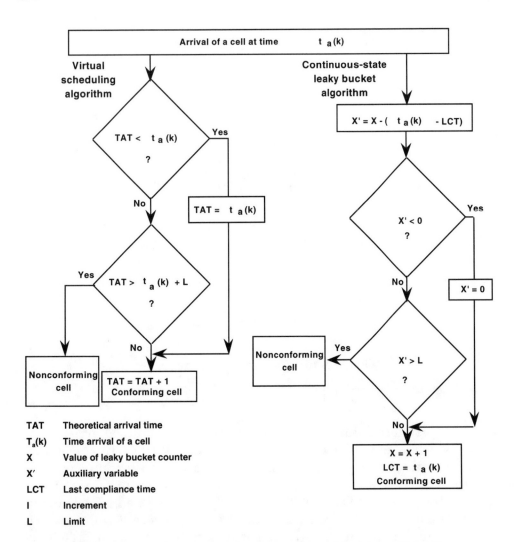

Figure 9–16 The generic cell rate algorithm (GCRA). [ATM94b]

industry. Notwithstanding, new papers appear each month in trade journals, and conferences are held in an attempt to work out this difficult issue. The reader is encouraged to study the IEEE and ACM publications and other trade journals for more detail. Indeed, a full book could be written on this subject.

The Peak Cell Rate Reference Model

The ATM Forum specification provides a reference model to describe the peak cell rate (PCR). This model is shown in Figure 9–17. It consists of an equivalent terminal, containing the traffic sources, a multiplexer (MUX), and a virtual shaper. The term equivalent terminal means a model of a user device that performs the functions described in this discussion.

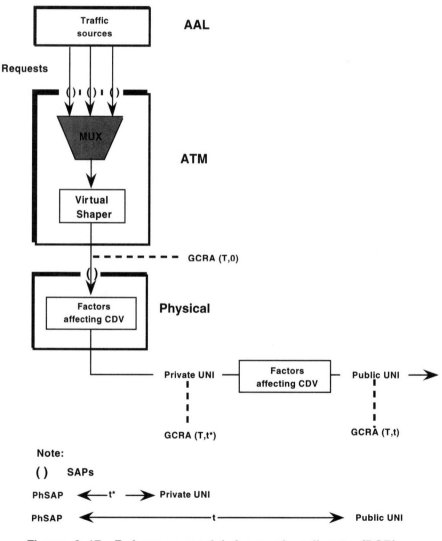

Figure 9–17 Reference model for peak cell rate (PCR). [ATM93a]

The traffic sources offer cells to a multiplexer (MUX), with each source offering cells at its own rate. Typically, the cells are offered from the AAL through the service access point (SAP). The MUX then offers all these cells to the virtual shaper. The job of the virtual shaper is to smooth the cell flow offered to the physical layer and the ATM UNI (private UNI). Moreover, the GCRA comes into play in this model at three interfaces: (1) the boundary between the ATM layer and the physical layer (the PhSAP), (2) the private UNI, and (3) the public UNI.

For this discussion, we define T as the peak emission interval of the connection, and the minimal interarrival time between two consecutive cells is greater than or equal to T. The PCR of the ATM connection is the inverse of the minimum arrival time between two cells.

The output of the virtual shaper at the PhSAP conforms to GCRA (T,0). The outputs at the private UNI and public UNI are different, because CDV will exist in the physical layer of the equivalent terminal (user device) and the node between this device and the network. Therefore, the private UNI conforms to GRCA (T,t*) and the public UNI conforms to GRCA (T,t), where t is the cell delay tolerance. The latter value takes into consideration the additional CDV between the PhSAP and the public UNI.

The ATM network does not set the peak emission interval T at the user device. T can be set to account for different profiles of traffic, as long as the MUX buffers remain stable. Thus, T's reciprocal can be any value that is greater than the sustainable rate, but (of course) not greater than the link rate.

Cell Delay Variation (CDV) Tolerance

A certain amount of delay is encountered when cells are vying for the same output port of the multiplexer, or when signaling cells are inserted into the stream. As a result, with the reference to the peak emission interval T, randomness is instilled in the interarrival time between consecutive cells ([ATM93a]; Appendix A).

1-point CDV. The 1-point CDV for cell $k(y_k)$ at the measurement point is the difference between the cell's reference arrival time (c_k) and the actual arrival time (a_k) at the measurement point: $y_k = c_k - a_k$. The reference arrival time (c_k) is:

$$c_0 = a_0 = 0$$

$$c_k + 1 = \begin{cases} c_k + T \text{ if } c_k \geq a_k \text{ otherwise} \\ a_k + T \end{cases}$$

2-point CDV.   The 2-point CDV, or cell k(v_k), between two measurement points MP_1 and MP_2 is the difference between the absolute cell transfer delay of cell k(x_k) between the two MPs and a defined reference cell transfer delay ($d_{1,2}$) between MP_1 and MP_2: $v_k = v_k - d_{1,2}$.

The absolute cell transfer delay (xk) of cell k between MP_1 and MP_2 is the same as the cell transfer delay defined earlier. The reference cell transfer delay (d1,2) between MP_1 and MP_2 is the absolute cell transfer delay experienced by a reference cell between the two MPs.

Figure 9–18 shows two examples of how the GCRA is applied [ATM94a]. Figure 9–18a shows smooth traffic with GCRA (1.5, .5). The vertical arrows connote the arrival of a cell across the UNI; the horizontal arrows connote time. The variables t– and t+ mean the following:

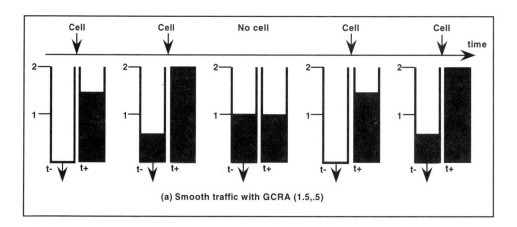

(a) Smooth traffic with GCRA (1.5,.5)

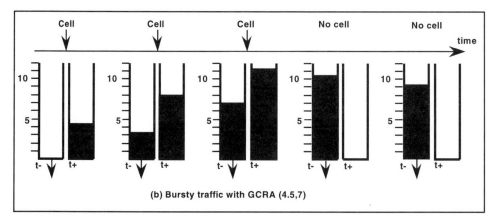

(b) Bursty traffic with GCRA (4.5,7)

Figure 9–18   Examples of the GCRA. [ATM94a]

t–: State of bucket just before the arrival of a cell

t+: State of bucket just after the arrival of a cell

For Figure 9–18a, with the bucket at 1, at t–, L prevents the sending of I cells. If they are sent, they are nonconforming.

The same definitions apply to Figure 9–18b, which shows bursty traffic for GCRA(4.5, 7). Once again, no cells are allowed (or if sent, they are nonconforming) if the bucket would overflow.

THE ATM SERVICES FOR LAN AND INTERNET TRAFFIC

Brief mention was made in Chapter 7 that the ATM Forum has defined other types of service that provide mechanisms for controlling traffic flow from LAN-based workstations and Internet routers that service these workstations. Since LAN and Internet devices have no "contract" with a network, no easy method is available to relate the CBR and VBR idea to a LAN/Internet environment.

Several proposals were considered for ABR. All entail a mechanism for informing a user about network conditions with a feedback loop from the network node to the user node. One proposal uses a backward explicit congestion notification (BECN) signal and the forward explicit congestion notification (FECN) signal to send to downstream and upstream devices respectively. This approach is borrowed from Frame Relay. Another proposal uses a credit scheme to control the user device's traffic. This section provides an introduction to ATM services for bursty LAN/internet traffic. The next section discusses the ATM Forum's Traffic Management Specification [ATM96b], the document that sets rules on how these services are implemented.

Examples of Feedback Operations

Currently, vendors are taking different approaches to the implementation of feedback loops. At the broadest level, the choices revolve around two approaches (with variations of these approaches discussed later):

1. Credit-based schemes
   a. Credits for each connection
   b. Credits aggregated for all connections (aggregate connections)

2. Rate-based schemes
a. Rates established for each connection
b. Rates established for all connections (aggregate connections)

Figures 9–19 and 9–20 show the credit-based and rate-based schemes operating on individual or aggregate connections. As depicted in Figures 9–19a and 9–20a, the credit-based scheme operates on a hop-by-hop (link-by-link) basis. Downstream nodes send credits to upstream nodes all the way to the source of the traffic. These credits allow a sending node to send

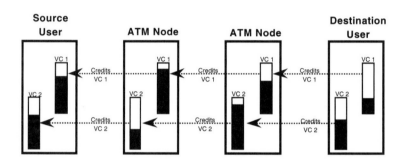

(a) Feedback loop: hop-by-hop

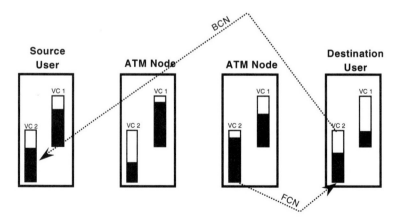

(b) Feedback loop: end-to-end

Note: Dashed lines in figure (b) show logical flow of feedback

Figure 9–19   Feedback on each connection.

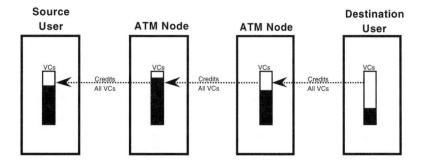

(a) Feedback loop: hop-by-hop

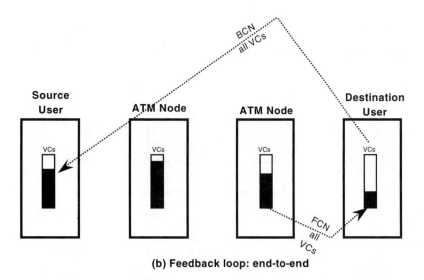

(b) Feedback loop: end-to-end

Figure 9–20   Aggregate feedback on all connections.

traffic down stream. If the sending node receives no credits, then it must wait (and stop sending) until credits arrive (if they do).

The rate-based scheme (shown in Figures 9–19b and 9–20b) is quite similar to Frame Relay congestion notification operations. An ATM node can send the destination a forward congestion notification signal. The destination user, in turn, sends to its source a backward notification congestion signal and through some algorithm, the source will back off from sending cells.

Both approaches have their advantages and disadvantages. Credit-based schemes are much more effective in regulating bandwidth immediately but they have more overhead. Rate-based schemes are cheaper to implement but the latency of acting upon forward and backward congestion notification could result in some oscillating behavior in the network.

The granularity of feedback is also a very important consideration in ABR. As shown in Figures 9–19 and 9–20, this feedback may be aggregated over multiple connections or on each connection. Obviously, the advantages and disadvantages for these operations are that aggregate feedback does not permit the monitoring of individual connections. Consequently, cells might be marked as congestion even though they may not be part of the problem. The per-connection feedback selects only those connections that are contributing to the problem.

In addition to the granularity and feedback, granularity of buffering is also an important consideration. Granularity of buffering simply means that connections are aggregated in one buffer or an individual buffer is reserved for each connection.

Types of Feedback

Several types of feedback information, depicted in Figure 9–21, can be implemented:

1. Binary rate feedback
2. Explicit rate feedback
3. Explicit burst feedback

With the binary rate feedback mechanism, a network node determines that congestion is occurring on a node and sets bits in a cell heading downstream to the destination. The destination uses these cells to send notifications back to the source. This means the source can stop, speed up, or slow down traffic based on receiving or not receiving this feedback. The term binary is used in this procedure because the amount of flow control that is performed is not determined. It is simply a binary yes or no to express if congestion is or is not occurring. Therefore, no further information is contained within the notification cell itself.

Explicit rate feedback allows a network node to examine each connection to determine that each connection receives its fair share of the available bandwidth. Periodically, a source node will send an OAM cell containing an initial bandwidth rate value for a particular connection. As the cell passes through a node, if the node's current storage of the fair share value of the connection is less than the value in the cell, the value in the cell is updated. The destination device returns this control cell

- **Binary Rate Feedback**
    Amount of flow not specified.
    A bit is on or off.

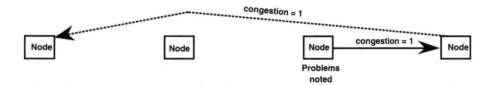

- **Explicit Rate Feedback**
    Each node determines each connection's fair share of resources.
    Periodically source device sends an OAM cell containing its current rate.
    Any node can reduce or expand this value, which is returned to the source.
    The source must adjust accordingly.

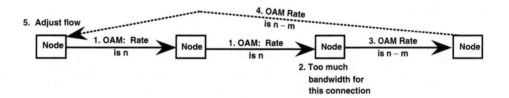

- **Explicit Burst Feedback**
    Number of cells a transmitter can send is limited by a burst size.
    Downstream node sends upstream node a credit.
    If upstream node uses up the credit, it must wait for a new credit.

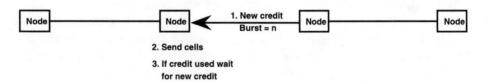

Figure 9–21   Types of feedback information.

back to the source. The source must adjust its flow relative to the point where the OAM cell was updated; i.e., to the most severe bottleneck in the virtual circuit. Thereafter, the source transmits at the new rate.

Explicit burst feedback is a credit-based scheme. A burst size is placed in an OAM cell and this burst size informs the transmitter (upstream node) its specified burst size. Therefore, when a network node has available buffer for forwarding cells, it forwards an OAM cell to the next upstream node. The upstream node uses this information to update its credit balance by forwarding cells. The upstream node reduces its credit balance by one with each cell sent. Therefore, once the node (or for that matter, the end user) has exhausted its balance, it must wait for the next credit update from the receiver.

Presently, vendors vary on how feedback is provided. The ATM Forum is working through the issues and will eventually publish a standard on feedback mechanisms. By the time this book is published, it is likely that the Forum will have decided on these issues.

THE ATM SERVICE ARCHITECTURE

The initial ATM specifications and standards published by the ITU-T focused on constant bit rate (CBR) and variable bit rate (VBR) applications. As more experience was gained with the ATM technology, it became evident that other "bit rate" categories should be defined, as well as methods and techniques to handle these other categories.

Two more service categories are now defined by the ATM Forum: unspecified bit rate (UBR) and available bit rate (ABR). The VBR category is further defined as real-time VBR and non-real-time VBR. Figure 9–22 shows the idea of all the ATM service categories and aspects of their operations. This figure also compares these classes of service in relation to bandwidth guarantee, delay variation guarantee, throughput guarantee, and congestion feedback.

The CBR service category is the need for a set amount of bandwidth, as defined by a peak cell rate (PCR) value. We have discussed this service category in earlier parts of this book and need not examine it again.

Real-time variable bit rate (rt-VBR) is intended for real-time applications requiring tight timing operations with low delay variation. Examples of these applications are bursty voice and video systems. The rt-VBR connections are described in terms of peak cell rate (PCR), sustainable cell rate (SCR), and maximum burst size (MBS).

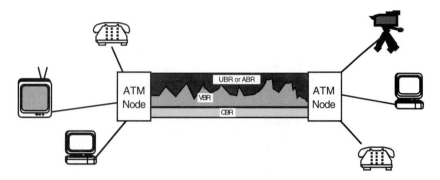

In order of priority:

Constant bit rate (CBR):   Assured steady supply of bandwidth, defined by PCR value

Variable bit rate (VBR):   Assured supply of bandwidth with:
                              rt = real-time, and nrt = non-real-time

Available bit rate (ABR):   Bandwidth to keep application running

Unspecified bit rate (UBR):   Bandwidth as available with no assurance

Quality of Service:

Service	Bandwidth Guarantee	Delay Variation Guarantee	Throughput Guarantee	Congestion Feedback
CBR	Yes	Yes	Yes	No
rt-VBR	Yes	Yes	Yes	No
nrt-VBR	Yes	No	Yes	No
ABR	Yes	No	Somewhat	Yes
UBR	No	No	No	No

Figure 9–22   ATM Forum service categories.

Non-real-time variable bit rate (nrt-VBR) is intended for non-real-time bursty applications with no delay bounds. The nrt-VBR connections are also described in terms of PCR, SCRk, and MBS.

The unspecified bit rate (UBR) service category is the lowest quality of service that an ATM network offers. A UBR user takes what is left on the channel (or logical connections) after CBR and VBR have had their go. As some people have described, UBR is like flying standby. UBR provides no way for a user to negotiate with the network, and the network provides no guarantee that the user's traffic will be delivered. PCR is not enforced, but it might be negotiated in order for the traffic source to know its bandwidth limitation. Examples of UBR traffic might be low-priority email, use group notices, and so on.

ABR is similar to UBR in that the user is not given as much preferential treatment as the users of the CBR and VBR services. However, the

Table 9–7   ATM Service Categories and Their Attributes [ATM96a]

Attribute	ATM Layer Service Category				
	CBR	**rt-VBR**	**nrt-VBR**	**UBR**	**ABR**
Traffic Parameters:					
PCR and CDVT (4,5)	specified			specified (2)	specified (3)
SCR, MBS, CDVT (4,5)	n/a	specified		n/a	
MCR (4)	n/a			n/a	specified
QOS Parameters:					
peak-to-peak CDV	specified		unspecified		
maxCTD	specified		unspecified		
CLR (4)	specified			unspecified	see Note 1
Other attributes:					
Feedback	unspecified				specified

Notes:
1. CLR is low for sources that adjust cell flow in response to control information. Whether a quantitative value for CLR is specified is network specific.
2. May not be subject to CAC and UPC procedures.
3. Represents the maximum rate at which the ABR source may ever send. The actual rate is subject to the control information.
4. These parameters are either explicitly or implicitly specified for PVCs or SVCs.
5. CDVT refers to the Cell Delay variation Tolerance. CDVT is not signaled. In general, CDVT need not have a unique value for a connection. Different values may apply at each interface along the path of a connection.

network provides enough bandwidth to keep the user application up and running. Additionally, flow control mechanisms are available to throttle the user's traffic in the event of problems. The ABR end-system is required to notify the network of its PCR and MCR requirements. The network can vary the bandwidth it gives the ABR user, but it cannot be less than MCR. Table 9–7 provides a more detailed view of the ATM service categories and their associated attributes.

EXAMPLES OF ABR OPERATIONS

In the ATM Forum deliberations on flow control, attention focused on two techniques, which are variations of the generic operations described Figures 9–16, 9–17, and 9–18. The ATM Forum chose a rate-based method for flow control, also called the Explicit Rate (ER) algorithm. It did not endorse the other method, which is called the credit-based scheme. These two methods of flow control operate in the following manner, and Figures 9–23, and 9–24 depict these operations: With the ER technique, resource management cells (RM) are sent by the source of the traffic cells through (perhaps) intermediate nodes to the end receiver for *each* VC. The RM cells contain values that describe the current rate the sender is transmitting cells (measured in cells per second) and the rate that the sender would like to increase this allowance. Any node that processes this cell (intermediate nodes or the end node) can reduce the requested rate (this value cannot be increased).

The end node reverses the RM cells, which are sent back to the originator. During this journey, any node can reduce further the requested cell rate. The final arbiter is the node next to the originating node, and this node reduces the requested rate, the sending node must so comply, regardless of the actions to the other nodes.

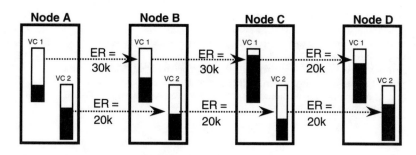

(a) Source node sends RM cell.

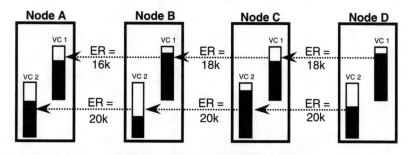

(b) Downstream nodes return RM cell.

Figure 9–23   Explicit rate approach.

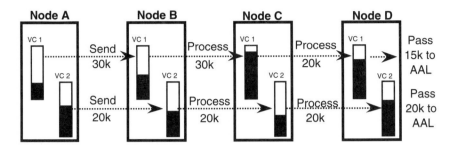

(a) Nodes process cells.

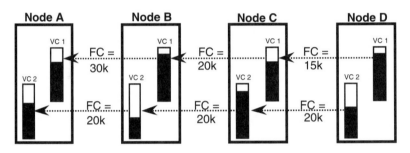

(b) Downstream nodes send fowarding counts (FC).

Figure 9–24 Quantum Flow Control Alliance (QFC) approach.

Although the intermediate nodes participate in the ER operations, the operations at these nodes are not burdensome. Therefore, the approach is attractive to switch vendors. Conceptually, only the source and destination nodes need keep book keeping operations. The transit nodes need not keep information about each VC, but simply modify the ER value in the RM cell as appropriate.

Thus, the ER mechanism has an end-to-end significance (certainly, more so than a hop-to-hop flavor).

Not all parties are in favor of the explicit rate feedback approach, and in 1995, the Quantum Flow Control (QFC) Alliance was formed to foster another approach, called the credit-based mechanism, depicted in Figure 9–24.

This technique has VC granularity, like the ER mechanism. But it differs from ER as follows. As an ATM node forwards cells (to the next node if it is a transit node, or to the AAL if it is the destination node), it sends an

RM cell containing a forwarding count in the reverse direction to the transmitting node. This count represents the cells that the node has released, and the related buffer space that is now available to receive more cells. The forwarding count is returned to the sender on a periodic basis.[4]

The RM cell is coded to contain forwarding counts for as many as seven VCs. If this cell is sent for every 20 cells processed, then 1/140 (20×7) of the bandwidth is expended for this operation.

The explicit rate (ER) and credit-based camps (mostly ATM switch vendors, and edge device vendors) have not been able to reach an agreement on flow control. Clearly, there are advantages and disadvantages to each approach (although further research after the ATM Forum vote casts favorable light on the credit-based scheme).

As stated earlier, the explicit rate design places minimal overhead on the intermediate ATM nodes (not an insignificant factor). Also, ER operates efficiently in a LAN environment where there may be relatively few intermediate ATM nodes, the distances between nodes is small, and there are few VCs to manage.

The proponents of the credit-based (CB) design assert that CB loses fewer cells (if done properly, none) than ER and reacts faster to congestion because the operations take place on a hop-by-hop basis (hop-by-hop is optional in ER).

Also, the intent of conventional CBR and VBR services is to "nail up" the bandwidth for these type of applications, and during times of inactivity, their unused capacity is not available to other users. The credit-based proponents claim that their approach allows an easy borrowing of bandwidth from unused VBR (and maybe CBR) traffic. Further claims from this camp estimate that 10 to 20 percent more capacity can be attained by the use of a credit based network.

So, what is the answer? There is no clear winner or loser. As a practical matter, a vendor should have both methods available in the product to meet differing demands from different customers.

ABR Service Parameters

We return to the ATM Forum Traffic Management Specification [ATM96a] to examine other aspects of the ABR service category. This

---

[4]The frequency in which this feedback is provided is not cast in stone. The QFC cites once for every 20 cells processed and released as a typical figure (see "New Prospects for ATM Flow Control," by Dr. James F. Mollenauer in *Business Communication Review,* March 1997).

Table 9–8   ABR Parameter Description [ATM96a]

Label	Description	Units and Range
PCR	The Peak Cell Rate (PCR) is the cell rate that the source may never exceed.	In cells/sec
MCR	The Minimum Cell Rate (MCR) is the rate at which the source is always allowed to send.	In cells/sec
ICR	The Initial Cell Rate (ICR) is the rate at which a source should send initially and after an idle period.	In cells/sec
RIF	Rate Increase Factor (RIF) controls the amount by which the cell transmission rate may increase upon receipt of an RM-cell.	RIF is a power of two, ranging from 1/32768 to 1
Nrm	Nrm is the maximum number of cells a source may send for each forward RM-cell.	Power of 2 Range: 2 to 256
Mrm	Mrm controls allocation of bandwidth between forward RM-cells, backward RM-cells, and data cells.	Constant fixed at 2
RDF	The Rate Decrease Factor (RDF) controls the decrease in the cell transmission rate.	RDF is a power of 2 from 1/32,768 to 1
ACR	The Allowed Cell Rate (ACR) is the current rate at which a source is allowed to send.	Units: cells/sec
CRM	Missing RM-cell count. CRM limits the number of forward RM-cells that may be sent in the absence of received backward RM-cells.	CRM is an integer. Its size is implementation specific.
ADTF	The ACR Decrease Time Factor is the time permitted between sending RM-cells before the rate is decreased to ICR.	Units: seconds ADTF range: 0.1 to 10.23 sec: with granularity of 10 ms
Trm	Trm provides an upper bound on the time between forward RM-cells for an active source.	Units: milliseconds Trm is 100 times a power of two Range: $100 * 2^{-7}$ to $100 * 2^0$
FRTT	The Fixed Round-Trip Time (FRTT) is the sum of the fixed and propagation delays from the source to a destination and back.	Units: 1 microseconds Range: 0 to 16.7 seconds
TBE	Transient Buffer Exposure (TBE) is the negotiated number of cells that the network would like to limit the source to sending during startup periods, before the first RM-cell returns.	Units: Cells Range: 0 to 16,777,215
CDF	The Cutoff Decrease Factor (CDF) controls the decrease in ACR associated with CRM.	CDF is zero, or a power of two in the range 1/64 to 1.
TCR	The Tagged Cell Rate (TCR) limits the rate at which a source may send out-of-rate forward RM-cells.	TCR is a constant fixed at 10 cells/second.

section provides a summary of the ABR service parameters, and the next section explains the coding of the resource management (RM) cell. Table 9–8 lists the ABR parameters and describes their functions. Table 9–9 lists the parameters that are signaled between ATM nodes and negotiated during the connection establishment operation. These parameters are mandatory. Table 9–10 lists other parameters that are optional.

The following parameters are computed or updated by the forward and backward sources upon completion of the call setup when FRTT and the other parameters are known.

CRM is computed as:

$$CRM = \left\lceil \frac{TBE}{Nrm} \right\rceil$$

ICR is updated after call setup is complete to insure TBE compliance as

$$ICR = \min\left(ICR, \frac{TBE}{FRTT} \right)$$

The ABR Resource Management (RM) Cell

Figure 9–25 shows the format and contents of the ABR resource management (RM) cell. A brief description (extracted from [ATM96a] of

Table 9–9   Mandatory Parameters to Be Signaled [ATM96a]

Name	Negotiation	Default
PCR	down	mandatory
MCR	down to MCRmin if MCRmin is signaled, else no	0
ICR	down	PCR
TBE	down	16,777,215
FRTT	accumulated	Note 1
RDF	down	1/16
RIF	down	1/16

Note 1: FRTT should be set by the source to the fixed source delay. FRTT is then accumulated during the call setup. FRTT is used to determine other parameters. It should be the sum of all the RM-cell fixed delays in the round trip call path.

Note 2: Because of the downward negotiation of RIF and RDF, a given switch may not be able to support the RIF and RDF values selected by switches farther from the source. This may occur because the RIF or RDF value is smaller than the given switch can support or because the ratio RIF/RDF is incompatible with other ABR connections using the given switch. When a switch cannot support the values negotiated during the forward pass of the call setup, it may decide to clear the call. Additionally, the specification of the QOS class may be signaled. If the QOS class is missing, the default is class zero.

Table 9-10   Optionally Signaled ABR Parameters [ATM96a]

Parameter	Negotiation	Default Value
Nrm	No	32
Trm	No	100
CDF	up	1/16
ADTF	down	0.5

each field in the cell should give the reader an idea of how the RM cell is used to control traffic flow:

- *Header:* The first five bytes are the standard ATM header with PTI=110 (binary) for a VCC, and additionally VCI=6 for a VPC. The CLP bit is 0 if the RM-cell is in-rate and 1 if it is out-of-rate.

- *ID:* The protocol ID identifies the service using the RM-cell. The ITU has assigned protocol ID=1 to ABR service.

- *Message Type Field:* Five bits of this octet are used as follows (the other are reserved):

  - *DIR:* The DIR bit indicates which direction of data flow is associated with the RM-cell. A forward RM-cell, indicated by DIR=0, is associated with data cells flowing in the same direction. A backward RM-cell, indicated by DIR=1, is associated with data cells flowing in the opposite direction. DIR is changed from 0 to 1 when an RM-cell is turned around at a destination.

  - *BN:* The BN bit indicates whether the RM-cell is a backward explicit congestion notification (BECN) cell (i.e., non-source-generated) or not. BN=0 indicates a source-generated RM-cell

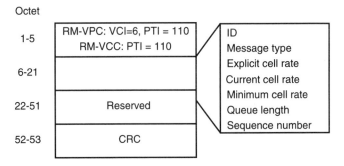

Figure 9-25   The ABR RM cell.

while BN=1 indicates a BECN RM-cell generated by a destination or a switch.

- *CI:* The congestion indication (CI) bit allows a network element to indicate that there is congestion in the network. When a source receives a backward RM-cell with CI=1 it decreases its ACR. When turning around a forward RM-cell, a destination will set CI=1 to indicate that the previous received data cell had the EFCI state set.

- *NI:* The no increase (NI) bit is used to prevent a source from increasing its ACR. In contrast to CI=1, NI=1 does not require any decrease. A network element might set NI to 1 to indicate impending congestion. Normally, a source will initialize NI to 0 so that it might be allowed to increase its ACR, but it can indicate that it does not need a higher ACR by initializing NI to 1.

- *RA:* The RA bit is not used for ATM Forum ABR.

- *ER:* The explicit rate (ER) field is used to limit the source ACR to a specific value. For each RM-cell ER is set by the source to a requested rate (such as PCR).

- *CCR:* The CCR field is set by their source to its current ACR.

- *MCR:* The MCR field carries the connection's minimum cell rate.

- *QL:* The QL field is not used for ATM Forum ABR.

- *SN:* The SN field is not used for ATM Forum ABR.

- *CRC-10:* The RM CRC is the same CRC used for all OAM cells.

Other Thoughts on the ABR Service Category

For the reader who is faced with installing and tuning an ATM network, I recommend you read the entire ATM Traffic Management Specification, version 4.0 [ATM96a]. We have only touched on its major features. Not explained in this general discourse are other important aspects of ABR such as the descriptions of how the source/destination switch behaves in sending and receiving the RM cells.

BUILDOUT DELAY PROCEDURES AT THE RECEIVING ENDPOINT

Most of this chapter has discussed how the ATM network manages user traffic at the UNI to the entrance of the network. At the receiving

UNI, the ATM network passes the cells to the user. The user processes the traffic based on the schemes explained earlier.

For voice packets, ITU-T Recommendation G.764 defines a method to define a maximum allowed time in an end-to-end transmission time. This method masks any delay that may have occurred in the network. The maximum delay must be less than 200 ms. Any packet that arrives at 200 ms or later is discarded. The reader may recall that this operation is described in some detail in Chapter 7 and can be reviewed again, if necessary (see the section titled "Packet Buildout at the Receiver" in Chapter 7).

WORK ON THE GUARANTEED FRAME RATE (GFR)

The ATM Forum has been working on a new traffic service category, called the guaranteed frame rate (GFR). The idea behind GFR is that there must be a method to guarantee a minimum rate for frame-based traffic, and frame-based guaranteed operations do not correlate with cell-based guarantees.

Rules exist in several specifications on how to correlate Frame Relay tagging, discard legibility operations, and congestion notification procedures to the ATM counterparts, and Q.933 Annex A, T1.617 Annex D provides guidance on QOS class mapping between Frame Relay and ATM, the determination of emission priority and discard priority decisions.

But these rules do not define how to handle peak cell rates (PCR) and how to handle cell delay variation (CDV) at each switch. Thus, the ATM Forum has tackled these issues and should have a draft agreement available in late 1998 or early 1999.

SUMMARY

A wide variety of methods have been proposed for the management of traffic in an ATM network. The manner in which traffic is managed will eventually become a standardized operation. Traffic policing functions have been published by the ATM Forum to provide guidance on how traffic can be tagged, but the decision on how to act upon the tag is not defined by the ATM Forum. Nor should it be. The manner in which a network manages user payload must rest with the network.

10

Call and Connection Control

This chapter examines the ATM call and connection control operations. Emphasis is placed on how connections are set up on demand between users and the ATM network. This procedure is also known as a *switched virtual call* (SVC) in older technology. The ITU-T Q.2931 connection control protocol is explained, and the Q.2931 messages and their contents are analyzed. The ATM address is also examined in this chapter, as is the ATM use of the OSI address.

The focus in the chapter is the ATM Forum's use of Q.2931, as published in the User-Network Interface (UNI), version 3.1 [ATM94c]. Version 4 is being developed as of this writing, and I will update you on this new version later in the chapter. However, version 3.1 is the Anchorage Accord specification, so it is emphasized here. The ITU-T Q.2931 specification is covered in Volume II of this series.

ATM CONNECTIONS ON DEMAND

Like all connections-on-demand (SVCs), a user-to-user session through an ATM network requires both a connection setup procedure and a disconnection procedure. With connection setup, the user must furnish the network with the calling and called party addresses and the

QOS needed for the session. In the event of a network failure, connection-on-demand sessions may not be automatically reestablished, although they may remain active for an arbitrary amount of time.

The ATM connection control procedures are organized around the ISDN Q.931 layer 3 operations (explained in Chapter 4), and a subset of Q.931, called Q.2931. Phase 1 signaling must support fourteen capabilities at the UNI. They are listed in Table 10–1, and summarized herein. Several of the descriptions of the demand connections are self-explanatory, others are not; more detail is provided for the ambiguous titles.

Connections on demand simply means that the ATM UNI must support switched channel connections. They are established with signaling procedures discussed shortly in this chapter. Permanent connections are not supported at this time, although they are under study.

The ATM UNI supports both point-to-point single connection and point-to-multipoint connections. A point-to-multipoint connection is defined as a collection of associated VC and VP links that are associated with endpoint nodes. One ATM link is designated as the root link, which serves as the root in a tree topology. When the root receives information, it sends copies of this information to all leaf nodes on the tree. Communications must occur between the leaf nodes through the root node. Connections are established initially through the root node and then one leaf

Table 10–1   Capabilities of ATM Demand Connections

- Connections on demand (switched)
- Point-to-point and point-to-multipoint connections
- Symmetric or asymmetric bandwidth requirements
- Single connection calls
- Specific procedures for call setup, request, answer, clear, and out-of-band signaling
- Support of class A, C, and X transport services
- Nonnegotiation of QOS between users
- Specification of VPI/VCI ranges
- Designation of an out-of-band signaling channel
- Mechanisms for error recovery
- Guidelines for addressing formats
- Client registration procedures
- Methods of identifying end-to-end capability parameters
- Nonsupport of multicasting operations

node, then other nodes can be added with "add party" operations, one leaf entry at a time.

The UNI supports either symmetric or asymmetric connections for bandwidth allocation. Bandwidth is specified independently in each direction across the virtual connection. Forward direction is from the calling party to the called party; backward direction is from the called party to the calling party.

The UNI also defines specific procedures for the requesting and setting up of connections and the clearing of the connections (and the reason for clearing) as well as an out-of-band channel used for control purposes.

Phase 1 supports ATM class A and class C transport services, as well as class X procedures, which are published by the ATM Forum. Class X is a user-defined QOS operation. The reader may wish to refer to the section titled "Classes of Traffic" in Chapter 7.

For phase 1, QOS cannot be negotiated between users. A user may request a certain level of service and can send the QOS parameters in the connection setup request. The receiver merely indicates if these values can be accommodated. It is not allowed to return any traffic suggesting a negotiation procedure.

The specification also defines a range for the use of VCI and VPI. For phase 1, there is a one-to-one mapping between a VCI and a VPI; therefore, values beyond 8 bits are not permitted. As part of the designation for the VPI/VCI ranges, an out-of-band signaling channel has been designated with the values of VCI = 5 and VPI = 0.

The phase 1 specification contains several mechanisms for handling error recovery procedures. Among these are provisions for the signaling of nonfatal errors (errors that can be recovered), procedures for recovering from resets, procedures for forcing VCCs into an idle state, and other diagnostic information pertaining to error recovery and call clearing.

One important capability at the UNI is the provision for addressing format guidelines. These guidelines are organized around OSI network service access points (NSAPs), which are specified in ISO 8348 and ITU-T X.213 Annex A. The phase 1 specification requires the use of these formats in accordance with registration procedures contained in ISO 10589. This feature of the standard will facilitate the interworking of different vendors' systems.

The ATM demand connections capabilities also include a client registration procedure that allows users to exchange address information across the UNI, as well as other administrative information. This procedure allows an ATM network administrator to load network addresses dynamically into the port.

Also supported is the ability to identify end-to-end capability para-meters. Capability means that provisions are available to identify what protocol is running inside the ATM PDU; that is to say, what protocols are operating above the ATM services. This capability allows the two end users to run various types of protocol families across an ATM-based net-work, and use this identifier to separate and demultiplex the traffic to the respective protocol families at the receiving machine.

Finally, the fourteenth capability is really not a capability, in that the phase 1 specification does not support multicast operations at this time.

THE ATM ADDRESS

With the addition of SVCs to ATM operations, it is important to have a standardized convention for coding destination and source ad-dresses. Addressing is not an issue with PVCs, because connections and endpoints (destination and source) are defined, and a user need only pro-vide the network with a preallocated VCI/VPI. However, for SVCs, the destination connection can change with each session; therefore, explicit addresses are required. After the call has been mapped between the UNIs, the VCI/VPI values then can be used for traffic identification.

The ATM address is modeled on the OSI network service access point (NSAP), which is defined in ISO 8348 and ITU-T X.213, Annex A. A brief explanation of the OSI NSAP and its relationship to ATM address-ing (see Figure 10–1) follows.

The ISO and ITU-T describe a hierarchical structure for the NSAP address, as well as the syntax for the NSAP address. It consists of four parts:

- *Initial domain part (IDP)*: Contains the authority format identifier (AFI) and the initial domain identifier (IDI).
- *Authority format identifier (AFI)*: Contains a one-octet field to identify the domain specific part (DSP). For ATM, the AFI field is coded as:
    39 = DCC ATM format
    47 = ICD ATM format
    45 = E.164 format
- *Initial domain identifier (IDI)*: Specifies the addressing domain and the network addressing authority for the DSP values. It is interpreted according to the AFI (where AFI = 39, 47, or 45). For

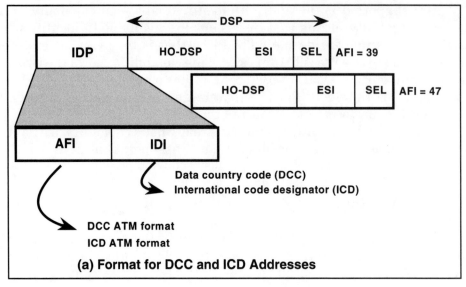

(a) Format for DCC and ICD Addresses

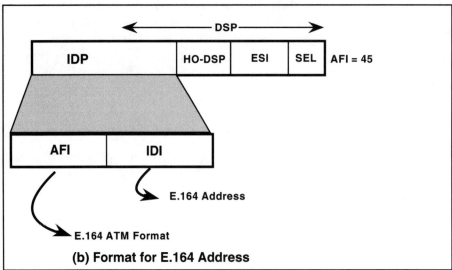

(b) Format for E.164 Address

Figure 10–1   The OSI/ATM address formats.

ATM, the IDI is coded as (1) a data country code (DCC) in accordance with ISO 3166; (2) the international code designator (ICD), which identifies an international organization and is maintained by the British Standards Institute; or (3) an E.164 address, which is a telephone number.

- *Domain specific part (DSP)*: Contains the address determined by the network authority. For ATM, the contents vary, depending on the value of the AFI. The domain format identifier (DFI) specifies the syntax and other aspects of the remainder of the DSP. The administrative authority (AA) is an organization assigned by the ISO that is responsible for the allocation of values in certain fields in the DSP.

The high order DSP is established by the authority identified by the IDP. This field might contain a hierarchical address (with topological significance, see RFC 1237), such as a routing domain and areas within the domain. The end system identifier (ESI) identifies an end system (such as a computer) within the area.

The selector (SEL) is not used by an ATM network. It usually identifies the protocol entities in the upper layers of the user machine that are to receive the traffic. Therefore, the SEL could contain upper layer SAPs.

ATM public networks must support the E.164 address and private networks must support all formats.

The Address Registration MIB

The Management Information Base (MIB) to support address registration is defined in the Integrated Local Management Interface (ILMI) Specification [ATM96a], which is explained in Chapter 13. The part of the ILMI MIB to support address registration consists of three MIB groups: (1) The NetPrefix Group contains the first 13 octets of the ATM address (AFI, IDI, and HO-DSP fields for a private address), and for a native E.164 address, it is the complete E.164 address. (2) The Address Group is the full 20 octets of the ATM address. (3) The Address Registration Admin Group explains if the other two groups are supported.

Address Registration

The ATM Forum UNI signaling specification provides a procedure for the user and the network to register the ATM address or addresses. The procedure begins with the network initializing its address table as empty. Then, as shown in Figure 10–2, it sends an SNMP ColdStart Trap message to the user side. It can issue GetNext Request to obtain addressing information. Next, it sends an SNMP SetRequest message to the user side, which contains a network prefix. The user side is expected to "register" this address in its address MIB. Although not shown in this figure, the user side can also send GetNext and Set responses to the network side to register addresses.

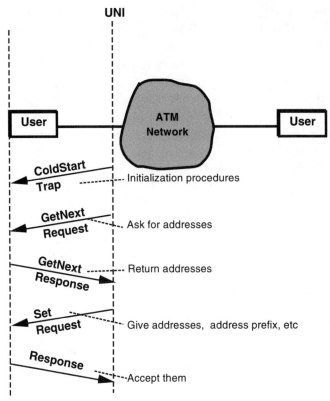

Note: Similar activities can occur in
the reverse direction

Figure 10–2   Address registration.

THE CONNECTION CONTROL MESSAGES

Table 10–2 lists the ATM messages and their functions employed for
demand connections at the UNI. Because these messages are derived
from Q.931, which was discussed in Chapter 4, this section will concentrate of the use of these messages vis-à-vis the ATM UNI operation.

These messages contain the typical Q.931 fields such as protocol discriminator, call reference, message type, and message length. The information content of the field, of course, is tailored for the specific ATM UNI
interface.

Table 10–2   ATM Connection Control Messages

Message	Function
Call establishment	
SETUP	Initiate the call establishment
CALL PROCEEDING	Call establishment has begun
CONNECT	Call has been accepted
CONNECT ACKNOWLEDGE	Call acceptance has been acknowledged
Call clearing	
RELEASE	Initiate call clearing
RELEASE COMPLETE	Call has been cleared
Miscellaneous	
STATUS ENQUIRY (SE)	Sent to solicit a status message
STATUS (S)	Sent in response to SE or to report error
Global call reference	
RESTART	Restart all VCs
RESTART ACKNOWLEDGE	ACKS the RESTART
Point-to-multipoint operations	
ADD PARTY	Add party to an existing connection
ADD PARTY ACKNOWLEDGE	ACKS THE ADD PARTY
ADD PARTY REJECT	REJECTS the ADD PARTY
DROP PARTY	Drops party from an existing connection
DROP PARTY ACKNOWLEDGE	ACKS THE DROP PARTY

CONNECTION SETUPS AND CLEARS

This section shows some examples of the use of the connection management messages. The connection establishment procedures begin by a user issuing the SETUP message (see Figure 10–3). This message is sent by the calling user to the network and is relayed by the network to the called user. This message contains several information elements (fields) to identify the message, specify various AAL parameters, calling and called party addresses, requirements for QOS, selection of the transit network (if needed), and a number of other fields. The notations in the boxes in Figure 10–3 depict the main information elements that are transferred in the messages. Other information elements may be present, depending on the specific implementation of a system.

Upon receiving the SETUP message, the network returns a CALL PROCEEDING message to the initiating user, forwards the SETUP message to the called user, and waits for the called user to return a CALL PROCEEDING message. The CALL PROCEEDING message is used to

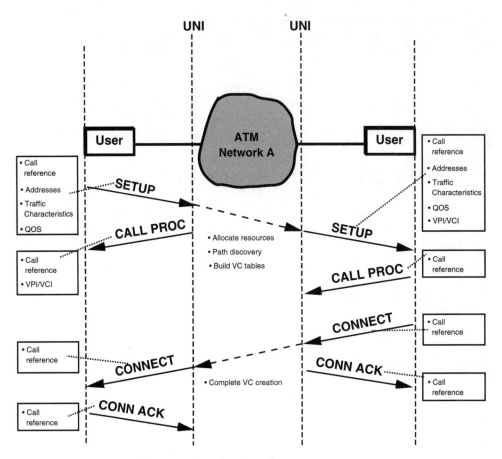

Figure 10–3   Connection setup.

indicate that the call has been initiated and no more call establishment information is needed, nor will any be accepted.

The called user, if it accepts a call, will then send to the network a CONNECT message. This CONNECT message will then be forwarded to the calling user. The CONNECT message contains parameters that deal with some of the same parameters in the SETUP message, such as call reference and message type, as well as the accepted AAL parameters and several other identifiers created as a result of the information elements in the original SETUP message.

Upon receiving the CONNECT messages, the calling user and the network return the CONNECT ACKNOWLEDGE to their respective parties.

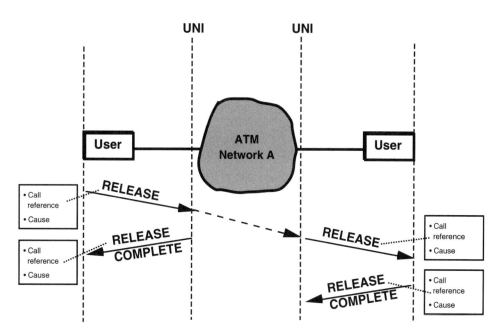

Figure 10–4   Connection release.

As Figure 10–4 illustrates, either user can initiate a disconnect operation. To do so requires the user to send to the network the RELEASE message. The effect of this message clears the end-to-end connection between the two users and the network. This message only contains the basic information to identify the message across the network. Other parameters are not included because they are not needed to clear the state tables for the connection. In consonance with the practice we established in Figure 10–3, the notations in the boxes in Figure 10–4 depict the main information elements that are transferred in the messages. Other information elements may be present, depending on the specific implementation of a system.

The receiving network and receiving user are required to transmit the RELEASE COMPLETE message as a result of receiving the RELEASE message.

Q.2931 TIMERS AND STATES

Most networks that provide connections on demand use timers at both the user and network nodes to define reasonable wait periods for completion of certain actions (such as completion of a setup, completion

Table 10–3   Timers in the Network Side

Timer Number	Cause for Start	Normal Stop
T301	Not supported in this Implementation Agreement	
T303	SETUP sent	CONNECT, CALL PROCEEDING, OR RELEASE COMPLETE received
T308	RELEASE sent	RELEASE COMPLETE or RELEASE received
T309	SAAL disconnection	SAAL reconnected
T310	CALL PROCEEDING	CONNECT or RELEASE received received
T316	RESTART sent	RESTART ACKNOWLEDGE received
T317	RESTART received	Internal clearing of call references
T322	STATUS ENQUIRY sent	STATUS, RELEASE, or RELEASE COMPLETE received
T398	DROP PARTY sent	DROP PARTY ACKNOWLEDGE or RELEASE received
T399	ADD PARTY sent	ADD PARTY ACKNOWLEDGE, ADD PARTY REJECT, or RELEASE received

of a restart, etc.). The ATM UNI signaling interface provides ten timers at the network side and ten timers at the user side. These timers and their general operations are summarized in Tables 10–3 and 10–4.

Each connection is controlled by states. For example, a user enters into a "call present" state when a call establishment request has been received but the user has not yet responded to the request. Various states can be entered and exited as a call is processed, some of which are governed by timers. In the event an action does not take place before a designated timer expires, various remedial actions are dictated, such as issuing retries and/or moving to other states.

CONNECTION CONTROL EXAMPLES

Before discussing and providing some examples of connection control operations, it is helpful to distinguish between three terms: (1) *connected virtual channels,* (2) *disconnected virtual channels,* and (3) *released virtual channels.* A virtual channel is considered connected when

Table 10–4   Timers in the User Side

Timer Number	Cause for Start	Normal Stop
T303	SETUP sent	CONNECT, CALL PROCEEDING, OR RELEASE COMPLETE received
T308	RELEASE sent	RELEASE COMPLETE or RELEASE received
T309	SAAL disconnection	SAAL reconnected
T310	CALL PROCEEDING	CONNECT or RELEASE received received
T313	CONNECT sent	CONNECT ACKNOWLEDGE received
T316	RESTART sent	RESTART ACKNOWLEDGE received
T317	RESTART received	Internal clearing of call references
T322	STATUS ENQUIRY sent	STATUS, RELEASE, or RELEASE COMPLETE received
T398	DROP PARTY sent	DROP PARTY ACKNOWLEDGE or RELEASE received
T399	ADD PARTY sent	ADD PARTY ACKNOWLEDGE, ADD PARTY REJECT, or RELEASE received

all parties, including network and users, have agreed to the connection. A virtual channel is disconnected when it is no longer a part of the connection but is not yet available for a new connection. A channel is considered to be released when not only is the channel not part of a connection, but is also available for another connection.

Connection Setup

Figure 10–5 shows the timers invoked for the establishment of a connection. Three timers are involved in the process and perform the following functions.

Timer T303 is invoked when ATM issues a SETUP message to the network on the local side of the network and is invoked by network node at the remote side when it passes the SETUP message to the user. The timer is stopped when the remote end user returns a CALL PROCEEDING message. This message is relayed to the local network side, which also sends it to the originating user. Although not illustrated in this figure, timer T303 can also be stopped if either a CONNECT message or a

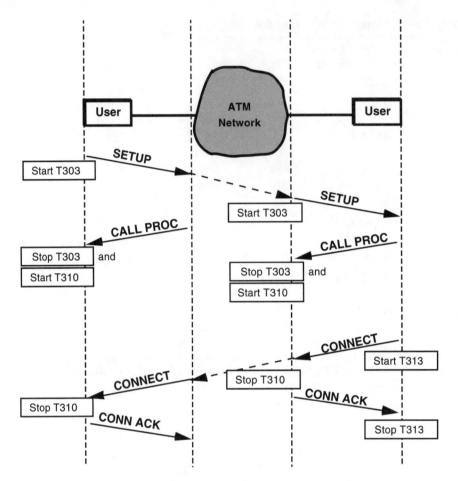

Figure 10–5   The connection setup procedure.

RELEASE COMPLETE message is received. If the timer expires before the reception of a CALL PROCEEDING message, a SETUP message may be retransmitted or, if the network does not support SETUP retransmissions, the potential connection is cleared and a null state is entered. The ATM specifications require that only one retry may be attempted after which a null state must be entered.

Upon receiving the CALL PROCEEDING message, the local user and remote network node turn off their T303 timers and turn on their T310 timers. This timer waits for the CONNECT message to be sent to either party. Upon successful reception of the CONNECT message, timer

T310 is turned off and the recipients of this message respond with a CONNECTION ACKNOWLEDGMENT of this message. If the CONNECTION ACKNOWLEDGMENT message is not received before timer T310 expires, the connection must be cleared.

The remote user also invokes timer T313 when it sends the CONNECT message to the network. This timer is turned off upon receiving the CONNECT ACKNOWLEDGMENT message.

The SETUP message must contain all the information required for the network and the called party to process the call. This information must include the QOS parameters, the cell rate parameters (called the traffic descriptor in more recent documents), and any bearer capabilities that the network may need at either side. The user is not allowed to fill in the connection identifier information element in the SETUP message. If it is included, the network ignores it. This means that the network selects the VPI/VCI for the connection. This information is returned to the user in the CALL PROCEEDING message.

A similar procedure is performed on the remote side of the network in that the network node is responsible for allocating the VPI/VCI value and placing this value in the SETUP message before it sends this message to the called user. Likewise, when the called user accepts the message, it maps these VPI/VCI values into its virtual circuit identifier (VCI) table and returns a CALL PROCEEDING message.

In the event a call is not completed, either party can send a number of diagnostics citing the reason for the inability to complete the connection.

Connection Release

As illustrated in Figure 10–6, the connection release operation entails only timer T308. Either the network or the user can invoke the connection release by sending the RELEASE message to the respective party. This operation turns on timer T308, which remains on until the RELEASE message is received. If T308 expires for the first time, the RELEASE message is retransmitted. If a response is not returned on this second try, the user must release the call reference and return to the null state (no connection exists). The manner in which this operation is then handled is not defined in the standard but is network- or user-specific.

In the event that a RELEASE message is received by the network or the user at the same time that the respective node sends a RELEASE (this procedure is called a clear-clear collision), the affected party stops

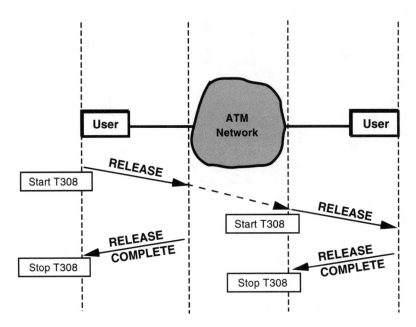

Figure 10–6   The release procedure.

timer T308, releases the call reference as well as the virtual channel, and enters into the null state.

Restart Procedure

The network or user can initiate restart operations for any number of reasons. Failure of any component can result in the restart procedure being invoked, and information elements in the header cite the reason for the restart. As illustrated in Figure 10–7, the initiation of the restart by the user invokes timer T316 by the originator's sending the RESTART message to the recipient. In turn, the recipient (network side shown) starts timer T317 upon receiving the RESTART message. After processing the RESTART message and taking any necessary actions, the recipient issues a RESTART ACKNOWLEDGE and stops T317.

Next, the network issues a RELEASE to the destination and starts timer T308. The destination acknowledges the RELEASE message by returning the RELEASE COMPLETE. A RESTART ACKNOWLEDGE is sent to the originator, which then stops T316. The field in the RESTART message labeled restart indicator determines if an indicated virtual channel is to be restarted or all channels controlled by this layer 3 entity are to be restarted.

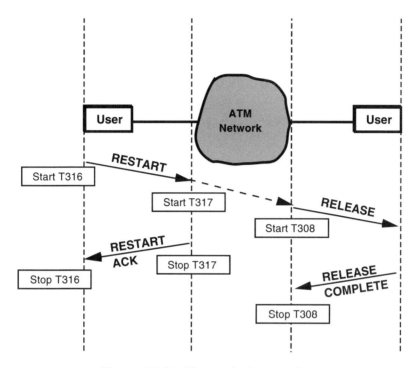

Figure 10–7 The restart procedure.

Status Inquiry

The status inquiry procedure is invoked by either the network or the user to determine the state of a connection, such as the call state, the type of connection being supported, or the end state of a point-to-multipoint connection. As indicated in Figure 10–8, timer T322 controls this procedure. Either party may invoke the STATUS INQUIRY message by turning T322 on. Upon receipt of the STATUS or STATUS COMPLETE message, this timer is turned off. Be aware that a status inquiry only operates on a link basis.

Add Party

Because of the importance and wide use of telephone conference calls and video conferencing operations, the ATM designers developed procedures to support these types of applications. This capability is implemented through the add-party procedure as shown in Figure 10–9. This illustration shows the addition of only one party, but multiple parties may be connected with this operation. The originating site issues an

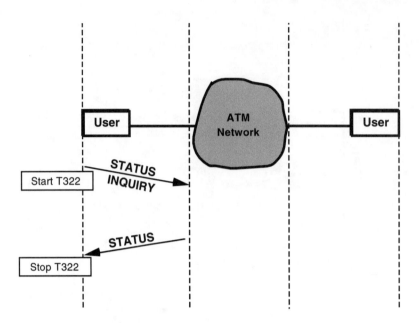

Figure 10–8   The status inquiry procedure.

ADD PARTY message across the UNI to the network. The network forwards this message to the destination in which the destination network
node issues a SETUP across the UNI to the destination user. The SETUP
message is used if procedures must begin from scratch. That is to say,
this UNI is currently not participating in the call. Not shown in this figure is the possibility of issuing the ADD PARTY message across the remote UNI for situations where a call is already in place and another calling party needs to be added.

   The operation is controlled with timer T399 at the sending site. This
timer is turned off upon receiving a CONNECTION ACKNOWLEDG-
MENT, an ADD PARTY, ADD PARTY ACK, REJECT, or a RELEASE.
In this example, the remote side uses the initial setup operation, discussed earlier. The point-to-multipoint operation is also controlled by
party-states. These states may exist on the network side or the user side
of the interface. They are summarized as follows:

  • *Null:* A party does not exist; therefore an endpoint reference value
    has not been allocated
  • *Add party initiated:* An ADD PARTY message or a SETUP mes-
    sage has been sent to the other side of the interface for this party

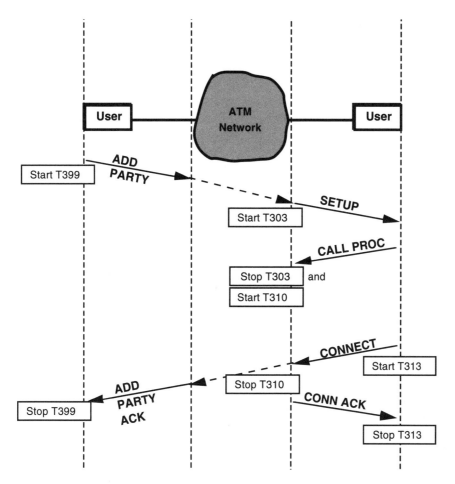

Figure 10–9   The add party procedure.

- *Add party received:* An ADD PARTY message or a setup message has been received by the other side of the interface for this party
- *Drop party initiated:* A DROP PARTY message has been sent for this party
- *Drop party received:* A DROP PARTY message has been received for this party
- *Active:* On the user side of the UNI, an active state is when the user has received an CONNECT ACKNOWLEDGE, ADD PARTY-ACKNOWLEDGE, or a CONNECT. On the network side an active state is entered when it has sent a CONNECT, CONNECT

ACKNOWLEDGE, or an ADD PARTY ACKNOWLEDGE; or when the network has received an ADD PARTY ACKNOWLEDGE from the user side.

Drop Party

As the reader might expect, the drop party procedure provides the opposite function of the add-party procedure discussed in the previous section. With this operation, one party or multiple parties can be dropped from the connection. These operations are illustrated in Figure 10–10. The activity is controlled by the T398 and T308 timers. In this example, the RELEASE and RELEASE COMPLETE messages are used at the remote side. Under certain conditions the drop party is also activated at the remote side.

Signaling AAL Reset and Failure

The AAL request operation occurs when the AAL entity issues a AAL-establish-indication primitive to ATM (no figure is shown). This resets a current connection but does not affect other connections on the interface. Another AAL operation is titled the AAL failure. In this situation any parties that are not in the active party state must be cleared.

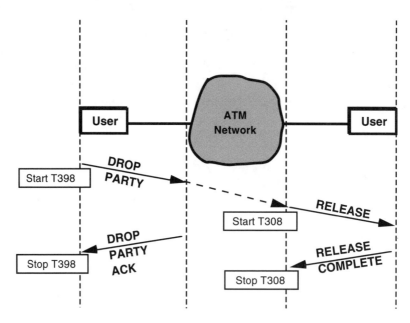

Figure 10–10   The drop party procedure.

FUNCTIONS OF Q.2931 MESSAGES AND INFORMATION ELEMENTS

We have learned that the messages for the ATM call and connection control are derived from the Q.931 protocol, the layer 3 specification for ISDN. The purpose of Q.931 is to establish connections for B channels at the ISDN basic rate interface (BRI). Q.2931 is used to set up and tear down a connection through the ATM network. The next three sections of this chapter provide a summary of the three major types of Q.2931 messages. Then, the fourth section describes the functions of the information elements that may reside in the messages. A fifth section shows coding examples of the messages and the information elements.

Messages for Call Control

Table 10–5 summarizes the information elements (fields) that are present in the messages. A key is provided with Table 10–5 to identify the message information elements. The reader will find this table handy as the information elements are described.

Messages for Restart Operations

The global call reference messages are used by the network or user to request the restart of a virtual channel or all virtual channels controlled by the signaling virtual channel. This channel is reserved with VCI = 5 and VPCI = 0.[1] It is used for all signaling in phase 1 of SVC. Metasignaling is not supported in phase 1.

The messages used for the global call reference are listed in Table 10–6, as well as the information elements that are used in these messages.

Messages for Adding and Dropping Parties

The ATM SVC supports both point-to-point connections and point-to-multipoint connections. The point-to-multipoint message allows one ATM link (the root link) to send information to any remaining nodes on the connection. These nodes are called leaf nodes and receive copies of all information sent by the root link. The add party messages (as their

---

[1]The ATM Forum uses the virtual path connection identifier (VPCI) instead of a VPI for certain forms of signaling. The issue is for further study. Currently, VPI and VPCI are the same.

Table 10–5   ATM Call and Connection Control Messages

Information Element	Message 1.	2.	3.	4.	5.	6.	7.	8.
Protocol discriminator	√	√	√	√	√	√	√	√
Call reference	√	√	√	√	√	√	√	√
Message type	√	√	√	√	√	√	√	√
Message length	√	√	√	√	√	√	√	√
AAL parameters		√		√				
AMT user traffic descriptor				√				
Broadband bearer capability				√				
Broadband high layer information				√				
Broadband repeat indicator				√				
Broadband low layer information		√		√				
Called party number				√				
Called party subaddress				√				
Calling party number				√				
Calling party subaddress				√				
Call state							√	
Cause					√	√	√	
Connection identifier	√	√		√				
QOS parameter				√				
Broadband sending complete				√				
Transit network selection				√				
Endpoint reference	√	√		√			√	√
Endpoint state							√	

1 CALL PROCEEDING	4 SETUP	7 STATUS
2 CONNECT	5 RELEASE	8 STATUS ENQUIRY
3 CONNECT ACKNOWLEDGE	6 RELEASE COMPLETE	

names imply) are to add a party to an existing connection and to acknowledge that the add party request was successful. The add party request can also be rejected.

The drop party messages (again, as the name implies) are used to drop a party from an existing point-to-multipoint connection.

The messages used with ATM point-to-multipoint call and connection control are shown in Table 10–7, as well as the information elements present in the messages.

Table 10–6   Global Call Reference Messages

Information Element	Restart	Restart Acknowledge	Status
Protocol discriminator	√	√	√
Call reference	√	√	√
Message type	√	√	√
Message length	√	√	√
Call state			√
Cause			√
Connection identifier	√	√	
Restart indicator	√	√	
Endpoint reference			√
Endpoint state			√

Table 10–7   Point-to-Multipoint Call and Connection Control Messages

Information Element	1.	2.	3.	4.	5.
Protocol discriminator	√	√	√	√	√
Call reference	√	√	√	√	√
Message type	√	√	√	√	√
Message length	√	√	√	√	√
AAL parameters	√				
Broadband high layer information	√				
Broadband low layer information	√				
Called party number	√				
Called party subaddress	√				
Calling party number	√				
Calling party subaddress	√				
Cause			√	√	√
Broadband sending complete	√				
Transit network selection	√				
Endpoint reference	√	√	√	√	√

1 ADD PARTY   4 DROP PARTY
2 ADD PARTY ACKNOWLEDGE   5 DROP PARTY ACKNOWLEDGE
3 ADD PARTY RESET

Descriptions of the Information Elements

This section describes the functions of the information elements, several of which are self-explanatory. To simplify matters, the functions of the information elements are summarized in Table 10–8, followed by additional comments on some of the entries in the table. Many of the entries listed in Table 10–8 are briefly explained following the table and are noted with the "see below" notation. The information in this section is amplified in the next section with examples.

Addresses and Other Identifiers in the Messages. ATM uses a number of labels, addresses, and identifiers to keep track of the various connections in the network. These values are placed in several of the ATM messages to be used for connection control. These values are listed in Table 10–5:

- Call reference
- Connection identifier
- Endpoint reference
- Called and calling party number
- Called and calling party subaddress

The call reference value identifies the call at the local UNI. It is used to associate incoming and outgoing messages with the proper connection. The call reference has local significance only and is not mapped to the other side of the network UNI. The values are assigned by the user on the originating side of the call and by the network on the other side of the call. They are unique at each local interface and exist only for the duration of the connection. Unlike other connection-oriented systems, such as X.25, identical call reference values may exist on the same virtual channel because the call reference value contains a flag identifying which end of the signaling channel originated the call. The originating side sets the call flag to 0 and the destination side sets the call flag to 1. This approach avoids call collisions (simultaneous use of the same value) that exist in older types of networks.

The connection identifier contains the VPI and VCI values. Within certain limitations (published by the ITU-T and ATM Forum), most of the VPI/VCI values can be used in any manner deemed necessary by the network.

Table 10–8 Functions of the Information Service Elements

Protocol discriminator	Distinguishes different types of messages within ITU-T standards and standards bodies throughout the world
Call reference	Uniquely identifies each call at the UNI (see below)
Message type	Identifies type of message, such as SETUP, STATUS, etc.
Message length	Length of message excluding the three elements above and this element
AAL parameters	AAL parameters selected by user
ATM user traffic descriptor	Specifies set of traffic parameters
Broadband and bearer capability	Indicates several network bearer services (end-to-end-timing, CBR, VBR, point-to-point, multipoint services) (see below)
Broadband high layer information	End-user codes, passed transparently through ATM network; identifies upper layer protocols or a vendor-specific application (see below)
Broadband repeat indicator	Used to allow repeated information elements to be interpreted correctly
Broadband low layer information	End-user codes, passed transparently through ATM network; identifies lower layer protocols and their configurations
Called party number	Called party of the call (see below)
Called party subaddress	Called party subaddress (see below)
Calling party number	Origin party number (see below)
Calling party subaddress	Calling party subaddress (see below)
Call state	One of 12 values to describe status of a call (active, call initiated, etc.)
Cause	Diagnostic codes (see below)
Connection identifier	The VPI and VCI for the call (see below)
QOS parameter	QOS class
Broadband sending complete	Indicates the completion of the called party number
Transit network selection	Identifies a transit network (an IXC in the U.S.) (see below)
Endpoint reference	Identifies endpoints in a point-to-multiplication connection
Endpoint state	Indicates state of each endpoint (add party initiated, received, active, etc.) (see below)
Restart indicator	For a restart, identifies which virtual channels are to be re-stated

The endpoint reference identifier is not an identifier as such but is used to identify a state of an endpoint in a point-to-multipoint connection. As examples, this value could indicate that an add party operation has been initiated, a drop party has been initiated, or that a party is now active.

The called and calling party numbers must be coded in messages dealing with connection setups. Without these numbers, the network would not know where to route the call. The party number is actually two fields, one for called party and the other for the calling party. These numbers are either a telephone number, which typically is an ISDN E.164 value, and/or an OSI address known as the network service access point (NSAP).

The last identifier is the network party called and calling party subaddress and is employed only if a network supports only an E.164 address. The purpose of the subaddress is to provide a field for the OSI NSAP address.

To clarify the difference between the party number and the party subaddress, the party number may have embedded in it the full OSI addressing plan, including NSAPs and E.164. If it does not have this full number and contains only the E.164 telephone number, then the additional party subaddress field can contain the OSI subaddress. The reason for this addition is that it is possible for traffic to be routed to an address signified by E.164 and delivered to the proper user station (computer, PBX, etc.) when the E.164 address is insufficient to define fully which entity inside the receiver station is to receive the traffic, such as file transfer server or an E-mail server. The OSI NSAP contains information that permits these operations to occur.

ATM AAL Parameters.   The parameters in the AAL information element indicate the AAL values for the connection. Listed below are some of the major parameters:

- Type of traffic (1, 3/4, 5, or user-defined)
- Subtype of traffic (circuit emulation, high-quality audio, video, etc.)
- Maximum SDU size for AAL 3/4
- CBR rate (64 kbit/s, DS1, E1, n ¥ 64 kbit/s, etc.)
- Clock recovery type for AAL 1
- Mode for AAL 5 (message mode or streaming mode)
- Error correction method for AAL 1

ATM User Traffic Descriptor. The parameters in the traffic descriptor information element indicate: (1) forward and backward peak cell rates, (2) forward and backward sustainable cell rates, and (3) forward and backward maximum burst sizes. The term forward describes the direction of traffic flow from the calling user to the called user, and the term backward indicates the direction of traffic flow from the called user to the calling user. A subfield in this information element allows the user to indicate if tagging is requested, for either forward or backward flows.

Broadband Bearer Capability and Higher Layer Information. Two information elements indicate a wide variety of services requested for the connection at a B-ISDN bearer service (the lower three layers of OSI) and the upper layers (the top four layers of OSI). These parameters have no effect on the ATM network, and are passed transparently to the end-user node.

Examples of the bearer parameters are an indication that timing is or is not required and an indication of CBR/VBR traffic. Examples of higher layer information are the identification of the user layers (protocol entities) that are to operate over ATM at the end-user station; or for X.25/X.75 traffic, the default packet size of the user payload or information on the layer 2 protocol, such as HDLC.

Chapter 11, Internetworking with ATM Networks, shows how these fields can be employed to facilitate internetworking between ATM and other networks, with ATM acting as the backbone transport network for the other networks.

Quality of Services (QOS). This information element contains values to request (and maybe receive) certain QOS operations. QOS is requested for both directions of the connection.

ATM QOS is organized around the ITU-T I.362 service classes A, B, C, and D (see Chapter 7). This information element is coded to request a QOS that meets one of the service class performance requirements. It may also be coded as unspecified, in which case the network may establish a set of objectives for the connection.

Cause Parameters. This information element contains diagnostic information and the reasons that certain messages are generated. Diagnostics such as user busy, call rejected, network out of order, QOS unavailable, user traffic descriptor not available, and the like are coded in this information element. Table 10–9 lists the cause values currently published [ATM93a].

Table 10–9   Cause Value Meaning

Unallocated (unassigned) number

No route to specified transit network

No route to destination

VPCI/VCI unacceptable

User busy

No user responding

Call rejected

Number changed

User rejects all calls with calling line identification restriction (CLIR)

Destination out of order

Invalid number format (address complete)

Response to STATUS ENQUIRY

Normal, unspecified

Requested VPCI/VCI not available

Network out of order

Temporary failure

Access information discarded

No VPCI/VCI available

Resource unavailable, unspecified

Quality of service unavailable

User traffic descriptor not available

Bearer capability not authorized

Bearer capability not presently available

Service or option not available, unspecified

Bearer capability not implemented

Unsupported combination of traffic parameters

Invalid call reference value

Identified channel does not exist

Incompatible destination

Invalid endpoint reference

Invalid transit network selection

Too many pending add party requests

AAL parameters cannot be supported

Mandatory information element is missing

Message type nonexistent or not implemented

Information element nonexistent or not implemented

Invalid information element contents

Message not compatible with call state

Recovery on timer expiry

Incorrect message length

Protocol error, unspecified

Transit Network Selection. This parameter is important in the United States for traffic that is sent across LATAs. It allows the user to choose the interexchange carrier (IXC) for the session.

EXAMPLES OF Q.2931 MESSAGES

The Q.2931 specification defines many rules for coding messages and information elements. This discussion will acquaint the reader with some of the principal features of the message coding, and will provide some examples of the information elements. Other examples can be found in Chapter 11. Be aware that this discussion does not explain all formats of all the messages.

It is recognized that some readers will not care to delve into the bit-level of these messages, and knowing the bit structure is not required to understand the functions of the messages. Other readers want the bit-level detail. Whatever the needs of the reader, an examination of these messages will help in understanding how the ATM connections are managed and will shed light on many of the functions of the ATM layer and the ATM adaptation layer.

One final point: It will become evident that the messages follow a common convention. Therefore, the first few examples will explain this convention, down to the bit level. Subsequent examples will elevate the level of detail. I hope this satisfies all readers.

Figure 10–11 shows the basic organization of the Q.2931 message. Most of the contents of this message have been explained earlier. Some additional comments are appropriate. The protocol discriminator field can be coded to identify the Q.2931 message, or other layer 3 protocols. Obviously, it is coded in this protocol to identify Q.2931 messages. The call reference identifies each call and is assigned by the originating side of the call (the user at the local side, and the network at the remote side). The message type identifies a SETUP, ADD PARTY, and other messages. The information elements contain the fields that are used to control the connection operation.

Coding Conventions

In order to understand the coding structure of the ATM messages, a few rules must be explained. All information elements contain a header, which identifies (1) the type of information element (IE), (2) a coding standard, (3) an IE instruction field, (4) a length field (length of the information elements), and (5) the actual information element (IE). The coding stan-

Bits

8	7	6	5	4	3	2	1	Octets
Protocol discriminator								1
0	0	0	0	Length of call reference				2
Flag	Call reference value							3
Call reference value (continued)								4
Call reference value (continued)								5
Message type								6
Message type (continued)								7
Message length								8
Message length (continued)								9
Variable length information elements								n

Figure 10–11   Organization of a Q.2931 message.

dard is usually set to 00 to identify an ITU-T standard. The IE instruction field values vary, depending on the specific information element. Generally, this field is not explained in our general description in this chapter.

An octet number may be repeated in the figure (for example, see Figure 10–13). The specific octet number identifies an octet group. Octets are extended in a group by appending .1, .2, .3, or .a, .b, .c, . . . behind the octet value. In Figure 10–13, octet 6 is extended by the notation 6.1. The groups can be identified and/or extended through the use of bit 8 in each octet as follows: 0 = another octet follows; 1 = last octet of this group.

AAL Parameters

Figure 10–12 illustrates the first six octets of the AAL information element. These octets are used for all AAL types. Octet 1 is coded as 01011000 to identify the information element. Octet 2 is preset or not significant. Octet 5 is coded to indicate the AAL type information that follows in octets 6 through n:

00000001   AAL 1
00000011   AAL 3/4

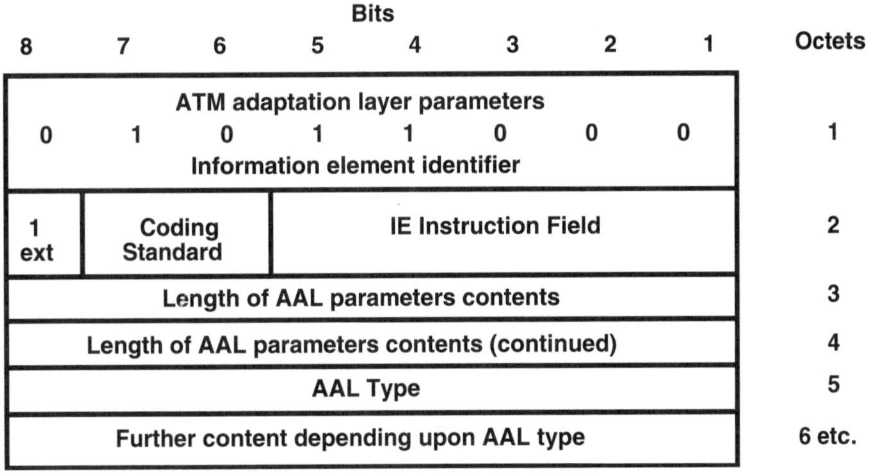

8	7	6	5	4	3	2	1	Octets

ATM adaptation layer parameters								
0	1	0	1	1	0	0	0	1
Information element identifier								

1 ext	Coding Standard	IE Instruction Field	2
Length of AAL parameters contents			3
Length of AAL parameters contents (continued)			4
AAL Type			5
Further content depending upon AAL type			6 etc.

Figure 10–12 AAL information element for all AAL types.

00000101	AAL 5
00010000	User-defined AAL

AAL 1. Figure 10–13 shows the parameters for octet groups 6–12 for AAL1. The subtype (octet 6.1) indicates:

00000000	Null/empty
00000001	Voiceband 64 kbit/s
00000010	Circuit emulation (synchronous)
00000011	Circuit emulation (asynchronous)
00000100	High-quality audio
00000101	Video

The CBR rate (octet 7.1) requests a bit rate for the session. It is coded as follows:

00000001	64 kbit/s
00000100	1544 kbit/s (DS1)
00000101	6312 kbit/s (DS2)
00000110	32064 kbit/s
00000111	44736 kbit/s (DS3)
00001000	97728 kbit/s
00010000	2048 kbit/s (E1)

Bits

8	7	6	5	4	3	2	1	Octets
Subtype identifer								6
1	0	0	0	0	1	0	1	
Subtype								6.1
CBR rate identifier								7
1	0	0	0	0	1	1	0	
CBR rate								7.1
Multiplier identifier								8 (Note 1)
1	0	0	0	0	1	1	1	
Multiplier								8.1 (Note 1)
Multiplier (continued)								8.2 (Note 1)
Source clock frequency recovery method identifier								9
1	0	0	0	1	0	0	0	
Source clock frequency recovery method								9.1
Error correction method identifier								10
1	0	0	0	1	0	0	1	
Error correction method								10.1
Structured data transfer blocksize identifier								11
1	0	0	0	1	0	1	0	
Structured data transfer blocksize								11.1
Partially filled cells identifier								12
1	0	0	0	1	0	1	1	
Partially filled cells method								12.1

These octets are only present if octet 7.1 indicates "n x 64 kbit/s."

Figure 10–13   Parameters for an AAL1 connection.

00010001   8448 kbit/s (E2)
00010010   34368 kbit/s (E3)
00010011   139264 kbit/s (E4)
01000000   n ¥ 64 kbit/s

The multiplier parameter is used to define a n × 64 kbit/s, with n ranging from 2 to $2^{16} - 1$. The clock recovery type parameter indicates the kind of clocking operation to be employed to recover and decode the signal (timestamp, etc.). The error correction parameter identifies the type of error correction method employed to detect errors at the terminating endpoint (none, FEC, etc.). The structured data transfer identifies that this connection will or will not use structured data transfer (see Chapter 7). The partially filled cells parameter states how many of the 47 octets in the cell are in use.

AAL3/4 and AAL5. Figure 10–14 shows the parameters for AAL3/4, and Figure 10–15 shows the parameters for AAL5. The functions represented in these fields are explained in Chapter 7. Briefly, then, the service specific CS (SSCS) and the common part CS (CPCS) parameters indicate (1) the maximum CPCS-SDU sizes (forward and backward), with values ranging from 1 to 65,535 ($2^{16} - 1$); (2) the ranges for the message identification field (1 to 1023); (3) a message or streaming mode; and (4) SSCS type (such as assured operations, a Frame Relay, SSCS, etc.).

				Bits				Octets
8	7	6	5	4	3	2	1	
Forward maximum CPCS-SDU size identifier								6
1	0	0	0	1	1	0	0	
Forward maximum CPCS-SDU size								6.1
Forward maximum CPCS-SDU size (continued)								6.2
Backward maximum CPCS-SDU size identifier								7
1	0	0	0	0	0	0	1	
Backward maximum CPCS-SDU size								7.1
Backward maximum CPCS-SDU size (continued)								7.2
MID range identifier								8
1	0	0	0	0	0	1	0	
MID range (lowest MID value)								8.1
MID range (lowest MID value) (continued)								8.2
MID range (highest MID value)								8.3
MID range (highest MID value)(continued)								8.4
SSCS type identifier								9
1	0	0	0	0	1	0	0	
SSCS type								9.1

Figure 10–14   Parameters for an AAL3/4 connection.

Bits

8	7	6	5	4	3	2	1	Octets
Forward maximum CPCS-SDU size identifier								6
1	0	0	0	1	1	0	0	
Forward maximum CPCS-SDU size								6.1
Forward maximum CPCS-SDU size (continued)								6.2
Backward maximum CPCS-SDU size identifier								7
1	0	0	0	0	0	0	1	
Backward maximum CPCS-SDU size								7.1
Backward maximum CPCS-SDU size (continued)								7.2
SSCS type identifier								8
1	0	0	0	0	1	0	0	
SSCS type								8.1

Figure 10–15   Parameters for an AAL5 connection.

User Traffic Descriptors

The user traffic descriptors indicate the characteristics the user wishes to use for the connection (no figure shown). The parameters (see Chapter 8) define the following traffic capabilities (the cell rates are expressed in cells per second, and the burst size is expressed as a cell):

Forward peak cell rate
Backward peak cell rate
Forward sustainable cell rate
Backward sustainable cell rate
Forward maximum burst size
Backward maximum burst size

These examples have given the reader an idea of the syntax and format of the Q.2931 messages. Chapter 11 examines those that are associated with internetworking operations.

THE PNNI MODEL

We are going to change our tack a bit and turn our attention to a switching system reference model for ATM, published in the Private Net-

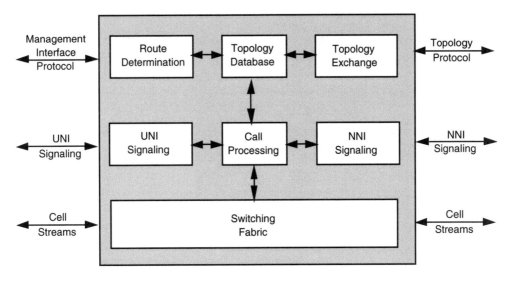

NNI   Network-to-network interface
UNI   User network interface

Figure 10–16   The ATM switching system reference model.

work to Network Interface (PNNI) specification from the ATM Forum, which is introduced here and explained further in subsequent chapters. Figure 10–16 illustrates the reference model for PNNI.

On the NNI side, the model is divided into three major areas of (1) cell streams, (2) NNI signaling, and (3) the topology protocol. On the UNI side, the model is divided into the (1) cell streams, (2) UNI signaling, and (3) the management interface protocol.

These operations are further divided into the components shown in the figure. The switching fabric is based on a cell technology switching elements. The call processing modules and signaling modules are based on the Q Series specifications, and the topology exchange and route determination functions are based on a shortest path route discovery technology.

Figure 10–17 shows how the switching model is used to set up a call.[2] In event 1, the call is received at the switch. UNI signaling is responsible for parsing the cell (for example, slicing the bits for parallel processing) and allocating resources for it. The call request is then

---

[2]This example is sourced from The *Bell Labs Technical Journal*, 3(1), "Scaleable Call Processing Architectures for ATM Switches," by Xiaoqiang Chen.

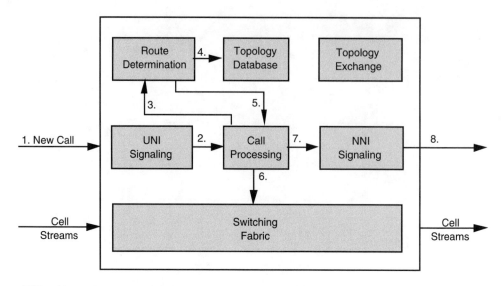

NNI   Network-to-network interface
UNI   User network interface

Figure 10–17   ATM call processing.

passed to call processing (event 2) where an identifier is assigned to the specific call. Call processing creates a table (block) for this call and passes it to route determination in event 3. This entity uses the called party address and the QOS values in the message to determine a route by examining the topology database (in event 4).

After the route is determined, call processing is informed in event 5 of the route and the outgoing link for the call. Additional information is added to the call's control table, such as the outgoing link and its associated physical port number. Assuming that call control processing has decided to accept the call, it reserves the bandwidth for the connection, and in event 6, programs the switching fabric to handle the ongoing cell transfers for the call. In event 7, call processing sends the call to the outgoing NNI link. Here, the call is assigned to an outgoing VPI/VCI. Finally, in event 8, the call is forwarded to the next hop on the selected path to the called party.

I recognize I have given short explanations (or none at all) to the PNNI route determination, topology database, and topology exchange procedures. A detailed description of PNNI is beyond the scope of this text. I refer you to Chapter 11 of this book, and *ATM Volume III* in this series for more information on PNNI.

UNI SIGNALING, VERSION 4.0, AND VOICE AND TELEPHONY OVER ATM TO THE DESKTOP

The UNI 3.1 contains the current signaling procedures for ATM signaling as established in the Anchorage Accord. In addition the ATM Forum publishes the ATM UNI Signaling Specification, Version 4.0, which defines several procedures not provided in the UNI 3.1 specification.[3]

Work is underway to define a desktop protocol called Voice and Telephony over ATM to the Desktop (VTOA). This protocol requires a subset of UNI Signaling 4.0.

To help the implementer in understanding the relationships of UNI 3.1, UNI 4.0, VTOA Desktop, as well as PNNI 1.0, the ATM Forum has published a worksheet, shown in Table 10–10. The table describes the messages, information elements or codepoints for these four specifications.

The following explanation of Table 10–10 is a summary of the tipsheet. It is intended for the reader who is tasked with implementing these procedures.

Notification Procedures

The NOTIFY message and Notification indicator information element are not supported in UNI 3.1, but are supported in PNNI 1.0, UNI Signaling 4.0, and Q.2931. UNI 3.1 is based on Q.2931, but it specifically excludes the notification procedures.

Notification of Interworking Procedures (Progress)

The PROGRESS message and Progress indicator information element are not supported in UNI 3.1, but are supported in PNNI 1.0, UNI Signaling 4.0, and Q.2931. UNI 3.1 is based on Q.2931, but it specifically excludes the notification of interworking procedures.

AAL Negotiation

Two AALs are supported for 64 kbit/s: "AAL for voice" which is a very simplified version of AAL1 and AAL5. AAL negotiation procedures

---

[3]UNI 4.0 is based on the ITU-T Q.2931 and Q.2931.1 Recommendations. These ITU-T specifications are explained in *ATM Volume II* of this series.

Table 10–10   Messages and Information Elements (from an ATM Forum Tipsheet)

Signaling Message, Information Element or Codepoint	UNI SIG 4.0	UNI 3.1	PNNI 1.0	VTOA Desktop
NOTIFY/Notification indicator	√	—	√	Note 1
PROGRESS/Progress	√	—	√	M
AAL for voice in AAL parameters	√	—	√	O
Cause value #93	√	Note 2	√	M
ALERTING	√	—	√	M
Narrowband bearer capability	√	—	√	M
Narrowband low layer capability	√	—	√	O
Narrowband high layer capability	√	—	√	O
Called party number	√	√	√	O
Called party subaddress	√	√	√	O
Calling party number	√	√	√	O
Calling party subaddress	√	√	√	O
Connected number	√	—	√	O
Connected subaddress	√	—	√	O
User-user information	√	—	√	O
AFI=x049 "Local ATM Format"	—Note 3—			O

Where:
 Messages, information elements or codepoint are supported (√)
 Messages, information elements or codepoint are not supported (—)
 Mandatory capability (M)
 Optional capability (O)
Note 1 - The Notification procedures are only necessary if adaptive timing recovery is used.
Note 2 - Cause valued #78 AND #93 have the same meaning in UNI 3.1.
Note 3 - Not explicitly mentioned, but in accordance with the principals of the specifications.

are required. AAL negotiation procedures require the use of UNI Signaling 4.0 cause value #93, "AAL parameters cannot be supported."

Call/Connection Alerting

The ALERTING message is not supported in UNI 3.1, but is supported in PNNI 1.0, UNI Signaling 4.0, and Q.2931. UNI 3.1 is based on Q.2931, but it specifically excludes the ALERTING message. The ALERTING message is described in 3.2.1/Q.2931 and 6.3.2.1/PNNI 1.0.

Narrowband Bearer Capability Information Element

The Narrowband bearer capability (N-BC) information element is not supported in UNI 3.1, but is supported in PNNI 1.0, UNI Signaling 4.0, and Q.2931.

Narrowband High Layer Compatibility Information Element

The Narrowband high layer compatibility (N-HLC) information element is not supported in UNI 3.1, but is supported in PNNI 1.0, UNI Signaling 4.0, and Q.2931. UNI 3.1 is based on Q.2931, but it specifically excludes the N-HLC information element.

The N-HLC information element is not essential for the support of any N-ISDN service, including VTOA to the Desktop. It is of end-to-end significance and transported transparently by the B-ISDN. Voice and Telephony over ATM to the Desktop does not make use of the N-HLC information element, but it could be used in the N-ISDN.

Narrowband Low Layer Compatibility Information Element

The Narrowband low layer compatibility (N-LLC) information element is not supported in UNI 3.1, but is supported in PNNI 1.0, UNI Signaling 4.0, and Q.2931. UNI 3.1 is based on Q.2931, but it specifically excludes the N-LLC information element.

The N-LLC information element is not essential for the support of N-ISDN services. It is of end-to-end significance and transported transparently by the B-ISDN. "Voice and Telephony Over ATM to the Desktop" does not make use of the N-LLC information element, but it could be used in the N-ISDN.

UNI Signaling 4.0 Supplementary Services

Although only UNI Signaling 4.0 explicitly supports these supplementary services, most of them do not have any extra signaling requirements over what is in UNI 3.1 or PNNI 1.0 because they support the required messages and information elements. All these services are optional.

Direct Dialing In (DDI). DDI uses the called address in the Called party number information element to route the call. Since delivery of the Called party number information element in the SETUP message is mandatory in both directions in UNI 3.1, UNI Signaling 4.0 and PNNI 1.0, there are no additional signaling requirements to support DDI.

Multiple Subscriber Number (MSN). MSN allows the use of more than one address for one endpoint using the called address in the Called party number information element to distinguish them. Since delivery of the called party number in the SETUP message is mandatory in both directions in UNI Signaling 4.0 and PNNI 1.0, there are no additional signaling requirements to support MSN.

Calling Line Identification Presentation (CLIP). Since the Calling party number and Calling party subaddress information elements are supported in UNI 3.1, there are no additional signaling requirements to support CLIP beyond including the Calling party number and possibly the Calling party subaddress information elements in the SETUP message.

Calling Line Identification Restriction (CLIR). To restrict presentation of the calling party number at the called party, the calling party shall set the "presentation indicator" in the Calling party number information element to "presentation restricted." To allow presentation of the calling party number at the called party, the calling party shall set the "presentation indicator" in the Calling party number information element to "presentation allowed."

Connected Line Identification Presentation (COLP). COLP requires the use of the Connected number and possibly the Connected subaddress information elements as defined in Q.2931. UNI Signaling 4.0 and PNNI 1.0 support the Connected number and Connected subaddress information elements, but not UNI 3.1.

Connected Line Identification Restriction (COLR). COLR requires the use of the Connected number information element as defined in Q.2931. UNI Signaling 4.0 and PNNI 1.0 support the Connected number information element, but not UNI 3.1. To restrict presentation of the Connected number at the Calling party, the connected party shall set the "presentation indicator" in the connected party number information element to "presentation restricted." To allow presentation of the Connected number to that Calling party, the connected party shall set the "presentation indicator" in the Connected number information element to "presentation allowed."

Subaddressing (SUB). SUB uses the called subaddress in the Called party subaddress information element to expand the addressing capabilities beyond the normal capabilities provided by the B-ISDN numbering plan. Since the Called party subaddress information element is supported in UNI 3.1, there are no additional signaling requirements to support SUB beyond including the Called party subaddress information element in the SETUP message.

SUMMARY

The ATM call and connection control operations define how connections are set up on demand between users and the ATM network. The Q.2931 connection control protocol, based on the ISDN Q.931, is used for these operations. The ATM address utilizes the OSI address syntax. Q.2931 supports point-to-point, unidirectional connections. Future releases of Q.2931 and the ATM Forum specifications will also support multipoint-to-multipoint connections.

11

Internetworking
with ATM Networks

This chapter examines how ATM internetworks with other networks. It explains the B-ISDN intercarrier interface (B-ICI). It also explains how several of the Q.2931 messages can be used to define network operations between networks that are using an ATM network as the backbone network between them. The ATM data exchange interface (DXI), Multiprotocol over ATM (MPOA), and Frame UNI (FUNI) are also examined. The reader who is not familiar with the basic operations of DS3 should review Chapter 4.

This chapter is an overview of the subject. See *ATM Volume III* of this series for more details.

THE ATM NETWORK AS THE BACKBONE
FOR OTHER NETWORKS

From the perspective of ATM vendors, the ATM Forum specifications, and other supporters of this technology, ATM is viewed as the backbone for interconnecting other networks. To this end, the standards bodies and the ATM Forum have published a number of recommendations and specifications that define (1) how traffic from different networks is transported through an ATM network, (2) how the header in the

PDUs of these different networks is (or is not) translated into the ATM cell, and (3) how the services offered by these networks are (or are not) mapped into the ATM services.

USING Q.2931 TO SUPPORT PROTOCOL CAPABILITY (TUNNELING)

As discussed in earlier chapters, the term *tunneling* refers to an operation in which a transport network, such as an ATM backbone, carries traffic from other protocols and networks transparently (or almost transparently) through the transport network. If possible, the transport network does not become involved with either the syntax or the interpretation of the transported traffic. Thus, the term refers to the notion of sending traffic (say a car) through a "tunnel" without anyone in the tunnel, stopping the car, rolling down the windows of the car, and checking the contents in the passenger space.

The tunneled information is passed transparently by the ATM network between the two user parties. ATM does not examine, interpret, or act on this traffic. Its intent is to allow the two end users to inform each other about the nature of some of the communications protocols operating in their machines. The goal is to stipulate or negotiate a compatible protocol stack for the exchange of traffic between the user applications. Tunneling in ATM is performed by using the Q.2931 operations and the broadband low-layer information element that is introduced in Chapter 10.

In some systems, such as the well-known point-to-point protocol (PPP), these services are accomplished with two methods. First, during the connection setup, two end users can inform each other about which protocols are to be invoked during the session. This procedure allows the two parties to negotiate an acceptable set of protocols to be used during the session. Second, during the transfer of traffic, a protocol identifier is conveyed to indicate what type of protocol payload is being sent in the service data unit (SDU).

While Q.2931 can be configured to accomplish either method, it does not stipulate any negotiation procedures. Additional software must be written to provide full negotiation operations.

Figure 11–1 shows how the Q.2931 messages (explained in Chapter 10) can be invoked and interpreted. The boundary of the message flow is between a calling user and a called user. In this example, the flow is between (in ITU-T terminology) interworking units (IWU)—or routers. Of course, the manner in which the end-user stations communicate with

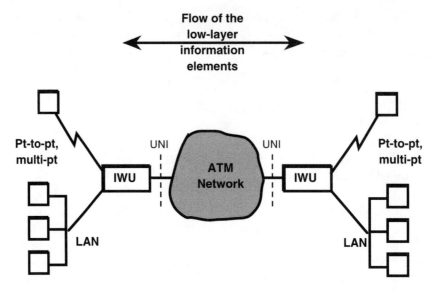

Figure 11–1   Flow of the Q.2931 low-layer information element.

the routers is not defined by ATM, since the information flow between the end-user station and the router is not part of the ATM UNI. Nonetheless, the user station-to-router operation is well-defined in other standards, and the router need only map the information received from the user stations into the Q.2931 message at the originating router and perform a complementary and reverse operation at the terminating router.

The identification of the layer 2 protocols must discern whether they are running on (1) point-to-point links, (2) multipoint links, or (3) LAN links. Some protocols, such as LAPD, can operate on a multipoint link; others operate on only point-to-point links, such as LAPB. Still others operate only on LAN links.

However, in this latter case for LAN links, these procedures do not identify the type of LAN (Ethernet, token ring, etc.), because the headers of the respective LANs are not carried across the ATM network—they are stripped away at the originating router and reconstituted at the terminating router. This approach allows the terminating router to place the traffic onto any type of LAN, which may be different than the LAN at the originating site.

Figure 11–2 illustrates the various layer 2 and 3 protocols and procedures that can be identified in the Q.2931 low-layer information element. Figure 11–2a depicts the layer 2 protocols, and Figure 11–2b de-

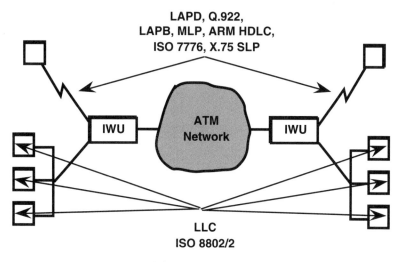

(a) Layer 2 Protocols

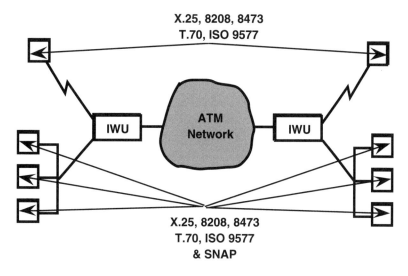

(b) Layer 3 Protocols

Figure 11–2   Layers 2 and 3 identifications.

picts the layer 3 protocols. The description of all these protocols is well beyond the subject of this book. The reader can study *X.25 and Related Protocols, Data Link Protocols,* and *Computer Networks: Protocols, Standards and Interfaces,* all by Uyless Black ([BLAC89], [BLAC91], and [BLAC93]) for information on these systems. All references are highly recommended by this writer.

For the layer 3 protocols, the LAN stations ordinarily support the Internet Protocol (IP), or some vendor-specific protocol, such as Novell's IPX. The approximate equivalent in this specification is ISO 8473, the connectionless network protocol, or CLNP.

Also, the subnetwork access protocol (SNAP) is usually employed in LANs (and not WANs) to identify the layer 3 protocol residing in the data unit. Nothing precludes using other methods. The most common approach is to use SNAP on LANs, as it was so designed, and to use PPP on point-to-point links, as it was so designed.

BROADBAND LOW-LAYER INFORMATION ELEMENT

Figure 11–3 shows the format and contents of the broadband low-layer information element. Octets 1-4 are explained in Chapter 10. Octet 5 is not supported at this time in the ATM Forum specification. Octet 6, bits 1–5, are coded in accordance with the conventions shown in Figure 11–4. Octet 6a uses the mode field to define if extended (0–127) or normal sequencing (0–7) is to be employed at layer 2 (if sequencing is employed). The Q.933 field is used, based on implementation-specific rules. The window size field (k) can range from 1 to 127. The next occurrence of 6a defines if a user-specified layer 2 protocol is employed.

Octet 7, bits 1–5, are coded in accordance with the conventions shown in Figure 11–5. The mode field in octet 7a defines if extended (0–127) or normal sequencing (0–7) is to be employed at layer 3 (if sequencing is employed). The default packet size field in octet 7b is used to define the default size of the X.25 packet (if X.25 is invoked). The packet window size is also employed for X.25 (octet 7c) for a range of 1 to 127.

The second occurrence of octet 7a is used to identify a user-specified layer 3 protocol, such as SNA Path Control or AppleTalk layer 3.

The remainder of the octets in this information element can be used to identify SNAP information. If so indicated by octets 7a, a 24-bit organization unique ID (OUI) and a 16-bit protocol ID (PID) are contained in the last octets of the information element. The OUI and PID are values that are registered under ISO, the IEEE, and the Internet.

Bits

8	7	6	5	4	3	2	1	Octets
Broadband low layer information								1
0	1	0	1	1	1	1	1	
1 ext	Coding standard		IE instruction field					2
Length of B-LLI contents								3
Length of B-LLI contents (continued)								4
1 ext	0 1 Layer 1 id		User information layer 1 protocol					5
0/1 ext	1 0 Layer 2 id		User information layer 2 protocol					6
0/1 ext	Mode		0 0 0 Spare			Q.933 use		6a
1 ext	Window size (k)							6b
1 ext	User specified layer 2 protocol information							6a
0/1 ext	1 1 Layer 3 id		User information layer 3 protocol					7
0/1 ext	Mode		0 0 0 0 0 Spare					7a
0/1 ext	0 0 0 Spare			Default packet size				7b
1 ext	Packet window size							7c
1 ext	User specified layer 3 protocol information							7a
0 ext	ISO/IEC TR 9577 Initial protocol identifier (IPI) (bits 8-2)							7a
1 ext	IPI (bit1)	0 0 0 0 0 0 Spare						7b
1 ext	0 0 SNAP ID	0 0 0 0 0 Spare						8
OUI Octet 1								8.1
OUI Octet 2								8.2
OUI Octet 3								8.3
PID Octet 1								8.4
PID Octet 2								8.5

Figure 11–3   The broadband low-layer information element.

Octet 6 Bits 54321	Meaning
00001	Basic mode ISO 1745
00010	CCITT Recommendation Q.921
00110	CCITT Recommendation X.25, link layer
00111	CCITT Recommendation X.25 multilink
01000	Extended LAPB; for half duplex operation
01001	HDLC ARM (ISO 4335)
01010	HDLC NRM (ISO 4335)
01011	HDLC ABM (ISO 4335)
01100	LAN logical link control (ISO 8802/2)
01101	CCITT Recommendation X.75, single link procedure (SLP)
01110	CCITT Recommendation Q.922
10000	User specified
10001	ISO 7776 DTE-DTE operation

Figure 11–4   Coding bits 1–5 of octet 6.

Octet 7 Bits 54321	Meaning
00110	CCITT Recommendation X.25, packet layer
00111	ISO/IEC 8208 (X.25 packet level protocol for data terminal equipment)
01000	X.223/ISO 8878 (use of ISO/ISO 8208 [41] and CCITT X.25 to provide the OSI-CONS)
01001	ISO/IEC 8473 (OSI connectionless mode protocol)
01010	CCITT Recommendation T.70 minimum network layer
01011	ISO/IEC TR 9577 (Protocol Identification in the Network Layer)
01000	User specified

Figure 11–5   Coding for bits 1–5 of octet 7.

THE NETWORK-TO-NETWORK INTERFACE

Presently, two network-to-network interfaces (NNI) are defined for ATM. (Some literature uses the term network-node interface; in this discussion, they mean the same thing). A public NNI is sponsored by the ITU-T, and a private NNI is sponsored by the ATM Forum (see Figure 11–6).

The private NNI (PNNI) is introduced in Chapter 10. It allows different vendors' ATM machines and different networks to communicate with each other. The communications utilize the standard UNI switched virtual call (SVC) procedures, with additional information added in the SVC messages. The major focus of the private UNI is on route discovery, address advertising, address aggregation, building routing tables, and

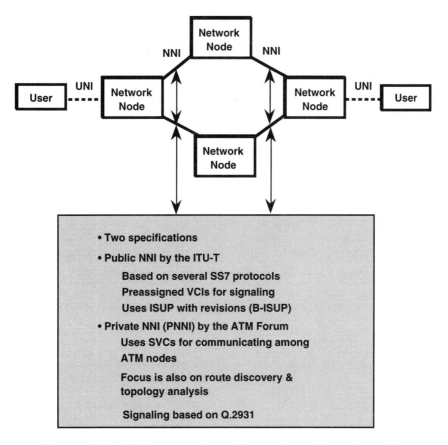

Figure 11–6   Major aspects of the network-to-network interface (NNI).

maintaining an awareness of "reachability" to other ATM nodes. It is based on hierarchical routing and hierarchical addresses. Advertisements are part of this specification, with information on link state metrics, and bandwidth availability.

The second major aspect of PNNI is connection management, and PNNI defines a version of Q.2931 for the setting up and tearing down of the ATM-based virtual circuits.

The public NNI was developed by the ITU-T. Signaling System No. 7 (SS7) has been adapted for use with this specification. As a general description, SS7's ISDN user part (ISUP), and message transfer part 3 (MTP 3) are modified for the public NNI. The modification is essentially one of managing ATM virtual circuits instead of DS0 channels. These protocols run on top of ATM and some type of physical layer. A special AAL called the signaling ATM adaptation layer (SAAL) rests between the ATM layer and the SS7 layers.

THE ATM B-ISDN INTERCARRIER INTERFACE (B-ICI)

The ATM Forum has published the broadband intercarrier interface (B-ICI) Version 1.0.[1] Figure 11–7 shows the relationships between the UNI and B-ICI and the idea that the B-ICI can operate with public local exchange carrier (LEC) networks and independent LECs (ILECs). This distinction is important, because B-ICI is an interface between public ATM networks, not private networks.

Figure 11–8 shows the relationship of the B-ICI to other interfaces and protocols, notably, Frame Relay service (FRS), circuit emulation service (CES) for CBR traffic, cell relay service (CRS), and SMDS. All these technologies, as well as ATM, provide for the user-to-network interface, which is called either a UNI or a subscriber-to-network (SNI).

The B-ICI is designed for multiservice operations. Traffic can be submitted to a network in ATM cells, DS1/DS3 frames, Frame Relay

---

[1]Some confusion exists regarding NNI. Some vendors/standards call it the network-node interface, and others call it the network-to-network interface. With either term, NNI is supposed to determine a switch-to-switch interface, which could be within a network or between networks. The major goal of an NNI is to allow ATM switches from different vendors to interwork with each other. Therefore, the ATM B-ICI is one aspect of an NNI specification: a carrier-to-carrier interface. Obviously (and eventually), the NNI and the B-ICI must coexist at the ICI. But the B-ICI need not exist between two switches in the same network.

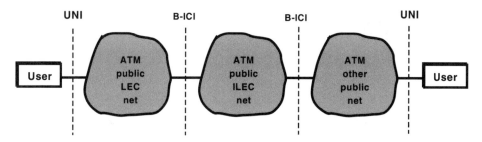

Figure 11–7 ATM and public carrier networks.

frames, or SMDSs L2_PDUs. This traffic is sent across the B-ICI in the form of (1) ATM cells over ATM connections, (2) DS1 or DS3 frames (CES), which are encapsulated into AAL 1 PDUs, (3) Frame Relay frames, which are encapsulated into AAL5 PDUs and mapped into ATM cells, or (4) SMDS L2_PDUs, which are encapsulated into AAL3/4 PDUs or mapped directly into ATM cells.

The capacity for each user is assigned based on the type of traffic. Consequently, access classes for SMDS, the committed information rate (CIR), and excess information rate (EIR) for Frame Relay pertain to this interface. Presently, dynamic bandwidth allocation is not provided.

The ATM B-ICI has considerable functionality. It is (in ITU-T terms) an interworking unit (IWU) that transmits and receives traffic from different systems. The term gateway is sometimes used to describe this function. The multiservice aspect of ATM is in keeping with ATM's design to support multimedia traffic.

For cell transfer between two ATM networks, the B-ICI specification requires that the two networks retain a relationship between a B-ICI connection and a UNI connection. For the transmission of DS1/DS3 frames, the DS1/DS3 VCCs should be translated to unique VCCs at the internetworking interface in order to avoid the use of duplicate VCC values (to those at the UNI). How this is performed is not defined in the standard but is left to the implementation of the carriers.

Frame relay frames are encapsulated into AAL5 cells, and the DLCI is sent transparently through the networks and translated at the receiving Frame Relay interface. Alternately, if frames are mapped to the ATM layer, a DLCI must be translated into a VPI/VCI. Finally, SMDS L2_PDUs can be encapsulated into AAL3 or 4 cells. Alternately, SMDS L2_PDUs can be mapped into specific VCC or VPC values.

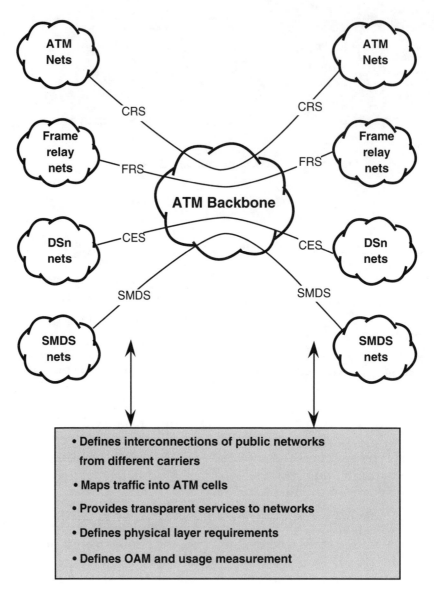

Figure 11–8   ATM B-ICI.

Physical Layer Requirements at the B-ICI

The B-ICI physical layer requirements are closely aligned with the ATM UNI requirements for 155.520 Mbit/s STS3-c, 622.080 Mbit/s STS-12c, and 44.736 Mbit/s DS3. Likewise, the ATM layer at the B-ICI is almost identical to the UNI. Since these requirements are covered in other parts of this book, they will not be repeated (see Chapter 14 for this information).

Traffic Management at the B-ICI

Like the UNI, the B-ICI stipulates a traffic contract between networks—a carrier-to-carrier service contract. With few modifications, the generic cell rate algorithm (GCRA) is used at the B-ICI.

For each direction of transmission, the traffic contract consists of several parameters (some optional and some required): (1) a connection traffic descriptor, (2) a requested QOS class, and (3) a definition of a compliant ATM connection. These parameters include: peak cell rate, sustainable cell rate, burst tolerance, cell delay variability tolerance, and conformance definition based on the GCRA. The cell loss priority CLP bit may be used at the B-ICI.

Reference Traffic Loads

The B-ICI specification provides guidance on how the network operator can identify and manage traffic loads in view of complying with the performance objectives of a service contract. The approach is to characterize traffic loads by a utilization factor for a specific type of physical circuit at the B-ICI, as well as the type of traffic being carried on the circuit. Table 11–1 shows the reference traffic loads for three types of traffic: Traffic load type 1 represents CBR traffic (DSn emulation), and traffic load types 2 and 3 represent VBR traffic. These traffic types are examined with three types of physical links: DS3 with PLCP cell mapping, SONET STS-3c, and SONET STS-12c. Table 11–1 also shows the number of active traffic sources that leads to the link utilization factor.

To illustrate how the reference traffic load is used, consider the requirement for generating reference traffic load type 1. Apply the number of active sources listed in Table 11–1 to each link being tested. The utilization factor is derived from the total traffic from the active sources, with each source producing cells at a rate of 4106 cells per second ([4106 = 1.544 Mbit/s] / [47 * 8 bits per cell]). For CBR traffic, the traffic from the same source must have a uniform distribution over a 244 µs interval

Table 11–1   Reference Traffic Loads for PVC Performance [ATM93a]

Reference Traffic Load Type	Link Capacity	Number of Active Traffic Sources to Provide Link Utilization Factor	Link Utilization Factor
1	DS3 PLCP	20	0.86
1	STS-3c	73	0.85
1	STS-12c	292	0.85
2	DS3 PLCP	Not applicable	0.85
2	STS-3c	Not applicable	0.85
2	STS-12c	Not applicable	0.85
3	DS3 PLCP	66	0.70
3	STS-3c	242	0.70
3	STS-12c	969	0.70

(244 µs = 1/4106 cells a second). This source traffic type is compatible with the requirements for AAL1, because of its support of 4106 cells/sec. Other reference traffic loads are explained in section 5.1 of the ATM Forum B-ICI documents.

B-ICI Layer Management Operations

The B-ICI layer management operations use the B-ISDN/ SONET/SDH F4 and F5 operations, administration, and maintenance (OAM) information flows. This topic is covered in Chapter 13 of this book, so it is not repeated here. On another level, the management operations are grouped into two categories of fault management and performance management. Fault management concerns itself with alarm surveillance and the verification of ongoing VP and VC connections. Performance management concerns itself with monitoring lost or misinserted cells, cell delay variations, and bit errors. The reader can refer to the section in Chapter 13 titled "Operation and Maintenance (OAM) Operations" for more information on the F4 and F5 information flows.

SPECIFIC INTERNETWORKING SERVICES

We now turn our attention to the four specific services supported by the B-ICI. These four services are examined in this order:

PVC cell relay service (CRS)

PVC circuit emulation service (CES)

PVC Frame Relay service (FRS)

SMDS service

PVC Cell Relay Service (CRS)

The CRS is the most straightforward of the B-ICI multiapplication services. The physical interfaces are the same as those for a UNI, and performance and QOS are based on ITU-T I.35B and the ATM Forum UNI, which include specifications on cell transfer delay, cell delay variation (CDV), misinsertion rate, error ratio, loss ratio, mean time between service outages, and mean time to restore. The interfaces and layers for CRS are depicted in Figure 11–9.

PVC Circuit Emulation Service (CES)

The CES supports operations for intercarriers DS1 and DS3 across the B-ICI. The grooming of these rates is not supported. Figure 11–10 shows three examples of CES configurations. These cases represent examples only, and other configurations are possible and permitted. In all three cases, AAL1 is required to support unstructured data transfer (UDT: Traffic is not organized into blocks). As described in the AAL chapter, the AAL1 convergence sublayer (CS) performs its typical operations of organizing the traffic into 47 octet PDUs, providing clocking operations and supporting sequencing functions. At the receiver, CS also generates dummy AAL_SDUs to the user application in the event of DS1

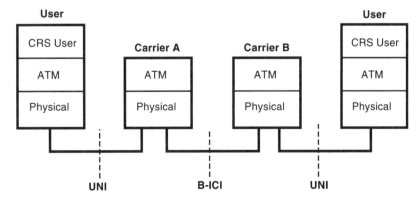

Figure 11–9   CRS layers and interfaces.

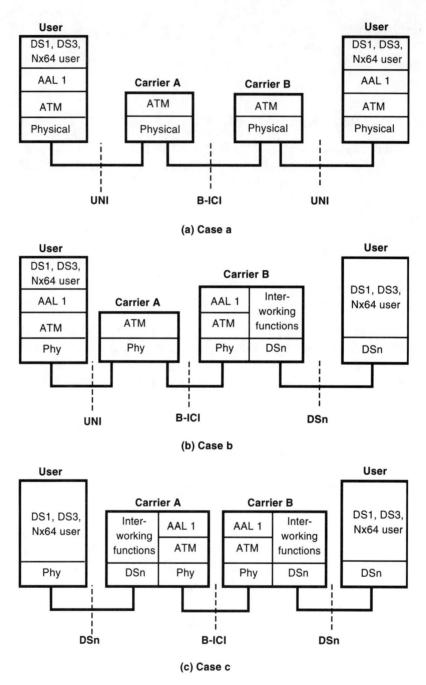

(a) Case a

(b) Case b

(c) Case c

Figure 11–10   CES layers and interfaces.

or DS3 alarm indication signals (AIS). The segmentation and reassembly layer (SAR) generates (at the sender) the 1-octet header and processes this header at the receiver.

Referring once again to Figure 11–10, in case a, the DSn operations and AAL1 occur at the user's customer premises equipment (CPE). For case b, Carrier B operates with an interworking unit (IWU). The reason for the placement of interworking functions in another machine is to monitor and measure (1) buffer overflows, (2) cell loss, (3) absence of user traffic (a starvation condition), and (4) length and time of the starvation on behalf of the CPE. Finally, for case c, IWUs are placed in the equipment of both carriers.

The interworking functions also compensate for loss of traffic that may occur when the ATM layer is not supporting the transfer rate of AAL1. The IWU must be able to detect the loss of signal (LOS), loss of frame (LOF), and alarm indication signals (AIS) signals on the DSn channel (discussed in Chapter 13). As illustrated in Figure 11–11, these detections are mapped into ATM OAM cells, transported through the ATM network(s), and mapped into DS3 alarm signals for receipt by the other DS3 interface component.

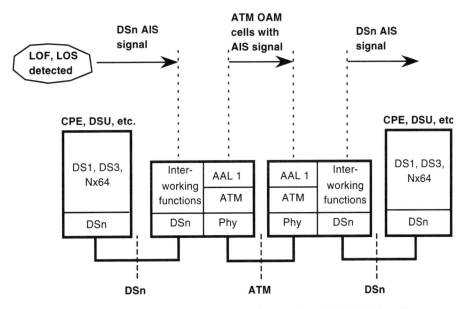

Figure 11–11   Mapping a DSn AIS into the ATM OAM cell.

PVC Frame Relay Service (FRS)

Figure 11–12 shows the structure and layers for internetworking Frame Relay networks with ATM networks. The interworking unit processes frames at the Frame Relay UNI with the user device using the Frame Relay Q.922 core procedures.

The IWF assumes the job of mapping functions between the Frame Relay network and the ATM network. At a minimum the following functions must be supported:

- *Variable length PDU formatting and delimiting:* Using AAL 5, support the Frame Relay 2 octet control field (required) and the 3 and 4 octet control field (optional)
- *Error detection:* Using CRC-32, provide error detection over the FR PDU
- *Connection multiplexing:* Associating one or multiple Frame Relay connections with one ATM VCC
- *Loss priority indication:* Mapping the Frame Relay discard eligibility bit and the ATM cell loss priority bit
- *Congestion indication:* Support of the Frame Relay forward and backward congestion notification features (within certain rules)

The FR-SSCS (Frame Relay-Service Specific Convergence Sublayer). FR-SSCS supports variable length frames at the FR UNI over

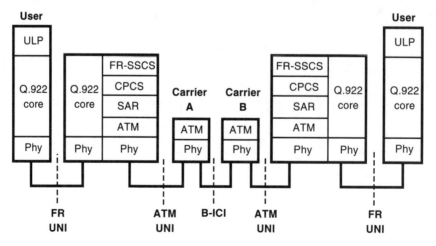

Figure 11–12   FRS layers and interfaces.

preestablished connections (i.e., PVCs). Each FR-SSCS connection is identified with a Frame Relay data link connection identifier (DLCI: equivalent to the ATM VPI/VCI). Multiple FR-SSCS connections can be associated with one common part CS (CPCS).

The principal job of FR-SSCS is to emulate the FR UNI. In so doing, it supports Frame Relay forward and backward congestion notification (FECN, BECN), as well as the discard eligibility (DE) bit.

The CPCS is responsible for the following operations:

- *Message support:* Support of message mode (fixed-length blocks) or streaming mode (variable-length blocks) operations
- *Assured operations:* CPCS is responsible for traffic integrity (retransmission of lost or corrupted PDUs
- *Nonassured operations:* CPCS is not responsible for traffic integrity

Figure 11–13 provides an example of the FRS operations. The interface between the Frame Relay entity and the AAL entity occurs through

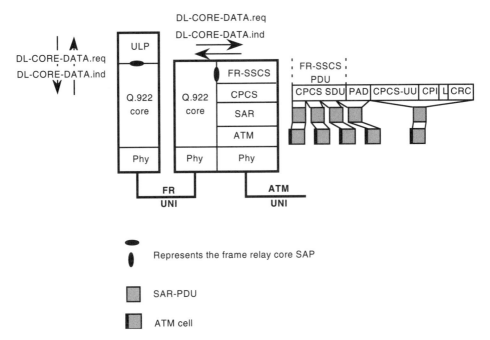

Figure 11–13 Relationships of frame relay and ATM.

the Frame Relay core SAP (service access point) defined in the Frame Relay specifications. Therefore, the IWF must accommodate to the Frame Relay service definitions at this SAP. Ideally, the Frame Relay entity has no awareness of the AAL and ATM operations.

In accordance with the Frame Relay specifications, the service primitives contain up to five parameters: core user data, discard eligibility (DE), congestion encountered (CE) backward, congestion encountered (CE) forward, and connection endpoint identifier (CEI).

The core user data parameter is used to convey data between the end-users in the Frame Relay service, and in Figure 11–13, it is represented by FR-SSCS PDU. The DE parameter is sent from the core service user to the service provider (FR-SSCS) and is mapped into the ATM CLP bit.

The two congestion parameters supply information about congestion that is encountered in the network. The congestion encountered forward parameter is used to indicate that congestion has occurred in transferring data to the receiving user. The congestion backward parameter indicates that the network has experienced congestion in transferring these units from the sending user.

The connection endpoint identifier (CEI) parameter is used to further identify a connection endpoint. For example, this parameter would allow a DLCI to be used by more than one user, and each user would be identified with a connection endpoint identifier value.

The AAL5 PDU introduced in Chapter 7 (see Figure 7–25) is used to support Frame Relay and ATM interworking. As before, the CPI field is not yet defined. The CPCS-UU field is passed transparently by the ATM network. The length field is checked for oversized or undersized PDUs. CRC violations are noted, and a reassembly timer can be invoked at the terminating endpoint.

Traffic Characterization at the B-ICI. Appendix A of the ATM Forum B-ICI specification provides guidelines on how to characterize Frame Relay traffic in terms of the ATM conformance parameters discussed in Chapter 9. The following parameters are described: (1) peak cell rate (PCR), (2) sustained cell rate (SCR), and (3) maximum burst size for CLP = 1 or 0. The reader is encouraged to read Appendix A of the ATM Specification if more detailed information is needed.

SMDS Service

Figure 11–14 depicts the configuration and layers for the SMDS service offered by the B-ICI. The services offered by the IWF to SMDS are similar in concept to those described in the Frame Relay service (FRS):

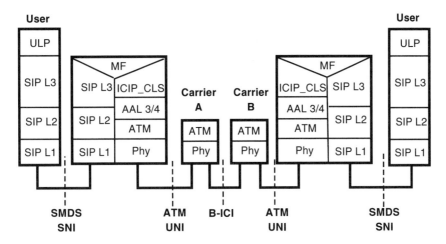

Figure 11–14   SMDS service layers and interfaces.

The IWF must transport SMDS traffic transparently through the ATM backbone network(s). It must map the SMDS PDUs into cells at the sending IWF and reassemble the cells into the SMDS PDUs at the terminating IWF. In addition, the IWF uses a specific, more detailed AAL3/4 for its AAL operations. For this operation, AAL3/4 invokes the common part convergence sublayer (CPCS), as well as the segmentation and reassembly sublayer (SAR). It uses the AAL3/4 PDU described in Chapter 7. Therefore, this operation is not described again here, because it is explained in the section titled "Type 3/4 Segmentation and Identification Operations" (specifically Figure 7–18).

Because SMDS is a connectionless service, the intercarrier interface protocol connectionless service (ICIP_CLS) layer maps the SMDS data units and the AAL PDUs. Its operations are consistent with the SMDS ICI specifications, as well as the ITU-T recommendations.

Figure 11–15 provides an example of the mapping between SMDS and ATM. This example shows the traffic flowing from the SMDS CPE to the ATM B-ICI. On the left side of the figure, the SMDS L3_PDU is processed by the SMDS interface protocol, layer 3 (SIP L3). Fields, such as BEtags, are discarded after all L2_PDUs have been reassembled into the L3_PDU.

Almost all the fields in the L3_PDU are simply mapped into the ICIP_CLS_PDU without alteration. In addition, these fields are also encapsulated into the ICIP_CLS_PDU user data field, as depicted by the dashed arrows in the figure.

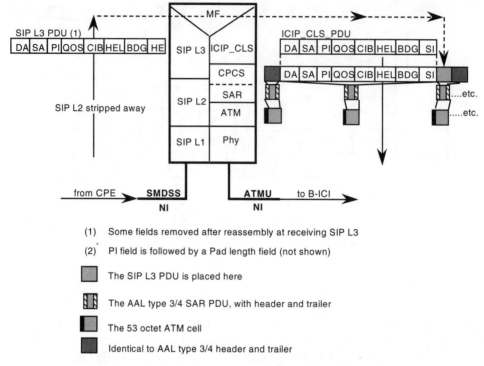

(1)   Some fields removed after reassembly at receiving SIP L3

(2)   PI field is followed by a Pad length field (not shown)

☐   The SIP L3 PDU is placed here

▨   The AAL type 3/4 SAR PDU, with header and trailer

◼   The 53 octet ATM cell

◼   Identical to AAL type 3/4 header and trailer

Figure 11–15   Relationships of SMDS and ATM.

The relationship of the SMDS L3_PDU fields and the ICIP_CLS_PDU fields is as follows. First, the destination address and source address are 8-octet fields. They each contain two subfields, the address type and the address. The address type field is 4 bits in length, the address is 60 bits in length. SMDS uses a 10-digit address with a prefix of 1 before the address in accordance with the ITU-T E.164 and the North American Numbering Plan (NANP). The address type field is coded as 1100 for an individual address and 1110 for group addresses. The bits that follow the 1100 code contain a prefix of 1 and then 10 digits of binary coded decimal (BCD) values. The remaining bits are coded as 1s. The ATM mapping functions (MF) simply map these addresses, without alteration, into the address fields of the ICIP_CLS_PDU.

The protocol identifier (PI) identifies the ICIP user, and (for the ATM B-ICI) service can range from the decimal values of 48 to 63. The PAD length (PL) field indicates that the octets in the PDU are 32-bit aligned, but is set to 0 for this operation.

The quality of service (QOS) field is not used and is present (and set to all 0s) to ensure alignment with SMDS—which includes it to ensure alignment with the metropolitan area network (MAN), which does not define how it is used . . . (I did not make this up). The CRC 32 indication bit (CIB) is used to indicate the absence or presence of the CRC32 field. For B-ICI, it is set to 0.

The header extension length (HEL) is a 3-bit field indicating the number of 32-bit words that exist in the header extension (HE) field. It is set to 011 to indicate a 12-octet header extension field.

The bridging (BDG) field is used to insure alignment with SMDS (and MAN). The HE field contains service specific information (SI), including the ICIP version (version is 1), as well as carrier and explicit selection subfields (which are not yet defined).

Finally, the information (I) field (not shown in figure) can contain ICIP-user data, which can range from 36 to 9288 octets.

The header and trailer shown at the common part convergence sublayer (CPCS) are identical to the AAL3/4 header (Chapter 7).

ATM LAN Emulation

As discussed in earlier chapters, ATM is a connection-oriented technology. It sets up virtual connections between two or more parties. The virtual connections are identified with virtual circuit IDs, known in ATM as virtual path identifiers and virtual channel identifiers.

Since LANs are connectionless and use media access control (MAC) addresses to identify communicating end stations (ES), some means must be provided to correlate MAC addresses with ATM identifiers. One approach is called *LAN emulation.* It is so named because an ATM backbone network operates between the LANs, and the LANs are unaware of this interface. The ATM network plays the role of a LAN. The approach is called LAN emulation, even though the ATM network may indeed be a LAN. But it does not use common LAN protocols, such as Ethernet.

As shown in Figure 11–16, the address resolution protocol (ARP) is used to translate and map the MAC addresses and ATM identifiers. A LAN emulation server (LES) provides the mapping service. When a LAN endstation sends a MAC frame to a router (which is called a LAN emulation client, or LEC), the router forms an ARP request with the destination MAC address in the target physical address of the ARP packet and sends it to the LES. The LES retrieves the ATM Id of the destination LES router and returns it to the inquiring LES in an ARP response.

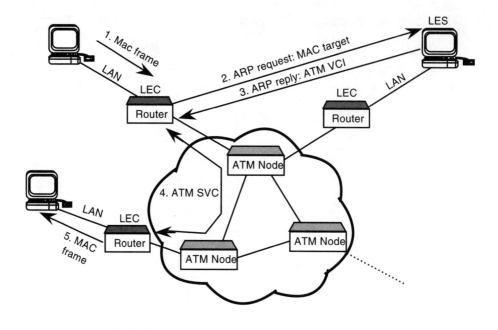

LES is LAN emulation server
LEC is LAN emulation client

Figure 11–16   ATM LAN emulation.

Next, this router sets up an ATM virtual connection with the destination router through the ATM switched virtual call protocol, Q.2931.
After the connection is established, traffic is placed into ATM cells and
relayed to the destination router, which then strips away the ATM headers, reassembles the MAC traffic into a MAC frame, and delivers it to the
destination ES.

RFC 1483 AND RFC 1577

The Internet authorities have released two requests for comments
(RFCs) that describe how an ATM network is used to carry traffic of
other protocols and networks. The ideas behind these RFCs are summarized in Figure 11–17. RFC 1483 describes two different methods for carrying connectionless network traffic over an ATM network. Paraphrasing
RFC 1483: The first method allows the multiplexing of multiple protocols

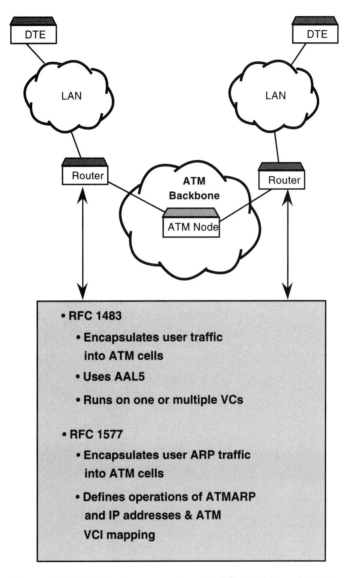

Figure 11–17   Major aspects of RFCs 1483 and 1577.

over a single ATM virtual circuit. The protocol family of a transported PDU is identified by prefixing the PDU by an IEEE 802.2 logical link control (LLC) header. This method is called "LLC Encapsulation." The second method performs higher-layer protocol multiplexing implicitly by ATM virtual circuits (VCs). It is called "VC Based Multiplexing."

RFC 1577 specifies how to carry IP datagrams and ATM address resolution protocol (ATM ARP) requests and replies over ATM adaptation layer type 5 (AAL5). It also defines the role of an ATM ARP server and the use of the ARP in resolving IP addresses and ATM virtual circuit IDs.

The ATM Data Exchange Interface (DXI)

The ATM data exchange interface (DXI) was developed to offload some of the more complex operations of ATM from a conventional customer CPE. This interface is abbreviated ATM DXI.

An additional piece of equipment, the data circuit-terminating equipment, for this operation is installed to support ATM DXI. It is usually implemented with a data service unit (DSU) (see Figure 11–18). Once this equipment is installed, the CPE is relieved of the requirements

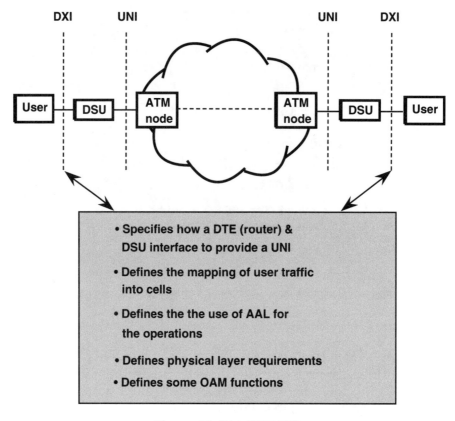

Figure 11–18   ATM DXI.

to support all the features of the ATM CS and the SAR. The CPE's principal job is to perform AAL3/4, or AAL5 CPCS encapsulation. Its only other requirement is to encapsulate this PDU into an ATM DXI frame. These operations are rather modest and do not require any significant "refitting" of the CPE. The DSU performs the SAR operations and acts as the interface to the ATM network at the ATM UNI.

DXI Modes

DXI operates with three modes: Mode 1a is used only for AAL5, mode 1b operates with AAL3/4 and AAL5, and mode 2 operates with AAL3/4 and AAL5.

The principal differences between these modes lie in how many virtual connections are allowed across the interface and the size of the user payload (SDU) that is permitted. Additionally, each mode defines slightly different headers and trailers that are created by the DTE and/or DCE at the CPCS sublayer. Table 11–2 summarizes the major features of the three DXI modes (not all modes are described in this section).

Figure 11–19 shows the relationship of the DTE layers and the DCE/SDU layers for AAL5 traffic. The DTE DXI data link layer is closely related to an HDLC interface. Indeed, the use of HDLC-type frames eases the task of the DTE because HDLC is well known and imple-

Table 11–2   ATM Data Exchange Interface (DXI)

• *Mode 1a*
Up to 1023 virtual connections
AAL5 only
Up to 9232 octets in DTE SDU
16-bit FCS between DTE and DCE

• *Mode 1b*
Up to 1023 virtual connections
AAL3/4 for at least one virtual connection
AAL5 for others
Up to 9232 octets in DTE SDU for AAL5
Up to 9224 octets in DTE SDU for AAL3/4
16-bit FCS between DTE and DCE

• *Mode 2*
Up to 16,777,215 virtual connections
AAL5 and AAL3/4 (2^{24-1}): one per virtual connection
Up to 65,535 (2^{16-1}) octets in DTE SDU
32-bit FCS between DTE and DCE

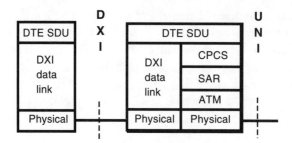

Figure 11–19   Layers for modes 1a and 1b for AAL5.

mented in many products. The task of the DTE is a relatively simple one—to create a header that will provide enough information for the DCE to create a virtual circuit in the ATM network. In essence, the DXI header contains a DXI frame address (DFA), which is used to convey the VPI and VCI values between the DTE and DCE. The DFA is 10 bits in length for modes 1a and 1b and 24 bits long in mode 2.

Figure 11–20 shows the activities for the support of AAL5 in modes 1a and 1b. The basic idea is to convey the DTE SDU across the ATM DXI to the DCE. The SDU is nothing more than the I field of the particular AAL protocol. This figure shows that the DTE encapsulates the DTE SDU into the DXI frame. The headers and trailers of this frame are then used by the DCE to receive the traffic and establish the virtual connection. The DCE is required to perform the ATM adaptation layer 5 common part convergence sublayer (AAL5 CPCS) as well as AAL segmentation and reassembly operations (AAL5 SAR). The DCE also contains the ATM layer, which is responsible for the management of the cell header.

This specification does not define the operations of the service specific convergence sublayer, which is defined in ITU-T recommendation I.363.

DXI Support for Frame Relay

The following requirements must be met at the DXI for Frame Relay:

Frame relay QOS will remain intact from end-to-end.
The Frame Relay user shall not be aware of the ATM operations.
The Frame Relay DLCI must be mapped to the ATM VPI/VCI and vice versa.
The Frame Relay DE bit must be mapped to the ATM CLP bit.

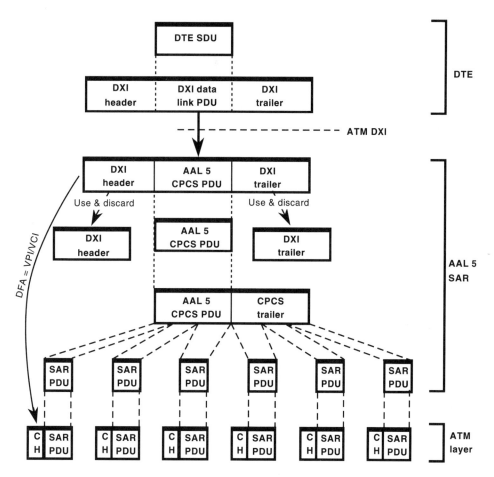

Figure 11–20   Modes 1a and 1b for AAL5.

QOS remains intact end-to-end.

Order of frames will remain intact end-to-end.

Congestion and flow control operations must be consistent end-to-end.

THE FRAME UNI (FUNI)

As discussed earlier, the DXI topology requires a data service unit (DSU, also known as channel service unit [CSU]) to rest between the user device and the ATM switch. This device provides several T1 functions such as the conversion of unipolar code to bipolar code, loopback testing, and other diagnostic operations. The DSU runs the ATM interface on the ATM side of the line, which relieves the end user from having to segment the traffic into cells and otherwise deal with the cell technology.

For the FUNI topology, the DSU is not required. The user runs its traffic directly between its device and the ATM switch. This approach is less expensive than the DXI option because the DSU is not necessary. The user frame is sent to the ATM switch, where AAL is executed to segment the frame into cells. So, the UNI is frame-based and not cell-based. However, the UNI is not a Frame Relay UNI; it is not as function-rich as Frame Relay.

The FUNI interface is quite simple. It requires a software setup between the user device and the ATM switch. Additionally, the FUNI payload (the I field) can be large (if necessary), which makes this interface attractive in relation to running the small cells across the communications line between the user and the ATM switch (as in the DXI option).

ARE DXI AND FUNI NEEDED?

The DXI and FUNI protocols were introduced to allow a user to use a high-speed ATM network but not have to install an ATM line card in the user equipment. ATM hardware is expensive, but its costs are falling. In the not too distant future, cost will not be a factor in deciding to place ATM in the user workstation, and solutions such as DXI and FUNI will no longer be used.

In addition, most user workstations in a typical company use Ethernet line cards to run on the LAN. The ATM interface is not an issue. The router runs the ATM UNI, and DXI and FUNI are not considered effective alternatives to a native mode ATM UNI between a router and the ATM switch.

MULTIPROTOCOL OVER ATM (MPOA)

The principal objective of MPOA is to support the transfer of intersubnet unicast traffic in an Internet environment, but through an ATM backbone. That is, MPOA provides mechanisms to circumvent a slower internet for a faster ATM network. It defines how layer three packets (typically, the Internet Protocol [IP]) are sent over ATM virtual channel connections (VCCs) without requiring routers in the data path. The goal of MPOA is to combine bridging and routing with ATM in a situation where diverse protocols and network topologies exist.

MPOA supports the concept of virtual routing, which is the separation of internetwork layer route calculation and forwarding. The idea behind virtual routing is to enhance the manageability of internetworking by decreasing the number of devices that are configured to perform route calculation. In so doing, virtual routing increases scalability by reducing the number of devices that participate in the internetwork layer route calculations.

Label-based switching can be employed by MPOA (see Chapter 8) to route the traffic. The most common name for the label identifier is a *tag*. The tag is a value of a few bits, used in place of the IP address for routing. It is examined on a complete value and not on a bit-by-bit closest match. Many of these operations can be performed in hardware, which further speeds up the process. The tag can be an ATM VPI/VCI or a separate field in the protocol data unit.

Companion Protocols to MPOA

MPOA is one of several ATM-based internetworking protocols that are designed for ATM to act as the backbone for multiple LANs and/or internets. Also, some of these systems are earlier efforts and represent an evolution to MPOA. In others, they are incorporated into the MPOA protocol.

First, Classical IP over ATM is part of the Logical IP Subnet (LIS) and is published as RFC 1577. It defines the operations for encapsulating IP datagrams and the ATM address resolution protocol (ATMARP) traffic over ATM and AAL5. Its principal concern is to specify the operation of IP over an ATM network and the resolving of IP addressees and ATM virtual channel Ids.

LAN emulation (LANE) was introduced earlier in this chapter. It is used when an ATM network connects multiple LANs. These LANs are unaware that LANE and ATM are involved in the process.

The Next Hop Resolution Protocol (NHRP) allows intermediate routers to be bypassed and traffic diverted to ATM. The MPOA uses NHRP, and embellishes it with added features.

Once again, I refer you to *ATM Volume III* for more information on ATM internetworking operations.

SUMMARY

ATM is viewed as a transport mechanism for user multiapplication traffic as well as traffic from other networks. Generally, ATM internetworking entails encapsulating user-network PDUs into the ATM cell through the invocation of AAL1, 3/4, and 5 modes.

The ATM DXI was published by the ATM Forum to provide a means of offloading some of the more complex AAL and ATM functions from a user DCE.

12

Synchronous Optical Network (SONET)

This chapter introduces the Synchronous Optical Network (SONET), also known as the Synchronous Digital Hierarchy (SDH). From the B-ISDN perspective, SONET and SDH provide the physical layer for ATM networks. For simplicity, the term SONET is used, instead of SONET/ SDH.

This chapter is a review of the SONET material introduced in the flagship book for this series, *Emerging Communications Technologies*. The reader familiar with SONET can skip this chapter and proceed to Chapters 13 and 14, which explain the OAM relationships of ATM and SONET, as well as other physical layer protocols and interfaces that are used by ATM. The reader should be familiar with the subject of networks and synchronization, discussed in Chapter 2, in the section entitled "Timing and Synchronization in Digital Networks."

PURPOSE OF SONET

SONET is an optical-based carrier (transport) network utilizing synchronous operations between the network components. The term SONET is used in North America, while the term SDH is used in Europe. SONET is:

- A carrier transport technology that provides high availability with self-healing ring topologies
- A multivendor approach allowing multivendor connections without conversions between the vendors' systems (with some exceptions)
- A network that uses synchronous operations with powerful, yet simple, multiplexing and demultiplexing capabilities
- A system that allows the direct access to low-rate multiplexed signals
- A network that is scalable to higher capacity as technologies improve
- A system that provides extensive OAM services to the network user and administrator

SONET provides a number of attractive features when compared with current technology. First, it is an integrated network standard on which all types of traffic can be transported. Second, the SONET standard is based on the optical fiber technology that provides superior performance vis-à-vis the older microwave or cable systems. Third, because SONET is a worldwide standard, it is now possible for different vendors to interface their equipment without conversion operations (with some exceptions—depending on how the optional headers in the SONET frame are implemented).

Fourth, SONET efficiently combines, consolidates, and segregates traffic from different locations through one facility. This concept, known as *grooming,* eliminates back hauling and other inefficient techniques currently being used in carrier networks. *Back hauling* is a technique in which user payload (say, from user A) is carried past a switch with a line to A and sent to another endpoint (say, user B). Then, the traffic for B is dropped, and user A's payload is sent back to the switch and relayed back to A. In present carrier network configurations, grooming can eliminate back hauling, but it requires expensive configurations (such as back-to-back multiplexers connected with cables, panels, or electronic cross-connect equipment).

Fifth, SONET eliminates back-to-back multiplexing overhead by using new techniques in the grooming process. These techniques are implemented in a new type of equipment, called an add-drop multiplexer (ADM).

Sixth, the synchronous aspect of SONET makes for more stable network operations. Later sections in this chapter explain how synchronous networks experience fewer errors than the older asynchronous networks and provide much better techniques for multiplexing and grooming payloads.

Seventh, SONET has notably improved OAM features relative to current technology. Approximately 5 percent of the bandwidth is devoted to OAM.

Eighth, SONET employs digital transmission schemes. Thus, the traffic is relatively immune to noise and other impairments on the communications channel, and the system can use the efficient time division multiplexing (TDM) operations.

PRESENT TRANSPORT SYSTEMS AND SONET

The present transport carrier system varies in the different geographical regions of the world. The structure is different in Japan than in North America, which is different than the structure in Europe. This disparate approach is complex and expensive and makes the interworking of the systems difficult. Moreover, companies that build hardware and software for carrier systems must implement multiple commercial platforms for what is essentially one technology.

While SONET does not ensure equipment compatibility, it does provide a basis for vendors to build worldwide standards. Moreover, as shown in Figure 12–1, SONET is backwards compatible, in that it supports the current transport carriers' asynchronous systems in North America, Europe, and Japan. This feature is quite important because it allows different digital signals and hierarchies to operate with a common transport system, which is SONET.

FOUNDATIONS FOR SONET

SONET did not just appear suddenly on the scene. Extensive research work has been underway for over a decade on many of the features that are found in SONET. One of these projects was Metrobus, an optical communications system developed at AT&T's Bell Labs in the early 1980s. Its name was derived from its purpose: to be placed in a metropolitan area to serve as a high-speed optical transport network.

Metrobus demonstrated the feasibility of effectively using several new techniques that found their way into SONET. Among the more notable were: (1) single-step multiplexing, (2) synchronous timing, (3) ex-

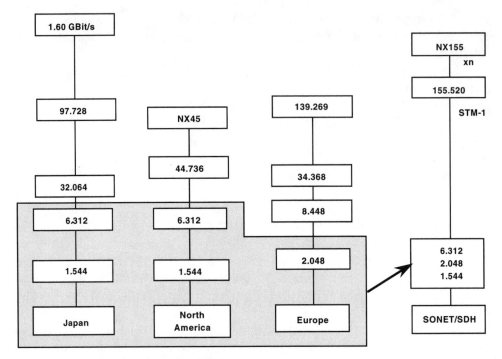

Note: Unless noted otherwise, speeds in Mbit/s

Figure 12–1   SONET support for current technologies.

tensive overhead octets, (4) accessing low-level signals directly, (5) point-to-multipoint multiplexing, and (6) the employment of 150 Mbit/s (146.432) media as the network transmission capacity. This latter decision, along with the ensuing research and testing, was important, because this signal rate can accommodate voice, video, and data signals, compressed HDTV, as well as exploit CMOS technology. Moreover, it permitted the use of relatively inexpensive graded-index, multimode fibers, instead of the more expensive single-mode fibers [LEE93], although single-mode fiber is now the media of choice for SONET.

SONET was developed in the early 1980s and was submitted to the T1 Committee during this period. This initial proposal had a bit rate of 50.688 Mbit/s, a 125 μs signal, and a frame format of 3 rows by 265 columns (264 octets ∗ 3 rows ∗ 8 bits per octet ∗ 8000 = 50,688,000). It did not arouse much interest until the Metrobus activity became recognized.

Later, using the innovative features of Metrobus, the SONET designers made modifications to the original SONET T1 proposal, principally in the size of the frame and the manner in which DS0, DS1, and DS3 signals were mapped into the SONET frame.

From 1984 to 1986, various alternatives were considered by the T1 Committee, which settled on the STS-1 rate as a base standard. During this time, the ITU-T had rejected the STS-1 rate as a base rate in favor of an STM-1 rate of 155.520 Mbit/s base rate. For a while, it appeared that the North American and European approaches might not converge, but the SONET frame syntax and structure were altered one more time to a rate of 51.84 Mbit/s, which permitted the rate to be multiplexed (concatenated) by an integer of three to the European preference of 155.52 Mbit/s. This work has resulted in almost complete compatibility between the North American and European approaches.

SYNCHRONOUS NETWORKS

Most digital networks in operation today have been designed to work as asynchronous systems. With this approach, each terminal (device) in the network runs with its own clock. These clocks are not synchronized from a central reference point.

The purpose of the terminal clock is to locate the digital 1s and 0s in the incoming data stream—a very important operation in a digital network. Obviously, if bits are lost in certain payloads, such as data, the traffic may be unintelligible to the receiver. What is more important, the loss of bits or the inability to locate them accurately can cause further synchronization problems. When this happens, the receiver usually does not deliver the traffic to the user, because it is simpler to discard the traffic than to initiate resynchronization efforts.

Because each clock runs independently of others, large variations can occur between the terminal's clock and the rate at which the data is received by the terminal. For example, experience has demonstrated that a DS3 signal may experience a variation of up to 1789 bit/s for a 44.736 Mbit/s signal.

Moreover, signals such as DS1s are multiplexed in stages up to DS2, DS3, and so on, and extra bits are added to the stream of data (bit stuffing) to account for timing variations in each stream. The lower level signals, such as DS1, are not accessible or visible at the higher rates. Consequently, the original stream of traffic must be demultiplexed if these signals are to be accessed.

SONET is based on synchronous transmission, meaning the average frequency of all the clocks in the network are the same (synchronous) or nearly the same (plesiochronous). As a result of this approach, the clocks are referenced to a stable reference point; therefore, the need to align the data streams or synchronize clocks is less necessary, because the synchronous signals, such as DS1/CEPT1, are accessible, and demultiplexing is not needed to access the bit streams. Also, the synchronous signals can be stacked together without bit stuffing. For those situations in which reference frequencies may vary, SONET uses pointers to allow the streams to "float" within the payload envelope. Indeed, synchronous clocking is the key to pointers; it allows a flexible allocation and alignment of the payload within the transmission envelope.

This concept of a synchronous system is elegantly simple. By holding specific bits in a silicon memory buffer for a defined and predictable period of time, it is possible to move information from one part of a PDU (a payload envelope) to another part. It also allows a system to know where the bits are located at all times. Of course, this idea is "old hat" to software engineers, but it is a different way of thinking for other designers. As one AT&T engineer put it, "Since the bits are lined up in time, we now know where they are in both time and space. So, in a sense, we can now move information in four dimensions, instead of the usual three."

The U.S. implementation of SONET uses a central clocking source—for example, from an end office. This central office must use a highly accurate clocking source known as stratum 3. Stratum 3 clocking requires an accuracy of 1.6 parts in 1 billion elements. Chapter 2 provides more detailed explanations of synchronization, and clocking operations, and the accuracy levels of the stratum 1–4n clocks.

OPTICAL FIBER—THE BEDROCK FOR SONET

It is likely that the reader has at least a general understanding and appreciation of the advantages of using optical fiber as the transmission medium for a telecommunications system. This section will summarize the major aspects of optical fiber, with a few thoughts.

- Optical transmission has a very large information capacity. Gigabit/s rates are easily obtainable in today's systems.
- Optical fibers have electrically nonconducting photons instead of the electrons found in metallic cables, such as wires or coaxial cables. This characteristic is attractive for applications in which the transmission path traverses hostile environments. For example,

optical cables are not subject to electrical sparks or interference from electrical components in a building or computer machine room.

- Optical fibers suffer less loss of signal strength than copper wire or coaxial cables. The strength of a light signal is reduced only slightly after propagation through several miles of cable.
- Optical fibers are more secure than copper cable transmission methods. Transmission of light does not yield residual intelligence that is found in electrical transmission.
- Optical cables are very small (roughly the size of a hair) and weigh very little. For example, 900 copper wire pairs pulled through 1000 feet in a building would weigh approximately 4800 pounds. Two optical fibers, with protective covers pulled the same distance, weigh only 80 pounds and yet yield greater capacity.
- Optical fibers are relatively easy to install and operate in high and low temperatures.
- Due to the low signal loss, the error rate for optical fibers is very low—a point made earlier in Chapter 6 in the discussion on the rationale for the size of an ATM cell.

Without further ado, we now examine how SONET exploits the performance of optical fiber.

PERTINENT STANDARDS

The SONET architecture is based on standards developed by the American National Standards Institute (ANSI) and the Exchange Carriers Standards Association (ECSA). In addition, Bellcore has been instrumental in the development of these standards. Although SONET has been designed to accommodate the North American DS3 (45 Mbit/s) signal, the ITU-T used SONET for the development and publication of the Synchronous Digital Hierarchy (SDH).

Due to the complexity of implementing a system such as SONET, the SONET implementation in the United States is divided into three phases. Phase 1 is divided into the implementation of the basic transfer rates, multiplexing scheme, and testing of the frame formats. Phase 2 consists of a number of mapping operations into the optical envelope from other tributaries such as FDDI and ATM. Phase 3 deals with more elaborate implementations to support operations, administration, maintenance, and provisioning (OAM).

The SONET standard has been incorporated into a synchronous digital hierarchy standard published by the ITU-T. In addition, Bellcore supports this standard on behalf of the United States Regional Bell Operating Companies (RBOCs). The relevant documents for SONET/ SDH are listed in Table 12–1.

Table 12–1   SONET/SDH Standards

SONET Add-Drop Multiplex Equipment (SONET ADM) Generic Criteria, TR-TSY-000496, Issue 2 (Bellcore, September 1989).

Integrated Digital Loop Carrier System Generic Requirements, Objectives, and Interface, TR-TSY-000303, Issue 1 (Bellcore, September 1986) plus Revisions and Supplements.

Digital Synchronization Network Plan, TA-NPL-000436, Issue 1 (Bellcore, November 1986).

Synchronous Optical Network (SONET) Transport Systems: Common Generic Criteria, TR-TSY-000253, Issue 1 (Bellcore, September 1989). (A module of TSGR, FR-NWT-0000440.)

Transport Systems Generic Requirements (TSGR): Common Requirements, TR-TSY-000499, Issue 3 (Bellcore, December 1989). (A module of TSGR, FR-NWT-000440.)

Synchronous Optical Network (SONET) Transport Systems: Common Generic Criteria, TA-NWT-000253, Issue 6 (Bellcore, September 1990), plus Bulletin No. 1, August 1991.

Generic Reliability Assurance Requirements for Fiber Optic Transport Systems, TA-NWT-000418, Issue 3 (Bellcore, to be issued).

ANSIT1.101, Synchronization Interface Standards for Digital Networks.

ANSIT1.106, Digital Hierarchy-Optical Interface Specifications (Single-mode).

ANSIT1.102, Digital Hierarchy-Electrical Interfaces.

G.700 Framework of the Series G.700, G.800, and G.900 Recommendations.

G.701 Vocabulary of Digital Transmission and Multiplexing, and Pulse Code Modulation (PCM) terms.

G.702 Digital Hierarchy Bit Rates.

G.703 Physical/Electrical Characteristics of Hierarchical Digital Interfaces.

G.704 Synchronous Frame Structures Used at Primary and Secondary Hierarchical Levels.

G.705 Characteristics Required to Terminate Digital Links on a Digital Exchange.

G.706 Frame Alignment and Cyclic Redundancy Check (CRC) Procedures Relating to Basic Frame Structures Defined in Recommendation G.704.

G.707 Synchronous Digital Hierarchy Bit Rates.

G.708 Network Node Interface for the Synchronous Digital Hierarchy.

G.709 Synchronous Multiplexing Structure.

TYPICAL SONET TOPOLOGY

Figure 12–2 shows a typical topology for a SONET network. End-user devices operating on LANs (FDDI, 802.3, 802.5, etc.) and digital transport systems (such as DS1, E1, etc.) are attached to the network through a SONET service adapter. This service adapter is also called an access node, a terminal, or a terminal multiplexer. This machine is responsible for supporting the end-user interface by sending and receiving traffic from LANs, DS1, DS3, E1, ATM nodes, and others. It is really a concentrator at the sending site, because it consolidates multiple user traffic into a payload envelope for transport onto the SONET network. It performs a complementary, yet opposite, service at the receiving site.

The user signals, whatever they are, T1, E1, ATM cells, and the like, are converted (mapped) into a standard format called the synchronous transport signal (STS), which is the basic building block of the SONET multiplexing hierarchy. The STS signal is an electrical signal, and the notation in Figure 12–2 of "STS-n" means that the service adapter can multiplex the STS signal into higher integer multiples of the base rate. The base rate is 51.84 Mbit/s in North America and 155.520 Mbit/s in Europe. Therefore, from the perspective of a SONET terminal, the SDH base rate in Europe is an STS-3 multiplexed signal (51.84 * 3 = 155.520 Mbit/s).

The terminal/service adapter (access node) shown in Figure 12–2 is implemented as the end-user interface machine, or as an add-drop multiplexer. The latter implementation multiplexes various STS-n input streams onto optical fiber channels, which now is called the optical carrier signal and designated with the notation OC-n, where n represents the multiplexing integer. OC-n streams can also be multiplexed and demultiplexed with this machine. The term "add-drop" means that the machine can add payload or drop payload onto one of the two channels. Remaining traffic passes straight through the multiplexer without additional processing.

The digital cross-connect (DCS) machine usually acts as a hub in the SONET network. Not only can it add and drop payload, but it can also operate with different carrier rates, such as DS1, OC-n, and CEPT1, as well as make two-way cross-connections between them. It consolidates and separates different types of traffic. The DCS is designed to eliminate devices called back-to-back multiplexers. As we learned earlier, these devices contain a plethora of cables, jumpers, and intermediate distribution frames. SONET does not need all these physical components because cross-connection operations are performed by hardware and software.

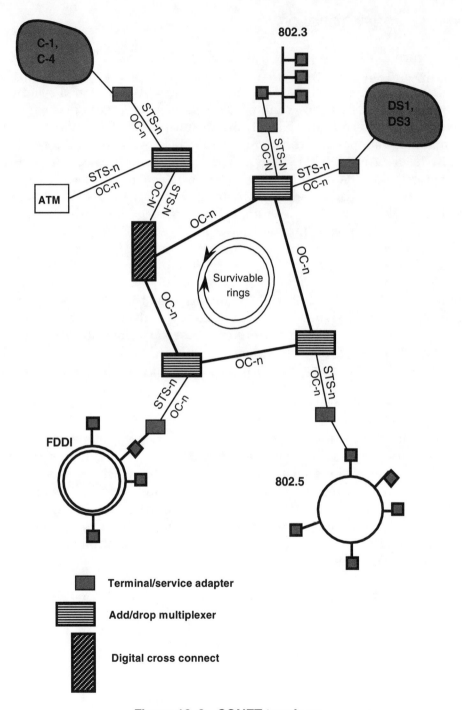

Figure 12–2   SONET topology.

The topology can be set up as either a ring or a point-to-point system. In most networks, the ring is a dual ring, operating with two optical fibers. The structure of the dual ring topology permits the network to recover automatically from failures on the channels and in the channel/machine interfaces. This is known as a self-healing ring and is explained later in this chapter.

While SONET establishes no strict requirements on how ATM operations relate to these SONET components, and, because implementations are vendor-specific, the ATM layer could reside at a SONET service adapter, an add-drop multiplexer, or a DCS. Later discussions in this chapter and in Chapters 13 and 14 explain the ATM and SONET relationships.

Figure 12–3 shows another example of a SONET topology and its multiplexing schemes. Service adapters can accept any signal ranging from DS1/CEPT1 to B-ISDN, as well as ATM cells. Additionally, sub-DS1 rates (such as DS0) are supported. The purpose of the service adapter is to map these signals into STS-1 envelopes or multiples thereof. As ex-

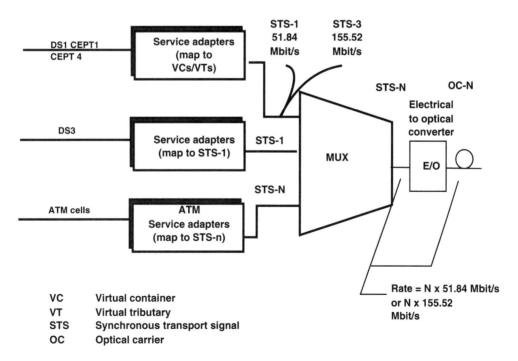

VC	Virtual container
VT	Virtual tributary
STS	Synchronous transport signal
OC	Optical carrier

Figure 12–3 SONET multiplexing.

plained earlier, in North America all traffic is initially converted to a synchronous STS-1 signal (51.84 Mbit/s or higher). In Europe, the service adapters convert the payload to an STS-3 signal (155.520 Mbit/s).

Lower-speed signals (such as DS1 and CEPT1) are first multiplexed into virtual tributaries (VTs, a North American term) or virtual containers (VCs, an European term), which are sub-STS-1 payloads. Then, several STS-1s are multiplexed together to form an STS-n signal. These signals are sent to an electrical/optical (E/O) converter where a conversion is made to a OC-n optical signal.

SONET Configuration

Figure 12–4 shows a simplified diagram of a SONET configuration. Three types of equipment are employed in a SONET system: (1) path terminating equipment, (2) line terminating equipment, and (3) section terminating equipment (regenerator). These components are introduced in this section and described in more detail later in the chapter.

The path terminating equipment is a terminal or multiplexer that is responsible for mapping the user payload (DS1, CEPT4, FDDI, etc.) into a SONET format. It must extend to the network elements that assemble

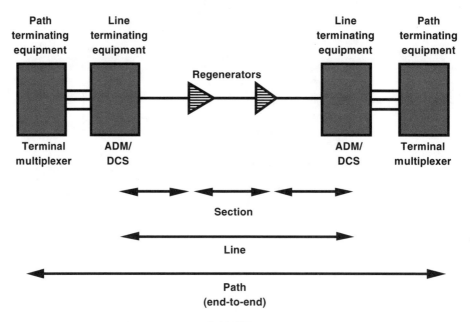

Figure 12–4   SONET configuration.

and disassemble the payload for the user CPE. The line terminating equipment is a hub. It provides services to the path terminating equipment, notably multiplexing, synchronization, and automatic protection switching. It does not extend to the CPE, but operates between network elements. The section terminating equipment is a regenerator. It also performs functions similar to HDLC-type protocols: frame alignment, scrambling, as well as error detection and monitoring. It is responsible for signal reception and signal regeneration. The section terminating equipment may be part of the line terminating equipment.

OAM at the Three Components.   Each of these components utilizes substantial OAM information (overhead). Path level overhead is inserted at the SONET terminal and carried end-to-end to the receiving terminal. The overhead is added to DS1 signals when they are mapped into virtual tributaries.

Line overhead is used for STS-n signals. This information is created by line terminating equipment such as STS-n multiplexers. The SONET line concept is important to network robustness, because a line span is protected in case of line or equipment failure, or a deterioration of conditions. Functions operate at the line level to provide for alternate paths—an operation called protection switching. Part of the line overhead is used for protection switching.

The section overhead is used between adjacent network elements such as the regenerators. It contains fields for the framing of the traffic, the identification of the STS payload, error detection, order wires, and a large variety of network-specific functions.

SONET LAYERS

ATM has been designated by the ITU-T to operate with SONET. Figure 12–5 shows the relationship of the ATM layers and the layers associated with SONET. The virtual channel and virtual path layers of ATM run on top of the SONET physical layer.

The physical layer is modeled on three major entities: transmission path, digital line, and the regenerator section. These layers correspond to the SONET section, line, and path operations that were introduced in the previous section.

The section and photonic layers comprise the SONET regenerators. The photonic layer is responsible for converting the electrical signal to an optical signal and then regenerating the optical signal as it is carried

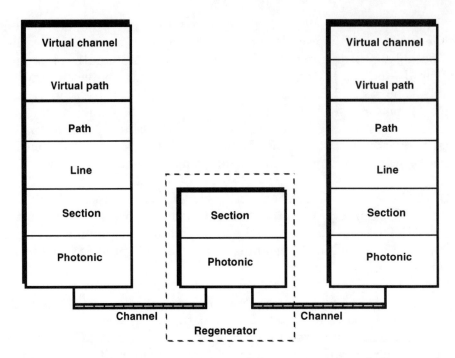

Note: Layer stacks may vary at multiplexers, switches, and other line terminating equipment

Figure 12–5   A SONET/ATM layer configuration.

through the network. This stack may vary in different implementations. For example, at an ATM switch, the SONET path layer might not be accessed because it is intended as an end-to-end operation. The manner in which the layers are executed depends on the actual design of the equipment.

AUTOMATIC PROTECTION SWITCHING (APS)

One of the more interesting aspects of SONET is the provision for automatic protection switching or APS. This feature permits the network to react to failed optical lines and/or interfaces by switching to an alternate facility (as illustrated in Figure 12–6). Protection switching operations are initiated for a number of reasons. As an example, the network manager may issue a command to switch the working facility operations to the protection facility for purposes of maintenance or testing. Or, more

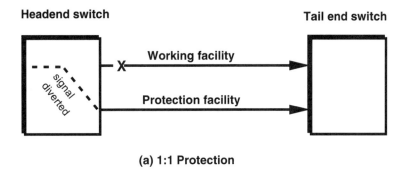

(a) 1:1 Protection

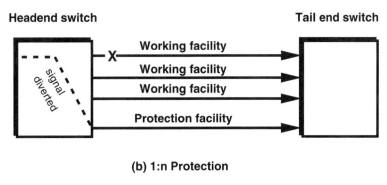

(b) 1:n Protection

Figure 12–6   Protection switching.

commonly, APS operations are initiated because of the loss of a connection or the deterioration in the quality of the signal.

APS can be provisioned for a 1:1 or a 1:n facility. With the 1:1 option, each working facility (fiber) is backed up by a protection facility
(fiber). With a 1:n option, one protection facility may service from one to
a maximum of fourteen facilities.

As a general practice, the 1:1 operation entails the transmission of
traffic on both the working and protection facilities. Both signals are
monitored at the receiving end (the tail end) for failures or degradation of
signal quality. Based on this analysis, the working or protection facility
can be selected, and switching operations can be sent back to the sender
(headend) to discern which facility is being employed for the transmission of the traffic.

For the 1:n APS, the switching is reverted. That is to say, the traffic
is sent across the working facilities and the protection facility is only em-

ployed upon the detection of a failure. So the protection facility is not employed until a working facility fails.

PAYLOADS AND ENVELOPES

SONET is designed to support a wide variety of payloads. Table 12–2 summarizes some typical payloads of existing technologies. The SONET multiplexer accepts these payloads as sub-STS-1 signals (or VTs).

Table 12–3 shows the relationships of the OC and STS levels. The synchronous transport signal-level 1 forms the basis for the optical carrier-level 1 signal. OC-1 is the foundation for the synchronous optical signal hierarchy. The higher-level signals are derived by the multiplexing of the lower-level signals. As stated earlier, the high-level signals are designated as STS-n and OC-n, where n is an integer number.

As illustrated in Table 12–3, OC transmission systems are multiplexed by the n values of 1, 3, 9, 12, 18, 24, 36, 48, and 192. In the future, multiplexing integrals greater than 192 will be incorporated into the standard. Presently, signal levels OC-3, OC-12, and OC-48 are the most widely supported multiples of OC-1.

Envelopes

The basic transmission unit for SONET is the STS-1 synchronous payload envelope (SPE or frame). SDH starts at the STS-3 level. All levels are comprised of 8-bit octets transmitted serially on the optical fiber. For ease of documentation, the payload is depicted as a 2-dimensional map (see Figure 12–7). The map is comprised of N rows and M columns. Each entry in this map represents the individual octets of an SPE. (The

Table 12–2 Typical SONET Payloads

Type	Digital Bit Rate	Voice Circuits	T1	DS3
DS1	1.544 Mbit/s	24	1	—
CEPT1	2.048 Mbit/s	30	—	—
DS1C	3.154 Mbit/s	48	2	—
DS2	6.312 Mbit/s	96	4	—
DS3	44.736 Mbit/s	672	28	1

Table 12–3   SONET Signal Hierarchy

OC Level	STS Level	Line Rate (Mbits/s)
OC-1*	STS-1	51.840
OC-3*	STS-3	155.520
OC-9	STS-9	466.560
OC-12*	STS-12	622.080
OC-18	STS-18	933.120
OC-24	STS-24	1244.160
OC-36	STS-36	1866.230
OC-48*	STS-48	2488.32
OC-96	STS-96	4876.64
OC-192	STS-19	9953.280

*Currently, the more popular implementations
(Note: Certain levels are not used in Europe, North America, and Japan.)

"F" is a flag and is placed in front of the envelope to identify where the envelope begins.)

The octets are transmitted in sequential order, beginning in the top left-hand corner through the first row, and then through the second row, until the last octet is transmitted—to the last row and last column (0_n).

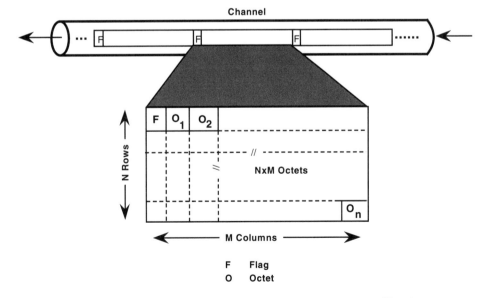

Figure 12–7   The synchronous payload envelope (SPE).

The envelopes are sent contiguously and without interruption, and the payload is inserted into the envelope under stringent timing rules. Notwithstanding, a user payload may be inserted into more than one envelope, which means the payload need not be inserted at the exact beginning of the part of the envelope reserved for this traffic. It can be placed in any part of this area, and a pointer is created to indicate where it begins. This approach allows the network to operate synchronously, yet accept asynchronous traffic.

Figure 12–8 depicts the SONET STS-1 envelope. It consists of 90 columns and 9 rows of 12-bit octets and carries 810 octets or 6480 bits. SONET transmits at 8000 frames/second. Therefore, the frame length is 125 microseconds (µs). This approach translates into a transfer rate of 51.840 Mbit/s (6480 × 8000 = 51,840,000).

The first three columns of the frame contain transport overhead, which is divided into 27 octets, with 9 octets allocated for section overhead and 18 octets allocated for line overhead. The other 87 columns comprise the payload or STS-1 SPE (although the first column of the envelope capacity is reserved for STS path overhead). The section overhead

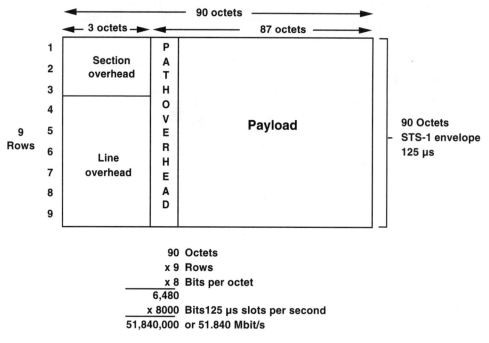

Figure 12–8   STS-1 envelope.

in this envelope is also known as region overhead in certain parts of the world, and the line overhead is also known as the multiplex section. The frame consists of two distinct parts: the user SPE part and the transport part.

Since the user payload consists of 86 columns or 774 octets, it operates at 49.536 Mbit/s (774 * 8 bits per octet * 8000 = 49,536,000). Therefore, the user payload can support VTs up to the DS3 rate (44.736 Mbit/s).

The SDH envelope begins at STS-3. As shown in Figure 12–9, it consists of three STS-1 envelopes and operates at a bit rate of 155.52 Mbit/s (51.840 × 3 = 155.52 Mbit/s). The STS-3 SPE has sufficient capacity to carry a broadband ISDN H4 channel.

The original SONET standard published by Bellcore had no provision for the European rate of 140 Mbit/s. Moreover, it was inefficient in how it dealt with the European 2.048 Mbit/s system. Bellcore and the T1 committee accommodated European requests and accepted the basic rate for SDH at 155.52 Mbit/s; other higher multiplexing rates were also approved. All parties worked closely to accommodate the different needs of

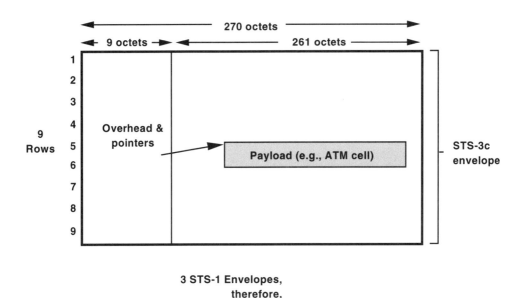

Figure 12–9   STS-3 envelope.

the various administrations and countries, which resulted in a worldwide multiplexing structure that operates with North American, European, and Japanese carrier systems.

Mapping ATM Cells into the SONET Envelope

Figure 12–9 shows that ATM cells can be mapped into the SONET envelope. The SONET header contains a byte called the H4 byte. It is used to point to the beginning of the first ATM cell in the payload. Since a 155.52 signal does not accommodate exactly an even multiple of 53 byte cells, ATM cells can run over an STS boundary. The H4 byte contains the position of the initial ATM cell. The position can vary from 0 to 52. In addition to the pointer operation for locating cells, an ATM receiver can also find the cells by checking any 5-octet sequence and determining if the fifth octet computes on the ATM header error control (HEC). The receiver continues to check 5-octet sequences until it computes on a valid HEC octet. This means the receiver has now found a cell, and after several other checks, the receiver achieves synchronization on the cells.

PAYLOAD POINTERS

SONET uses a new concept called *pointers* to deal with timing variations in a network. The purpose of pointers is to allow the payload to "float" within the envelope area. As Figure 12–10 shows, the SPE can occupy more than one frame. The pointer is an offset value (a variable) that shows the relative position of the first octet of the payload. During the transmission across the network, if any variations occur in the timing, the pointer is increased or decreased to compensate for the variation. While SONET is designed to be a synchronous network, different networks may operate with different clocks at slightly different rates. So, the pointers and the floating payload allow the network to make adjustments to these variations. In effect, payload pointers allow the existence of asynchronous operations within a synchronous network.

Traffic must be synchronized in the SONET network equipment before it is multiplexed. For example, as individual transport signals arrive at a multiplexer, they may be misaligned due to timing and bit rate differences. The bit rate variation could occur because of asynchronous operations between other equipment. The SONET equipment will synchronize the traffic such that: (1) the individual transport overhead octets are aligned, and (2) payload pointers have been changed to adjust the user

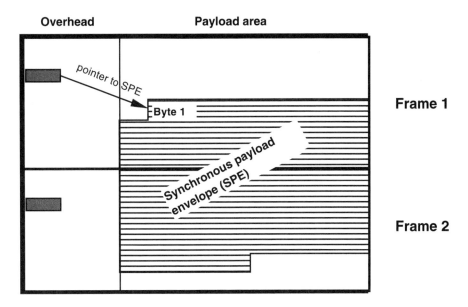

Figure 12–10   Floating payloads.

payload within the envelope. Therefore, two types of timing adjustments take place. One timing adjustment takes place within the SPE with pointers, and the other takes place with buffer adjustments at the receiver.

SONET makes pointer adjustments on a full octet (8 bits). Therefore, this large compensation requires complex and precise operations. The problem leads to jitter and has not yet been solved satisfactorily. Chapters 13 and 14 discuss this issue further.

MAPPING AND MULTIPLEXING OPERATIONS

This section expands the explanations in the previous sections and shows more examples of the SONET mapping and multiplexing functions. One idea should be kept in mind when reading this section: A principal function of these operations is to create a payload format and syntax that is the same for any input (DS1, CEPT1, etc.) after the initial multiplexing and pointer processing is complete. Therefore, the T1 and CEPT1 rates of 1.544 Mbit/s and 2.048 Mbit/s respectively are mapped and multiplexed into a 6.912 Mbit/s frame. Then these signals are multiplexed further into higher levels.

This section does not show all the mapping and multiplexing possibilities, but concentrates on the VT 1.5 group (1.544 Mbit/s) and the VC-12 group (2.048 Mbit/s). Figure 12–11 shows the VT 1.5, which multiplexes four DS1 systems. First, the bipolar code (BI) is converted to unipolar code (UNI). Each 1.544 Mbit/s DS1 signal is converted to a 1.728 Mbit/s virtual tributary. The additional bits are created to provide flags, buffering bits, conversion bits, and VT headers.

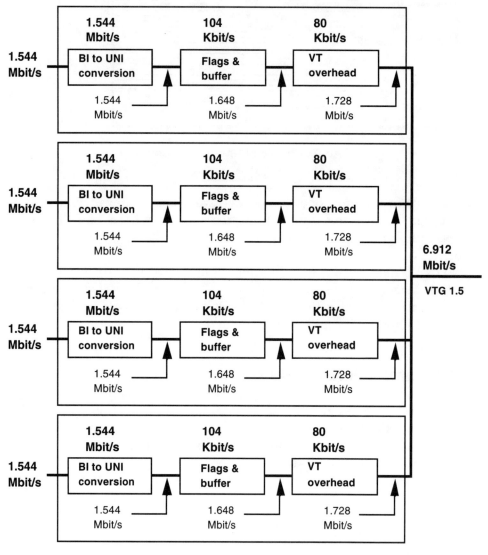

Figure 12–11   Virtual tributary (VT) 1.5.

Even though bit stuffing is usually associated with asynchronous systems in which the bits compensate for speed differences between the input and output, SONET also uses the technique. The intent is to create constant output stream of 6.912 Mbit/s, which requires insertion of the stuffed bits.

The four DS1s are multiplexed to equal a 6.912 Mbit/s VT 1.5 output. Then the 6.912 Mbit/s output is input into additional multiplexing functions in which each VT has path, line, and section overhead bits added. In addition, pointer bits are added to align the VT payload in the SONET envelope. The result of all these operations is a 51.840 Mbit/s STS-1 signal.

The European CEPT1 is converted to a VT 2.0 (called VC-12 in Europe) signal of 6.912 Mbit/s (see Figure 12–12). It can be seen that the

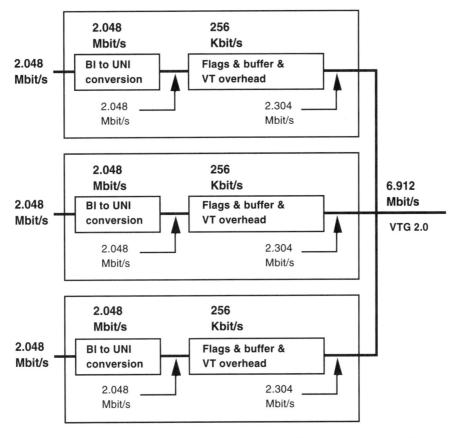

Figure 12–12 Virtual tributary 2 (VT 2.0) or tributary unit group 2 (TUG-2).

approach of the multiplexing scheme is to provide a preliminary payload output of 6.912 Mbit/s for all input streams.

For the CEPT1 conversion, 3 CEPT transmissions of 2.048 Mbit/s are input into the SONET conversion operation. The operation adds flags, buffering bits, and VT overhead bits, which equal 256 kbit/s. Therefore, each CEPT signal is converted to a 2.304 Mbit/s signal. 3 CEPT1 signals at 2.304 equal the desired 6.912 Mbit/s output stream. This stream is called the transmission unit group 2 (TUG-2) in the SDH standards.

Figure 12–13 shows how 28 DS1s are mapped into the DS1 payload, and how a DS3 transmission is mapped into the STS-1 payload. The two mappings in Figure 12–13 are taken from two separate operations on two separate input streams. They are shown together to illustrate how both

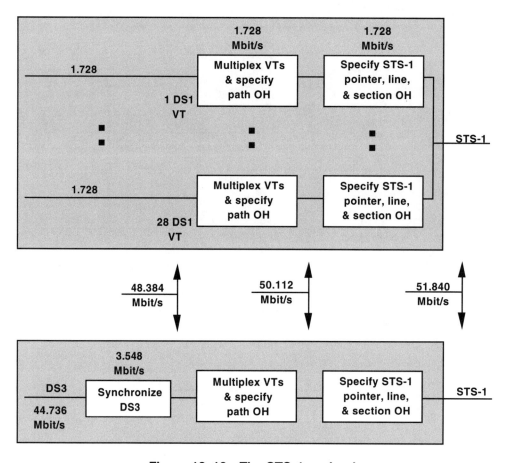

Figure 12–13   The STS-1 payload.

input streams are mapped first to 48.384 Mbit/s, second to 50.112 Mbit/s, and finally to 51.840 Mbit/s.

The purpose of the initial multiplexing and mapping is to create an intermediate stream of 48.384 Mbit/s; thereafter, both DS1, CEPT, and DS3 transmissions are treated the same. All these transmissions have path, line, and section overhead bits added as well as the STS-1 pointer. The result is shown on the right-hand side of the figure as the 51.840 Mbit/s STS-1 envelope.

The Control Headers and Fields

Figure 12–14 provides a general view of the control fields used by the SONET equipment for control and signaling purposes. The section

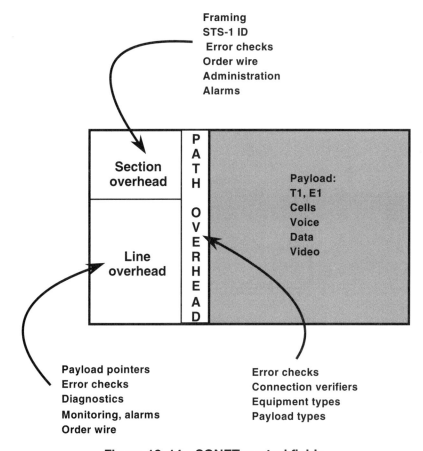

Figure 12–14   SONET control fields.

overhead and the line overhead make up the transport overhead that consumes nine rows of the first three columns of each STS-1 payload. This equals 27 octets allocated to the transport overhead. Nine octets are allocated for the section overhead and 18 octets are allocated for the line overhead. These fields are explained in the next chapter. On a more general note, headers are used to provide OAM functions such as signaling control, alarms, equipment type, framing operations, and error checking operations.

SONET EQUIPMENT

The next set of figures show the major equipment that is used in SONET networks. The terminal multiplexer, ADM, and building integrated timing system (BITS) are shown in Figure 12–15. The terminal multiplexer is used to package incoming T1, E1, and other signals into STS payloads for network use. The architecture of the terminal multi-

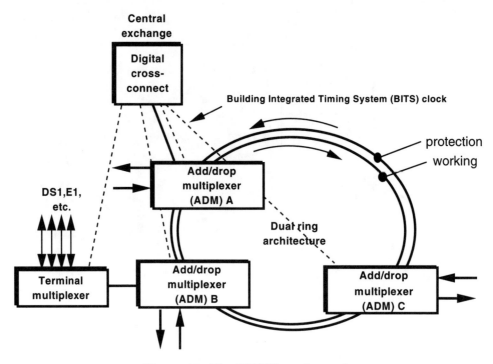

Figure 12–15   SONET equipment.

plexer consists of a controller, which is software driven; a transceiver, which is used to provide access for lower-speed channels; and a time slot interchanger (TSI), which feeds signals into higher-speed interfaces.

The add drop multiplexer (ADM) replaces the conventional back-to-back M13 devices in DS1 cross-connections. ADM is actually a synchronous multiplexer used to add and drop DS1 signals onto the SONET ring. The ADM is also used for ring healing in the event of a failure in one of the rings. The ADM can be reconfigured for continuous operations.

The ADM must terminate both OC-n connections as well as conventional electrical connections. The ADM can accept traffic from incoming OC-n and insert it into an outgoing OC-n. ADMs can also provide groom and fill operations, although this capability is not defined in the current Bellcore standards manuals.

The ADM multiplexers are required to convey the DS-n signals as they are—without alteration. They operate bidirectionally, which means they can add-drop DS1, E1, and other signals from either direction. The ADM uses both electrical and optical interfaces, which are specified in great detail in the ITU-T and ANSI/Bellcore documents.

Timing is distributed to the network elements with the building integrated timing system (BITS), which is used at these elements to synchronize the output onto the lines.

It is conceivable that ADMs will become protocol converters as the technology matures. This means that instead of only providing simple multiplexing and bridging functions, they may also perform protocol conversion functions by internetworking SONET with LANs, SMDS, Frame Relay, and others.

The topology for the ring can take several forms. Figure 12–16 shows a simple arrangement, known as a unidirectional self-healing ring (USHR). Two fibers are used in this example; one is a working fiber, and the other is a protection fiber. In the event of a failure on a fiber or at an interface to a node, the ring will take corrective action (self-heal) and cut out the problem area. An example of this operation is provided shortly.

Although not shown in Figure 12–16, the topology can also be established to include four fibers and operate with a second arrangement, known as bidirectional SHR (BSHR), in which case traffic shares the working and protection fibers between two nodes and traffic is routed over the shortest path between nodes.

Path protection switching (PPS) is achieved by using fields in the overhead headers. During normal operations (Figure 12–16a), STS-1 signals are placed on both fibers, so the protection fiber carries a duplicate copy of the payload, but in a different direction, and as long as the sig-

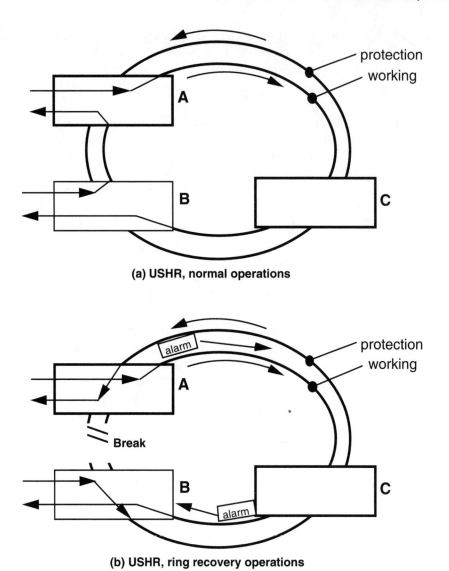

(a) USHR, normal operations

(b) USHR, ring recovery operations

Figure 12–16   Normal operations and ring recovery operations.

nals are received at each node on these fibers, it is assumed all is well. When a problem occurs, such as a fiber cut between nodes A and B, the network changes from a ring (loopback) network to a linear network (no loopbacks). In this example, node A detects a break in the fiber and sends an alarm to the other nodes on the working fiber. The effect of the signal is to notify node B of the problem. Since node B is not receiving traffic on the protection fiber from node A, it diverts its traffic onto the fiber, as shown in Figure 12–16b.

The digital cross-connects (DCSs) systems are used to cross-connect VTs, (see Figure 12–17). One of their principal jobs is to process certain of the transport and path overhead signals and map various types of tributaries to others. In essence, they provide a central point for grooming and consolidation of user payload. The DCS is also tasked with trouble isolation, loopback testing, and diagnostic requirements. It must respond to alarms and failure notifications. The DCS performs switching at the VT level, and the tributaries are accessible without demultiplexing. It can segregate high bandwidth traffic from low bandwidth traffic and send them out to different ports.

Figure 12–18 shows the traffic on one ring (the outer ring of the two dual rings). Some traffic is relayed around the same ring and other traffic is diverted and cross-connected to the other ring.

For some applications, it may be necessary to provide extra capacity in the system. For others, it may be necessary to ensure survivability of

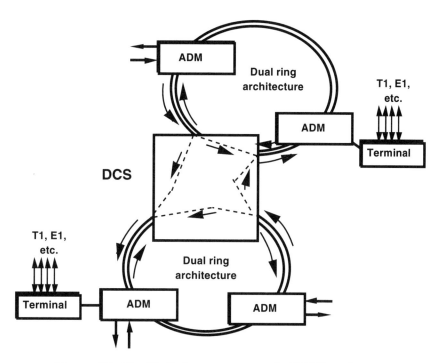

Figure 12–17   Digital cross-connects (DCS) systems.

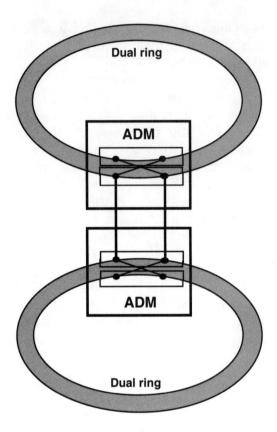

Figure 12–18   Multiple rings.

the network in the event of problems. In either case, path protection switching (PPS) and self-healing rings (SHRs) are employed, and in some instances multiple PPS rings may be employed. An SHR is a collection of nodes joined together by a duplex channel. This arrangement is quite flexible. The rings are connected together, but they are independent of each other and can operate at different speeds. The rings can be expanded by adding other ADMs, DCSs, and PPS rings to the existing topology. The ADMs are called serving nodes. Any traffic that is passed between the rings is protected from a failure in either of the serving nodes. The small boxes within the ADM in Figure 12–18 depict selectors that can pass the signals on to the same ring, or to the other ring.

Figure 12–19 shows one example of how SONET is being deployed. Figure 12–19a is a typical non-SONET access network using the current optical fiber technology. Most of the connections are point-to-point between high-density metropolitan areas that employ optical fiber termi-

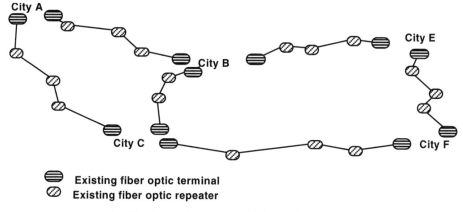

Existing fiber optic terminal
Existing fiber optic repeater

(a) Typical structure of the network

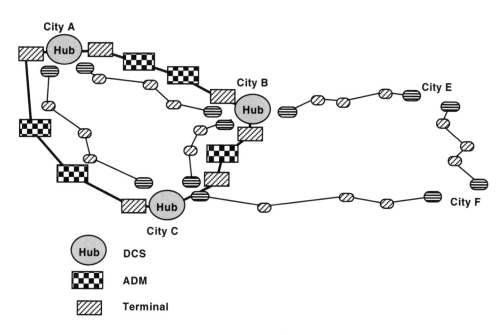

Hub   DCS

ADM

Terminal

(b) Overlaying the network

Figure 12–19   SONET development.

nals at each end, and, if necessary, repeaters on the line. Figure 12–19b shows how SONET is being used to improve and modernize the network. SONET is deployed between cities A, B, and C. This deployment occurs for a number of reasons: (1) growth of the subscriber base between these cities, (2) exhaustion of the current network's capacity, or (3) the desire to modernize the current T1/E1 system. Eventually, a SONET network could connect cities E and F.

PROGRESS IN SONET PENETRATION

SONET and SDH installations are used mostly for new or expanding systems. Older carrier systems are being rewired and replaced with SONET systems. T1 and E1 will still be quite prevalent through the end of this century. But recent announcements and deployments of SONET technology (as well as the drop in prices) lead this writer to think that most of the older technology (in backbone networks) will be replaced by SONET by the year 2000.

SUMMARY

Modern telecommunications and applications need increased carrier capacity for wide area transport service. Broadband WANs provide the answer, and SONET is being positioned to provide this high-speed transport service. From the perspective of the ITU-T and other standards groups, ATM will provide the switching operations for a B-ISDN with the underlying physical operations of the ATM traffic supported by the SONET operations.

13

Operations, Administration, and Maintenance (OAM)

This chapter describes the network management operations for ATM, generally known as operations, administration, and maintenance (OAM) or in some installations, simply signaling. Since ATM and SONET are interrelated, the ATM and SONET OAM information flows F1–F5 are examined, as well as the section, line, and path overhead octets. The SONET alarm surveillance operations, including yellow signals and red alarms, are explained. The interim local management interface (ILMI) and the ATM MIB are also included in this chapter.

A brief note is in order about two terms used in this chapter. The term *far-end receive failure* (FERF) means the same as a newer term, *remote detect indicator* (RDI). I shall continue to use the term FERF because this term is used in more installations and specifications at this time.

THE NETWORK MANAGEMENT MODEL

Work is underway on many aspects of the ATM network management standards. Currently, five areas have been defined for an ATM network management model, which are illustrated in Figure 13–1. They are labeled M1 through M5 and are focused on the following activities:

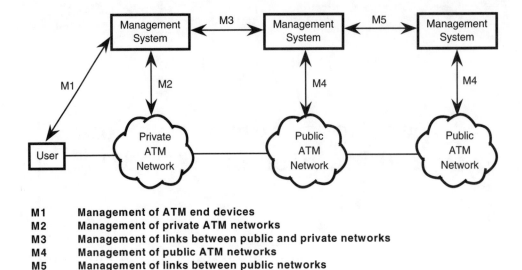

M1	**Management of ATM end devices**
M2	**Management of private ATM networks**
M3	**Management of links between public and private networks**
M4	**Management of public ATM networks**
M5	**Management of links between public networks**

Figure 13–1   ATM network management model.

M1 Management of ATM end devices

M2 Management of private ATM networks

M3 Management of links between public and private networks

M4 Management of public ATM networks

M5 Management of links between public networks

This figure shows the placement of these operations in the context of the ATM interfaces. Later discussions in this chapter will focus on some of these management interfaces.

OPERATION AND MAINTENANCE (OAM) OPERATIONS

The OAM functions are associated with the hierarchical layered design of SONET/SDH and ATM. Figure 13–2 shows the five levels of the corresponding OAM operations, which are labeled F1, F2, F3, F4, and F5. F1, F2, and F3 functions reside at the physical layer; F4 and F5 functions reside at the ATM layer.

The Fn tags depict where the OAM information flows between two points. This numbering scheme is part of the B-ISDN architecture defined by the ITU-T I.610 and is a convenient tool to readily identify the

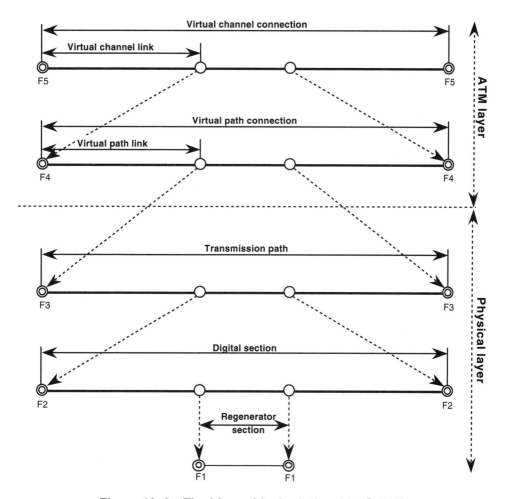

Figure 13–2   The hierarchical relationship. [I.311]

originating and terminating endpoint of an OAM message. The five OAM flows occur as follows (see also Figure 13–3):

F5   OAM information flows between network elements (NEs) performing VC functions. From the perspective of a B-ISDN configuration, F5 OAM operations are conducted between B-NT2/B-NT1 endpoints. F5 deals with degraded VC performance, such as late arriving cells, lost cells, and cell insertion problems.

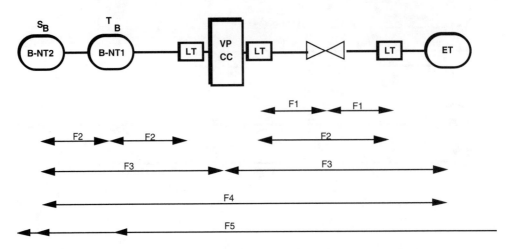

Figure 13–3   Information flows in the B-ISDN.

F4	OAM information flows between NEs performing VP functions. From the perspective of a B-ISDN configuration, F4 OAM flows between B-NT2 and exchange termination (ET. F4) OAM reports on an unavailable path or a virtual path (VP) that cannot be guaranteed.
F3	OAM information flows between elements that perform the assembling and disassembling of payload, header, and control (HEC) operations and cell delineation. From the perspective of a B-ISDN configuration, F3 OAM flows between B-NT2 and VP cross-connect and ET.
F2	OAM information flows between elements that terminate section endpoints. It detects and reports on loss of frame synchronization and degraded error performance. From the perspective of a B-ISDN configuration, F2 OAM flows between B-NT2, B-NT1, and LT, as well as from LT to LT.
F1	OAM information flows between regenerator sections. It detects and reports on loss of frame and degraded error performance. From the perspective of a B-ISDN, F1 OAM flows between LT and regenerators.

Figure 13–4 shows the SONET and ATM OAM flows from the context of their layers. F1, F2, and F3 OAM flows pertain to the SONET section, line, and path layers respectively. ATM does not distinguish be-

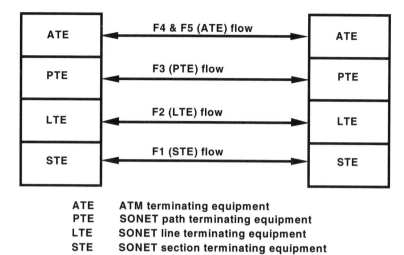

ATE	ATM terminating equipment
PTE	SONET path terminating equipment
LTE	SONET line terminating equipment
STE	SONET section terminating equipment

Figure 13–4   SONET and ATM OAM flows.

tween a VP and VC "layer," but F4 and F5 still describe the OAM flows between a VP and VC respectively.

ATM FUNCTIONS AT THE U- AND M-PLANES

The ATM layer management functions occur at the user plane (U-plane) and the management plane (M-plane) in the B-ISDN reference model.

U-Plane Operations

U-plane operations are discussed in several parts of this book. This section concentrates on management operations for the U-plane.[1]

The U-plane provides several UNI support services. The information for these services are conveyed in the ATM cell header. The contents of this header are explained in Table 13–1. The reader should study the footnotes of this table to obtain a more detailed understanding of these UNI operations. Many of the code points are somewhat generic, and their

---

[1]U-plane operations (and metasignaling) are not used in all ATM switches. The reader should check the specific vendor offering.

Table 13–1   Predefined Header Field Values

Use	Value[1,2,3,4]			
	Octet 1	Octet 2	Octet 3	Octet 4
Unassigned cell indication	00000000	00000000	00000000	0000xxx0
Metasignaling (default)[5,7]	00000000	00000000	00000000	00010a0c
Metasignaling[6,7]	0000yyyy	yyyy0000	00000000	00010a0c
General broadcast signaling (default)[5]	00000000	00000000	00000000	00100aac
General broadcast signaling[6]	0000yyyy	yyyy0000	00000000	00100aac
Point-to-point signaling (default)[5]	00000000	00000000	00000000	01010aac
Point-to-point signaling[6]	0000yyyy	yyyy0000	00000000	01010aac
Invalid pattern	xxxx0000	00000000	00000000	0000xxx1
Segment OAM F4 flow cell[7]	0000aaaa	aaaa0000	00000000	00110a0a
End-to-end OAM F4 flow cell[7]	0000aaaa	aaaa0000	00000000	01000a0a

[1] "a" indicates that the bit is available for use by the appropriate ATM layer function (for example, ILMI).

[2] "x" indicates "don't care" bits.

[3] "y" indicates any VPI value other than 00000000.

[4] "c" indicates that the originating signaling entity shall set the CLP bit to 0. The network may change the value of the CLP bit.

[5] Reserved for user signaling with the local exchange.

[6] Reserved for signaling with other signaling entities (e.g., other users or remote networks).

[7] The transmitting ATM entity shall set bit 2 of octet 4 to zero. The receiving ATM entity shall ignore bit 2 of octet 4.

[8] "0" in VPI/VCI fields means VPI/VCI values can be present.

specific use is defined in other specifications or left to a user-specific implementation.

The ATM header is predefined for these operations. Metasignaling is used by a metasignaling protocol for the establishment and releasing of virtual channel connections. For PVCs, metasignaling is not used.

General broadcast signaling, as its name implies, is used to send broadcast information. How it is employed is network-dependent. It is not used in PVC operations. The F4 information flow is for OAM operations, discussed earlier.

The three bits in the cell header that identify the payload type are called the payload type identifier (PTI) (see Table 13–2). As the name suggests, the main function of the PTI is to identify the type of informa-

Table 13–2   Payload Type Indicator (PTI) Encoding

PTI Coding (MSB first)	Interpretation
000	User data cell, congestion not experienced, SDU-type = 0
001	User data cell, congestion not experienced, SDU-type = 1
010	User data cell, congestion experienced, SDU-type = 0
011	User data cell, congestion experienced, SDU-type = 1
100	Segment OAM F5 flow-related cell
101	End-to-end OAM F5 flow-related cell
110	Reserved for future traffic control and resource management
111	Reserved for future functions

Note: PTI values of 000–011 indicate user information
      PTI values of 100–111 indicate management information or are reserved

tion residing in the payload of the cell. It also is used for congestion notification and OAM operations. Code points 0–3 identify user cells, and the other code points identify OAM cells and indicate if congestion has or has not been experienced. Interestingly, the generic flow control field of the ATM cell header does not contain the congestion notifications, which are coded in the PTI field.

M-Plane Operations

M-plane operations are divided into three major categories for OAM services and are supported with the parameters in the cell header as shown in Table 13–3. This section will explain each of these services.

Table 13–3   OAM Services in the ATM Cell

Function	Services
Fault	Alarm surveillance with AIS (alarm indication signal)
Fault	Alarm surveillance with FERF (far-end receive failure)
Fault	Loopback
Fault	Continuity check
Performance	Forward monitoring
Performance	Backward reporting
Performance	Monitoring/reporting
Activation/deactivation	Performance monitoring (activation/deactivation)
Activation/deactivation	Continuity check

Fault management cells are sent to indicate a problem, such as a loss of a connection, a failed interface, or a failed component. Fault management cells are also used to provide loopback tests.

Performance management cells are used to monitor and report on the performance of connections. Statistics—such as errored cells, lost cells, or severely damaged cells—are reported with performance management operations.

The activation/deactivation function performs performance monitoring and continuity check of connections. It allows the activating and deactivating of cells for VPC/VCC management.

End-to-End and Segment Flows

Figure 13–5 shows the manner in which the OAM layer management traffic flows between a user device, a public ATM switch, and/or a private ATM switch. The flows are called F4 and F5 in accordance with the B-ISDN standards. The F4 flow is used for segment or end-to-end VP termination management, whereas the F5 flow is used for segment or end-to-end VC termination management. F4 is identified with VCI values 3 and 4; and F5 is identified by using the payload type identifier (PTI) code points of 4 and 5 (in Table 13–2).

The distinction between end-to-end and segment flow is defined in ITU-T I.610. Segment flow is considered one in which a single VP or VC

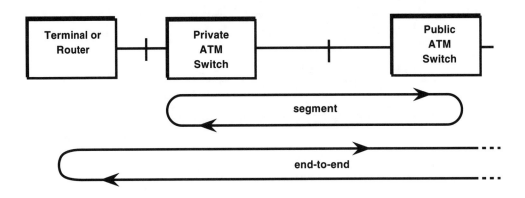

Notes:
    Segment flow can take other forms: eg, within networks, etc.
    F4 flow is for VPs
    F5 flow is for VCs

Figure 13–5   OAM traffic flows.

link is identified, or a group of VPs or VCs are identified that fall within administration of a single network provider. So, an end user may or may not see any aspect of segment flows, since they are managed independently by the network provider.

The OAM layer management information flows may occur end-to-end, between private and public switches, or between the private switch and the user terminal/router.

The F4 and F5 Operations. The F4 and F5 OAM information cell formats are illustrated in Figure 13–6. They are quite similar, and the basic differences pertain to the values in the VPI/VCI and PTI fields.

The F4 OAM cell format uses the VPI value that is the same as the user's cells and identifies the F4 information flow as segment flow with VCI = 3, or end-to-end flow with VCI = 4. For the latter, this value identifies the connection between two end-to-end ATM layer management entities (LMEs).

For the F5 flow, both the VPI and VCI values are the same as the user cells, and the payload type (PT) field identifies the flow as segment flow (PT = 100), or end-to-end flow (PT = 101).

The OAM cell type is identified as fault management (0001) for both information flows. The function specific fields are coded in accordance

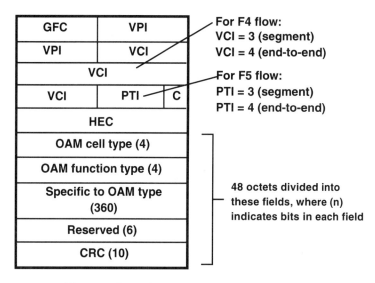

Figure 13–6   F4 and F5 information flows.

with ITU-T recommendation I.610. Table 13–4 shows the coding for the function type field and the associated OAM type field.

The 360 bits are coded to provide more information about the specific OAM message. As of this writing, the ITU-T had not defined all the variations for this field. Later discussions provide examples of how this field is coded. The reserved field is not defined at this time and is filled with zeroes. The 10-bit cyclic redundancy check (CRC) field detects an error in the 48-octet cell SDU. The receiving ATM entity will not process any corrupted OAM data units.

THE SONET OAM FUNCTIONS

Before proceeding further with the ATM F4 and F5 OAM flows, it is necessary to examine the OAM flows provided by the physical layer. This section introduces the SONET OAM operations and the F1, F2, and F3 operations. After this discussion, the F4 and F5 flows are examined in more detail.

Maintenance and Alarm Surveillance

SONET maintenance functions include trouble detection, repair, and restoration. To support these functions, SONET is designed with a

Table 13–4   Coding for Function Field

Function (cell type)	Value	Operation	Value
Fault management	0001	Alarm surveillance with alarm indication signal (AIS)	0000
Fault management	0001	Alarm surveillance with far end receive failures (FERF)*	0001
Fault management	0001	Cell loopback for connectivity verification	0010
Fault management	0001	Continuity check	0100
Performance management	0010	Forward monitoring	0000
Performance management	0010	Backward reporting	0001
Performance management	0010	Monitoring/reporting	0010
Activation/deactivation	1000	Performance monitoring	0000
Activation/deactivation	1000	Continuity check	0001

*Also called remote defect indicator (RDI) in some specifications

number of alarm surveillance operations to detect a problem or a potential problem. Before the surveillance operations are explained, the terms *state, indication,* and *condition* must be defined.

The term state describes an occurrence in the network that must be detected. A network element (NE) enters a state when the occurrence is detected and leaves the state when the occurrence is no longer detected. The detection of an occurrence may lead to an alarm being emitted by the NE, which is called an indication. An indication represents the presence of a condition.

Indications sometimes are not reported, but are available for later retrieval by an operating system (OS). Others may be reported immediately, as an alarm or a non-alarm indication.

Failure States

Several failure states are monitored by SONET NEs:

- Loss of signal (LOS): The LOS state is entered when a signal loss is detected. State is exited when two valid frame alignment flags are detected. Flags are introduced in Chapter 12.
- Loss of frame (LOF): The LOF state is entered when a NE detects four consecutive framing errors and is exited when alignment is detected for 3 ms.
- Loss of pointer (LOP): The LOP state is entered when a NE cannot interpret an STS or floating VT pointer in eight consecutive frames of VT super frames, or if eight consecutive new data flags are detected. The state is exited when a valid pointer with a correct new data flag is detected.
- Equipment failures: Equipment failures are vendor-specific, and include conditions such as CPU failure, and power failure.
- Loss of synchronization: Loss of synchronization is reported to OS upon detection of the loss of a primary or secondary reference.

Alarm Indication Signals (AISs), FERF, and Yellow Signals

The purpose of alarm indication signals (AISs) is to alert downstream equipment that a problem at an upstream NE has been detected. Different types of AISs are reported for the various layers. Figure 13–7 shows the relationships between the layers and AIS.

This figure shows two aspects of OAM. To address the first aspect, on the left of the figure are vertical (↑) arrows and their associated OAM

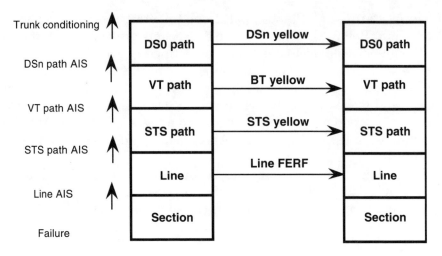

Figure 13–7   Maintenance signals and layers.

indications. Their purpose is to inform the downstream entity of a failure. The position of the vertical arrows is meant to convey the following events (note that the AIS OAM flow is upstream to downstream):

1. An upstream section terminating equipment (STE) informs a downstream line terminating equipment (LTE) of a failure (a line AIS).

2. An upstream STE informs a downstream path terminating equipment (PTE) of a failure (an STS path AIS).

3. Upon detection of a failure, a line AIS, an STS path AIS, or an upstream STS PTE informs a downstream STS DTE of the failure (a VT path AIS, DS3 AIS, or DS0 AIS, depending on the specific STS-SPE).

4. If DSn signals are being transported, an NE informs a downstream NE of the failure, or a termination of the DSn path (DSn AIS).

To address the second aspect, line far-end receive failure (FERF) is a SONET line-layer maintenance signal, and yellow signals are STS and VT path-layer signals. Yellow signals can be used for trunk conditioning and are used by a downstream terminal to report an upstream terminal's failure to initiate trunk conditioning on the failed circuit. These signals are used for troubleshooting and trouble sectionalization [BELL89a].

The position of the horizontal arrows ($\rightarrow$) in Figure 13–7 is meant to convey the following events (note this OAM flow is the opposite AIS OAM flow; it is downstream to upstream):

1. A downstream LTE informs an upstream LTE of a failure along the downstream line (line FERF).
2. A downstream PTE informs an upstream PTE that a downstream failure indication has been declared along the STS path (STS path yellow).
3. A downstream VT PTE informs an upstream VT PTE that a failure indication has been detected along the downstream BT path (VT path yellow).
4. DSn yellow signals are generated for failures or for DSn paths that are terminated (DSn yellow).

A number of factors lead to the use of DSn yellow signals, which is beyond our general descriptions for this chapter. The interested reader should consult Bellcore TR-TSY-000499 for more information.

Examples of Remedial Actions upon Entering a Failure State

Figure 13–8 provides an example of how NEs react to a failure. This example shows only a few actions among a wide array of possible actions. Obviously, the various types of AIS, FERF, and yellow signals sent between the NEs will vary, depending upon the nature of the failure.

Two parts of Figure 13–8 have not been explained—the red alarm and performance monitoring parameters. The red alarm is generated if an NE detects a failure state that persists for 2.5 seconds, or if the NE is subject to continuous, intermittent failures. The collection of performance monitoring parameters is suspended during the handling of a failure state—after all, there is no meaningful performance on which to report.

THE OAM HEADERS

With a few exceptions, the alarm surveillance signals and other OAM signals are conveyed in the SONET headers. Figure 13–9 illustrates the three headers for a SONET frame. Each box in this figure is one octet of information.

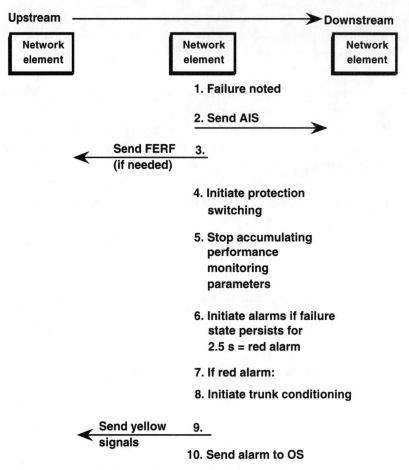

Figure 13–8   Example of OAM actions.

Section Overhead

The A1 and A2 octets are the framing octets. They are provided with all STS-1 and STS-n signals. The bit pattern is always 1111011000101000 in binary, or F628 in hexadecimal. The purpose of these octets is to identify the beginning of each STS-1 frame. The receiver initially operates in a search mode and examines bits until the candidate A1 and A2 pattern is detected. Afterwards, the receiver changes to the maintenance mode, which correlates the received A1 and A2 values with the expected values. If this mode detects the loss of synchronization, the search mode is then executed to once again detect the framing bits.

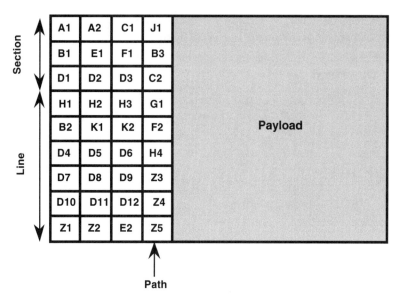

Figure 13–9   SONET overhead octets.

The C1 bit is used for STS-1 identification. It is a unique number that is assigned to each STS-1 of an STS-n signal. The C1 octet in the STS-1 is set to a number that corresponds to its order in the STS-n frame. The C1 value is assigned to each STS-1 signal before the signal is byte-interleaved into an STS-n frame. The C1 octet is simply incremented from zero through n to indicate the first, second, third, through n STS-1 signals to appear in the STS-n signal. The identifying number does not change in the STS-1 signal until byte-deinterleaving occurs.

The B1 octet is the bit interleaved parity (BIP-8) byte. SONET/SDH performs a parity check on the previously sent STS-1 frame and places the answer in the current frame. The octet checks for transmission errors over a section. It is defined only for the first STS-1 of the STS-n signal.

The E1 octet is an order wire octet. It is a 64 kbits/s voice path that can be used for maintenance communications between terminals, hubs, and regenerators.

The F1 octet is the section-user channel octet and is set aside for the network provider to use in any manner deemed appropriate, but it is used at the section terminating equipment within a line.

The D1, D2, and D3 octets are for data communications channels and are part of 192 kbits/s operations used for signaling control, administrative alarms, and other OAM. The contents of these octets are left to the manufacturer-specific implementation.

Line Overhead

The line overhead occupies the bottom six octets of the first three columns in the SONET/SDH frame (shown in Figure 13–9). It is processed by all equipment except for the regenerators. The first two octets (labeled H1 and H2) are pointers that indicate the offset in octets between the pointer and the first octet of the synchronous payload envelope (SPE). This pointer allows the SPE to be allocated anywhere within the SONET/SDH envelope, as long as capacity is available. These octets also are coded to indicate if any new data are residing in the envelope.

The pointer action (H3) octet is used to frequency justify the SPE. It is used only if negative justification is performed. The B2 octet is a BIP-8 parity code that is calculated for all bits of the line overhead.

Octets K1 and K2 are the automatic protection switching (APS) octets. They are used for detecting problems with line terminating equipment (LTE) for bidirectional traffic and for alarms and signaling failures. They are used for network recovery as well.

All the data communications channel octets (D4–D12) are used for line communication and are part of a 576 kbits/s message to be used for maintenance control, monitoring, alarms, and so on.

The Z1 and Z2 octets had been reserved for further growth and are now partially defined. The Z2 octet is now defined to support a line layer for n block error operation on a broad band ISDN UNI. Finally, the E2 octet is an order wire octet.

STS Path Overhead (STS POH)

The path overhead remains with the payload until the payload is demultiplexed finally at the end MUX (the STS-1 terminating equipment). Path overhead appears once in the first STS-1 of the STS-Nc. The path overhead octets are processed at all points of the SONET/SDH system. SONET/SDH defines four classes provided by path overhead:

Class A   Payload independent functions (required)

Class B   Mapping dependent functions (not required for all payload types)

Class C   User specific overhead functions

Class D   Future use functions

All path terminating equipment must process class A functions. Specific and appropriate equipment also processes class B and class C functions.

For class A functions, the path trace octet (J1) is used to repetitively transmit a 64-octet fixed-length string in order for the recipient path terminating equipment to verify a connection to the sending device.

The BIP-8 (B3) is also a class A field. Its function is the same as that of the line and section BIP-8 fields, to perform a BIP-8 parity check calculated on all bits in the path overhead.

The path signal label (C2) is used to indicate the construction of the STS payload envelope (SPE). The path signal label can be used to inform the network that different types of systems are being used, such as SMDS or FDDI—something like a protocol identifier for upper-layer protocols. For ATM traffic that is loaded into the frame C2 is set to 00010011. It is also coded to indicate if path-terminating equipment is not sending traffic; that is to say, that the originating equipment is intentionally not sending traffic. This signal prevents the receiving equipment from generating alarms.

The path status octet (G1) carries maintenance and diagnostic signals such as an indication for block errors for class A functions. For class B functions, a multiframe indicator octet (H4) allows certain payloads to be identified within the frame. It is used, for example, for VTs to signal the beginning of frames. It also can be used to show a DS0 signaling bit, or as a pointer to an ATM cell.

G1 is used when cells are transported over DS3 facilities. It serves to inform a receiving upstream node that a failure indication has been detected by a downstream node on the DS3 path.

For class B functions, the multiframe indicator octet (H4) is used for certain payloads to indicate the phase of the STS SPE in different length super frames. It can be coded to indicate up to forty-eight 125 ms phase boundaries.

For class C functions, the one F2 octet is used for the network provider. For class D functions, the growth octets of Z3 through Z5 are available.

ATM Use of the OAM Octets

It is evident from these discussions that the physical layer OAM is quite important to ATM. To reinforce this thought, Figure 13–10 shows an example of several OAM flows in relation to an ATM interface. These octets perform the following services:

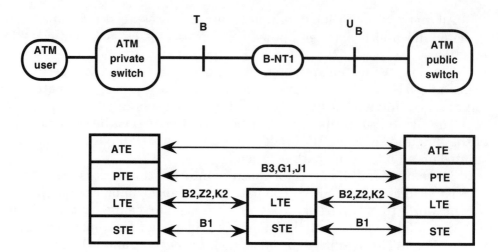

Figure 13–10   Example of OAM flow at the physical layer.

J1   Verifies a continued connection between the two ATM switches (contents = user defined)

G1   Indicates an STS yellow signal (contents = the value 1 in bit 5)

B3   A BIP-8 calculation results on the previous STS SPE (contents = even parity calculation)

B2   A BIP-8 calculation results on the previous line overhead and STS-1 envelope (contents = even parity calculation)

Z2   Conveys back to the originator (as an FEBE, far-end block error) the error counts from the B2 calculations (contents = count in the Z2 octet of third STS-1)

K2   Indicates a line FERF (far-end receive failure) and that the LTE is entering a LOS or LOF state (contents = 100 in bits 6, 7, and 8)

B1   A BIP-8 calculation results on all bits of the previous STS-N frame (contents = even parity calculation)

Using Payload Pointers for Troubleshooting Timing Problems

Chapter 2 describes how timing inconsistencies can create clocking variations in the network components, and Chapter 12 also introduces the SONET pointers, which are used to compensate for the variations. Chapter 14 explains how the pointers keep track of the payload. If problems

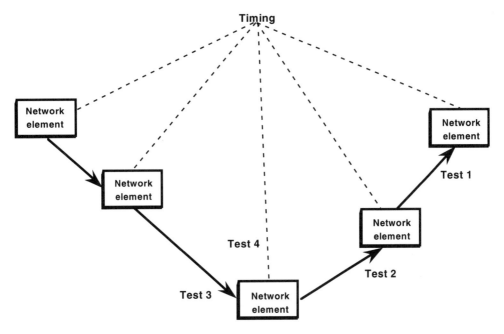

Figure 13–11   Troubleshooting timing problems.

occur, the network manager looks for two possible sources—an NE or the timing feed. As depicted in Figure 13–11, tests can be conducted with test sets to determine where pointer adjustments are being made. By working back toward the upstream NEs (test 1, test 2, test 3), the tests reveal a point where pointer adjustments are not being made; the NE will exhibit pointer adjustments on the output side, but not at the input side (test 2 and test 3). The next task is to determine if the clock recovery board in the NE is faulty, or if the BITS timing has been isolated from the NE (test 4).

OAM AT THE ATM LAYER

We now return to OAM at the ATM layer. This section shows some examples of ATM OAM operations. The examples are not exhaustive, but will give the reader an idea of how ATM OAM is implemented. Figures 13–4 and 13–5 provide useful references for our examination of ATM-layer OAM operations. The reader should review Tables 13–3 and 13–4 as well.

Fault Management

AIS and FERF.   The physical layer OAM alarms can trigger ATM layer alarms. This relationship can be demonstrated by reviewing Figure 13–7, which is redrawn in Figure 13–12. The physical layer informs the ATM layer about a problem, which permits ATM to issue AIS/FERF cells. In this situation, the ATM alarms would identify a physical problem.

Figure 13–13 shows the relationships of the physical, VP, VC AIS, and FERF operations. Be aware that this example represents only one combination of how these OAM operations are implemented. That is to say, physical-layer OAM actions do not necessarily have to invoke ATM-layer actions. Likewise, certain ATM actions can be generated independently of the physical-layer actions. For this example, ATM VPC and VCC AIS and FERF operations should be generated due to the physical-layer defect.

Loopbacks.   Figure 13–14 shows how ATM OAM loopbacks are performed. A network element generates the OAM cells and forwards them to another network element which is responsible for returning them (the loopback) to the generating network element. The cells are used to isolate faults on channels and network elements and to make certain the path is fully connected. They are used to perform a variety of tests, both for preservice and after the service has been initiated.

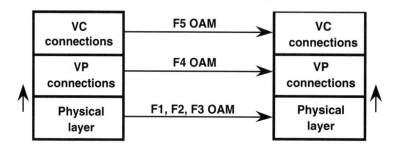

Figure 13–12   Relationship of physical and ATM layer OAM.

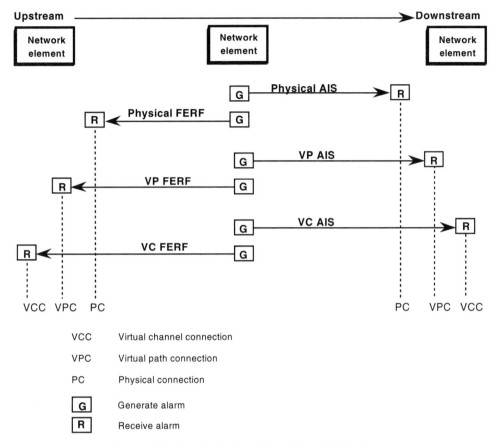

Figure 13–13   Relationship of the OAM alarms.

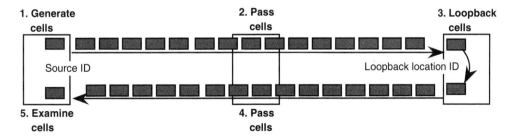

Figure 13–14   Loopback testing.

Each loopback cell contains the Id of the generating network element and the ID of the network element that is to loop the cells back to the originator. Any intermediate site must pass the cells on to the loopback site (as cells go forward), and the generating site (as cells are returned). Each cell contains an identifier that is used to correlate related OAM cells, in case multiple loopbacks are occurring on the same connection.

Figure 13–15 shows the format for an OAM loopback cell. The OAM cell type is coded as 0001; the OAM function type is coded as 0010. The 360 bits specific to the OAM type are divided into the following fields:

- *Loopback indication:* A bit that is set to 1 before the cell is looped back. The loopback node sets the bit to 0, indicating it has been looped back.
- *Correlation tag:* Used to identify (correlate) related OAM cells within the same connection.
- *Loopback location ID:* An optional field that identifies the site that is to loop back the cell.
- *Source ID:* An optional field that identifies the site generating the cell.

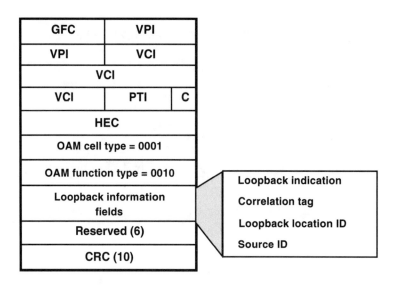

Figure 13–15   The OAM loopback cell.

Performance Management

Performance management entails the periodic evaluation of an ATM equipment and software. The goal is to assess the ATM system in a systematic way in order to determine how the network is performing, if components are deteriorating, and if error conditions are acceptable. VPC and VCC monitoring can be performed end-to-end or on VPC/VCC segments. Recall that a segment represents one part of a connection, such as one network provider (say, out of several that are part of the virtual circuit).

Performance management consists of:

- *Forward monitoring:* Generating cells from one network element to a receiving network element
- *Backward monitoring:* At the receiving network element, checking the cells and reporting back to the generating network element
- *Monitoring/reporting:* Storing the results of the monitoring activities based on filtering selected parameters and thresholds

Figure 13–16 depicts the performance monitoring operations. A block of cells on one connection is sent to an endpoint. These cells are bounded by OAM cells, which are not part of the block. Each user cell in the block has a BIP-16 calculation performed on the user payload. An OAM cell (a forward monitoring cell), which contains the same VPC/VCC as the user cells, is inserted behind the block of cells containing the result of the BIP-16 calculation, as well as other information (explained shortly). In addition, the OAM cell contains a count of the number of user cells in the block. The blocks can vary in size, and an OAM cell can be inserted at times that do not interfere with ongoing operations.

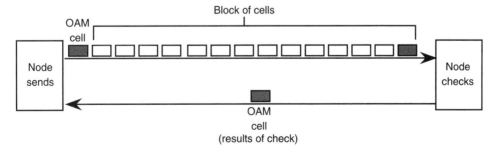

Figure 13–16 Performance monitoring.

The receiving network element receives the user and OAM cells and compares the BIP-16 value in the forward monitoring OAM cell to a BIP-16 calculation it executed over the user cells. It also counts the number of cells in the block and compares this count with the count in the OAM header to determine if any cells have been lost or if extra cells have been inserted. This information is stored and later sent back to the originator in the form of a backward reporting OAM cell.

These operations may occur in both directions, if the performance management system has been so configured.

Figure 13–17 shows the format for an OAM performance monitoring cell. The OAM cell type is coded as 0010; the OAM function type is coded as 0000, 0001, or 0010 in accordance with Table 13–4. The 360 bits specific to the OAM type are divided into the following fields:

- *Monitoring sequence number:* A sequence number in forward monitoring cells to detect missing or inserted cells
- *Total user cell number:* Number of user cells in the block sent before this OAM cell
- *BIP-16 value:* Value of the BIP-16 calculation on the user cells that have been sent since the last OAM cell

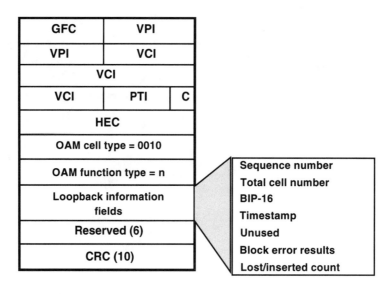

n = 0000, 0001, or 0010

Figure 13–17   The OAM performance monitoring cell.

- *Timestamp:* An optional field to indicate when the OAM cell was inserted
- *Unused:* Not used and coded to all 6A hex
- *Block error result:* Used in a backward reporting cell to indicate how many errored parity bits were received in the forward monitoring OAM cell
- *Lost or inserted cells:* Used in backward reporting to indicate how many cells were lost or inserted

Activation/Deactivation

Before the ATM VP/VC connections can be monitored, an end user or a network management system must initiate the OAM operations with a handshake (an activation). After the OAM operations are complete, another handshake is required to terminate these operations (a deactivation). The monitoring begins when one party (user, network management) sends an activate PDU. This party is called A. The responding party is called B. If this PDU is ACKed by B, the parties can execute the OAM described in the previous sections. If it is NAKed, no OAM can take place.

Figure 13–18 shows the format for an OAM performance monitoring cell. The OAM cell type is coded as 1000; the OAM function type is coded

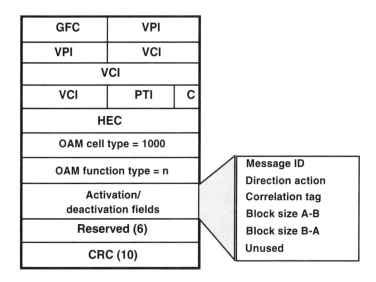

n = 0000 or 0001

Figure 13–18 Activation/deactivation cell.

as 0000 or 0001 in accordance with Table 13–4. The 360 bits specific to the OAM type are divided into the following fields:

- *Message ID:* Identifies the type of message, coded as shown in Figure 13–18
- *Directions of action:* Identifies the A-B, B-A, or two-way direction for the activation/deactivation
- *Correlation tag:* Value to correlate requests and responses
- *PM block sizes A-B:* Indicates the size of the performance monitoring block; can be set to indicate block sizes of 128, 256, 512, or 1024 cells
- *PM block sizes B-A:* Same as above, except for the B-A direction
- *Unused:* Not defined

THE ATM MANAGEMENT INFORMATION BASES (MIBs)

The ATM network management activities have focused on the efforts of the ITU-T and the ATM Forum. The ITU-T has published several specifications on operations, administration, and maintenance (OAM) that deal with alarms and performance monitoring.

Since the ITU-T work has not been completed, the ATM Forum has published several documents that deal with network management at the UNI and the NNI.

Theoretically, the ATM Forum specifications are "interim," in that they will go away when formal international standards are in place. Realistically, once interim standards are in place, it is difficult to dislodge them.

The management information base (MIB) is one of the most important parts of a network management system. The MIB identifies the network elements (managed objects) that are to be managed. It also contains the unambiguous names that are to be associated with each managed object.

Network management protocols (such as CMIP and SNMP) rely on the MIB to define the managed objects in the network. The MIB defines the contents of the information carried with the network management protocols. It also contains information describing each network management user's ability to access elements of the MIB. For example, user A might have read-only capabilities to a MIB, while another user may have read/write capabilities.

THE INTEGRATED LOCAL MANAGEMENT INTERFACE (ILMI)

This section explains the Integrated Local Management Interface (ILMI) Specification, Version 4.0, published by the ATM Forum. This section assumes the reader has a general understanding of MIBs.

While ATM OAM specifies a number of management operations, it is not complete, and does not provide enough diagnostic, monitoring, and configuration services at the UNI. Therefore, the ATM Forum has published an integrated local management interface, known as the ILMI.[2] It uses the Simple Network Management Protocol (SNMP), and a management information base (MIB).

As depicted in Figure 13–19,[3] the operations revolve around an ATM interface management entity (IME), which resides at each device that supports the ILMI. The IME accesses the ATM MIB through SNMP. SNMP runs on a well-known VPI/VCI value.

Each IME contains an SNMP agent and perhaps a management application. Adjacent IMEs must contain the same MIB. The MIB is specified in the Internet's registration tree (RFC 1212). It is prefixed by 1.3.6.1.4.1.353.

The ATM management information at the UNI is represented in the MIB. Figure 13–20 shows the tree structure of the ATM UNI ILMI MIB. It is organized into seven major categories. The physical-layer category contains objects common to all VPCs and VCCs, as well as objects that are unique to VPCs and VCCs. The bottom part of the figure shows the values used to identify each major grouping.

SNMP is used to manipulate the information in the MIB with Get, Get-Next, Set, and Trap operations. This part of the ILMI operates in accordance with Internet RFCs.

The ILMI MIB Tree Structure

The types of information that are available in the ATM Interface MIB are as follows:

---

[2]The term interim was the "I" in the ILMI title, but it is no longer appropriate. It was thought that ILMI would be temporary, but this is no longer the case. The ILMI specification from the ATM Forum (see [ATM96a]) states that ILMI procedures will be used indefinitely.

[3]This figure is a simplification of a more detailed figure in [ATM96a], but is sufficient for our overview.

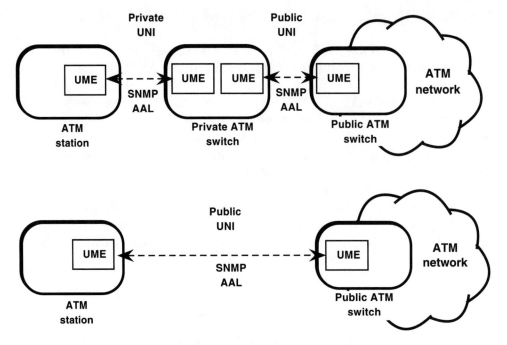

Figure 13–19　Interim local management interface (ILMI).

- System parameters
- Physical layer
- ATM layer
- Virtual path (VP) connections
- Virtual channel (VC) connections
- Network prefix
- Address registration information
- Service registry

System.　The System group from RFC 1213 [MIB-II] is included to support seven objects:

- sysDescr　A textual description of the entity. This value includes the full name and version identification of the system's hardware type, software operating system, and networking software. It is mandatory that this only contain printable ASCII characters.

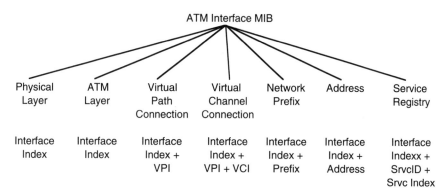

Figure 13–20 The ATM UNI ILMI MIB tree structure. [ATM96a]

- sysObjectID   The vendor's authoritative identification of the network management subsystem contained in the entity. This value is allocated within the SMI enterprises subtree (1.3.6.1.4.1) and provides an easy and unambiguous means for determining what kind of box is being managed.

- sysUpTime   The time (in hundredths of a second) since the IME was last reinitialized.

- sysContact   The textual identification of the contact person for this managed node, together with information on how to contact this person.

- sysName   An administratively assigned textual name for this managed node.

- sysLocation   A textual description of the physical location of this device.

- sysServices   A value that indicates the set of services that this entity primarily offers. The value is a sum of individual values, each representing a particular switching function.

Physical Layer.   The ILMI provides access to management information identifying the Physical Layer interface. When ILMI communication takes place over a physical link, there is one Physical Layer group for that physical interface. When ILMI communication takes place over a virtual link (i.e., a Virtual Path Connection used by PNNI), the physical layer management information is present and represents the virtual interface. Each physical or virtual interface has a set of specific attributes and information associated with it.

ATM Layer.   The ATM layer provides access to management information about the ATM Layer, and there is one ATM layer group per physical or virtual interface. Certain attributes of the ATM layer are common across all Virtual Path Connections (VPCs) and Virtual Channel Connections (VCCs) at this ATM Interface. Configuration information at the ATM layer relates to the size of the VPI and VCI address fields in the ATM cell header, number of configured permanent VPCs and permanent VCCs, and maximum number of VPCs and VCCs allowed at this ATM Interface.

ATM Layer Statistics.   The ATM Layer Statistics Group specified in versions 3.1 and older of the User-Network Interface Specification provided statistics for the ATM layer. This group has now been deprecated. This information is now available via standard Network Management MIBs.

Virtual Path Connections.   A point-to-point Virtual Path Connection (VPC) extends between two ATM interfaces that terminate the VPC. On the local ATM layer interface, the VPC is uniquely identified by the VPI value, when ILMI communication takes place over a physical link. The status information indicates the IME's knowledge of the VPC status. Configuration information relates to the QOS parameters for the VPC local end point.

Virtual Channel Connections.   A point-to-point Virtual Channel Connection (VCC) extends between two ATM Interfaces that terminate the VCC. On the local ATM layer interface, the VCC is uniquely identified by the VPI and VCI value, when ILMI communication takes place over a physical link. When ILMI communication takes place over a virtual link (i.e. a Virtual Path Connection used by PNNI), the VPI value is not used. In this case, the VPI value should be transmitted as zero and ignored upon reception. The status information indicates the IME's knowledge of the VCC status. Configuration information relates to the QOS parameters for the VCC local end point.

Network Prefix.   The ILMI provides an Address Registration mechanism that allows switches to automatically configure Network Prefixes in end-systems.

Address. The ILMI provides an Address Registration mechanism that allows end-systems to automatically configure ATM Addresses for ATM Interfaces on switches.

Service Registry. The ILMI provides a general-purpose Service Registry for locating ATM network services such as the LAN Emulation Configuration Server (LECS).

ILMI MIBs

The ILMI version 4.0 now contains four MIBs. They are: (a) The Textual Conventions MIB, (b) the Link Management MIB, (c) the Address Registration MIB, and (d) the Service Registry MIB.

The Textual Conventions MIB. The Textual Conventions MIB defines several Textual Conventions and Object Identifiers that can be imported to other MIBs. This MIB also contains types that were in earlier versions of ILMI, but are no longer used in version 4.0.

Link Management MIB. This MIB defines objects for each ATM interface, as well as procedures that describe methods to detect the establishment and loss of ILMI connectivity between ATM entities. The Link Management MIB contains the following MIB groups:

• *Per-Physical Interface Attributes:* These attributes are located in the Physical Port Group (atmfPhysicalGroup), with each physical interface identified by the interface index (atmfPortIndex). However, the atmfPortIndex is set to zero for ILMI, and all ILMI messages (SNAP messages) are related to the physical link on which they are transmitted. Most of the objects are deprecated from previous versions. One set of objects is required, referred to as Adjacency Information; these objects contain information about ATM neighbor nodes and are used to aid in autodiscovery and connection tracing through a network.

• *Per-ATM Layer Interface Attributes:* These attributes are located in the ATM Layer Group (atmfAtmLayerGroup), and each interface is identified by the interface index (atmfAtmLayerIndex). The information in this part of the MIB contains 15 objects that define the maximum number of VPI/VCI bits that can be active for this interface, as well as the maximum number of VPCs and VCCs that can be supported. The objects also contain information on the configured connections, if the associated ATM device in a public/private type, a user/node device, the ILMI version in operation, and the versions of the UNI and NNI signaling protocols.

• *Per-ATM Layer Interface Statistics:* The ATM Layer Statistics Group (atmfAtmStatsGroup) is deprecated and is used only for backward compatibility.

• *Per-Virtual Path Attributes:* These attributes are located in the Virtual Path Group (atmfVpcGroup), which is indexed by the interface index (atmfVpcPortIndex) and the VPI value (atmfVpcVpi). They have atmfAtmLayerConfiguredVPCs entries. Only permanent virtual path connections are represented in this group. The MIB information at this level includes:

The *Interface Index* object (atmfVpcPortIndex) is the same at that for the Physical interface. The *VPI* object (atmfVpcVpi) is the value of the Virtual Path Identifier (VPI) for this VPC. The *Operational Status* object (atmfVpcOperStatus) represents the state of the VPC as known by the local device. If the end-to-end status is known, then a value of end2endUp(2) or end2endDown(3) is used. If only the local status is known, then a value of localUpEnd2endUnknown(4) or localDown(5) is used.

The *Transmit* and *Receive Traffic Descriptors* are specifications of the conformance definition and associated source traffic descriptor parameter values in the ATM Forum's traffic management specification that are applicable to the transmit and receive sides of this interface for this VPC.

The *Best Effort Indicator* object (atmfVpcBestEffortIndicator) specifies whether best effort is requested for this VPC.

The *Transmit* and *Receive QOS* Class objects (atmfVpcTransmitQOSClass and atmfVpcReceiveQOSClass) specified I versions 3.1 and older of the User-Network Interface Specification are deprecated.

The *Service Category* object (atmfVpcServiceCategory) indicates the service category of this VPC.

• *Per-Virtual Path ABR Attributes:* ABR virtual path connections are tuned on a per-connection basis via a set of attributes. These attributes are located in the Virtual Path ABR Group (atmfVpcAbrGroup). This group is indexed by the interface index (atmfVpcAbrPortIndex) and the VPI value (atmfVpcAbrVpi). Every entry in the Virtual Path ABR Group has a one-to-one correspondence to an entry in the Virtual Path Group. The MIB information at this level includes:

The *Interface Index object* (atmfVpcAbrPortIndex) is the same as
that for the Physical interface. The *VPI* object (atmfVpcAbrVpi) is
the value of the Virtual Path Identifier (VPI) for this VPC. The *ABR
VPC table* (atmfVpcAbrTable) and *ABR VCC table* (atmfVccAbr-
Table) contain the ABR parameters which govern the ABR source
and destination behaviors. The objects in Table 13–5 are the ABR
parameters defined in the ATM Forum traffic management specifications (with some minor exceptions).

• *Per-Virtual Channel Attributes:* These attributes are located in the
Virtual Channel Group (atmfVccGroup). This group is indexed by the interface index (atmfVccPortIndex), VCC VPI value (atmfVccVpi) and VCC

Table 13–5   ABR Operational Parameters.

Name	Meaning	Description
ICR	Initial Cell Rate	Upper bound on the source's transmission rate, im- posed at initial start-up and after an idle period. The unit is an integer number of cells/second. The value must not exceed PCR and is usually lower.
Nrm	Number of data cells per forward RM-cell	The maximum number of data cells a source may send between forward RM-cells. Allowed values are: 2, 4, 8, 16, 32, 64, 138, and 256.
Trm	Maximum time between forward RM-cells	Upper bound on the time between forward RM-cells for an active source (in milliseconds).
CDF	Cutoff Decrease Factor	Controls the required decrease in source transmission rate associated with lost or delayed backward RM- cells. Larger values cause a faster decrease.
RIF	Rate Increment Factor	Controls the allowed increase in source transmission rate associated with the receipt of a backward RM-cell that indicates no congestion in the network (i.e., CI=0 and NI=0). Larger valued permit a faster increase.
RDF	Rate Decrease Factor	Controls the required decrease in source transmission rate associated with the receipt of a backward RM-cell indicating congestion in the network (i.e., CI=1). Larger values cause a faster decrease.
ADTF	ACR Decrease Time Factor	Allowed time between the transmission of forward RM-cells, before the source is required to decrease its transmission rate to ICR. Larger values allow a source to retain its rate longer, during periods of relative in- activity.
CRM	RM-Cells before Cutoff	Limits the number of forward RM-cells that may be sent in the absence of received backward RM-cells.

VCI value (atmVccVci). They have atmfAtmLayerConfiguredVCCs entries. Only permanent virtual channel connections are represented in this group, including all standard permanent VCCs (e.g., the Signaling, ILMI, and LECS VCCs) and non-standard permanent VCCs that are configured for use, but not including any standard permanent VCCs that are not configured for use. The MIB information at this level includes:

The *Interface Index* object (atmfVccPortIndex) is the same as that for the Physical interface. The *VPI* object (atmfVccVpi) is the value of the Virtual Path Identifier (VPI) for this VCC. For virtual interfaces (i.e., Virtual Path Connections used by PNNI), this object has the value zero in all SNM messages (e.g., GetRequest, GetNextRequest, GetResponse, SetRequest, and Trap) and implicitly identifies the VPI over which ILMI messages are received. The *VCI* object (atmfVccVci) is the value of the Virtual Channel Identifier (VCI) for this VCC.

The *Operational Status* object (atmfVccOperStatus) represents the state of the VCC as known by the local device. The *Transmit* and *Receive Traffic Descriptors* are a specification of the conformance definition and associated source traffic descriptor parameter values described in the ATM Forum's traffic management specification that are applicable to the transmit and sides of this interface for this VCC.

The *Best Effort Indicator* object (atmfVccBestEffortIndicator) specifies whether best effort is requested for this VCC, as defined in the ATM Forum's traffic management specification.

The *Transmit* and *Receive QOS Class* objects (atmfVccReceiveQOSClass and atmfVccTransmitQOSClass) specified in versions 3.1 and older of the User-Network Interface Specification are deprecated.

The *Transmit* and *Receive Frame Discard Indication* objects (atmfVccTransmitFrameDiscrd and atmfVccReceiveFrameDiscard) specify whether the network is allowed to invoke frame discard mechanisms in the receive direction of the associated connection as specified in the ATM Forum's traffic management specification.

The *Service Category* object (atmfVccServiceCategory) indicates the service category of this VCC.

• *Per-Virtual Channel ABR Attributes*: The Virtual Channel ABR source and destination behaviors are "tuned" on a per-connection basis via a set of attributes. These attributes are located in the Virtual Channel ABR Group (atmfVccAbrGroup). This group is indexed b the interface index (atmfVccAbrPortIndex), VCC VPI value (atmfVccAbrVpi) and VCC

VCI value (atmfVccAbrVci). Every entry in the Virtual Channel ABR Group must have a one-to-one correspondence to an entry in the Virtual Channel Group. The MIB information at this level includes:

The *Interface Index* object (atmfVccAbrPortIndex) is the same as that for the Physical interface.

The *VPI Value* object (atmfVccAbrVpi) is the value of the Virtual Path Identifier (VPI) for this VPC. For virtual interfaces (i.e., Virtual Path Connections used by PNNI), this object has the value zero in all SNMP messages (e.g., GetRequest, GetNextRequest, Get-Response, SetRequest, and Trap) and implicitly identifies the VPI over which ILMI messages are received.

The *VCI Value* object (atmfVccAbrVci) is the value of the Virtual Channel Identifier (VCI) for this VCC.

The *ABR Operational Parameters* used with VCCs are identical to those used with VPCs.

• *Link Management Traps:* Two traps (atmfVpcChange and atmf-VccChange) have been defined for the ILMI in order to indicate a newly configured, modified, or deleted permanent VPC or permanent VCC. The atmfVpcChange trap provides the Virtual Path Identifier (VPI) value of the new or deleted configured VPC at the ATM interface. The atmfVcc-Change trap provides the Virtual Channel Identifier (VCI) and the VPI values of the new or deleted configured VCC at the ATM Interface.

The Address Registration MIB. The Address Registration MIB supports the procedures for address registration, a set of operations that allows the user and the network to know each other's ATM address(es) in effect at the UNI. Later, these addresses can be associated with VPIs/VCIs, with the connection identifiers used in place of the addresses. Addresses and Address registration are described in Chapter 10, so we will not examine these subjects here.

The Service Registry MIB. This MIB is used to define a general service registry for locating ATM services, such as name servers, LAN Emulation (LANE) servers, and Multiprotocol over ATM (MPoA) servers.

MIB (RFC 1695)

The IETF AToM MIB Working Group's efforts have been published as the ATM MIB in RFC 1695. Its purpose is to define a virtual store for ATM objects for network management operations. This section provides an overview of the ATM MIB (it is almost a book unto itself, running 73 pages in length). Our focus is to gain a general understanding of RFC 1695; you can then study the RFC if more detailed information is needed. Figure 13–21 shows the structure of this MIB in relation to its object groups. Other objects are defined in the MIB, and will be explained shortly.

The ATM MIB Groups

Interface Configuration Group. The interface configuration group contains ATM layer information on local interfaces. The atmInterface-ConfTable contains this information, with one entry in the table per physical interface port. In this table are (as examples):

- The maximum number of VCCs/VPCs supported at each interface
- The number of active VCC/VPI bits in the cell header
- The values of VCI and VPI supporting the ILMI at each interface
- The type of address used at the interface (private, E.164, etc.)
- The IP address and textual name of the neighbor (the far-end node on this interface)

DS3 PLCP Group. The DS3 PLCP group contains DS3 PLCP configuration and state variable for ATM interfaces running over DS3. The atmInterfaceDs3PlcpTable contains this information, with one entry per port. In this table are:

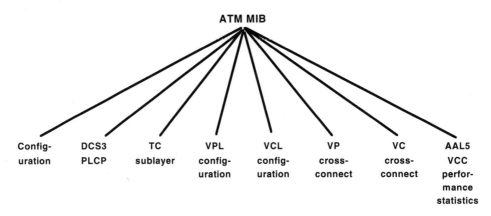

ATM MIB

| Config-
uration | DCS3
PLCP | TC
sublayer | VPL
config-
uration | VCL
config-
uration | VP
cross-
connect | VC
cross-
connect | AAL5
VCC
perfor-
mance
statistics |

Figure 13–21   The ATM MIB object groups.

- The number of DS3 PLCP severely errored framing seconds (SEFS)
- Indication if an alarm is present for the interface (yellow signal, loss of frame, none)
- The number of unavailable seconds encountered by the PLCP

TC Sublayer Group. The TC sublayer group contains TC sublayer configuration and state variable for ATM interfaces using the TC sublayer over SONET or DS3. The atmInterfaceTC Table contains this information, with one entry per port. In this table are:

- The number of times the out-of-cell delineation events occur
- Indication if an alarm is present for the TC sublayer

The VPL and VCL Groups. The virtual path link group contains configuration and state information on each bidirectional virtual path link (VPL) at an ATM node. Likewise, the virtual channel link group contains similar information of virtual channel links (VCL). In this situation, a link is a segment of a VPC or a VCC. The concatenation of the VPLs or VCLs collectively form a VPC or VCC respectively. This idea is shown in Figure 13–22.

Each VPC/VCC is bidirectional. A virtual path and virtual channel identifier are used to identify the incoming and outgoing cells on each connection at the ATM device. Figure 13–23 shows this idea. As just explained, the associated VPLs for a connection form a VPC. The ATM switch must map the VPI from an incoming port to an associated VPI on the outgoing port. This concept was explained in Chapter 8 (see Figure 8–5).

The VPL and VCL groups are defined by tables, with the OBJECT IDENTIFIERS of atmVplTable and atmVclTable respectively. They contain information on VPI and VCIs, as well as the values of the VPIs and VCIs.

In addition, another table is used in conjunction with these tables. It is the traffic descriptor table and is identified as atmTrafficDexcr-ParamTable. It contains information on traffic parameters and QOS classes for the receive and transmit directions for each ATM virtual link.

Figure 13–24 shows a general example of the traffic descriptor table and the VPL table. Be aware that this figure shows only parts of these tables, and "readable" names have been substituted for OBJECT IDENTIFIERS. The tables are referenced to each other with index pointers. The attractive aspect of this arrangement is that traffic parameters and

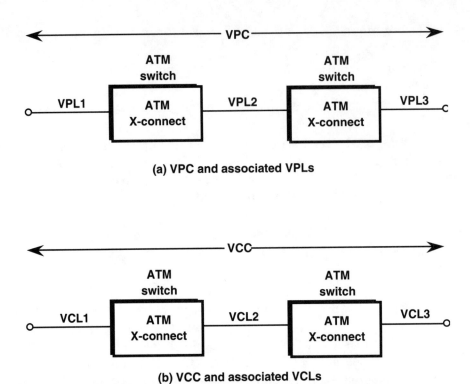

(a) VPC and associated VPLs

(b) VCC and associated VCLs

Figure 13–22 Associations of connections and links.

QOS values need not be stored for each connection. The VPL (and VCL, not shown) have an index value that points to the relevant row of the traffic descriptor table. With this arrangement, traffic descriptor values can be changed easily and are not hard-coded to each connection.

In addition, each VPL and VCL can have different values for each direction of traffic flow (asymmetrical traffic flow). These directions are noted in Figure 13–23 as the Receive descriptor index and the Transmit descriptor index. The traffic descriptor table also contains the traffic de-

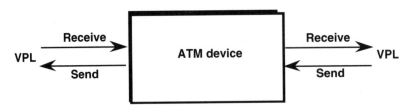

Figure 13–23 Bidirectional associations.

Traffic Descriptor Table

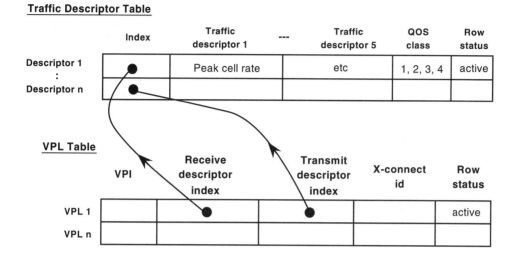

Notes:

Column names are "readable" forms of **OBJECT IDENTIFIERS** in the MIB

Row entries are instances of the objects

Only selected parts of tables are shown

Figure 13–24   Example of tables in the ATM MIB.

scriptors for the connection, such as peak cell rate and sustained rate, as well as the QOS classes of 1, 2, 3, 4, which map to the AAL classes of A, B, C, D respectively. The row status column indicates if the connection is active, in a set up condition, and so on. For the VPL table, the column labeled X-connect ID is a value implemented only for a VPL that is cross-connected to other VPLs that belong to the same VPC.

The VP and VC Cross-connect Groups.   The VP cross-connect group contains information on all VP cross-connects. It is used to cross-connect VPLs together in the ATM node. A unique value named atm-VpCrossConnect Index is used to associate all related VPIs that are cross-connected. This table reflects three types of cross connects: (1) point-to-point; (2) point-to-multipoint, and (3) multipoint-to-multipoint.

Figure 13–25 shows an abbreviated, general view of the VP cross-connect table, which is named atmVpCrossConnectTable. Be aware that an identical table exists for VCs. As with the previous example, I have shown only part of this table, and "readable" names have been substituted

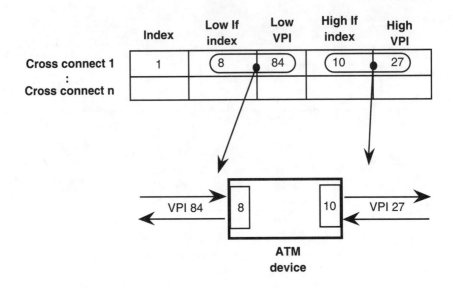

Note: Column names are "readable" forms of OBJECT IDENTIFIERS in the MIB

Figure 13–25   Example of the ATM cross-connect table.

for their OBJECT IDENTIFIERS. The terms low and high are used to represent the numerical values of the physical interfaces associated with the VPC cross connect (the IfIndex in this figure). VPI 84 is associated with IfIndex 8, and VPI 27 is associated with IfIndex 10. Other parts of this table (not shown) are used with these entries to provide directional information. For example, the object atmVpCrossConnectL2HOperStatus applies to the low-to-high direction, and the atmVpCrossConnectH2LOper-Status applies to the high-to-low status.

An entry to the cross-connect table is generated by a manager when a new connection is created at the ATM node. The row or rows in the table in Figure 13–24 are created, and a row status column is set to "create and wait." An agent then checks the requested ATM traffic parameters, QOS classes, and requested topology to ascertain if they are all consistent. As an example, the parameters for 8.84 that receive direction must be equal to the parameters for 10.27 send direction. If all checks are satisfactory, the manager will set the row status column to "active." Then, an adminStatus column in set to "up" for all rows, which allows traffic flow to commence. Similar procedures are followed for setting up the VC cross -connect table.

The AAL5 Connection Performance Statistics Group. The ATM MIB also contains objects pertaining to the performance statistics of a VCC at the interface associated with an AAL5 entity. The aal5VccTable contains:

- The VPI value associated with the AAL5 VCC
- The VCI value associated with the AAL5 VCC
- Number of CRC-32 errors
- Number of discarded AAL5 CPCS PDUs that were discarded because they were not fully reassembled during a required time
- Number of discarded AAL5 CPCS PDUs that were discarded because the AAL5 SDUs were too large

THE ILMI MIB AND THE ATM MIB

The ILMI MIB is intended for use at the UNI and not between the ATM switches. The ATM MIB is intended for use between ATM switches and also contains LMI objects. Both MIBs contain many entries that are the same, even though the objects have different OBJECT IDENTIFIERS. The major differences is that the ILMI MIB does not have objects pertaining to: (1) VP/VC cross-connect configurations, (2) VCC AAL5 CPCS layer performance, and (3) AAL5 entity performance and configuration parameters.

It may be desirable to access both the RFC 1695 MIB, as well as the ILMI MIB. Annex A of the ILMI defines a proxy mechanism to obtain this service, and I refer you to this document if you wish more information.

THE LAYER MANAGEMENT/ATM PRIMITIVES

Earlier discussions in this book have explained the concepts of B-ISDN layer management (specifically, Chapter 5, Figure 5–2). The layer management service definitions are implemented with nine primitives. These primitives define the interactions between the ATM management entity and the ATM entity. The text below Figure 13–26 describes the functions of each of the primitives, so we shall not need to explain further.

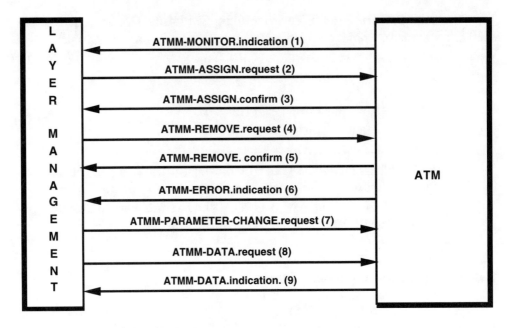

1. Issued by an ATM layer management entity (LME) to deliver the content of an ATM_PDU, to facilitate an OAM function

2. Issued by an ATM LME to request the establishment of an ATM link

3. Issued by an ATM to confirm the establishment of an ATM link

4. Issued by an ATM LME to request the release of an ATM link

5. Issued by an ATM to confirm the release of an ATM link

6. Issued by an ATM to indicate an error event and invoke appropriate management actions

7. Issued by an ATM LME to request a change in a parameter of the ATM link

8. Issued by an ATM LME to request transfer of a management ATM_SDU

9. Issued to an ATM to indicate the arrival of a management ATM_SDU

Figure 13–26   Layer management and ATM primitives.

**Table 13–6   Network Management Specifications included
in the Anchorage Accord**

LAN Emulation Client Management Specification v 1.0

Customer Network Management (CNM) for ATM Public Network Service (M3 Specification)

M4 Interface Requirements and Logical MIB

CMIP Specification for the M4 Interface

M4 Network View Interface Requirements and Logical MIB

M4 Network View Requirements & Logical MIB Addendum

Circuit Emulation Services Interworking Requirements Logical CMIP MIB

M4 Network View CMIP MIB Specification v 1.0

AAL Management for the M4 "NE View" Interface

OTHER ATM FORUM SPECIFICATIONS
FOR NETWORK MANAGEMENT

We have only touched the tip of the ATM network management iceberg. There are many other considerations that the ATM network manager must take into account. For the reader who needs more information on this subject, the ATM Forum specifications listed in Table 13–6 should prove helpful.

SUMMARY

ATM networks implement extensive network management services, generally known as operations, administration, and maintenance (OAM). The ATM and SONET F1–F5 information flows provide a formal model for OAM messages.

The section, line, and path overhead octets of the SONET frame are used for alarm surveillance operations, as well as yellow signals and red alarms. The integrated local management interface (ILMI) and the ATM MIB are published by the ATM Forum and the Internet, respectively.

14

Physical Layer Services for ATM

This chapter examines the B-ISDN concept of using SONET at the physical layer to support the ATM operations. In addition, the ATM Forum has defined three other physical layer operations to act as service providers to ATM. They are DS-3 for 44.736 Mbit/s operations, FDDI for 100 Mbit/s operations, and a private 155.52 Mbit/s UNI on twisted pair. This chapter examines each of these physical layer operations. The analysis begins with a look at the primitives that are passed between ATM and the physical layer. The chapter also shows and explains several examples of payload mappings.

Several of the operations described in this chapter make use of the OAM features supported in the SONET headers. We shall explain their contents briefly here, because they were covered in more detail in Chapter 13.

PHYSICAL LAYER OPTIONS FOR ATM

SONET/SDH is not the only physical layer that ATM can use. Indeed, it is likely that shielded twisted pair, unshielded twisted pair, and the FDDI physical (PHY) sublayer and physical media dependent (PMD)

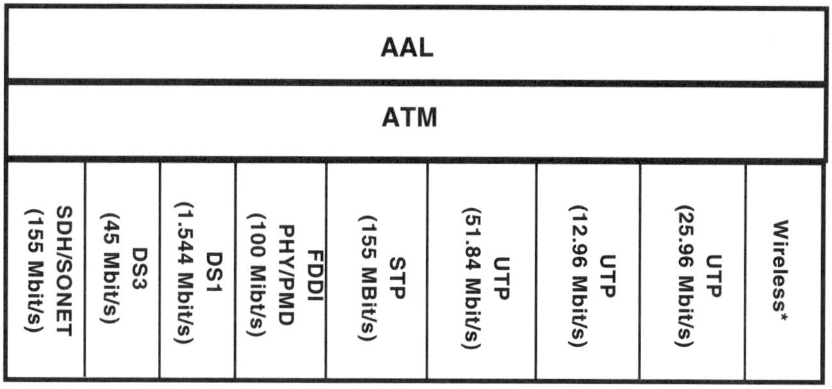

AAL								
ATM								
SDH/SONET (155 Mbit/s)	DS3 (45 Mbit/s)	DS1 (1.544 Mbit/s)	FDDI PHY/PMD (100 Mbit/s)	STP (155 MBit/s)	UTP (51.84 Mbit/s)	UTP (12.96 Mbit/s)	UTP (25.96 Mbit/s)	Wireless*

*Not yet developed as a standard

FDDI	Fiber distributed data interface
PHY	Physical sublayer
PMD	Physical media dependent sublayer
STP	Shielded twisted pair
UTP	Unshielded twisted pair

Figure 14–1   Physical layer options.

sublayer will used more than SONET/SDH. Figure 14–1 shows the choices that are emerging in the marketplace for an ATM physical layer.

The ATM Forum has released specifications on all these physical layer interfaces and protocols, with the exception of the wireless medium. Some vendors will run ATM over current wireless systems. For example, SONET radio interfaces will support ATM traffic.

THE ATM/PHYSICAL LAYER PRIMITIVES

As the reader might expect, physical layer primitives (service definitions) for ATM are part of the B-ISDN architecture. However, the physical layer might be non-B-ISDN systems, such as DS3, FDDI, or others. So, be aware that this section reflects the view of B-ISDN and may or may not be found in other physical layer operations.

Figure 14–2 shows the primitives operating between ATM and the physical layer. Chapter 3 explained that an OSI-type protocol entity can send and receive four types of primitives: (1) request, (2) indication, (3) response, and (4) confirm. The ATM/B-ISDN uses two of them, the re-

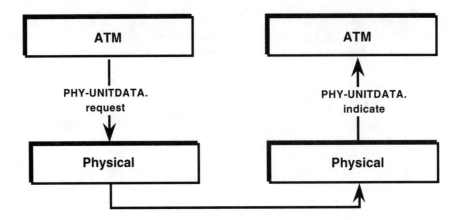

The ATM-entity passes one cell per PHY-UNITDATA.request and accepts one cell per PHY-UNITDATA.indicate.

Figure 14–2   ATM—physical layer primitives.

quest and indication primitives. The interface is quite simple, and as the figure shows, a request primitive results in one cell being passed from the ATM layer to the physical layer; an indication primitive results in one cell being passed from the physical layer to the ATM layer.

ATM MAPPING INTO SONET STS-3c

Chapter 13 introduced SONET payloads and STS-3c. This section continues this discussion, and covers both a public and private UNI. The focus is on the physical layer operations for the U-plane. The M-plane operations are covered in Chapter 13.

Operations are supported through two sublayers of the U-plane model: the physical media dependent (PMD) sublayer, and the transmission convergence (TC) sublayer. As expected, the PMD is responsible for bit timing and line coding. The TC is responsible for HEC operations, identification of the cells in the payload, cell delineation within the payload, pointer processing, cell scrambling/unscrambling (if necessary), frequency justification, and multiplexing.

The 155.52 Mbit/s frame supports a transfer rate of 149.760 Mbit/s for the actual cells in the payload. The other bits in the frame are overhead. The cells do not compute to an even integer multiple of the cell length, so a cell can cross into another SPE frame.

The format for the ATM payload in STS-3c is shown in Figure 14–3. Since the functions of these fields were explained in Chapter 13, this discussion will only describe any special considerations for their use for cell payloads.

The boxes with Xs denote that the STS-3c field is not defined. The C2 octet is used to indicate that the payload is loaded with ATM cells when it is set to 00010011.

The A1 and A2 octets are the conventional framing octets. The C1 octets are also used in the conventional manner, and are set to 00000001-00000010-00000011 respectively in the three C1 octets. Likewise, the B1 and B2 octets perform BIP-8 operations for section and line monitoring, respectively. The H octets support the pointer and concatenation functions, and the remainder of the octets are used for diagnostics, alarms, and so on.

The G1 octet is used to alert an upstream node of an out-of-cell delineation (OCD) using the HEC operations. The exact method for use of G1 is under study.

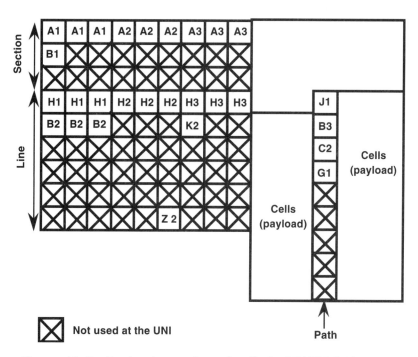

Figure 14–3 Payload mapping of cells in SONET STS-3c at the UNI.

ATM MAPPING INTO DS3

Because of widespread use, the DS3 carrier system is emerging as the preferred transport mechanism for ATM traffic. In order for this feature to be implemented, a physical layer convergence protocol (PLCP) quite similar to the PLCP in IEEE 802.6 and the SMDS specifications has been defined.

ATM cells are carried in the DS3 frame by mapping 53-byte ATM cells into a DS3 PLCP payload. The PLCP is then further mapped into the DS3 information payload. This concept is illustrated in Figure 14–4, which depicts a DS3 PLCP transmission stream. As the reader might expect, it consists of a 125 µs frame running within a DS3 payload. The

PLCP framing		POI	POH	PLCP payload	
A1	A2	P11	Z6	First ATM cell	
A1	A2	P10	Z5	ATM cell	
A1	A2	P9	Z4	ATM cell	
A1	A2	P8	Z3	ATM cell	
A1	A2	P7	Z2	ATM cell	
A1	A2	P6	Z1	ATM cell	
A1	A2	P5	X	ATM cell	
A1	A2	P4	B1	ATM cell	
A1	A2	P3	G1	ATM cell	
A1	A2	P2	X	ATM cell	
A1	A2	P1	X	ATM cell	
A1	A2	P0	C1	Twelfth ATM cell	Trailer
1 octet	1 octet	1 octet	1 octet	53 octets	13 or 14 nibbles

Object of BIP-8
calculation

POI   Path overhead indicator

POH   Path overhead

BIP-8   Bit interleaved parity—8

X   Unassigned—Receiver required to ignore

Note: Overhead of PLCP yields a cell transport rate of 40.704 Mbit/s: 424 bits per cell x 12 cells per frame x 8000 = 40,704,000 bit/s, with 96k cells per second in throughout (8000 x 12 = 96,000)

Figure 14–4   Running ATM over DS3.

frame consists of twelve rows of ATM cells with each cell preceded by four octets of overhead. The overhead is used for framing, error checking, bit stuffing (if necessary), alarm conditions, path overhead identifiers, and reserved octets. These fields are described shortly. Cell delineation is accomplished in a simple manner by placing the cells in predetermined locations within the PLCP.

As Figure 14–4 shows, the following PLCP overhead octets are used for the UNI operation. The framing octets (A1, A2) use the conventional framing pattern employed in SONET and SDH. The bit interleaved parity-8 field (B1) is also used in the conventional manner to support the monitoring of path errors. The BIP-8 field is calculated over the entire envelope structure, including the path overhead and the associated 648 octets of the ATM cells of a previous PLCP frame.

The cycle/stuff counter (C1) provides the minimal nibble stuffing cycle and length indicator for the PCLP frame. Its purpose is to frequently justify the 125 μs PLCP frame. This operation is implemented for every third frame of a 375 μs stuffing. Bit stuffing is not used in this scheme. Either 13 or 14 nibbles (4 bits) are inserted into the third frame.

The PLCP path status field (G1) is used to indicate a far-end block error (FEBE), based on the contents of BIP-8 in the previous frame. It can be coded to indicate how many BIP-8 errors were detected in that frame during its traversing the path from the source node. This field contains one bit for signaling that a failure indication has been declared along the DS3 path.

The path overhead identifier (P0–P11) is used to index the adjacent path overhead octet of the DS3 PLCP. The specification provides rules for the coding of the POI with the associated POH. For example, P11 is coded as 00101100 to identify an associated POH of Z6. The growth octets (Z1-Z6), as their name suggests, are reserved for future use. Finally, the nibbles were explained earlier.

Figure 14–5 provides a example of the order of byte transmission of the PLCP frame. The order is, in relation to Figure 14–4, left to right, and top to bottom with the most significant bits (MSB) on the left and the least significant bits (LSB) on the right.

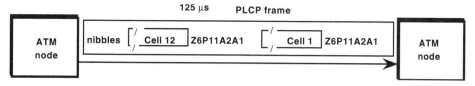

Figure 14–5   Order of byte transmission of the PLCP frame.

Other Aspects of the DS3 Scheme

Scrambling may be performed to compensate for bit patterns that create problems for equipment. If performed, the operation is based on ITU-T I.432. The PLCP frame must have its timing traced to a primary reference source (PRS). Cell delineation using HEC is not necessary, because the cells are placed in fixed locations in the PLCP. HEC operations must still be performed in accordance with ITU-T 1.432.

CIRCUIT EMULATION SERVICE INTEROPERABILITY (CES-IS) SPECIFICATION

Since the DS1/DS3 and E1/E3 technology is quite pervasive throughout the world, the ATM Forum has published a specification defining how an ATM network transports CBR traffic. It is titled, "Circuit Emulation Service Interoperability" (CES-IS) Specification [ATM97], and this summary is an extraction of the specification.

CES-IS supports the following types of CBR traffic:

- Structured DS1/E1 Nx64 kbit/s (Fractional DS1/E1) service
- Unstructured DS1/E1 (1.544 Mbit/s, 2.048 Mbit/s) service
- Unstructured DS3/E3 (44.736 Mbit/s, 34.368 Mbit/s) service
- Structured J2 Nx64 kbit/s (Fractional J2) service
- Unstructured J2 (6.312 Mbit/s) service

The Structured Nx64 and Unstructured DS1/E1/J2 services provide two ways to connect DS1/E1/J2 equipment across emulated circuits carried on an ATM network. The Structured DS1/E1/J2 Nx64 service is modeled after a Fractional DS1/E1/J2 circuit and is useful in the following situations:

- The Nx64 service can be configured to minimize ATM bandwidth, by only sending the timeslots that are actually needed.
- The Nx64 service provides clocking to the end-user equipment.
- The Nx64 service can provide accurate link quality monitoring and fault isolation for the DS1/E1 link between the ATM network and the end-user equipment.

The Unstructured DS1/E1/J2 Service provides transparent transmission of the DS1/E1/J2 data stream across the ATM network and is modeled after an asynchronous DS1/E1 leased private line. It supports the following situations:

- End-user equipment may use either standard ITU-T or on-standard framing formats.
- When end-to-end communication of the Data Link or Alarm status is important.
- When timing is supplied by the end-user DS1/E1/J2 equipment and carried through the network. The end-user equipment may or may not be synchronous to the network.

The Unstructured DS3/E3 Service provides basic DS3/E3 Circuit Emulation Service and allows for the following situations:

- Standard or non-standard framing may be used by the end-user DS3/E3 equipment.
- End-to-end communication of channels is provided.
- Timing is supplied by the end-user DS3/E3 equipment and carried through the network. The end-user equipment may or may not be synchronous to the network.

For all the CBR traffic, CES-IS defines the following operations:

- Clocking
- Jitter and wander
- The Facility Data Link (FDL) and the use of the Extended Superframe (ESF)
- Downstream and upstream alarms
- T1 signaling bits
- Use of the AAL types
- Error ratios
- Electrical interfaces

The CES-IS specification is a welcome addition to the ATM specs family. I refer you to [ATM97] for more details.

ATM MAPPING INTO THE 100 MBIT/S MULTIMODE FIBER INTERFACE

The ATM Forum UNI also specifies the interface for an ATM/FDDI configuration across the U-plane. This interface is not a full FDDI operation. Only the physical layer of FDDI is used, and the interface is on a private UNI. It does not have (or need) the elaborate OAM schemes for long-distance public communications lines, such as SONET. Therefore, OAM is provided by the interim local management interface (ILMI) (see Chapter 13). The media access control (MAC) layer of FDDI is not used in this implementation. This interface is shown in Figure 14–6.

This physical layer adheres to the FDDI physical media dependent (PMD) specification (ISO DIS 9314-3). The network interface unit (NUI) must provide the functions for AAL3/4 traffic.

Functions of the U-Plane Physical Layer

The functions of this interface are grouped into two sublayers: the physical media dependent (PMD) sublayer and the transmission convergence (TC) sublayer. The TC is responsible for cell delineation through the use of FDDI control codes and header error control (HEC) generation and verification. HEC is calculated for the four octets of the cell header and the results are inserted in the HEC field.

The PMD is responsible for the actual timing of the bits and the coding of these bits onto the physical medium. The physical media sublayer operates at 100 Mbit/s with a 125 Mbaud rate, which is the same rate used on conventional FDDI networks.

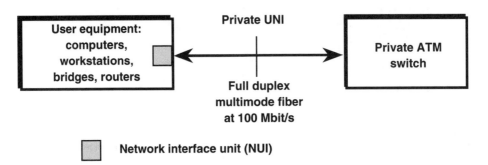

Figure 14–6   The ATM private UNI local fiber topology.

PMD Sublayer.   This sublayer uses 62.5 micron multimode fiber at 100 Mbits/s with the 125 Mbaud 4B/5B encoding scheme (ANSI X3T9.5) (FDDI). The FDDI control codes are used in a limited manner. The mnemonic JK is used to signal an idle line and the mnemonic TT is used to signify the beginning of a cell. That is to say, TT is used for cell delineation. The cell octets then follow contiguously on the channel, and the cell and its start of cell code (TT) must also be contiguous to each other on the channel. Other mnemonics shown in Table 14–1 are either reserved or not recommended for usage. The only other FDDI mnemonic is QQ, which is used to code a loss of signal indication.

TC Sublayer.   These sublayer operations are independent of the PMD, and thus not concerned with the characteristics of the medium. Their principal job is the generation and receiving of the control codes and the cells. The TC operations are depicted in Figure 14–7.

TC generates the TT code and the cell. It uses the JK code for synchronization purposes. In the event of the loss of synchronization, the JK code is used to regain octet alignment. Therefore, a least one JK code is

Table 14–1   Control Codes for a 100 Mbit/s Link

Mnemonic	Definition
JK (sync)	Idle
II	Reserved
TT	Start of cell
TS	Reserved
IH	Not recommended
TR	Reserved
SR	Reserved
SS	Unused
HH	Not recommended
HI	Not recommended
HQ	Not recommended
RR	Unused
RS	Reserved
QH	Not recommended
QI	Not recommended
QQ	Loss of signal

Figure 14–7   Example of cell transmission of the fiber link.

inserted between each cell, which ensures that only one cell will be lost in the event of a synchronization problem. Otherwise, this interface follows the pertinent ISO and ANSI specifications.

ATM MAPPING INTO THE 155.52 MBIT/S PRIVATE UNI

ATM mapping is designed to allow the ATM switch to act as a hub in a local area network (LAN) environment. Two options are available for this interface: optical fiber and shielded twisted pair.

Multimode Fiber Interface

This interface is a point-to-point multimode fiber, and operates full duplex between an ATM switch and a host. The fiber is 62.5/125 micron, graded index, multimode fiber (using a wavelength of 1300 nm), with an option of 50 micron core fiber available. At 62.5, the distance between the switch and the host is up to 2 km. This interface uses the conventional STS-3c coding and mapping schemes that were described earlier in this chapter and in Chapter 13.

Shielded Twisted Pair Interface

This interface is a point-to-point shielded twisted pair (STP) and operates full duplex between an ATM switch and a host. The cable is a 150W connection, as specified in EIA/TIA 568, 1991. The maximum distance between the STP interfaces is 110 m, using either Type 1 or Type 2 cable in accordance with ANSI/IEEE 802.5 (Type 6 cable can be used for short patches). The physical connector is shown in Figure 14–8 and is based on ANSI/IEEE 802.5 standard.

Figure 14–9 shows how the cells are organized for transport across the STP interface. A set of 26 cells is preceded by an OAM cell, which is also 53 octets in length. The first five octets in the OAM cell are coded to

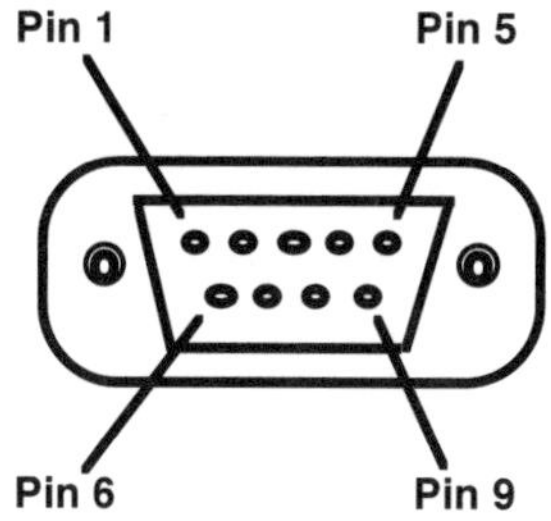

	Pin #	Signal
	1	Transmit +
	2	Not used
	3	Not used
	4	Not used
	5	Receive +
	6	Transmit −
	7	Not used
	8	Not used
	9	Receive −
	Shell	Chassis

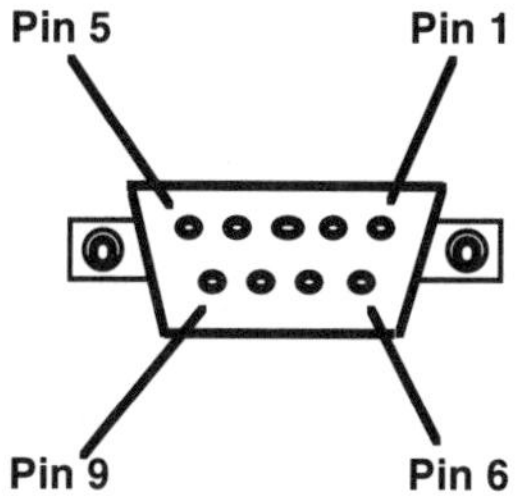

	Pin #	Signal
	1	Receive +
	2	Not used
	3	Not used
	4	Not used
	5	Transmit +
	6	Receive −
	7	Not used
	8	Not used
	9	Transmit −
	Shell	Chassis

Figure 14–8 Plug and jack pin assignments for shielded twisted pair interface.

provide octet and frame synchronization. Most of the octets in the remainder of the OAM cell are not defined. The sixth octet contains three bits used for OAM (discussed in Chapter 13) for far-end receive failure (FERF), errored frame indicator (EFI), and alarm indication signal (AIS).

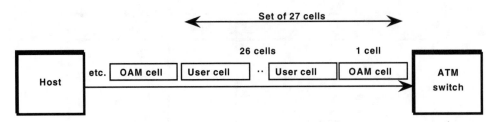

Figure 14–9 Example of cell transmission on shielded twisted pair.

PRIVATE UNI FOR 51.84 MBIT/S AND SUBRATES

The ATM Forum has also published specifications for running ATM over Category 3 unshielded twisted pair cabling for the following rates [ATM94b]: (1) 51.84 Mbit/s, (2) 25.92 Mbit/s, and (3) 12.96 Mbit/s. In addition, alternative cable types may be used. Table 14–2 summarizes the permissible rates and distances for Categories 3 and 5 cable.

The bit rate of 51.84 Mbit/s is the SONET STS-1 rate as defined in ANSI T1.105. The physical medium dependent (PMD) sublayer uses a carrierless amplitude modulation/phase modulation (CAP) for bit transmission and timing. This technique is used in many high speed modems, and the constellation map is almost identical to V.22 bis, a widely used modem in personal computers. Of course, the symbol rate for V.22 bis is only 1200 baud. The symbol rate for the 51.84 Mbit/s interface is 12.96 Mbaud, and 4 data bits are mapped into a 16-CAP constellation diagram, as shown in Figure 14–10. The lower rates of 25.92 Mbit/s and 12.96 Mbit/s use a 4-CAP code and 2-CAP code respectively. For more information on these three interfaces, refer to [ATM94b], part II.

Table 14–2 Cable Lengths and Bit Rates for Categories 3 and 5 Cable

Cable Type	Bit Rates		
	51.84 Mbit/s	*25.92 Mbit/s*	*12.96 Mbit/s*
3	100m	170m	200m
5	160m	270m	320m

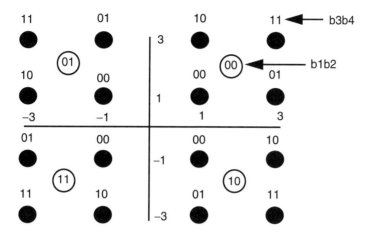

Figure 14–10 Constellation map for 51.84 mbit/s twisted pair interface.

MAPPING DS1, DS3, AND CEPT PAYLOADS INTO SONET FRAMES

This section provides the reader with examples of how several user payloads are mapped into the SONET SPE. The focus of this section is carrier payloads such as DS1, DS3, and CEPT1. During this discussion, keep in mind that SONET can carry today's carrier payloads. However, the reverse case is not true; today's carriers cannot always carry SONET payloads.

SONET is designed to be "backward compatible" with the carrier technologies in Europe, North America, and Japan. Therefore, the DSn and CEPTn payloads are supported and carried in the SONET envelope. These payloads range from the basic DS0/CEPT0 of 64 kbit/s up to the higher speed rates of DS4 and CEPT5.

In addition, cells are also carried in the SONET envelope, which results in the technology being both backward compatible (supporting current technology) and forward compatible (supporting cell technology).

The VT/VC Structure

SONET supports a concept called virtual tributaries (VT) or virtual containers (VC)—the former phrase is used in SONET, and the latter phrase is used in SDH (see Figure 14–11).

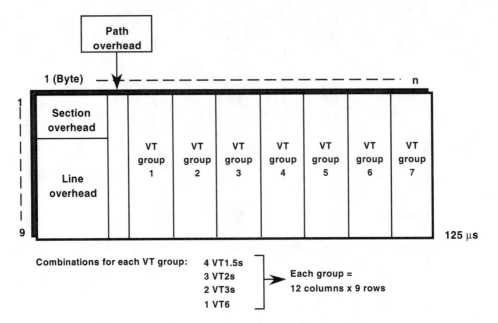

Figure 14–11 Virtual containers (VCs)/virtual tributaries (VTs).

Through the use of pointers and offset values, VTs/VCs, such as DS1, DS3, and CEPT1, can be carried in the SONET envelope. The standard provides strict and concise rules on how various VTs/VCs are mapped into the SONET envelope.

VT/VCs are used to support sub-STS-1 levels, which are lower-speed signals. To support different mixes of VTs/VCs, the STS-1 SPE can be divided into seven groups. As seen in Figure 14–12, each group occupies columns and rows of the SPE and may actually contain 4, 3, 2, or 1 VTs/VCs. For example, a VT group may contain one VT 6, two VT 3s, three VT 2s, or four VT 1.5s. Each VT/VC group must contain one size of VTs/VCs, but different groups can be mixed in one STS-1 SPE.

The four sizes of the VT supported by SONET are: VT 1.5 = 1.728 Mbit/s, VT 2 = 2.304 Mbit/s, VT 3 = 3.456 Mbit/s, and VT 6 = 6.912 Mbit/s. If the reader adds the number of columns that should exist in Figure 14–11, the total number of columns shown is only 88, not the 90 columns explained earlier. Shortly, we will see that two more columns are added to compensate for the differences between the bandwidth required in the payloads and the bandwidth available in the STS-1 envelope.

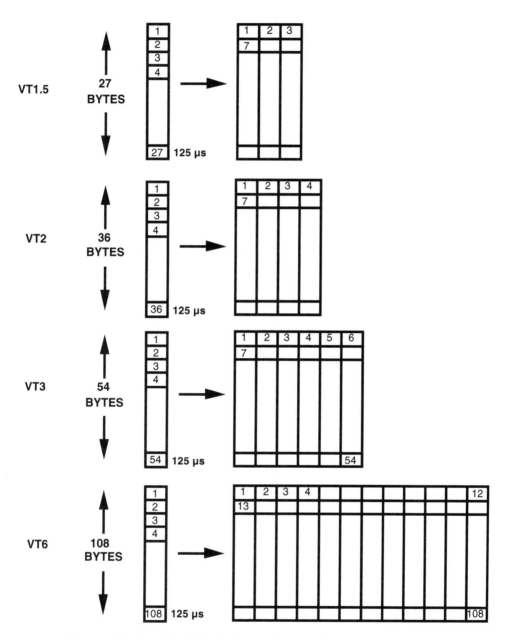

Figure 14–12   The tributaries and containers to accommodate regional multiplexing schemes.

VT1.5 is called VC1-11 in Europe and it accommodates the T1 rate. VT2 is called VC-12 in Europe. It accommodates the Europe CEPT1 rate of 2.048 Mbit/s. VT3 is not employed in Europe. It is used in North America to optimize multiplexing DS1c transport signals. VT6 is called VC-2 in Europe and it accommodates the 6.912 Mbit/s rate from all three regions.

The various administrations and standards groups from Japan, North America, and Europe worked closely together to accommodate the three different regional signaling standards. The initial SONET standards published in the United States in 1984 were reviewed by Japan and the European PTTs to see if these requirements would meet their needs. During this time, the ANSI T1 committee had become involved with Bellcore in the development of SONET.

Discussions continued through the European Telecommunications Standard Institute (ETSI), and agreement was reached on a subset of the multiplexing schemes of the three regions. ETSI stressed the importance of the intermediate rates of 8 and 34 Mbit/s in contrast to the ease of doing international networking. Reason prevailed, compromises were reached, and the importance of international internetworking came to the fore with multiplexing schemes based on 1.5, 2.48, and 6.312 Mbit/s capabilities.

Floating and Locked VT Mode

Two options dictate how the VT payload is mapped into the frame. One option is called the floating mode, for obvious reasons. Floating mode provides a convenient means to cross-connect transport signals in a network. Floating mode allows each VT SPE to float with respect to the complete envelope. This approach also obviates the use of slip buffers, which have been used in the past to phase-align the individual multiplexed signals as required. While the use of the slip buffers allows the system to repeat or delete a frame to correct for frequency variations: They should be avoided, if possible, because they impose additional complexity and may further impair the system. Payload pointers eliminate the need for slip buffers.

Another option is called the locked mode. With this approach, the pointers are not used and the payload is fixed within the frame. It cannot float. Locked mode is simpler, but it requires that timing be maintained throughout the network. Because all signals have a common orientation, the processing of the traffic is performed efficiently. However, slip buffers must be employed to adjust to any timing and synchronization differences that may be present in the system.

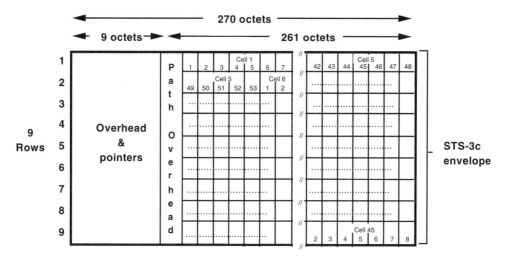

Note: Example shows first cell aligned exactly in beginning of payload area.
May be positioned anywhere in the payload.

Figure 14–13   Running ATM in SONET envelopes.

Figure 14–13 shows how ATM cells are mapped into a SONET or SDH payload envelope. The payload pointers can be used to locate the beginning of the first cell. Additionally, cell delineation is achieved by the receiver locking onto the 5 bytes that satisfy the HEC operations. In this manner, the receiver knows where a cell is positioned in the envelope. The receiver also is able to detect an empty cell.

It is unlikely that cells would be positioned at the first byte of the payload. If they are, an STS-3c system can carry 44 cells and bytes 1–8 of the 45th cell. The remainder of the 45th cell is placed in the next SONET frame.

INTERWORKING ATM AND SONET

The specific implementations and topologies for interfaces between SONET and ATM are not defined in the international standards. Vendors are free to build their architecture based on their own design preferences. Notwithstanding, a possible scheme is depicted in Figure 14–14. As discussed in earlier parts of this book, an add-drop multiplexer (ADM) is used to add and drop payload at various locations in a network. Therefore, an ADM must be able not only to extract ATM cells from incoming

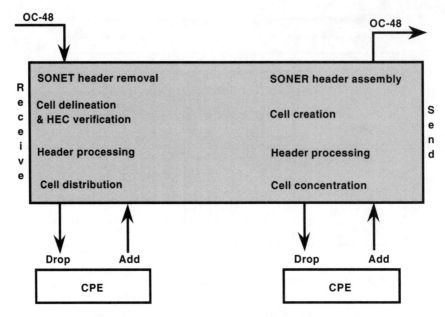

Figure 14–14   ATM and SONET interworking.

SONET frames and drop off to a local node, but also to add ATM cells at this same node for transmission downstream. This example shows the reception and transmission of a SONET OC-48 envelope.

The first task is to receive the SONET envelope, examine the SONET overhead, act upon it, and then remove it. Thereafter, the payload, consisting of ATM cells, is examined to determine if the cells are to be dropped at this site or forwarded to the next site.

The ADM is responsible for checking the cell header (VPI and perhaps VCI) and making decisions as to the processing of the traffic. It may drop the cell at this node or relay the cell to another node.

The architecture is based on four major operations. The first operation converts the STS-3c payload to an ATM stream at the input and performs a complementary function at the output. The second operation locates the cells within the payload for an incoming transmission, and places the cells inside the SONET envelope for an outgoing transmission. The third operation examines the label in the ATM cell header (the VPI and perhaps VCI). The fourth operation distributes the cells to the outlets at this node or passes the cells to an outlet at this node. In its simplest form, these operations make decisions on whether traffic is passed or dropped at this node.

THE 2.4 GBIT/S PHYSICAL LAYER SPECIFICATION

Due to the increased use of SONET/SDH networks, the ATM Forum has published a draft specification for the support of ATM cells on the SONET/SDH OC-48 payload and the SDH VC-4-16c payload. It is titled the 2.4 Gbit/s Physical Layer Specification [ATM98], from which I have extracted this survey:

The specification defines six single mode fiber interfaces, in accordance with ITU-T G.957:

- One short-reach interface (2 km target distance, 0–7 dB span loss, 1310 nm region on single mode fiber)
- Two intermediate reach interfaces (15 km target distance, 0–12 dB span loss, 1310 or 1550 nm region on single mode fiber)
- Three long reach interfaces (40–80 km target distance, 10–24 dB span loss, 1310/1550 nm region on single mode fiber, 1550 nm region on dispersion shifted single mode fiber)

Mapping of ATM cells into the SONET/SDH frame occurs by scrambling the ATM cell payload and mapping the resulting cell stream into a synchronous payload envelope (SPE) or a VC-4-16c, then mapping the SPE into the SONET/SDH frame using the H1-H2 pointer. The SONET/SDH frame synchronous scrambler is applied to the resulting frame.

Table 14–3 depicts the status for the overhead functions for the OC-48/STM-16 interface.

These overhead functions are described in more detail in Annex A of [ATM98].

INVERSE MULTIPLEXING FOR ATM (IMA)

Inverse multiplexing for ATM (IMA) is used to provide a transport service at rates between the existing DS1/E1 and DS3/E3 rates. IMA gives network administrators more flexibility in buying and using bandwidth. IMA is published by the ATM Forum as Inverse Multiplexing for ATM (IMA) Specification, Version 1.0 [ATM97a].

This specification defines the inverse multiplexing of an ATM cell stream over multiple physical links and the retrieval of the original stream at the far-end from these links. The concept is shown in Figure 14–15. The idea revolves around an IMA group. The circular arrows depict the multiplexing and demultiplexing of cells in a cyclical fashion

Table 14–3   SONET SDH Overhead Functions

Overhead	Status
A1, A2	R
B1	R
D1, D2, D3	N/A
J0	R
Z0	N/A
E1	N/A
F1	N/A
B2	R
D4-D12	N/A
E2	N/A
H1, H2, H3	R
K1, K2 (APS)	O
K2 (6-8) AIS-L	R
K2 (6-8) RDI-L	R
S1 (sync msg)	R
M1 Line REI	R
H1, H2 (AIS-P)	R
J1	R
B3	R
C2	R
G1	R
H4	N/A
F2	N/A
Z3, Z4, Z5	N/A

where:
  R = required
  O = optional
  N/A = not applicable

across physical links whose aggregate bandwidth is used to form a logical link of an intermediate rate between DS1/E1 and DS3/E3.

Rules for IMA Operations

The specification sets for the following rules (see section 1.1 of [ATM97a]:

IMA groups must terminate at each end of the IMA virtual link. In the transmit direction, the ATM cell stream received from the ATM layer

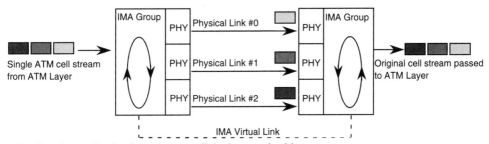

Tx direction cells distributed across links in round robin sequence
Rx direction cells recombined into single ATM stream

Figure 14–15   Inverse multiplexing. [ATM97a]

is distributed on a cell-by-cell basis, across the multiple links within the
IMA group. At the far-end, the receiving IMA must recombine the cells
from each link, on a cell-by-cell basis, recreating the original ATM cell
stream. The aggregate cell stream is then passed to the ATM layer.

The transmit IMA periodically transmits special cells that contain
information that permit reconstruction of the ATM cell stream at the receiving IMA end after accounting for the link differential delays, smoothing CDV introduced by the control cells, etc. These cells, defined as IMA
Control Protocol (ICP) cells, provide the definition of an IMA frame. The
transmitter must align the transmission of IMA frames on all links (see
Figure 14–16). This allows the receiver to adjust for differential link de-

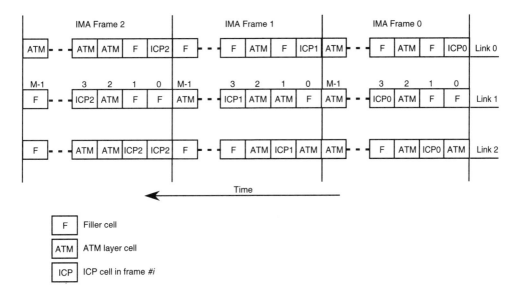

Figure 14–16   Illustration of IMA frames. [ATM97a]

lays among the constituent physical links. Based on this required behavior, the receiver detects the differential delays by measuring the arrival times of the IMA frames on each link.

At the transmitting end, the cells are transmitted continuously. If there are no ATM layer cells to be sent between ICP cells within an IMA frame, then the transmit IMA sends filler cells to maintain a continuous stream of cells at the physical layer. The insertion of filler cells provide cell rate decoupling at the IMA sublayer. The filler cells should be discarded by the receive IMA.

A new OAM cell is defined for use by the IMA protocol. This cell has codes that define it as an ICP or filler cell.

		User Plane Functions	Layer Management Functions	Plane Management Functions
ATM Layer				
Physical Layer	IMA Transmission Convergence Sublayer	• ATM cell stream splitting and reconstruction • ICP cells insertion/ removal • Cell rate decoupling • IMA Frame Synchronization • Stuffing • Discarding of cells with bad HEC	• IMA Connectivity • ICP Cell Errors (OIF, LIF) • LIF/LODS/RDI-IMA defect processing • RDI-IMA alarm generation • Tx/Rx IMA Link State Report	• IMA group configuration • Link addition/deletion • ATM cell rate change • IMA group failure notification • IMA statistics
	Interface Specific Transmission Convergence Sublayer	• Cell scrambling/ descrambling (if required) • No cell discarding • Cell delineation • Header error correction (if required) • HEC generation/ verification	• HEC Error Indication • LCD-RDI alarm generation (if required)	• LCD failure notification • TC stats
	Physical Medium Dependent Sublayer	• Bit timing • Line coding • Physical Medium	• Local alarm processing • RDI alarms generation	• Link failure notification • PMD stats

Figure 14–17   IMA OSI Layer Reference Model.

The IMA Sublayer in the Layered Model

Figure 14–17 shows how IMA fits into the physical layer of the OSI Reference Model. It rests between the ATM layer and the transmission convergence sublayer. (Figure 14–17 is a redrawing of Figure 5–5).

Figure 14–18 shows yet another view of IMA, from the standpoint of the layers and the functional blocks. This section provides a general description of the functional blocks, based on IMA, Section 4.

The Source Interface provides the connection to an internal data bus (e.g., an ATM switch, router, computer), which might be a standard interface (e.g., DXI over HSSI, RS442, RS449). There is no requirement that a particular Source Interface must be supported. The Source choice is vendor specific. There is also no requirement that the Source Interface on one side match the Source Interface on the other (e.g., one side could be a direct interface to a data bus in an ATM switch and the other could be an ATM DSU supporting the IMA function).

The Cell Function is dependent upon the Source Interface:

- If the Source Interface emits ATM cells, the Cell Function is null (traffic shaping, if any, may be accomplished outside the unit). In this case, OAM cells, RM cells, and so on, must be passed transparently through the Source Interface.
- If the Source Interface does not emit ATM cells, the Cell Function must arrange for the output of the Source Interface to be converted into ATM cells. There is no limitation on the Cell Function other than it must emit ATM cells. This requirement does not pre-

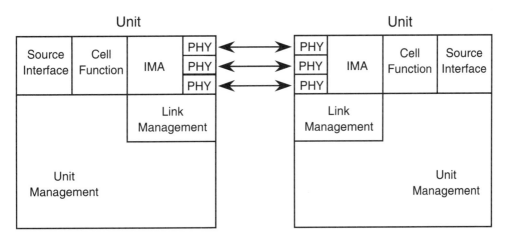

Figure 14–18   Functional blocks and layers.

clude the cell function implementing traffic shaping, buffering for frames/cells, and so on. Support within the cell function is an implementation issue (e.g., OAM cell flows, RM cells, VPI/VCI to frame-level mapping).

- There is no requirement that the Cell Function on one side match the cell function on the other (e.g., one side could be null, as would be the case with a direct interface to a data bus in an ATM switch, and the other could support full AAL1, AAL3/4, AAL5 SAR functions, as might be the case for an ATM DSU supporting the IMA function).

Link management manages the physical links, including the initialization of the links, instantiating link MIB objects, network management and link integrity checks. Finally, unit management entails the overall management of the complete IMA unit.

The IMA specification is quite detailed (it consists of 133 pages), so I refer you to [ATM97a] if you need more information.

SUMMARY

The B-ISDN concept uses SONET at the physical layer to support the ATM operations. The ATM Forum has defined three other physical layer operations that act as service providers to the ATM layer. They are DS3 for 44.736 Mbit/s operations, FDDI for 100 Mbit/s operations, and a private twisted pair UNI. Cells are mapped into these systems, based on the use of special line codes to identify the position of the cells on the media.

The SONET SPE can be used in a wide variety of ways to support various combinations of DSn virtual tributaries (VTs) and CEPTn virtual containers (VCs).

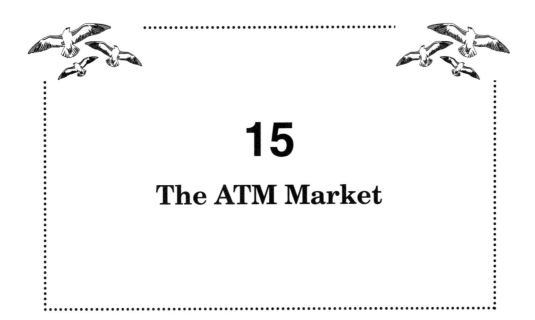

15

The ATM Market

A SOFT MARKET, INITIALLY

The market for ATM has not developed as quickly as some people predicted. Several factors have contributed to the slow introduction of ATM into the marketplace. First, the success of Frame Relay in wide area networks has meant that substantial markets for ATM have been usurped by Frame Relay. Second, "ATM to the desktop" has not occurred on a large scale due to (a) the expense of ATM line cards and software, (b) the difficulty of replacing legacy Ethernet interfaces on the workstation, and (c) the upgrading of these Ethernet interfaces with point-to-point Ethernet and/or Fast Ethernet capabilities. Third, many user devices, such as personal computers and workstations, do not need the speed and features that ATM offers. And fourth, most new, complex technologies take a while to be integrated into the industry.

RECENT SUCCESSES AND PROJECTIONS

ATM is now experiencing more success. For example, ATM now makes up about 11 percent of the LAN backbone market, and the Yankee Group predicts that over the next five years, that market should grow to about 30 percent of the total (with Gigabit Ethernet capturing about

70%) [YANK98]. Most of this market will be for 155 Mbit/s ATM LAN backbone switches.

The market projections for deployment of ATM to support wide area and metropolitan area backbones is larger because Gigabit Ethernet is not deployed in wide areas. Furthermore, ATM is more attractive than the current MAN and WAN options of FDDI and private lines. Thus, the connections of LANs (Fast Ethernets and Gigabit Ethernets) in a "transparent LAN service" (TLS) will be dominated by ATM, according to another market forecast by the Yankee Group (YANK98a]. The Yankee group also projects TLS revenues and backbones to 2001 as follows:

Revenues (in millions of dollars):

FDDI and private lines	$98m
Packet over SONET (POS)	$166m
ATM	$842m

Backbone platforms (in percent):

FDDI and private lines	11%
Packet over SONET (POS)	15%
ATM	74%

ATM AND IP

Even though ATM consumes more overhead than Packet over SONET (POS), it has many more features and is a more mature technology (for example, ATM over SONET is already in the market).

Notwithstanding, some people see IPv6 (IP version 6) over SONET as an attractive alternative to ATM, especially with the use of the Resource Reservation Protocol (RSVP) and IPv6's source routing, priority, and flow label capabilities. In addition, IP operates on the desktop as well as in the network (routers) and provides a convenient and relatively seamless way for placing a standardized multimedia capability into user devices and networks (assuming the IPv4 to IPv6 migration issues are solved).

I agree with this view, but IPv6 is not yet being deployed, and my clients are not eager to move away from the stable IPv4 platform as long as private IP addresses, classless addressing, and network address translation (NAT) capabilities keep their systems going. Clearly, they are looking to the future and learning about IPv6 and the associated migration issues, such as address resolution, socket management, and so on. But in the meantime, ATM *is* being deployed, and gaining market share.

Moreover, the current trend in the industry is to migrate away from traditional IP routing and use label switching (as examples, tag switching and IP switching). Most of these techniques are also using ATM as the label switching fabric.

ATM IN RESIDENTIAL BROADBAND

Some people view ATM as a good candidate to handle the bandwidth management operations on the emerging residential broadband link (the local loop). Others think ATM has too much overhead to be effective. Whatever one's view, bandwidth management must be examined in relation to the twisted pair local loop and the CATV local loop.

For twisted pair, ADSL is assuming the lead role in defining the physical operations on the loop (coding, modulation, and so on). ADSL (see ANSI T1.413) also defines the frame structure for the ADSL traffic. However, ADSL does not define mechanisms for requesting and negotiating bandwidth. So, a technology is needed to support ADSL, and ATM is a candidate.

For CATV, the IEEE has published IEEE 802.14. This specification defines several bandwidth managers; ATM is provided as one option, but it operates within the confines of other IEEE 802.14 protocols.

ATM'S FUTURE

I leave ATM's projections to the market experts. From the technical standpoint, I think ATM will succeed. But for the foreseeable future, it will meet stiff competition from the emerging Fast/Gigabit Ethernet technologies and perhaps the IPv6 platform.

In a touch of irony, ATM is starting to succeed in an area that many Internet watchers never considered: IP/label switching. Indeed, some IP supporters (ATM detractors) have stated that the initials ATM mean "another telecommunications mistake." Yet, ATM is coming along at a very opportune time to rescue the saturated IP routers and their longest match rules. It appears ATM's small header, small payload size, and label switching philosophy are not such bad ideas after all.

IN CONCLUSION

We shall have to wait a bit longer to see what happens to ATM, as well as the other technologies cited here. When I penned the first edition of this book, I thought ATM's position in the marketplace would have been known by now. Well, not yet. So, in the meantime, my advice is to use ATM if it fulfills your needs, don't use it if it does not, and worry about more important matters, such as the progress on your backhand, what your elected politicians are up to, and other weighty subjects.

I welcome your correspondence; you can reach me at uyless@infoinst.com. My web page is at http://www.infoinst.com.

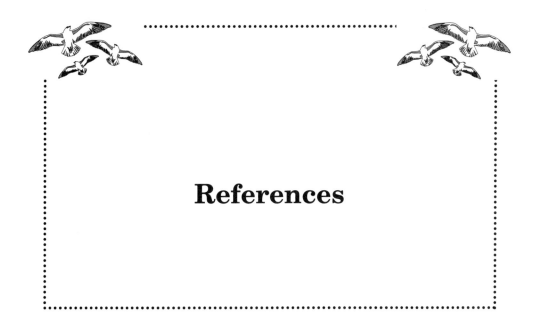

References

In addition to the formal standards for the systems described in this book, these references should prove useful to the reader. Many of them were used for the development of this material.

[AHMA93] Amhad, R., and Halsall, F. (1993). Interconnecting high-speed LANs and backbones, *IEEE Network*, September.

[AMOS79] Amos, J.E., Jr. (1979). Circuit switching: Unique architecture and applications. *IEEE Computer*, June.

[ARMT93] Armitage, G.J., and Adams, K.M.(1993). Packet reassembly during cell loss, *IEEE Network*, September.

[ATM88] ATM Forum (October, 1998), The 2.4 Gbit/s *Physical Layer Specification* (Draft).

[ATM92a] ATM Forum. (June 1, 1992). *ATM user-network interface specification, Version 2.0.*

[ATM93a] ATM Forum. (August 5, 1993). *ATM user-network interface specification, Version 3.0.*

[ATM94a] ATM Forum. (March, 1994). *Education and training work group*, ATM Forum Ambassador's Program.

[ATM94b] ATM Forum. (July 21, 1994). *ATM user-network interface specification, Version 3.1.*

[ATM94c] ATM Forum (September, 1994) *ATM User-Network Interface* (UNI) Specification, Version 3.1.

[ATM96a] ATM Forum (September, 19960 *Integrated Local Management Interface* (ILMI) Specification, Version 4.0

[ATM96b] ATM Forum (April, 1996), *Traffic Management Specification,* Version 4.0.

[ATM97a] ATM Forum (May, 1997), Inverse Multiplexing for ATM (IMA) Specification, Version 1.0.

[ATM97] ATM Forum (January, 1997), Circuit Emulation Service Interoperability Specification (CES-IS), Version 2.0.

[ATT89a] (January, 1989). Observations of error characteristics of fiber optic transmission systems, CCITT SGXVIII, San Diego, CA.

[BELL82] Bellamy, J. (1982). *Digital Telephony*, New York, NY: John Wiley and Sons.

[BELL90a] (May, 1993). Generic requirements for frame relay PVC exchange service, TR-TSV-001369, Issue 1.

[BELL89a]. (September, 1989). Synchronous optical network (SONET) transport systems: common generic criteria, TR-TSY-000253, Issue 1.

[BELL94] Bellman, R.B. (1994). Evolving traditional LANs to ATM, *Business Communications Review*, October.

[BLAC89] Black, U. (1989). *Data Networks, Concepts, Theory and Practice*, Prentice Hall.

[BLAC91] Black, U. (1991). *X.25 and related protocols*, IEEE Computer Society Press.

[BLAC93] Black, U. (1993). *Data link protocols*, Prentice Hall.

[BLAI88] Blair, C. (1988). SLIPs: Definitions, causes, and effects in T1 networks, *A Tautron Application Note, Issue 1*, September. (Note: my thanks to this author for a lucid explanation of slips.)

[BNR92a] Bell Northern Research. (1992). Global systems for mobile communications, *Telesis*, 92.

[BNR94a] Discussions held with Bell Northern Research (BNR) designers during 1993 and 1994.

[BROW94] Brown, P.D. (ed.). (1994). The price is right for ATM to become a serious competitor, *Broadband Networking News*, May.

[CCIT90a] (1990). Voice packetization-packetized voice protocols, CCITT Recommendation G.764, Geneva.

[CDPD93] (July 19, 1993). Cellular digital packet data system specification, *Release 1.0*.

[CHER92] Cherukuri, R. (August 26, 1992). Voice over frame relay networks, A technical paper issued as Frame Relay Forum, FRF 92.33.

[CHEU92] Cheung, N.K. (1992). The infrastructure of gigabit computer networks, *IEEE Communications Magazine*, April,.

[COMM94a] Korostoff, K. (April 18, 1994). Wide-area ATM undergoes trial by MAGIC, *Communications Week*.

[DAVI91] Davidson, R.P., and Muller, N.J. (1991). *The Guide to SONET*, Telecom Library, Inc.

[DELL92] Dell Computer, Intel, and University of Pennsylvania, A study compiled by Marty Baumann, *USA Today*, date not available.

[dePr91] dePrycker, M. (1991). *Asynchronous Transfer Mode*. Ellis Harwood Ltd.

[dePR92] de Prycker, M. (1992) ATM in Belgian Trial. *Communications International*, June.

[DUBO94] DuBois, D. Simnet Inc., Palo Alto, CA. A recommendation from a reviewer of *Emerging Communications Technologies*. (Thank you Mr. DuBois.)

[ECKB92] Eckberg, A.E. (1992). B-ISDN/ATM traffic and congestion control, *IEEE Network*, September.

[EMLI63] Emling, J.W., and Mitchell, D. (1963). The effects of time delay and echoes on telephone conversations. *Bell Systems Technical Journal*, November.

[FORD93] Ford, P.S., Rekhter, Y., and Braun, H.-W. (1993). Improving the routing and addressing of IP. *IEEE Network*, May.

[FORU92] Frame Relay Forum Technical Committee. (May 7, 1992). ÒFrame relay network-to-network interface, phase 1 implementation agreement, Document Number FRF 92.08R1–Draft 1.4.

[GASM93] Gasman, L. (1993). ATM CPE—Who is providing what?, *Business Communications Review*, October.

[GOKE73] Goke, L.R., and Lipovski, G.J. (1973). Banyan networks for partitioning multiprocessor systems. First Annual Symposium on Computer Architecture.

[GRIL93] Grillo, D., MacNamee, R.J.G., and Rashidzadeh, B. (1993). Towards third generation mobile systems: A European possible transition path. *Computer Networks and ISDN Systems*, 25(8).

[GRON92] Gronert, E. (1992). MANS make their mark in Germany. *Data Communications International*, May.

[HAFN94] Hafner, K. (1994). Making sense of the internet. *Newsweek*, October 24.

[HALL92] Hall, M. (ed.). (1992). LAN-based ATM products ready to roll out. *LAN Technology*, September.

[HERM93] Herman, J., and Serjak C. (1993). ATM switches and hubs lead the way to a new era of switched internetworks. *Data Communications*, March.

[HEWL91] Hewlett Packard, Inc. (1991). Introduction to SONET, A tutorial.

[HEWL92] Hewlett Packard, Inc. (1992). Introduction to SONET networks and tests, An internal document.

[HEYW93] Heywood, P. (1993). PTTs gear up to offer high-speed services. *Data Communications*, August.

[HILL91] SONET, An overview. A paper prepared by Hill Associates, Inc., Winooski, VT, 05404.

[HUNT92] Hunter, P. (1992). What price progress?, *Communications International*, June.

[ITU93a] ITU-TS (1993). ITU-TS draft recommendation Q93.B ÒB-ISDN user-network interface layer 3 specification for basic call/bearer control. May.

[JAYA81] Jayant, N.S., and Christensen, S.W. (1981). Effects of packet losses on waveform-coded speech and improvements due to an odd-even interpolation procedure. *IEEE Transactions of Communications*, February.

[JOHN91] Johnson, J.T. (1991). Frame relay mux meets cell relay switch. *Data Communications*, October.

[JOHN92] Johnson, J.T. (1992). ÒGetting access to ATM. *Data Communications LAN Interconnect*, September 21.

[KING94] King, S.S. (1994). Switched virtual networks. *Data Communications*, September.

[KITA91] Kitawaki, N., and Itoh, K. (1991). Pure delay effects of speech quality in telecommunications. *IEEE Journal of Selected Areas in Communications*, May.

[LEE89] Lee, W.C.Y. (1989). *Mobile cellular telecommunications systems*. McGraw-Hill.

[LEE93] Lee, B.G., Kang, M., and Lee, J. (1993). *Broadband telecommunications technology*. Artech House.

[LISO91] Lisowski, B. (1991). Frame relay: what it is and how it works. *A Guide to Frame Relay, Supplement to Business Communications Review*, October.

[LIZZ94] Lizzio, J.R. (1994). Real-time RAID stokrage: the enabling technology for video-on-demand. *Telephony*, May 23.

[LYLE92] Lyles, J.B., and Swinehart, D.C. (1992). The emerging gigabit environment and the role of the local ATM. *IEEE Communications Magazine*, April.

[McCO94] McCoy, E. (1994). SONET, ATM and other broadband technologies. TRA Document # ATL72 16.9100, *Telecommunications Research Associates*, St. Marys, KS.

[MCQU91] McQuillan, J.M. (1991). Cell relay switching. *Data Communications*, September.

[MINO93] Minoli D. (1993). Proposed Cell Relay Bearer Service Stage 1 Description, T1S1.1/93-136 (Revision 1), ANSI Committee T1 (T1S1.1), June.

[MODA97] "Here Comes UBR+", by Houman Modarres, *Telephony,* October 6, 1987.

[MORE9] Moreney, J. (1994). ATM switch decision can wait, *Network World*, September 19.

[NOLL91] Nolle, T. (1991). Frame relay: Standards advance, *Business Communications Review*, October.

[NORT94] Northern Telecom. (1994). Consultant Bulletin 63020.16/02-94, Issue 1, February.

[NORT98] Nortel (1998), *Nortel 1-Meg Modem: Next Generation Data Access, File Technology II-General Hardware,* 50167.16/07-98, Issue 2.

[[NYQU24] Nyquist, H. (1924). Certain factors affecting telegraph speed. *Transactions A.I.E.E.*

[PERL85] Perlman, R. (1985). An algorithm for distributed computation of spanning tree in an extended LAN. *Computer Communications Review*, 15(4) September.

[ROSE92] Rosenberry, W., Kenney D., and Fisher, G. (1992). *Understanding DCE.* OÕReilly & Associates.

[SALA92] Salamone, S. (1992). Sizing up the most critical issues. *Network World*.

[SAND94] Sandberg, J. (1994). Networking. *Wall Street Journal*, November 14.

[SHAN48] Shannon, C. (1948). Mathematical theory of communication, *Bell System Technical Journal, 27*, July and October.

[SRIR90a] Sriram, K. (1990a). Dynamic bandwidth allocation and congestion control schemes for voice and data integration in wideband packet technology, *Proc. IEEE. Supercomm/ICC Õ90, 3*, April.

[SRIR90b] Sriram, K. (1990b). Bandwidth allocation and congestion control scheme for an integrated voice and data network. *US Patent No. 4, 914650*, April 3.

[SRIR93a] Sriram, K. (1993). Methodologies for bandwidth allocation, transmission scheduling, and congestion avoidance in broadband ATM networks. *Computer Networks and ISDN Systems, 26*(1), September.

[SRIR93b] Sriram, K., and Lucantoni, D.M. (1993). Traffic smoothing effects of bit dropping in a packet voice multiplexer. *IEEE Transactions on Communications*, July.

[STEW92] Steward, S.P. (1992). The world report Õ92. *Cellular Business*, May.

[WADA89] Wada, M. (1989). Selective recovery of video packet loss using error concelment. *IEEE Journal of Selected Areas in Communications*, June.

[WALL91] Wallace, B. (1991). Citicorp goes SONET. *Network World*, November 18.

[WERK92] Wernik, M., Aboul-Magd, O., and Gilber, H. (1992). Traffic management for B-ISDN services. *IEEE Network*, September.

[WEST92] Westgate, J. (1992).*OSI Management*, NCC Blackwell.

[WILL92] Williamson, J. (1992). GSM bids for global recognition in a crowded cellular world. *Telephony*, April 6.

[WU93] Wu, T.-H. (1993). Cost-effective network evolution. *IEEE Communications Magazine*, September.

[YANK98a] *"Transparent LAN Service: A Clear Winner in MANs?"* "Yankee Group Report, Vol. 13, No. 6, April 1998.

[YANK98] *"1998 LAN Switch and Hub Market ANalysis",* Yankee Group Report, Vol. 13, No. 5, April, 1998.

[YAP93] Yap, M.-T., and Hutchison (1993). An emulator for evaluating DQDB performance. *Computer Networks and ISDN Systems,* 25(11).

[YOKO93] Yokotani, T., Sato, H., and Nakatsuka, S. (1993). A study on a performance improvement algorithm in DQDB MAN. *Computer Networks and ISDN Systems,* 25(10).

Abbreviations

2 B+D B, B and D channels
AA Administrative authority
AAL CP AAL common part
AAL ATM adaptation layer
ABR available bit rate
ACK positive acknowledgments
ACR allowed cell rate
ADM Add-drop multiplexer
ADPCM Adaptive differential pulse code modulation
AFI Authority Format Identifier
AIS Alarm indication signals
AL alignment field
ANSI American National Standards Institute
AP DPCM Adaptive Predictive DPCM
APS Automatic protection switching
ASE application service element
ATM Asynchronous transfer mode
ATMARP ATM address resolution protocol
BAMM Bidirectional asymmetric multipoint-to-multipoint
BAPM Bidirectional asymmetric point-to-multipoint
BECN backward explicit congestion notification
B-ICI B-ISDN Intercarrier Interface

B-ISDN broadband ISDN
B-ISDN Broadband-Integrated Services Digital Network B-ISDN
B_c Committed burst rate
B_e Excess burst rate
BECN Backward explicit congestion notification
BER Basic encoding rules; Bit error rate
BI Bipolar code
BIP-8 Bit interleaved parity 8 field
BITS Building integrated timing system
BLER Block error rate
BOG bridging
BRI Basic rate interface
BSHR Bi-directional SHR
BSMM Bidirectional symmetric multipoint-to-multipoint
BSPM Bidirectional point-to-point
BSPP Bidirectional symmetric point-to-point
C Cell loss priority
C-Plane Control-plane
C/R Command/response
C/S or C/SAR Convergence services and segmentation and reassembly
CAC Connection admission control
CB credit-based

CBR Constant bit rate
CDF cutoff decrease factor
CDV cell delay variation
CDV Cell delay variation
CE congestion encountered
CEI Connection endpoint identifier
CES Circuit emulation service
CI congestion identification
CID channel identifier
CIR Committed information rate
CLIP callin line identification presentation
CLIR calling line idnetification restriction
CLNP Connectionless Network Layer Protocol
CLP Cell loss priority
CMIP Common Management Information Protocol
CMR cell misinsertion rate
COFA change of frame alignment
COLP connected line identification presentation
COLR connected line identification restriction
CPCS Common part of convergence sublayer (aka Common part CS)
CPE Customer premises equipment
CPI common part identifier
CRBS Cell relay bearer service
CRC Cyclic redundancy check
CRS Cell relay service
CS capability set
CS Convergence sublayer
CSU Channel service unit
CT cordless telephony
CUG closed user group
DCC Data country code
DCE Data circuit-terminating equipment
DCS Digital cross connect
DDI direct dialing in
DE Discard eligibility
DFA DXI frame address
DFI Domain format identifier
DLCI Data link connection identifier
DPCM Differential pulse code modulation
DQDB Distributed queue dual bus
DSP Domain specific part
DSU Data service unit
DXI Data exchange interface

E/O Electrical/optical
EA Address extension
ECSA Exchange Carriers Standards Association
EFI Errored frame indicator
EIM External interface module
EIR Excess information rate
ER explicit rate
ERR exhaustive round robin algorithm
ES end station
ESF T1 extended superframe
ESI end system identifier
FDDI fiber distributed data interface
FDL facility data link
FEC forward error correction
FECN Forward explicit congestion notification
FERF Far-end receive failure
FIFO First-in, first-out
FISU fill-in signal unit
FRS Frame relay service
FRTT fixed round-trip time
FUNI frame user interface
GCRA Generic cell rate algorithm
GFC Generic flow control
GFR guaranteed frame rate
HDLC High level data link control
HDTV high definition television
HE header extension
HEC Header error control
HEL leader extension length
ICD International code designator
ICI Intercarrier interface
ICIP ICI protocol
ICR initial cell rate
ID Identifier
IDI Initial domain identifier
IDN integrated digital network
IDP Initial Domain Part
IE Information element
ILMI Interim local management interface
IME interface management entity
IP internet protocol
ISDN Integrated services digital network
ISO International Standards Organization
ISUP ISDN user part
ITU-T or ITU-TS Formerly known as CCITT

IWF Interworking functions
IWU Interworking unit
IXC Interexchange carrier
LAN Local area network
LANE LAN emulation
LAPD Link access procedure for the D
    channel
LAPM link access procedure for modems
LAPB link access procedure, balanced
LATA Local access and transport area
LCNs Logical channel numbers
LECS LAN emulation configuration
    server
LI Length indicator
LIS logical IP subnet
LLC logical link control
LMEs Layer management entities
LMI Local management interface
LOF Loss of frame
LOP Loss of pointer
LOS Loss of signal
LSB Least significant bit
LSSU link status siganl unit
LTE line terminating equipment
M bit More data bit
M-plane Management plane
MAN Metropolitan Area Network
MAC medium access control
MBS maximum burst size
MCR minimum call rate
MIB Management information base
MID Message identification
ms Millisecond ms
MPOA multipoint over ATM
MSB Most significant bit
MSN multiple subscriber number
MSU message signal unit
MTP message transfer part
MUX multiplexer
NANP North American Numbering Plan
NAKs negative acknowledgments
NAT network address translation
N-BC narrowband bearer capability
NE Network element
N-HLC narrowband high layer compata-
    bility
NHRP next hop resolution protocol

N-LLC narrowband low layer compatabil-
    ity
NNI Network-to-network interface
NSAP network service access points
NT Network termination
NUI Network interface unit
OAMP Operation, administration, mainte-
    nance, and provisioning services
OAM or OAMP Operation, administration,
    and maintenance services or Opera-
    tion, administration, maintenance,
    and provisioning services
OC-n Optical carrier signal
OC Optical carrier
OCD out-of-cell delineation
OS Operating system
OSI Open Systems Interconnection
OSF offset field
OUI Organization unique ID
P parity
PA Pre-arbitrated access
PAD padding bytes
PAM Pulse amplitude modulation
PC protocol control
PCI Protocol control information
PCM Pulse code modulation
PCR Peak cell rate
PD Propagation delay
PDH Plesiochronous digital hierarchy
PDUs Protocol data units
PH packet header
PHY physical
PL Physical layer
PLCP Physical layer convergence protocol
PLP packet layer procedure
PM Physical medium (sublayer)
PMD Physical media dependent
PNNI private network-network interface
POS packet over SONET
PPS Path protection switching
PRS primary reference source
PRI Primary rate interface
PT portable terminal
PTE path terminating equipment
PTI Payload type identifier
PTOs Public Telecommunications Opera-
    tors

PTTs Postal Telephone and Telegraph Ministries
PVCs Permanent virtual circuits
QA Queued arbitrated access
QD Queuing delay
QFC quantum flow control
QLR RR queue length-weighted round robin algorithm
QOS Quality of service
RAM random access memory
RBB residential broadband
RBOCs Regional Bell Operating Companies
RDF redirect flush
RDI remote detect indicator
RFC request comments
RIF rate increase factor
RJE remote job entry
RNR receive not ready
RR receive ready
RSVP resource reservation protocol
RTS Return to send
rt-VBR real-time variable bit rate
SAAL Signaling ATM adaptation layer
SAPI service access point identifier
SAPs Service access points
SAR Segmentation and reassembly
SCP service control points
SCR Sustainable cell rate
SD Switching delay
SDH Synchronous Digital Hierarchy
SDT structured data transfer
SDU Service data unit
SECBR severely errored cell block ratio
SEFS severely errored framing seconds
SFM Switch fabric module
SHR self-healing rings
SI specific information
SMDS Switched Multi-megabit Data Services
SN Sequence number
SNAP subnetwork access protocol
SNI Subscriber-to-network
SNMP Simple Network Management Protocol
SNP Sequence number protection
SONET Synchronous Optical Network

SPE Synchronous payload envelope
SRTS synchronous residual time stamp
SS7 Signaling system #7
SSCF Service specific coordination function
SSCOP Service specific connection-oriented part
SSCP service switching and control point
SSCS Service specific CS
SSP service switching point
STE section terminating equipment
STDM Statistical time division multiplexer
STP Shielded twisted pair
STS Synchronous transport signal
SU siganl units
SVC Switched virtual calls
TA Terminal adapter
TAT Theoretical arrival time
TBE transient buffer exposure
TC Transmission convergence
T_c Time interval
TCAP transaction capabilities application part
TCP transmission control protocol
TCP Transaction Control Protocol
TCP/IP Transaction Control Protocol/Internet Protocol
TCR tagged cell rate
TDM Time division multiplexing
TE Terminal equipment
TEI Terminal endpoint identifier
TE1 terminal equipment type 1
TE2 terminal equipment type 2
TMM Transmission monitoring machine
TS Timestamp
TSI Time slot interchanger
U-plane User plane
UBR unspecifies bit rate
UDT unstructures data transfer
UDP User datagram protocol
UIH header check
ULP upper layer protocols
UME UNI management entity
UMM unidirectional multipoint-to-multipoint
UNI User-to-network interface

UP user part
UPC Usage parameter control
UPM unidirectional point-to-multipoint
UPP unidirectional point-to-point
UUI user-to-user identification
VBR Variable bit rate
VC Virtual channel
VC Virtual container
VCC Virtual channel connection
VCI Virtual circuit identifier

VDR voice digitization rate
VP virtual path
VPC Virtual path connection
VPI virtual path identifier
VPN Virtual private network
VT Virtual tributary
VSLI very long scale integrated
VTOA voive and telephony over ATM
WAN Wide area network

Index

ATM, Volume II

**Prentice Hall Series In
Advanced Communications Technologies**

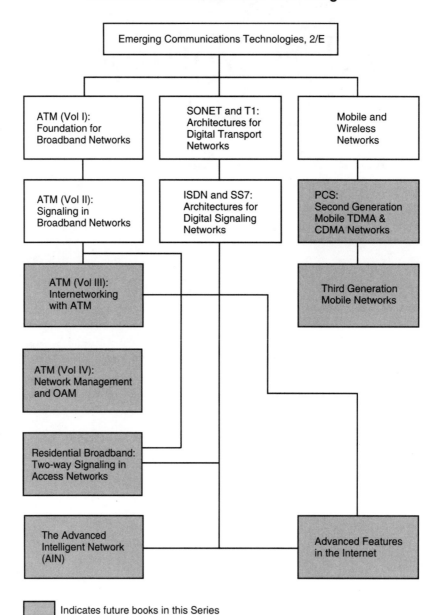

Emerging Communications Technologies, 2/E

ATM (Vol I):
Foundation for
Broadband Networks

SONET and T1:
Architectures for
Digital Transport
Networks

Mobile and
Wireless
Networks

ATM (Vol II):
Signaling in
Broadband Networks

ISDN and SS7:
Architectures for
Digital Signaling
Networks

PCS:
Second Generation
Mobile TDMA &
CDMA Networks

ATM (Vol III):
Internetworking
with ATM

Third Generation
Mobile Networks

ATM (Vol IV):
Network Management
and OAM

Residential Broadband:
Two-way Signaling in
Access Networks

The Advanced
Intelligent Network
(AIN)

Advanced Features
in the Internet

Indicates future books in this Series

ATM, Volume II
SIGNALING
IN BROADBAND
NETWORKS

UYLESS BLACK

To join a Prentice Hall PTR Internet mailing list, point to:
http://www.prenhall.com/mail_lists/

Prentice Hall PTR
Upper Saddle River, New Jersey 07458

Library of Congress Cataloging-in-Publication Data

Black, Uyless D.
   ATM—foundation for broadband networks / Uyless Black.
     p. cm.
   Includes bibliographical references and index.
   ISBN 0–13–571837–6
   1. Asynchronous transfer mode. 2. Broadband communication
systems. I Title.
TK5105.35.B53 1995
621.382—dc20   95–5961
                                        CIP

Acquisitions editor: Mary Franz
Cover designer: Scott Weiss
Cover design director: Jerry Votta
Manufacturing manager: Alexis R. Heydt
Marketing manager: Miles Williams
Compositor/Production services: Pine Tree Composition, Inc.

Published by Prentice Hall PTR
Prentice-Hall, Inc.
A Simon & Schuster Company
Upper Saddle River, New Jersey 07458

Prentice Hall books are widely-used by corporations and government agencies for training,
marketing, and resale.

The publisher offers discounts on this book when ordered in bulk quantities. For more
information contact:

        Corporate Sales Department
        Phone: 800–382–3419
        Fax: 201–236–7141
        E-mail: corpsales@prenhall.com

        Or write:

        Prentice Hall PTR
        Corp. Sales Dept.
        One Lake Street
        Upper Saddle River, New Jersey 07458

Printed in the United States of America
10 9 8 7 6 5 4 3 2 1

ISBN: 0-13-571837-6

Prentice-Hall International (UK) Limited, *London*
Prentice-Hall of Australia Pty. Limited, *Sydney*
Prentice-Hall Canada Inc., *Toronto*
Prentice-Hall Hispanoamericana, S.A., *Mexico*
Prentice-Hall of India Private Limited, *New Delhi*
Prentice-Hall of Japan, Inc., *Tokyo*
Simon & Schuster Asia Pte. Ltd., *Singapore*
Editora Prentice-Hall do Brasil, Ltda., *Rio de Janeiro*

*This book is dedicated to my good friend
and goddaughter Holly Gillen*

During the time that I was writing this book about communications and signaling in broadband networks, I happened to watch a film about dolphins. The film demonstrated how dolphins communicate among themselves with certain types of audible signals, and how they use different signals for selected purposes such as location detection and mating rituals.

I was taken by the nature of their communication signals. At times they seemed to send digital "clicks"—something like the binary pulses employed by modern computer-based networks. At other times, they emitted different audible signals similar to the squeal of a high-pitched analog whistle. In a remarkable display of communications versatility, they alternated between transmitting "digital" and "analog" signals depending upon the occasion. These capabilities are performed by human-made systems with great difficulty and awkwardness (for example, the Digital AMPS technology).

Upon further study, I discovered that the digital clicks are also used as sonar signals and through a process called echolocation, dolphins can navigate and stay aware of their location and surroundings (something like our use of the global positioning system [GPS]).

Some researchers even claim that dolphins can use their signals to stun or kill a prey of another species with an acoustic shock (something like our use of a boom box on our own species).

The dolphins are quite social and scientists state that they possess an intelligence level far above most other mammals. They are said to be great imitators and some can imitate parts of human speech.

But in the final analysis, it is we humans who are the imitators. For time and time again, we find that our human creations and inventions are antedated by the natural world, in this case, the dolphin.

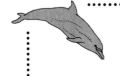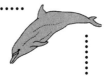

Contents

CHAPTER 3   **ATM Architecture**   **24**

CHAPTER 4   **Signaling System Number 7 (SS7) Architecture**   **39**

CHAPTER 9   **Operations Between UNI and NNI**   **144**

CHAPTER 10   **Other Broadband Signaling Operations
               and Performance Requirements**   **148**

CHAPTER 11   **Private Network–Network Interface (PNNI)**   **159**

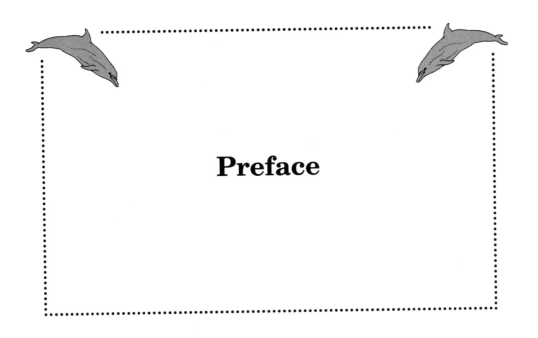

Preface

This book is one in a series of books called *Advanced Communications Technologies*. It is a companion book to *ATM: Foundation for Broadband Networks*. In the first volume, a chapter was devoted to ATM-based signaling operations at the UNI. Since the publication of that book, there has been an increased interest in the industry in signaling, both at the user-network interface (UNI) and the network-network interface (NNI). In addition, most of the specifications that define broadband signaling have now been released, and were not available when I wrote Volume I.

This book is written in response to the general interest of the public and provides a detailed description of the broadband signaling specifications. As the name of Volume I implies, ATM serves as a foundation for broadband networks. These broadband networks may or may not use signaling techniques in their operations, but the term broadband signaling does imply the use of signaling operations in a broadband network.

A separate book in this series is devoted to "narrow band signaling" and it is titled, *ISDN and SS7, Architectures for Digital Signaling Networks*. While this book is a useful reference guide when reading the book you have in your hands, I have included enough tutorial information in *ATM, Volume II* for you to deal with narrowband signaling. I also provided comparisons of narrowband and broadband signaling in this book.

I hope you find this book a valuable addition to your library and I hope you find it fulfills your needs. You can reach me at:

102732.3535@compuserve.com.

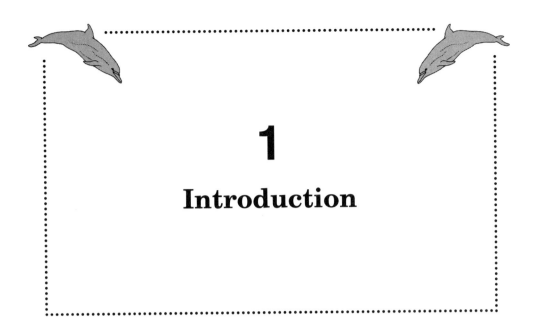

1

Introduction

INTRODUCTION

This chapter introduces the concept of a signaling system and compares a signaling system with a transport system. Early signaling systems are explained and compared to current systems (which are the focus of this book). Narrowband signaling systems are defined and are compared to broadband signaling systems. We also examine the role of the Asynchronous Transfer Mode (ATM) and Signaling System Number 7 (SS7) in broadband signaling networks.

PURPOSE OF A SIGNALING SYSTEM

The purpose of a signaling system is to transfer control information (signaling units) between elements in a telecommunications network. The elements are switches, operations centers, and databases. This information includes signaling units (also called messages) to establish and terminate connections (e.g., a voice call, a data connection) and other information such as directory service and credit card messages.

Originally, signaling systems were designed to set up connections between telephone offices and customer premises equipment (CPE) in order to transport only voice traffic through a voice-oriented, analog network. Today, they are designed to set up connections between service provider offices and CPE in order to transport not only voice but video or data signals through either an analog or a digital network.

TRANSPORT SYSTEMS AND SIGNALING SYSTEMS

A transport system is different from a signaling system. A transport system provides the physical facilities over which the signaling system operates. For example, a transport system defines the physical channel and the electrical/optical nature of the signals that operate on the channel. Examples of transport systems are T1 and the Synchronous Optical Network (SONET).

A signaling system defines how the physical channels are used and how they are allocated and provisioned to fit the user's needs. Signaling networks possess traits that allow the provisioning of bandwidth (capacity) on the physical channels to meet varying user throughput and delay requirements.

Signaling systems allow a user to request the network to provide certain quality of service (QOS) features to the user. They also provide a means for the user to convey certain QOS information to another end user, which the signaling network may act upon or pass (as a courtesy) directly to another user.

Figure 1–1 shows the relationships of a signaling system and a transport system between two machines labeled A and B. The transport

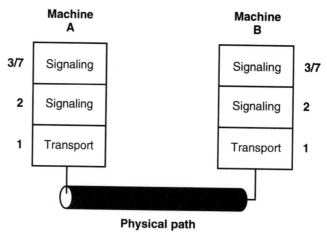

Figure 1–1   Signaling and transport systems.

system operates at layer 1 of the layered model and the signaling system operates at layer 2 or perhaps layers 2 and 3, or layer 7.

The Blurring of the Distinction between Transport and Signaling Networks

The distinction between transport and signaling networks may be blurred in some systems, because they may do some of both. For example, SONET is primarily a transport technology, but it does have some signaling capabilities, and the narrowband Integrated Services Digital Network (ISDN) exhibits both transport and signaling characteristics. I will clarify and amplify this point in later discussions.

NARROWBAND TRANSPORT AND SIGNALING NETWORKS

The T1 System

In 1962 the U.S. Bell System (as it was known in the predivestiture days) installed the first commercial digital voice system in Chicago, Illinois. The system was known as T1 and carried 24 voice channels over copper wire between Bell's telephone offices. (This book uses the terms T1 and DS1 synonmously.)

T1 is designed to act principally as a transport network. Its signaling capabilities are very few, and the provisioning of channels (in the original T1 networks) was a labor-intensive, manual operation in which cables, dip switches, and other hardware had to be altered each time a new or revised user requirement developed.

T1 was designed to support fairly modest requirements for user applications, at least when compared to modern applications' needs. For example, the T1 systems support a transfer rate of 1.544 Mbit/s, and 28 T1s (called T3) operate at approximately 45 Mbit/s. These bit transfer rates may seem high to the reader, but remember that a 45 Mbit/s transport system like T3 only supports 672 voice calls—a lot of T3s have to be in operation to support the public telephone network.

These systems are often called narrowband signaling networks due to their limited capacity, typically no greater than 1.544 Mbit/s or 2.048 Mbit/s.

The T1 systems were designed to set up physical circuits (connections) for a call between two parties. These circuits were provisioned through hardware registers and by apportioning a physical circuit (which is usually called a DS0 channel, with a bit rate of 64 kbit/s) or a part of a physical circuit capacity (part of the circuit's bandwidth) for a call. Once the bandwidth was set up, it was fixed and could not be used by anyone else, even though the original customer would not be using the bandwidth. These networks suffered from bandwidth waste, because of the rigid manner in which bandwidth is allocated. Expensive and time-consuming tasks were involved in modifying and reprovisioning the bandwidth on these earlier systems.

Increasingly, many applications require bandwidth only when sending and receiving information. The vast part of the 64 kbit/s DS0 channel is wasted with a typical user needing only a fraction of the 64 DS0 slice of bandwidth.

X.25 and Packet Switching Systems

In the early 1970s, another technology, called packet switching, was deployed to support data networks. Unlike the T1 networks, which were designed for voice applications, packet switching networks have become the foundation for the majority of data networks.

Unlike T1, packet switching has a more flexible way of allocating bandwidth to users. First, bandwidth is not charged on a fixed basis; a user pays for what is used. Second, bandwidth need not be "nailed-up"; it can be allocated on a more dynamic basis to meet the varying needs of the user. And third, the network has more flexibility in managing bandwidth for all users and can make better use of network resources. Most of the functions came through the use of software to support user requirements instead of the T1 focus on hardware. Experience demonstrates that packet switched systems can be engineered to support up to eight times as many data users on the same T1 channel.

At about the same time that packet switching networks were being deployed, the International Telecommunications Union-Telecommunication Standardization Sector (ITU-T, formerly, the CCITT) published the X.25 specification. X.25 defines the procedures for user computers to communicate with network machines (packet switches) to transport data to another user computer. X.25 has become a widely used industry standard and has facilitated the building of standardized communications interfaces between different vendors' machines.

X.25 was designed for data systems that operate at only a few bit/s or a few hundred bit/s—typically 600 to 9600 bit/s. Although X.25 can be placed on very high-speed media and can operate efficiently at high speed, a substantial amount of subscriber equipment and software has been designed for modest transfer rates—typically no greater than 19.2 kbit/s.

Once again, sending data at a rate of 19.2 kbit/s may seem fast. After all, it translates to a transfer rate of 2400 characters per second (19,200/8 bits per character), and no one can type in an E-mail message that fast. However, for other applications, this speed is not sufficient. File transfers, database updates, and color graphics (to mention a few) need much greater transfer rates.

X.25 does have powerful signaling capabilities. A wide variety of signaling messages can be exchanged between network nodes and user devices to allocate, manage, and deallocate channel capacity for the user.

The Virtual Circuit Concept.   In comparison to T1, X.25 uses a different approach in its operations, called a virtual circuit (as opposed to a physical circuit). The term virtual circuit is used to describe a shared circuit (or circuits) wherein the sharing is transparent to the circuit users. The term was derived from computer architecture (in the 1960s) in which an end user perceives that a computer has more memory than actually exists and the capacity is shared by other users. The idea of a virtual circuit is to allow the bandwidth of physical circuits to be shared on a more flexible basis than what is available in a conventional physical circuit arrangement.

Inband and Out-of-Band Signaling.   Another aspect of X.25 is noteworthy: inband signaling. With this approach, signaling and user traffic share the same physical channel, with part of the channel capacity used for signaling traffic and the remainder of the bandwidth allocated for user traffic. Thus, signaling traffic and user traffic compete with each other for the channel capacity. In contrast, out-of-band signaling employs a separate physical channel for signaling.

Fixed and Variable Length Messages.   The X.25 signaling messages that are sent on the channel are variable length. The size of the message can range from 16 octets to 4096 octets; T1 uses fixed length messages (called frames). With fixed length units, transmission delay is more predictable as is queuing delay (if any) inside the switches. In addition, fixed length buffers are easier to manage than variable length buffers. In essence, a fixed-length system is more deterministic than the use of a technology with variable length data units.[1]

---

[1]There are also several disadvantages to the use of fixed-sized messages, but for this discussion the issue is moot, since broadband signaling is based partly on ATM, which uses fixed length units called cells. The first volume (*ATM: Foundation for Broadband Networks*) on ATM in this series examines this issue in more detail.

SS7 Systems

Newer signaling systems such as SS7 are classified as out-of-band signaling systems because they use a separate channel for signaling information. These systems are also called common channel signaling (CCS) systems because a shared (common) channel is used for signaling. SS7 is designed to be a pure signaling system and provides no features for a transport system. It relies on a transport system such as T1 or SONET to support the signaling services.

Problems with Narrowband Signaling

Some of the systems just described are quite specialized: As examples, T1 is designed for circuit-switched systems and X.25 is designed for packet-switched systems. This approach results in duplicate signaling systems, which is an expensive approach.

The older circuit-switched T1 systems provision bandwidth and do not allow it to be shared. Packet-switched systems are more flexible, but they are designed for data traffic only. Moreover, X.25 introduces considerable delay in the network because it is designed to perform extensive error-checking and editing operations on the traffic.

BROADBAND SIGNALING NETWORKS

A better approach is to combine some of the attractive characteristics of circuit switching, packet switching, and common channel signaling, and that is exactly what broadband signaling networks are designed to do. Their principal characteristics are:

- The provisioning of virtual circuits onto physical circuits to allow a more efficient allocation of network bandwidth.
- The use of out-of-band signaling channels, which translates into a more reliable system and ensures that critical signaling messages are delivered safely across the signaling link between the exchanges.
- Provisioning operations are performed more in software and less in hardware, which, again, provides more flexibility and leads to a more responsive reaction to user requirements and changes.
- The provisioned bandwidth can be accessed (borrowed) by other users (bandwidth is furnished dynamically to another user if one user is not using it).

- Provisioned bandwidth can be asymmetrical; that is, different bandwidth in each direction on the circuit. This feature is attractive for client-server applications wherein one end of the connection sends more traffic than the other end.
- The underlying technology is based on fixed length ATM cells.

This last statement warrants a few more comments. From the perspective of most of the telecommunications standards groups and telecommunications providers, ATM acts as the switching, multiplexing, and virtual circuit mechanism for broadband signaling networks. Technically, nothing precludes the use of other non-ATM options, but the broadband signaling systems that are described in this book allocate virtual circuits based on ATM virtual circuit concepts (for example, the fields in an ATM cell header) and ATM-based bandwidth requirements (for example, sustained and peak cell rate requirements for the virtual circuit).

WHY NOT JUST USE SS7?

Since SS7 is a very powerful and flexible signaling system, why not use it for broadband signaling? The answer is that SS7 is used and is an important part of a broadband signaling system. However, the original SS7 specification is designed for setting up, managing, and tearing down *physical* circuits (or parts of a physical circuit; e.g., a DS0 slot in a DS1 channel). It has no provisions for setting up, managing, and tearing down *virtual* circuits. To support broadband signaling, SS7 is modified to support not only virtual circuits but the operations that are associated with the ATM technology as well.

SUMMARY

Originally, signaling systems were designed to set up physical circuits (connections) between users. Narrowband signaling systems set up fixed slots (DS0 channels) with symmetrical bandwidth of 64 kbit/s in each direction.

Broadband signaling systems still set up connections, but the bandwidth can vary depending upon the individual needs of each user. These connections are based on ATM virtual circuits.

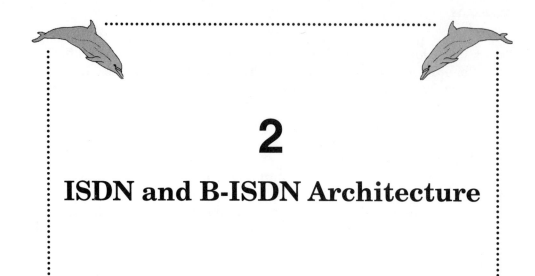

2

ISDN and B-ISDN Architecture

INTRODUCTION

This chapter provides an overview of the Integrated Services Digital Network (ISDN) and Broadband ISDN (B-ISDN) architectures. For detailed information on ISDN, the reader should refer to *ISDN and SS7: Foundation for Digital Signaling Networks*, published as part of this series. The emphasis in this chapter is B-ISDN.

Reference points and functional groups are explained with examples of typical implementations. ISDN logical and physical channels are introduced, as well as the ISDN and B-ISDN logical channels. A review is provided of the ITU-T view of B-ISDN services and the layers that comprise B-ISDN.

INTERFACES AND FUNCTIONAL GROUPINGS

An end user device connects to an ISDN node through a user network interface (UNI protocol) (see Figure 2–1). The UNI provides a connection to the network node (a switch, multiplexer, and the like), that can then support the user traffic flow through a network. At a remote UNI, the process is reversed, with the user traffic presented to the destination user across the UNI.

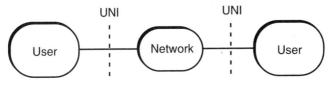

Figure 2–1   The UNI.

Two definitions are in order (and refer to Figure 2–2). Functional group-ings are a set of capabilities needed in an ISDN user-access interface. Specific functions within a functional grouping may be performed by multiple pieces of equipment or software. Second, reference points are the interfaces dividing the functional groupings. Usually, a reference point corresponds to a physical interface between pieces of equipment. The reference point also defines the protocol that runs between the func-tional groupings.

The reference points labeled R, S, T, and U are logical interfaces be-tween the functional groupings, which can be either a terminal equip-ment (TE) type 1, a terminal equipment type 2, or a network termination (NT) grouping. One other purpose of the reference points is to delineate where the responsibility of the network operator ends or begins.

The U reference point is the reference point for the 2-wire side of the NT1 equipment. It separates a NT1 from the line termination (LT) equip-ment. The U interface is a national standard, while interfaces imple-mented at reference points S and T are international standards. The R ref-erence point represents non-ISDN interfaces, such as RS-422 and V.35.

The end-user ISDN terminal is identified by the ISDN term TE1. The TE1 connects to the ISDN through a twisted pair 4-wire digital link. The TE2 connects to a terminal adapter (TA), which is a device that al-lows non-ISDN terminals to operate over ISDN lines. The TA and TE2 devices are connected to either an ISDN NT1 or NT2 device. The NT1 is a device that connects the 4-wire subscriber wiring to the conventional 2-wire local loop. ISDN allows up to eight terminal devices to be ad-dressed by NT1. The NT1 is responsible for the physical layer functions, such as signaling synchronization and timing. NT1 provides a user with a standardized interface.

The NT2 is a more intelligent piece of equipment. It may be found in a digital PBX and contains the layer 2 and 3 protocol functions. It can multiplex 23 B+D channels onto the line at a combined rate of 1.544 Mbit/s or 31 B+D channels at a combined rate of 2.048 Mbit/s.

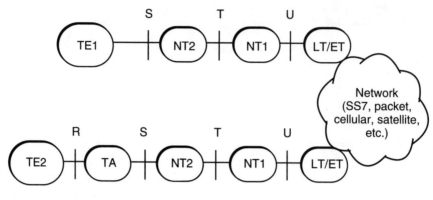

where:
    ET Exchange termination
    LT Line termination
    NT Network termination
    TA Terminal adapter
    TE Terminal equipment

Figure 2–2   ISDN model: Interfaces and functional groupings.

Reference Points

Figure 2–3 provides another view of the ISDN reference points. The purpose of the reference points is to define (1) the mechanical connectors, (2) the electrical signals, and (3) the procedures (protocols) that take place between the functional groupings. The S and T reference points are standardized internationally, and the U reference point is based on national standards within countries.

Depending on national or vendor implementations, network provider responsibilities end at the S, T, or U reference points:

1. At the S reference point, the network provider is responsible for NT2 and NT1

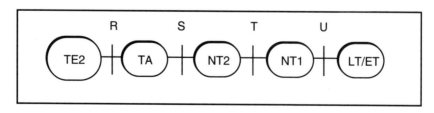

Figure 2–3   Reference points.

2. At reference point T, the network provider is responsible for NT1 only

3. At reference point U, the network provider is responsible for neither NT1 or NT2.

The S and T reference points may be the same (combined) if functional group NT2 is not implemented (that is, no NT2 is used, known as zero NT2). For this arrangement, reference point S operates at reference point T.

The R reference point defines conventional interfaces, such as the ITU-T V Series Recommendations, EIA-232-E, RS-442, and so on. As shown in this figure, the R reference point delineates the boundary between the non-ISDN world and the ISDN world.

ISDN LOGICAL CHANNEL CONCEPT

ISDN employs time division multiplexing (TDM) operations on its physical channels. The TDM slots contain user traffic (such as a voice signal, data signal, etc.), or control traffic (such as a call setup, network management message, etc.). These slots are structured in accordance with concise rules to keep the traffic on the physical channel organized into discrete, identifiable signals. This approach is quite important, because it enables the receiving machine to discern the type of traffic in each of the received slots and react accordingly.

As depicted in Figure 2–4, each slot is part of a "logical channel" that resides on the physical channel. The term logical channel is used to convey the idea of a logical association of TDM slots. On the physical media, the slots are discrete binary 1s and 0s. For ISDN, these slots are called D or B channels.

The B channel is similar to the DS0 slot in a DS1 (T1) system. As a general practice, the B channel at the UNI is mapped into a corresponding DS0 slot for transport across a higher capacity DS1 link. The mapping occurs at the customer premise equipment (CPE) if the customer subscribes to a primary rate (1.544 Mbit/s), or at the central office if the customer subscribes to a basic rate (64 kbit/s).

Each D channel is used to carry control/signaling information or user data. The B channels carry user voice, video, or data traffic. As shown in the figure, a D channel can operate at 16 or 64 kbit/s. In most commercial ISDN deployments, the D channel has not been made available to the end user; it is there but the customer cannot access it.

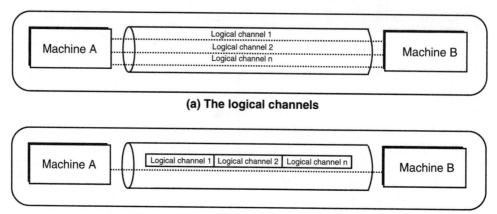

(a) The logical channels

(b) The logical channels on the physical channel

Examples:
• D Channel: 16 or 64 kbit/s
• B Channel: 64 kbit/s
• H Channel: Aggregates of B channels
        H0: 384 kbit/s (6 B channels)
        H11: 1536 kbit/s (24 B channels)
        H12: 1920 kbit/s (30 B channels) etc.

Figure 2–4   ISDN logical channels.

With the recent problems of obtaining bandwidth and connections from the local telephone exchange and the Internet Service Provider (ISP), some companies are re-examining this practice. Although 16 kbit/s is not a lot of bandwidth, it beats having no bandwidth at all.

The B channel operates at 64 kbit/s, although a number of B channels can be aggregated together to provide a user application more transmission capacity. For example, an H0 channel is an aggregation of six B channels, and operates at 384 kbit/s. In North America, these aggregated B channels are known as Fractional T1.

TYPICAL ISDN CONFIGURATION

The TE1 connects to the ISDN through a twisted pair 4-wire digital link (Figure 2–5). This link uses TDM to provide three channels, designated as the B, B and D channels (or 2 B+D). The B channels operate at a speed of 64 kbit/s; the D channel operates at 16 kbit/s. The 2 B+D is designated as the basic rate interface (BRI), and ISDN allows up to eight TE1s to share one 2 B+D link. The purpose of the B channels is to carry

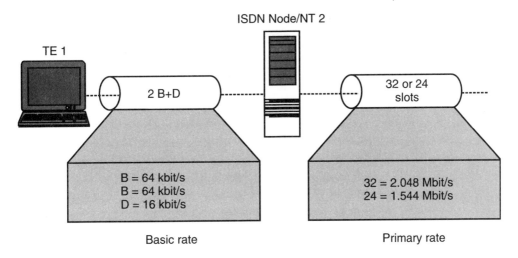

Figure 2–5   An ISDN configuration.

the user payload in the form of voice, compressed video, and data. The purpose of the D channel is to act as an out-of-band control channel for setting up, managing, and clearing the B channel connections.

In other configurations, the user DTE is called a TE2 device. As explained earlier, it is current equipment in use such as workstations and personal computers. The TE2 connects to a TA, which is a device that allows non-ISDN terminals to operate over ISDN lines. The user side of the TA typically uses a conventional physical layer interface such as EIA-232–D, RS-422 or the V-series specifications. It is packaged like an external modem or as a board that plugs into an expansion slot on the TE2 devices.

THE ISDN LAYERS

The ISDN approach is to provide an end user with full support through the seven layers of the OSI Model, although ISDN confines itself to defining the operations at layers 1, 2, and 3 of this model, as shown in Figure 2–6. In so doing, ISDN is divided into two kinds of services: the bearer services, responsible for providing support for the lower 3 layers of the seven-layer standard; and teleservices (for example, telephone, Teletex, Videotex message handling), responsible for providing support through all 7 layers of the model and generally making use of the underlying lower-layer capabilities of the bearer services. The services are referred to as low-layer and high-layer functions, respectively. The ISDN functions are allocated according to the layering principles of the OSI Model.

Figure 2–6 shows the ISDN layers. Layer 1 (the physical layer) uses either the basic rate interface (BRI) or 2 B+D, or the PRI, which is either 23 B+D or 31 B+D. These standards are published in ITU-T's I Series as I.430 and I.431, respectively. Layer 2 (the data link layer) consists of LAPD and is published in the ITU-T Recommendation Q.921. Layer 3 (the network layer), is defined in the ITU-T Recommendation Q.931.

WHAT IS B-ISDN?

B-ISDN cannot be described in one sentence. But it can be defined with a few definitions, numbered 1–9 in the following information.

1. B-ISDN's transfer rate on a communications link is anything beyond narrowband ISDN (N-ISDN). In other words, it is above the

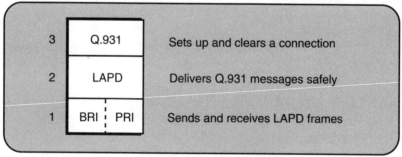

(a) Functions of the layers

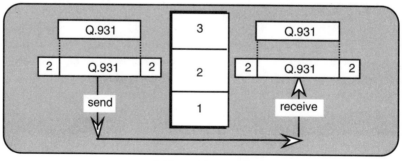

(b) Layer interaction

Figure 2–6   The ISDN layers.

1.544 Mbit/s and 2.048 Mbit/s rates of the N-ISDN primary rate. This declaration does not mean that B-ISDN does not use the lower rates, but the term "broadband" implies higher transfer rates. B-ISDN supports the lower rates as well.

2. B-ISDN continues to use the N-ISDN "model". Therefore, functional entities, reference points are used in all the B-ISDN specifications, but each is appended with a "B", to connote broadband. (See Figure 2–7 for an example of this notation.)

3. B-ISDN continues to use some of the N-ISDN protocols (with modifications), such as the N-ISDN layer three Q.931. This protocol is modified in B-ISDN to set up connections on demand (switched virtual calls [SVCs]) in an ATM network.

4. B-ISDN expands on the N-ISDN Model of layers and planes to accommodate full multiservice capabilities.

5. In a very broad context, B-ISDN describes the types of applications supported in a B-ISDN. A later discussion in this chapter expands on this idea.

6. The technical underpinnings of B-ISDN are ATM and SDH/SONET. They act as the bearer services to the applications that they support.

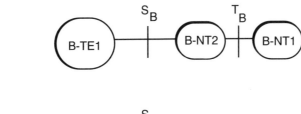

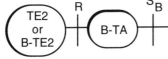

where:
B   Broadband
NT   Network termination (ISDN devices)
S/T ISDN reference points
TA   Terminal adapter (interfaces non-ISDN devices into ISDN interfaces)
TE   Terminal equipment (user devices)
    TE1 ISDN device
    TE2 Non-ISDN device

Figure 2–7   B-ISDN functional groups and reference points.

7. Provisioning of connections is performed on virtual circuits and not DS0 slots.

8. Bandwidth can be set up on a symmetrical or asymmetrical basis.

9. Bandwidth is provisioned on ATM performance parameters, such as peak cell rate, cell delay variation, ect.

B-ISDN FUNCTIONAL ENTITIES AND REFERENCE POINTS

In the early 1980s when ISDN standards were being established, the ITU-T concentrated on the H1 channel for the primary rate interface (PRI) and the 2 B+D interface for the basic rate interface (BRI). Interest shifted in the mid-1980s to higher speed channels due to the recognition of the need and the inadequacies of the BRI and PRI technologies. The various standards groups recognized the value of the architecture of ISDN and believed that higher capacity specifications could use the basic concepts of the work performed in the 1980s.

Thus, B-ISDN started out as an extension of ISDN and has many concepts similar to ISDN. For example, functional groupings still consist of TE1, TE2, NT1, NT2, and TA. Reference points are still R, S, and T. These are conveniently tagged with the letter B in front of them to connote the broadband architecture.

It should be emphasized that the similarities between ISDN and B-ISDN are only in concept and work well enough for a general model. In practice, the ISDN and B-ISDN interfaces are not compatible. It is impossible to upgrade an ISDN interface by simply supplementing it with B-ISDN functional groups and reference points. Therefore, the reader should consider these terms as abstract conceptions that are still useful for understanding the overall B-ISDN architecture.

Another point that should be noted is that most of the specifications (recommendations) developed by the ITU-T are written from the view of the network provider, and not the network user. This approach merely reflects the slant of the ITU-T, which, historically, has been to publish standards for use by public telecommunications operators (PTOs, such as AT&T, British Telecom, MCI, Sprint, etc.).

The B-ISDN Planes and Layers

The rather abstract view of B-ISDN and ATM can be viewed in a more pragmatic way. The three planes (control, user, and management)

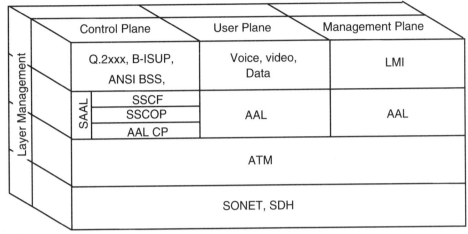

where:
AAL   ATM adaptation layer
LMI   Local management interface
SAAL   Signaling AAL
SSCOP   Service Specific Connection-Oriented Part
SSCF   Service Specific Coordination Function

Figure 2–8   Examples of protocol placement in the B-ISDN layers.

are shown in Figure 2–8 with the placements of protocols residing in the layers. Strictly speaking, the B-ISDN model defines SDH for the physical layer, although this figure shows other choices.

The ATM Adaptation Layer (AAL) is designed to support different types of applications and different types of traffic, such as voice, video, and data. The AAL plays a key role in the ability of an ATM network to support multi-application operations. It isolates the ATM layer from the myriad operations necessary to support diverse types of traffic. The ATM chapter will explain that AAL is divided into a convergence sublayer (CS) and a segmentation and reassembly sublayer (SAR). CS operations are tailored, depending on the type of application it is supporting. SAR operations entail the segmentation of payload into 48-octet SDUs at the originating SAR and reassembling the SDUs into the original payload at the receiver.

In the B-ISDN Signaling Model, the signaling AAL (SAAL) is designed to support the control plane. It is in this plane that the signaling operations take place

The ATM layer's primary responsibility is the management of the sending and receiving of cells between the user node and the network node. It adds and processes the 5-octet cell header.

The control plane contains the Q.2931 and B-ISDN signaling protocols that are used to set up connections in the ATM network (Q.2931 is a variation of Q.931). It also contains a variety of ITU-T X.2xxx Recommendations. The layer below Q.2931 is the signaling ATM adaptation layer (SAAL). SAAL contains three sublayers. Briefly, they provide the following functions. The AAL common part (AAL CP) detects corrupted traffic transported across any interface using the control plane procedures. The service-specific connection-oriented part (SSCOP) supports the transfer of variable length traffic across the interface and recovers from erred or lost service data units. The service-specific coordination function (SSCF) provides the interface to the next upper layer, in this case, Q.2931.

In the middle of Figure 2–8 is the user plane, which contains user- and applications-specific protocols, such as Transmission Control Protocol/Internet Protocol (TCP/IP) and the File Transfer Protocol (FTP). These protocols are chosen arbitrarily as examples of typical user protocols.

The management plane provides the required management services and is implemented with the ATM Local Management Interface (LMI). The Internet Simple Network Management Protocol (SNMP) and/or the OSI Common Management Information Protocol (CMIP) can also reside in the C-plane.

Figure 2–9 shows how the layers in the planes in the user machine communicate with the network machine or another user machine. The user device is represented by the stacks of layers on the left side of the figure, and the network node is represented by the stacks of the right side.

In accordance with conventional OSI concepts, each layer in the user machine communicates with its peer layer in the network node and vice versa. The one exception to this statement is at the U-plane. The ATM node (and ATM network) does not process the PDUs of the AAL and the user-specific protocols. This traffic is passed through the network to the corresponding peer layers on the remote side of the network. Once again, this concept is in the spirit of the OSI Model and its encapsulation/decapsulation techniques and the notion of the transparent aspect of a service data unit (SDU). To the ATM network, AAL and upper layer operations are SDUs.

MAJOR FUNCTIONS OF THE LAYERS

Figure 2–10 summarizes the ITU-T I.321 view of the major functions of the layers and sublayers of B-ISDN. The functions are listed on the left side of the figure, and the layers or sublayers in which the functions operate are shown in the right side of the figure.

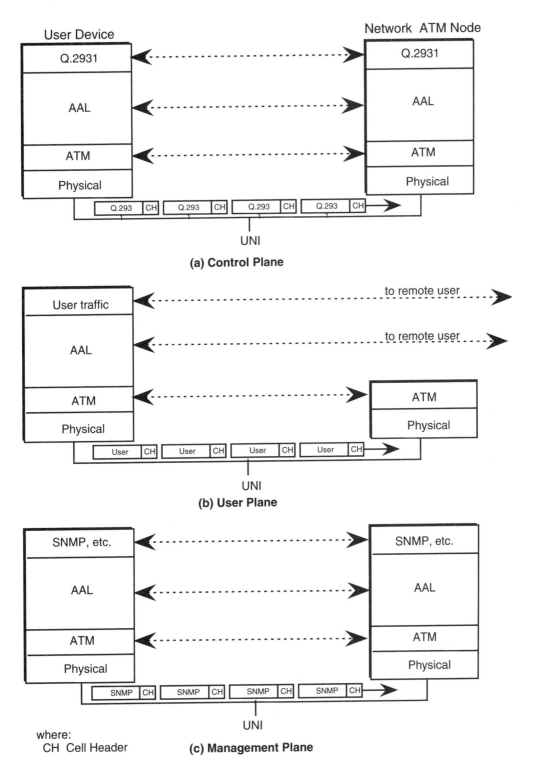

User Device

Network ATM Node

Q.2931	Q.2931
AAL	AAL
ATM	ATM
Physical	Physical

| Q.293 | CH | Q.293 | CH | Q.293 | CH | Q.293 | CH |

UNI

(a) Control Plane

User traffic	to remote user
AAL	to remote user
ATM	ATM
Physical	Physical

| User | CH | User | CH | User | CH | User | CH |

UNI

(b) User Plane

SNMP, etc.	SNMP, etc.
AAL	AAL
ATM	ATM
Physical	Physical

| SNMP | CH | SNMP | CH | SNMP | CH | SNMP | CH |

UNI

where:
CH Cell Header

(c) Management Plane

Figure 2–9   Relationships of the B-ISDN peer layers.

19

	Higher Layer Functions		Names of Higher Layers	
Layer Management	Convergence	CS	AAL	
	Segmentation and reassembly	SAR		
	Generic flow control	ATM		
	Cell header processing			
	VPI/VCI processing			
	Cell muxing and demuxing			
	Cell rate decoupling	TC	PL	
	HEC header processing			
	Cell delineation			
	Transmission frame adaptation			
	Transmission frame generation/recovery			
	Bit timing	PM		
	Physical medium			

where:
AAL   ATM adaptation layer
ATM   Asynchronous transfer mode
CS   Convergence sublayer
PL   Physical layer
PM   Physical medium sublayer
SAR   Segmentation and reassembly sublayer
TC   Transmission convergence sublayer
VPI   Virtual path identifier
VCI   Virtual channel identifier

Figure 2–10   B-ISDN layer functions.

The physical layer (PL) contains two sublayers: the physical medium sublayer (PM) and the transmission convergence sublayer (TC). PM functions depend upon the exact nature of the medium (single mode fiber, microwave, etc.). It is responsible for typical physical layer functions, such as bit transfer/reception and bit synchronization. TC is responsible for conventional physical layer operations that are not medium dependent. It is organized into five major functions.

Transmission frame generation/recovery is responsible for the generation and recovery of PDUs. Transmission frame adaptation is responsible for placing and extracting the cell into and out of the physical layer frame. Cell delineation is responsible for the originating endpoint to define the cell boundaries in order for the receiving endpoint to recover all cells. Cell header processing is responsible for generating a header error check (HEC) field at the originating endpoint and processing it at the terminating endpoint in order to determine if the cell header has been damaged in transit. Cell rate decoupling inserts idle cells at the sending end and extracts them at the receiving end in order to adapt to the physical level bandwidth capacity.

The ATM layer is independent of the physical layer operations and, conceptually, does not care what medium an ATM cell is running on. The ATM layer is organized into four major functions.

Cell muxing and demuxing is responsible for multiplexing (combining) cells from various virtual connections at the originating endpoint and demultiplexing them at the terminating endpoint. VPI/VCI processing is responsible for processing the labels/identifiers in a cell header at each ATM node. ATM virtual connections are identified by a virtual path identifier (VPI) and a virtual channel identifier (VCI). Cell header processing creates the cell header (with the exception of the HEC field) at the originating endpoint and interprets/translates it at the terminating endpoint. The VPI/VCI may be translated into a SAP at this receiver. Generic flow control is responsible for creating the generic flow control field in the ATM header at the originator and acting upon it at the receiver.

The functions of the AAL, CS, and SAR were described earlier in this chapter.

CLASSIFICATION OF BROADBAND SERVICES

The ITU-T Recommendation I.211 describes the services offered by B-ISDN. The services are classified as either interactive services or distribution services. Interactive services, as the name implies, entail an ongoing dialogue between the service user and service provider. The distribution services also entail a dialogue between the service provider and service user but the dialogue is oriented toward a batch or remote job entry (RJE) basis.

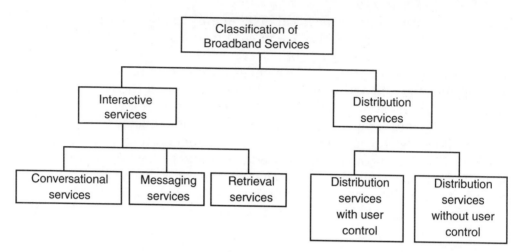

Figure 2–11   Classification of broadband services.

As depicted in Figure 2–11, interactive services are further classified as (1) conversational services, (2) messaging services, and (3) retrieval services. Distribution services are further classified as distribution services without user individual presentation control and distribution services with user individual presentation control.

Conversational services are interactive dialogues with real-time operations. In this context, real-time means that there are no store-and-forward operations occurring between the service user and service provider. For example, interactive teleshopping, ongoing message exchanges between two people, LAN-to-LAN communications, and building surveillance fall into the conversational services category.

Messaging services include user-to-user communications, such as video mail service or document mail service, which can be done on a conversational basis or on demand.

Retrieval services fall into the store-and-forward category where a user can obtain information stored for pubic use. This information can be retrieved on an individual basis from the service provider to the service user. Archival information is a good example of retrieval services.

Distribution services without user individual presentation control include conventional broadcast services such as television and radio. As the reader might expect, this service provides continuous flows of information where service users can obtain unlimited access to the information.

In contrast, distribution services with user individual presentation control allows the central source to distribute the information to a large or small number of users based on some type of cyclical repetition. Obviously, the B-ISDN category of interest here is the emerging video-on-demand market.

SUMMARY

ISDN is designed to be an all-digital user network interface (UNI). It is intended to be vendor and application independent. It supports user traffic on its B channels and allocates part of its bandwidth for signaling and control with its D channel. Through the use of TEIs and SAPIs, it can support and identify multiple workstations and applications within the workstations. And through the use of the terminal adapter (TA), it can support non-ISDN interfaces.

B-ISDN is based on the ISDN model, but is concerned with virtual circuits instead of DS0 slots. The B-ISDN virtual circuits are provisioned based on ATM performance parameters, such as peak rate, sustained cell rate, and cell delay variation.

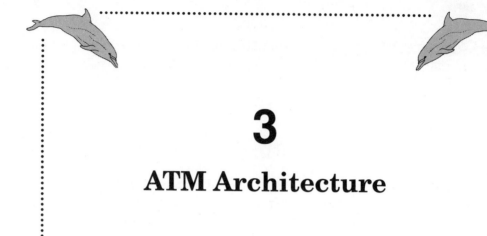

3

ATM Architecture

INTRODUCTION

This chapter provides an overview of the major functions of ATM networks. The initial part of the chapter describes how ATM supports different types of traffic and manages connections. The chapter also explains how ATM users are identified to the network through virtual connections.

ATM ARCHITECTURE

The Asynchronous Transfer Mode (ATM) forms the basis for many broadband networks, and it forms part of the foundation for B-ISDN networks. ATM uses multiplexing, switching, and segmentation/reassembly operations to support a high-speed transport network.

In an ATM network, all traffic is divided into small fixed-size units, called cells, and is sent over one channel and switched based on information in the cell header. The cell header contains two values, called the virtual path and virtual channel identifiers, which identify the cell to distinguish it unambiguously from other connections' cells.

ATM supports a multimedia environment; therefore, it must guarantee limits for delay and loss for different applications. It is also designed to exhibit high throughput and low delay by maximizing switch-

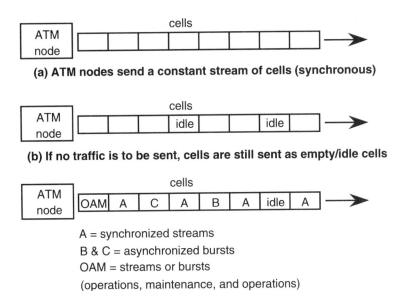

(a) ATM nodes send a constant stream of cells (synchronous)

(b) If no traffic is to be sent, cells are still sent as empty/idle cells

A = synchronized streams

B & C = asynchronized bursts

OAM = streams or bursts

(operations, maintenance, and operations)

(c) All traffic fills the cells synchronously or asynchronously

Figure 3–1   ATM transmission streams.

ing speed with the use of (1) short headers, (2) predefined paths, and (3) no link-to-link error recovery.

Newcomers to ATM often wonder why ATM has the term "asynchronous" as part of its title, especially since it supports synchronous traffic, such as voice and video applications. As depicted in Figure 3–1, the term is used because traffic is not necessarily assigned to fixed slots (cells) on the transmission channel, such as in a conventional time division multiplexing (TDM) system. Therefore, the cells of an application are not always in a fixed position in the channel. Because of this asynchronous aspect of the scheme, each cell must have a header attached to it that identifies each application's traffic in the cell stream. The scheme permits either synchronous or asynchronous allocation of the cells.

Even synchronous traffic, such as voice, can be placed into an ATM network in an asynchronous (bursty) fashion, as long as the receiving user machine "smooths" the asynchronous, bursty cell flow to a TDM-type presentation at the receiving application.

In Figure 3–1a, the ATM nodes send and receive a constant stream of cells. If the cells contain no traffic, they are identified as idle cells (Figure 3–1b). As stated previously, the cells can be filled either synchronously or asynchronously (as shown in Figure 3–1c).

WHY THE INTEREST IN ATM?

Without question, ATM has attracted considerable attention in the telecommunications industry. Other than the fact that new technologies attract articles in trade magazines, why has ATM drawn so much attention?

First, ATM is one of the few technologies that supports the transport of voice, video, and data applications over one media and one platform. Second, ATM is one of the few technologies to support LAN, WAN, and MAN traffic with one platform. It also allows a user to negotiate quality of service (QOS) features with the network, such as delay, CBR, VBR, ect.

ATM is designed to facilitate the implementation of many of these services in hardware, which translates to fast processing of all traffic and low delay through switches and networks.

ATM also allows a user to obtain scalable bandwidth and bandwidth on demand. A user need not be allocated fixed bandwidth, as in a time division multiplexed system. Since ATM does not define a specific port speed at the ATM and user devices, an ATM device can support different link speeds, and the switching fabric can be upgraded (made faster) as more devices (and/or more traffic) are added to the system. Lastly, ATM is a telecommunications transport technology that is a worldwide standard.

These statements are not meant to imply that other technologies are not designed to provide the same attractive services, but ATM offers an attractive combination of them.

ATM AND B-ISDN

ATM is designed for use with B-ISDN, which, in turn, is designed to support public networks. However, ATM can also be employed in private networks and therefore comes in two forms for the user-network interface (UNI):

- A public UNI defines the interface between a public service ATM network and a private ATM switch.
- A private UNI defines an ATM interface with an end user and a private ATM switch.

This distinction may seem somewhat superficial, but it is important because each interface will likely use different physical media and span different geographical distances.

It is obvious from a brief glance at Figure 3–2 that the ATM interfaces

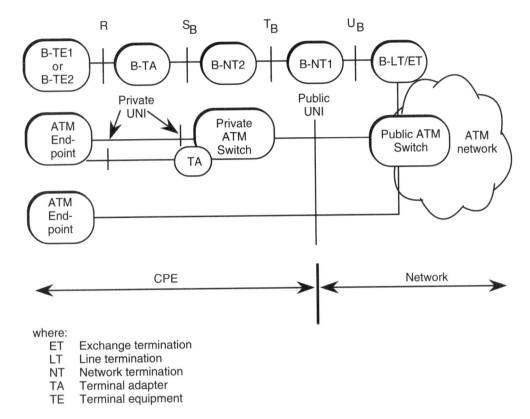

Figure 3–2   Asynchronous Transfer Mode (ATM) B-ISDN model.

and topology are organized around the ISDN model. As just stated, the UNI can be either public or private, and can span across S_B, T_B, and U_B interfaces. Internal adapters may or may not be involved. If they are involved, a user device (the B-TE1 or B-TE2) is connected through the R reference point to the B-TA. B-NT2s and B-NT1s are also permitted at the interface, with B-NT2 considered to be part of the CPE. For purposes of simplicity, the picture shows only one side of an ATM network. The other side could be a mirror image of the side shown in the figure, or it could have variations of the interfaces and components shown in the figure.

THE ATM LAYERS

As depicted in Figure 3–3, ATM provides convergence functions at the ATM adaptation layer (AAL) for connection-oriented and connection-

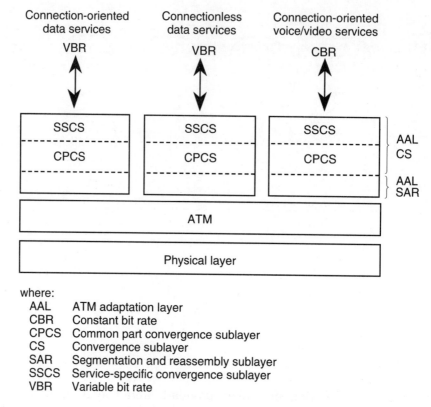

Figure 3–3   The ATM layers.

less variable bit rate (VBR) applications. It supports isochronous applications (voice, video) with constant bit rate (CBR) services.

A convenient way to think of the AAL is that it is actually divided into two sublayers, as shown in Figure 3–3. The segmentation and reassembly (SAR) sublayer, as the name implies, is responsible for processing user PDUs that are different in size and format into ATM cells at the sending site and reassembling the cells into the user-formatted PDUs at the receiving site. The other sublayer is called the convergence sublayer (CS), and its functions depend upon the type of traffic being processed by the AAL, such as voice, video, or data.

The SAR and CS entities provide standardized interfaces to the ATM layer. The ATM layer is then responsible for relaying and routing the traffic through the ATM switch. The ATM layer is connection-oriented and cells are associated with established virtual connections. Traffic must be segmented into cells by the AAL before the ATM layer can process the traffic. The switch uses the VPI/VCI label to identify the connection to which the cell is associated.

Broadband virtual private networks (VPNs) may or may not use the services of the ATM adaptation layer. The decision to use this service depends on the nature of the VPN traffic as it enters the ATM device.

The ATM layers do not map directly with the OSI layers. The ATM layer performs operations typically found in layers 2 and 3 of the OSI Model. The AAL combines features of layers 2 and 4 of the OSI Model. It is not a clean fit, but then, the OSI Model is over thirteen years old and it should be changed to reflect the emerging technologies.

The physical layer can be a SONET or SDH carrier. It may also be other carrier technologies, such as DS3, E3, or FDDI.

Whatever the implementation of AAL at the user device, the ATM network is not concerned with AAL operations for the ongoing processing of user traffic. Indeed, the ATM bearer service is "masked" from these CS and SAR functions. The ATM bearer service includes the ATM and physical layers. The bearer services are application independent, and AAL is tasked with accommodating to the requirements of different applications.

These ideas are amplified in Figure 3–4. For the transfer of user payload, upper layer protocols (ULP) and AAL operations are not invoked in the ATM network functions. The dotted arrows indicate that logical operations occur between peer layers at the user nodes and the ATM nodes. Therefore, the ULP headers, user payload, and the AAL headers are passed transparently through the ATM network. Of course, AAL must be invoked for the C-plane and M-plane because AAL must be available to assemble the payload in the cells back to an intelligible ULP PDU.

However, the bottom part of the figure shows that these upper layers are invoked by the network of SVC and OAM traffic. Whether the node inside the network invokes these layers depends upon the nature of the traffic. For example, if the traffic is a network management message between the user and its local node, then of course the "internal" network nodes will not participate in the operation.

VIRTUAL CIRCUITS WITH THE VPCI, VPI, AND VCI

Earlier discussions explained that an ATM connection is identified through two labels called the virtual path identifier (VPI) and virtual channel identifier (VCI). In each direction, at a given interface, different virtual paths are multiplexed by ATM onto a physical circuit. The VPIs and VCIs identify these multiplexed connections (see Figure 3–5).

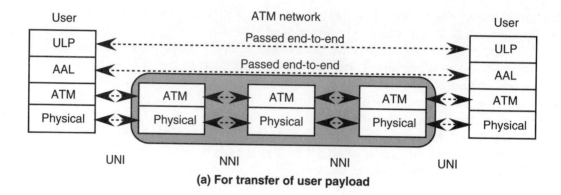

(a) For transfer of user payload

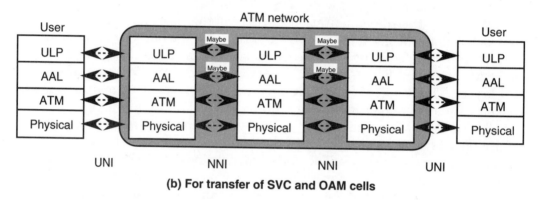

(b) For transfer of SVC and OAM cells

where:
  OAM   Operations, administration, and maintenance
  SVC   Switched virtual calls
  ULP   Upper layer protocols

Figure 3–4   Relationship of user and network layers.

    Virtual channel connections can have end-to-end significance be-
tween two end users, usually between two AAL entities. The values of
these connection identifiers can change as the traffic is relayed through
the ATM network. For example, in a switched virtual connection, the
specific VCI value has no end-to-end significance. It is the responsibility
of the ATM network to "keep track" of the different VCI values as they
relate to each other on an end-to-end basis. Perhaps a good way to view
the relationship of VCIs and VPIs is to think that VCIs are part of VPIs;
they exist within the VPIs.

    Routing in the ATM network is performed by the ATM switch exam-
ining both the VCI and VPI fields in the cell or only the VPI field. This

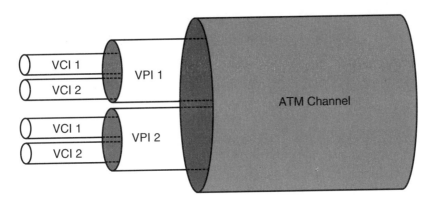

where:
VCI = Virtual channel identifiers
    VC link = terminated by points where VCI is assigned, translated or removed
VPI = Virtual path identifiers
    VP link = terminated by points where VPI is assigned, translated or removed

Figure 3–5   The ATM connection identifiers.

choice depends on how the switch is designed and if VCIs are terminated within the network.[1]

The VCI/VPI fields can be used with switched or nonswitched ATM operations. They can be used with point-to-point or point-to-multipoint operations. They can be pre-established (PVCs) or set up on demand, based on signaling procedures, such as the B-ISDN network layer protocol (Q.2931).

Additionally, the value assigned to the VCI at the user-network interface (UNI) can be assigned by the network, the user, or through a negotiation process between the network and the user.

To review briefly, the ATM layer has two multiplexing hierarchies: the virtual channel and the virtual path. The virtual path identifier (VPI) is a bundle of virtual channels. Each bundle must have the same end points. The purpose of the VPI is to identify a group of virtual channel (VC) connections. This approach allows VCIs to be "nailed-up" end-to-end to provide semi-permanent connections for the support of a large number of user sessions. VPIs and VCIs can also be established on demand.

---

[1]Some ATM implementations pass the VCI value unaltered through the network and use only the VPI to identify and switch the cell. The VCI is "fixed" and is transported transparently by the ATM network. This technique is called transparent VP service in the ATM Forum UNI specification (version 4.0). It is also known as VP switching.

The VC is used to identify a unidirectional facility for the transfer of the ATM traffic. The VCI is assigned at the time a VC session is activated in the ATM network. Routing might occur in an ATM network at the VC level, or VCs can be mapped through the network without further translation. If VCIs are used in the network, the ATM switch must translate the incoming VCI values into outgoing VCI values on the outgoing VC links. The VC links must be concatenated to form a full virtual channel connection (VCC). The VCCs are used for user-to-user, user-to-network, or network transfer of traffic.

The VPI identifies a group of VC links that share the same virtual path connection (VPC). The VPI value is assigned each time the VP is switched in the ATM network. Like the VC, the VP is unidirectional for the transfer of traffic between two contiguous ATM entities.

Referring to Figure 3–5, two different VCs that belong to different VPs at a particular interface are allowed to have the same VCI value (VCI 1, VCI 2). Consequently, the concatenation of VCI and VPI is necessary to uniquely identify a virtual connection.

Virtual Path Connection Identifier (VPCI)

The reader may have heard of or read about another label called the VPCI. It is used in broadband signaling, but the ATM layer is not concerned or aware of its presence (it is in another layer). The VPCI is explained in Chapter 5 (see the section entitled, "Virtual Path Connection Identifier [VPCI]").

THE ATM CELL AND CELL HEADER

The ATM PDU is called a cell (Figure 3–6). It is 53 octets in length, with 5 octets devoted to the ATM cell header and 48 octets used by AAL and the user payload. As shown in this figure, the ATM cell is configured slightly differently for the UNI than for the NNI. Since flow control and OAM operate at the UNI interface, a flow control field is defined for the traffic traversing this interface, but not at the NNI. The flow control field is called the generic flow control (GFC) field. If GFC is not used, this 4-bit field is set to zeros.

Most of the values in the 5-octet cell header consist of the virtual circuit labels of VPI and VCI. Most of the VPI and VCI overhead values are available to use as the network administrator chooses. Herein are some examples of how they can be used.

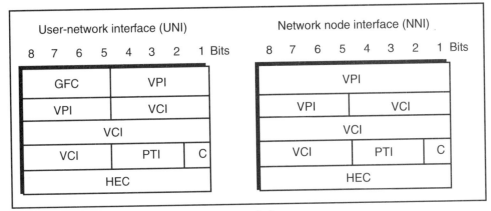

(a) A general view

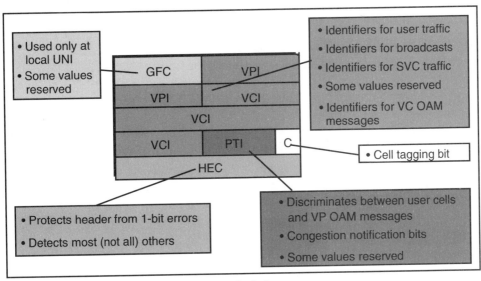

(b) A detailed view

where:
C: Cell loss priority
GFC: Generic flow control
HEC: Header error control
PTI: Payload type identifier
VCI: Virtual channel identifier
VPI: Virtual path identifier

Figure 3–6   The ATM protocol data units-PDUs (cells).

Multiple VCs can be associated with one VP. This approach can be used to assign a certain amount of bandwidth to a VP and then allocate it among the associated VCs. "Bundling" VCs in VPs allows one OAM message to be transmitted that provides information about multiple VCs, by using the VPI value in the header. Some implementations do not use all the bits of VPI/VCI to avoid processing all the bits in the VP and VC fields. Some implementations examine only the VPI bits at intermediate nodes in the network.

A payload type identifier (PTI) field identifies the type of traffic residing in the cell. The cell may contain user traffic or management/control traffic. The standards bodies have expanded the use of this field to identify other payload types (OAM, control, etc.). Interestingly, the GFC field does not contain the congestion notification codes, because the name of the field was created before all of its functions were identified. The flow control fields (actually, congestion notification bits) are contained in the PTI field.

The cell loss priority (C) field is a 1-bit value. If C is set to 1, the cell has a better chance of being discarded by the network. Whether the cell is discarded depends on network conditions and the policy of the network administrator. The field C set to 0 indicates a higher priority of the cell to the network.

The header error control (HEC) field is an error check field, which can also correct a 1-bit error. It is calculated on the 5-octet ATM header, and not on the 48-octet user payload. ATM employs an adaptive error detection/correction mechanism with the HEC. The transmitter calculates the HEC value on the first four octets of the header.

A CLOSER LOOK AT AAL

AAL is organized around a concept called service classes, which are summarized in Table 3–1. The classes are defined with regard to the following operations:

- Timing between sender and receiver (present or not present)
- Bit rate (variable or constant)
- Connectionless or connection-oriented sessions between sender and receiver
- Sequencing of user payload
- Flow control operations

Table 3–1   Support Operations for AAL Classes (Note: Work is underway to redefine AAL type 2)

Class	A	B	C	D
Timing	Synchronous	Scnchronous	Asynchronous	Asynchronous
Bit transfer	Constant	Variable	Variable	Variable
Connection mode	Connection-oriented	Connection-oriented	Connection-oriented	Connection-less
AAL type	1	2	3/4 and 5	3/4 and 5

- Accounting for user traffic
- Segmentation and reassembly (SAR) of user PDUs

As of this writing, the ITU-T had approved four classes, with labels of A through D. We will now summarize these classes and their major features. Table 3–1 summarizes the following thoughts.

Classes A and B require timing relationships between the source and destination. Therefore, clocking mechanisms are utilized for this traffic. ATM does not specify the type of synchronization—it could be a time stamp or a synchronous clock. This function is performed in the application running on top of AAL. Classes C and D do not require precise timing relationships. A constant bit rate (CBR) is required for class A, and a variable bit rate (VBR) is permitted for classes B, C, and D. Classes A, B, and C are connection-oriented, while class D is connection-less.

It is obvious that these classes are intended to support different types of user applications. For example, class A is designed to support a CBR requirement for high-quality video applications. On the other hand, class B, while connection-oriented, supports VBR applications and is applicable for VBR video and voice applications. For example, the class B service could be used by information retrieval services in which large amounts of video traffic are sent to the user and then delays occur as the user examines the information.

Class C services are the connection-oriented data transfer services such as X.25-type connections. Conventional connectionless services such as datagram networks are supported with class D services. Both of these classes also support (final decisions by ITU-T still pending) the multiplexing of multiple end users' traffic over one connection.

As of this writing, other classes are under study and undergoing revisions through ITU-T working groups. This work has been published in ITU-T Recommendation I.363 Annex 5.

Formats of the AAL PDUs

Figure 3–7 illustrates the formats of the AAL PDUs. AAL uses type 1 protocol data units (PDUs) to support applications requiring a constant bit rate transfer to and from the layer above AAL. It is also responsible for the following tasks:

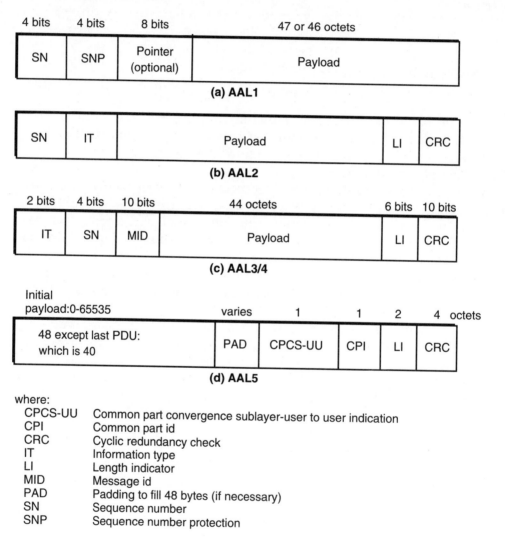

(a) AAL1

(b) AAL2

(c) AAL3/4

(d) AAL5

where:
CPCS-UU	Common part convergence sublayer-user to user indication
CPI	Common part id
CRC	Cyclic redundancy check
IT	Information type
LI	Length indicator
MID	Message id
PAD	Padding to fill 48 bytes (if necessary)
SN	Sequence number
SNP	Sequence number protection

Figure 3–7 The AAL PDUs.

1. Segmentation and reassembly of user information
2. Handling the variable cell delay
3. Detecting lost and mis-sequenced cells
4. Providing source clock frequency recovery at the receiver

The AAL1 PDU consists of 48 octets with 47 octets available for the user's payload. As shown in Figure 3–7a, the first header field is a sequence number (SN) and is used for detection of mistakenly inserted cells or lost cells. The other header field is the sequence number protection (SNP) that is used to provide for error detection and correction operations. AAL1 is responsible for clock recovery for both audio and video services.

AAL type 2 was designed for variable bit rate (VBR) services where a timing relationship is required between the source and destination sites. For example, class B traffic, such as variable bit rate audio or video, would fall into this category. This category of service requires that the timing information be maintained between the transmitting and receiving site. It is responsible for handling variable cell delay as well as the detection and handling of lost or missequenced cells.

The PDU for AAL2 consists of both a header and a trailer (see Figure 3–7b). The header consists of a sequence number (SN) as well as an information type (IT) field. The length of these fields and their exact functions have not been determined as of this writing. Obviously, the SN will be used for detection of lost and mistakenly inserted cells. The IT field can contain the indication of beginning of message (BOM), continuation of message (COM), or end of message (EOM). It may also contain timing information for audio or video signals.

The AAL2 trailer consists of a length indicator (LI) that is used to determine the number of octets residing in the payload field. Finally, the cyclic redundancy check (CRC) is used for error detection.

The original AAL2 has just been described. It has not been used, and as of this writing, work is underway to use AAL2 for multiplexing small packets over ATM.

The original ATM standards established AAL3 for VBR connection-oriented operations and AAL4 for VBR connectionless operations. These two types have been combined and are treated as one type. As the AAL standard has matured, it became evident that the original types were inappropriate. Therefore, AAL3 and AAL4 were combined due to their similarities and shown as AAL3/4.

As shown in Figure 3–7c, the AAL3/4 PDU carries 44 octets in the payload and 5 fields in the header and trailer. The 2-bit information type

(IT) is used to indicate the beginning of message (BOM), continuation of message (COM), end of message (EOM), or single segment message (SSM). The sequence number is used for sequencing the traffic. It is incremented by one for each PDU sent, and a state variable at the receiver indicates the next expected PDU. If the received SN is different from the state variable, the PDU is discarded. The message identification (MID) field is used to reassemble traffic on a given connection. The length indicator (LI) defines the size of the payload. Finally, the cyclic redundancy check (CRC) field is a 10-bit field used to determine if an error has occurred in any part of the cell.

AAL5 was conceived because AAL3/4 was considered to contain unnecessary overhead. It was judged that multiplexing could be handled by any upper layer, and that the operations to preallocate buffers at the receiver were not needed.

Figure 3–7d shows the format of the AAL5 PDU. It consists of an 8-octet trailer. The PAD field acts as a filler to fill out the PDU to 48 octets. The CPCS-UU field is used to identify the user payload. The common part indicator (CPI) has not been fully defined in ITU-T I.363. The length indicator (LI) field defines the payload length, and the CRC field is used to detect errors in the SSCS PDU (user data).

Type 5 is a convenient service for frame relay because it supports connection-oriented services. In essence, the frame relay user traffic is given to an ATM backbone network for transport to another frame relay user.

SUMMARY

ATM is a high-speed, low-delay, multiplexing and switching technology that supports any type of user traffic, such as voice, data, and video applications. ATM uses small, fixed-length units called cells that are identified with VPIs and VCIs that are contained in the cell header.

ATM provides limited error detection operations, provides no retransmission services, and few operations are performed on the small header. ATM also has a layer that operates above it, called the ATM adaptation layer (AAL), which performs convergence as well as segmentation and reassembly operations on different types of traffic.

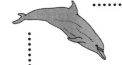

4

Signaling System
Number 7 (SS7) Architecture

INTRODUCTION

This chapter introduces the Signaling System Number 7 network, known simply as SS7. The concepts behind the SS7 design are explained and SS7 nodes are examined. The relationship of SS7 and the OSI Model are clarified, as well as the SS7 topologies and link (communications channel) types. SS7 addresses are explained and we show some examples of these addresses. The chapter concludes with a discussion of internetworking and international SS7 networks.

EARLY SIGNALING

Early signaling systems used a technique called per-trunk, in-band signaling. With this approach, the call control path is the same physical circuit as the speech path. Consequently, call control competes with voice traffic for use of the channel. This is not an efficient technique, since the traffic of the telephone calls and the traffic of the control signals are competing with each other. Supervisory functions, such as on-hook and off-hook; call information, such as dial tone and busy signals; and addressing information, such as the called number, must be interspersed with the voice traffic.

COMMON CHANNEL SIGNALING

In contrast to per-trunk signaling, common channel signaling (CCS) divides the call control path from the speech path. As a consequence, call control does not compete with voice traffic for use of the channel. Moreover, this approach reduces call setup time and provides the opportunity to build redundant links between offices, which improves reliability. Another advantage of CCS is the ability to look ahead when setting up a connection. Therefore, resources do not have to be reserved until it is determined that a connection can be made. Thus, the high reliability coupled with faster operations and increased capabilities provide both local exchange carriers (LECs) and interchange carriers (ICs or IXCs) with a powerful tool for enhancing telephone operations.

There are two types of communications employed in common channel signaling, associated signaling and quasi-associated signaling. With associated signaling, common channel signaling messages pertaining to a particular operation are conveyed over communication links that are connected directly between the network nodes. With quasi-associated signaling, the messages are transferred indirectly through at least one tandem point usually known as the signaling transfer point (STP). Even though intermediate nodes are involved in the transfer of the messages, the messages always take a fixed, predetermined path between the two communicating entities.

SS7 FUNDAMENTALS

Common channel signaling (CCS) systems were designed in the 1950s and 1960s for analog networks and later adapted for digital telephone switches. In 1976, AT&T implemented the Common Channel Interoffice Signaling (CCIS) into its toll network. This system is referred to as CCS6 and was based on the CCITT Signaling System No. 6 Recommendation. SS6 and CCS6 were slow and designed to work on low bit rate channels. Moreover, these architectures were not layered, which made changing the code a complex and expensive task.

Consequently, the CCITT began work in the mid-1970s on a new generation signaling system. These efforts resulted in the publication of SS7 in 1980, with extensive improvements published in 1984 and again in 1988. Today, SS7 and variations are implemented throughout the world. Indeed, SS7 has found its way into other communications architectures such as personal communications services (PCS) and global systems for mobile communications (GSM).

SS7 defines the procedures for the setup, ongoing management, and clearing of a call between telephone users. It performs these functions by exchanging telephone control messages between the SS7 components that support the end users' connection.

The SS7 signaling data link is a full duplex, digital transmission channel operating at 64 kbit/s. Optionally, an analog link can be used with either 4 or 3 kHz spacing. The SS7 link operates on both terrestrial and satellite links. The actual digital signals on the link are derived from pulse code modulation (PCM) multiplexing equipment or from equipment that employs a frame structure. The link must be dedicated to SS7. In accordance with the idea of clear channel signaling, no other transmission can be transferred with these signaling messages.

EXAMPLE OF AN SS7 TOPOLOGY

Figure 4–1 depicts a typical SS7 topology. The subscriber lines are connected to the SS7 network through the service switching points (SSPs). The SSPs receive the signals from the CPE and perform call processing on behalf of the user. SSPs are implemented at end offices or access tandem devices. They serve as the source and destination for SS7 messages. In so doing, SSP initiates SS7 messages either to another SSP or to a signaling transfer point (STP).

FUNCTIONS OF THE SS7 NODES

SSP, STP, and service control points (SCP) are all SS7 nodes that are also known as signaling points. The STP is tasked with the translation of the SS7 messages and the routing of those messages between network nodes and databases. The STPs are switches that relay messages between SSPs and SCPs as well as other STPs. Their principal functions are similar to the layer 3 operations of the OSI Model.

The SCPs contain software and databases for the management of the call. For example, 800 services and routing are provided by the SCP. They receive traffic (typically requests for information) from SSPs via STPs and return responses (via STPs) based on the query.

Although Figure 4–1 shows the SS7 components as discrete entities, they are often implemented in an integrated fashion by a vendor's equip-

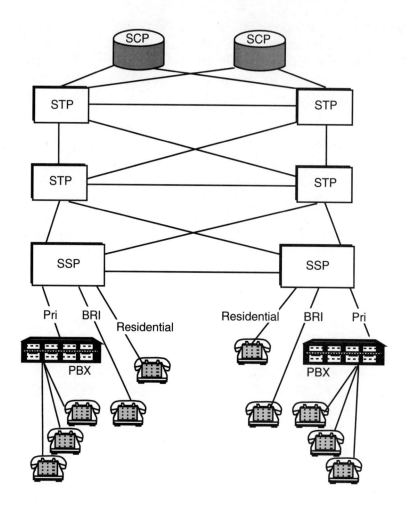

where:
BRI	Basic rate interface
PBX	Private branch exchange
PRI	Primary rate interface
SCP	Service control point
SSP	Service switching point
STP	Signaling transfer point

Figure 4–1   Example of an SS7 topology.

ment. For example, a central office can be configured with a SSP, a STP, and a SCP or any combination of these elements. These SS7 components are explained in more detail later in this section.

The Service Switching Point (SSP)

The SSP is the local exchange to the subscriber and the interface to the telephone network. It can be configured as a voice switch, an SS7 switch, or a computer connected to a switch.

The SSP creates SS7 signal units at the sending SSP and translates them at the receiving SSP. Therefore, it converts voice signaling into the SS7 signal units, and vice versa. It also supports database access queries for 800/900 numbers

The SSP uses the dialed telephone numbers to access a routing table to determine a next exchange and the outgoing trunk to reach this exchange. The SS7 connection request message is then sent to the next exchange.

The Signaling Transfer Point (STP)

The STP is a router for the SS7 network. It relays messages through the network but it does not originate them. It is usually an adjunct to a voice switch and does not usually stand alone as a separate machine.

The STP is installed as a national STP, an international STP, or a gateway STP. Even though SS7 is an international standard, countries may vary in how some of the features and options are implemented. The STP provides the conversions of the messages that flow between dissimilar systems. For example, in the United States the STP provides conversions between ANSI SS7 and ITU-T SS7.

STPs also offer screening services, such as security checks on incoming and/or outgoing messages. The STP can also screen messages to make certain they are acceptable (conformant) to the specific network.

Other STP functions include the acquisition and storage of traffic and usage statistics for OAM and billing. If necessary, the STP provides an originating SCP with the address of the destination SCP.

The Service Control Point (SCP)

The SCP acts as the interface into the telephone company databases. These databases contain information on the subscriber, 800/900 numbers, calling cards, fraud data, and so on. The SCP is usually linked to computer and/or databases through X.25. The SCP address is a point code, and the address of the database is a subsystem number (addresses are explained shortly).

The SS7 Levels (Layers)

Figure 4–2 shows the levels (layers) of SS7. The right part of the figure shows the approximate mapping of these layers to the OSI Model. Beginning from the lowest layers, the message transfer part (MTP) layer 1 defines the procedures for the signaling data link. It specifies the functional characteristics of the signaling links, the electrical attributes, and the connectors. Layer 1 provides for both digital and analog links al-

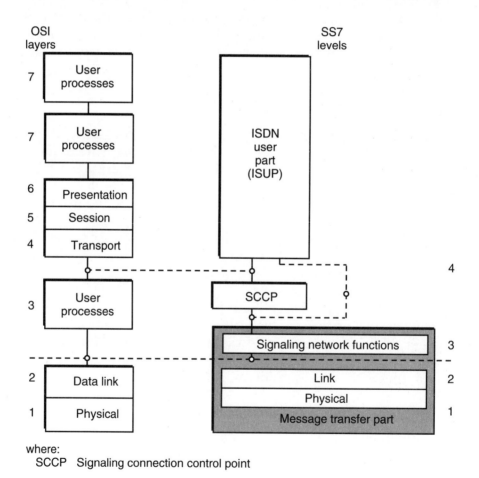

where:
 SCCP   Signaling connection control point

Figure 4–2   A general view of the SS7 levels (layers).

though the vast majority of SS7 physical layers are digital. The second layer is labeled MPT layer 2. It is responsible for the transfer of traffic between SS7 components. It is quite similar to an HDLC-type frame and indeed was derived from the HDLC specification. The MPT layer 3 is somewhat related to layer 3 of ISDN and X.25 in the sense that this layer provides the functions for network management, and the establishment of message routing as well as the provisions for passing the traffic to the SS7 components within the SS7 network. Many of the operations at this layer pertain to routing, such as route discovery and routing around problem areas in an SS7 network.

The signaling connection control point (SCCP) is also part of the network layer and provides for both connectionless and connection-oriented services. The main function of SCCP is to provide for translation of addresses, such as ISDN and telephone numbers to identifiers used by MTP 3 to route traffic.

The ISDN user part (ISUP) is responsible for transmitting call control information between SS7 network nodes. In essence, this is the call control protocol, in that ISUP sets up, coordinates, and takes down trunks within the SS7 network. It also provides features such call status checking, trunk management, trunk release, calling party number information, privacy indicators, detection of application of tones for busy conditions, and so on. ISUP works in conjunction with ISDN Q.931. Thus, ISUP translates Q.931 messages and maps them into appropriate ISUP messages for use in the SS7 network.

Figure 4–3 provides a more detailed description of the SS7 levels and will serve as an introduction to subsequent material on these levels. The three MTP levels serve as a connectionless transport system. With this approach, each SS7 message is routed separately from other messages, and there is no connection setup for the message transport.

MTP level 1 performs the functions of a traditional OSI physical layer. It generates and receives the signals on the physical channel. MTP level 2 relates closely to the OSI layer 2. It is a conventional data link level, and is responsible for the delivery of traffic on each link between SS7 nodes. The traffic in the upper layers of SS7 are encapsulated into MTP 2 "signal units" (this term is used by SS7 instead of the conventional HDLC "frame" term) and sent onto the channel to the receiving node. This node checks for errors that may have occurred during transmission and, if necessary, takes remedial action (discussed later).

MTP 3 is the connectionless routing part of the MTP levels. MTP level 3 performs OSI layer 3 functions, notably, the routing of messages between machine and between components within a machine. It per-

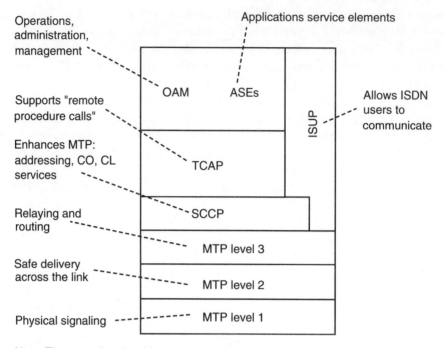

Note: The terms level and layer are used interchangably.

where:
CL   Connectionless
CO   Connection-oriented
ISUP   ISDN user part
MTP   Message transfer part
SCCP   Signaling connection control point
TCAP   Transaction capabilities application part

Figure 4–3   The SS7 levels in more detail.

forms load-sharing operations across multiple links and reconfiguration operations in the event of node or link failure.

SCCP corresponds to several of the operations associated with OSI layer 3 (and although not generally discussed in literature, OSI layer 4, as well). Some of its principal jobs are: (1) supporting the MTP levels with global addressing, (2) providing connectionless or connection-oriented services, and (3) providing sequencing and flow-control operations.

The transaction capabilities application part (TCAP) corresponds to several of the functions of the OSI layer 7. It uses the remote operations service element (ROSE). As such, it performs connectionless, remote procedure calls on behalf of an "application" running on top of it.

The ISDN user part (ISUP) provides circuit-related services needed to support applications running in an ISDN environment. Non-ISDN originated calls are also supported by ISUP

The transaction capabilities application part (TCAP) is an OSI application layer. It can be used for a variety of purposes. One use of TCAP is the support of 800 numbers (in North America) that are transferred between SCP databases. It is also used to define the syntax between the various communicating components, and it uses a standard closely aligned with OSI transfer syntax, called the basic encoding rules (BER). Finally, the OMAP and ASEs are used respectively for network management and user-specific services.

SS7 IDENTIFIERS AND NUMBERING SCHEME

SS7 nodes (signaling points) are identified with an address and each node must have a unique address. The SS7 addresses are called point codes (PCs) or signaling point codes. The PC is kept transparent to entities operating outside the SS7 network; no direct correlation is made between a PC and a telephone number or an ISDN address. Any correlation between these identifiers is made by each network. The PC is placed inside the L_3 MTP message and used to route the message to the appropriate signaling point.

The PC is a hierarchical address consisting of (1) a network identifier, (2) a network cluster, and (3) a network cluster member. The network identifier, as its name implies, identifies a signaling network. The network cluster identifies a cluster of nodes that belong to a network. Typically, a cluster of signaling nodes consists of a group that home in on a mated pair of STPs. They can be addressed as a group. The network cluster member code identifies a single member (signaling point) operating within a cluster. The structure of the point code system and its relationship to signaling points is depicted in Figure 4–4. For example, a PC could be 123.2.4 to identify cluster member 4, which belongs to cluster 2, which belongs to network 123.

The structure of the PC fields is different in United States, ITU-T, and other national specifications. Each country may implement its own PC structure, but is expected to support an ITU-T structure at the international gateway (between two countries).

In addition to the PC used by MTP for routing to a node in the network, SS7 also utilizes a subsystem number (SSN). This number does not pertain to a node but to entities within a node, such as an application or

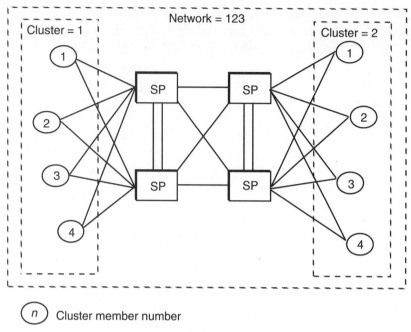

Figure 4–4   SS7 numbering plan.

some other software entity. As examples, it could identify enhanced 800 (E800) services running in a node, an automated calling card service (ACCS) module operating in the node, ISUP, and so on.

SS7 also supports the global title (GT) identifier, which could be the dialed digits of a telephone number. Perhaps the best way to view the GT is that it is mapped to an SS7 network address of PC + SSN.

As we shall see later, an SS7 subsystem operates as a user to SCCP. Therefore, SCCP "routes" traffic to and from the proper subsystem operating on top of SCCP.

The assignment of the codes is governed by each country's telecommunications administrations. The assignment scheme provides for three types of registration: (1) network code; (2) network code and cluster code; and (c) network code, cluster code, and cluster member codes, which is called a signaling point code block. For large networks, registration type (a) is used. Large networks must have more than 75 signaling points and 5 STPs in the first five years of operation, and several other requirements in outgoing years.

For small networks, registration type (b) is used. Registration type (c) is used for a group of signaling points that are not part of a network and have no STP.

Global Title Addressing and Translation

Obviously, the telephone user is not concerned with SS7 addresses. This customer need only enter a called party telephone number, and SS7 will set up the call. To the SS7 network, the telephone number is a global title, and as such, does not contain sufficient information for routing in the signaling network. Furthermore, a user may not use a conventional telephone number as a called address. Other identifiers may be used—as examples, 911 number, a mobile phone number, a telex number, or an 800 number.

SS7 is adaptable enough to accept these logical addresses and translate them to a routing address in order to support the call. Typically, an SS7 network contains sites that are responsible for these translations, and most systems place these operations at designated STPs. As we shall see in later discussions, SCCP is the SS7 entity that provides for global title translations.

SUMMARY

SS7 is the international standard for out-of-band signaling systems. Most systems in the world are quite similar, with some minor variations on a national or regional basis. Initially employed for use by the telephone network, SS7 is now used in mobile, wireless networks, and ATM networks, and broadband signaling networks.

5

Addressing, SAPs, Primitives, and PDUs

INTRODUCTION

This chapter examines the addresses and identifiers used in a broadband signaling network. Since the OSI Model plays a key role in this network, the subjects of service access points (SAPs), primitives, and protocol data units (PDUs) are also explained. We also compare addresses to labels (virtual circuit identifiers).

The only addresses used in ATM broadband signaling that are not discussed in this chapter are the SS7 point codes and global titles that are covered in Chapter 4.

EXPLICIT ADDRESSES AND LABELS

In order for the end user application's traffic to be sent to the proper destination (the terminating end point), a control field in the traffic must contain an identifier of the destination. If this identifier is not understood by a node that is supposed to relay it to the destination, the traffic cannot be delivered. Therefore, it is important that these identifiers be understood by all communicating parties: the originating party, the terminating party, and the network (and its switches). Most systems use one or two kinds of identifiers called explicit addresses or labels.

A specific address is one that has a location associated with it. As an example, the telephone numbering plan has a structure that permits the identification of a geographical region in the world, an area within that region, a telephone exchange within the area, and the telephone that is connected to the exchange. As another example, the CCITT X.121 has a structure that permits identification of a country, a network within that country, and a device within that network. Further values are used with these structures for applications running within the host, such as file servers and message servers. Explicit addresses are used by switches, routers, and bridges as an index to look up tables as to how to route the traffic.

Another identifying scheme is known by the term label although the reader may be more familiar with other terms such as logical channel number (LCN) or virtual circuit identifier (VCI). A label contains no information about network identifiers or locations. It is simply a value that is assigned to a user's traffic that identifies each data unit of that user's traffic.

The most common practice is to reserve a label such as a VCI for permanent virtual circuits (PVCs). This means that the user of the PVC need only submit to the network the label in the header associated with the user's traffic. The network then uses this label to examine tables to determine explicit location information. For a switched virtual call (SVC), also called connections on demand, the typical practice is to provide a label and an explicit address to the network, and this information is mapped into tables for the management of the ongoing call. Once this mapping has occurred, the user need only submit to the network the label, which is used as a lookup into a table to find an explicit address.

A SHORT TREATISE ON ROUTING

Upon receiving traffic from an incoming link, the network switch examines an address or a virtual circuit id in the traffic header and matches it with an entry in a routing table to determine where to route the traffic.

This routing decision is based on an entry in the routing table that identifies the next node (switch) in the path to the final destination. The switch then places the traffic onto the outgoing link that is attached to that next node. Upon receiving the traffic, this next switch goes through the same process, which is repeated until the traffic arrives at the terminating endpoint. Here, the traffic is passed to the destination application, through the use of other identifiers that distinguish which user application is to receive the traffic. These "other" identifiers are coded in the form of service access points (SAPs) and are explained later in this chapter. For this narration, the emphasis is on the identifiers that are used to route the traffic to the terminating end point.

THE ATM ADDRESS SCHEME

With connection on demand operations in ATM networks, it is important to have a standardized convention for coding destination and source addresses. Addressing is not an issue with PVCs since connections and endpoints (destination and source) are defined, and a user need only provide the network with a preallocated VCI/VPI. However, for SVCs, the destination connection can change with each session; therefore, explicit addresses are required. After the call has been mapped between the UNIs, the VCI/VPI values then can be used for traffic identification.

The ATM address is modeled on the OSI network service access point (NSAP), which is defined in ISO 8348 and ITU-T X.213, Annex A (Figure 5–1a). A brief explanation of the OSI NSAP and its relationship to ATM addressing follows.

The ISO and ITU-T describe a hierarchical structure for the NSAP address, as well as the structure for the NSAP address. It consists of four parts:

Initial Domain Part (IDP): Contains the authority format identifier (AFI) and the initial domain identifier (IDI).

Authority Format Identifier (AFI): Contains a 1-octet field to identify the domain specific part (DSP).

Initial Domain Identifier (IDI): Specifies the addressing domain and the network addressing authority for the DSP values; it is interpreted according to the AFI.

Domain Specific Part (DSP): Contains the address determined by the network authority; for ATM, the contents vary, depending on value of the AFI.

Figure 5–1b shows typical contents of the DSP. It can contain a variety of identifiers. It is used by ATM to identify a private or public address, as well as the end station, such as a user computer. It may also contain information on which protocols are to be invoked at the destination end station. Since a user device may be operating with different stacks of protocols, an SVC operation can identify which protocols are to receive the incoming traffic.

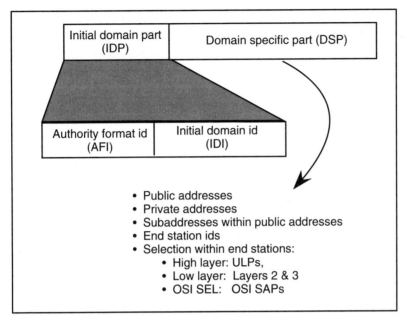

(a) Format

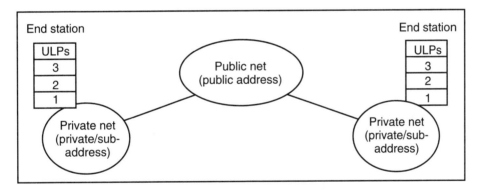

(b) Example

where:
SAPs   Service access points
ULPs   Upper layer protocols

Figure 5–1 The OSI address format.

Figure 5–2 shows the conventions for coding the OSI address for ATM operations. For ATM, the AFI field is coded as:

39 = DCC ATM format
47 = ICD ATM format
45 = E.164 format

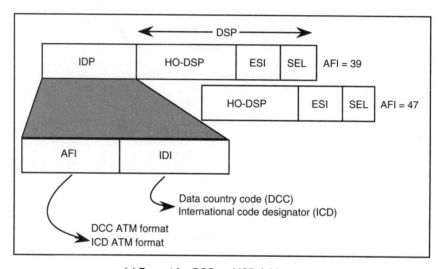

(a) Format for DCC and ICD Addresses

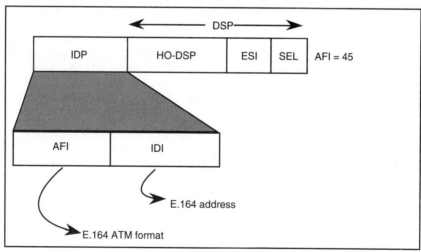

(b) Format for E.164 Address

Figure 5–2 The OSI/ATM address formats.

The IDI is interpreted according to the AFI (where AFI = 39, 47, or 45). For ATM, the IDI is coded as (1) a data country code (DCC) in accordance with ISO 3166; (2) the international code designator (ICD), which identifies an international organization and is maintained by the British Standards Institute; or (3) an E.164 address, which is a telephone number.

The domain specific part identifier (DFI) specifies the syntax and other aspects of the remainder of the DSP. The administrative authority (AA) is an organization assigned by the ISO that is responsible for the allocation of values in certain fields in the DSP. The R field is a reserved field.

The high-order DSP is established by the authority identified by the IDP. This field might contain a hierarchical address (with topological significance, see RFC 1237) such as a routing domain and areas within the domain. The end system identifier (ESI) identifies an end system (such as a computer) within the area.

The selector (SEL) is not used by an ATM network. It usually identifies the protocol entities in the upper layers of the user machine that are to receive the traffic. Therefore, the SEL could contain upper layer service access points (SAPs), which are explained shortly.

ATM public networks must support the E.164 address and private networks must support all formats. E.164 is covered in the next section of this chapter.

THE E.164 ADDRESS SCHEME

The ITU-T E.164 Recommendation is the prevalent standard for addresses in telecommunications systems throughout the world. E.164 is a variable length of decimal digits arranged in specific field. The fields are the country code (CC) and the national (significant) number (Figure 5–3).

The CC is used to select the destination country and varies in length as outlined in Recommendation E.163.

The national (significant) number N(S)N is used to select the destination subscriber. In selecting the destination subscriber, however, it may be necessary to select a destination network. To accomplish this selection, the N(S)N code field comprises a national destination code (NDC) followed by the subscribers number (SN).

The NDC field will be variable in length depending upon the requirements of the destination country. Each NDC may have one of the following structures:

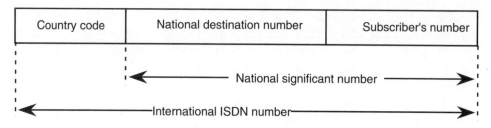

Figure 5–3   E.164.

1. A destination network (DN) code, which can be used to select a destination network serving the destination subscribers.
2. A trunk code (TC), the format of which is defined in Recommendation E.160.
3. Any combination of DN and TC.

The international number may be of variable length. The maximum number length shall be fifteen digits. However, some administrations may wish to increase their register capacity to sixteen or seventeen digits. The decision on register capacity is left to individual administrations.

The length does not include prefixes, language digit, address delimiters (e.g., end of pulsing signals, etc.) since these items are not considered as part of the international ISDN number.

SERVICE ACCESS POINTS (SAPS)

The services invoked at a layer are dictated by the upper layer's passing primitives (transactions) to the lower layer. In Figure 5–4, users A and B communicate with each other through a lower layer.

Services are provided from the lower layer to the upper layer through a service access point (SAP). The SAP is an identifier. It identifies the entity in layer N+1 that is performing the service(s) for layer N.

An entity in machine A can invoke some services in machine B through the use of SAPs. For example, a user that sends traffic can identify itself with a source SAP id (SSAP). It identifies the recipient of the traffic with a destination SAP value (DSAP).

It is the responsibility of the receiving lower layer N (in concert of course with the operating system in the receiving machine) to pass the traffic to the proper destination SAP in layer N+1. If multiple entities

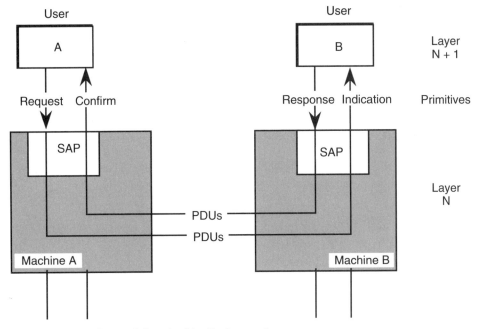

Note: The lower layers follow the identical procedures.

where:
SAP   Service access point

Figure 5–4   SAPs and primitives (service definitions).

(e.g., processes) exist in the machine, the DSAP serves to properly identify the process.

Some people view the SAP as a software "port." It is akin to the
socket concept found in the UNIX operating system environment.

How Primitives (Service Definitions) Are Used

The primitive is used by the layer to invoke the service entities and
create any headers that will be used by the peer layer in the remote station. This point is quite important. The primitives are received by adjacent layers in the local site and are used to create the headers used by
peer layers at the remote site. At the receiving site, the primitive is used
to convey the data to the next and adjacent upper layer and to inform
this layer about the actions of the lower layer.

The OSI Model uses four types of primitives to perform the actions
between the layers (Figure 5–4; Table 5–1. The manner in which they are
invoked varies. Not all four primitives must be invoked with each opera-

Table 5–1   Functions of Primitives

At user A:

- *Request*. A primitive initiated by a service user to invoke a function.
- *Confirm*. A primitive response by a service provider to complete a function previously invoked by a request primitive. It may or may not follow the response primitive.

At user B:

- *Indication*. A primitive issued by a service provider to (a) invoke a function, or (b) indicate a function has been invoked.
- *Response*. A primitive response by a service user to complete a function previously invoked by an indication primitive.

---

tion. For example, if the remote machine has no need to respond to the local machine, it need not return a response primitive. In this situation, a request primitive would be invoked at the local site to get the operation started. At the remote site, the indication primitive would be invoked to complete the process.

Of course, if the remote station were to send traffic back, it would invoke the operation with a response primitive, which would be mapped to the confirm primitive at the local machine.

Relationships of Service Definitions and Protocol Specifications

The ITU-T and ISO use two key terms in describing the OSI standards. This figure describes these terms as they relate to the material discussed in earlier parts of this chapter. In summary, they are:

- *Service Definitions*: Defines the services and operations that take place between the layers of the model within the same machine. The service definitions are implemented with primitives.
- *Protocol Specifications*: Actions taken within or between peer layers of the model across different machines (or two peer layers within the same machine) These actions taken are based on the service definitions.

CONNECTION MAPPING

The OSI Model specifies several procedures to manage connections between protocol entities. In Figure 5–5a, a direct or one-to-one mapping is shown. For this operation, one (N+1) connection is mapped directly to one (N) connection.

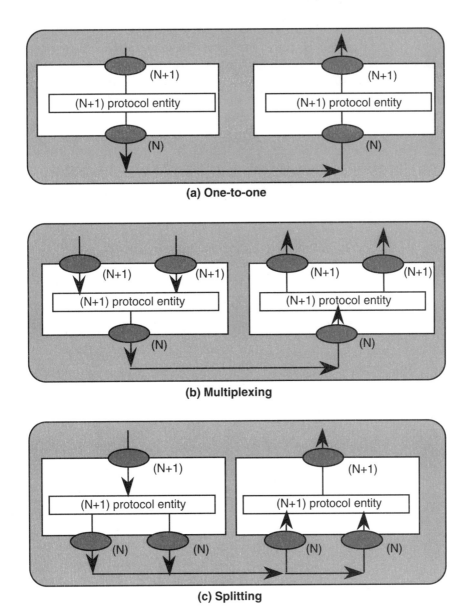

(a) One-to-one

(b) Multiplexing

(c) Splitting

Figure 5–5   Connection mapping.

In Figure 5–5b, the multiplexing of many-to-one connection mapping is shown. This is a common practice in the industry to mapping multiple users onto one network connection. If these users need the same quality of service from a network, and if they are connected to the same endpoint, one connection can be set up to manage all their connections.

This approach has several advantages. For example, it permits users (at the upper layers) to set up and tear down connections without requiring network intervention and provisioning. As another example, the network can signal OAM (operations, administration, and maintenance) to multiple users with one message that is identified with one SAP, and this signal is pertinent to multiple connections.

In Figure 5–5c, the splitting of one connection to multiple connections is also a useful function. For example, a user (upper layer) may need more bandwidth than is available on a single connection at a lower layer. The user can "fool" the lower layer (say, the network layer—representing the network itself), by obtaining multiple connections to improve the user's throughput.

OTHER KEY CONCEPTS

Figure 5–6 depicts the relationship of the layers from the standpoint of how data are exchanged between them. Three terms are important to this discussion.

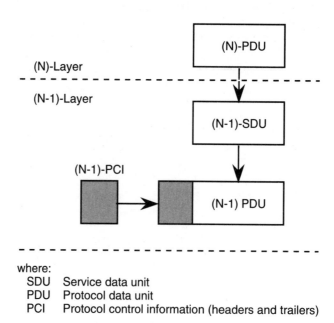

where:
  SDU   Service data unit
  PDU   Protocol data unit
  PCI   Protocol control information (headers and trailers)

Figure 5–6   Mapping between layers.

- *SDU (service data unit):* Consists of user data and control information created at the upper layers that is transferred transparently through a primitive by layer (N+1) to layer (N) and subsequently to (N-1). The SDU identity is preserved from one end of an (N)-connection to the other end.
- *PCI (protocol control information):* Information exchanged by peer (the same) entities at different sites on the network to instruct the peer entity to perform a service function (PCI is also called by these names: headers and trailers).
- *PDU (protocol data unit):* The PDU is a combination of the SDU and PCI.

This process repeats itself at each layer. At the transmitting site, the PDU becomes larger as it passes through each layer. At the receiving site, the PDU becomes smaller as it passes (up) through each layer.

ATM'S USE OF THE OSI MODEL

Figure 5–7 shows the conventions for the ATM and AAL layers, as well as the placement of service access points (SAPs) and the naming conventions.

This figure is largely self-explanatory. It can be seen that the naming conventions follow the OSI conventions and use the concepts of service data units (SDUs), protocol data units (PDUs), primitives, encapsulation, decapsulation, and protocol control information (PCIs).

THE BROADBAND SIGNALING STACKS AND THE USER LAYERS

To wrap up this chapter, Figure 5–8 shows how the layers of ATM and SDH/SONET relate to the user layer(s). We have learned that the layers communicate with each other between two machines through the use of PDUs. At the ATM layer, the PDUs are called cells; at the physical layer, the PDUs are called frames.

The service definitions define the interactions between adjacent layers in the same machine and use service access points (SAPs) to identify the source and destination communicating parties. The service definitions are known as primitives and are actually implemented with computer-specific operations, such as C function calls, UNIX system li-

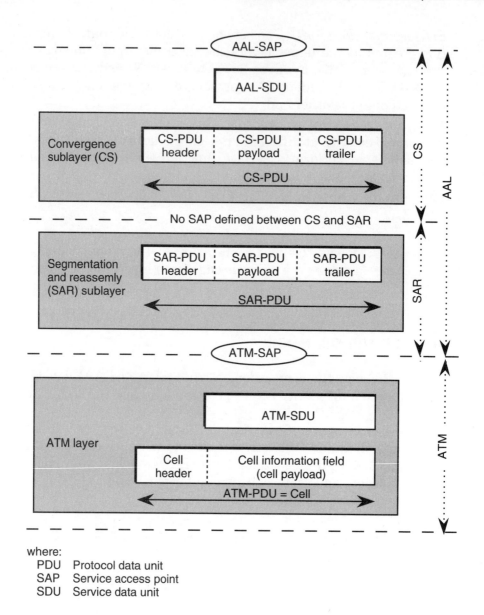

where:
    PDU   Protocol data unit
    SAP   Service access point
    SDU   Service data unit

Figure 5–7   AAL general data unit conventions.

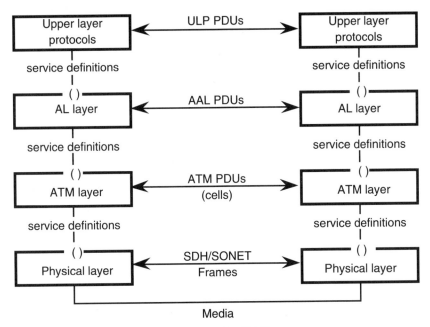

Note: ( ) represents a service access point (SAP)

Figure 5–8   Broadband signaling and the user layer(s).

brary calls, and so on. The user layer (or layers) rest on top of AAL and are known as upper layer protocols.

SUMMARY

ATM is organized into layers, SAPs, and service definitions, along the lines of the OSI Model. The SAPs and service definitions are a useful tool for designers and programmers, because they provide guidance on how to build the interfaces between the layers.

The use of OSI addresses is required in a broadband signaling network when a connection is requested by an ATM user. The ATM address can take several forms; the E.164 address is the most common form at this time.

6

SAAL, SSCOP, and SSCF

INTRODUCTION

This chapter examines the signaling ATM adaptation layer (SAAL) and its associated sublayers, the service-specific coordination function (SSCF), and the service-specific connection oriented protocol (SSCOP). The relationship of these entities to each other and to ATM layer management is also explored.

Since most of the interactions of SAAL entities within an exchange occur through primitives, an explanation is provided of the primitives' operations. The messages that are transferred between exchanges are explained and several examples are provided to show how SAAL services are used in the broadband signaling network.

Due to the many interfaces between SAAL and its upper and lower layers as well as those between the sublayers of SAAL and the many primitives and signals that are invoked between them, it is not practical to compare the differences between the ANSI and ITU-T specifications. For purposes of continuity and simplicity, I will explain the ANSI specifications.

POSITION OF SAAL IN THE BROADBAND SIGNALING LAYERS

Figure 6–1 compares the broadband signaling stacks (protocol stacks) for UNI and NNI operations and the placement of SAAL in these stacks.

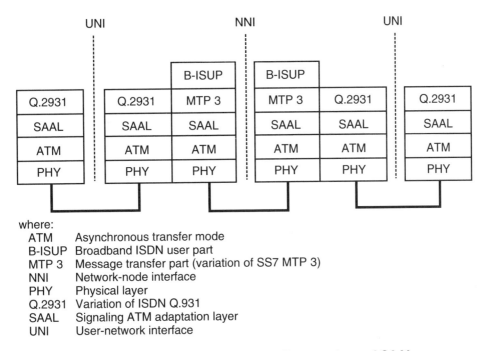

where:

ATM   Asynchronous transfer mode
B-ISUP   Broadband ISDN user part
MTP 3   Message transfer part (variation of SS7 MTP 3)
NNI   Network-node interface
PHY   Physical layer
Q.2931   Variation of ISDN Q.931
SAAL   Signaling ATM adaptation layer
UNI   User-network interface

Figure 6–1   The broadband signaling stacks and SAAL.

For the UNI, Q.2931 (a variation of ISDN's layer 3 Q.931) is used to set up and tear down a connection. It operates over an AAL designed especially for Q.2931, which is called the signaling AAL (SAAL). These layers operate over the conventional ATM layer and a selected physical layer.

For the NNI, the broadband ISUP (B-ISDN) and message transfer part 3 (MTP 3) are variations of their counterparts in the SS7 signaling standard. They rely on the SAAL to support their operations. These layers also operate over the conventional ATM and a selected physical layer.

The UNI and NNI SAALs have some similarities and differences. Both contain a common part convergence sublayer (CPCS) and a segmentation and reassembly sublayer (SAR). However, in actual implementations, the NNI SAAL is likely to be more complex than the UNI SAAL and performs a wide array of support services for B-ISUP and MTP 3. These services are described later in this chapter.

The Protocol Stack in More Detail

Figure 6–2 is yet another level of detail and shows the protocol stack for the signaling part of the NNI. The CES notations identify connection endpoints (with connection endpoint suffixes) that are used in conjunc-

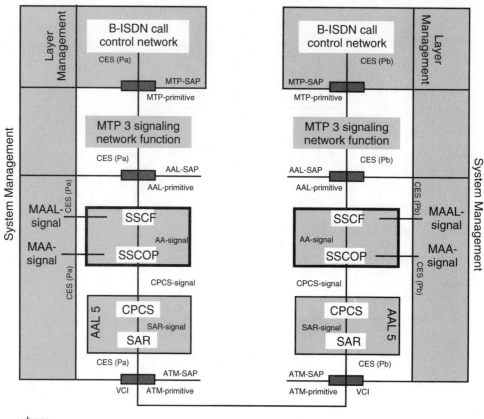

where:
CES   Connection end points
CPCS   Common part convergence sublayer
SAR   Segmentation and reassembly sublayer

Figure 6–2   Signaling stack for the NNI.

tion with service access points (SAPs) to identify a connection. SAPs are explained in Chapter 5. A one-to-one relationship exists between a connection endpoint within the AAL-SAP and a connection endpoint within the ATM-SAP. The communications between the entities in each exchange occur through the primitive and signaling operations, also described in Chapter 5. Remember, signals are used between layer entities that have no SAPs defined between them.

The layers above the ATM AAL (SSCF and SSCOP) are B-ISDN call control and MTP 3. B-ISDN call control is responsible for connection management, and MTP 3 is responsible for routing traffic between NNI nodes.

FUNCTIONS OF SAAL

The overall functions of the SAAL can be summarized as follows. SAAL is responsible for the correct transfer of data on a point-to-point ATM connection. One of its primary functions is to relieve the user (the upper layers in the signaling stack, B-ISUP and MTP 3) from any concern for data errors, loss, duplications, or insertions that may occur on the signaling link. SAAL restricts the length of user data from 5 to a maximum of 4096 octets.

SAAL provides a link monitoring service, that is similar to MTP 2 in a narrowband signaling stack. It "proves" that links are stable and error-free enough to be used (with alignment procedures). It can also take a link out of service when it becomes unreliable.

SAAL also provides for flow control procedures and employs mechanisms to insure that two exchanges do not create congestion problems with each other.

The sublayers of SAAL contribute to these overall functions. Let us take a brief look at them as a prelude to more detailed discussions.

Functions of SSCF

SSCF acts as a go-between for MTP 3 and SSCOP. As such, it maps primitives from MTP 3 to the required SSCOP signals and vice versa. In essence, it passes signals back and forth between SSCOP and MTP 3. As such, it does not send much information (PDUs) to its peer entity in the receiving exchange, but relies on SSCOP to convey its information in the SSCOP PDUs. Notwithstanding, it has other responsibilities as well. They are summarized here:

Flow Control: SSCF notifies the user about levels of congestion (or if no congestion exists) in order to prevent cell loss. It also regulates its flow of PDUs to the lower layers to prevent congestion at the other end.

Link Status: Based on primitives it receives from MTP 3 and SCCOP, SSCF maintains information (local state variables) about the status of the link, such as "aligned ready," "out of service," and so on. Using this information, it may generate primitives/signals to MTP 3 and SSCOP to aid in managing the link.

Layer Management: SSCF reports to layer management when a link is released. It relies upon layer management to help it in error monitoring functions.

Alignment Procedures: SSCF maintains the information (state variables) about all the alignment procedures that are taking place when a link is brought into service or taken out of service. These procedures are summarized below.

Alignment Procedures.   A link is brought into service by a request from the user. The user is the upper layer resting above SSCF, typically MTP 3. At the request of the user (through the issuance of a request primitive), SSCF sends a PDU to its peer entity in the receiving exchange to start the process and moves from the "out of service" state to the "alignment" state for this link.

These operations require SSCOP to set up the link between two exchanges. When the link setup is finished, SSCF so indicates to layer management, which initiates error monitoring operations. SSCF then enters into the "proving" state for this link.

At this time, proving PDUs are transferred between the two exchanges. If the proving operation occurs successfully (transferring a specific number of PDUs across the link within a set time), SSCF instructs layer management to terminate the proving operations and sends a PDU to its peer to indicate that proving was successful. When it sends this PDU, SSCF enters into the "aligned-ready" state and upon receiving a confirmation of this PDU, it enters into the "in service" state.

A link is proved by the successful transfer of n number of proving PDUs during time period T3 (which is controlled by a timer). After T3 expires, if C_n number of proving PDUs have been sent successfully with no indications of problems, the link is considered aligned and placed into service.

Like MTP 2, SSCF alignment procedures provide for normal or emergency proving. With normal proving, a link must prove itself (determine it is reliable) for a set proving period before it is allowed to transmit live signals. Emergency proving is invoked from either MTP 3 or layer management. If it is invoked from MTP 3, proving is performed. If it is invoked from layer management, it means that layer management requests no proving.

Proving Algorithm.   The ITU-T Q.2144 Recommendation defines the proving algorithm. Bellcore GR-2878-CORE provides an overview of the operation, which I have included here. The proving algorithm for SAAL links is based on of the alignment error rate monitor used for proving 56/64 kbit/s CCS links. Test PDUs are sent over the link at a specified rate r over a proving period of 1 minute. If the link suffers from one or more errors during this time, the proving is tried again. If no errors occur, the link is returned to service. The test PDU sending rate r is determined such that the proving procedure is in consonant with the in-service error monitor.

According to ITU-T Q.2144, if the existing error rate is such that the error monitor will take the link out of service in a matter of eight minutes or less, the proving algorithm should have almost zero probability of proving the link in 8 minutes (the craft alerting timer). The parameter r depends on the link speed, as specified in Section 9.4 of draft recommendation Q.2144. For a 1.5 Mbit/s link, $r = 1322$ cells/second, which corresponds to 0.365 Erlang load.

The SSCF PDU.   SSCF entities exchange only one PDU. It contains information on the status of the sending SSCF and is coded to indicate one of the following states or to indicate a problem: (1) out of service, (2) processor outage, (3) in service, (4) normal, (5) emergency, (6) alignment not successful, (7) management initiated, (8) protocol error, and (9) proving not successful.

Functions of SSCOP

One might wonder why another lower layer protocol is needed to support a signaling network. After all, earlier signaling networks performed well enough with MTP 2 at one of the lower layers (layer two) to support the upper layer signaling protocols (such as ISUP). The answer is that MTP 2, while well-designed and powerful in its functions, contains some operations and fields that are not needed in an ATM-based broadband signaling system. In retrospect, MTP 2 has also been found to be deficient in how it handles certain sequencing, flow control, and acknowledgments operations on the signaling link. Therefore, the standards groups decided that a new protocol was needed.

Like MTP 2, SSCOP keeps all signaling units (messages) that flow across the link in sequential order, and it also provides for retransmission of erred traffic. To make certain the communicating nodes (exchanges) are operational, each node executes a "keep alive" procedure with its neighbor node. SSCOP also contains a procedure that allows the local user to look at the SSCOP queue for purposes of determining the status of messages. The SSCOP also provides a number of status reporting operations.

SSCOP and AAL5.   Figure 6–3 shows the relationship of the SSCOP service data unit (SDU), the AAL5 CPCS service data unit, and the ATM cell. Beginning at the top part of the figure, the B-ISUP message is encap-

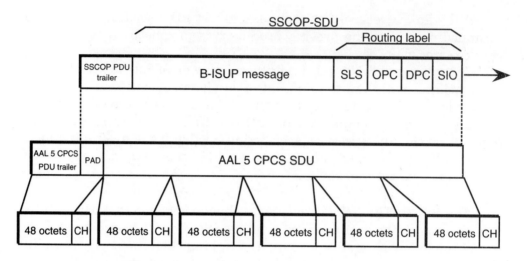

**Figure 6–3   SSCOP SDU, AAL 5 SDU, and the ATM cells.
(See footnote 1)**

sulated into the MTP 3 header (shown in this figure as the routing label). Then, the SSCOP trailer is placed behind these fields and sent to AAL5.[1] AAL5 adds its trailer and any PAD characters to ensure an even 48-byte (octet) boundary alignment. Traffic is then passed to segmentation operations and then to the ATM layer (depicted at the bottom part of this figure) where it is segmented into 48-byte traffic. Each 48-byte payload is appended with a cell header. This process is reversed at the receiver in accordance with conventional OSI depcapsulation operations.

Functions of SSCS Layer Management (LM)

The SSCS LM is the service specific convergence sublayer layer management entity. It interacts with the layers directly to perform a variety of operations, administration, and maintenance (OAM) functions. Thus, it is depicted as an entity that interacts with all the SAAL layers, except for CPCS and SAR (AAL type 5) where no interactions are defined. SSCS LM is tasked with the following responsibilities.

---

[1]Figure 6–3 shows the SSCOP PDU placed behind the B-ISUP, which I derived from the ANSI specifications. In practice, most systems place a L_2 header (SSCOP) in front of the MTP 3 routing label since the L_2 header is examined at the receiver before the routing label and the B-ISUP message. However, the figure is correct, and SSCOP is actually a logical L_2 protocol. The traditional L_2 functions of "frame delineation" with flags/preambles are performed by a layer operating below the ATM layer. (For example, a media access control [MAC] layer or the SONET physical layer.)

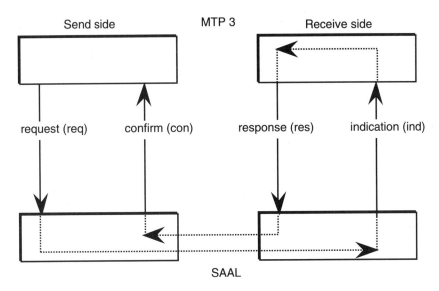

Figure 6–4   Primitives' relationships to the layers (MTP 3 and SAAL used in this example).

Layer management determines if a signaling link should be taken out of service or put into service (the latter function is called link proving). As part of these operations, links are monitored for excessive delays in the delivery of traffic. Layer management also permits a certain number of errors to occur on the link in order to avoid unnecessary changeovers to alternate links.

A number of ongoing measurements are taken by layer management. As examples, counters are maintained on how long each link has been in service, how often it has failed, how often and how many times the link has experienced congestion, and other information.

THE SAAL PRIMITIVES AND SIGNALS OPERATIONS

SAAL (and the ATM architecture in general) is organized around the OSI Model. As such, the layers in each ATM node interact with each other through primitives or signals.[2] Figure 6–4 shows how the primitives operate (MTP 3 and SAAL are used as the examples). Four transac-

---

[2]As a reminder, the term signal is used in place of a primitive if there is no service access point (SAP) defined between the user and provider (between the SAAL entities).

tions (primitives) are invoked to and from a layer through service access points (SAPs). (Primitives are explained in Chapter 5.) While the OSI Model defines four primitives, not all of them need be invoked to carry out an operation. Later discussions will explain how each of them is used by the SAAL sublayers.

Depictions of the Layers and Their Associated Primitives and Signals

Due to the variety of interfaces that exist between the SAAL sublayer entities, several sets of primitives and signals are defined, one for each interface. An understanding of these operations is fundamental to understanding the architecture of SAAL. To that end, Figure 6–5 shows all the primitives/signals and at which interface they operate. This figure will be a helpful reference tool for the material in this section of the chapter.

Two sets of primitives are not shown in Figure 6–5 and are explained in subsequent chapters. The primitives between Q.2931 and SAAL are described in Chapter 7. The primitives between MTP 3 and B-ISUP are explained in Chapter 8.

Primitives and Signals between SSCF and MTP 3

Table 6–1 lists the primitives that operate between SSCF and MTP 3 as well as the parameters that are passed with the primitives. The parameter labeled FSNC is the forward sequence number of the last message signal unit that was accepted by the remote peer entity. The parameter labeled BSNT is the backward sequence number that is transmitted to the remote peer entity. The congestion parameter is explained in Note 3 in Table 6–1. The message unit (mu) parameter contains the traffic passed between SSCF and MTP 3.

Many of the primitives are self-descriptive, but I will provide a summary of their use. Data are sent between MTP 3 and SSCF through the AAL-MESSAGE_FOR_TRANSMISSION and the AAL-RECEIVED_MESSAGE primitives. The former primitive is used by the AAL user to send data to SSCF, and the latter is used by AAL to deliver data to SSCF.

If the signaling link becomes congested, SSCF can notify the user with the AAL-LINK_CONGESTED primitive. Conversely, when the link is no longer congested, SSCF informs the user with the AAL-LINK_CONGESTION_CEASED primitive. (This latter primitive is not used in North America.) In addition, the congestion parameter in the AAL-LINK_CONGESTION primitive must indicate one of four levels of congestion numbered zero through three with zero meaning no congestion.

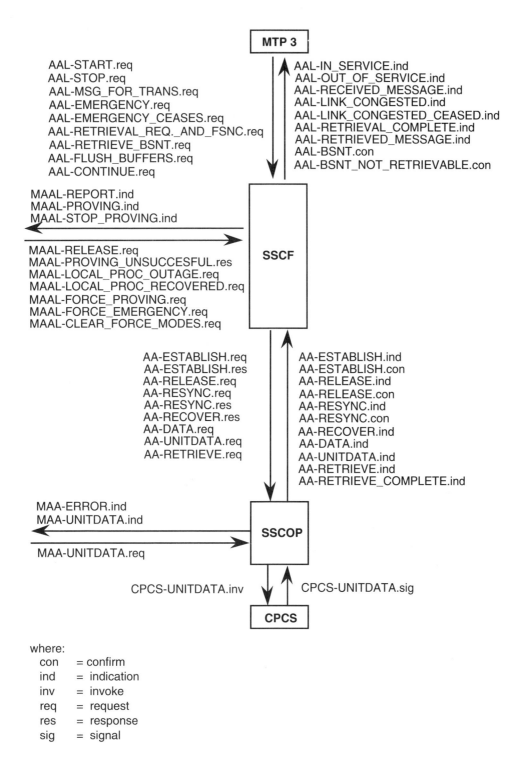

MTP 3

AAL-START.req
AAL-STOP.req
AAL-MSG_FOR_TRANS.req
AAL-EMERGENCY.req
AAL-EMERGENCY_CEASES.req
AAL-RETRIEVAL_REQ._AND_FSNC.req
AAL-RETRIEVE_BSNT.req
AAL-FLUSH_BUFFERS.req
AAL-CONTINUE.req

AAL-IN_SERVICE.ind
AAL-OUT_OF_SERVICE.ind
AAL-RECEIVED_MESSAGE.ind
AAL-LINK_CONGESTED.ind
AAL-LINK_CONGESTED_CEASED.ind
AAL-RETRIEVAL_COMPLETE.ind
AAL-RETRIEVED_MESSAGE.ind
AAL-BSNT.con
AAL-BSNT_NOT_RETRIEVABLE.con

MAAL-REPORT.ind
MAAL-PROVING.ind
MAAL-STOP_PROVING.ind

MAAL-RELEASE.req
MAAL-PROVING_UNSUCCESFUL.res
MAAL-LOCAL_PROC_OUTAGE.req
MAAL-LOCAL_PROC_RECOVERED.req
MAAL-FORCE_PROVING.req
MAAL-FORCE_EMERGENCY.req
MAAL-CLEAR_FORCE_MODES.req

SSCF

AA-ESTABLISH.req
AA-ESTABLISH.res
AA-RELEASE.req
AA-RESYNC.req
AA-RESYNC.res
AA-RECOVER.res
AA-DATA.req
AA-UNITDATA.req
AA-RETRIEVE.req

AA-ESTABLISH.ind
AA-ESTABLISH.con
AA-RELEASE.ind
AA-RELEASE.con
AA-RESYNC.ind
AA-RESYNC.con
AA-RECOVER.ind
AA-DATA.ind
AA-UNITDATA.ind
AA-RETRIEVE.ind
AA-RETRIEVE_COMPLETE.ind

MAA-ERROR.ind
MAA-UNITDATA.ind

MAA-UNITDATA.req

SSCOP

CPCS-UNITDATA.inv

CPCS-UNITDATA.sig

CPCS

where:
  con   = confirm
  ind   = indication
  inv   = invoke
  req   = request
  res   = response
  sig   = signal

Figure 6–5 The SAAL NNI interface architecture.

73

Table 6–1   Primitives between SSCF and MTP 3

	Primitive Type				Parameters in Primitive			
	res	ind	res	con	Message Unit	FSNC	BSNT	Congestion Parameter
AAL-MESSAGE_FOR TRANSMISSION	X				X			
AAL-RECEIVED_MESSAGE		X			X			
AAL-LINK_CONGESTED		X						X[1]
AAL-LINK_CONGESTION_CEASED[2]		X						
AAL-EMERGENCY	X							
AAL-EMERGENCY_CEASES	X							
AAL-STOP	X							
AAL-START	X							
AAL-IN_SERVICE		X						
AAL-OUT_OF_SERVICE		X						
AAL-RETRIEVE_BSNT	X							
AAL-RETRIEVAL_REQUEST_AND_FSNC	X					X		
AAL-RETRIEVED_MESSAGES		X			X			
AAL-RETRIEVAL_COMPLETE		X						
AAL-BSNT			X				X	
AAL-FLUSH_BUFFERS[3]	X							
AAL-CONTINUE[3]	X							
AAL-BSNT_NOT_RETRIEVABLE				X				

Notes:
1. In North American networks, the AAL-LINK_CONGESTED primitive must indicate one of four levels of congestion in the congestion parameter, levels 0 through 3, with 0 meaning no congestion.
2. The AAL-LINK_CONGESTION_CEASED primitive is not used in North American networks.
3. If these primitives occur they must be ignored (i.e., not implemented in ANSI specifications).
where:
  BSNT = Backward sequence number
  FSNC = Forward sequence number

MTP 3 can curtail link proving by sending the AAL-EMERGENCY primitive to SSCF, and it can request that SSCF return to its normal link proving operations by sending to SSCF the AAL-EMERGENCY_CEASES primitive.

To establish communications with another exchange, MTP 3 issues the AAL-START primitive, and when it wishes to inhibit further communications with the exchange, it sends the AAL-STOP primitive.

SSCF can inform MTP 3 about the status of a signaling link. It uses the AAL-IN_SERVICE primitive to inform MTP 3 that a link is available and the AAL-OUT_OF_SERVICE to indicate a link is not available.

In the ANSI specifications, AAL-FLUSH_BUFFERS and AAL-CONTINUE primitives are not implemented.

For ongoing management of the link, MTP 3 and SSCF have access to several primitives to request and inform each other about a number of operations. MTP 3 invokes the AAL-RETRIEVE_BSNT primitive to request the BSNT value to be retrieved and SSCF responds with the AAL-BSNT.confirm. If the BSNT value is not available, SSCF will send MTP 3 the AAL-BSNT_NOT_RETRIEVABLE.

Finally, MTP 3 can request nonacknowledged messages to be delivered by presenting the AAL-RETRIEVAL_REQUEST_AND_FSNC primitive to SSCF. In turn, SSCF delivers nonacknowledged messages to MTP 3 with two primitives: AAL-RETRIEVED_MESSAGES and AAL-RETRIEVAL_COMPLETE.

Table 6–2   Signals between SSCF and SSCOP and SSCOP and Layer Management

Signal	Type and Associated Parameters			
	Request	*Indication*	*Response*	*Confirm*
AA-ESTABLISH	SSCOP-UU, BR	SSCOP-UU	SSCOP-UU, BR	SSCOP-UU
AA-RELEASE	SSCOP-UU	SSCOP-UU Source	Not defined	—
AA-DATA	MU	MUSN	Not defined	Not defined
AA-RESYNC	SSCOP-UU	SSCOP-UU	—	—
AA-RECOVER	Not defined	—	—	Not defined
AA-UNITDATA	MU	MU	Not defined	Not defined
AA-RETRIEVE	RN	MU	Not defined	Not defined
AA-RETRIEVE COMPLETE	Not defined	—	Not defined	Not defined
MAA-ERROR	Not defined	Code, Count	Not defined	Not defined
MAA-UNITDATA	MU	MU	Not defined	Not defined

—: The signal has no parameters
Note: The SSCF PDU can be placed in the MU parameter of AA-DATA.req or in the SSCOP-UU of the AA-ESTABLISH.req or AA-RELEASE.req
where:

BR	Buffer release
MU	Message unit
MUSN	Message unit sequence number
RN	Retrieval number
UU	User-to-user

Signals between SSCOP-SSCF and SSCOP-Layer Management

Table 6–2 lists the signals that are exchanged between SSCOP and SSCF and SSCOP and layer management. The specific operations pertaining to the signals are explained next, and several examples of the use of these signals and parameters are provided in the next section of this chapter.

In order to establish connections between two exchanges and release these connections, SSCF and SSCOP exchange the AA-ESTABLISH and AA-RELEASE signals respectively. The AA-RESYNC signals are used to resynchronize the SSCOP connection and the AA-RECOVER signals are used to recover from an error occurring during an ongoing operation.

The AA-DATA signals are used for assured transfer of data between the exchanges.

In contrast, the AA-UNITDATA signals are used for nonassured transfer of data between layer management and SSCOP. The AA-UNITDATA signal also supports broadcast operations between multiple exchanges. The other signal exchanged between layer management and SSCOP is the MAA-ERROR signal. It is used to indicate the type of protocol error that has occurred. The reader should refer to Annex A of ANSI T1.637-1994 for information on these error conditions. As a general statement, they cover problems dealing with timer expirations, receiving erroneous PDUs, unsuccessful retransmissions, and others.

The AA-RETRIEVE and AA-RETRIEVE_COMPLETE signals are used to exchange data from SSCOP to SSCF.

Parameters in the Signals.   The parameters that are associated with these signals are also listed in Table 6–2. They have the following functions.

The message unit (MU) parameter contains user information. For the request signals, the parameter is mapped directly into the information field of the SSCOP PDU. For the indication signals, this field is derived from the contents of the information field of an incoming SSCOP PDU. The one exception to these comments pertains to the AA-RETRIEVE.indication signals, in which case the MU parameter contains a message that is returned to the SSCOP user from a queue containing data awaiting transmission.

The SSCOP user-to-user (SSCOP-UU) parameter contains end user traffic. The parameter correlates directly with the SSCOP-UU field in the SSCOP PDU.

The message unit sequence number (MUSN) parameter is derived from the N(S) field of the incoming SD PDU.

The retrieval number (RN) parameter, as its name implies, is used to retrieve data. It is sent by SSCF to request that SSCOP retrieve data from the transmission buffer. It can be coded to obtain the following services:

- Identification of the first SD PDU to be retrieved
- Retrieval of only those SD PDUs that have not yet been transmitted
- Indication that all SD PDUs are to be retrieved

The buffer release (BR) parameter is used during the connection setup to indicate if the transmitting SSCOP is allowed to release its buffers when the connection is released. It can be coded also to allow the release of selectively acknowledged messages from the transmission buffer.

The code parameter is an error code that indicates what type of problem has occurred during an ongoing operation, (Table 6–5).

The source parameter indicates to the SSCOP user whether the local or remote exchange originated a connection release.

And, finally, the count parameter indicates the number of SD PDUs that have been retransmitted.

Signals between Layer Management and SSCF

Table 6–3 lists the signals that are exchanged between layer management and SSCF. This section provides a summary of the functions of these signals. The MAAL-PROVING. ind is sent by SSCF to initiate error monitoring by layer management; it is part of the link proving process. If the proving is not successful, layer management sends the MAAL-PROVING_UNSUCCESSFUL.res to SSCF. If proving is to be terminated, SSCF sends the MAAL-STOP_PROVING.ind to layer management.

Layer management (LM) can also initiate forced proving by sending the MAAL-FORCE_PROVING.req to SSCF, and proving can be omitted by layer management sending SSCF the MAAL-FORCE_EMERGENCY.req signal. If layer management does not care which proving mode is used, it sends SSCF the MAAL-CLEAR_FORCE_MODES.req signal.

If a local processor fails or if a failed processor has been placed back into service, layer management sends to SSCF the MAAL-LOCAL_PROCESSOR_OUTAGE.req and MAAL-LOCAL_PROCESSOR_RECOVERED.req signals respectively.

Table 6–3   Signals Between Layer Management and SCCF.

	Signal Type and Associated Parameters			
Signals	*Request*	*Indication*	*Response*	*Confirm*
MAAL-PROVING		X		
MAAL-CLEAR_FORCE_MODES	X			
MAAL-FORCE_EMERGENCY	X			
MAAL-FORCE_PROVING	X			
MAAL-STOP_PROVING		X		
MAAL-PROVING_UNSUCCESSFUL			X	
MAAL-RELEASE	X			
MAAL-LOCAL_PROCESSOR_OUTAGE	X			
MAAL-LOCAL_PROCESSOR_RECOVERED	X			
MAAL-REPORT		X		

Note: For an explanation of the parameters in these signals, refer to "Parameters in the Signals"

SSCF can notify layer management about a variety of events with the MAAL-REPORT.ind signal. Its purpose is to give layer management a clear view of the status of SSCF. As examples, this signal can contain information (1) on the state of a SSCOP connection, (2) about whether the connection has been released or an indication of the origination of the release (local or remote), (3) about congestion, and (4) types of errors that have been encountered on the link.

Finally, layer management can instruct SSCF to release a connection by sending it the MAAL-RELEASE.req signal.

Parameters in the Signals.   The large number of parameters in the signals precludes a detailed discussion (many of them deal with the state transitions of SSCF, which is described in an 11-page table [Table 6] in ANSI T1.645-1995). As a general description, the parameters describe the state of an SSCOP connection (in service alignment not successful, etc.) and the reasons for the transitions from one state to another.

SIGNALS BETWEEN SSCOP AND CPCS

Two signals are passed between SSCOP and CPCS, (Table 6–4). The CPCS-UNITDATA.invoke is used by SSCOP to send SSCOP PDUs to its peer, by placing the PDU in the interface data (ID) parameter of CPCS-

Table 6–4   Signals between SSCOP and CPCS

Name	Parameters
CPCS-UNITDATA.invoke	ID, LP, CI, CPCS-UU
CPCS-UNITDATA.signal	ID, LP, CI, CPCS-UU

Note: Only ID is used at this time. The terms LP, CI, UU are not explained in either the ANSI or ITU-T specifications. I have notified these organizations of this omission.

ID	Interface data
LP	Ignored or not defined
CI	Ignored or not defined
UU	Ignored or not defined

UNITDATA.invoke. Conversely, the CPCS-UNITDATA.signal is used to receive messages from the peer; the SSCOP PDUs also reside in the ID parameter. The other parameters in the signals are ignored or not defined.

THE ERROR CODES

As explained in the previous section, a code parameter is used to indicate the type of problem that has occurred during an SSCOP operation. Table 6–5 shows the error codes that SSCOP may pass to layer management via the MAA-ERROR.ind signal. (The right-most column is explained in the next section of this chapter.)

THE SSCOP OPERATIONS IN MORE DETAIL

Before we analyze SSCOP operations, it will be helpful to briefly digress to explain the rationale for some of SSCOP's behavior. First, you will notice that SSCOP performs many conventional layer two functions, such as the sequencing and acknowledgment of traffic. Second, SSCOP employs a rather elaborate sequencing and acknowledgment scheme to do its job, in comparison to other protocols that perform similar services, such as MTP 2, LAPD, or LAPB.

The reason for these measures is that SSCOP is more efficient than its predecessors in managing the link. This link efficiency translates into a more "elaborate" protocol, but as we shall see, it is well-designed and elegantly simple.

Before the SCCOP operations are demonstrated, it is necessary to examine the SSCOP PDUs (messages).

Table 6–5   Error Codes in the code parameter

Type of Error	Code	PDU or Other Event That Creates Error Condition
Receipt of unsolicited or inappropriate PDU	A	SD PDU
	B	BGN PDU
	C	BGAK PDU
	D	BGREJ PDU
	E	END PDU
	F	ENDAK PDU
	G	POLL PDU
	H	STAT PDU
	I	USTAT PDU
	J	RS
	K	RSAK PDU
	L	ER
	M	ERAK
Unsuccessful retransmission	O	VT(CC) >= MaxCC
	P	Timer_NO-RESPONSE expiry
Other list elements error type	Q	SD or POLL, N(S) error
	R	STAT N(PS) error
	S	STAT N(R) or list elements error
	T	USTAT N(R) or list elements error
	U	PDU length violation
SD loss	V	SD PDUs must be retransmitted
Credit condition	W	Lack of credit
	X	Credit obtained

SSCOP PDUs

Table 6–6 lists the SSCOP PDUs that are exchanged between SSCOP peer-entities in two different ATM signaling nodes. The function of each PDU is shown as well as a brief description of the PDU's operations. Later material explains these PDUs in more detail with some examples. Table 6–6 is a summary of the following explanations of the PDUs.

- Begin (BGN): This PDU establishes a connection between two peer SSCOP entities. It is a housekeeping function in that it clears buffers and initializes transmit and receive counters.
- Begin acknowledge (BGAK): This PDU acknowledges the connection request; that is, the BGN PDU.

- Begin reject (BGREJ): This PDU rejects the connection request; once again, the BGN PDU.
- End (END): This PDU releases the connection between the two communicating parties.
- End acknowledge (ENDAK): This PDU confirms the release; that is, the END PDU.
- Resynchronization (RS): This PDU acts as a conventional connection-oriented reset found in other connection-oriented protocols. It resynchronizes the buffers as well as the transmitter and receiver state variables (counters).
- Resynchronization acknowledge (RSAK): This PDU acknowledges the resynchronization request by the peer entity; that is, the RS PDU.
- Error recovery (ER): This PDU recovers from errors occurring during the connection operations.

Table 6–6   Summary of the SSCOP Protocol Data Units (PDUs)

Function	PDU Name	Description
Establishment	BGN	Request initialization
	BGAK	Request acknowledgment
	BGREJ	Connection reject
Release	END	Disconnect command
	ENDAK	Disconnect acknowledgment
Resynchronization	RS	Resynchronization command
	RSAK	Resynchronization acknowledgment
Recovery	ER	Recovery command
	ERAK	Recovery acknowledgment
Assured data transfer	SD	Sequenced connection-mode data
	POLL	Transmitter state information with request for receive state information
	STAT	Solicited receiver state information
	USTAT	Unsolicited receiver state information
Unacknowledged data transfer	UD	Unnumbered user data
Management data transfer	MD	Unnumbered management data

- Error recovery acknowledge (ERAK): This PDU acknowledges the recovery request; that is, the ER PDU.
- Sequenced data (SD): This PDU transfers user traffic (traffic from the upper layers) to the peer entity.
- Status request (POLL): This PDU requests status information about the operations at the peer SSCOP entity.
- Solicited status response (STAT): This PDU responds to the POLL PDU. It is used to inform the polling entity about the correct reception of traffic (SD PDUs). It is also used for window control and contains a credit value to provide guidance to the poller about how much more traffic it can or cannot send. This PDU also contains the sequence number that was transmitted in the POLL PDU (N(PS)).
- Unsolicited status response (USTAT): This PDU is transmitted to the peer entity when missing SDUs are detected, which is based on comparing the sequence numbers of the incoming SD PDUs. This PDU also contains the credit field for window control.
- Unnumbered data (UD): This PDU is used to transmit unsequenced traffic between the SSCOP users. It does not affect the ongoing connection-oriented sequencing nor does it alter any counters or states between the two entities. This type of traffic may be discarded or lost without either party being notified of the event.
- Management data (MD): This PDU transmits non-sequenced management information between two SSCOP management entities. It carries the same risks (regarding possible loss) as the UD PDU.

It is also important to explain the parameters (fields) that are carried in the PDUs. You should refer to this section in conjunction with the operations that are described next.

- *N(SQ)*: This field is a connection sequence value. It is carried in a BGN, RS, or ER PDU. It is used with a counter at the receiver to identify any retransmissions of these three types of PDUs.
- *N(S):* This is a send sequence number that is placed in each newly transmitted SD or POLL PDU.
- *N(PS):* This field is carried in a POLL PDU at the transmitting site. The receiver of the POLL maps this field into a returned STAT PDU. In this manner, each POLL and its associated STAT can be correlated with each other.

- *N(R):* This field is carried in a STAT or USTAT PDU. It is a receive sequence number and is used to acknowledge transmissions.
- *N(MR):* This field is carried in the following PDUs: STAT, USTAT, RS, RSAK, ER, ERAK, BGN, BGAK. It is used to indicate if the peer SSCOP entity can send (a grant credit) or not send more traffic.

Examples of SSCOP "Housekeeping" Operations

This section should tie together many of the concepts that have been explained thus far in this chapter. Several examples are shown shortly, and the reader is encouraged to study Annexes D and E of ANSI T1.637 for more detailed explanations.

We have examined several aspects of SAAL and discussed briefly about the relationships between primitives and PDUs. Let us now see how they are used together.

An Example of the Relationship of SSCF/SSCOP Primitives and the SSCOP PDUs. As shown in Figure 6–6, to set up a connection between two SAAL entities, SSCF issues an AA-ESTABLISH.req primitive to SSCOP. This primitive contains the SSCOP-UU and BR parameters, which are used by SSCOP to create the BGN message. This message is sent to the receiving SSCOP where it is decoded, acted upon, and mapped to the AA-ESTABLISH.ind primitive sent to the receiving SSCF. This SSCF responds with the AA-ESTABLISH.res primitive to its SSCOP, which also contains the SSCOP-UU and BR parameters. In turn, the SSCOP sends the BGAK message back to the originating SSCOP, which decodes it, acts upon it, and passes it to its SSCF. These actions set up the connections at the two SAAL entities in the two broadband signaling exchanges.

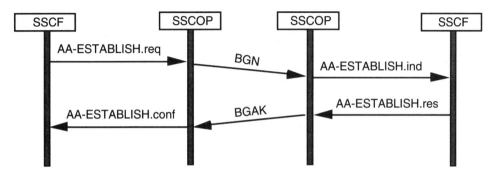

Figure 6–6   Example of SSCF and SSCOP operations.

Other housekeeping operations are part of SAAL and SSCOP activities, and follow similar procedures shown in the time sequence diagram in Figure 6–6, but one time sequence diagram should suffice.

Examples of SSCOP Transferring Signaling Traffic

As examples of how some of the PDU fields are used, ANSI provides a useful table in ANSI T1.637-1994 Annex D. The reader should use Table 6–7 as a reference as you study this section. Generally speaking, the purpose of the acknowledgments is to selectively reject, and/or accept the received PDUs. The "x" in the table means the PDU was not received correctly, or not received. The numbers between the { } are list elements and inform the receiver of the message which PDUs are acceptable, and which PDUs must be resent.

Figure 6–7 provides a general example of SSCOP operations in which no errors occur. A poll timer (called the TIMER_POLL in the specifications) is used to control the sending of periodic polls. Another timer (NO-RESPONSE) is used in parallel with the poll timer. During its interval, at least one STAT PDU must be received or the connection is aborted. The POLL PDU invokes the STAT PDU; the purpose of the STAT PDU is to find out about the status of the sequenced data units it had previously sent to its peer SSCOP entity (SCCOP B).

Next, the receiving of the AA-DATA.req signal from SSCF A directs SCCOP A to send an SD PDU. Recall from Table 6–2 that this signal contains the message unit (MU), which is traffic from MTP 3 and B-ISUP, and the MU sequence number (MUSN). Thus, SSCF is responsible for the sequencing operations on the signaling link.

Table 6–7   The SSCOP List

Received PDUs	Received POLL PDU	Responding PDU[1]
1,x,x,4	For USTAT	USTAT(N(R)=2{2,4})
1,x,x,4	POLL(N(S)=5)	STAT(N(R)=2{2,4,5})
1,x,x,x	POLL(N(S)=5)	STAT(N(R)=2,{2,5})
1x,x,4,5	POLL(N(S)=6)	STAT(N(R)=2{2,4,6})
1,x,x,4,5,x,x	POLL(N(S)=8)	STAT(N(R)=2,{2,4,6,8})
1,x,x,4,5,x,x,8,9	POLL(N(S)=10)	STAT(N(R)=2,{2,4,6,8,10})

[1]Odd elements in the list indicate first PDU of a missing gap. Even elements indicate first PDU of a received sequence, except possibly the last one.

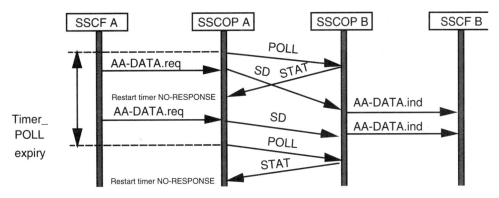

Figure 6–7   Data transfer with polls.

The initial POLL operation from SSCOP A begat the STAT PDU from SCCOP B. Upon receiving this PDU, SSCOP A restarts the NO-RESPONSE timer (which is restarted each time a STAT PDU is received). The issuance of POLL PDUs at SSCOP A is controlled by the POLL timer.

Figure 6–7 shows SSCOP operating in its active phase. It operates in the active phase as long as an SD or an ACK is outstanding. If the TIMER_POLL expires and there are no SDs or ACKs outstanding, but a STAT PDU is still outstanding, SSCOP enters into the transit phase.

Upon entering the transit phase, SSCOP starts the KEEP_ACTIVE timer (and continues to use the NO-RESPONSE timer). Upon receiving the STAT PDU, SSCOP stops the KEEP_ACTIVE and NO_RESPONSE timers, starts the IDLE timer and enters into the idle phase. During this phase SSCOP sends no polls and sends/receives no SD PDUs. Upon either a poll or SD being sent or received, SSCOP once again enters the active phase.

There is not much more to be said about the operations in Figure 6–7 except that the SD PDU message units are delivered to SSCF B (and then to MTP 3 and B-ISUP) by the AA-DATA.ind signals.

Figure 6–8 shows an SSCOP operation in more detail, with the primitives between SSCF and SSCOP excluded. SD PDUs are sent, with each succeeding PDU having its $N(S)$ field incremented by one. The $N(R)$ field in the PDU is set to 0, because the SSCOP A is expecting the SSCOP B to send its first PDU, which would be numbered $N(S) = 0$ (assuming it would be the first PDU sent since initialization, or that operations had wrapped that counter around to 0 again).

The POLL PDU solicits a STAT PDU. The $N(S)$ field is also used in the POLL and is set to 3 in the POLL. The $N(PS)$ value must be the same

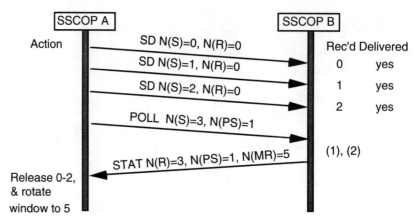

Notes:
1. Receiver of POLL maps *N(PS)* into field of STAT *N(PS)*
2. STAT *N(R)* = 3 is acknowledging SD PDUs, not the POLL.

Figure 6–8 Data transfer, with credit.

in the POLL and STAT, in order to correlate the two PDUs together.[3] The $N(MR) = 5$ is the credit value and rotates the send window to 5. So, SSCOP A can send PDUs up to 5, without waiting for a response.

At SSCOP B, the successful reception of SD PDUs 0, 1, and 2 allow SSCOP to deliver the message units to SSCF, noted by the "delivered" entries in Figure 6–8.

Figure 6–9 shows how SSCOP recovers from an error. SSCOP A sends four SD PDUs to SSCOP B, which are sequenced with $N(S) = 0$ through 3. All PDUs arrive at SSCOP correctly except PDU 1. SSCOP is not allowed to deliver out-of-sequence traffic to its user, so SSCOP B holds PDUs 2 and 3 in its buffer, and delivers PDU 0 to the user. It sends a USTAT PDU to SSCOP with $N(R) = 1$. This value informs SSCOP that PDU 1 should be retransmitted. (The $N(MR) = n$ is the credit value and not discussed in this example.)

The list element (LE) is set to 1,2, which conveys the following information. The odd element (the value of 1) specifies the PDU of a missing gap, which in this simple example is 1 (and the same value of the $N(R)$ value). The even element (the value of 2) specifies the first PDU of the next correctly received sequence. This information tells SSCOP A that:

---

[3]There is a conflict in the ANSI T1.637 document regarding the incrementing of $N(S)$ for the POLL PDU. Clause 7.4 a) (page 22) states that it is updated only for a SD PDU, but examples and clause 7.4 b) (page 23) contradict the former clause. I have notified ANSI, and this chapter assumes $N(S)$ is incremented for both PDUs.

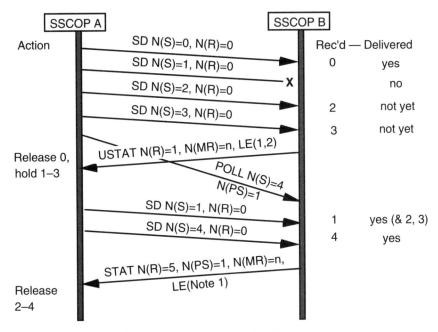

Note 1: List element (LE) is not needed in this PDU.

Figure 6–9   Recovery from an error.

(1) It must resend PDU 1; (2) it can release PDU 0 from its buffer; and (3) it must continue to hold PDUs 1, 2, and 3, because it does not yet have enough information about the fate of PDUs 2 and 3.

Before SSCOP A received the USTAT PDU from SSCOP B, it sent a POLL PDU. This message contains $N(S) = 4$, which represents the $N(S)$ value of the next new SD PDU (that is, an SD PDU that is to be transmitted for the first time). The POLL also contains $N(PS) = 1$. As discussed earlier, this is a sequence number of the POLL PDU. Upon receiving the USTAT PDU, SSCOP A resends SD 1, and sends SD 4 for the first time. These PDUs are received correctly by SSCOP B, which can now release PDUs 1, 2, 3, and 4 to the user. SSCOP B responds to the POLL PDU with the USTAT PDU which is coded with $N(R) = 5$ to inclusively acknowledge PDUs 1–4, and indicate it is expecting PDU 5 next. The $N(PS)$ field in the USTAT must be the same value as the $N(PS)$ field in the associated POLL PDU (a value of 1 in this example). As the note explains, no LEs need be coded in the PDU since there are not missing PDUs. The $N(R) = 4$ is sufficient to account for all traffic.

The final example (Figure 6–10) of SSCOP operations shows how the protocol recovers from multiple errors. SSCOP A sends eleven PDUs (with

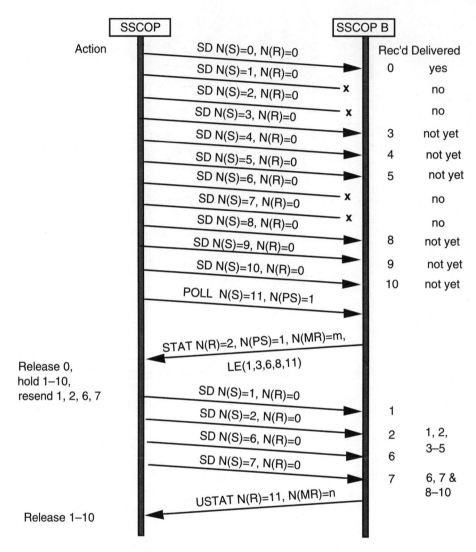

Figure 6–10   Recovery from multiple errors.

$N(S)$ = 0 through 10) to SSCOP B. PDUs 1, 2, and 6, 7 are not received correctly and are not delivered to the SSCOP B user. The PDUs that are received correctly are either delivered to the user (PDU 1) if their delivery keeps them in sequential order, or are held to await the retransmissions of the erred PDUs. So, PDUs 3, 4, 5, and 8, 9, 10 are held by SSCOP B.

SSCOP A sends a POLL PDU to SSCOP B, with N(S) set to 11. This value means that SSCOP has sent PDUs of 0–10 inclusive and intends to send PDU 11 next. The POLL PDU asks SSCOP to respond with a status message about which PDUs it has or has not received correctly.

SSCOP B responds with the STAT PDU. The list of elements (LEs) is coded to indicate the missing gaps. Remember the list is interpreted as: Odd elements identify the first PDU of a missing gap, and even elements identify the first PDU of a received sequence of PDUs, except possibly the last.

SSCOP A uses the information to resend PDUs 1, 2, 6, and 7, which are received correctly by SSCOP B. This entity responds with the USTAT PDU with the N(R) value set to 11, which inclusively acknowledges all the PDUs sent from SSCOP A.

RELATIONSHIPS OF THE SAAL ENTITIES AND MTP 3

Finally, Figure 6–11 shows one example of the relationships of the SAAL entities and MTP 3. This example is the initiation of a connection setup between two exchanges. MTP 3 at exchange A starts the process for sending an AAL-START.req primitive to SSCF A, which uses this information to form an AA-ESTABLISH.req primitive to send to SSCOP A. In turn, SSCOP A uses this information to create a BGN PDU to send to its peer SSCOP entity at exchange B. Notice that SSCF A returns the

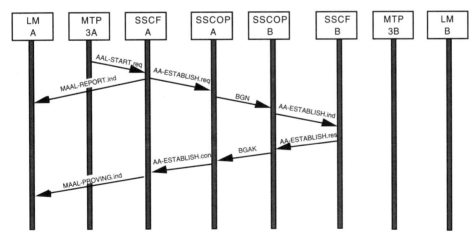

Note: The same set of procedures occur from exchange B (and MTP 3B), but are not shown in this figure.

Figure 6–11   Example of SAAL entity relationships.

MAAL-REPORT.ind signal to layer management A (LM A). Since link proving has just begun, this signal contains information that the link is not (yet) in service.

The BGN PDU parameters are used by SSCOP B to create an AA-ESTABLISH.ind primitive for transferal to SSCF B. No further information is sent to the entities at exchange B, but as the note in Figure 6–11 states, an identical operation is invoked at exchange B, but not shown in this example.

SSCF B examines the AA-ESTABLISH.req primitive and parameters, and responds with the AA-ESTABLISH.res primitive. This primitive is used by SSCOP B to create the BGAK PDU, which is sent to SSCOP A. The end result of this exchange is to notify LM A of the proving operations with the MAAL-PROVING.ind primitive.

Parameters in the Primitives and PDUs

Figure 6–12 shows the parameters that are associated with the primitives and PDUs. Their functions are as follows:

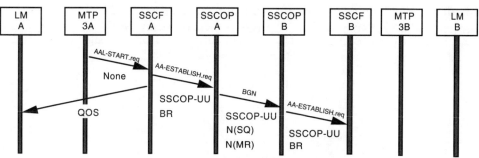

(a) Parametets in the forward directions

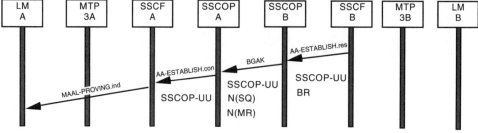

(b) Parameters in the backward direction

Figure 6–12   Parameters in the primitives.

- *SSCOP-UU*: This parameter is a user-to-user message. Its contents are application-dependent and may be null (not present).
- *BR*: This parameter is the buffer release. It indicates if the sender can release its buffers after the connection is released. It is also used during ongoing operations to release selectively acknowledged messages from the transmit buffer.
- *N(SQ)*: This parameter contains a connection sequence number. It is used to identify retransmitted BGN, RS, or ER PDUs.
- *N(MR)*: This parameter is used to set up the initial flow control operations (it is a window size parameter). The value establishes an initial credit between the SSCOPs to govern how many PDUs they can send to each other.
- *QOS* (quality of service): Optional features, that are tailored to a specific implementation.

SUMMARY

SAAL is responsible for the correct transfer of signaling data on a broadband signaling link. It relieves the user of concern about data errors, loss, duplicates, or insertions that may occur on the signaling link.

SAAL provides a link monitoring service, and "proves" that links are stable and error-free enough to be used (with alignment procedures). It can also take a link out of service if it becomes unreliable. SAAL also provides for flow control procedures and employs mechanisms to insure that two exchanges do not create congestion problems.

SSCF and SSCOP are the protocol entities that make up the SAAL operations, and these overall operations are coordinated by layer management (LM).

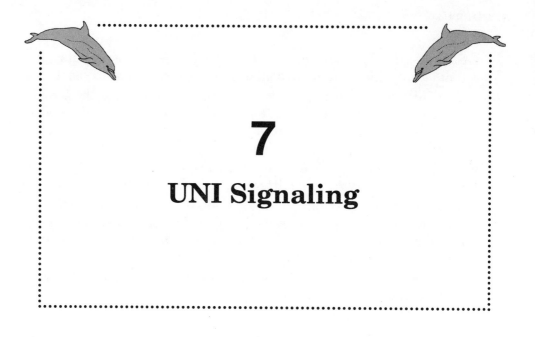

7

UNI Signaling

INTRODUCTION

This chapter examines the ATM signaling operations at the UNI. The operations deal with call and connection control procedures. Emphasis is placed on how connections are set up on demand between users and the ATM network. This procedure is also known as a switched virtual call (SVC) in older technology. The Q.2931 connection control protocol is explained, and the Q.2931 messages and their contents are analyzed.

This chapter is organized around the ITU-T Q.2931 Recommendation. The ATM Forum UNI Signaling Specification (version 4.0) is based on Q.2931, but has several variations of Q.2931. The major variations are also explained in this chapter.

BROADBAND SIGNALING STACKS

Figure 7–1 compares the ATM signaling stacks (protocol stacks) for UNI and NNI operations. For the UNI, Q.2931 (a variation of ISDN's layer 3 Q.931) is used to set up and tear down a connection. It operates over an AAL designed especially for Q.2931, which is called the signaling AAL (SAAL). I explain more about SAAL shortly. These layers operate over the conventional ATM layer and a selected physical layer.

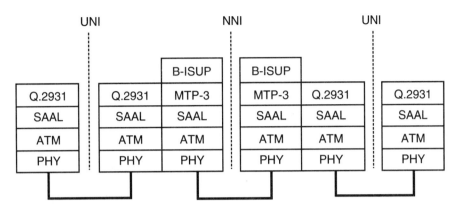

where:
ATM   Asynchronous transfer mode
B-ISUP Broadband ISDN user part
MTP-3   Message transfer part (variation of SS7 MTP-3)
NNI   Network node interface
PHY   Physical layer
Q.2931 Variation of ISDN Q.931
SAAL   Signaling ATM adaptation layer
UNI   User network interface

Figure 7–1   Broadband signaling stacks.

For the NNI, the broadband ISDN (B-ISDN) and message transfer part 3 (MTP 3) are variations of their counterparts in the SS7 signaling standard. They rely on the SAAL to support their operations. These layers also operate over the conventional ATM and a selected physical layer.

The UNI and NNI SAALs have some similarities and differences. Both contain a common part convergence sublayer (CPCS) and a segmentation and reassembly sublayer (SAR). However, the NNI SAAL is more complex than the UNI SAAL, and performs wide array of support services for B-ISUP and MTP 3. These services are described later in this chapter.

UNI MESSAGES AND INFORMATION ELEMENTS

Signaling at the UNI requires that a wide variety of information be exchanged between the user and the network. This section provides a description of the messages and parameters that are used in these exchanges.

Message Format

Figure 7–2 shows the format of the Q.2931 message. The protocol discriminator field can be coded to identify the Q.2931 message, or other layer 3 protocols, such as ISDN Q.931, a frame relay SVC message in a frame relay network. Obviously, it is coded in this protocol to identify Q.2931 messages and is set to 00010001.

The call reference identifies each call and is assigned by the originating side of the call (the user at the local side, and the network at the remote side); therefore, it does not have end-to-end significance. Its purpose is to keep the different calls uniquely identified, and it remains fixed for the duration of the call. The call reference field contains a 1-bit call reference flag, which is used to identify which end of the signaling virtual channel originated the call reference. The origination side sets this bit to 0 and the destination side sets it to 1. Thus, this flag is used to avoid simultaneous attempts to allocate the same call reference value.

The message type identifies the specific type of message, such as a SETUP, ADD PARTY, and so on.

The information elements contain the fields that are used to control the connection operation. They contain information of the AAL and QOS operations that are to be supported during the connection.

				Bits				
8	7	6	5	4	3	2	1	Octets
Protocol discriminator								1
0	0	0	0	Length of call reference				2
Flag	Call reference value							3
Call reference value (continued)								4
Call reference value (continued)								5
Message type								6
Message type (continued)								7
Message length								8
Message length (continued)								9
Variable length information elements								n

Figure 7–2   Contents of the Q.2931 message.

The Messages

Table 7–1 lists the ATM messages and their functions employed for demand connections at the UNI. Since these messages are derived from Q.931, they contain the typical Q.931 fields such as protocol discriminator, call reference, message type, and message length. The information content of the field, of course, is tailored for the specific ATM UNI interface.

The Information Elements (IEs)

The functions of the information elements are summarized in Table 7–2. Many of the information elements are optional. It is the job of the ATM switch to map the contents of these information elements into operations at the NNI, and to map them back at the remote UNI.

OVERVIEW OF UNI OPERATIONS

As depicted in Figure 7–3, the connection establishment procedures begin by a user issuing the SETUP message. This message is sent by the calling user to the network and is relayed by the network to the called

Table 7–1   ATM Connection Control Messages

Message	Function
Call establishment	
SETUP	Initiate the call establishment
CALL PROCEEDING	Call establishment has begun
CONNECT	Call has been accepted
CONNECT ACKNOWLEDGE	Call acceptance has been acknowledged
Call clearing	
RELEASE	Initiate call clearing
RELEASE COMPLETE	Call has been cleared
Miscellaneous	
STATUS ENQUIRY (SE)	Sent to solicit a status message
STATUS (S)	Sent in response to SE or to report error
Global call reference	
RESTART	Restart all VCs
RESTART ACKNOWLEDGE	ACKS the RESTART
Point-to-multipoint operations	
ADD PARTY	Add party to an existing connection
ADD PARTY ACKNOWLEDGE	ACKS the ADD PARTY
ADD PARTY REJECT	REJECTS the ADD PARTY
DROP PARTY	Drops party from an existing connection
DROP PARTY ACKNOWLEDGE	ACKS the DROP PARTY

Table 7–2   Functions of the Information Service Elements

Element	Function
Protocol discriminator	Distinguishes different types of messages within ITU-T standards and standards bodies throughout the world
Call reference	Uniquely identifies each call at the UNI
Message type	Identifies type of message, such as SETUP, STATUS, etc.
Message length	Length of message excluding the three elements above and this element
AAL parameters	AAL parameters selected by user
ATM user cell rate	Specifies set of traffic parameters
Broadband bearer capability	Indicates several network bearer services (end-to-end timing, CBR, VBR, point-to-point, multipoint services)
Broadband high layer information	End-user codes, passed transparently through ATM network; identifies upper layer protocols or a vendor-specific application
Broadband repeat indicator	Used to allow repeated information elements to be interpreted correctly
Broadband low layer information	End-user codes, passed transparently through ATM network; identifies lower layer protocols/configurations
Called party number	Called party of the call
Called party subaddress	Called party subaddress
Calling party number	Origin party number
Calling party subaddress	Calling party subaddress
Call state	One of 12 values describing status of a call (active, call initiated, etc.)
Cause	Diagnostic codes
Connection identifier	The VPI and VCI for the call
QOS parameter	QOS class
Broadband sending complete	Indicates the completion of the called party number
Transit network selection	Identifies a transit network (an IXC in the United States)
Endpoint reference	Identifies endpoints in a point-to-multipoint connection
Endpoint state	Indicates state of each endpoint (add party initiated, received, active, etc.)
Restart indicator	Identifies which virtual channels are to be restated

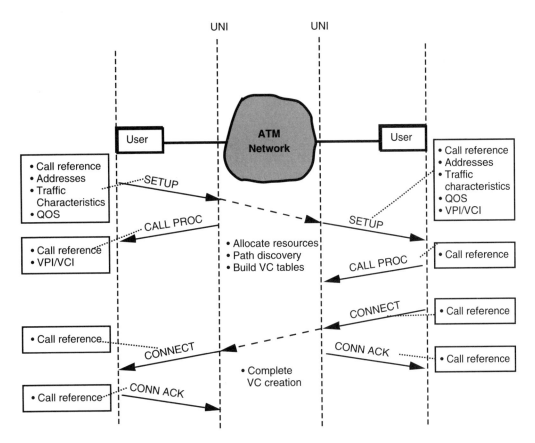

Figure 7–3 Connection setup.

user. This message contains several information elements (fields) to: (a) identify the message, (b) specify various AAL parameters, (c) identify the calling and called party addresses, (d) establish requirements for QOS, (e) select the transit network (if needed), and (f) specify a number of other requirements.

Upon receiving the SETUP message, the network returns a CALL PROCEEDING message to the initiating user, forwards the SETUP message to the called user, and waits for the called user to return a CALL PROCEEDING message. The CALL PROCEEDING message is used to indicate that the call has been initiated and no more call establishment information is needed, nor will any be accepted.

The called user, if it accepts a call, will then send to the network a CONNECT message. This CONNECT message will then be forwarded to the calling user. The CONNECT message contains parameters that deal with some of the same parameters in the SETUP message such as call reference and message type, as well as the accepted AAL parameters and several other identifiers that are created as a result of the information elements in the original SETUP message.

Upon receiving the CONNECT messages, the calling user and the network return the CONNECT ACKNOWLEDGE to their respective parties.

Either user can initiate a disconnect operation (see Figure 7–4). To do so requires the user to send the RELEASE message to the network. This message clears the end-to-end connection between the two users and the network. This message only contains the basic information to identify the message across the network. Other parameters are not included because they are not needed to clear the state tables for the connection.

The receiving network and receiving user are required to transmit the RELEASE COMPLETE message as a result of receiving the RELEASE message.

The Q.2931 Timers

The vast majority of networks that provide connections on demand use timers at both the user and network nodes to define reasonable wait periods for completion of certain actions (such as completion of a setup,

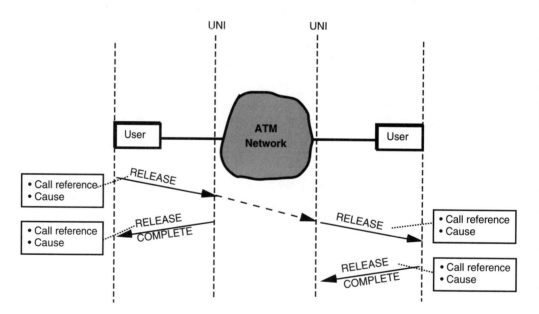

Figure 7–4   Connection release.

completion of a restart, etc.). The ATM UNI signaling interface provides ten timers at the network side and ten timers at the user side (see Table 7–3).

Each connection is controlled by states. For example, a user enters into a "call present" state when a call establishment request has been received but the user has not yet responded to the request. Various states can be entered and exited as a call is processed, some of which are governed by timers. In the event an action does not take place before a designated timer expires, various remedial actions are dictated, such as issuing retries or moving to other states.

Table 7–3 Timers

Timer Network Side	Number User Side	Cause for Start	Normal Stop
T301		Not supported in this Implementation Agreement	
T303	T303	SETUP sent	CONNECT, CALL PROCEEDING, or RELEASE COMPLETE received
T308	T308	RELEASE sent	RELEASE COMPLETE or RELEASE received
T309	T309	SAAL disconnection	SAAL reconnected
T310	T310	CALL PROCEEDING received	CONNECT or RELEASE received
	T313	CONNECT sent	CONNECT ACKNOW-LEDGE received
T316	T316	RESTART sent	RESTART ACKNOW-LEDGE received
T317	T317	RESTART received	Internal clearing of call references
T322	T322	STATUS ENQUIRY sent	STATUS, RELEASE, or RELEASE COMPLETE received
T398	T398	DROP PARTY sent	DROP PARTY ACKNOWLEDGE or RELEASE received
T399	T399	ADD PARTY sent	ADD PARTY ACKNOWLEDGE, ADD PARTY REJECT or RELEASE received

THE UNI OPERATIONS IN MORE DETAIL

We continue our analysis of the Q.2931 UNI with a more detailed examination of the operations. In this section, I show how the Q.2931 timers and the parameters in the messages are used. I will focus on all the mandatory parameters and several optional parameters that warrant our interest.

The Connection Establishment Operation

Figure 7–5 shows the timers invoked for the establishment of a connection. Three timers are involved in the process and perform the following functions.

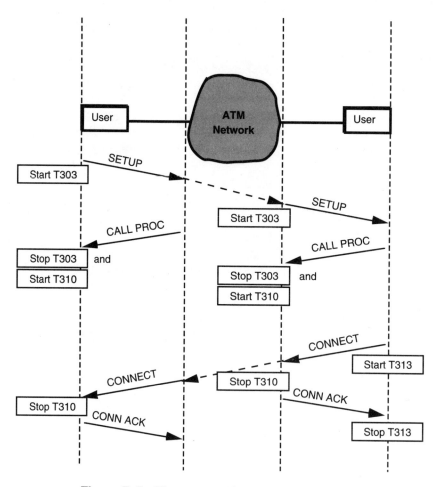

Figure 7–5   The connection setup procedure.

Timer T303 is invoked when ATM issues a SETUP message to the network on the local side of the network and is invoked by network node at the remote side when it passes the SETUP message to the user. The timer is stopped when the remote end user returns a CALL PROCEEDING message. This message is relayed to the local network side, which also sends it to the originating user. Although not illustrated in this figure, timer T303 can also be stopped if either a CONNECT message or a RELEASE COMPLETE message is received. If the timer expires before the reception of a CALL PROCEEDING message, a SETUP message may be retransmitted or, if the network does not support SETUP retransmissions, the potential connection is cleared and a null state is entered. The ATM specifications require that only one retry may be attempted after which a null state must be entered.

Upon receiving the CALL PROCEEDING message, the local user and remote network node turn off their T303 timers and turn on their T310 timers. This timer waits for the CONNECT message to be sent to either party. Upon successful reception of the CONNECT message, timer T310 is turned off and the recipients of this message respond with a CONNECTION ACKNOWLEDGMENT of this message. If the CONNECTION ACKNOWLEDGMENT message is not received before timer T310 expires, the connection must be cleared.

The remote user also invokes timer T313 when it sends the CONNECT message to the network. This timer is turned off upon receiving the CONNECT ACKNOWLEDGMENT message.

The SETUP message must contain all the information required for the network and the called party to process the call. This information must include the QOS parameters, the cell rate parameters, and any bearer capabilities that the network may need at either side. The user is not allowed to fill in the connection identifier information element in the SETUP message. If it is included, the network ignores it. This means that the network selects the VPI/VCI for the connection. This information is returned to the user in the CALL PROCEEDING message.

A similar procedure is performed on the remote side of the network in that the network node is responsible for allocating the VPI/VCI value and placing this value in the SETUP message before it sends this message to the called user.

The Connection Release Operation

The connection release operation entails only timer T308 (see Figure 7–6). Either the network or the user can invoke the connection release by sending the RELEASE message to the respective party. This op-

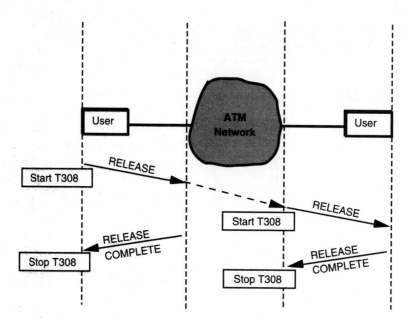

Figure 7–6   The release procedure.

eration turns on timer T308 which remains on until the RELEASE message is received. If T308 expires for the first time, the RELEASE message is retransmitted. If a response is not returned on this second try,
the user must release the call reference and return to the null state (no
connection exists). The manner in which this operation is then handled is
not defined in the standard but is network or user specific.

In the event that a RELEASE message is received by the network or
the user at the same time that the respective node sends a RELEASE
(this procedure is called a clear-clear collision), the affected party stops
timer T308 and releases the call reference as well as the virtual channel
and enters into the null state.

The Restart Operation

The network or user can initiate restart operations for any number
of reasons (see Figure 7–7). Failure of any component can result in the
restart procedure being invoked, and information elements in the header
cite the reason for the restart. The initiation of the restart invokes timer
T316 by the originator sending the RESTART message to the recipient.
In turn, the recipient starts timer T317 upon receiving the RESTART
message. After processing the RESTART message and taking any neces-

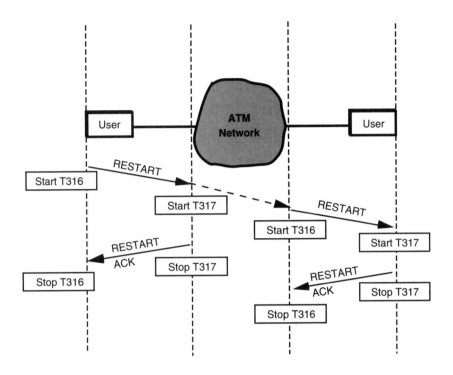

Figure 7–7   The restart operation.

sary actions, the recipient issues a RESTART acknowledge and stops T317. A RESTART acknowledge is sent to the originator, which then stops T316. The field in the RESTART message labeled restart indicator determines if an indicated virtual channel is to be restarted or all channels controlled by this layer 3 entity are to be restarted.

The Status Inquiry Operation

The status inquiry procedure depicted in Figure 7–8 is invoked by either the network or the user to determine the state of a connection, such as the call state, the type of connection being supported, the end state of a point-to-multipoint connection, and so on. As indicated in this figure, timer T322 controls this procedure. Either party may invoke the STATUS INQUIRY message by turning T322 on. Upon receipt of the STATUS or STATUS COMPLETE message, this timer is turned off.

The Add Party Operation

Because of the importance and wide use of telephone conference calls, multicasting data traffic, and video conferencing operations, the ATM de-

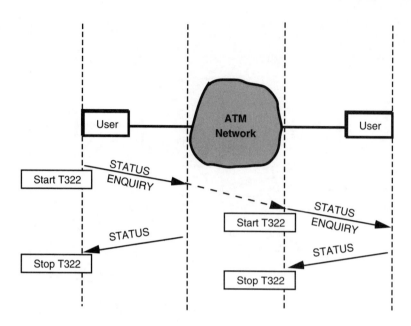

Figure 7–8   The status enquiry operation.

signers developed procedures to support these types of applications. It is anticipated that most initial implementations will be data only.

This capability is implemented through the add-party procedure as shown in Figure 7–9. This illustration shows the addition of only one party, but multiple parties may be connected with this operation. The originating site issues an ADD PARTY message across the UNI to the network. The network forwards this message to the destination in which the destination network node issues a SETUP across the UNI to the destination user. The SETUP message is used if procedures must begin from scratch. That is to say, this UNI is currently not participating in the call. Not shown in this figure is the possibility of issuing the ADD PARTY message across the remote UNI for situations where a call is already in place and another calling party needs to be added.

The operation is controlled with timer T399 at the sending site. This timer is turned off upon receiving a CONNECTION ACKNOWLEDG-MENT, an ADD PARTY, ADD PARTY ACK, REJECT, or a RELEASE. In this example, the remote side uses the initial setup operation, discussed earlier. The point-to-multipoint operation is also controlled by party-states. These states may exist on the network side or the user side of the interface. They are summarized as follows:

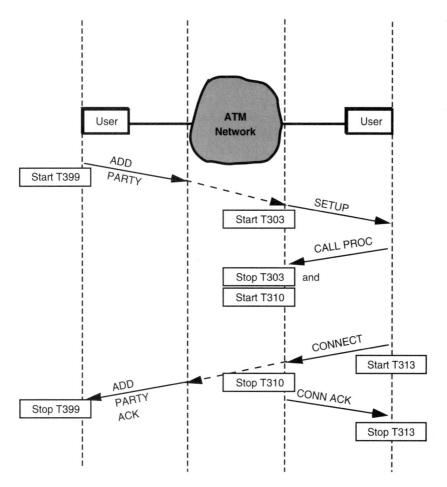

Figure 7–9   The add party procedure.

- *Null:* A party does not exist; therefore an endpoint reference value has not been allocated.
- *Add party initiated:* An ADD PARTY message or a SETUP message has been sent to the other side of the interface for this party.
- *Add party received:* An ADD PARTY message or a setup message has been received by the other side of the interface for this party.
- *Drop party initiated:* A DROP PARTY message has been sent for this party.
- *Drop party received:* A DROP PARTY message has been received for this party.
- *Active:* On the user side of the UNI, an active state is when the

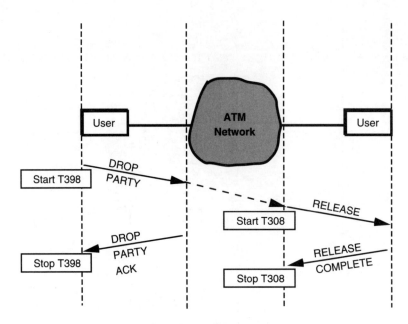

Figure 7–10   The drop party procedure.

user has received an CONNECT ACKNOWLEDGE, ADD PARTY
ACKNOWLEDGE, or a CONNECT. On the network side, an active state is entered when it has sent a CONNECT, CONNECT
ACKNOWLEDGE, or an ADD PARTY ACKNOWLEDGE, or when
the network has received an ADD PARTY ACKNOWLEDGE from
the user side.

The Drop Party Operation

As the reader might expect, the drop party operations provide the
opposite function of the add party procedure discussed in the previous
section (see Figure 7–10). With this operation, one party or multiple parties can be dropped from the connection. The activity is controlled by the
T398 and T308 timers. In this example, the RELEASE and RELEASE
COMPLETE messages are used at the remote side. Under certain conditions the drop party is also activated at the remote side.

THE Q.931 MESSAGE INFORMATION ELEMENTS
IN MORE DETAIL

This section explains the Q.2931 information elements that are
mandatory and those that are optional but are needed to support several

important operations. The structure of the elements is illustrated in several figures, but I have not described all the coding rules and bit-structure of the information elements. This practice is in keeping with the overall theme of the book, and the reader should study *ATM Forum User-Network Interface Specification* (V.4.0) and ITU-T Q.2931 if more detal is needed.

AAL Information Element

Figure 7–11 illustrates the first 6 octets of the AAL information element. These octets are used for all AAL types. Octet 1 is coded as 01011000 to identify the information element. Octet 2 is preset or not significant. Octet 5 is coded to indicate the AAL type information that follows in octets 6 through n:

00000001   AAL type 1
00000011   AAL type 3/4
00000101   AAL type 5
00010000   User-defined AAL

AAL Type 1.   Figure 7–12 shows the information elements for octet groups 6–12 for AAL type 1. The subtype identifier indicates:

00000000   Null/empty
00000001   Voice-band 64 kbit/s

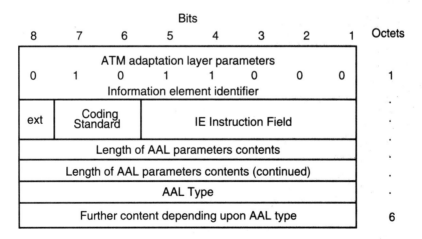

Figure 7–11   AAL information element for all AAL types.

Bits

8	7	6	5	4	3	2	1	Octets
Subtype identifer								6
Subtype								
CBR Rate Identifier								.
CBR Rate								.
Multiplier Identifier								.
Multiplier (Note 1)								.
Multiplier (continued)								.
Source Clock Frequency Recovery Method Identifier								.
Source Clock Frequency Recovery Method								.
Error Correction Method Identifier								.
Error Correction Method								.
Structured Data Transfer Blocksize Identifier								.
Structured Data Transfer Blocksize								.
Partially Filled Cells Identifier								.
Partially Filled Cells Method								n

These octets are only present if CBR rate indicates "n x 64 kbit/s".

Figure 7–12   Information elements for an AAL Type 1 connection.

00000010   Circuit emulation (synchronous)
00000011   Circuit emulation (asynchronous)
00000100   High-quality audio
00000101   Video

The CBR rate requests a bit rate for the session. It is coded as follows:

00000001   64 kbit/s
00000100   1544 kbit/s (DS1)
00000101   6312 kbit/s (DS2)

```
00000110   32064 kbit/s
00000111   44736 kbit/s (DS3)
00001000   97728 kbit/s
00010000   2048 kbit/s (E1)
00010001   8448 kbit/s (E2)
00010010   34368 kbit/s (E3)
00010011   139264 kbit/s (E4)
01000000   n × 64 kbit/s
```

The multiplier parameter is used to define a $n \times 64$ kbit/s, with n ranging from 2 to $2^{16} - 1$. The clock recovery type parameter indicates the kind of clocking operation to be employed to recover and decode the signal (timestamp, etc.). The error correction parameter identifies the type of error correction method employed to detect errors at the terminating end-point (none, FEC, etc.). The structured data transfer identifies that this connection will or will not use structured data transfer. The partially filled cells parameter states how many of the 47 octets in the cell are in use.

AAL Type 3/4. Figure 7–13 shows the parameters for AAL types 3/4 and 5 The functions represented in these fields were explained previously. Briefly, then, the service specific CS (SSCS) and the common part of CS (CPCS) parameters indicate (1) the maximum CPCS-SDU sizes (forward and backward), with values ranging from 1 to 65,535 ($2^{16} - 1$); (2) the ranges for the message identification field (1 to 1023); (3) a message or streaming mode; and (4) SSCS type (such assured operations, a frame relay SSCS, etc.).

Broadband Low Layer Informaton Element

Figure 7–14 shows the parameters of the broadband low layer information element. The mode field defines if extended (0–127) or normal sequencing (0–7) is to be employed at layer 2 (if sequencing is employed). The Q.933 field is used, based on implementation-specific rules. The window size field (k) can range from 1–127.

The next parameters define if user-specified layer 2 and layer 3 protocols are employed. The mode field defines if extended (0–127) or normal sequencing (0–7) is to be employed at layer 3 (if sequencing is employed). The default packet size field is used to define the default size of the X.25 packet (if X.25 is invoked). The packet window size is also employed for X.25 for a range of 1–127.

AAL Type 3/4

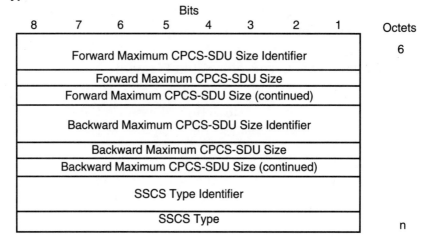

AAL Type 5

Figure 7–13   Parameters for AAL Types 3/4 and 5.

Bits								Octets
8	7	6	5	4	3	2	1	
Broadband low layer information								1
ext	Coding Standard		IE Instruction Field					
Length of B-LLI contents								
Length of B-LLI contents (continued)								
ext	Layer 1 id		User information layer 1 protocol					
ext	Layer 2 id		User information layer 2 protocol					
ext	Mode		Spare			Q.933 use		
ext	Window size (k)							
ext	User specified layer 2 protocol information							
ext	Layer 3 id		User information layer 3 protocol					
ext	Mode		Spare					
ext	Spare			Default Packet Size				
ext	Packet window size							
ext	User specified layer 3 protocol information							
ext	ISO/IEC TR 9577 Initial Protocol Identifier (IPI)							
ext	IPI		Spare					
ext	SNAP ID		Spare					
OUI Octet 1								
OUI Octet 2								
OUI Octet 3								
PID Octet 1								
PID Octet 2								n

Figure 7–14   The broadband low layer information element.

The remainder of the octets in this information element can be used to identify Subnetwork Access Protocol (SNAP) information. If so indicated by octets 7a, a 24-bit organization unique ID (OUI) and a 16-bit protocol ID (PID) are contained in the last octets of the information element. The OUI and PID are values that are registered under ISO, the IEEE, and the Internet.

ATM FORUM UNI VERSION 4.0 VARIATIONS

The ITU-T specifications do not allow a leaf to joint an ADD PARTY Connection without the intervention of the root. The ATM Forum UNI establishes procedures for the leaf to initiate an ADD PARTY request, which is handled by the network. The root is not involved in this operation. This operation is called the leaf initiated join capability (LIJ).

UNI 4.0 also provides for an ATM group address, which is a collection of ATM end systems. The idea of the group address is to identify related end stations that provide well known services (for example, ATM LAN emulation services).

Group addressing also allows an ATM end system to define a membership scope during the address registration procedure, which is used to determine the range of routing. For example, a limited scope can restrict routing to a single Ethernet network (including bridges and repeaters).[1]

In conjunction with group addressing, version 4.0 defines the Anycast operation. This procedure allows a single ATM end system to request a point-to-point connection to a single ATM end system that is part of an ATM group.

SUMMARY

Broadband signaling at the UNI establishes call and connection control operations and defines how connections are set up on demand between users and the ATM network. The Q.2931 connection control protocol, based on the ISDN Q.931, is used for these operations.

Q.2931 utilizes the OSI address syntax and supports point-to-point, point-to-multipoint, and multipoint-to-multipoint connections.

---

[1]As explained later in this book the most limited scope would correlate to the bottom level of the PNNI routing heirarchy.

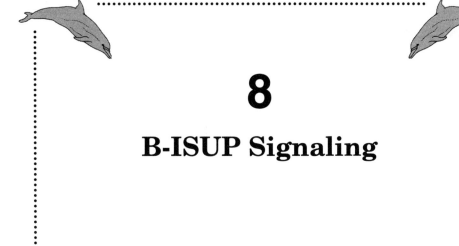

8

B-ISUP Signaling

INTRODUCTION

This chapter examines the Broadband ISDN user part (B-ISUP), one of the key applications used in a broadband signaling network. The relationships of B-ISUP, ISUP, and SS7 are explained, as well as how they interwork with each other. The B-ISUP entities (sublayers) are examined as well, and due to the close relationships of these B-ISUP entities, it will be necessary to examine the primitives that are exchanged between them.

The ANSI T1.648 and ITU-T Q.2764 and Q.2763 standards are examined in this chapter. They are quite similar to each other and I will point out their major differences during this analysis.

A few more comments before we proceed. The UNI and NNI message parameters are closely associated with each other. Therefore, I have included this information as Appendix 8A and will not repeat the descriptions of the parameters that are the same, but will refer you to Chapter 7. Finally, the interfaces and primitives between the B-ISUP entities are quite varied and complex and might be of interest only to the reader who is a programmer. I describe the major aspects of these operations in one section of this chapter and provide more details in Appendix 8B.

PURPOSE OF B-ISUP

The principal function of B-ISUP is to provide the signaling functions necessary to set up, manage, and terminate a virtual circuit in the broadband network. It provides functions to support both basic bearer and supplementary services and is based on ISUP. In addition, ANSI B-ISUP is based on (with some minor exceptions) the same procedures as the ITU-T specifications that are published in ITU-T Recommendations Q.276, Q.2764 and Q.2730.

As its name implies, B-ISUP is related to ISUP, and draws most of its features from its narrowband counterpart. The B-ISUP developers took this approach because ISUP has proven to be an effective signaling protocol, and many designers and programmers have used it. It makes little sense to start from scratch when existing technology can be modified to accomplish the job.

Like ISUP, B-ISUP is designed to transfer control information between elements in a telecommunications network. The principal elements are switches, but B-ISUP can operate between other signaling points as well, such as operations centers and switches and their associated databases. The control information is used to establish and terminate virtual circuits and to manage the bandwidth of the virtual circuits.

WHAT B-ISUP DOES NOT DO

While B-ISUP is the mechanism for transferring signaling information between network nodes, it does *not* become involved in the following operations:

- Bandwidth capacity analysis (at the network nodes)
- Path discovery through the network (and through the network nodes)
- Setting up the routing and mapping tables (cross-connect tables) for the virtual circuits
- Ongoing operations, administration, and maintenance (OAM) of the existing virtual circuits

The first two operations are not defined in any of the broadband signaling standards and are left to the network operator and switch supplier to implement. The Internet RFC 1695 provides a model for building cross-connect tables, and separate standards deal with OAM (these two subjects are discussed in Volume I of this series). We will spend a few moments here on the subjects of bandwidth analysis and path discovery.

Bandwidth Analysis and Path Discovery

In order for a broadband network to support the rapid setup of a connection, it must have a means to know quite quickly which network nodes can or cannot support the connection. The best approach to set up connections in a timely manner is for the nodes to perform ongoing bandwidth analysis and path discovery with each other. The nodes send messages to each other about their spare capacity and capability to support connections. The messages may be exchanged on a periodic basis or when a node experiences an unusual condition, such as reaching a threshold in its utilization.

It is also possible for bandwidth determination to be made upon receiving a call request from a user, with each successive node requesting bandwidth from its downstream neighbor until a complete path has been set up between the calling and called parties. This approach entails more delay in setting up the connection but cuts down on the number of messages that must be exchanged in comparison to an ongoing analysis.

Assuming path discovery has been an ongoing process, when the originating node (originating exchange) receives a Q.2931 SETUP message from a user, it is aware of the ability (or inability) of the other network nodes to support the connection. When this exchange sends a B-ISUP "setup" message to a neighboring node, it knows that its neighbor exchange can support the connection, since these nodes have been keeping each other informed about their ongoing operations.

These types of operations are often called route advertisements, or route discovery, and are a common aspect of most advanced networks. Some networks have moved to the use of a link state protocol, known generally as a shortest path first (SPF). The term is inaccurate; a better term is optimum path, but the former term is now accepted. These protocols are based on well-tested techniques that have been used in the industry for a number of years.

Ideally, communications networks are designed to route user traffic based on a variety of criteria, generally referred to as a least-cost routing. The name does not mean that routing is based solely on obtaining the least-cost route in the literal sense. Other factors are often part of a network routing algorithm, and for broadband networks, advertising bandwidth availability and delay are key parts of the advertisement.

Even though networks vary in least-cost criteria, three constraints must be considered: (1) delay, (2) throughput, and (3) connectivity. If delay is excessive or if throughput is too little, the network does not meet the needs of the user community. The third constraint is quite obvious; the exchanges must be able to reach each other; otherwise, all other least-cost criteria are irrelevant.

POSITION OF B-ISUP IN THE BROADBAND SIGNALING LAYERS

Previously, we examined the overall architecture of broadband signaling networks, which included a description of where B-ISUP fits into this architecture. The reader may wish to review Figures 6–1, 6–2, and 6–3.

THE SS7 MTP SUPPORT TO B-ISUP

B-ISDN is a fundamental part of SS7 architecture and relies on MTP 3 for support services. B-ISUP and MTP 3 interact through conventional OSI primitives. The information transferred between these protocols is summarized in Figure 8–1 and Table 8–1. Only request and indication primitives are invoked and only four primitives are needed for

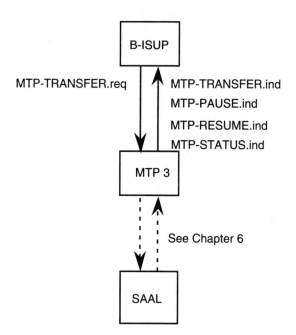

Figure 8–1   MTP 3 and B-ISUP interface.

Table 8–1   MTP 3 and B-ISUP Primitives

Primitive	Req	Ind	Res	Con	Parameters
MTP-TRANSFER	x	x			OPC, DPC, SLS, SIO, signaling information
MTP-PAUSE		x			Affected DPC
MTP-RESUME		x			Affected DPC
MTP-STATUS		x			Affected DPC, cause

B-ISUP to obtain the services of MTP 3. A brief description of the primitives follows.

The MTP_TRANSFER primitive is used by B-ISUP (request) to obtain the message handling functions of MTP 3 and by MTP 3 (indication) to deliver signaling information to B-ISUP. Both primitives contain the originating point code (OPC), destination point code (DPC), signaling link selection code (SLS), service information octet (SIO), and signaling information, which is discussed later in this chapter.

The MTP-PAUSE is sent only as an indication primitive by MTP 3 to inform B-ISUP that MTP 3 is not able to transfer messages to the specified DPC.

The MTP_RESUME is also sent only as an indication primitive by MTP 3 to inform B-ISUP that MTP 3 has resumed its ability to transfer messages to the specified DPC.

As shown in Table 8–1, the MTP_PAUSE and MTP_RESUME primitives contain only one parameter, the affected DPC.

The MTP_STATUS primitive is sent by MTP 3 as an indication primitive to B-ISUP to specify that a signaling route is congested or the destination B-ISUP is not available. The primitive contains the affected DPC and cause parameter that identifies: (1) the signaling network is congested, (2) the User Part is unavailable because a remote user is unequipped, (3) the user is inaccessible, or (4) the User Part is unavailable for unknown reasons.

OVERVIEW OF THE B-ISUP OPERATIONS

Q.2931 and B-ISUP are separate protocols, and they perform different operations in the signaling network architecture. But they are "partners" in that Q.2931 assumes B-ISUP will set up the virtual connections within a network, and B-ISUP assumes Q.2931 will set up the virtual

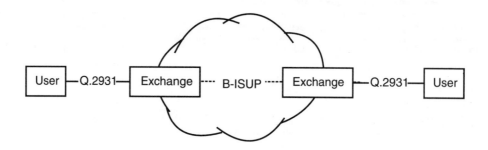

Figure 8–2   Relationship of Q.2931 and B-ISUP.

connections at the network boundaries (outside the network). As depicted in Figure 8–2, Q.2931 is viewed as a user-network interface (UNI) operating between the user device and the network node, and B-ISUP is viewed as part of the network-node interface (NNI) operating between the nodes within the network.

Trunk Groups and VPCIs

The "trunk group" is a key concept in narrowband signaling. It consists of one or more trunks that connect two switches. In ATM broadband signaling, a virtual path connection (VPC) is analogous to a narrowband trunk group. The VPC is assigned a specified amount of bandwidth, which may be an entire link (say, an OC-3) or a subset of it (part of an OC-3).

To allocate and identify bandwidth for SVCs, the concept of a virtual path connection identifier (VPCI) is used. The VPCI identifies the specific VPC that is used for a connection—it must be unique over a particular destination point code (DPC) and originating point code (OPC) combination within the broadband signaling system. There must be a unique VPCI and VPI at a physical interface.

Therefore, a VPCI/DPC/OPC is defined as the broadband equivalent of a narrowband trunk group, and the broadband equivalent of a narrowband channel is the virtual channel, which is identified by the VCI. The VCI needs to be unique only within a VPCI.

In a narrowband system, an idle trunk must be available within a trunk group before a connection is granted and, once granted, the bandwidth is fixed. In the broadband system, there is no fixed bandwidth for a VCI, although the total number of VCIs associated with each VPCI cannot exceed the allocated bandwidth for that VPCI.

Setting up the Virtual Circuits

B-ISUP is responsible for assigning bandwidth to connections in the network, putting routes into service, and managing the VPCI/VCI values for these connections. These procedures include the following activities.

Before a route is put into service between two exchanges, the VPCIs to be used are assigned unambiguously and identically at both ends of each VPC. For every VPCI, B-ISUP defines which exchange controls this VPCI. This exchange is responsible for assigning bandwidth and the VPCI/VCI for this VPCI.

B-ISUP uses a default mechanism that is defined for determining this designation. Each exchange will be the assigning exchange for one-half of the VPCI values. The exchange with the higher signaling point code will be the assigning exchange for all even numbered VPCI values, and the other exchange will be the assigning exchange for all odd numbered VPCI values.

The assigning exchange must perform the following actions:

- From several available VPCs, it must select one VPC that is able to provide the requested bandwidth according to the requested ATM cell rate.
- It must assign bandwidth and a VCI value to the call/connection, and it must update the bandwidth and VCI value of the selected VPCI.

The *assigning* exchange assigns both VPCI/VCI and bandwidth (according to its connection admission control (CAC) procedures for outgoing and incoming calls. The non-assigning exchange does not assign but requests the assigning exchange to assign both VPCI/VCI and bandwidth.

The virtual circuits must undergo a VPCI/VCI consistency check in order to verify the correct allocation of a VPCI to an interface in both of the connected exchanges. This check uses the loopback F4 flow described in Volume I of this series (and specified in ITU-T I.610).

B-ISUP NNI MESSAGES AND PARAMETERS

This section provides an overview of B-ISUP and the parameters in these messages. After they are described, we will provide several examples of how B-ISUP uses these messages to support users' connections in the broadband network.

The Messages

This section provides an summary description of the B-ISUP messages, which are listed in Table 8–2. For ease of reference, they are listed in alphabetical order.

Address Complete Message (ACM). This message is sent in the backward direction to indicate that all addressing information has been

Table 8–2   B-ISUP Messages

Address complete (ACM)

Answer (ANM)

Blocking (BLO)

Blocking acknowledgment (BLA)

Call progress (CPG)

Confusion (CFN)

Consistency check end (CCE)

Consistency check request acknowledgment (CCEA)

Consistency check request (CSR)

Exit (EXM) (2)

Forward transfer (FOT)

IAM acknowledgment (IAA)

IAM reject (IAR)

Initial address (IAM)

Network resource management (NRM) (1)

Release (REL)

Release complete (RLC)

Reset (RSM)

Reset acknowledgment (RAM)

Resume (RES)

Segmentation (SGM)

Subsequent address (SAM) (1)

Suspend (SUS)

Unblocking (UBL)

Unblocking acknowledgment (UBA)

User part available (UPA)

User part test (UPT)

User-to-user information (USR) (1)

(1) Defined in the ITU-T Q.2763; not in the ANSI T1.648
(2) Defined in the ANSI T1.648, not in the ITU-T Q.2763

received to complete the call to the called party. It also conveys that the call is being processed.

Answer Message (ANM). This message is sent in the backward direction to indicate that the called party has answered the call.

Blocking Message (BLO). This message is typically used for maintenance purposes and is sent to the exchange at the other end of the virtual circuit to block outgoing calls at that remote end. The affected exchange should still be able to receive incoming calls on the affected resource.

Blocking Acknowledgment Message (BLA). This message acknowledges the BLO and signals that the resource has been blocked.

Call Progress Message (CPG). This message indicates that an event has occurred in the processing of a call. It can be sent in the forward or backward direction and usually indicates that the call is being processed without problems.

Confusion Message (CFN). This message is a catch-all (which most software-based systems have) that is sent by an exchange in response to receiving a message that it does not understand (either the message, the fields in the message, or both).

Consistency Check Request End Message (CCE). This message terminates the consistency check operation and the ATM cell monitoring operations.

Consistency Check Acknowledgment Message (CCEA). This message is sent in response to the consistency check request message.

Consistency Check Request Message (CSR). This message requests that the other end of the virtual connection verify the correct VPCI for a VP. The message requires that receiving exchange activate an ATM cell monitoring operation.

Exit Message (EXM). This message is sent by an outgoing gateway exchange in the backward direction to signal that call setup has occurred successfully to the adjacent network. The message is exchanged only within a network.

Forward Transfer Message (FOT).   This message in sent in the forward direction on semi-automatic calls when the assistance of an operator is needed. The operator may be recalled when the call is completed.

IAM Acknowledgment Message (IAA).   This message is sent in response to an initial address message to indicate that resources are available, the IAM has been accepted, and that the requested bandwidth (on this incoming leg, for both directions) is available.

IAM Reject Message (IAR).   This message is sent in response to an initial address message to indicate that the call is refused due to the unavailability of resources.

Initial Address Message (IAM).   This message is the first message sent to begin the call connection process. It initiates the seizure of the outgoing virtual circuit.

Network Resource Management Message (NRM).   This message is used to convey echo control information.

Release Message (REL).   This message is sent (in either direction) to begin the release of the circuit, and to free the resources that had been reserved for the connection.

Release Complete Message (RLC).   This message acknowledges the REL message. It indicates that the virtual circuit has been released.

Reset Message (RSM).   If an exchange loses its knowledge about the state of a connection (register problem, memory loss, signaling identifier, whatever), it sends this message to the far-end exchange (in either direction).

Reset Acknowledgment Message (RAM).   This message acknowledges the RSM.

Resume Message (RES). This message is sent in the backward direction and is used to indicate that a calling or called party has been reconnected after having been suspended.

Segmentation Message (SGM).   In the event a message must be divided into smaller parts, this message indicates that it is part of the original oversize message.

Subsequent Address Message (SAM).   This message is used if a subsequent number is to be passed to a node.

Suspend Message (SUS).   This message indicates that the calling or called party has been temporarily suspended.

Unblocking Message (UBL). This message unblocks the resource that was blocked by the blocking message (BLO).

Unblocking Acknowledgment Message (UBA). This message acknowledges the UBL and indicates that the resource is unblocked.

User Part Available Message (UPA). This message acknowledges the user part test message (UPT).

User Part Test Message (UPT). B-ISUP can test entities to determine if a particular user part is available. This message is sent to an exchange to make this test.

User-to-User Information Message (USR). This message is used to pass information between the users, but not to any network node.

Parameters in the Messages

One could ask why yet another protocol has been defined for signaling when the conventional ISUP for the narrowband NNI is already written and in operation. Indeed, some people (developers of products that use these protocols) have complained that ISUP could have been modified to handle any special signaling needs for a broadband network. That is exactly what happened with ISUP; it was modified and named B-ISUP to distinguish it from the narrowband ISUP counterpart.

We shall see that B-ISUP is needed because it carries parameters that do not pertain to a conventional circuit-based network, on which ISUP operates. Likewise, ISUP carries parameters that are not pertinent to a virtual circuit-based network. Appendix 8A (at the end of this chapter) provides a summary of the parameters that are carried in the B-ISUP messages. Some of them are mapped transparently from Q.2931 to B-ISUP at the ingress node to the network and back to Q.2931 at the egress node. These parameters are described in Chapter 7. The next section shows a example of B-ISUP operations and will explain how some of the more widely used parameters are employed.

EXAMPLES OF B-ISUP OPERATIONS

Figure 8–3 shows the flow of messages that occur in a typical call setup between two exchanges. Several to many parameters can be coded into these messages. I describe those that are of the most importance for the call and, as just mentioned, Appendix 8A explains each parameter. Table 8–3 lists

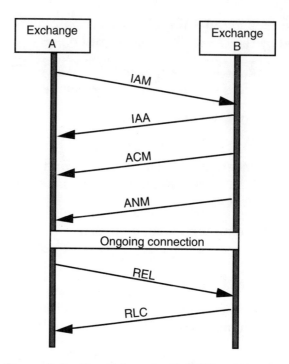

Figure 8–3   Examples of a B-ISUP operation.

and describes the timers used in B-ISUP operations, and several will be explained in this section. The "Timer Expires" column lists the actions that occur when the timer is not turned off by receipt of the expected message.

The operations begin when exchange A issues an initial address message (IAM). During this procedure, exchange A assigns an origination signaling id (OSID) for this side of the connection and turns on timer T40b.

Also during this operation, the virtual circuit is set up along an appropriate route. The decisions on how a route is selected is not defined by B-ISUP, but is left to the discretion of the B-ISUP implementor. However the route is chosen, its selection must depend on the parameters furnished to it by the user. These parameters are the called party number, broadband bearer capability, ATM cell rate, and—if the maximum end-to-end transit delay parameter is used—the propagation delay counter must also be considered. Other parameters can be placed in this message and/or sent unaltered to the end destination. These include: AAL parameters, broadband bearer capability (as we just learned, also used for route selection), broadband low layer information, broadband high layer information, narrowband high layer compatibility, narrowband low layer compatibility, OAM traffic descriptor, and progress indicator.

Table 8–3 The B-ISUP Timers

Name (Symbol)	Timer Started	Timer Stopped	Timer Expires
Await Release Complete (T1b)	When Release message is sent	Receipt of Release Complete Message	Release resources, alert maintenance and send Reset message
User Part Availability (T4b)	At receipt of MTP-STATUS primitive coded with cause "remote user unavailable"	Receipt of User Part Available message	Send User Part Test message and start T4b
Await Network Resume (T6b)	When controlling network receives Suspend message	At the receipt of Resume or Release message	Initiate release procedure
Await Address Complete (T7b)	When the latest address message is sent	At the receipt of Address complete, Answer messages	Release all equipment and connection and send Release message
Await answer (T9b)	Exchange receives Address Complete message	At the receipt of Answer message	Release connection and send Release message
Await Blocking Acknowledge (T12b)	When Blocking message is sent	At receipt of Blocking Acknowledgment	Alert Maintenance system
Await Unblocking Acknowledge (T14b)	When Unblocking message is sent	At receipt of Unblocking Acknowledgment	Alert Maintenance system
Await Reset Acknowledge (T16b)	When Reset message is sent	At receipt of Reset Acknowledgment message	Resend Reset message
Repeat Reset (T17b)	When Reset Acknowledgment is not received within timer "Await Reset Acknowledgment"		Resend Reset message, alert maintenance
Segmentation (T34b)	When indication of a segmented message is received	At receipt of a segmentation message	Proceed with call
Await Network Resume-International (T38b)	When the incoming international exchange sends to the preceding exchange a Suspend (network) message	At Receipt of Resume (network) message or Release message	Send Release message

(continued)

Table 8–3 Continued

Name (Symbol)	Timer Started	Timer Stopped	Timer Expires
Await IAM Acknowledge (T40b)	When Initial Address Message is sent	At receipt of IAM Acknowledgment or IAM Reject	Release resources, alert maintenance system, send Reset message
Await Consistency Check Request Acknowledgment (T41b)	When Consistency Check Request message is sent	At receipt of Consistency Check Request Acknowledgment	Alert Maintenance system
Await Consistency Check end Acknowledgment (T42b)	When Consistency Check End message is sent	At receipt of Consistency Check End Acknowledgment	Alert Maintenance system

The calling party number may be included depending on the implementation and is subject to bilateral agreements among networks. If present, it may be used for address screening.

When the IAM arrives at exchange B, this exchange must perform the VPCI/VCI assignments and allocate bandwidth. Of course, these operations assume the called party number is valid and the called party can be connected. If the connection is allowed, exchange B will offer the call to the called party.

In addition, upon successful receipt of the IAM at exchange B, this exchange assigns an origination signaling id (OSID). Therefore, exchange A and exchange B each have assigned an OSID to this connection. These values will be used hereafter to keep track of this specific connection.

Upon successful assignment procedures and other processing at exchange B, this exchange returns an IAM acknowledge message (IAA) to exchange A. The IAA message contains: (1) a connection element id, (2) the destination signaling id (which is the OSID assigned by exchange A), and (3) the origination signaling id (which is the OSID assigned by B). The connection element id contains the VPCI and the VCI. Also, the receipt of IAA results in turning off timer T40b.

At exchange B, the address complete message (ACM) is issued to exchange A to indicate that the IAM is complete and sufficient to process the call. Several parameters are coded in the ACM; some of the more significant ones are the backward narrowband interworking indicators, the called party's indicators, the charge indicator, and the destination signaling indicator. At exchange A, the receipt of the ACM turns on timer T9b.

When the called party answers, exchange B removes ringing tone from the line (if applicable) and sends the answer message (ANM) to the originating exchange. As this message transits from exchange B to exchange A, any resources at intermediate exchanges that were in a "wait state" must be activated. For example, cross-connect tables containing entries about the virtual connection must have these entries set to "active." As a general statement, the ANM operation results in resources in the network being reserved for the virtual connection, but they may not be activated until the ANM is received from the terminating exchange. After the ANM is received at exchange A, the bidirectional virtual circuit is open to both the called and calling parties, and the exchange of information can begin. The receipt of ANM also turns off timer T9b.

Either party can terminate the connection by issuing a release (REL) message (turning on timer T1b), which is acknowledged with a release complete (RLC) message (turning off timer T1b). Upon receiving an RLC, an exchange (including any intermediate exchanges) must release the associated VPCI/VCI, the reserved bandwidth, and the associated OSID. Also, the process (the application entity instance) in each exchange, that supported this specific connection, is released.

THE B-ISUP ARCHITECTURE IN MORE DETAIL

The B-ISUP architecture is built around the Open Systems Interconnection (OSI) Model, as depicted in Figure 8–4.

The applications process (AP) is a set of capabilities within an open system that performs services on behalf of the end user (the application resting on top of the application layer). In B-ISUP, the term exchange application process describes all the application layer functions, and B-ISUP is part of the exchange application process.

In the OSI model, the APs use an application entity (AE) to communicate with each other. The AEs are invoked at run time to setup a connection between two or more APs. The B-ISUP AE provides all the capabilities needed at an exchange, and to simplify matters, only one single association object (SAO) and its single association control function (SACF) is contained in B-ISUP.

The SAO in the B-ISUP AE is classified as one of four application service elements (ASEs), which is the software that is invoked to perform B-ISUP functions. These ASEs are: (1) call control (CC), (2) bearer con-

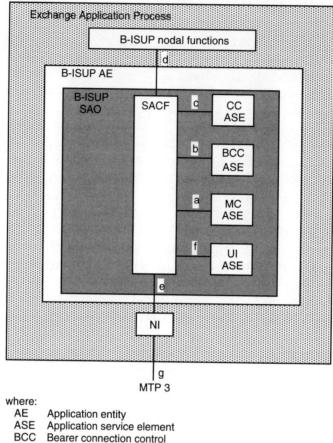

where:
    AE   Application entity
    ASE   Application service element
    BCC   Bearer connection control
    CC   Call control
    MC   Maintenance control
    NI   Network interface
    SACF Single association control function
    SAO   Single association object
    UI   Unrecognized information

Figure 8–4   The B-ISUP internal layer architecture.

nection control (BCC), (3) maintenance control (MC), and (4) unrecognized information (UI). We will have more to say about these ASEs shortly.

In the OSI Model, a unique and specific process is called an application process invocation, which starts an application entity invocation (AEI). An AE invocation is identified with an AEI identifier.

Each instance of the B-ISUP AE within each exchange is identified with a signaling identifier value (SID); it is allocated when the application entity invocation (AEI) is created and deallocated when the AEI is deleted. It is similar to the OSI service access point (SAP) or a UNIX socket.

Table 8–4 Mapping at the AP and ASE Interfaces

Interface (d) from AP	Interface (c) to CC ASE	Interface (b) to BCC ASE	Interface (a) to MC ASE
Set_Up req	Call_Set_Up req	Link_Set_Up req	
Address_Complete req	Call_Address_ Complete req	Link_Information req	
Incoming_Resources_ Accepted req		Link_Accepted req	
Incoming_Resources_ Rejected req		Link_Rejected req	Congestion_Level req
Release req/res	Call_Release req	Link_Release req/res	Congestion_Level req
Answer req	Call_Answer req	Link_Information req	
Progress req	Call_Progress req	Link_Information req	
Suspend req	Call_Suspend req		
Resume req	Call_Resume req		
Forward_Transfer req	Call_Forward_ Transfer req		
Segment req	Call_Segment req	Link_Information req	
Block_Resource req/res			Block req/res
Unblock_Resource req/res			Unblock req/res
Reset_Resource req/res			Reset req/res
User_Part_ Available req/res			User_Part_Test req/res
Check_Resource_ Begin req/res			Check_Begin req/res
Check_Resource_ End req/res			Check_End req/res
	Interface(f) to UI ASE		
Unrecognized Message_Type req	Unrecognized_ Message req		
Confusion req	Confusion req		

Table 8–5   Mapping of the Primitives and B-ISUP Messages

Interface (c) CC to ASE	Interface (b) to BCC ASE	Interface (a) to MC ASE	Message Type
Call_Set_Up req	Link_Set_Up req		Initial address
	Link_Accepted req		IAM Acknowledge
	Link_Accepted req	Congestion_Level req	IAM Reject
Call_Release req	Link_Release req	Congestion_Level req	Release
	Call_Release res		Release Complete
Call_Address_ Complete req	Link_Information req		Address Complete
Call_Answer req	Link_Information req		Answer
Call_Progress req	Link_Information req		Call Progress
Call_Suspend req			Suspend
Call_Resume req			Resume
Call_Forward_Transfer req			Forward transfer
Call_Segment req	Link_Information req		Segmentation

Figure 8–4 uses notations (a) to (g) to identify where primitives are exchanged between the B-ISUP entities. Primitives are valuable documentation tools that are used by designers to lay out the interfaces between the entities. The B-ISUP specification also provides guidance on how these primitives and their parameters are mapped into the messages that are transferred between exchanges.

Two tables help explain the overall architecture and relationships of the AP and ASEs and the relationships of the key primitives to B-ISUP messages. Table 8–4 provides a summary of the primitives invoked at interfaces (a) through (d) and (f). Table 8–5 shows the mapping relationship of these primitives to B-ISUP messages. Appendix 8B provides a description of all these and the other interfaces, their associated primitives, and the parameters associated with the primitives.

SUMMARY

B-ISUP and SS7 are partners in supporting the end users' connection. ATM's Q.2931 is a user-network interface (UNI) operating between the user device and the network node, and B-ISUP is a network-node interface (NNI) operating between the nodes within the network or between networks. B-ISUP is also employed as an internetworking interface allowing two networks to communicate with each other.

APPENDIX 8A: PARAMETERS USED IN B-ISUP MESSAGES

This appendix provides a summary of the parameters that are coded into the B-ISUP messages. The reader should study ANSI T1.648-1995 if more detailed information is needed. Also, several of these parameters are described in Chapter 7, and I refer you to that chapter where appropriate.

ATM adaptation layer (AAL) parameters: These parameters are described in Chapter 7. Be aware that although they have end-to-end significance, they are also processed by the users' local exchanges, but transferred transparently between local exchanges.

Access delivery information: Defined in ITU-T Recommendations only. It is coded in the address complete, answer, or release message to indicate if a setup message was or was not generated for this connection. (It usually is generated.)

Additional calling party number: Defined in ITU-T Recommendations only. It is used to provide an additional calling party number in case more than one party is involved in the initiation of a call.

Additional connected number: Defined in ITU-T Recommendations only. This parameter is present in an answer, initial address, or segmentation message if more than one connected number must be identified.

ATM cell rate: This parameter contains the cell rate (in number of cells per second) requested in the forward and backward directions for both cell loss priority = 0 and cell loss priority = 0 + 1.

Automatic congestion level: This parameter is sent to the exchange at the other end of a virtual path to indicate that a predefined level of congestion has occurred. Currently, congestion levels 1 and 2 can be coded in the field, but their meanings are not defined in B-ISUP, but left to specific implementations.

Backward narrowband interworking indicator: Since B-ISUP, ISUP and ISDN are far from being universal signaling protocols (dial-tone signaling will predominate for many years), this parameter is sent in the backwards direction to indicate that a non-ISDN node has been encountered within the network connection. It can also indicate if a non-SS7 node has been encountered.

Broadband bearer capability: This parameter is described in Chapter 7.

Broadband high layer information: This parameter is described in Chapter 7.

Broadband low layer information: This parameter is described in Chapter 7 and amplified with a field stating if the parameters are or are not in a prioritized order.

Call diversion information: Defined in ITU-T Recommendations only. See the next parameter.

Call diversion may occur: Defined in ITU-T Recommendations only. In the event a call is diverted (redirected), this parameter and the parameter above stipulates if the call can indeed be diverted and the reason for the diversion (user busy, mobile subscriber not available, etc.).

Call history information: This parameter is sent in the backward direction and contains information on the accumulated propagation delay encountered for this connection. The value is coded in binary form and represents ms.

Called party number: This parameter contains the identification of the called party. The address is coded as a 4-bit BCD digit for each value in the address. The actual numbering plan can vary and a field in this parameter identifies the type of numbering plan used in the message. With few exceptions, the ISDN telephony numbering plan is used (ITU-T Recommendation E.164). The parameter also contains a field called the "nature of address indicator," which provides the following information:

- Subscriber number
- Unknown (national use)
- National (significant) number
- International number
- Reserved for national use
- Subscriber number, operator requested
- National number, operator requested
- International number, operator requested
- No number present, operator requested
- No number present, cut-through call to barrier
- 950+ call from local exchange carrier public station, hotel/motel, or non-exchange access end office
- Test line test code
- Reserved for network specific use (no interpretation)

Called party subaddress: This parameter is described in Chapter 7.

Called party's indicators: This parameter is sent in the backwards direction and is used to indicate (1) if the called party is an ordinary subscriber or a pay phone, and (2) if the called party status is that of alerting or of no indication.

Calling party number: This parameter identifies the calling party and is coded with the same conventions as the called party number discussed earlier, except that the "nature of address" indicator may have slightly different values. The nature of address values are as follows:

- Subscriber number
- Unknown (national use)
- National (significant) number
- International number
- Reserved for national use
- Non-unique subscriber number
- Non-unique national (significant) number
- Non-unique international number

This parameter also contains fields to indicate if the calling party number is complete/incomplete, if it can be displayed or not, and if it is subject to screening.

Calling party subaddress: This parameter is described in Chapter 7.

Calling party's category: This parameter provides several types of information about the category of the calling party and (where operators must participate in the call) the service language that is to be spoken by the assistance operators. It provides the following additional information:

- Operator, language (French, English, German, Russian, Spanish)
- Reserved for administration's use
- Reserved for national use
- Ordinary calling subscriber
- Calling subscriber with priority
- Data call
- Test call
- Pay phone

Carrier identification code: This parameter is sent in the forward direction to identify the carrier selected by the calling party.

Carrier selection information: This parameter is used in conjunction with the carrier identification code to indicate if the transit network was selected by pre-prescription or by dialed input.

Cause indicators: This parameter is described in Chapter 7.

Charge indicator: This parameter is sent in the backward direction to indicate if the call is chargeable.

Charge number: If the call is chargeable, this parameter contains the number to which the call is to be charged.

Closed user group information: Defined in ITU-T Recommendations only. Closed user groups (CUGs) are used to filter access to a subscriber or a group of subscribers. They are also used to prevent someone from making a call on a facility.

Connected line identity request: Defined in ITU-T Recommendations only. This parameter is coded in the initial address message (IAM) to request the identity of the connected line.

Connected number: Defined in ITU-T Recommendations only. This parameter is used to identify the connected number.

Connected subaddress: Defined in ITU-T Recommendations only. This parameter is used for the same purpose as the connected number parameter.

Connection element identifier: This parameter is sent in the backwards direction to identify the ATM virtual connection. It contains the virtual path connection identifier (VPCI) and the virtual channel identifier (VCI). The VPCI represents a VPI on a given interface and is not the same as the value of the VPI in the ATM cell header in which the B-ISUP message resides. As stated in previous chapters, the VPCI is used instead of the VPI since virtual path cross-connects allow multiple interfaces to be controlled by a single signaling virtual channel. The values of VCI=5 and VPCI=0 are reserved for the signaling virtual channel.

Consistency check request information: This parameter is sent in the backward direction to provide information about the virtual circuit connection (the VPCI). It indicates if the VPCI check was successful, was not successful, or not performed.

Destination signaling identifier (DSID): This parameter identifies the call control association at the receiving end of the virtual circuit. It is used to correlate related messages to an ongoing call sequence.

Echo control information: This parameter is sent in the backward or forward direction to indicate if an echo control device is requested for the connection.

Egress service: This parameter is sent in the forward direction to provide network specific parameters associated with the terminating exchange.

Forward narrowband interworking indicator: This parameter is sent in the forward direction to indicate the signaling capabilities within the network connection when interworking with a N-ISDN unit has occurred. The fields indicate the following information:

- ISDN user part preferred all the way
- ISDN user part not required all the way

- ISDN user part required all the way
- Originating access non-ISDN
- Originating access ISDN
- ISDN user part not used all the way
- ISDN user part used all the way
- No interworking encountered
- Interworking encountered

Generic address: This parameter defines the type of address (such as dialed number, destination number, ITU-T spare, ASNI spare, etc.).

Generic digits: This parameter defines the type of digits; that is, how they are coded (examples: IA5, binary, BCD, etc.).

Generic name: This parameter defines whether a name can or cannot be presented to a party. If it is a calling name, this parameter indicates which one is it (i.e., original called name, redirecting name, or a connected name).

Inband information indicator: This parameter is sent in the backward direction to indicate that inband information is or is not available.

Jurisdiction information: This parameter is coded as an address.

Location number: Defined in ITU-T Recommendations only. This parameter is coded in the initial address message (IAM) to indicate: (1) if routing to a particular number is/is not allowed, (2) if the presentation of the number is allowed, (3) if screening of the number is provided. It also contains the number in question.

Maximum end-to-end transit delay: This parameter establishes the maximum acceptable transit delay for the call.

MLPP Precedence: This parameter (multilevel precedence and preemption) contains several fields and is sent in the forward direction to contain the following information:

- LFB allowed
- Path reserved
- LFB not allowed
- Flash override
- Flash
- Immediate
- Priority
- Routine

MLPP user information: This parameter is sent in the backward direction to identify that the called user is an MLPP user.

Narrowband bearer capability: This parameter is sent in the forward or backward direction to identify a requested or proposed N-ISDN bearer capability. This information is coded in the same form as the bearer capability information elements described in Q.2931 (see Chapter 7).

Narrowband high layer compatibility: This parameter is described in Chapter 7.

Narrowband low layer compatibility: This parameter is described in Chapter 7.

National/international call indicator: This parameter is coded to stipulate that the call is to be treated as a national or international call.

Notification: Defined in ITU-T Recommendations only. This parameter provides a wide variety of information about a call. Here are some examples:

- Other party added, disconnected, reattached
- Conference call is established, disconnected
- Call transfer
- Remote hold

OAM traffic descriptor: This parameter is coded in the same format as its counterpart in Q.2931 to indicate the number of cells per second for OAM traffic and whether traffic shaping is permitted.

Original called number: This parameter is sent in the forward direction when a call is redirected and it identifies the original call party. It is coded in the same format as the called party number described earlier.

Origination IC Point code: Defined in ITU-T Recommendations only. This parameter is simply the SS7 point code of the origination signaling point. It can be useful to determine where the call emanated (the MTP 3 label does not retain the origination point code).

Origination signaling identifier (OSID): The value in this parameter is assigned by the node initiating a call control or maintenance operation. It is used to identify the signaling association at the calling end.

Outgoing facility identifier: This parameter contains several fields and is sent in the backward direction to identify a facility selected at an outgoing gateway. It must contain a VPCI and an SS7 point code. The SS7 point code identifies the far-end switch.

Progress indicator: This parameter is sent in the forward or backward direction to describe any chosen event that has occurred during the lifetime of the connection. It contains the same information as its companion information element in Q.2931.

Propagation delay counter: This parameter is sent in the forward direction to provide information on the propagation delay encountered in the processing of a connection. The field is increased as the message is transferred through the network. The counter increments in integer multiples of 1 ms.

Redirecting number: This parameter is sent in the forward direction if a call is diverted and it indicates the number from which the call was diverted.

Redirection information: In the event that a call is diverted, this parameter contains information about the call rerouting or redirection. It yields the following information:

- Unknown/not available
- User busy (national use)
- No reply (national use)
- Unconditional (national use)
- No redirection (national use)
- Call rerouted (national use)
- Call rerouted, all redirection information presentation restricted (national use)
- Call diversion
- Call diversion, all redirection information presentation restricted
- Call rerouted, redirection number presentation restricted (national use)
- Call diversion, redirection number presentation restricted
- Deflection during alerting
- Deflection immediate response
- Mobile subscriber not reachable

Redirecting number: This parameter contains the number of the party that set up a redirection operation.

Redirection number: Defined in ITU-T Recommendations only. This parameter contains the number of the redirected number.

Redirection number restriction: Defined in ITU-T Recommendations only. This parameter stipulates if the redirected number can be presented to the called party.

Resource identifier: In the event resources in the network must be reset, blocked or unblocked, this parameter identifies those resources. It identifies if the source is (1) a local signaling identifier, (2) a remote signaling identifier, (3) a VPCI/VCI, or (4) a VPCI.

Segmentation indicator: This parameter is sent in the forward or backward direction to indicate if additional messages will or will not be sent pertaining to the full logical message.

Special processing request: This parameter is sent in the forward direction and specifies if the call requires special processing. The processing depends on the specific implementation in a B-ISUP network.

Suspend / resume indicators: As this name implies, this parameter is used in the B-ISUP suspend and resume messages to identify if the suspend or resume was initiated by the network or the network subscriber.

Transit network selection: This parameter is sent during the call setup to identify the transit network that is to be used to process the call.

User-network interaction indicator: This parameter is sent in the backward direction to indicate that the exchange is collecting more information from the calling party about the called party before proceeding further with the call.

User-to-user indicators: This parameter is sent in a request or a response to a request and provides user-to-user signaling supplementary services.

User-to-user information: This parameter is not processed by the interexchange network but is transferred transparently between the originating and terminating local exchanges.

APPENDIX 8B: B-ISUP INTERFACES, PRIMITIVES, AND PRIMITIVE PARAMETERS

This appendix provides a summary of the B-ISUP interfaces, primitives, and primitive parameters. The reader should study ANSI T1.648-1995 and ITU-T Q.2764 if more detailed information is needed.

The (a) interface is concerned with maintenance operations such as connection resets, blocking/unblocking, checking for resource availability, message compatibility checking, and so on. The primitives shown in Table 8B–1 are used to support these operations. The parameters used in the primitives are listed at the bottom of the table.

The (b) interface is concerned with setting up and clearing of connections between exchanges and is not concerned with user virtual connections. Table 8B–2 lists the primitives used for link management and their associated parameters. The table should be self-explanatory, if the reader has studied this chapter. Many of the parameters are mapped into the B-ISUP message information elements (explained in Appendix 8A.)

Table 8B–1   Primitives and Parameters at the (a) Interface

| | Primitive Type and Associated Parameters | | | |
Primitive Name	*Request*	*Indication*	*Response*	*Confirm*
Block	MCI/RI	MCI/RI	MCI	MCI
Unblock	MCI/RI	MCI/RI	MCI	MCI
Reset	MCI/RI	MCI/RI	MCI	MCI
User_Part_Test	MCI	MCI	MCI	MCI
Error	(1)	None	(1)	(1)
Congestion_Level	ACI	ACI	(1)	(1)
Check_Resource_Begin	MCI/RI	MCI/RI	MCI	MCI
Check_Resource_End	MCI	MCI	MCI/CCRI	MCI/CCRI

where:
MCI:	Message compatibility information
RI:	Resource identifier
ACL:	Automatic congestion level
CCRI:	Consistency check result information
(1):	Primitive not used
None:	No parameter is contained in the primitive

Table 8B–2   Primitives and Parameters at the (b) Interface

| | Primitive Contents for Associated Parameters | | | | | | | | | | | | | |
Primitive Name	1	2	3	4	5	6	7	8	9	10	11	12	13	14
Link_Set_Up	QI	QI	QI		QI	QI	QI	QI	QI	QI	QI	QI	QI	
Link_Accepted	QI						QI							
Link_Rejected	QI													QI
Link_Information	QI	QI		QI	QI			QI		QI	QI	QI		
Link_Release	QIRC													QIRC
Link_Error														I

where:
QIRC:	Stands for Request, Indication, Response, Confirmation, respectively and

1:	Message compatibility information	8:	Echo control information
2:	AAL parameters	9:	Maximum end-to-end transit delay
3:	ATM cell rate	10:	Narrowband bearer capability
4:	Call history information	11:	Narrowband low layer capability
5:	Broadband low layer information	12:	OAM traffic descriptor
6:	Broadband bearer capability	13:	Propagation delay counter
7:	Connection element identifier	14:	Cause

Table 8B–3   Primitives and Parameters at the (c) Interface

Primitive Name	Primitive Contents for Associated Parameters																		
	1	2	3	4	5	6	7	8	9	10	11	12	13	14	15	16	17	18	19
Call_Set_Up	QI					QI	QI			QI	QI		QI	QI	QI	QI	QI		QI
Call_Address_Complete	QI	QI		QI				QI	QI				QI	QI		QI	QI		
Call_Release	QI							QI								QI	QI		
Call_Answer	QI	QI	QI						QI				QI	QI		QI	QI		
Call_Progress	QI	QI		QI				QI	QI				QI	QI		QI	QI		
Call_Suspend	QI																	QI	
Call_Resume	QI																	QI	
Call_Forward_Transfer	QI																		
Call_Exit																			
Call_Segment	QI		QI										QI			QI			
Call_Error								I											

where:

QIRC: Stands for Request, Indication, Response, Confirmation, respectively and

1: Message compatibility information
2: Backward narrowband interworking indicator
3: Broadband high layer information
4: Call history information
5: Called party indicators
6: Called party number
7: Calling party's category
8: Cause indicators
9: Charge indicator
10: Exchange type*
11: Forward narrowband interworking indicator
12: Inband information indicator
13: Narrowband high layer capability
14: National/international call indicator
15: Origination ISC point code
16: Progress indicator
17: Segmentation indicator
18: Suspend/resume indicators
19: Transit network selection

*The exchange type parameter is passed to the ASE so that the protocol can be varied depending on the role that the exchange is performing for this call/connection. Unlike the other parameters, it does not relate to a protocol information element.

Table 8B–4   Primitives and Parameters at the (d) Interface

Where following primitive is either M for mandatory, O for optional or — for not known for the related parameter in B-ISDN:

		PRIMITIVES			
		Request	*Indication*	*Response*	*Confirm*
1:	Set_Up	X	X		
2:	Address_Complete	X	X		
3:	Incoming_Resources_Accepted	X	X		
4:	Incoming_Resources_Rejected	X	X		
5:	Release	X	X		
6:	Release			X	X
7:	Answer	X	X		
8:	Progress	X	X		
9:	Suspend	X	X		
10:	Resume	X	X		
11:	Forward_Transfer	X	X		
12:	Segment	X	X		

Primitive Contents for Associated Parameters

Parameter Name	1	2	3	4	5	6	7	8	9	10	11	12
Message compatibility information	M	M	M	M	M	M	M	M	M	M	M	M
AAL parameters	O						O					
ATM cell rate	M											
Automatic congestion level					O	O		—				
Backward narrowband interworking indicator		M						—				
Broadband bearer capability	M											
Broadband low layer information	O						O				O	
Broadband high layer information	O											O
Call history information							O					
Called party indicators		M						O				
Called party number	M											
Calling party's category	M											
Cause indicators		M			M	M	O	O				
Charge indicator		M					O	O				
Connection element identifier	O		O									
Echo control information	O	M										

(continued)

Table 8B–4 Continued

Parameter Name	Primitive Contents for Associated Parameters											
	1	2	3	4	5	6	7	8	9	10	11	12
Exchange type*	M											
Forward narrowband interworking indicator	—											
Inband information indicator	—			—	—							
Maximum end-to-end transit delay	O											
Narrowband bearer capability	—	—		—	—							
Narrowband bearer capability prime	—											
Narrowband high layer capability	—	—					—	—				O
Narrowband low layer capability	—						—					O
National/international call indicator	O											
OAM traffic descriptor	O					O						
Progress indicator	O	O			O		O	O				O
Propagation delay counter	M											
Segmentation indicator	O	O			O		O	O				
Suspend/resume indicators										M	M	
Transit network selection	O											

*The exchange type parameter is passed to the ASE so that the protocol can be varied depending on the role that the exchange is performing for this call/connection. Unlike the other parameters, it does not relate to a protocol information element.

The (c) and (d) interfaces are concerned with supporting a user's call. Most of the primitives in Tables 8B–3 and 8B–4 are mapped into corresponding B-ISUP messages and the parameters are mapped into the information elements of the messages. Once again, these tables are self-explanatory.

The primitives shown in Table 8B–5 pertain to the (e) interface and are concerned with the transfer of signaling units from SACF through its MTP 3 to another exchange.

The MTP_Transfer primitives are distributed to the connect AEIs based on the destination SID parameter according to the following rules (established in ANSI T1.648.4):

- If the Destination SID corresponds to an existing B-ISUP AEI, the message is distributed to that AEI.
- If the Destination SID does not correspond to an existing B-ISUP AEI, a new instance of B-ISUP, including an AEI, is created. This new instance is allocated with a new SID value.
- If the message does not contain a Destination SID parameter but

Table 8B–5   Primitives and Parameters at the (e) Interface

Primitive Name	Types			
	Request	*Indication*	*Response*	*Confirm*
1: Transfer	X	X		
2: Remote_Status		X		
3: Destination_Unavailable		X		
4> Destination_Available		X		

	Mappings			
	(g) from MTP 3	*(e) to SACF*	*(e) from SACF*	*(g) to MTP 3*
MTP_Transfer indication	X			
MTP_Status indication	X			
MTP_Pause indication	X			
MTP_Resume indication	X			
Transfer request			X	
MTP_Transfer request				X

Table 8B–6   Primitives and Parameters at the (f) Interface

Primitive Name	Types			
	Request	*Indication*	*Response*	*Confirm*
1: Unrecognized_Message	X	X		
2: Unrecognized_Parameter	X	X		
3: Confusion	X	X		

Parameter Name	Primitive Contents for Associated Parameters		
	1	2	3
Message compatibility information			M
Cause			M

it does contain an Origination SID parameter, a new instance of B-ISUP, including an AEI, is created. This new instance is allocated a new SID value.

The primitives shown in Table 8B–6 play a limited role dealing with the inability to recognize a message, a parameter in the message, or anything else (confusion) that cannot be processed.

Finally, interface (g) is concerned with the MTP 3/B-ISUP interface. This interface is described in the main body of this chapter (see Figure 8–1).

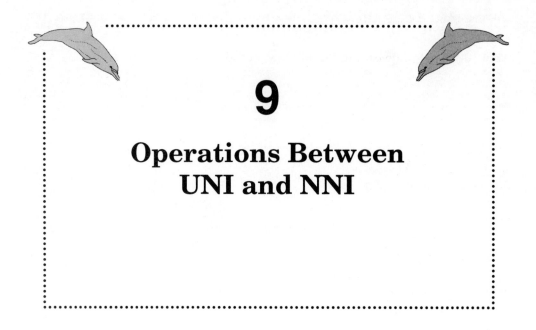

9

Operations Between
UNI and NNI

INTRODUCTION

This chapter pieces together the UNI and NNI operations and explains how the messages and parameters are interworked across these interfaces.

Due to the rather extensive analysis of the UNI and NNI operations in Chapters 7 and 8, respectively, I will not rehash timers or the details of the information elements in the messages. I will explain how the information elements in the messages correlate (map) to each other.

TYPICAL CALL SETUP AND RELEASE OPERATIONS

Figure 9–1 shows a typical call setup and release operation at both the UNI (with Q.2931) and NNI (with B-ISUP). User A initiates the connection by sending the Q.2931 SETUP message to its exchange (exchange A). At this switch, the Q.2931 message and its information elements are used to set up the virtual circuit and create the B-ISUP initial address message (IAM). After sending the CALL PROCEEDING message to user A, exchange A sends the IAM message through the network across intermediate exchanges (in this example, exchange B) to the terminating exchange (exchange C). The exchanges return IAAs upon receiving the IAM. At exchange C, the IAM is used to create the virtual circuit across the

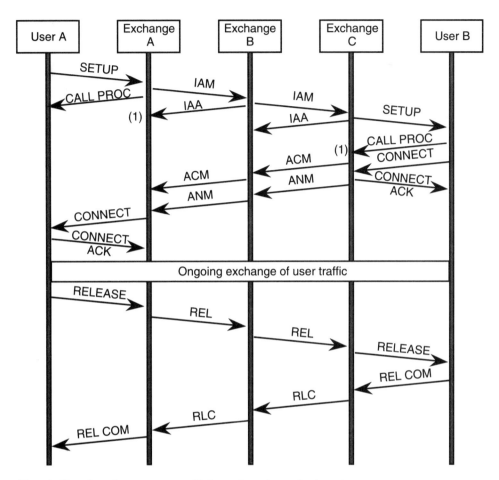

Note 1: Mapping of messages and information elements do not occur.

Figure 9–1   UNI and NNI operations.

UNI to user B by the issuance of the Q.2931 SETUP message, and user B returns the CALL PROCEEDING MESSAGE to its exchange.

If the user decides to accept the call, it sends an ALERT (optional) message and/or the CONNECT message. The ALERT message is mapped to the B-ISUP ACM and back to the Q.2931 ALERT at the originating UNI. The ALERT operations are not shown in this example, which uses the CALL PROCEEDING message instead.

The CONNECT is mapped to the B-ISUP and back to the Q.2931 CONNECT at the originating UNI. The CONNECT ACK messages acknowledge the CONNECT messages.

Table 9–1   SETUP ↔ IAM Mapping

SETUP Is Mapped to	IAM Is Mapped to	SETUP
AAL parameters	AAL parameters	AAL parameters
ATM traffic descriptor	ATM cell rate Additional ATM cell rate	ATM traffic descriptor

Broadband bearer
  capability
	Broadband bearer
	  capability
		Broadband bearer
		  capability

Broadband high layer
  information
	Broadband high layer
	  information
		Broadband high layer
		  information

Broadband sending complete	Not carried	No mapping
Called party number	Called party number AESA for called party	Called party number
Called party subaddress	Called party subaddress Calling party number AESA for calling party	Called party subaddress Calling party number
Calling party subaddress	Calling party subaddress	Calling party subaddress
Transit network selection	Transit network selection	
Quality of service	Quality of service	Quality of service

During these operations, the users and the exchanges are involved in creating each segment of the virtual circuit and allocating the resources that will be needed to support the call. After the successful completion of these operations, the users' exchange their traffic with each other.

In this example, user A initiates the release of the connection by sending a Q.2931 message to exchange A. The successful receipt of this message begins the disconnection of the virtual circuit and its associated resources by mapping the RELEASE message and its parameters into the B-ISUP REL, which is mapped back into the Q.2931 RELEASE message at the exchange C-user B UNI.

Table 9–2   CONNECT ↔ ANM Mapping

CONNECT Is Mapped to	ANM Is Mapped to	CONNECT
AAL parameters	AAL parameters	AAL parameters

Broadband low layer
  information
	Broadband low layer
	  information
		Broadband low layer
		  information

Table 9–3   RELEASE ↔ REL Mapping

RELEASE Is Mapped to	REL Is Mapped to	RELEASE
Cause	Cause indicators	Cause

The next section of this chapter describes the message mapping operations between Q.2931 and B-ISUP. For this example, it should be noted that the IAA message is not mapped to the CALL PROCEEDING message at the originating UNI (note 1 in Figure 9–1). Likewise, there is no mapping between CALL PROCEEDING and ACM at the terminating UNI.

MAPPING BETWEEN THE UNI AND NNI MESSAGES AND INFORMATION ELEMENTS

The mapping of the messages and information elements for the operations in Figure 9–1 are depicted in Tables 9–1 through 9–3. Table 9–1 shows the mapping of the SETUP and IAM, Table 9–2 shows the mapping of the CONNECT and ANM, and Table 9–3 shows the mapping of the RELEASE and REL messages.

Other mapping operations occur for other operations (i.e., ALERT). If you need more details of each mapping operation, I refer you to Bellcore GR-1417-CORE, Issue 2, November 1995. The ITU-T and ANSI specifications provide similar information.

SUMMARY

The protocols at the broadband UNI and NNI have been designed to interwork gracefully with each other. They are quite similar to each other, but different enough to warrant different specifications. Fortunately, the broadband signaling specifications provide mapping tables to define the relationships of the UNI/NNI messages and the information elements in the messages.

10

Other Broadband
Signaling Operations
and Performance Requirements

INTRODUCTION

This chapter examines other aspects of the UNI and NNI operations and how they are used in a Broadband Switching System (BSS). This term is introduced in this chapter due to its use by Bellcore. We will also examine some Bellcore specifications. Several configuration options are examined pertaining to the interworking of current systems and broadband signaling systems. In addition, point-to-multipoint calls are explained along with add services. The chapter concludes with an examination of performance requirements for a BSS.

CONFIGURATION OPTIONS

There are several ways that a BSS can be configured, and the decision on a configuration is left to the service provider. Figure 10–1 will be used during this discussion.

One approach, called an overlay, is shown in Figure 10–2. The existing CCS network is connected to the ATM-based network at ATM nodes through a CCS interface (CSS I/F), which acts as a gateway between the systems. B-ISUP messages conveyed between the BSS and the CCS SPs are provided by the MTP layers, which use the layer operation shown in Figure 10–1b. This approach is attractive because the BSS has access to

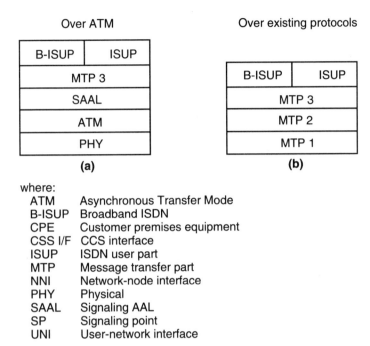

where:

ATM	Asynchronous Transfer Mode
B-ISUP	Broadband ISDN
CPE	Customer premises equipment
CSS I/F	CCS interface
ISUP	ISDN user part
MTP	Message transfer part
NNI	Network-node interface
PHY	Physical
SAAL	Signaling AAL
SP	Signaling point
UNI	User-network interface

Figure 10–1   Layers for configuration options.

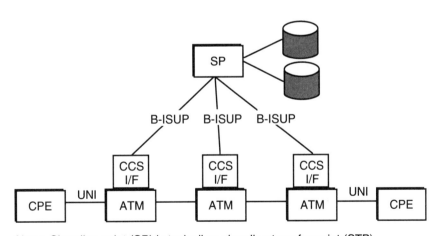

Note: Signaling point (SP) is typically a signaling transfer point (STP).

Figure 10–2   Overlay network, using B-ISUP with existing CCS network.

other resources (signaling points, databases) in the SS7 network. There-fore, this approach uses SCCP and TCAP for address translation and database access. The complexity arises because B-ISUP must be inte-grated into the signaling points, which forces the integration of the vir-tual circuit technology into the current physical circuit technology.

Another option is shown in Figure 10–3. In this situation, the CCS is not accessed. The BSSs are connected directly with ATM virtual chan-nel connections over which the NNI signaling ATM adaptation layer (SAAL) is utilized. B-ISUP operates over SAAL to exchange messages be-tween the BSSs. This approach uses the options shown in Figure 10–1a. It may be necessary to implement a subset of MTP 3 with this arrange-ment, because some of MTP 3 functions only come into play when mes-sages are exchanged between STPs. With this approach, B-ISUP mes-sages need only be exchanged between BSSs. But of course, it does not provide access to existing SS7 networks. I view this option as an interim measure, because it makes little sense to not draw on the resources of the current SS7 databases.

It is possible to use a hybrid configuration, as depicted in Figure 10–4. Both protocol stacks in Figure 10–1 are utilized. Access to the SS7 network is limited to one BSS hub. This configuration is attractive be-cause it limits the number of links that connect the BSSs and the SPs, but it must be configured carefully due to the vulnerability of a single failure. As the BSS evolves and draws more heavily on the use of the SPs

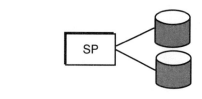

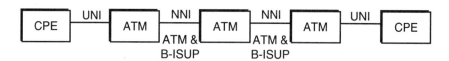

Figure 10–3 CCS network is not used.

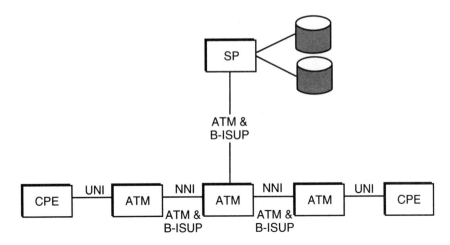

Figure 10–4   A hybrid configuration.

and databases, a fully meshed topology between the two systems is essential. A possible set of configurations is discussed next.

A likely configuration for the near future is shown in Figure 10–5. The ATM BSS machines (ATM BSS A, ATM BSS B, and ATM BSS C) interconnect through ATM virtual circuits. These machines are hooked up through signaling points (SPs), which are actually signaling transfer points (STPs) in this more detailed example.

This view represents one of Bellcore's approaches, which includes the signaling between two networks, labeled in Figure 10–5 as networks ABC and XYZ. This scenario would exist if a local exchange carrier (LEC) connected with an interexchange carrier (IXC).

This configuration is based on SS7 architecture and uses the quasi-associated signaling mode. An STP pair (STP A1, STP A2) is connected to another STP pair (STP B1, STP B2) in the other network through four D-link sets (known as a D-link quad[1]).

For this example, network ABC is the originating or terminating LEC network and network XYZ is the IXC network. The ATM BSS B is the gateway between the networks (the intermediate BSS).

Connections between the mated STPs are with C-links and connections between the ATM BSS machines are the STPs are with A-links.

---

[1]The SS7 links are explained in a companion book, *ISDN and SS7: Architectures for Digital Signaling Networks.*

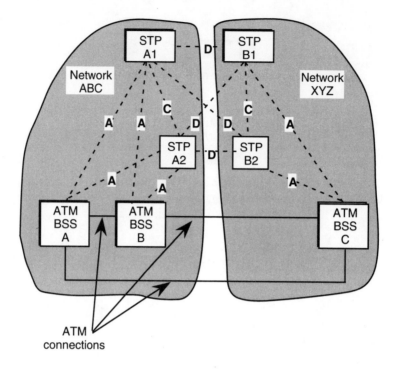

where: A = A links, C = C links, D = D links, and BSS = broadband switching system

Figure 10–5   Signaling network architecture.

POINT-TO-MULTIPOINT CALLS[2]

Because of the importance and wide use of telephone conference calls, multicasting data traffic, and video conferencing operations, broadband signaling networks have procedures to support these types of applications. The procedures are known as multicasting in most point-to-multipoint calls.

SIGNALING IDENTIFIERS (SIDs)

Thus far in this book, our discussions have concentrated on two identifiers: labels (VPIs, VCIs, VPCIs) and addresses (OSI, E.164, etc.).

---

[2]This example is derived from Bellcore GR-1431–CORE, Issue 2, November 1995. Some of the parameters and messages vary between Bellcore, ANSI, and ITU-T specifications.

Another identifier needs to be brought to our attention—the signaling identifier (SID), which is placed as a parameter in B-ISUP messages and used to identify a signaling association between a pair of BSSs.

The SIDs must remain constant for the life of the signaling connection and must be established for each BSS association. The SIDs are independently chosen and maintained by each BSS, and these BSSs may be in the same or different networks.

Figure 10–6 provides an example of how the SIDs are set up, used during the connection, and cleared. Exchange A selects SID = abc for the connection. This value is placed into the originating SID (OSID) parameter of the IAM and sent to exchange B. Upon receiving this message, exchange B selects SID = xyz for the connection and places this value in the OSID parameter of the IAA. Exchange B must also place SID = abc in the parameter of the IAA. Exchange destination SID (DSID) of the message to enable exchange A to correlate the two SIDs and the subsequent messages.

After the connection has been established, the two exchanges use the SIDs to identify all call control messages. These messages do not need to contain an OSID parameter; they contain the DSID of the recipient of the message. This rule holds true for the connection release messages, as well.

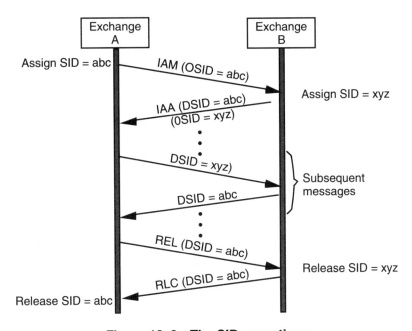

Figure 10–6   The SID operations.

Add Party Operations

This capability is implemented through the point-to-multipoint procedure as shown in Figure 10–7, which is an extension of Figure 7–10. This illustration shows the inclusion of three parties, but multiple parties may be connected with this operation.

The originating site issues a SETUP message across the UNI to the network. The network forwards this message to the destination in which the destination network node issues a SETUP across the UNI to the destination user.

The originating party (user A) is called the root party; this party is the source of the point-to-multipoint call. The destinations are called the

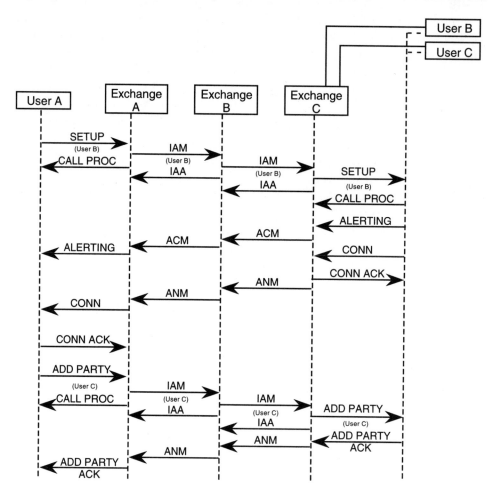

Figure 10–7 Point-to-multipoint operations.

leaf entries. It is the responsibility of the root to initiate the joining (adding) of all leaf entries to the call.

The originating exchange that receives the Q.2931 SETUP message determines if the call can be made and, if so, sends an IAM to the next (intermediate) exchange. The operations proceed in the ongoing manner discussed in Chapters 7 and 8. At the terminating exchange (exchange C), the B-ISUP messages are translated back to Q.2931 messages and vice versa between exchange C and user A.

Notice that an ALERTING message is sent in the backward direction (which is mapped into the B-ISUP ACM). The ALERTING message is optional; as explained in Chapter 7, it is not part of the ATM UNI specification (Version 3.1).

The addition of new leaf entries takes place from the root party through the use of the ADD PARTY message instead of the SETUP message. This message is invoked in Figure 10–7 to add party C to the connection.

The IAM for the call must contain the leaf party type parameter, and the origination connection link identifier parameter (containing the link identifier). In addition, the broadband bearer capability parameter must indicate in the user plane connection configuration field the "point-to-multipoint" operation. The other parameters that are required are ATM cell rate, quality of service, called party number, calling party's category, and origination signaling identifier.

For adding user C to this existing connection, the IAM must contain the destination connection link identifiers instead of the origination connection link identifier, and the connection element identifier parameter (VPCI/VCI).

PERFORMANCE REQUIREMENTS FOR THE SIGNALING VIRTUAL CHANNEL CONNECTION (VCC)

It was explained earlier that the VCI value of 5 is reserved for each virtual path connection (VPC) that is used for signaling. It is important that the signaling channel be provided with adequate bandwidth to support the broadband network. The various standards define the following requirements:

- At a minimum, the signaling systems shall support a peak cell rate of the signaling virtual channel ranging from $n \times 173$ cells/second (where $1 \leq n \leq 23$) and 4140 cells/second.

- As options, peak cell rates may be greater: (1) 5520 cells/second, (2) 8280 cells/second, or (3) 11040 cells/second.
- Cells transmitted through the signaling system must conform to a cell delay variation tolerance of 1000 μsec for peak cell rates below 4140 cells/second and 250 μsec for peak cell rate higher than 4140 cells/second.

These performance requirements are calculated on the 48 octets of the ATM cell and discount the AAL headers that reside in these 48 octets. (The network considers these 48 octets as user traffic). The peak cell rates contain "padding" to account for the overhead of OAM (operations, administration, and maintenance) cells that consume part of the channel bandwidth.

The values are inflated to reflect the OAM traffic. For example, a cell user payload (48 octets/cell) needs slightly over 166 cells/second (166.67) to support a 64 kbit/s application. But the figures cited above show that 173 cells/second are allocated to accommodate the OAM cells.

Table 10–1   PCR Values to Be Supported by Equivalent Bandwidth

PCR Value (cells/second)	Equivalent Bandwidth (bits/second)
0	0
152	56 kbit/s + OAM cells
$n \times 173$ where $n = 1,2, ..., 23$	$n \times 64$ kbit/s + OAM cells
3,622	1.39 Mbit/s including OAM cells
$n \times 690$ where $n = 7, 8, 9, 10, 11, 13, 14, 15, 16,$ 17, 19, 20, 21, 22, 23, 25, 26, 27, 28, 29, 31, 32 33, 34, 35, 37, 38, 39, 40, 41, 42, 44, 45, 46, 47	Approximately $n \times 256$ kbit/s
$n \times 4,140$ where $n = 1,2, ..., 23$	$n \times 1.544$ Mbit/s + OAM cells
$n \times 4,140$ where $n = 24, 25, ..., 85$	$n \times 1.544$ Mbit/s + OAM cells
96,111	36.86 Mbit/s including OAM cells
104,268	40.04 Mbit/s including OAM cells
$n \times 119,910$ where $n = 1, 2$	$n \times 44.763$ Mbit/s + OAM cells
353,207	135.63 Mbit/s including OAM cells

Note: Equivalent bandwidth entries for 56 kbit/s, $n \times$ DS0, $n \times$ DS1, and $n \times$ DS3 allow overhead for the Type 1 ATM Adaptation Layer (AAL) and OAM cells. The OAM cell overhead allows up to 1 OAM cell for every 128 User Information cells plus 1 cell/second for reporting Alarm Indicate Signal (AIS) and Far End Receive Failure (FERF) information.

Table 10–2   Cell Delay Variation Tolerance (CDVT) at the UNI

CDVT for DS1	CDVT for DS3	CDVT for STS-3c or STS-12c
—	—	50 microseconds
100 microseconds	100 microseconds	100 microseconds
150 microseconds	150 microseconds	150 microseconds
200 microseconds	200 microseconds	200 microseconds
250 microseconds	250 microseconds	250 microseconds
350 microseconds	350 microseconds	—
500 microseconds	500 microseconds	—

These figures also contain some extra padding to account for the varying use of AAL1 or AAL5 protocol data units, which consume different amounts (in the headers/trailers) of the 48 octet payload.

Bellcore provides some useful information (Bellcore GR-1110-CORE, Issue 1, September 1994) to correlate the ATM peak cell rate (PCR) to the required equivalent bandwidth. Table 10–1 is a summary of the PCR in cells/second and the equivalent bandwidth in bits/sec. Table 10–2 shows the amount of cell delay variation tolerance (CDVT) for user traffic in the ingress direction at the UNI (based on the two-point CDV definition in ITU-T Recommendation I.356). Table 10–3 correlates the sustainable cell rate (SCR) for VBR traffic to an equivalent bandwidth.

Table 10–3   Sustained Cell Rate (SCR) and Equivalent Bandwidth

SCR Value (cells/second)	Approximate Equivalent Bandwidth
0	0
152	56 kbps
$n \times 173$ where $n = 1, 2, ..., 23$	$n \times 64$ kbps
$n \times 690$ where $n = 7, 8, 9, 10, 11, 13,$ 14, 15, 16, 17, 19, 20, 21, 22, 23, 25, 26, 27, 28, 29, 31, 32, 33, 34, 35, 37, 38, 39, 40, 41, 43, 44, 45, 46, 47	Approximately $n \times 256$ kbps
$n \times 4,140$ where $n = 1, 2, ..., 85$	$n \times 1.544$ Mbps
$n \times 119,910$ where $n = 1, 2$	$n \times 44.736$ Mbps + OAM cells

158 BROADBAND SIGNALING OPERATIONS AND PERFORMANCE REQUIREMENTS

SUMMARY

The evolution to an ATM-based broadband signaling network is underway. For the foreseeable future, overlay and hybrid networks will be prevalent.

As the broadband switching networks mature, more multimedia services will be created and the point-to-multipoint operations will become essential to the success of broadband signaling.

11

Private Network–Network Interface (PNNI)

INTRODUCTION

This chapter examines the Private Network–Network Interface (PNNI), a specification that is published by the ATM Forum. We learn the reason PNNI was developed as well as the PNNI operations. Two categories of PNNI protocols are described. One deals with route advertising and the other deals with signaling. The latter is the main focus of this chapter since this book concentrates on signaling protocols.

WHY ANOTHER NNI PROTOCOL?

One can reasonably ask why yet another set of specifications is required to define another protocol in the ATM environment. Indeed, for the ATM implementer or the user of the ATM equipment, the proliferation of new specifications creates more complexity in a network (the PNNI specification by itself is 365 pages in length). But PNNI is published for a very good reason. The ITU-T does not concern itself with the operations of private networks. (From the ITU-T perspective, the Internet is considered to be a private network.) Additionally, the ITU-T does not concern itself with the distribution of routing information, route discovery, or topology analysis. These operations have been left to the implementation of individual telecommunications administrations.

This approach is not the case with PNNI. The PNNI philosophy is that these important considerations cannot be left to individual implementations. For full interworking to occur between ATM-based networks and ATM switches, there must be standards in place to define how information is distributed between switches in an ATM network. Thus, PNNI consists of two major parts. The first part defines a protocol to exchange routing information for route discovery. It defines the operations for the distribution of topology and routing information between ATM switches. It allows the switches to compute paths through a network. The second part of PNNI is the focus on this book. It is used for signaling and defines the procedures to establish point-to-point or point-to-multipoint connections through an ATM network. In this regard, we will see that the PNNI signaling operations are quite similar to many of the other protocols described in this book because they are based on the Q.2931 specification.

OVERVIEW OF PNNI PROTOCOL

Figure 11–1 illustrates the reference model for PNNI. On the network side, it is divided into the three major areas of cell stream, NNI signaling, and the topology protocol. On the user side, it is divided into the cell stream, UNI signaling, and the management interface protocol. These operations are further divided into the components shown in the figure. The switching fabric is based on a cell technology switching elements. The call processing modules and signaling modules are based on

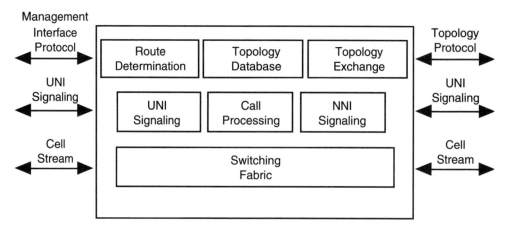

Figure 11–1   The PNNI reference model.

the Q Series specifications, and the topology exchange and route determination functions are based on shortest path route discovery technology.

Phase one of PNNI is designed to support all of the UNI release 3.1
capabilities and some of the UNI 4.0 capabilities. It is designed to support large networks, hierarchical routing, a wide variety of QOS, multiple routing metrics, source routed connection setups, and dynamic routing. In addition, it supports tunneling over virtual path connections
(VPCs) and unicasting operations.

The signaling part of PNNI is derived from Q.2931 from which the
ATM Forum's UNI signaling protocol was also derived. In this chapter,
we will examine the unique aspects of the PNNI signaling protocol and
refer to Q.2931 when appropriate. We will not revisit all the PNNI operations that use Q.2931 since this protocol was covered in Chapter 7.

I mentioned earlier that PNNI has two major aspects: that of signaling, which is the subject of this chapter, as well as that of route discovery, routing exchange, and topology analysis. For these latter operations,
PNNI fills in the void left by the other signaling protocols published by
the ITU-T, Bellcore, and ANSI. For those specifications, it is left to the
vendor or designer to determine how these important operations are carried out. The ATM Forum has done a laudable job in forging this aspect
of the PNNI to completion.

UNIQUE ASPECTS OF PNNI SIGNALING VIS-À-VIS Q.2931

Before we examine the PNNI signaling protocol, it will be useful to
describe unique features not found in other signaling protocols described
in this book. First, PNNI provides for a *crankback* operation. This allows
for the release of the connection setup in progress when it encounters a
failure at a node. The procedure allows the PNNI to perform alternate
routing to find a nonblocked or better path through the network.

PNNI uses *link metrics* to determine a route. The link metric uses conventional shortest path first operations and may also employ Dykstra's algorithm to compute a spanning tree topology in the network. The link metric parameter requires that the values of the parameter for all links along a
specific path be combined (summed) to determine whether the path is acceptable and/or optimal to carry the traffic to the destination address.

PNNI uses a *routing control channel*, which is a VCC employed for
the exchange of PNNI routing protocol messages.

A *restricted transit node* is a node that can be used only under restricted and identified circumstances. It must always be an intermediate

node in the call, because a restricted transit node is free to originate or terminate a call.

In addition, PNNI defines a *logical link* concept. Logical links exist between nodes in the network and can be a physical link or a VPC between two nodes. A logical link becomes operational when the attached nodes of the link initiate the exchange of information through a well known VCC, which we learned earlier is called the routing control channel (RCC). Logical link awareness is maintained through a procedure called the *Hello*, which stipulates the transmission of messages that are sent periodically between the two nodes to determine if the logical link is operational. These hello messages are exchanged between all intermediate neighbors to determine if all is well and the local state information of the neighbor nodes.

All the nodes in the PNNI network store *topology state parameters* (which are known as link state parameters in other route discovery protocols). This information is used in making routing decisions and also is used to accumulate the values to determine the shortest path based on the link metrics. Of course, certain types of topology state information such as delay and bandwidth may change. On the other hand, other information such as security may remain static. PNNI makes no distinction between dynamic or static parameters when it advertises routes between nodes.

PNNI SIGNALING SPECIFICATION MODEL

Figure 11–2 shows the topology and model for the PNNI interfaces. A calling user is called the *preceding side* and the called user is called the *succeeding side*. PNNI uses the same term, *forward direction,* as the other specifications in this book to connote the calling user to called user and the term *backward direction* to connote the called user to the calling user. In addition, the network that originates the call from the user is called the *preceding network* and the network that receives the call is called the *succeeding network.*

The PNNI model is further depicted in Figure 11–3, which is almost identical to the NNI signaling stack defined by other standards organizations. One difference pertains to the PNNI call control and PNNI protocol control. The call control layer services the upper layers for functions such as routing, routing exchange, and allocation of resources. The PNNI protocol control layer rests below the call control layer and thus provides services to call control. The PNNI call control layer is responsible for pro-

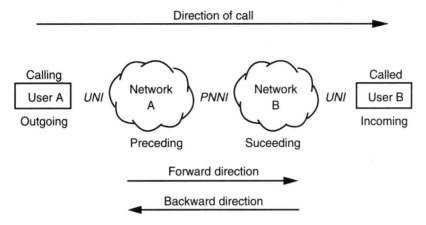

Figure 11–2   The PNNI interface and associated terms.

cessing the signaling. It operates with state machines for the incoming and outgoing calls. The layers below these two layers are based on the ITU-T Q.2xxx specifications described in earlier chapters in this book, and therefore, we shall not revisit those specifications here.

TERMS AND CONCEPTS

In order to grasp the basic concepts of how PNNI operates, we must first deal with several terms. In this section, I introduce the terms, and

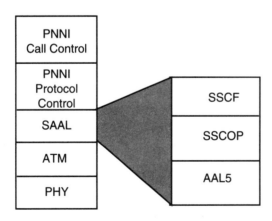

Figure 11–3   The PNNI control plane

then I explain them in more detail later in this chapter. Refer to Figure 11–4 during this discussion.

Figure 11–4 shows the PNNI hierarchy. It is so named because PNNI is designed for hierarchical routing. With this technique, nodes and their attached links at a given hierarchical level can be aggregated to a higher level, and this higher level can be once again aggregated into the next higher level.

This recursive aggregation is performed to (1) reduce the amount of routing information that is passed through a network, and (2) hide (if needed) topology information for privacy or security purposes.

At the lowest level in the hierarchy (shown in this figure as small black or white circles) is a relay node (an ATM switch, for example). These switches are connected by physical links (an OC-12 SONET link, for example). A collection of these switches form a hierarchy to the next higher level.

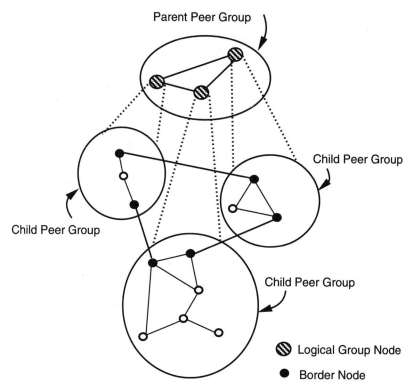

Figure 11–4   PNNI hierarchy.

The nodes at the same hierarchical level are known as a peer group. All nodes in a peer group exchange topology information with each other. As shown in this figure, a peer group may represent a lower-level peer group, or stated another way, lower peer groups can be aggregated to a higher peer group. The lower-level peer group is called a child peer group, and the upper-level group is called a parent peer group.

A group of nodes can be represented by one single node, which is called a logical node. Each child peer group is associated with (represented by) a logical group node inside the parent peer group. This relationship means that a logical group node represents a lower level peer group (the entire peer group). This relationship is depicted in this figure with the dashed lines.

Within the peer group, one logical group node is elected to be a peer group leader. This entity is responsible for route advertisements and topology aggregation for all the nodes in the peer group.

Another concept needs to be emphasized. The logical node is an abstract representation of a group of physical nodes. Therefore, the aggregated topology information associated with this logical node is actually a representation of the connectivity of the physical nodes.

The figure also shows the border node (black circles). This node is so defined if it has at least one attachment to another peer group. No restriction is placed on how many border nodes are configured in a PNNI network.

PNNI METRICS

Modern routing technology is based on a number of criteria called type of service factors (TOS), an Internet term for quality of service factors (QOS). These factors are defined by the network administrators and users and may include criteria such as delay, throughput, or security needs. The path through an internet is chosen based on the ability of the routers and networks to meet a required service.

This technique is also called link state routing, because the TOS values are applied to each communication link in the internet. A link metric is defined as the sum of a link state parameters (based on TOS) along a given path from a source address to a destination address. One of the purposes of PNNI is to provide means to advertise these metrics in order for a node to choose a "best" path (known as the shortest path) between two nodes. The length of the shortest path between the nodes is known as the distance between the nodes.

In typical large networks, there will be more than one path available from one node to another. Moreover, the various combinations of paths in a network may make the advertisements of all possibilities an onerous task. However, if a node in the network (say, a PNNI logical group node) somehow aggregates these many metrics to a shorter summary, and then advertises this summary, the task becomes feasible.

However, metric aggregation has a price to pay for this usefulness. In many situations, it will not lead to the optimum route. In these systems, one must weigh the amount of aggregation versus the accuracy of the aggregation.

To illustrate this point, consider Figure 11–5, which is extracted from the topology from the previous figure. Four nodes are connected to each other with four physical links. I change the topology in the bottom part of the figure to a meshed topology to make some points regarding metric aggregation. Nodes A, B, C, and D are now fully connected with

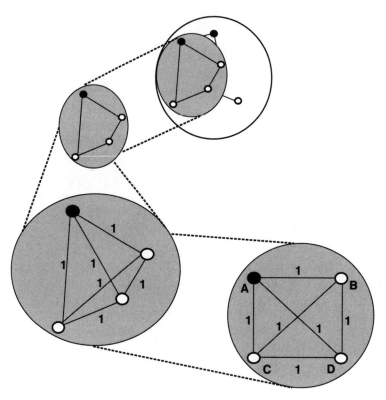

Figure 11–5   Link metrics.

six links.[1] Link state parameters of 1 are assigned to each link for this simple example.

Metric Aggregation

The metrics for the fully meshed 6-link network in Figure 11–6a, (the original graph) are aggregated to a 5-link network (Figure 11–6b, which is a subgraph). The dashed lines in the Figure 11–6 indicate that links have been eliminated from the network logical topology. Stated another way, they have been aggregated out of the graph.

A key goal in metric aggregation is to create a fully connected subgraph that has small stretch factor. The stretch factor is the maximum ratio of the distance in the subgraph to the distance in the original graph. For the 5-link subgraph, the stretch factor is 2, and five links are used to maintain the logical full-mesh topology. The compromise from the original graph is that the distance between B and C is now 2, but the aggregation translates to fewer variables in an advertisement. Furthermore, due to costs, it may be preferable to not have a physical link between B and C. Let's assume the links are T1 channels, for example. These links are expensive to lease, and the nature and amount of traffic between B and C may not warrant the cost of the T1 link.

To continue this example, Figure 11–6c shows another possibility for aggregating the metrics for this network. The 3-link aggregation still provides full connectivity, with the stretch factor remaining at 2. The compromise is that the distances between nodes A–C and B–C is now 2. Once again, this compromise may or may not be desirable, depending upon the nature of traffic between these nodes and the costs to provide direct links between them.

PNNI does not tell the network manager how to make the decisions on the physical topology, but it does provide a tool for advertising the topology and for using the network effectively.

---

[1] This analysis is based on several papers on the subject. I recommend for the reader who wishes more details: (1) David Peleg and Alejandro A. Schaffer, "Graph Spanners," *Journal of Graph Theory*, 13 (1), 1989. (2) Numerous ATM Forum working papers. See ATM Forum Contributions 94-0606, 95-0153, 94-0449. (3) Whay C. Lee (whay@prospero.dev.cdx.mot.com) is a noted expert in this field, and any of his papers are recommended. Mr. Lee contributed to most of the ATM papers, and (4) Whay C. Lee, "Topology Aggregation for Hierarchical Routing in ATM Networks," *Computer Communication Review*, 25 (2) April, 1995.

(a) Fully meshed nodes:

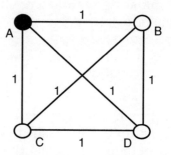

(b) Logically meshed with five links and stretch factor = 2:

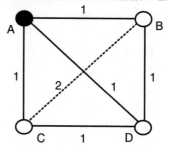

(c) Logically meshed with two links and stretch factor = 2:

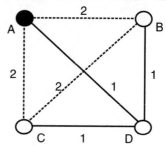

Figure 11–6   Metric aggregation.

In ATM networks, it is likely that the link attributes may vary from node to node. Even if the links are the same (for example, all OC-12 links), their utilization may vary, with some links carrying more traffic than others. This situation gives rise to different TOS values with regard to delay and throughput.

Figure 11–7 shows examples of metric aggregation with varying link attributes. Figure 11–7a shows a fully meshed network; Figure 11–7b shows a 5-link aggregation; and Figure 11–7c represents a minimum spanning tree with a 3-link aggregation.

This example illustrates that shorter paths may be available between physically adjacent nodes through nonadjacent nodes. The direct physical path between nodes A and C is 4, yet the aggregated path distance between A and C through B is 3. This situation can occur if, as examples, (1) node A's link to C is congested, (2) the link is operating at a low bit-rate, (3) the metric represents a high cost in relation to the error rate on the link, and so on.

Routing exchange information is advertised in a PNNI system by each node flooding PNNI topology state elements (PTSEs) within a desig-

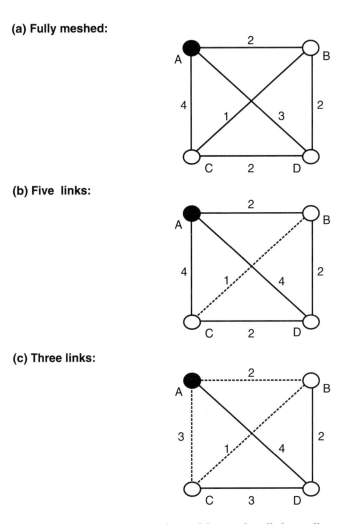

(a) Fully meshed:

(b) Five links:

(c) Three links:

Figure 11–7   Metric aggregation with varying link attributes.

nated part of the overall network, which is called a peer group (see Figure 11–8). The information includes the node identity and the status of its links to its neighbors.

This information is used to keep a topology database updated at each node in the peer group. In effect, the topology database is a reflection of the information in the PTSEs and contains all the needed information to calculate a route from any node in the peer group to any other node. The PTSEs contain link state parameters (also called topology state parameters) and nodal state parameters. The former describes the state of each link at a node; the latter describes the state and characteristics of the node.

Topology state parameters are classified as follows (and they may be static or dynamic; PNNI does not care):

- *Attribute:* A single value, considered individually when making a routing decision (for example, link failure attribute that causes a link not to be selected for a route)
- *Metric:* An accumulation of values along a path (for example, a delay metric on each link that is added up for the end-to-end path.

The PTSEs are transmitted in a PNNI topology state packet (PTSP) and they must be acknowledged by the receiving node. Upon receiving a PTSP, a node examines it and performs the following actions:

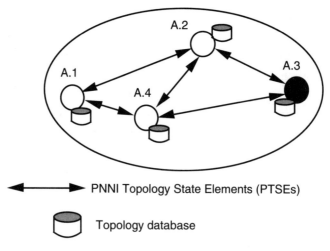

Figure 11–8   Exchanging information within a peer group (PG).

- If the PTSE is new or more recent than the current copy that is in the topology database, it is placed in the database.
- This PTSE is sent out on all the node's links except the link from which the information was received.

These operations are an ongoing activity, and a PTSE is sent whenever something changes, or on a periodic basis. At the topology database, entries are removed if they are not refreshed within a specific period. A node can only resend a PTSE that it originated.

HORIZONTAL AND OUTSIDE LINKS

Between lowest level nodes, connections are made by "logical links," which are either physical links or virtual path connections (VPCs) (see Figure 11–9). Links between two lowest level nodes in the same peer group cannot be aggregated. For example, if two physical links connect a pair of lowest level nodes, they are represented by two separate logical links. Two terms are important in this discussion: logical links inside a peer group are called horizontal links and logical links that connect two peer groups are called outside links.

When a logical link is set up and becomes operational, the neighbor nodes exchange information though a well-known VCC. This VCC is

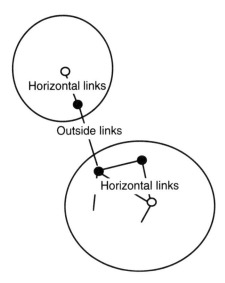

Figure 11–9   Horizontal links and outside links.

called a PNNI routing control channel (RCC). As we shall see later, a special protocol called the *Hello* protocol sends *Hello* packets across the RCC to keep neighbor nodes aware of each other's existence and the state of their communications channels. We shall also see that the PNNI *Hello* protocol allows a node to determine if it belongs to a peer group or not.

PNNI HIERARCHY EXAMPLE

As we just learned, the PNNI architecture is based on a hierarchical structure. Nodes are associated with level in a hierarchy and nodes that belong to the same hierarchy are in the same peer group. An example of the PNNI hierarchy, which I have derived from the ATM Forum PNNI specification, is provided in Figure 11–10. The numbers and alphanumerics in this figure represent addresses. They are drawn in place of specific addresses for ease of explanation. The highest hierarchy of this figure is peer group A, identified with the address of A. The nodes inside the group are identified as A1, A4, and so on. Within each peer group, there is a peer group leader whose responsibility is to receive topology information from all nodes in the group and advertise this information to other groups. The information that is advertised is "filtered" in that summary information is given to the other groups.

The next level of the PNNI hierarchy is shown with peer groups A.1, A.2, and so on. Within these peer groups are other nodes labeled as A.1.3, A.4.1, and so on. PNNI establishes rules about how messages can be sent up and down the hierarchy based on the functions of the nodes in a peer group. Once again, this concept is to place restrictions on how many route advertisements can be sent between nodes.

A logical group node represents a peer group in the next PNNI routing hierarchy. In Figure 11–10, logical group node A.2 represents peer group A.2 in the next higher level of the hierarchy, in this case, peer group A (PG (A)).

The functions and characteristics of the logical group node are as follows (and see Figure 11–11):

- Aggregates and summarizes information about its child peer group
- Floods this information to its own peer group

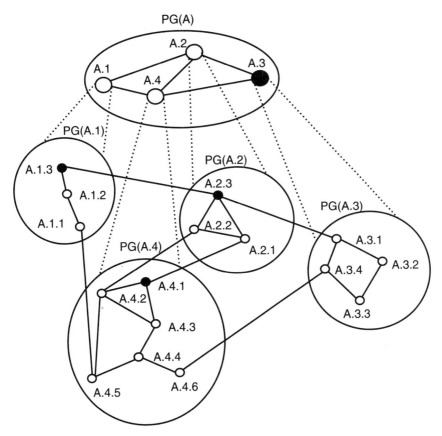

Figure 11–10   The PNNI hierarchy.

- Passes information about its peer group to the peer group leader (PGL) of the child peer group (this PGL floods this information within the peer group)
- Does not participate in the signaling operations
- The functions that define—for example, PGL A—are located in node A.2, which is implemented in a physical switching system (e.g., an ATM switch) containing the lowest level node (for example, A.2.3)
- Any node can become a peer group leader (if it is so configured)

The information flow up to the peer group leader is reachability, which contains summarized address information that is used to decide

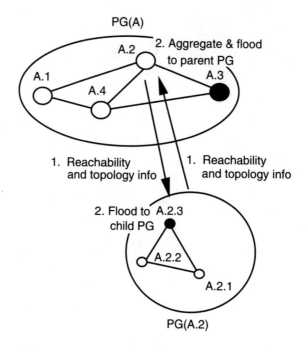

Figure 11–11   PNNI information exchange.

which addresses can be reached through the lower level peer group, and topology aggregation, which is summarized topology information that is used to route in and across the peer group.

The purpose of topology aggregation is to reduce the amount of information that is exchanged between nodes (or nodes between networks) about routes between nodes. The aggregation of routing information reduces the overhead in the network or networks by eliminating or decreasing the amount of information that must be exchanged to determine an efficient route between two endpoints.

Topology aggregation is also used to hide the details of a specific topology from another node that, for example, has no need to know about the minutiae of each individual route in the node's network. This aspect of topology aggregation may stem from security/privacy considerations, or the well-founded design principle of keeping network-specific operations within that network.

Whatever the rationale may be for link aggregation, Figure 11–12 shows the ideas behind it. In peer group A, noted as PG(A), the link between A.2 and A.4 is a logical link, because two physical links connect A.2 and A.4. They are the links between (1) A.2.2 and A.4.2, and (2) A.2.2 and A.4.1.

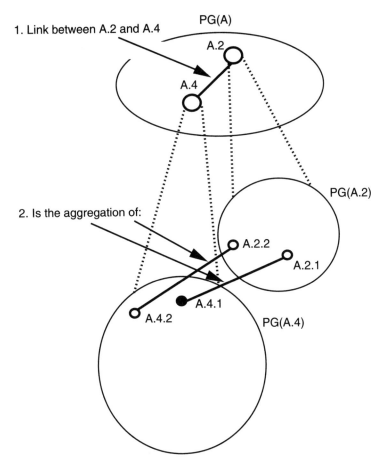

Figure 11–12   Link aggregation.

PNNI SIGNALING MESSAGES

The basic messages for PNNI signaling are derived from Q.2931. Table 11–1 lists these messages and their major functions. You can refer to earlier chapters for a detailed description of these messages. My intent in this section is to describe parameters in the messages that are unique to PNNI that are not defined in the other signaling specifications in this book.

A Look at the SETUP Message Information Elements

In this section we examine the SETUP message information elements that are unique to PNNI and not found in the other specifications.

Table 11–1   The PNNI Messages for Call and Connection Control (Point-to-Point)

Message	Function
Call establishment	
SETUP	Initiate the call establishment
CALL PROCEEDING	Call establishment has begun
CONNECT	Call has been accepted
ALERTING	Called party has been alerted
Call clearing	
RELEASE	Initiate call clearing
RELEASE COMPLETE	Call has been cleared
Miscellaneous	
STATUS ENQUIRY (SE)	Sent to solicit a status message
STATUS (S)	Sent in response to SE or to report error
NOTIFY	Sent to provide additional information about a call

Calling Party Soft (permanent virtual path connection [PVPC] or permanent virtual channel connection [PVCC]). This information element indicates the VPI or VPI/VCI values used for the PVC segment for the calling connecting point. If no VPCs are configured for the use of logical links on a physical interface, a signaling channel designated as VPI = 0 controls all the virtual paths on the interface. Multiple virtual path connections (VPCs) are supported by PNNI to multiple destinations through a single physical interface. In this configuration, each VPC that is configured for use as a logical link must have a signaling channel associated with it. The virtual channels of these VPCs are controlled by the associated signaling pertaining to that particular VPC. This means that the signaling channel (which is the default channel of VPI = 0) on the same physical interface does not control the virtual channels that are used as logical links within PVCs. However, this default signaling channel does control all the remaining virtual channels and virtual paths on the physical link.

Called Party Soft (PVPC or PVCC). This information element indicates the VPI or VPI/VCI values of the PVC segment between the called connecting point and the user of a PVPC or PVCC, respectively.

Available Bit Rate (ABR) Parameters. The values in this information element pertain to the ABR class of service that is defined by the

ATM Forum in its UNI specification. This class of service was established by the ATM Forum because the ITU-T basic documentation did not provide for this feature.

In accordance with ATM Forum UNI 4.4, the parameter defaulting for the ABR parameters is performed by the network side of the calling user UNI. In the case of a soft PVPC or PVCC setup, it is the responsibility of the originating switch to send the setup message containing the ABR parameters. PNNI permits the ABR parameters to be adjusted by each switching system in the PNNI network hierarchy. This feature allows a network to protect resources or to modify the request so that the resources can meet the ABR parameters.

PNNI Available Bit Rate (ABR) Descriptors

Parameter values in each direction can be negotiated by either side for peak cell rate (PCR), initial cell rate (ICR), transit buffer exposure (TBE), rate increase factor (RIF), and rate decrease factor (RDF). If the network node is able to provide the requested PCR and ABR parameter values, the node must progress the call towards the called user with the original parameters. If it is not able to provide the requested PCR, but it is able to provide at least MCR value, then the node shall also progress the call towards the called user after it adjusts the PCR value to what it can handle. The adjusted PCR value must be greater or equal to MCR.

The PNNI node is allowed, if required, to also adjust either in the forward or backward directions the ABR setup parameters, ABR initial cell rate, ABR transfer buffer exposure, rate increase factor and rate decrease factor. Table 11–2 summarizes the changes that can be made by a PNNI node.

The succeeding side must adjust the accumulative RM fixed round-trip parameter within the ABR information element. The adjustment amount is the sum of the forward and reverse direction fixed portion of

Table 11–2   Permissible Modifications

Parameter for a Given Direction	Modification by the Network
PCR	Decrease only
ICR	Decrease only
TBE	Decrease only
RIF	Decrease only
RDF	Increase only

the RM cell relay including forward and reverse link propagation delays and any fixed processing delays that would be encountered within each PNNI switching system. The adjustment value is added to the cumulative RN fixed round trip-time parameter.

The cumulative RM fixed round-trip parameter will be adjusted in the first and last switching systems of full call path of the network side of the UNI. Once again, the amount of the adjustment is the sum of the forward and reverse direction fixed portion of the RM cell delay at the UNI. Additionally, it includes the forward and reverse link propagation delays up to network boundary and fixed processing delays at the UNI.

DESIGNATED TRANSIT LIST (DTL)

The designated transit list includes the logical nodes (and perhaps logical links) that a connection traverses through a peer group at some level of a PNNI hierarchy. The DTL list is coded in the SETUP and ADD PARTY messages within a designated transit list information elements. When the DTL is processed in each node in the path, the node determines whether any DTLs need to be added to the DTL stack (a stack is a representation of the hierarchically complete source route with the last-in/first-out list of DTLs). During this determination, the PNNI node determines whether any DTLs need to be removed from the stack and then processes the remaining stack to prepare it for transmission to the next node.

With regard to the crankback, if the call cannot be forwarded within a PNNI domain, then it can be cranked back. If the call goes all the way to the called user and gets rejected, this is not a crankback. In such cases the RELEASE or RELEASE COMPLETE message is sent by the called user. Crankback is used when reachability cannot be obtained, resource problems occur, or an error in DTL processing occurs. It is also possible for a crankback to occur because the path selection of sum nodes determines that no paths meet the quality constraints for the connection.

Crankbacks may result in alternate routing being attempted. But, this is an implementation decision based on the network. Crank back may also crank back to the next level in a PNNI hierarchy.

SOFT PERMANENT VIRTUAL CONNECTION PROCEDURES

Two network interfaces that serve the permanent virtual connection will establish and release a soft PVPC/PVCC. The influence of this connection are identified by assigning unique ATM addresses, which must include the SEL octet in the ATM address field.

One of the network interface endpoints owns the PVPC/PVCC and, therefore, assumes the responsibility for establishing and releasing the connection. This interface is called the calling endpoint. In order to establish a PVPC/PVCC, the endpoints must be identified. The calling endpoint is identified in the calling party number information element and the network management system provides the ATM addresses of the endpoints for the connection as well as the necessary information about the VPI/VCI that are used at the two endpoints.

It is important to note that parameters of the PVPC or PVCC are established administratively. They are separate from a process that establishes the soft PVPC/PVCC. Therefore, negotiation of these end-to-end parameters is not permitted.

Crank back

As we discussed earlier in this chapter, the crankback information element indicates that crankback procedures have been initiated. The information element also identifies the node or link where the connection could not be accepted. It also contains an identifier to note the level within the PNNI hierarchy at which crankback is being executed.

INFORMATION ELEMENTS FOR THE SUPPORT OF OTHER SERVICES

PNNI defines the support of other services, such as 64 kbit/s-based circuit mode services. These capabilities and information elements have been described in the material in this book dealing with Q.2931.

SUMMARY

The private network–network interface performs two major services in the broadband network. First, it provides a protocol for route advertising and guidance on link aggregation procedures. Second, it defines the signaling operations that are to be imployed in a private network based on Q.2931.

PNNI should play a valuable role in broadband networks since, heretofore, there has been no specification defining how routing exchange information is to be exchanged between switches. PNNI has not yet seen implementation in commercial systems since it is a relatively new specification.

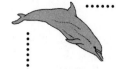

Abbreviations

AAL CP: AAL common part
AAL5: ATM adaptation layer, type 5
ACL: Automatic congestion level
AESA: ATM end system address
ARP: Address Resolution Protocol
AA: Administrative authority
AAL: ATM adaptation layer
ACCS: Automated calling card service
ACM: Address complete message
AE: Application entity
AEI: Application entity invocation
AFI: Authority format identifier
AIS: Alarm indicate signal
AP: Applications process
ASE: Application service element
ATM: Asynchronous Transfer Mode
B-ISDN: Broadband-ISDN
B-ISUP: Broadband-ISDN user part
BC: Bearer capability
BCC: Bearer connection control
BER: Basic encoding rules
BGAK: Begin acknowledge
BGN: Begin
BGRE: Begin reject
BOM: Beginning of message
BR: Buffer release
BRI: Basic rate interface

BSS: Broadband Switching System
C: Cell loss priority
CAC: Connection admission control
CBR: Constant bit rate
CC: Call control
CC: Country code
CCIS: Common channel interoffice signaling
CCRI: Consistency check result information
CCITT: International Telecommunications Union-Telecommunication Standardization Sector (see also ITU-T)
CCS: Common channel signaling
CCS I/F: CCS interface
CMIP: Common management information protocol
COM: Continuation of message
CPCS: Common part convergence sublayer
CPCS: Common part CS
CPCS-UU: Common part convergence sublayer-user-to-user
CPE: Customer premises equipment
CPI: Common part id
CPI: Common part indicator
CRC: Cyclic redundancy check
CS: Convergence sublayer

CUG: Closed user group
DCC: Data country code
DFI: Domain specific part identifier
DN: Destination network
DPC: Destination point code
DSAP: Destination SAP
DSID: Destination signaling identifier
DSP: Domain specific part
DSS: Digital subscriber signaling system
ENDAK: End acknowledge
E800: Enhanced 800
EOM: End of message
ER: Error recovery
ERAK: Error recovery acknowledge
ESI: End system identifier
FEC: Forward error correction
FERF: Far End Receive Failure
FOT: Forward transfer message
GFC: Generic flow control
GSM: Global systems for mobile communications
GT: Global title
HEC: Header error check
HEC: Header error control
HO DSP: High order domain specific part
IAA: IAM acknowledgment
IAM: Initial address
IC: Interchange carrier
ICD: International code designator
ICI: Intercarrier interface
ID: Interface data
id: Identification
IDI: Initial domain identifier
IDP: Initial domain part
IE: Information elements
IP: Internet Protocol
IPI: Initial protocol identifier
ISDN: Integrated Services Digital Network
ISUP: ISDN user part
IT: Information type
ITU-T: International Telecommunications Union-Telecommunication Standardization Sector (ITU-T, formerly, the CCITT)
IXC: Interchange carrier
LCN: Logical channel number
LE: List element
LEC: Local exchange carrier
LI: Length indicator

LLC: Low layer compatibility
LM: Layer management
LMI: Local management interface
MC: Maintenance control
MCI: Message compatibility information
MD: Management data
MID: Message id
MTP 3: Message transfer part 3
MTP: Message transfer part
MU: Message unit
MUSN: MU sequence number
N-BC: Narrowband bearer capability
N-HLC: Narrowband high layer capability
N-ISDN: Narrowband Integrated Services Digital Network
N-LLC: Narrowband low layer compatibility
NDC: National destination code
NNI: Network-node interface
NNI: Network-to-network interface
NSAP: Network service access point
N(S)N: National (significant) number
OSI Model: Open Systems Interconnection Model
OAM: Operations, administration, and maintenance
OUI: Organization unique ID
OPC: Originating point code
OSID: Origination signaling identifier
PAD: Padding
PBX: Private branch exchange
PC: Point code
PCI: Protocol control information
PCM: Pulse code modulation
PCR: Peak cell rate
PCS: Personal communications services
PDU: Protocol data unit
PHY: Physical layer
PID: Protocol id
PL: Physical layer
PM: Physical medium sublayer
PRI: Primary rate interface
PTI: Payload type identifier
PTO: Public telecommunications operators
PVC: Permanent virtual circuit
QOS: Quality of service
REL: Release
RES: Resume
RJE: Remote job entry

RLC: Release complete
ROSE: Remote operations service element
SAAL: Signaling ATM adaptation layer
SACF: Single association control function
SAO: Single association object
SAP: Service access point
SAR: Segmentation and reassembly
SCCP: Signaling connection control point
SCP: Service control point
SD: Sequenced data
SDU: Service data unit
SE: Status enquiry
SEL: Selector
SID: Signaling identifier
SIO: Service information octet
SLS: Signaling link selection code
SN: Sequence number
SN: Subscribers number
SNAP: Subnetwork access protocol
SNMP: Simple Network Management Protocol
SNP: Sequence number protection
SONET: Synchronous Optical Network
SP: Signaling point
SPF: Shortest path first
SPI: Subsequent protocol identifier
SS7: Signaling System Number 7
SSAP: Source service access point
SSCF: Service-specific coordination function
SSCOP: Service-specific connection-oriented protocol
SSCOP-UU: SSCOP user-to-user

SSCS LM: Service specific convergence sublayer layer management
SSCS: Service specific convergence sublayer
SSM: Single segment message
SSN: Subsystem number
SSP: Service switching point
STAT: Solicited status response
STP: Signaling transfer point
SUS: Suspend message
SVC: Switched virtual call or channel
TA: Terminal adapter
TCAP: Transaction capabilities application part
TC: Transmission convergence sublayer
TC: Trunk code
TCP/IP: Internet Protocols
TDM: Time division multiplexing
TUP: Telephone user part
UD: Unnumbered data
UI: Unrecognized information
ULP: Upper layer protocol
UNI: User-network interface
USTAT: Unsolicited status
VBR: Variable bit rate
VC: Virtual channel
VCC: Virtual channel connection
VCI: Virtual channel identifier
VCI: Virtual circuit identifier
VPC: Virtual path connection
VPCI: Virtual path connection identifier
VPI: Virtual path identifier
VPN: Virtual private network

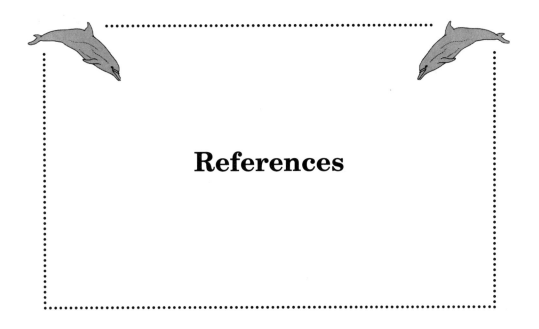

References

In addition to the formal standards for the systems described in this book, these references should prove useful to the reader. Many of them were used for the development of this material.

[AHMA93] Amhad, R., and Halsall, F. (1993). Interconnecting high-speed LANs and backbones, *IEEE Network*, September.

[AMOS79] Amos, J.E., Jr. (1979). Circuit switching: Unique architecture and applications. *IEEE Computer*, June.

[ARMT93] Armitage, G.J., and Adams, K.M.(1993). Packet reassembly during cell loss, *IEEE Network*, September.

[ATM92a] ATM Forum. (June 1, 1992). *ATM user-network interface specification*, Version 2.0.

[ATM93a] ATM Forum. (August 5, 1993). *ATM user-network interface specification, Version 3.0.*

[ATM94a] ATM Forum. (March, 1994). *Education and training work group*, ATM Forum Ambassador's Program.

[ATM94b] ATM Forum. (July 21, 1994). *ATM user-network interface specification, Version 3.1.*

[ATT89a] (January, 1989). Observations of error characteristics of fiber optic transmission systems, CCITT SGXVIII, San Diego, CA.

[BELL82] Bellamy, J. (1982). *Digital Telephony*, New York, NY: John Wiley and Sons.

[BELL90a] (May, 1993). Generic requirements for frame relay PVC exchange service, TR-TSV-001369, Issue 1.

[BELL89a]. (September, 1989). Synchronous optical network (SONET) transport systems: common generic criteria, TR-TSY-000253, Issue 1.

[BELL94] Bellman, R.B. (1994). Evolving traditional LANs to ATM, *Business Communications Review*, October.

[BLAC89] Black, U. (1989). *Data Networks, Concepts, Theory and Practice*, Prentice Hall.

[BLAC91] Black, U. (1991). *X.25 and related protocols*, IEEE Computer Society Press.

[BLAC93] Black, U. (1993). *Data link protocols*, Prentice Hall.

[BLAI88] Blair, C. (1988). SLIPs: Definitions, causes, and effects in T1 networks, *A Tautron Application Note, Issue 1*, September. (Note: my thanks to this author for a lucid explanation of slips.)

[BNR92a] Bell Northern Research. (1992). Global systems for mobile communications, *Telesis*, 92.

[BNR94a] Discussions held with Bell Northern Research (BNR) designers during 1993 and 1994.

[BROW94] Brown, P.D. (ed.). (1994). The price is right for ATM to become a serious competitor, *Broadband Networking News*, May.

[CCIT90a] (1990). Voice packetization-packetized voice protocols, CCITT Recommendation G.764, Geneva.

[CDPD93] (July 19, 1993). Cellular digital packet data system specification, *Release 1.0*.

[CHER92] Cherukuri, R. (August 26, 1992). Voice over frame relay networks, A technical paper issued as Frame Relay Forum, FRF 92.33.

[CHEU92] Cheung, N.K. (1992). The infrastructure of gigabit computer networks, *IEEE Communications Magazine*, April,.

[COMM94a] Korostoff, K. (April 18, 1994). Wide-area ATM undergoes trial by MAGIC, *Communications Week*.

[DAVI91] Davidson, R.P., and Muller, N.J. (1991). *The Guide to SONET*, Telecom Library, Inc.

[DELL92] Dell Computer, Intel, and University of Pennsylvania, A study compiled by Marty Baumann, *USA Today*, date not available.

[dePr91] dePrycker, M. (1991). *Asynchronous Transfer Mode*. Ellis Harwood Ltd.

[dePR92] de Prycker, M. (1992) ATM in Belgian Trial. *Communications International*, June.

[DUBO94] DuBois, D. Simnet Inc., Palo Alto, CA. A recommendation from a reviewer of *Emerging Communications Technologies*. (Thank you Mr. DuBois.)

[ECKB92] Eckberg, A.E. (1992). B-ISDN/ATM traffic and congestion control, *IEEE Network*, September.

[EMLI 63] Emling, J.W., and Mitchell, D. (1963). The effects of time delay and echoes on telephone conversations. *Bell Systems Technical Journal*, November.

[FORD93] Ford, P.S., Rekhter, Y., and Braun, H.-W. (1993). Improving the routing and addressing of IP. *IEEE Network*, May.

[FORU92] Frame Relay Forum Technical Committee. (May 7, 1992). "Frame relay network-to-network interface, phase 1 implementation agreement, Document Number FRF 92.08R1–Draft 1.4.

[GASM93] Gasman, L. (1993). ATM CPE—Who is providing what?, *Business Communications Review*, October.

[GOKE73] Goke, L.R., and Lipovski, G.J. (1973). Banyan networks for partitioning multiprocessor systems. First Annual Symposium on Computer Architecture.

[GRIL93] Grillo, D., MacNamee, R.J.G., and Rashidzadeh, B. (1993). Towards third generation mobile systems: A European possible transition path. *Computer Networks and ISDN Systems*, 25(8).

[GRON92] Gronert, E. (1992). MANS make their mark in Germany. *Data Communications International*, May.

[HAFN94] Hafner, K. (1994). Making sense of the internet. *Newsweek*, October 24.

[HALL92] Hall, M. (ed.). (1992). LAN-based ATM products ready to roll out. *LAN Technology*, September.

[HAND91] Handel, R., and Huber, M.N. (1991). *Integrated broadband networks: An introduction to ATM-based networks*. Addison-Wesley.

[HERM93] Herman, J., and Serjak C. (1993). ATM switches and hubs lead the way to a new era of switched internetworks. *Data Communications*, March.

[HEWL91] Hewlett Packard, Inc. (1991). Introduction to SONET, A tutorial.

[HEWL92] Hewlett Packard, Inc. (1992). Introduction to SONET networks and tests, An internal document.

[HEYW93] Heywood, P. (1993). PTTs gear up to offer high-speed services. *Data Communications*, August.

[HILL91] SONET, An overview. A paper prepared by Hill Associates, Inc., Winooski, VT, 05404.

[HUNT92] Hunter, P. (1992). What price progress?, *Communications International*, June.

[ITU93a] ITU-TS (1993). ITU-TS draft recommendation Q93.B "B-ISDN user-network interface layer 3 specification for basic call/bearer control. May.

[JAYA81] Jayant, N.S., and Christensen, S.W. (1981). Effects of packet losses on waveform-coded speech and improvements due to an odd-even interpolation procedure. *IEEE Transactions of Communications*, February.

[JOHN91] Johnson, J.T. (1991). Frame relay mux meets cell relay switch. *Data Communications*, October.

[JOHN92] Johnson, J.T. (1992). "Getting access to ATM. *Data Communications LAN Interconnect*, September 21.

[KING94] King, S.S. (1994). Switched virtual networks. *Data Communications*, September.

[KITA91] Kitawaki, N., and Itoh, K. (1991). Pure delay effects of speech quality in telecommunications. *IEEE Journal of Selected Areas in Communications*, May.

[LEE89] Lee, W.C.Y. (1989). *Mobile cellular telecommunications systems*. McGraw-Hill.

[LEE93] Lee, B.G., Kang, M., and Lee, J. (1993). *Broadband telecommunications technology*. Artech House.

[LISO91] Lisowski, B. (1991). Frame relay: what it is and how it works. *A Guide to Frame Relay, Supplement to Business Communications Review*, October.

[LIZZ94] Lizzio, J.R. (1994). Real-time RAID stokrage: the enabling technology for video-on-demand. *Telephony*, May 23.

[LYLE92] Lyles, J.B., and Swinehart, D.C. (1992). The emerging gigabit environment and the role of the local ATM. *IEEE Communications Magazine*, April.

[McCO94] McCoy, E. (1994). SONET, ATM and other broadband technologies. TRA Document # ATL72 16.9100, *Telecommunications Research Associates*, St. Marys, KS.

[MCQU91] McQuillan, J.M. (1991). Cell relay switching. *Data Communications*, September.

[MINO93] Minoli D. (1993). Proposed Cell Relay Bearer Service Stage 1 Description, T1S1.1/93-136 (Revision 1), ANSI Committee T1 (T1S1.1), June.

[MORE9] Moreney, J. (1994). ATM switch decision can wait, *Network World*, September 19.

[NOLL91] Nolle, T. (1991). Frame relay: Standards advance, *Business Communications Review*, October.

[NORT94] Northern Telecom. (1994). Consultant Bulletin 63020.16/02-94, Issue 1, February.

[[NYQU24] Nyquist, H. (1924). Certain factors affecting telegraph speed. *Transactions A.I.E.E.*

[PERL85] Perlman, R. (1985). An algorithm for distributed computation of spanning tree in an extended LAN. *Computer Communications Review, 15*(4) September.

[ROSE92] Rosenberry, W., Kenney D., and Fisher, G. (1992). *Understanding DCE.* O'Reilly & Associates.

[SALA92] Salamone, S. (1992). Sizing up the most critical issues. *Network World.*

[SAND94] Sandberg, J. (1994). Networking. *Wall Street Journal*, November 14.

[SHAN48] Shannon, C. (1948). Mathematical theory of communication, *Bell System Technical Journal, 27*, July and October.

[SRIR90a] Sriram, K. (1990a). Dynamic bandwidth allocation and congestion control schemes for voice and data integration in wideband packet technology, *Proc. IEEE. Supercomm/ICC '90, 3*, April.

[SRIR90b] Sriram, K. (1990b). Bandwidth allocation and congestion control scheme for an integrated voice and data network. *US Patent No. 4, 914650*, April 3.

[SRIR93a] Sriram, K. (1993). Methodologies for bandwidth allocation, transmission scheduling, and congestion avoidance in broadband ATM networks. *Computer Networks and ISDN Systems, 26*(1), September.

[SRIR93b] Sriram, K., and Lucantoni, D.M. (1993). Traffic smoothing effects of bit dropping in a packet voice multiplexer. *IEEE Transactions on Communications*, July.

[STEW92] Steward, S.P. (1992). The world report '92. *Cellular Business*, May.

[WADA89] Wada, M. (1989). Selective recovery of video packet loss using error concelment. *IEEE Journal of Selected Areas in Communications*, June.

[WALL91] Wallace, B. (1991). Citicorp goes SONET. *Network World*, November 18.

[WERK92] Wernik, M., Aboul-Magd, O., and Gilber, H. (1992). Traffic management for B-ISDN services. *IEEE Network*, September.

[WEST92] Westgate, J. (1992).*OSI Management*, NCC Blackwell.

[WILL92] Williamson, J. (1992). GSM bids for global recognition in a crowded cellular world. *Telephony*, April 6.

[WU93] Wu, T.-H. (1993). Cost-effective network evolution. *IEEE Communications Magazine*, September.

[YAP93] Yap, M.-T., and Hutchison (1993). An emulator for evaluating DQDB performance. *Computer Networks and ISDN Systems, 25*(11).

[YOKO93] Yokotani, T., Sato, H., and Nakatsuka, S. (1993). A study on a performance improvement algorithm in DQDB MAN. *Computer Networks and ISDN Systems, 25*(10).

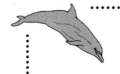
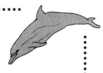

Index

ATM, Volume III

ISBN 0-13-784182-5

90000

9 780137 841820

Prentice Hall Series In
Advanced Communications Technologies

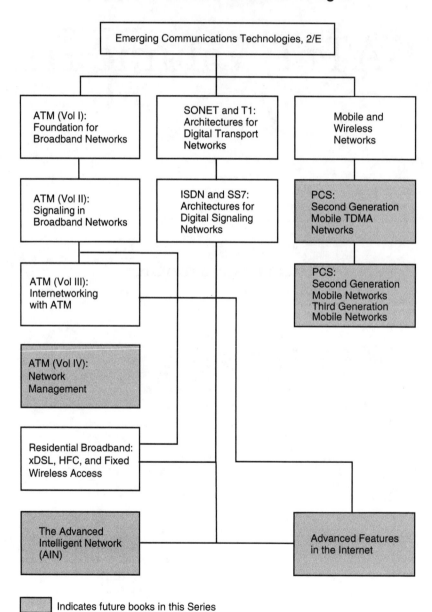

Emerging Communications Technologies, 2/E

ATM (Vol I):
Foundation for
Broadband Networks

SONET and T1:
Architectures for
Digital Transport
Networks

Mobile and
Wireless
Networks

ATM (Vol II):
Signaling in
Broadband Networks

ISDN and SS7:
Architectures for
Digital Signaling
Networks

PCS:
Second Generation
Mobile TDMA
Networks

ATM (Vol III):
Internetworking
with ATM

PCS:
Second Generation
Mobile Networks
Third Generation
Mobile Networks

ATM (Vol IV):
Network
Management

Residential Broadband:
xDSL, HFC, and Fixed
Wireless Access

The Advanced
Intelligent Network
(AIN)

Advanced Features
in the Internet

Indicates future books in this Series

ATM, Volume III
INTERNETWORKING
WITH ATM

UYLESS BLACK

To join a Prentice Hall PTR Internet mailing list, point to:
http://www.prenhall.com/mail_lists/

Prentice Hall PTR
Upper Saddle River, New Jersey 07458

Library of Congress Cataloging-in-Publication Data

Black, Uyless D.
   ATM—Vol.III: Internetworking with ATM / Uyless Black.
     p. cm.
   Includes bibliographical references and index.
   ISBN 0–13–784182–5
   1. Asynchronous transfer mode.   2. Broadband communication
systems. I Title.
   TK5105.35.B53   1995
   621.382—dc20   95–5961
                                          CIP

Acquisitions editor: Mary Franz
Cover designer: Scott Weiss
Cover design director: Jerry Votta
Manufacturing manager: Alexis R. Heydt
Marketing manager: Miles Williams
Compositor/Production services: Pine Tree Composition, Inc.

© 1998 by Uyless Black

 Published by Prentice Hall PTR
Prentice-Hall, Inc.
A Simon & Schuster Company
Upper Saddle River, New Jersey 07458

Prentice Hall books are widely-used by corporations and government agencies for training, marketing, and resale.

The publisher offers discounts on this book when ordered in bulk quantities. For more information contact:

        Corporate Sales Department
        Phone: 800–382–3419
        Fax: 201–236–7141
        E-mail: corpsales@prenhall.com

        Or write:

        Prentice Hall PTR
        Corp. Sales Dept.
        One Lake Street
        Upper Saddle River, New Jersey 07458

Printed in the United States of America
10 9 8 7 6 5 4

ISBN: 0-13-784182-5

Prentice-Hall International (UK) Limited, *London*
Prentice-Hall of Australia Pty. Limited, *Sydney*
Prentice-Hall Canada Inc., *Toronto*
Prentice-Hall Hispanoamericana, S.A., *Mexico*
Prentice-Hall of India Private Limited, *New Delhi*
Prentice-Hall of Japan, Inc., *Tokyo*
Simon & Schuster Asia Pte. Ltd., *Singapore*
Editora Prentice-Hall do Brasil, Ltda., *Rio de Janeiro*

During the writing of this book, I happened to attend my 40th high school class reunion, and re-renewed some fine friendships.

This book is dedicated to the Lovington, New Mexico High School class of 1957. This dedication is also to acknowledge those class members of '57 that I have known since my childhood, and who went through "all the grades" with me. I enjoyed seeing you again at the reunion.

This book has one other dedication. It is to our English teacher, Frances Campbell.

Any errors in grammar or paragraph composition in this book should be directed straight to Ms. Campbell, which is in order with the culture of the 1990s of blaming someone else for our shortfailings.

No, Ms. Campbell, I was kidding. Any semblance in this book to a logical and well-constructed composition, I owe largely to you (and your diagramming exercises).

The effective internetworking of computers, switches, routers, and bridges requires a great deal of cooperative interaction between these machines. In a sense, they must have some type of social structure in order for the networks that they create to be able to transport information. Since they may be in different geographical areas, perhaps far-apart from each other, a process called path discovery is executed between them in order to build an efficient route between the machines. Furthermore, the route, once learned, must be retained, and if necessary, updated to reflect changing conditions in the system.

In conducting research for the books in this series, and as part of my interest in nature, I have noticed the similarities of computer networks' behavior to that of creatures in the natural world. For this book, I have chosen the common ant as an analogy to computer networking.

Like computer networks, the ant's "social" behavior in building and maintaining their networks of colonies and nests is quite complex, one of the most elaborate in the insect world. But the scientists who study ants are not certain how the ants decide how to build (or abandon) some of these networks. Indeed, the communications between ants occurs through a perplexing combination of smell, taste, touch, and antennae movement.

One of the most fascinating aspects of computer networking is route discovery, and I have wondered how the ant performs this feat—how they know where their home base is, after wondering about in their foraging labors. Generally, the ant finds its way, largely by environmental clues. But on occasion, it operates like a first-generation route discovery protocol; not very efficient. For example, some ants use a process called light-compass orientation, and take their clues from the sun's angle to them. Try placing a box on top of an ant that is walking about. If the box is left over the ant for say an hour, and then removed, the ant will strike out in a different direction from its original course, by an angle equal to the number of degrees the sun moved during the ant's confinement. Well, not too impressive. Maybe something like looping packets through a network again-and-again.

One of the most remarkable attributes of ants is their prodigious strength. Some can lift a stone some 60 times their own weight. That impressive fact led me to use them for the cover of this book, symbolized by their carting-around Frame Relay, ATM, and other networks.

The ant is quite efficient; it does not waste much time hauling non-productive things to its colony. So, even though virtual networks are part of the subject matter of this book, I chose not to show this term on the cover. After all, no self-respecting ant would waste its time transporting something that doesn't exist.

Contents

CHAPTER 7   Introduction to LAN Emulation   114

**CHAPTER 8   Service Specification and Protocol Data Units
(PDUs)   139**

CHAPTER 9   **Configuration, Registration, and ARP Procedures and LNNI   157**

CHAPTER 10   **Next Hop Resolution Protocol (NHRP)   173**

Purpose of MPOA   186
    Advantages of L_3 Operations   186
Intra-Subnet and Inter-Subnet Operations   187
    Virtual Routing   190
MPOA Requirements   191
MPOA Cache   191
    Ingress Cache   191
    Egress Cache   191
MPOA Clients and Servers   192
    The MPC   193
The Use of Tags   195
MPOA Information Flows   195
Major MPOA Operations   197
Examples of MPOA Operations   197
    MPOA Host-to-MPOA Host   198
    Edge Device-to-MPOA Host   200
    Edge Device-to-Edge Device   200
Roles of MPS and MPC in More Detail   200
The MPOA Protocol Data Units (PDUS) Formats   204
Format and Syntax for the MPOA Messages   205
Other MPOA Operations   206   Summary   207

Appendix A **Basics of Internetworking   208**

Appendix B **Addressing Conventions   221**

Appendix C **Lane Parameters   227**

    Abbreviations   231
    Other References   234
    Index   239

Preface

This book is one in a collection of books titled Advanced Communications Technologies. It is also a companion to two Asynchronous Transfer Mode (ATM) books in this series, volumes I and II, titled *ATM: Foundation for Broadband Networks,* and *ATM: Signaling in Broadband Networks,* respectively.

This volume deals with a major issue in the industry: integrating the ATM technology into existing systems. The approach taken is called internetworking (or interworking): connecting ATM networks to existing systems. In so far as possible, the internetworking operations makes the presence of ATM transparent to the existing systems.

If ATM is to be successful, prominent technologies must be supported by ATM, or integrated into the ATM technology. Several of these technologies are discussed in this book. They are: (a) Frame Relay, (b) Ethernet and Token Ring local area networks, and (c) Internet Protocol (IP)-based internets and intranets.

Many issues surrounding the subject of ATM internetworking must be resolved, such as migration plans, deployment schedules, and acquisition decisions. Moreover, the tradeoffs of ATM vs. Fast Ethernet, and ATM vs. IPv6 (IP, version 6) are far from settled. In many network situations, these technologies provide attractive alternatives to ATM.

However, the majority of the technical issues pertaining to the internetworking of ATM to Frame Relay, Ethernet, Token Ring, and IP have been resolved, due to the work of the ATM Forum, the Frame Relay

Forum, several Internet Task Forces, and some of the formal standards bodies. It is this subject that this book addresses.

I hope you find this information useful, and this book a welcome addition to your library. I can be reached at:

102732.3535@compuserve.com.

1

Introduction

This chapter introduces ATM internetworking and describes why having ATM as part of an internetworking operation can provide benefits to an organization. Key internetworking concepts are explained, and ATM is compared to the major systems with which it may interwork.

REASONS FOR INTERNETWORKING

Internetworking is the sharing of computer resources by connecting the computers through a number of data communications networks. The networks can be public or private networks; they can be local or wide area networks. Perhaps the most common shared resources are the computing cycles on a machine and software, typically on some type of "server" computer. Common databases are also shared through internetworking.

Reasons for Internetworking with ATM

As just stated, internetworking allows the users of different networks to exchange information with each other. For this book, one of the networks is an ATM system. One might ask why an organization would want to add ATM to the internetworking picture.

First, the deployment of ATM to support other networks is consistent with the trend toward increased use of ATM in multiservice (voice, data, video) networks. Second, carriers and service providers can accommodate the continuing growth of Frame Relay and LAN services (as two examples) and the more modest growth of ATM services. Third, carriers and service providers can support the trend toward service consolidation at the customer premises. Fourth, ATM offers high-speed trunks that permit the negotiation of quality of service (QOS) features, such as delay, throughput, and peak burst rate. These features are not supported by most other technologies.

Internetworking also permits the distribution of resources—an important element in load leveling and backup operations. Indeed, distributed processing is made possible through internetworking.

TERMS AND DEFINITIONS

Internetworking and Interworking

The term *internetworking (or interworking) unit (IWU)* is used to describe a machine that performs relaying functions between networks. Other terms are explained shortly.[1]

The networks are often called *subnetworks*. The term does not mean that they provide fewer functions than a conventional network. Rather, it means that the subnetworks contribute to the overall operations for internetworking. Stated another way, subnetworks comprise an internetwork or an internet.

An internetworking unit is designed to remain transparent to the end user application. Typically, the end user application resides in the host machines connected to the networks; rarely are user applications placed in the IWU. This approach is attractive from several standpoints. First, the IWU need not burden itself with application layer protocols. Since they are not invoked at the IWU, the IWU can dedicate itself to fewer tasks, such as managing the traffic between networks. It is not concerned with application layer functions such as database access, electronic mail, and file management.

---

[1]The terms internetworking and interworking are used to describe the relaying of traffic between networks. Some specifications use one term; other specifications use the other. They are synonymous and this book uses both terms.

L_2 and L_3 Protocol Data Units (PDUs)

This book uses the notation L_2 to describe a layer 2 protocol, also known as a data link layer protocol. The notation L_3 describes a layer 3 protocol operating at the network layer. The network layer is also called the internetwork(ing) layer in many of the Internet and ATM Forum specifications.

Also, the term *PDU* (for protocol data unit) describes the unit of traffic sent across the communications link. Some of the standards and specifications discussed in this book use other terms in place of PDU, such as packet, message, or frame.

This book equates a *frame* to either a L_1 (physical layer) PDU or a L_2 PDU. It equates a *datagram* to a connectionless L_3 PDU, and a *packet* to a connection-oriented L_3 PDU.

The term *message* is used generally to describe any type of PDU. The term *cell* is used exclusively for the ATM PDU. The term *segment* will describe a L_4 PDU (notably a TCP or UDP segment). A *fragment* will describe any type of PDU that has been broken up into smaller PDUs.

Addresses[2] and Virtual Circuit Identifiers

Whether a PDU is a cell, datagram, or frame, it must have some type of an identifier in its header in order for the IWU to relay it to the correct destination. This identifier also distinguishes the PDU from PDUs associated with different end-to-end data flows.

Two types of identifiers are used in most computer-based networks: an address and a virtual circuit identifier (ID). An address has (or can be made to have) geographical significance and hence is inherently routable. Examples are a telephone number (area code and exchange code) and the IP address (a network and subnetwork identifier). Virtual circuit IDs are simply labels attached to the PDU to uniquely identify one PDU from another. The virtual circuit ID is not inherently routable, but the common practice is to construct routing tables (usually called cross-connect tables) in the IWU for the purpose of using the virtual circuit ID for just that—routing.

Why have two identifiers? Simply put, it comes down to a difference in opinion on how to identify traffic. It is also a result of how the industry and different network technologies evolved over the past twenty-five years.

---

[2]Appendix B provides a description of the addresses commonly used in the industry.

Routing and Switching

Currently in vogue is the debate on the difference between routing and switching. Here are some definitions:

- Routing is performed in software while switching is performed in hardware.
- Routing uses addresses while switching uses virtual circuit IDs.

These definitions are clouded by two terms: IP switching and tag switching. Vendors/operators vary on their definitions of these two terms.

IP switching is the use of fast processors to relay IP datagrams and uses a mix of hardware and software, but it is designed to reduce the latency in processing the IP datagram through the IWU. Tag switching uses a label to assist in processing the PDU at the IWU. Indeed, the label may be a virtual circuit ID. Therefore, in IP-based systems, tag switching is a form of IP switching.

Specific Terms for the Virtual Circuit ID

A rose by any other name is still a rose and a virtual circuit ID by any other name is still a virtual circuit ID. Here are the terms used in the industry:

- ATM   Virtual path ID (VPI)/virtual channel ID (VCI)
- Frame Relay   Data link connection ID (DLCI)
- X.25   Logical channel number (LCI)

Correlating Addresses and Virtual Circuit IDs

In several of the networks discussed in this book, both addressing and virtual circuit IDs are used. A common practice in ATM is to set up a connection first, by using a source and destination address; second, during the connection setup process, associating these addresses with a VPI/VCI; and third, constructing appropriate entries in the cross-connect table. Thereafter, high-speed switching can take place by using the short VPI/VCI instead of a lengthy, cumbersome address.

ATM INTERNETWORKING EXAMPLES

Figure 1–1 shows the relationship of the an ATM internetworking interface to other interfaces and protocols. All these technologies, as well

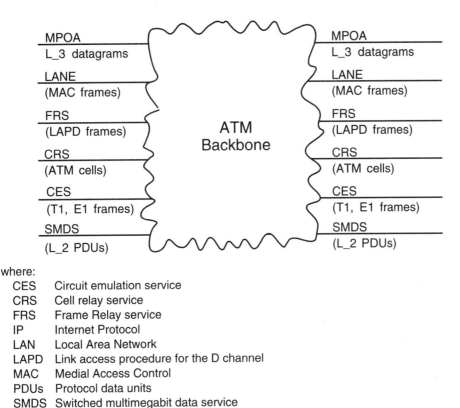

where:

CES	Circuit emulation service
CRS	Cell relay service
FRS	Frame Relay service
IP	Internet Protocol
LAN	Local Area Network
LAPD	Link access procedure for the D channel
MAC	Medial Access Control
PDUs	Protocol data units
SMDS	Switched multimegabit data service

Figure 1–1   ATM internetworking examples.

as ATM, provide for the user-to-network interface, which is called either a UNI, or a subscriber-to-network (SNI).[3]

Traffic can be submitted to a network in ATM cells, E1/T1 frames, LAN frames, Frame Relay frames, or SMDS (PDUs). This traffic is sent across the interface in the form of (1) ATM cells over ATM connections; (2) E1/T1 frames (CES), which are encapsulated into AAL type 1 PDUs; (3) Frame Relay frames, which are encapsulated into AAL type 5 PDUs and mapped into ATM cells; (4) SMDS PDUs, which are encapsulated into AAL type 3/4 PDUs and mapped into ATM cells, or LAN frames which are encapsulated into AAL5 PDUs and ATM cells. The LAN frames typically carry IP or IPX datagrams.

The ATM backbone has considerable functionality. It contains interworking units, which transmit and receive traffic from different systems.

---

[3]Internetworking ATM and T1 (CES) and ATM and SMDS are covered in Volume I of this series.

The term gateway is sometimes used to describe this function. This aspect of ATM is in keeping with ATM's design to support multiservice traffic.

Frame Relay frames can be encapsulated into AAL type 5 PDUs and the Frame Relay data link connection identifier (DLCI) is sent through the networks and translated at the receiving Frame Relay interface. Alternately, if frames are mapped to the ATM layer, a DLCI must be translated into an ATM VPI/VCI. Finally, SMDS PDUs can be encapsulated into AAL type 3/4 PDUs.

Through a process called LAN Emulation (LANE), ATM can act as a backbone to multiple LANs. In effect, the ATM nodes emulate bridges because they process LAN frames and the MAC addresses in the frames. Finally, with Multiprotocol Over ATM (MPOA) network layer traffic (IP, IPX) can be passed to/from the ATM backbone.

COMPARISON OF ATM AND FRAME RELAY

While we assume that the reader is familiar with Frame Relay and ATM operations, it is a good idea to pause briefly and compare some of the major attributes of these two technologies. Table 1–1 makes such a comparison. It consists of three columns: the first column is labeled attribute, which describes the characteristics (attributes) of the technology in a short phrase; the next two columns, labeled Frame Relay and ATM, describe how these technologies use or do not use the attribute. Further comparisons for these technologies is available in the flagship book for this series, *Emerging Communications Technologies,* second edition.

The ATM and Frame Relay Headers

Figure 1–2 illustrates the headers for Frame Relay and ATM. They are more alike than different, in that each contains a virtual circuit id, which is called the data link connection identifier (DLCI) in Frame Relay and the virtual path identifier/virtual channel identifier (VPI/VCI) in ATM. Both contain bits to allow the traffic to be tagged in the event of problems; for Frame Relay this is called the discard eligibility (DE) bit and for ATM it is called cell loss priority (CLP).

Both technologies provide for congestion notification. For Frame Relay this feature is provided in the forward explicit congestion notification (FECN) and the backward explicit congestion notification (BECN) bits. For ATM, this feature is provided in the bits residing in the payload type identifier (PTI), which is known generically as congestion notifica-

Table 1–1   Major Attributes of Frame Relay and ATM

Attribute	Frame Relay	ATM
Application support?	Asynchronous data (with voice gaining in use [but not designed for voice])	Asynchronous, synchronous voice, video, data
Connection mode?	Connection-oriented	Connection-oriented
Congestion management?	Yes, congestion notification, traffic tagging (DE bit), and possible traffic discard	Yes, congestion notification, traffic tagging (CLP bit), and possible traffic discard
Method of identifying traffic?	Virtual circuit id: the DLCI	Virtual circuit id: The VPI/VCI
PVCs?	Yes	Yes
SVCs (connections on demand)?	Yes	Yes
Congestion notification technique?	The FECN and BECN bits	The CN bits in the PTI field
Traffic tagging technique?	The discard eligibility (DE) bit	The cell loss priority (CLP) bit
LAN or WAN technology?	WAN based	Either
PDU size?	Variable (PDU is called a frame)	Fixed at 53 bytes (PDU is called a cell)
Sequencing of traffic?	No	Cell header, no; for AAL payload, depends on AAL type
ACKs/NAKs retransmissions?	No	Only for signaling traffic on SVCs

BECN	Backward explicit congestion notification
CLP	Cell loss priority
DE	Discard eligibility
DLCI	Data link connection identifier
FECN	Forward explicit congestion notification
LAN	Local area network
PDU	Protocol data unit
SVC	Switched virtual call
VCI	Virtual channel identifier
VPI	Virtual path identifier
WAN	Wide area network

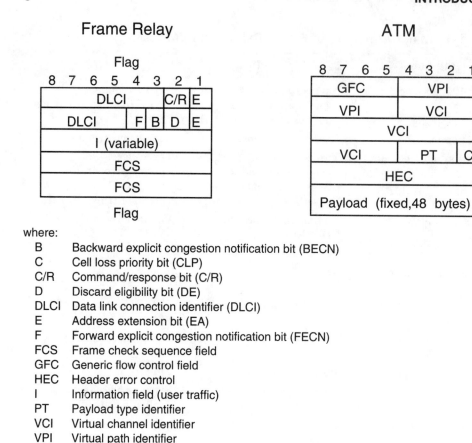

Figure 1–2   The Frame Relay and ATM headers.

tion. ATM provides no mechanism for identifying forward or backward congestion notification with these bits.

Figure 1–2 provides other information that is pertinent to this discussion. Notice that the Frame Relay header is actually embedded into another protocol data unit (PDU), which is considered part of the overall Frame Relay header and trailer (protocol control information [PCI]). This PCI is nothing more than flags that are used to delineate the beginning and ending of traffic, and the frame check sequence field (FCS) is used to perform an error check at the receiver to determine if the information between the flags were damaged while in transit.

In contrast, ATM does not contain flag-type fields and its error checking is performed with the fifth byte of the header, called the header error correction (HEC) field. This field error corrects any one-bit error in the header and will detect most others. But it operates differently from the Frame Relay FCS field in that it performs forward error correction. The Frame Relay FCS only does error detection and not error correction.

COMPARISON OF ATM AND LAN TECHNOLOGIES

While we also assume that the reader is somewhat familiar with LAN and ATM operations, it is a good idea to pause briefly and compare some of the major attributes of these technologies. Table 1–2 makes such a comparison. It consists of four columns: The first column is labeled attribute and describes the characteristics (attributes) of the technology in a short phrase; the next four columns, labeled Ethernet, IEEE 802.3, IEEE 802.5, and ATM, describe how these technologies use or do not use the attribute. For ease of reference, I include the ATM information that is also in Table 1–1.

One key concept to note in this table is that LANs are connectionless and ATM is connection-oriented. LANs do not create connections with each other; they send and receive traffic without regard to a connection setup. In contrast, ATM is connection-oriented and sets up virtual circuits before sending traffic.

Additionally, ATM nodes are identified with an ATM address, and LAN nodes are identified with the 48-bit MAC address. This aspect—different addresses—means an IWU must be able to map or correlate these addresses in an ATM/LAN interworking operation. This operation is called address resolution and is one of the principal subjects of this book. It is introduced in Chapter 2, and explained further in sebsequent chapters.

Notice also that LANs do not provide much in the way of value-added services, such as sequencing, congestion notifications, and so on; whereas, ATM provides for a number of these services.

Also, notice the attribute "Encapsulation header." It too is a major part of this book and is explained in Chapter 2.

COMPARISON OF ATM AND IP

To complete the comparisons of the technologies discussed in this book, Table 1–3 compares the major features of IP and ATM. The ATM column in Tables 1–1 and 1–2 is repeated for the convenience of the reader.

Once again, the different technologies use different identifiers ("method of identifying traffic") and different encapsulation headers ("Encapsulation header"). These features are also explained in Chapter 2.

Table 1–2 Comparisons of ATM and LAN Technologies

Attribute	Ethernet	IEEE 802.3	IEEE 802.5	ATM
Application support?	Asynchronous data (with some voice, but not designed for voice)	Asynchronous data (with some voice [but not designed for voice])	Asynchronous data	Asynchronous, synchronous voice, video, data
Connection mode?	Connectionless	Connectionless	Connectionless	Connection-oriented
Congestion management?	Collision detection	Collision detection	Priority (8 levels), and the passing of a token	Congestion notification, traffic tagging (CLP bit), and possibly traffic discard
Method of identifying traffic?	48-bit MAC address	48-bit MAC address	48-bit MAC address	Virtual circuit id: The VPI/VCI and an ATM address during connection setup
Congestion notification technique?	None	None	None	The CN bits in the PTI field
Traffic tagging technique?	None	None	None	The cell loss priority (CLP) bit
PDU size?	Variable	Variable	Variable	Fixed at 53 bytes (PDU is called a cell)
Sequencing of traffic?	No	No	No	Cell header, no; for payload, depends on payload type
Encapsulation header?	Yes, Ethertype	Yes, LLC header	Yes, LLC header	Typically LLC header
ACKs/NAKs/ retrans-missions?	No	No	No	Only for signaling traffic (SVCs)

CLP	Cell loss priority	MAC	Media access control	
CN	Congestion notification	PDU	Protocol data unit	
DE	Discard eligibility	SVC	Switch virtual calls	
LAN	Local area network	VCI	Virtual channel identifier	
LLC	Logical link control	VPI	Virtual path identifier	

Table 1–3   Comparisons of IP and ATM Technologies

Attribute	IP	ATM
Application support?	Asynchronous data (with some voice and video, but not so designed)	Asynchronous, synchronous voice, video, data
Connection mode?	Connectionless	Connection-oriented
Congestion management?	None	Congestion notification, traffic tagging (CLP bit), and possibly traffic discard
Method of identifying traffic?	32-bit IP address	Virtual circuit id: The VPI/VCI and an ATM address
Congestion notification technique?	None	The CN bits in the PTI field
Traffic tagging technique?	None	The cell loss priority (CLP) bit
PDU size?	Variable	Fixed at 53 bytes (PDU is called a cell)
Sequencing of traffic?	No	Cell header, no; for payload, depends on payload type
Encapsulation header?	Yes, IP Protocol ID (IP PID)	Typically LLC header
ACKs/NAKs/ retransmissions?	No	Only for signaling traffic (SVCs)

CONVENTIONS FOR ATM INTERFACES AND DATA UNITS

Figure 1–3 shows the conventions for the ATM and AAL layers, as well as the placement of service access points (SAPs) and the naming conventions. This information is discussed in more detail in Volume I of this series, but we revisit SAPs in Chapter 2.

Figure 1–3 is largely self-explanatory. It can be seen that the naming conventions follow the OSI conventions and use the concepts of service data units (SDUs), protocol data units (PDUs), primitives, encapsulation, decapsulation, and protocol control information (PCIs).

The AAL type 5 structure contains the convergence sublayer, which is divided into the common part convergence sublayer (CPCS) and the service specific convergence sublayer (SSCS) and is shown in Figure 1–4. The SSCS is used to support different user applications, and thus, multiple

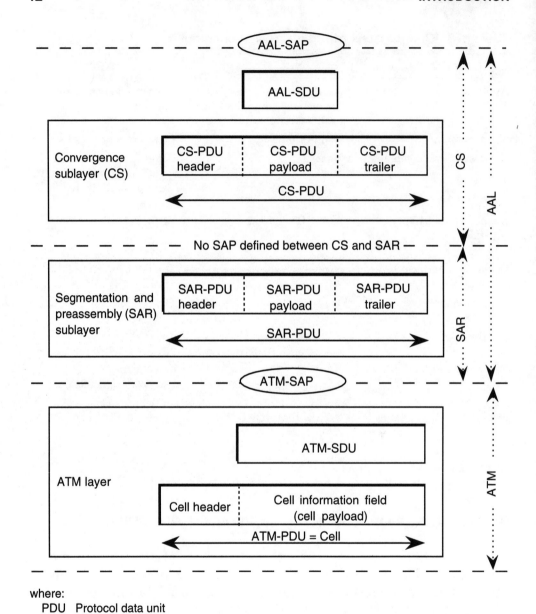

Figure 1–3   AAL general data unit conventions.

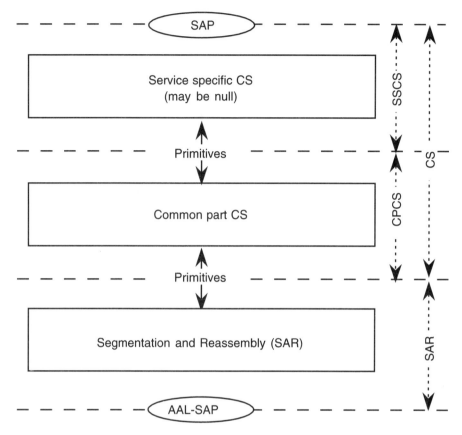

Figure 1–4 The AAL 5 structure.

SSCSs may exist. The SSCS may be null if it is not needed. In this case, it is used only to map primitives of the user upper layer to/from CPCS.

SUMMARY

Internetworking allows the users of different networks to exchange information with each other, and the deployment of ATM backbones to support other networks is consistent with the trend toward the increased use of ATM.

Carriers and service providers can accommodate the continuing growth of Frame Relay, LAN, and Internet services and integrate ATM features at the same time. ATM offers high-speed trunks that permit the negotiation of quality of service (QOS) features, such as delay, throughput, and peak burst rate features that most other technologies do not offer.

2

Encapsulation and Address Mapping Operations

This chapter describes the works of the standards bodies that have published a number of specifications defining (a) how traffic from different networks is transported through another network (for example, an ATM network), and (b) how the header in the PDUs of these different networks is (or is not) translated into the transporting network header.

This chapter also explains how MAC L_2 addresses, IP L_3 addresses, Frame Relay addresses, ATM addresses, and ATM/Frame Relay virtual circuit IDs are correlated with each other through address resolution protocols.

Some of the specifications that are examined in this chapter are generic, in that they do not define ATM per se. We will examine these specifications from the generic standpoint, as well as how they are used in ATM networks.

ENCAPSULATION CONCEPTS

The term encapsulation refers to an operation in which a transport (backbone) network, such as Ethernet, ATM, or Frame Relay, carries traffic (PDUs) from other protocols through the transport network. The other protocols could be IP, AppleTalk, SNA, DECnet, and so on that operate at the upper layers of the OSI layered model, typically at layer 3 and above. The transport network performs lower layer bearer services, typically at layers 1 and 2, and perhaps layer 3 of the model (but not always . . . nothing is simple in internetworking . . .).[1]

If possible, the transport network does not become involved with either the syntax or the format of the transported traffic. The term encapsulation refers to the notion of the interworking unit (say, a router) "wrapping" the *transport* PDU around the *user* SDU, without consideration to its contents.

Some people use the terms encapsulation and tunneling synonymously. Others use the term tunneling to describe the notion of sending traffic (say a car) through a "tunnel," and periodically stopping the car, rolling down the windows of the car and checking the contents in the passenger space. In other words, some definitions of tunneling suggest that the contents of the PDU may be examined during the transport operations. In this book, I will use the term encapsulation to describe both of these concepts.

To invoke encapsulation operations, the user must furnish the network with a specific identifier to distinguish the type of traffic that is to be sent through the transport network. This identifier is important, because the IWU and the receiving user machine must invoke support procedures that apply to the specific type of traffic; that is, a specific protocol family, such as X.25, IP, or SNA. After all, an IWU, such as a router, cannot process the PDU until it knows the type of PDU, such as its header contents and syntax.

These identifiers are depicted in Figure 2–1. They are known by various names, and vary in how they are used. They are examined in the next section of this chapter.

As we examine these encapsulation identifiers, keep in mind that some of them perform the same functions, and indeed are redundant. The reason that overlapping identifiers exist is that they have been developed by different standards groups and have evolved and changed over time.

Anyway, after each of these identifiers are examined, we will then learn about the overlaps of their functions, and how this overlap is handled in ATM encapsulations.

---

[1]Bearer services is a term used by most standards bodies to describe the basic telecommunications services that are available to the user of a network. They support services such as throughput (in bit/s) and delay (in ms).

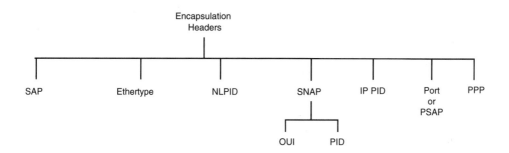

where:
IP PID   IP Protocol ID
NLPID   Network level protocol ID
OUI   Organization unique ID
PID   Protocol ID
PPP   Point-to-Point Protocol
PSAP   Presentation layer SAP
SAP   Service access point
SNAP   Subnetwork access protocol

Figure 2–1   Options for encapsulation headers.

SERVICE ACCESS POINTS (SAPS)

In most systems, the services invoked at a layer are requested by the upper layers passing primitives (transactions) to the next lower layer. The primitives are usually coded into program function calls or system library calls and are used to identify the type of service needed, such as a connection or the transfer of traffic over the connection. Services are provided from the lower layer to the upper layer through a service access point (SAP). The SAP is an identifier. It identifies the entity or process in (say) layer $N - 1$ that is performing the service(s) for layer N (see Figure 2–2).

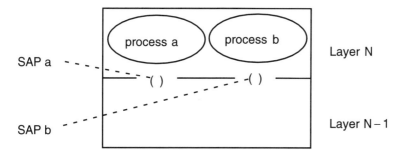

Figure 2–2   OSI service access points (SAPs).

An entity in machine A can invoke some services in machine B through the use of SAPs. For example, a user that sends traffic can identify itself with a source SAP id (SSAP). It identifies the recipient of the traffic with a destination SAP value (DSAP).

Some people view the SAP as a software "port." It is akin to the socket concept found in the UNIX operating system environment. In Figure 2–2, SAP a identifies a process (process a) in layer N, and SAP b identifies another process (process b). Examples of processes and their associated processes are (1) a signaling module, such as ATM's Q.2931, (2) a route discovery module, such as the Intermediate System-to-Intermediate System (IS-IS) protocol, and (3) the Connectionless Network Layer Protocol (CLNP).

LLC and LSAPs

The IEEE 802 LAN standards require the use of Link SAPs (LSAPs). As shown in Figure 2–3, an LSAP identifies the entity that resides above logical link control (LLC). Likewise, a MAC SAP (MSAP) identifies a particular LSAP entity operating above MAC, and a physical layer SAP (PLSAP) identifies a process operating above the physical layer (in the MAC layer).

In many installations, the PLSAPs and MSAPs are not employed. However, the LSAP is a common tool used by many vendors to provide interfaces into and out of LLC from the vendor network layer entities

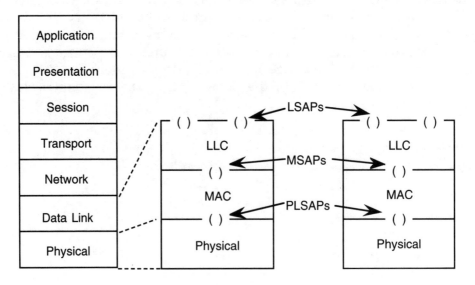

Figure 2–3   The SAPs.

such as IP, CLNP, and so on. In effect, the LSAP performs the same function as Ethertype, discussed next.

ETHERTYPE (TYPE)

The Ethertype (also called type or protocol type) field in an Ethernet frame is used to identify different protocols that are running on the Ethernet network (see Figure 2–4). Well-known protocols are registered and given a reserved value. As examples, IP is Ethertype = 0x0800, X.25 = 0x0805, ARP = 0x0806, RARP = 0x0835, AppleTalk = 0x8098, ect.

SUBNETWORK ACCESS PROTOCOL (SNAP)

Due to the separate evolution of the Ethernet, TCP/IP, and IEEE LAN standards, it has been necessary to define additional procedures to provide guidance on the use of IP datagrams over Ethernet and IEEE networks. Figure 2–5 shows the approach specified by RFC 1042 (A Standard for the Transmission of IP Datagrams over IEEE 802 Networks). RFC 1042 defines an extension to the LLC header, called the Subnetwork Access Protocol (SNAP).

The LLC destination and source service access points (DSAP and SSAP, respectively) are each set to a decimal value of 170 (0xAA). The LLC control field is not affected by this standard. This control field is

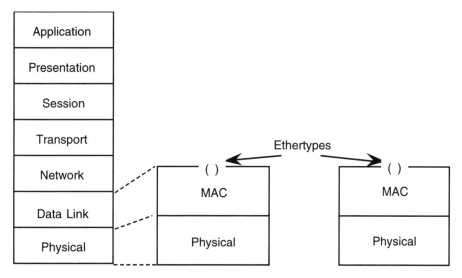

Figure 2–4   The Ethertype field.

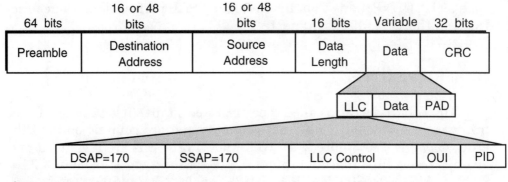

Figure 2–5   The Subnetwork Access Protocol (SNAP) format (RFC 1042).

based on the L_2 protocol, High Level Data Link Control (HDLC). In most LLC systems, this field is coded as 0x03 to identify an LLC type 1 PDU, which is an HDLC unnumbered information (UI) control field.

The SNAP control field identifies an organization unique ID (OUI) and a specific protocol ID (PID). Thereafter, the Ethertype field is often coded to describe the type of protocol running on the LAN. The Ethertype field is coded in accordance with the standard conventions. This figure shows the convention for coding the LSAP values (i.e., 170) for the SNAP convention.

The SNAP OUI and PID contents can vary, depending upon the technology using SNAP. For example, the original RFC 1042 sets OUI to 0 to indicate the PID is an ethertype value, but other implementations of SNAP use the field to identify how the field is employed, such as the enterprise or technology that is using the code for its own purposes. Many examples are provided in this book on the use of the SNAP OUI and PID.

ISO/IEC TR 9577 (NETWORK LEVEL PROTOCOL IDENTIFIER [NLPID])

The network level protocol identifier (NLPID) contains values to identify common protocols that are used in the industry, such as Connectionless Network Layer Protocol (CLNP), X.25, ect. It is administered by the International Standards Organization (ISO). The purpose of this field is to inform the receiver which protocol is being carried inside the transporting PDU frame.

The reader can obtain ISO/IEC TR 9577 for the values that are currently administered by the ISO. Examples of NLPIDs values are as follows. Note the provision for the use of the SNAP header (0x80), and IP(0xCC).

0x00 Null network layer
0x80 IEEE SNAP
0x81 ISO CLNP
0x82ISO ES-IS
0x83 ISO IS-IS
0xCC IP
0x08ISDN Q.933

EXAMPLES OF JOINT USE OF NLPID AND SNAP

Some protocols do not have an assigned NLPID. In this situation, the subnetwork access protocol (SNAP) header can be used, and the NLPID is set to indicate that a SNAP header is present. Figure 2–6

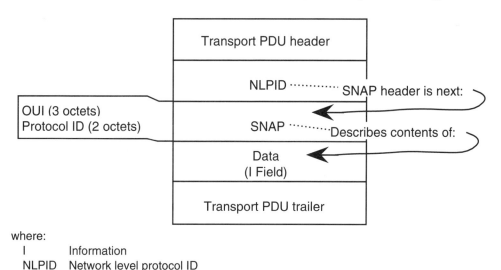

where:
I   Information
NLPID Network level protocol ID
OUI   Organization unique ID
SNAP   Subnetwork access protocol

Figure 2–6   Use of the NLPID and SNAP headers.

shows the PDU for this approach. If the SNAP header is used, it is placed into the PDU immediately following the NLPID field.

IP PROTOCOL ID

The IP protocol field (IP PID) resides in the IP datagram header (a layer 3 header) and is used to identify the next protocol beyond IP that is to receive the IP datagram (see Figure 2–7). It is similar in function to the Ethertype field found in the Ethernet frame, but identifies the "next" entity beyond IP that is to receive and process the traffic, whereas Ethertype identifies an entity such as IP. The Internet standards groups have established a numbering system to identify widely used upper-layer protocols. As examples, TCP is 6 and UDP is 17.

The IP PID may also indicate the presence of another layer 3 header, in which case, the traffic is passed to it. For example, the Open Shortest Path First (OSPF) is a layer 3 protocol, and OSPF PDUs are transported through an internet with IP headers. At the receiving OSPF entity, the IP PID is used to pass the OSPF PDU to the OSPF module.

PORTS/PSAPS

Yet another encapsulation header is a port (an Internet term) or a presentation layer SAP (PSAP, an OSI term). This value is used to iden-

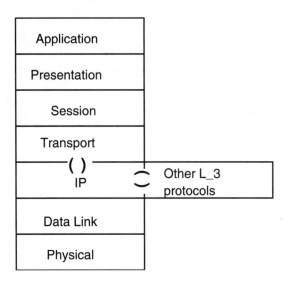

Figure 2–7   The IP protocol ID.

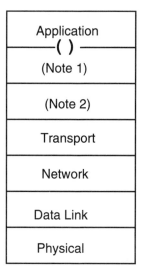

Application
─( )─
(Note 1)
(Note 2)
Transport
Network
Data Link
Physical

Note 1: For OSI, the presentation layer. For Internet, TCP, or UDP.
Note 2: For OSI, the session layer. For Internet, session layer not used.

Figure 2–8   The Port.

tify a process residing in the application layer (layer 7) of the conventional layered model.

The port operation is used more often than the PSAP, because it is part of the Internet protocol stack. Figure 2–8 shows that the layer under layer 7 uses the port number to identify the next (and last) process to receive the traffic.

The Internet reserves ports 1–1023 for common layer 7 protocols with "well-known ports". Some examples are: Telnet = 23, FTP = 20 and 21, and Domain Name System = 53.

THE POINT-TO-POINT PROTOCOL (PPP)

The Point-to-Point protocol (PPP) was implemented to solve a problem that evolved in the industry during the last decade. With the rapid growth of internetworking, several vendors and standards organizations developed a number of network layer protocols. The Internet Protocol (IP) is the most widely used of these protocols. However, machines (such as routers) typically run more than one network layer protocol. While IP is a given on most machines, routers also support network layer protocols developed by companies such as Xerox, 3Com, IBM, etc. Machines communicating with each other did not know which network layer protocols were available during a session.

In addition, until the advent of PPP, the industry did not have a standard means to define a point-to-point encapsulation protocol. The PPP standard solves these two problems.

PPP is used to encapsulate network layer datagrams over a serial communications link. The protocol allows two machines on a point-to-point communications channel to negotiate the particular types of network layer protocols (such as IP) that are to be used during a session. It also allows the two machines to negotiate other types of operations, such as the use of compression and authentication procedures. After this negotiation occurs, PPP is used to carry the network layer protocol data units (PDUs) in the I field of an HDLC-type frame.

This protocol supports either bit-oriented synchronous transmission, byte-oriented, or asynchronous (start/stop) transmission. It can be used on switched or dial-up links. It requires a full duplex capability.

PPP Layered Architecture

As shown in Figure 2-9, PPP operates over the High Level Data Link Control protocol (HDLC), and consists of two major protocols, explained in the following material.

The Link Control Protocol (LCP) is the first procedure that is executed when a PPP link is set up. It defines the operations for configuring the link, and for the negotiation of options. As part of LCP, another procedure, the authentication option (AUTH), can be invoked to validate the users of the PPP connnection.

In addition, PPP uses the Network Control Protocol (NCP) to negotiate certain options and parameters that will be used by a L_3 protocol. The IPCP (The IP Control Protocol) is an example of an specific NCP, and is used to negotiate various IP parameters, such as IP addresses, compression, etc.

The PPP PDU uses the HDLC frame as stipulated in ISO 3309-1979 (and amended by ISO 3309-1984/PDAD1). Figure 2-10 shows this format. The flag sequence is the standard HDLC flag of 01111110 (Hex 7E), the address field is set to all 1s (Hex FF) which signifies an all stations address. PPP does not use individual station addresses because it is a point-to-point protocol. The control field is set to identify a HDLC unnumbered information (UI) command. Its value is 00000011 (Hex 03).

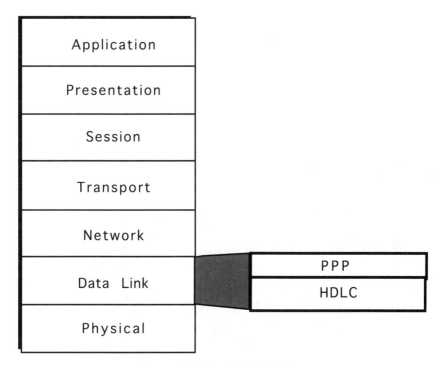

Figure 2-9.The PPP Entities

The protocol field is used to identify the PDU that is encapsulated into the I field of the frame. The field values are assigned by the Internet, and the values beginning with a 0 identify the network protocol that resided in the I field. Values beginning with 8 identify a control protocol that is used to negotiate the protocols that will actually be used.

The PPP frame I field is used to carry the link control protocol packet. The protocol field in the frame must contain hex C021 to indicate the I field carries link control protocol information. The format for the field is shown in this figure. The code field must be coded to identify the type of LCP packet that is encapsulated into the frame. As examples, the code would indicate if the frame contains a configure request, which would likely be followed by a configure ACK or NAK. Additionally, the code could indicate (for example) an echo request data unit. Naturally, the next frame would probably identify the echo reply. Each of the packets discussed in the previous section are described with codes.

The identifier field is a value that is used to match requests and replies to each other. The length field defines the length of the packet which includes code, identifier, and data fields. The data field values are determined on the contents of the code field.

The NCP identifiers are numbered 8000-BFFF, and 8021 is assigned to the IPCP. Another set of numbers identifies the specific protocol, and 0021 is used of the IP traffic.

The rule for using these numbers is that the L_3 identifiers are the same as negotiation identifiers, less 8000.

LCP was introduced briefly earlier in this discussion. To iterate, its purpose is to support the establishment of the connection and to allow for certain configuration options to be negotiated. The protocol also main-

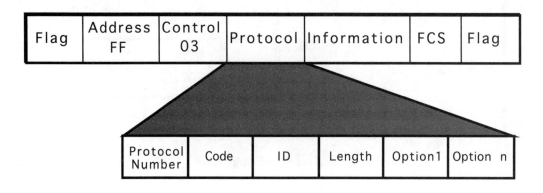

Figure 2-10. The PPP Frame Format

tains the connection and provides procedures for terminating the connection. In order to perform these functions, LCP is organized into three phases:

PPP requires that LCP be executed to open the connection between two stations before any network layer traffic is exchanged. This requires a series of packet exchanges which are called configure packets. After these packets have been exchanged and a configure acknowledge packet has been sent and received between the stations, the connection is considered to be in an open state and the exchange of datagrams can begin. LCP confines itself only to link operations. It does not understand how to negotiate the implementation of network layer protocols. Indeed, it does not care about the upper layer negotiations relating to the network protocols.

Link quality determination is optional and allows LCP to check to see if the link is of sufficient quality to actually bring up the network layer. Although the link quality determination phase is defined in the standard, the actual implementation procedures are not specified. This tool exists to provide an LCP echo request and an LCP echo-type packet. These packets are defined within the protocol and exist within the state transition tables of the protocol. The user should simply realize that how they are implemented is not defined in the standard.

After the link establishment (and if the link quality determination phase is implemented), the protocol configuration allows the two stations to negotiate/configure the protocols that will be used at the network layer. This is performed by the appropriate network control protocol (NCP). The particular protocol that is used here depends on which family of NCPs is implemented.

LCP is also responsible for terminating the link connection. It is allowed to perform the termination at its discretion. Unless problems have occurred which creates this event, the link termination is usually provided by a upper layer protocol or a user-operated network control center.

Figure 2-11 shows an example of how PPP can be used to support network configuration operations. Routers, hosts, etc. exchange the PPP frames to determine which network layer protocols are supported. In this example, two machines negotiate the use of the Internet Protocol (IP) and its OSI counterpart, ISO 8473, the Connectionless Network Protocol (CLNP). The LCP operations are invoked first to setup and test the link. Next NCP operations are invoked to negotiate which network protocols (and associated procedures) are to be used between the machines. After this negotiation is complete, datagrams are exchanged. At any point, either node can terminate the session.

PUTTING IT ALL TOGETHER

As stated earlier, some of these encapsulation headers perform the same functions. We will use Figure 2–12 to explain these redundancies and the overall relationships of the encapsulation headers. The figure illustrates the layered architecture for an internet system that operates with five layers of the conventional OSI Model. The layers are listed in the legend to the figure. User traffic is sent through the layers, as illustrated on the left side of the figure, from the sending side and is

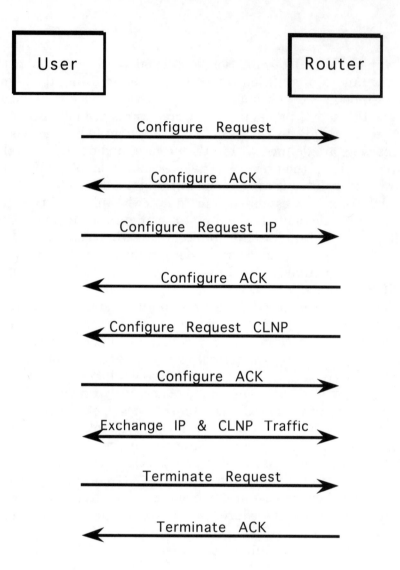

Figure 2-11. Example of PPP Operations

processed through the receiving protocol stack, which is illustrated on the right side of the figure.

The sending side performs conventional encapsulation functions by placing protocol control information (PCI) (headers and/or trailers) around the data unit that it is processing. At the receiving side, conventional decapsulation operations are performed with the PCI stripped away at the respective layer and processed by an identified entity in the layer. The bottom part of Figure 2–12 shows how the traffic is trans-

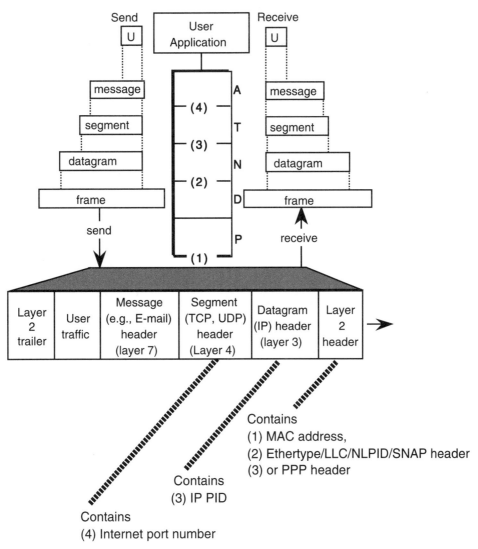

Figure 2–12   The encapsulation headers.

ported across the communications link in relation to the position of the headers and trailers.

The previous paragraph stated that an identified entity in a layer processes its respective header and that is the purpose of the encapsulation header: identify that entity. This idea is illustrated in Figure 2–12 with the use of the numbered notations (1), (2), (3), and (4). They are placed at the layer boundaries to symbolize where the interpretation of each encapsulation header is performed. Also notice that these numbers identify the specific encapsulation headers shown at the bottom of the figure. For the encapsulation header identified as (2), it should now be evident that there are several encapsulation headers performing the same or nearly the same function. But as I stated earlier, nothing is straightforward with this methodology. For example, an NLPID header could be coded to connote that a SNAP header follows in the PDU. Further, the SNAP header could indicate that an Ethertype field follows in the next field of the PDU. This rather confused approach is the result of the evolution of these methods through different standards groups with different agenda.

As we shall see as we proceed through this book, many of the internetworking operations must translate between the different encapsulation methods that are employed with a specific technology. For example, when internetworking ATM with Frame Relay the NLPID-based approach in Frame Relay must be mapped to the LLC-based approach in ATM.

Example of Encapsulation Operations

We proceed further to show how internetworking encapsulation operations are performed by using Figure 2–13 as an illustration. Remember that internetworking is performed for local area, wide area, and point-to-point or multipoint systems, as shown in Figure 2–13a. Regardless of the source or destination networks, the traffic passed to an IWU must contain an encapsulation header that identifies the type of traffic in the PDU (such as SNA, IP, X.25, etc.). This process is depicted in Figure 2–13b.

Figure 2–14 shows how the user traffic can be interpreted and transported through the ATM network. The boundary of the message flow is between a calling user and a called user. In this example, the flow is between interworking units (IWU)—that is, routers.

The manner in which the end-user stations communicate with the routers is not defined by ATM, since the information flow between the end-user station and the router is not part of the ATM interface (at this

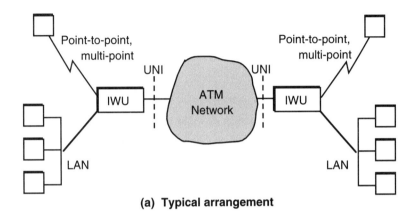

(a) Typical arrangement

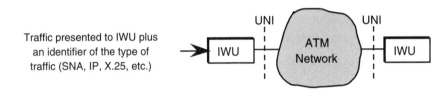

(b) Getting started

where:
  IWU   Interworking unit

Figure 2–13   Using ATM as the transport network.

time). Nonetheless, the user station-to-router operation is well defined in other standards, and the router need only map the information received from the user stations into the ATM AAL PDU at the originating router and perform a complementary and reverse operation at the terminating router.

Figure 2–14 also shows the operations for a LAN-to-LAN transmission with event-by-event notations, so I shall not elaborate further, but later discussions will focus in more detail on these operations.

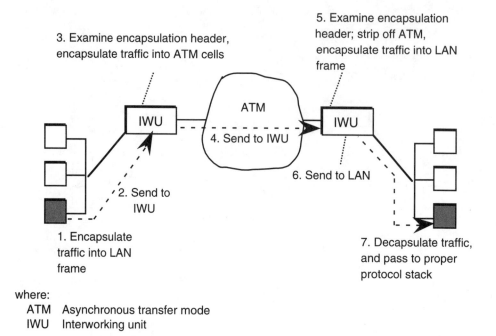

Figure 2–14   Example of an encapsulation procedure (a LAN-to-LAN example).

SUPPORT FOR LAYER 2 AND 3 PROTOCOLS

Figure 2–15 illustrates the various layer 2 and 3 protocols and procedures that can be identified in the encapsulation operations. Figure 2–15a depicts the layer 2 protocols, and Figure 2–15b depicts the layer 3 protocols.

For the layer 3 protocols, the LAN stations ordinarily support the Internet Protocol (IP), or some vendor-specific protocol, such as Novell Netware IPX. The approximate equivalent in this specification is ISO 8473, the connectionless network protocol, or CLNP.

Also, the subnetwork access protocol (SNAP) is employed in some systems to identify the layer 3 protocol that resides in the data unit. Nothing precludes using other methods. The most common approach is to use SNAP on LANs, as it was so designed, and to use the Point-to-Point (PPP) protocol on point-to-point links, as it was so designed.

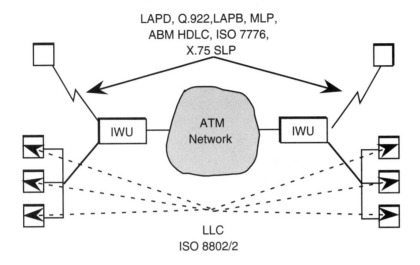

LAPD, Q.922,LAPB, MLP,
ABM HDLC, ISO 7776,
X.75 SLP

ATM
Network

IWU

IWU

LLC
ISO 8802/2

(a) Layer 2 protocols

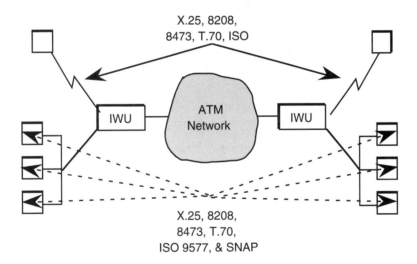

X.25, 8208,
8473, T.70, ISO

ATM
Network

IWU

IWU

X.25, 8208,
8473, T.70,
ISO 9577, & SNAP

(b) Layer 3 protocols and SNAP

where:
ABM   Asynchronous balanced mode
HDLC   High level data link protocol
LAPD/B   Link access procedure, D channel/balanced
LLC   Logical link control
MLP   Multilink procedure
SLP   Single link procedure
SNAP   Subnetwork access protocol

Figure 2–15   Layers 2 and 3 identifications.

ENCAPSULATION RULES FOR FRAME RELAY (RFC 1490)

The Internet standard Request for Comments (RFC) 1490 establishes the rules for how protocols are encapsulated within the Frame Relay frame and transported across a network. This proposal is based on the encapsulation standards published in ANSI T1.617, Annex F. The Frame Relay Forum has used these documents as the basis for its Implementation Agreements (IAs).

This section provides a broad overview of RFC 1490. Be aware that RFC 1490 has many features and provides for various encapsulation operations. This section shows one option with the use of the NLPID. More options are described in Chapter 6.

As shown in Figure 2–16, traffic is carried in the Frame Relay frame, with the network level protocol identifier (NLPID) field used to identify which protocol family is contained in the I field of the frame. The

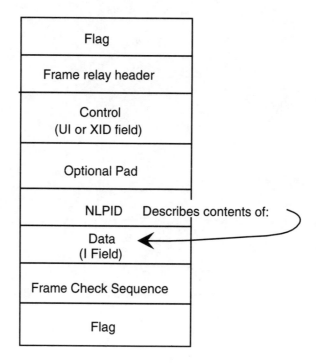

where:

I	Information
NLPID	Network level protocol ID
UI	Unnumbered information
XID	Exchange ID

Figure 2–16   Encapsulation scheme for Frame Relay.

control field contains the HDLC unnumbered information (UI) field, or the XID field. The pad field is used to align the full frame to a 2-octet boundary.

For ongoing traffic, the UI control field is used. The XID control field can be employed during an initialization operation between the user stations to negotiate (1) maximum frame size, (2) the retransmission timer, and (3) the window size (maximum number of permitted outstanding I frames allowed).

We leave RFC 1490 for the time being. More detailed examples of Frame Relay encapsulation are provided in Chapter 6 (see "Bridged PDUs", "Routed IP PDUs", and "Routed OSI PDUS" sections).

ENCAPSULATION RULES FOR ATM (RFC 1483)

The Internet standard Request for Comments (RFC) 1483 establishes the rules for how protocols are encapsulated within the AAL 5 PDU and transported across a network. RFC 1483 supports a number of options and is similar to its Frame Relay counterpart, RFC 1490, just discussed. It uses the conventional AAL 5 PDU format that is described in Volume I of this series, with some special rules that are summarized here.

In the same manner that we examined RFC 1490, this section provides a broad overview of RFC 1483, which has many features and provides for various encapsulation operations. This section shows one option with the use of AAL 5. Once again, Chapter 6 depicts some more options. Also, Chapter 3 has other information on RFC 1483 (See "Guidance from RFC 1483").

Figure 2–17 shows the format of the type 5 PDU. It consists of an 8-octet trailer. The PAD field acts as a filler to fill out the CPCS-PDU to

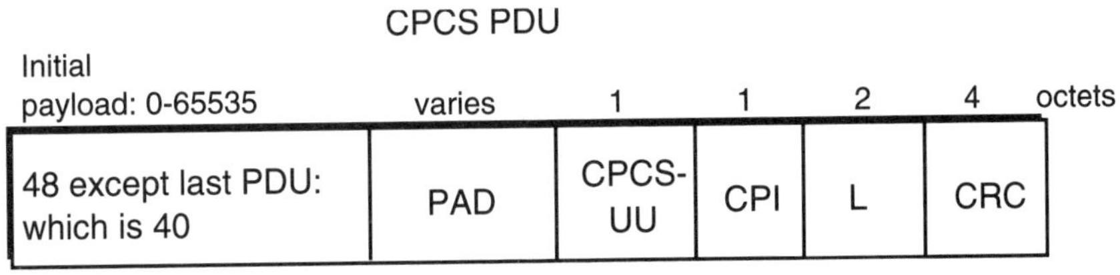

CPCS PDU

Initial payload: 0-65535	varies	1	1	2	4	octets
48 except last PDU: which is 40	PAD	CPCS- UU	CPI	L	CRC	

where:

CPCS-UU	Common part convergence sublayer-user to user indication
CPI	Common part indicator
CRC	Cyclic redundancy check
L	Length
Payload	CPCS-PDUs

Figure 2–17   The AAL type 5 PDU.

48 octets. The CPCS-UU field not processed, since it has no function under RFC 1483. The common part indicator (CPI) has not been fully defined in ITU-T I.363. The length field (L) defines the payload length, and the CRC field is used to detect errors in the SSCS PDU (user data).

Type 5 is a convenient service for Frame Relay because it supports connection-oriented services. In essence, the Frame Relay user traffic is given to an ATM backbone network for transport to another Frame Relay user.

Options in RFC 1483

RFC defines two methods of sending connectionless traffic over ATM (this traffic can be bridged PDUs (L_2) or routed PDUs (L_3)). The first method supports multiplexing multiple protocols over a single ATM virtual circuit. Using this method, the PDU protocol is identified by an LLC header. The second method requires that the transported protocol be identified by the ATM VC.

The values and meanings for the LLC encapsulation method are shown in Table 2–1. The PID for bridged PDUs can have more than one value. One value indicates that the FCS (frame check sequence) in the PDU is to be preserved. The other value indicates that the FCS is not preserved.

We leave RFC 1483 for a while, but revisit it in the chapters/sections cited earlier, and show several detailed examples in Chapter 6. (See "Bridged PDUs", "Routed IP PDUs", and "Routed OSI PDUs" sections).

Table 2–1   LLC Values

LLC Value	Meaning
0xFE-FE-03	Routed ISO PDUs (1)
0xAA-AA-03	Presence of SNAP header (2)
0xAA-AA-03	Presence of SNAP header (3)

(1) Routed ISO protocol is identified by NLPID that is part of the PDU

(2) OUI of 0x00-00-00 indicates that the following SNAP PID is an Ethertype valve

(3) OUI of 0x00-80-02 identifies the IEEE 802.1 organization code followed by PID which identifies the type of bridged media: (a) 802.3 (b) 802.4, (c) 802.5, (d) FDDI, (e) 802.6 and (f) a bridge PDU

THE ADDRESS RESOLUTION PROTOCOL (ARP)

The Internet publishes a protocol for resolving addresses. Resolving addresses means the association (correlation) of one address to another. The Address Resolution Protocol (ARP) is used to take care of the translation of L_3 addresses to physical addresses (also known as hardware addresses, link addresses, and L_2 addresses) and hide these addresses from the upper layers.

The operation of ARP is important because most networks use more than one address. In the TCP/IP suite, for example, the IP L_3 address is used to route traffic through a wide area internet (and must be available for TCP/IP to function correctly), whereas a MAC L_2 address is used to reach a host attached to a LAN. Both addresses are required for the two systems to communicate with each other.

Generally, ARP works with mapping tables (referred to as ARP cache). For example, the table provides the mapping between an IP address and a physical address. The term physical address is used in ARP to describe a lower layer address. This book uses the terms, MAC and L_2 address for physical address. In a LAN (like Ethernet or an IEEE 802 network), ARP takes a target IP address and searches for a corresponding "target" physical address (a 48-bit MAC address) in a mapping table. If it finds the address, it returns the 48-bit MAC address back to the requester, such as a work station or server on a LAN. However, if the needed address is not found in the ARP cache, the ARP module sends a broadcast onto the network (assuming the network is a LAN).

The broadcast is called the ARP request. The ARP request contains a target IP address. Consequently, if one of the machines receiving the broadcast recognizes its IP address in the ARP request, it will return an ARP reply back to the inquiring host. This message contains the hardware address of the queried host and its IP address. Upon receiving this datagram, the ARP requestor places this address mapping into the ARP cache. Thereafter, datagrams sent to this particular IP address can be translated to the physical address.

The ARP protocol thus allows an inquiring node to find the physical address of another node by using the IP address.

The concepts of ARP requests and replies are shown in Figure 2–18. Host A wishes to determine C's physical address (say, an Ethernet address). It broadcasts to B, C, and D. Only C responds because it recognizes its IP address in the incoming ARP request message. Host C places its IP and MAC addresses in the ARP reply. The other hosts, B and D, do not respond.

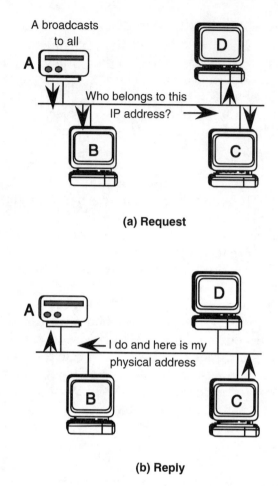

(a) Request

(b) Reply

Figure 2–18   The Address Resolution Protocol (ARP) request and reply.

In addition to the mapping of IP addresses to physical addresses, ARP also allows the designation of specific hardware types. Therefore, when an ARP message is received by the queried host, it can use a field in the datagram to determine if the machine is using a particular type of hardware such as an Ethernet interface, packet radio, and so on.

The operations shown in Figure 2–18 can be invoked at a host by issuing a function called gethostbyname. This routine uses a name server operation (the Domain Name System [DNS]) to map a name to a L_3 address (an IP address).

The entries in the ARP cache are managed with a timer. Most systems will time-out the entry after 20 minutes, although entries can be entered by the system administrator that do not time-out.

The ARP Protocol Data Units (PDUs)

The format for the ARP message is shown in Figure 2–19. The first part of the message is the header of the Ethernet frame, consisting of the MAC addresses and the Ethertype field. Thereafter, the hardware type and protocol type describe the types of addresses that are to be "resolved." The term hardware refers to a physical, link layer address, and the term protocol refers to an upper layer address, typically a L_3 address, such as IP, X.25, or IPX .

The length fields explain how long the address fields are, and for Ethernet and IP addresses, they are 6 and 4 octets respectively. The sending address fields identify the addresses of the sending entity. The target addresses are those that need resolving. In a typical ARP request, the target hardware address is left blank, and in the reply, it is filled in by the responding station.

	Octets
Destination Address	6
Source Address	6
Ethertype	2
Hardware type	2
Protocol type	2
Hardware length	1
Protocol length	1
Op code	2
Sending hardware address	6
Sending protocol address	4
Target hardware address	6
Target protocol address	4

Figure 2–19   The ARP PDU.

FRAME RELAY ARP

Address resolution in a Frame Relay network works in a similar manner as I just described in a conventional environment. Figure 2–20 shows how ARP is used with Frame Relay. Be aware that the approach described here does not use ARP in its conventional manner. The hardware address fields in the ARP messages are used to contain Frame Relay DLCIs, and pure, modular OSI layering concepts are not used. Also, the ARP hardware type is 15 (0x00-0F), which is assigned to Frame Relay.

Keep in mind for this operation that Frame Relay DLCIs have local significance, and a user device (such as a router) uses a DLCI based on an agreement with the network.

To begin the process, user A forms an ARP request message. Since hardware addresses are not used initially in this process, the hardware address fields are undefined in the ARP request message. The source and destination protocol addresses (for example, IP addresses) are filled in as usual. In this example, the source IP address is A (for user A) and the destination IP address is D (for user D).

User A encapsulates its L_3 traffic into a frame and places DLCI 15 in the frame header. This value was assigned previously (usually by the network). The object is to associate DLCI 15 and IP address D with a remote DLCI. When user D receives the ARP request, it is encapsulated into the frame header, which contains the local DLCI value of 56 (placed into the frame by the Frame Relay network). User D extracts this value from the header and places it in the source hardware address of the incoming ARP request message. This process allows user D to associate protocol address A (in the source protocol address field) with DLCI 56. The box on the right side of the figure shows where the correlation takes place.

Next, user D forms the ARP response message (exchanges the source and destination values in the message), but leaves the destination hardware address undefined (which of course becomes defined when the source and destination addresses are exchanged). When user A receives this frame, it has DLCI 15 in the Frame Relay header. Thus, user A extracts this value and places it in the source hardware address field of the message. This operation allows user A to correlate DLCI 15 to protocol address D. Once again, the two boxes in this figure highlight where the correlations take place.

After these operations have taken place, users A and B know the following facts:

- User A knows that address D is correlated with its local DLCI 15
- User D knows that address A is correlated with its local DLCI 56

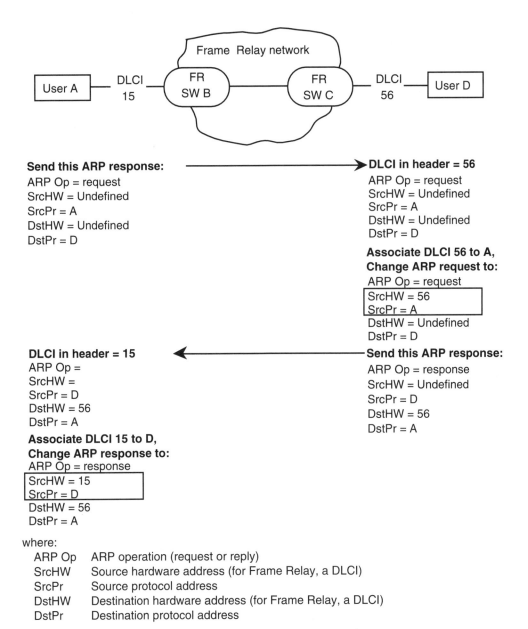

Figure 2–20 Frame Relay ARP operations.

CLASSICAL IP AND ARP OVER ATM (RFC 1577)

RFC 1577 defines the operations for encapsulating IP datagrams and ATM address resolution protocol (ATMARP) traffic over ATM and AAL5. Its principal concern is to specify the operation of IP over an ATM network and the resolving of IP addressees and ATM addresses. The idea is to allow ATM to replace (1) a LAN backbone, such as FDDI; (2) dedicated links between routers; (3) LANs (such as Ethernet, Token Ring, etc.); or (4) Frame Relay networks. The environment is established as a logical IP subnetwork (LIS).

RFC 1577 views ATM acting as a layer 2 transport service, which simply uses the IP over Ethernet idea and extends the concepts to ATM (IP over ATM).

IP subnetworks become LISs, which are internetworked by routers, as shown in Figure 2–21.

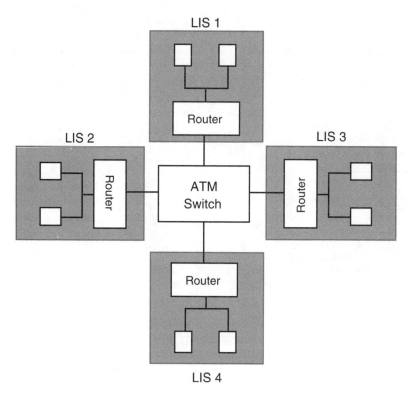

Figure 2–21   Logical IP subnets (LISs).

THE LIS CONFIGURATION

The LIS is configured with hosts and routers within a logical IP subnetwork. Each LIS communicates with each other through the same ATM network, although each LIS is independent of each other. Communication occurs through an IP router, which is configured as an ATM end point connected both to the ATM network and to one or more LISs. As a result of this configuration, multiple LISs might operate over the same ATM network. However, RFC 1577 requires that hosts operating on different LISs must communicate with each other through an intermediate router, even if they are attached to the same ATM network. This rule exists even though it is possible to establish a direct virtual channel between the two IP members over the ATM network. This rule is based on previous Internet standards dealing with IP host requirements, and relies on conventional protocols to interwork LISs. See RFC 1122.

Given this basic scenario, the operations are established with the following rules:

1. All IP members (which consist of hosts and routers) are directly connected to the ATM network.
2. All members must use the same IP network/subnetwork number as well as address mask.
3. Any member that is outside the LIS must be accessed via a router.
4. All members must be able to resolve IP addresses to ATM addresses through ATMARP.
5. All LIS members must be able to communicate via ATM with other members within the same LIS (this means that within a list membership connection topologies are fully meshed).
6. Address resolution must be performed for both PVCs and SVCs.

Each IP station connected to the ATM network must be configured with an ATM address (which is the ATM address of the individual station) as well as an ATMARP request address. This value is the ATM address of an ATMARP server located at the LIS. The idea is to permit this server to resolve IP and ATM addresses. The server must be able to resolve all ATMARP requests for all IP members in the LIS.

In addition, all operations must support the IEEE 802.2 LLC/SNAP encapsulation operations defined in RFC 1483.

A default maximum transmission unit size (MTU) for IP members is 9180 octets. Since the LLC/SNAP header consists of 8 octets, the default

AAL5 PDU is 9188 octets. Values other than the default can be used if all members of the LIS have be so configured.

RULES FOR ADDRESS RESOLUTION

The address resolution operations make use of the ATM address resolution protocol (ATMARP) and the inverse address resolution protocol (InATMARP). These specifications are published in RFC 826 and RFC 1293, respectively. The ATMARP is an extension of the original ARP protocol. Inverse ATMARP is the same protocol as the original inverse ARP published in RFC 1293 but altered for ATM operations.[2] The system also uses ATMARP servers, and clients, as shown in Figure 2–22.

InARP operates like ARP except InARP does not use broadcasting, since the hardware address of the destination station is already known. Therefore, for the InARP (and the ATM extension, InATMARP) operation, the requesting station constructs a request by placing its source ATM address, its source protocol address, and the known target destination ATM (AKA hardware) address in these fields. The responding station fills in the destination protocol address in the reply and uses the source addresses in the request as the target addresses for the reply. This completes the resolution of the L_3 and ATM addresses.

As stated earlier, the classical IP operations must support both PVCs and SVCs. For operations with PVCs, the IP members must use inverse ATMARP for the PVCs with LLC/SNAP, SNAP encapsulation. If the ATM source and/or target address is not known, the corresponding address length in the inverse ATM packet is set to zero, which indicates a no length. Otherwise, the address is filled into the field.

For switched virtual connections (SVCs), classical IP requires that an ATMARP server must be located within the LIS and it must have the responsibility for resolving any ATMARP requests with all members of the LIS. It is not the responsibility of the server to establish connections, but will depend on the clients within the LIS to initiate the ATMARP registration operations when a client connects to the ATMARP server with a point-to-point VC. Upon the completion of an ATM connection, the server will transmit an inverse ATMARP request to determine the IP address of the client. The client then will reply in the ATMARP reply message the information that the ATMARP server will need to build its

---

[2]RFC 1293 was published to resolve Frame Relay and L_3 addresses, but it applies to ATM, as well.

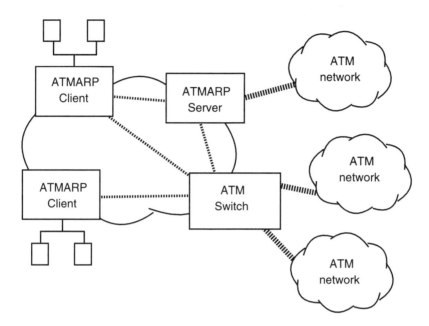

Figure 2–22   ATMARP clients and servers.

ATMARP table cache. Afterwards, this information is used to generate replies to the ATMARP queries that the server receives. Only one ATMARP server is allowed to operate per logical IP subnet, and the ATMARP server should also be an IP station. In addition, the ATMARP server must be configured with an IP address for each logical IP subnet that it serves in order to support all the inverse ATMARP requests.

Figure 2–23 shows these ideas in more detail (examples use IP class B addresses). An ATM backbone connects three subnetworks: 176.16.2, 176.16.3, and 176.16.4. Routers act as the interworking units between the legacy (conventional) LANs and the ATM backbone. The routers are also configured as LIS clients and access the LIS ARP server to obtain mappings between IP and ATM addresses.

Figure 2–24 provides another level of detail to Figure 2–23. Each node in the ATM network is configured with an ATM address and an IP address as follows:

	ATM Address	**IP Address**
LIS server	HIJ	172.16.1.1
LIS router/client	DEF	172.16.1.4
LIS router/client	ABC	172.16.1.3
LIS router/client	KLM	172.16.1.2

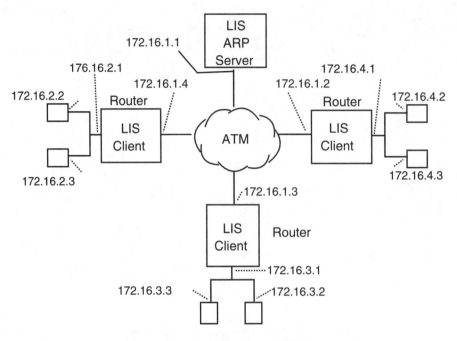

Figure 2–23   LIS clients and servers.

Figure 2–24 shows examples of entries in the routing table and ARP table stored at router KLM/172.16.1.2. The routing table contains the next node that is to receive the datagram based on the destination IP address in the IP datagram. The ARP table (cache) contains the IP and ATM address mappings (resolutions).

The creation of the routing table is through conventional route discovery protocols, such as OSPF. The creation of the ARP table is through ATMARP.

OPERATIONS AT THE ATMARP SERVER AND CLIENT

Operations at the Server

As mentioned earlier, the ATMARP server communicates with other ATM endpoints over ATM VCs shown in Figure 2–25. At the call setup operation, the ATMARP server will transmit to each originating ATM station the inverse ARP request message (InATMARP). A request is sent for each logical IP subnet that the server is configured to serve (bear in mind, configuration is required beforehand). The server then receives the InATMARP reply and examines the IP address and the correlated ATM

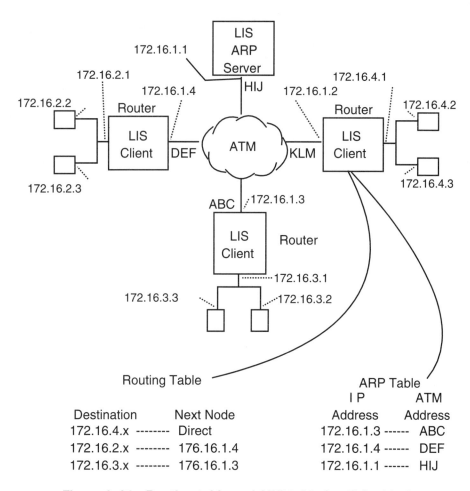

Figure 2–24   Routing table and ARP table (partial tables).

address. Based on this examination, the server then adds or deletes the ATM address, IP address entry into its ATMARP table. It also adds a timestamp to this entry at this time.

Thereafter, as mentioned earlier, the ATMARP server is responsible for receiving ATMARP requests and generating an appropriate ATMARP reply, if it has a proper entry in its ATMARP table. If it does not have an entry in this table, it will generate a negative ATMARP reply to the client.

Operations at the ATMARP Client Site

The ATMARP client must contact the ATMARP server to register its own information and to refresh any information that it has sent earlier.

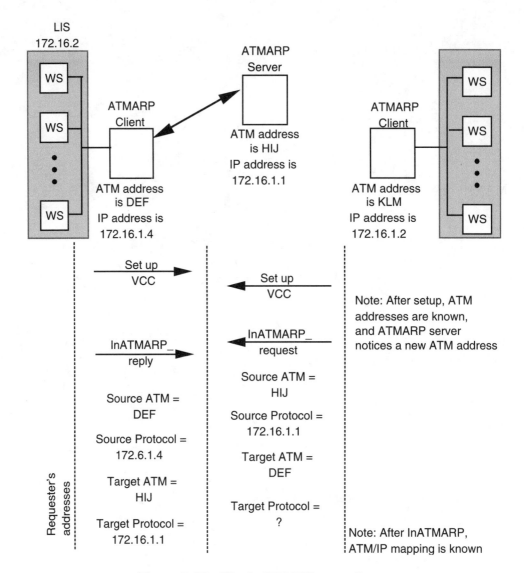

Figure 2–25   The InATMARP operations.

Consequently, the ATMARP client must be configured beforehand with the address of the ATMARP server. Once these configuration operations are put in place, the ATMARP client is responsible for the following:

- As just stated, it must initiate the VC connection to the ARP server.
- It must respond to ARP request and inverse ARP request packets.

- It must generate and transmit ARP request packets to the server and process ARP reply and ARP NAK packets from the server.
- The ARP reply packets must be used to refresh its own table entry.
- It must generate and transmit inverse ARP request packets as needed and to process inverse ARP reply packets as needed.
- It must provide an ATMARP table with an appropriate agent function in order to remove old entries after a period of time.

Figure 2–26 provides one final example of ATMARP (not InAT-MARP) operations. We assume that router A (also an ATMARP client)

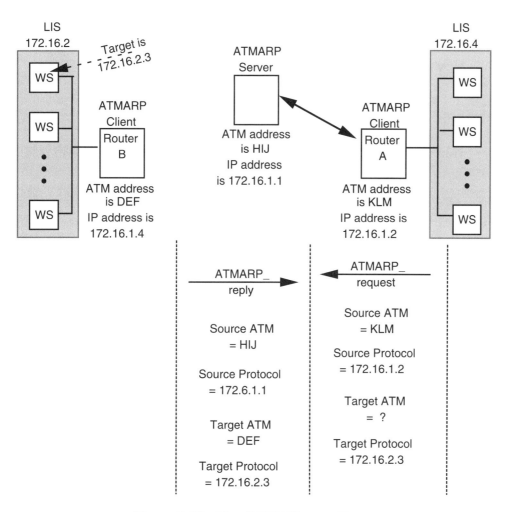

Figure 2–26   The ATMARP operations.

identified as KLM/172.16.1.2 receives a datagram from one of its workstations (WS) with an IP destination address of 172.16.2.3. This datagram should be forwarded across the ATM network to router B (DEF/172.16.1.4) for delivery to the destination workstation. If router A has the entry IP = 172.16.2—ATM = DEF in ARP cache, it knows the path to the destination. If it has no such entry, it constructs an ATMARP request message as shown in Figure 2–26 and sends the message to the ATMARP server. Because router B had previously registered its address with the server, this server can send back the ATMARP reply to router A, which now knows the path to the destination.

Notice that the ATMARP operation in Figure 2–26 is the opposite of the InATMARP operation in Figure 2–25:

InATMARP request: Target Protocol address is sought
ATMARP request: Target ATM address is sought

ATMARP AND INVERSE ATMARP PACKET FORMATS

Table 2–2 shows the formats for the ATMARP and inverse ATMARP packets. The formats are quite similar to the conventional ARP and inverse ARP protocols referenced earlier. Indeed, the hardware type, protocol type, and operation code are the same between the two sets of protocols, and the location of these fields within the ATMARP packet are in the same position as in the ARP and inverse ARP packets. For ATMARP, a unique hardware type has been assigned and also ATMARP uses an additional operation code for ARP NAK.

ATMARP AND INATMARP PACKET ENCAPSULATION

The ATMARP and inverse ATMARP packets must be encoded in AAL5 PDUs using LLC/SNAP encapsulation. Figure 2–27 shows the format for these encapsulations. The LLC of 0xAA-AA-03 indicates the presence of a SNAP header. The OUI of 0x00-00-00 indicates the next two bytes are the Ethertype field, and the Ethertype field is coded as 0x08-06 to indicate ATMARP or InATMARP packets.

As stated earlier, the restriction of this simple classical model is due to its adherence to RFC 1122 ("Requirement for Internet hosts—Communication Layers"): any datagram with a destination address other than the originator's subnet must go through a *default* router, even if a better

Table 2–2 Formats for ATMARP Packets

Name	Function	Size
Hardware type	Assigned to ATM Forum (0x00-13)	2
Protocol type	Based on Assigned numbers for protocol type using ATM. For example, IP is 0x08-00	2
Source ATM address/type length	Type and length of source ATM number (q)	1
Source ATM subaddress type/length	Type and length of source ATM subaddress (r)	1
Operation code	Operation code for packet (see Table 2–3)	2
Source protocol address length	Length of source protocol address (s)	1
Target ATM address/type length	Type and length of target ATM number (x)	1
Target ATM subaddress type/length	Type and length of target ATM subaddress (y)	1
Target protocol address length	Length of target protocol address (s)	1
Source ATM address	ATM source address	q
Source ATM subaddress	ATM source subaddress	r
Source protocol address	Protocol source address	s
Target ATM address	ATM target address	x
Target ATM subaddress	ATM target subaddress	y
Target protocol address	Protocol target address	z

path exists, say through an ATM backbone to hosts on multiple LISs. Also, the datagram must pass through the *intermediate* routers of any other LISs.

These deficiencies are addressed with other internetworking specifications, notably the next Hop Resolution Protocol, discussed in Chapter 10.

Table 2–3 Coding for the Operation Type

OP Code	Value
ARP_REQUEST	1
ARP_REPLY	2
InARP_REQUEST	8
InARP_REPLY	9
ARP_NAK	10

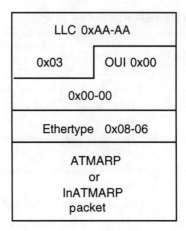

Figure 2–27   Encapsulation into AAL5 PDUs.

MULTICAST ADDRESS RESOLUTION SERVER (MARS)

Until recently, the ATM internetworking operations have focused on unicast operations. But for ATM to be an effective transport network it must support multicasting since LANs use multicasting extensively. Furthermore, IP multicasting is common today, especially with the use of Mbone (multicasting backbone), the Internet multicasting protocol.

To fix this problem (at least partially) the Multicast Address Resolution Server (MARS) specification is being developed. As of this writing, all issues surrounding MARS had not been resolved, but its definition is stable enough to warrant a discussion of its operations.

MARS is an extension to ARP and ATMARP. It maps L_3 multicast addresses to one or more ATM addresses. The mapping record is called a host map and contains the IP multicast address to/from the ATM addresses.

The MARS configuration is shown in Figure 2–28. The multicast server and client communicate initially through a bi-directional point-to-point (pt-pt) ATM VC, which is setup at the initiative of the client. The VC is used to transmit multicast resolution queries to the server. Each server manages a cluster of ATM end-points (clients), which represent a set of ATM interfaces.

Two types of VCs are defined for MARS operations. The first is the Cluster Control VC and is used to connect MARS to all end systems (cluster members). This link is a point-to-multipoint (pt-mpt) VC, and all

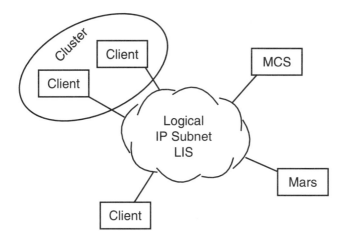

where
  MARS: Multicast Address Resolution Protocol Server
  MCS: Multicast Server

Figure 2–28   The MARS configuration.

members are leaf nodes. The second VC is the Server Control VC, which links MARS to all multicast servers (MCSs)—if MCSs are used. MARS does not define the role of the MCS. For more information on multicasting servers, see M. Macedonia and D. Brutzman. mBone, The Multicast Backbone, http://www.cs.ucl.ac.uk/mice/mbone_review.html

Before a datagram is sent by a client, it is determined if a multicast outbound path currently exists for the multicast address. If no path exists, the MARS is queried in a MARS_REQUEST message by the client for the appropriate ATM addresses for the operation. The paths could be to MCSs or the actual members of the multicast group. The MARS responds to the request message in one of two ways:

- Sends a MARS_NAK message: MARS has no mapping for the multicast address
- Sends a MARS_MULTI message: A match is found and the host map is sent to the client

Thereafter, a pt-mpt VC is created and the ATM endpoints in the host map are added to a multicast group.

Nodes can join and leave multicasting groups with the MARS_JOIN and MARS_LEAVE messages, that are sent via the Cluster Control VC. MCSs can also join and leave the system by using these messages.

Pros and Cons of MARS

MARS is a simple and effective approach for small environments with few nodes. It handles registration, queries, and "de-registration" in an efficient manner. However, several studies conclude that MARS will not scale well to larger systems, since multicast traffic must transit to a single multicast server. The problem also stems from the likely expanding of hosts and/or MCSs that must be connected with pt-mpt SVCs. IP multicast routing can reduce the magnitude of the problem, but the provisioning and management of the MARS mapping information still translates into considerable overhead.[3]

Notwithstanding, MARS is another useful tool and one more supplementary instrument in the ATM internetworking tool box.

SUMMARY

We learned in this chapter that encapsulation operations are used to identify the types of traffic that are carried in a protocol data unit. We have also learned that the concept of encapsulation is quite simple but overlapping encapsulation conventions and standards complicate the process.

The chapter also introduced address resolution with the focus on the Address Resolution Protocol (ARP) and its variations. This protocol is essential in internetworking operations because of its ability to resolve (correlate/map) from one address to another.

---

[3]For more information on this subject see G. Armitage, "VENUS—Very Extensive Non-Unicast Service", Internet Draft, 1997.

3

ATM/Frame Relay
Interworking Operations

This chapter introduces the basic operations for ATM/Frame Relay interworking. It sets the stage for more detailed discussions in subsequent chapters. Several interworking models are explained and a comparison is made between protocol encapsulation/protocol mapping and network interworking/service interworking.

The chapter also explains the use of the Frame Relay core service access point (CSAP), which provides guidance on building an application programming interface (API) on top of the Frame Relay layers. This chapter concludes by revisiting RFC 1483 (which was introduced in Chapter 2) in more detail.

ATM/FRAME RELAY INTERWORKING MODELS

The FR/ATM interworking function (IWF) can be implemented in two configurations:

- As a interworking service application, in which frame-to-cell adaptation is done at the edge of the subnet
- As a gateway between the frame and ATM subnetworks within a network

Using these two basic configurations, FR-ATM interworking can be deployed with three different models. Most implementations reflect this model, which is derived from Nortel's Magellan ATM Family.

1. *Frame Relay network leveraging another carrier's ATM network.* The frame-to-cell adaptation is done on the edge of the Frame Relay network, between the Frame Relay network and the carrier ATM network. This application is a FR-ATM gateway (see Figure 3–1a).

2. *Interconnected Frame Relay and ATM networks.* The frame-to-cell adaptation is done in the middle of the mixed network configuration, outside of the subnetworks. This application is also a gateway (see Figure 3–1b).

3. *ATM centric network.* The frame-to-cell adaptation is performed at the edge of the ATM network. This application uses the IWF in a FR-ATM interworking service implementation (see Figure 3–1c).

The FR-ATM IWF can be deployed within a single network in any combination and number of these models. Since networks are not static, most network topologies evolve from one model to another, or evolve to incorporate additional models, as traffic volumes, services, and tariffs evolve.

INTERNETWORKING DEFINITIONS

Protocol Encapsulation and Protocol Mapping

Before we begin an analysis of the internetworking relationships of Frame Relay and ATM, several definitions are in order. These definitions are extracted from ITU-T Recommendation I.555. First, *protocol encapsulation* describes an interworking function in which the conversions in the network or terminals are such that the protocols used to provide one service make use of the layer service provided by another protocol. This means that at the interworking point, the two protocols are stacked. In effect, this means that a protocol is encapsulated by either the network or the terminal.

In contrast, *protocol mapping* actually performs conversion. By this I mean that the protocol information of one protocol is extracted and mapped onto the protocol information of another protocol. This also means that each terminal can support different protocols and a common layer service is provided by the functions that are common to the two protocols.

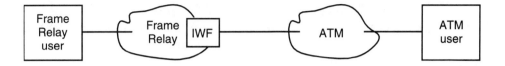

(a) Adaptation at edge of Frame Relay network

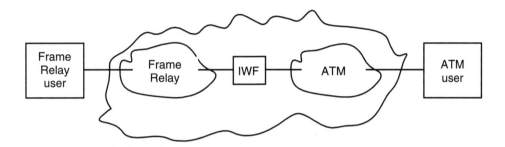

(b) Adaptation at middle of a mixed network

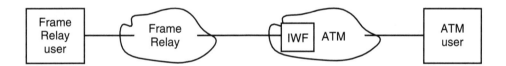

(c) Adaptation at edge of ATM network.

Figure 3–1   Deployment model.

Network and Service Interworking

Two other definitions that are used in this book are network interworking and service interworking.

Network interworking is an operation in which an ATM network connects two Frame Relay users *through* the ATM backbone.

Service interworking is similar to network interworking, but the ATM backbone connects a Frame Relay user to an ATM user.

GUIDES FOR THE USER INTERFACE

The ITU-T has published Annex C to I.233, which defines the relationship of the relaying bearer service to the OSI network layer service. This bearer service is intended to support the network layer service, in accordance with ITU-T Recommendation X.213. The value of this specification is that it defines the interface between a user application and the Frame Relay layer. Thus, it aids the programmer who is writing the application's programming interface (API) between a user application and Frame Relay.

OSI network service consists of three phases: (1) connection establishment, (2) data transfer, and (3) connection release. The connection establishment and release services are provided by Q.930 series, and the data transfer phase is provided by the Q.922 series, which is the ITU-T Frame Relay standards.

ITU-T requires that several functions be supported above Q.922: (1) segmentation/reassembly, (2) RESET, (3) a protocol discriminator, (4) expedited data, and (5) qualified data indication.

The actual transfer phase must be provided by a protocol that resides in the user end systems. This protocol must reside above the data link layer. That is to say, it must reside above Q.922. This end user protocol could be an existing X.25 protocol, a user specific protocol, or a connectionless protocol (such as ISO 8473, the connectionless network protocol [CLNP]).

The core service is made available through the core service access point (CSAP). The core service provides connection-oriented transparent transfer of data between core users. The core service must provide independence from any type of underlying physical layer. It is the function of core service to keep the user transparent from the physical layer with the exception of certain QOS features that depend on the physical layer (such as basic or primary data rates).

As depicted in Figure 3–2, the core service must also provide transparency of information transfer. This means that the user need not be concerned with the core layer interpreting the content of its data. Conversely, the core layer does not care about the content, syntax, coding, or format of the data it receives. Its only concern in this regard is that of the length of the core service data unit.

Primitive Operations

The core service must provide several features to the user above it. It must support connections that remain transparent to the end user (see Figure 3–3). Additionally, it must support certain QOS parameters that have been coordinated by the user through the use of the C-plane and perhaps the systems management plane.

It must provide a transparent connection and transfer of CSDUs on behalf of the user through the network. It must also be able to measure

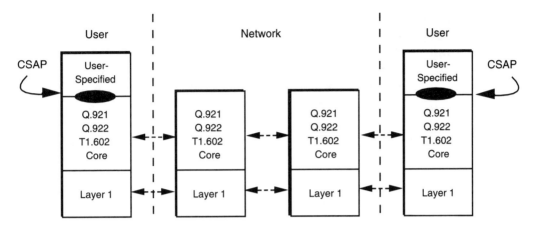

Figure 3–2 Core service access point (CSAP).

certain QOS features to see if they are being met in regard to the user's requested QOS. It must be able to provide congestion information to the core service user and it also must be able to provide some type of information about the release of the connection in the event of problems.

The OSI Model requires the use of primitive calls between the core service user and core service provider. These primitives are core data request and core data indication primitives and are mapped in operating system specific calls between the two software elements.

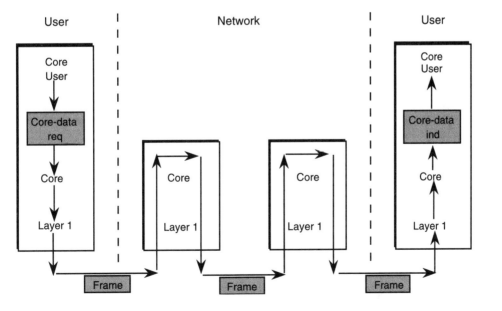

Figure 3–3 The primitives in the data transfer.

The core data request and indication primitives contain up to five parameters. These parameters are used to provide the transfer of the following information: The core service is provided through the use of service primitives and parameters. Two primitives are involved, the core data request and the core data indication. These primitives are passed between the core service user and core service provider. All primitives are passed as unconfirmed services. This means no confirmation is given the core service user that the core data has been accepted either by the service provider or by the peer user. No responses are provided either by the provider or by the other user.

Parameter Primitives

The service primitives contain up to five parameters: core user data, discard eligibility, congestion encountered backward, congestion encountered forward, and connection endpoint identifier (see Figure 3–4).

The core data parameter is used to convey data between the end users in the Frame Relay service. This data must be transferred in accordance with OSI's SDU (service data unit) concept, which means it must be transmitted without modification. The discard eligibility parameter is sent from the core service user to the service provider. It is used by the

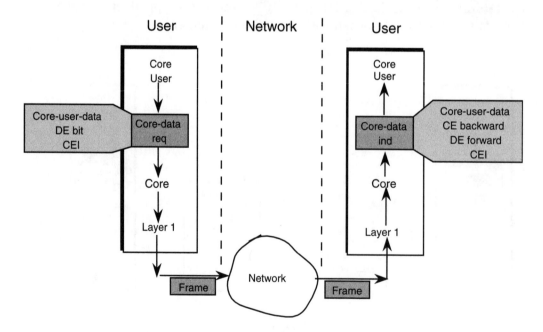

Figure 3–4   The parameters in the primitives.

provider to select CSDUs that may be discarded, assuming that the Frame Relay network decides that discarding is required.

The two congestion parameters are sent by the core data service provider to the core data service user to supply information about congestion that has been encountered in the network. The congestion encountered forward parameter is used to indicate that the provider has determined that congestion has occurred in transferring data to its user. The congestion backward parameter indicates that the provider has experienced congestion in transferring these units from the user.

The connection endpoint identifier parameter is used to further identity a connection endpoint. For example, this parameter would allow a DLCI to be used by more than one user and each user would be identified with a connection endpoint identifier value.

ONE SCENARIO FOR ATM FRAME RELAY INTERWORKING

Figure 3–5 provides an example of the ATM and Frame Relay internetworking operations. The interface between the Frame Relay entity and the AAL entity occurs through the Frame Relay core SAP (service access point) that is defined in the Frame Relay specifications. Therefore, the IWF must accommodate to the Frame Relay service definitions at this SAP. Ideally, the Frame Relay entity has no awareness of the AAL and ATM operations.

In accordance with the Frame Relay specifications, the service primitives contain up to five parameters: core user data, discard eligibility (DE), congestion encountered (CE) backward, congestion encountered (CE) forward, and connection endpoint identifier (CEI).

The *core user data* parameter is used to convey data between the end users in the Frame Relay service and is represented by FR-SSCS PDU. The DE paramcter is sent from the core service user to the service provider (FR-SSCS) and is mapped into the ATM CLP bit.

The two congestion parameters supply information about congestion that is encountered in the network. The *congestion encountered forward* parameter is used to indicate that congestion has occurred in transferring data to the receiving user. The *congestion encountered backward parameter* indicates that the network has experienced congestion in transferring these units from the sending user.

The *connection endpoint identifier (CEI)* parameter is used to further identify a connection endpoint. For example, this parameter would

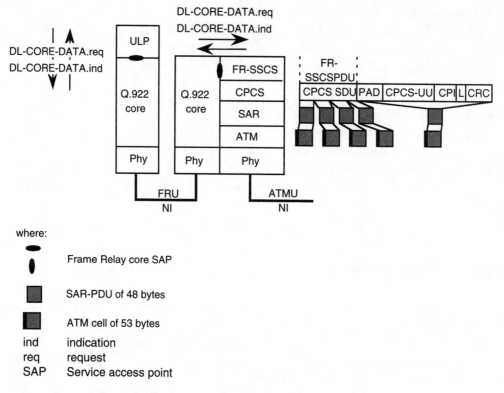

Figure 3–5   ATM and Frame Relay internetworking.

allow a DLCI to be used by more than one user and each user would be identified with a connection endpoint identifier value.

The AAL type 5 PDU is used to support Frame Relay and ATM interworking. As before, the CPI field is not yet defined. The CPCS-UU field is passed transparently by the ATM network. The length field is check for oversized or undersized PDUs. CRC violations are noted, and a reassembly timer can be invoked at the terminating endpoint.

GUIDANCE FROM RFC 1483

RFC 1483 defines two methods for carrying network interconnect traffic over an ATM network. The first method multiplexes multiple protocols over a single ATM virtual circuit. The second carries each protocol over a different ATM virtual circuit (VC). The gateway assumes the job of mapping functions between the Frame Relay network and the ATM network. At a minimum the following functions must be supported:

- *Variable length PDU formatting and delimiting:* Using AAL type 5, support the Frame Relay 2-octet control field (required), and the 3- and 4-octet control field (optional).
- *Error detection:* Using CRC-32, provide error detection over the FR PDU.
- *Connection multiplexing:* Associating one or multiple Frame Relay connections with one ATM VCC.
- *Loss priority indication:* Mapping the Frame Relay discard eligibility bit and the ATM cell loss priority bit.
- *Congestion indication:* Support of the Frame Relay forward and backward congestion notification features (within certain rules)

An FR-SSCS PDU consists of Frame Relay address field followed by an information field (I). The Frame Relay frame flags and the FCS are omitted, since the FCS functions are provided by the AAL, and the flag operations are supported by the underlying physical layer. Figure 3–6 shows an FR-SSCS-PDU encapsulated in the AAL5 CPCS PDU.

Routed and bridged traffic is carried inside the FR-SSCS-PDU as defined in RFC 1490. The protocol of the carried PDU is identified by prefixing the PDU by a network level protocol ID (NLPID).

The FR-SSCS supports variable length frames at the FR UNI over preestablished connections (PVCs). Each FR-SSCS connection is identified with a Frame Relay data link connection identifier (DLCI: equivalent to the ATM VPI/VCI). Multiple FR-SSCS connections can be associated with one Common Part CS (CPCS). The principal job of FR-SSCS is to emulate the FR UNI. In so doing, it supports Frame Relay forward and backward congestion notification (FECN, BECN), as well as the discard eligibility (DE) bit.

The CPCS is responsible for the following operations:

- Support of message mode (fixed-length blocks) or streaming mode (variable-length blocks) operations.
- Assured operations: CPCS is responsible for traffic integrity (retransmission of lost or corrupted PDUs.
- Non-assured operations: CPCS is not responsible for traffic integrity.

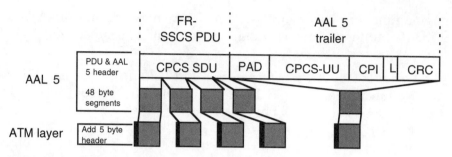

Note: CPCS PDU contains Q.922 header and user data.

where:

AAL	ATM adaptation layer
CPCS	Common part convergence sublayer
CPI	Common part identifier
CRC	Cyclic redundancy check
FR	Frame Relay
L	Length
PDU	Protocol data unit
RFC	Request for Comments
SSCS	Service specific part convergence sublayer
UU	User to user

Figure 3–6   RFC (Request for Comments) 1483.

The interface between the Frame Relay entity and the AAL entity occurs through the Frame Relay core SAP.

SUMMARY

The basic operations for internetworking Frame Relay and ATM were introduced in this chapter. These operations provide options for protocol encapsulation or protocol mapping and network interworking or service interworking.

The Frame Relay core service access point (CSAP) is a useful tool for the programmer in that it provides guidance on building an application programming interface (API) on top of the Frame Relay layers.

4

DXI and FUNI

In this chapter we examine the operations of the Data Exchange Interface (DXI) and the Frame User Network Interface (FUNI). We learn why DXI and FUNI were developed and cite the advantages and disadvantages of their use. A comparison is made of the DXI and FUNI headers in relation to the Frame Relay header. The role of the data service unit (DSU) is explained as well as the DXI and FUNI topologies.

WHY DXI AND FUNI WERE DEVELOPED

Until recently, there were few products that supported ATM interfaces and for the products that did exist, the ATM interface was quite expensive. In addition, some machines require significant architectural changes to support ATM operations.

The net effect was a reluctance to install ATM in end-user equipment. Notwithstanding these problems, the early ATM systems were viewed as effective candidates as basic backbone transport networks, yet there remained the problem of how to interface an end-user device into these ATM backbones. The DXI and FUNI standards were developed to address these issues and solve the problems just described. We can understand this statement better by examining the DXI and FUNI topologies.

DXI AND FUNI TOPOLOGIES

Figure 4–1 shows the topologies for DXI and FUNI. Figure 4–1a shows the DXI topology and Figure 4–1b shows the FUNI topology.

The DXI topology requires a data service unit (DSU, also known as channel service unit [CSU]) to rest between the user device and the ATM switch. This device provides several T1 functions such as the conversion of unipolar code to bipolar code, loopback testing, and other diagnostic operations. The DSU runs the ATM interface on the ATM side of the line, which relieves the end user from having to segment the traffic into cells and otherwise dealing with the cell technology.

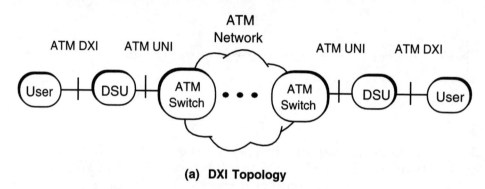

(a) DXI Topology

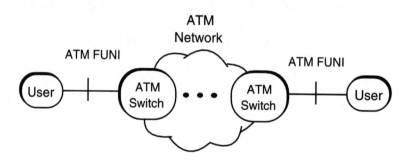

(b) FUNI Topology

Note: User device is usually a router and not a workstation/host.
where:

ATM   Asynchronous transfer mode
DSU   Data service unit
DXI   Data exchange interface
FUNI   Frame UNI
UNI   User network interface

Figure 4–1   DXI and FUNI topologies.

Figure 4–1b shows the FUNI topology, in which the DSU is not required. The user runs its traffic directly between its device and the ATM switch. This approach is less expensive than the DXI option because the DSU is not necessary.

The FUNI interface is quite simple, as we will see later in this chapter. It requires a software setup between the user device and the ATM switch. Additionally, the FUNI payload (the I field) can be large (if necessary), which makes this interface attractive in relation to running the small cells across the communications line between the user and the ATM switch (as in the DXI option).

A LOOK AT THE HEADERS

Figure 4–2 depicts the structure and format of the Frame Relay UNI (FUNI) and Data Exchange Interface (DXI) headers. They are quite simi-

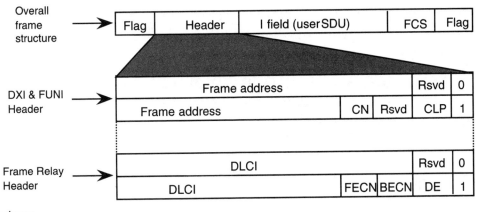

where:
BECN   Backward explicit congestion notification bit
C/R   Command/response bit
CLP   Cell loss priority bit
CN   Congestion notification bit
DCLI   Data link connection identifier (10 bits)
DE   Discard eligibility bit
FCS   Frame check sequence (16 or 32 bits)
FECN   Forward explicit congestion notification bit
Rsvd   Reserved bit
SDU   Service data unit (length varies)

Figure 4–2   Comparison of Frame Relay, Data Exchange Interface (DXI), and Frame UNI (FUNI) Headers.

lar to each other and the minor variations are explained here. First, notice that the header structure for DXI and FUNI are identical and the frame address for these two headers is in the same position as the Frame Relay DLCI. The command response (C/R) bit in the Frame Relay header is not instituted in DXI or FUNI, but is reserved for future use. The discard eligibility (DE) bit in the Frame Relay header is related to the DXI and FUNI cell loss priority (CLP) bit.

The Frame Relay BECN does not have a similar function in FUNI or DXI, or for that matter, it has no similar function in ATM either. As we learned earlier, the BECN is sent in the backward direction to indicate that traffic problems have occurred. The FECN bit of Frame Relay maps to the congestion notification (CN) bit of the DXI and FUNI headers, the FECN bit also maps to the CN bits in an ATM header. This information is forwarded to the recipient of the traffic, and it is assumed the destination end user will act upon these bits by sending some type of congestion notification to its sending user.

Finally, the CLP bit performs the same function as the DE bit, which is used for traffic tagging.

DXI MODES

DXI operates with three modes: Mode 1a is used only for AAL5, mode 1b operates with AAL3/4 and AAL5, and mode 2 operates with AAL3/4 and AAL5.

The principal differences between these modes lie in how many virtual connections are allowed across the interface and the size of the user payload (SDU) that is permitted. Additionally, each mode defines slightly different headers and trailers that are created by the DTE and/or DCE at the CPCS sublayer. Table 4–1 provides a summary of these modes.

EXAMPLE OF MODES 1A AND 1B

Figure 4–3 shows the relationship of the DTE layers and the DCE/SDU layers' modes 1a, 1b, and for AAL 5 traffic. The DTE DXI data link layer is closely related to an HDLC interface. Indeed, the use of HDLC-type frames eases the task of the DTE because HDLC is well known and implemented in many products. The task of the DTE is a relatively simple one to create a header that will provide enough information for the DCE to create a virtual circuit in the ATM network. In essence, the DXI header contains a DXI frame address (DFA), which is

Table 4–1 ATM Data Exchange Interface (DXI)

- *Mode 1a*
  Up to 1023 virtual connections
  AAL5 only
  Up to 9232 octets in DTE SDU
  16-bit FCS between DTE and DCE

- *Mode 1b*
  Up to 1023 virtual connections
  AAL3/4 for at least one virtual connection
  AAL5 for others
  Up to 9232 octets in DTE SDU for AAL5
  Up to 9224 octets in DTE SDU for AAL3/4
  16-bit FCS between DTE and DCE

- *Mode 2*
  Up to 16,777,215 virtual connections
  AAL5 and AAL3/4 (2^{24-1}): one per virtual connection
  Up to 65,535 (2^{16-1}) octets in DTE SDU
  32-bit FCS between DTE and DCE

---

used to convey the VPI and VCI values between the DTE and DCE. The DFA is 10 bits in length for modes 1a and 1b and 24 bits long in mode 2.

Figure 4–4 shows the activities for the support of AAL5 in modes 1a and 1b. The basic idea is to convey the DTE SDU across the ATM DXI to the DCE. The SDU is nothing more than the I field of the particular AAL protocol. This figure shows that the DTE encapsulates the DTE SDU into the DXI frame. The headers and trailers of this frame are then used by the DCE to receive the traffic and establish the virtual connection. The DCE is required to perform the ATM adaptation layer 5 common part

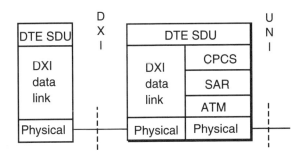

where:
  CPCS   Common part convergence sublayer
  SDU   Service data unit

Figure 4–3   Layers for modes 1a and 1b and AAL 5.

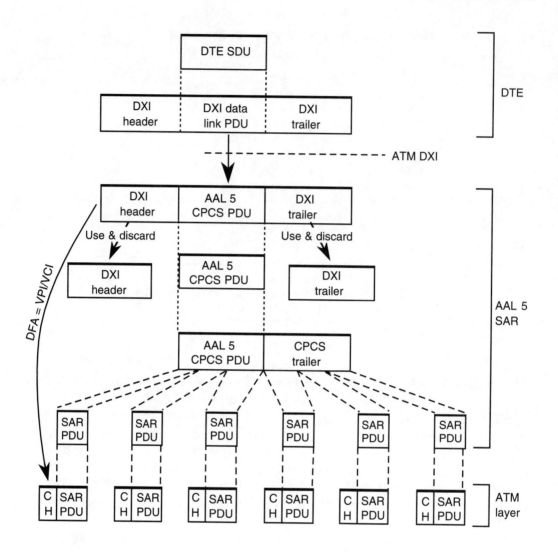

Notes:

The Frame Relay data link connection identifier in the DFA must be mapped into an ATM VPI/VCI.

The Frame Relay discard eligibility bit must be mapped to the ATM cell loss priority bit. Frame Relay congestion notification of FECN/BECN must be mapped into ATM congestion notification bits.

where:

BECN   Backward explicit congestion notification bit
DFA   DXI frame address
FECN   Forward explicit congestion notification bit

Figure 4–4   Modes 1a and 1b for AAL5.

convergence sublayer (AAL5 CPCS) as well as AAL segmentation and re-assembly operations (AAL5 SAR). The DCE also contains the ATM layer, which is responsible for the management of the cell header.

This specification does not define the operations of the service specific convergence sublayer, which is defined in ITU-T recommendation I.363.

EXAMPLES OF DXI FRAMES

Figure 4–5 shows examples of several of the frames transported across the DXI. Figure 4–5a illustrates modes 1a and 1b for AAL5. Figure 4–5b

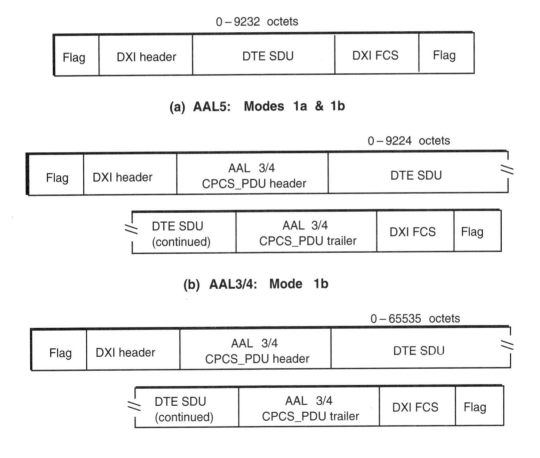

(a) AAL5: Modes 1a & 1b

(b) AAL3/4: Mode 1b

(c) Mode 2 data link frame

Figure 4–5   ATM DXI frames.

illustrates mode 1b with AAL3/4. The intent of the operations in Figures 4–5a and 4–5b is to emulate Frame Relay encapsulation, which, once again, requires few changes to the installed DTE devices in the industry. Finally, Figure 4–5c shows the contents of the mode 2 data link frame.

As Figure 4–6 shows, the DXI header and trailer are variations of the HDLC/LAPD header and trailer. The leading and trailing flags and the FCS fields are used in accordance with conventional HDLC operations. The DXI frame address (DFA) carries the bits for the VPI and VCI. Bits 6 through 3 of octet 1 represent the four least significant bits (LSBs) of the VPI. Bits 8 and 7 of octet 1 and bits 8 through 5 of octet 2 represent the six least significant bits of the VCI.

The four most significant bits (MSBs) of the VPI are set to 0 by the DCE on sending and ignored on receiving. Obviously, they are not coded in

Bit	8	7	6	5	4	3	2	1	Octet
Flag	0	1	1	1	1	1	1	0	0
DXI Header	DFA						RSVD	0	1
	DFA				CN	RSVD	CLP	1	2

(a) DXI Header

DXI Trailer	2^8	2^9	2^{10}	2^{11}	2^{12}	2^{13}	2^{14}	2^{15}	n–1
(FCS)	2^0	2^1	2^2	2^3	2^4	2^5	2^6	2^7	n
Flag	0	1	1	1	1	1	1	0	n+1

(b) DXI Trailer

where:
CLP   Cell loss priority
CN   Congestion notification
DFA   DXI frame address
FCS   Frame check sequence
RSVD   Reserved

Figure 4–6   DXI header and trailer for AAL5.

the DFA field. The ten MSBs of the VCI are set to 0 by the DCE on sending and ignored on receiving; they are not coded in the DFA field, either.

The congestion notification (CN) bit is used by the DCE if the last ATM cell that composes the DXI frame has the payload type identification (PTI) field set to 01x. The cell loss priority (CLP) bit is copied from the CLP bit sent from the DTE into the ATM cell header. The DCE does not see this bit when traffic is sent from the DCE to the DTE.

DXI FRAME ADDRESS MAPPINGS

Since DXI modes 1a and 1b restrict the number of virtual connections that can be established to 1023, 10 bits are sufficient for the VPI/VCI labels (2^{10-1} = 1023). And, since mode 2 permits 16,777,215 virtual connections, 24 bits are sufficient for the VPI/VCI (2^{24-1} = 16,777,215). Table 4–2 shows the mappings of the modes 1a and 1b 10-bit DFA and the mode 2 24–bit DFA to the VPI/VCI mappings.

COMPARISONS OF DXI AND FUNI

Table 4–3 provides a summary of the differences between DXI and FUNI. They are similar in their operations, but have some significant differences. FUNI is more flexible and does not require the installation of an SDU. It also allows the user of fractional T1.

For FUNI operations, the network is tasked with executing AAL to segment and reassemble the user's traffic. However, this arrangement allows the user link to/from the network to use frames and takes advantage of the variable (potentially large) information field in the frame. Thus, the overhead of the small payload in the ATM cell is not visible at the UNI. The network must absorb this overhead as part of its operations.

FRAME RELAY VS. DXI/FUNI

DXI and FUNI were developed as Frame Relay was maturing and becoming a major communications technology. Since Frame Relay is widely available, efficient and simple, this writer sees no compelling reason to use DXI or FUNI in place of Frame Relay, especially if it would mean the installation of another interface technology at the customer premises.

Table 4–2 DXI DFA Mappings to ATM VPI/VCI

Address Mapping	DFA Octet	DFA Bit	VPI Octet	VPI Bit	VCI Octet	VCI Bit
Modes 1A and 1B	1	6	2	8		
	1	5	2	7		
	1	4	2	6		
	1	3	2	5		
	1	8			3	2
	1	7			3	1
	2	8			4	8
	2	7			4	7
	2	6			4	6
	2	5			4	5
Mode 2	1	8	1	4		
	1	7	1	3		
	1	6	1	2		
	1	5	1	1		
	1	4	2	8		
	1	3	2	7		
	2	6	2	6		
	2	5	2	5		
	2	8			2	4
	2	7			2	3
	3	8			2	2
	3	7			2	1
	3	6			3	8
	3	5			3	7
	3	4			3	6
	3	3			3	5
	3	2			3	4
	4	8			3	3
	4	7			3	2
	4	6			3	1
	4	5			4	8
	4	4			4	7
	4	3			4	6
	4	2			4	5

Table 4-3   DXI and FUNI

DXI	FUNI
• DSU/CSU is required	• DSU/CSU is not required
• Cells still operate on the link	• Cells are created at the ATM switch
• Does not support Fractional T1	• Supports Fractional T1
• Does not supports SVCs	• Supports SVCs
• Supports SNMP	• Supports SNMP
• Uses a MIB	• Uses a MIB (a subset of the DXI MIB)
• Uses AAL 5 or 3/4	• Requires AAL5 with 3/4 optional
• Protocol encapsulation supported	• Protocol encapsulation supported

SUMMARY

We have seen that ATM can act as a transport mechanism for user multi-application traffic within and between networks and that ATM internetworking entails encapsulating user-network PDUs into the ATM cell through the invocation of AAL type 1, 3/4, and 5 modes. In addition, we've observed that the ATM DXI offloads some of the more complex AAL and ATM functions from a user device, while FUNI is based on DXI and provides a less complex and less expensive operation for the end user.

5

Network Interworking

This chapter describes the ATM Forum's Network Interworking specification, published as Document FRF.5. The emphasis is on how an ATM network is used to support transmission of traffic between Frame Relay systems. The network-interworking combinations are explained as well as the configuration options. The correlation of the Frame Relay quality of service features and those of ATM are also explored.

NETWORK INTERWORKING CONCEPTS

Figure 5–1 shows three Frame Relay service configurations for network A and network B through an ATM backbone. The configurations are labeled A1 through A3 for network A and B1 through B3 for network B. This is known as the Frame Relay internetworking scenario 1. It conforms to ITU-T I.555 (Frame Relay bearer service internetworking) and I.365.1 (Frame Relay service specific convergence sublayer, FR-SSCS). Several combinations of these interconnections are permitted. They are: (1) A1 to B1, (2) A1 to B2, (3) A1 to B3, (4) A2 to B2, (5) A2 to B3, and (6) A3 to B3.

ATM/Frame Relay network interworking does not stipulate any physical location for the interworking function (IWF). Figure 5–2 shows the possible placements of the IWF in relation to the access configura-

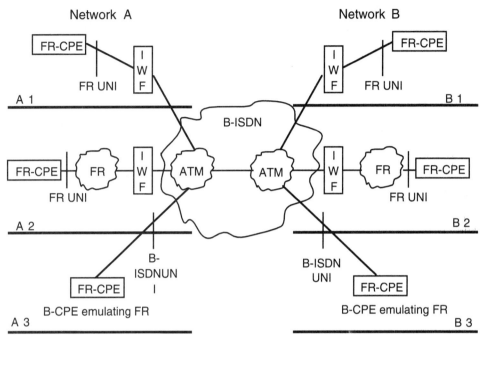

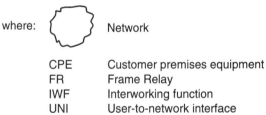

where: Network

CPE   Customer premises equipment
FR   Frame Relay
IWF   Interworking function
UNI   User-to-network interface

Figure 5–1   Network interworking topologies.

tions. Also, refer to Chapter 3, Figure 3–1. The IWF can be located at the Frame Relay network, the ATM network, at the customer premises equipment (CPE), or as a stand-alone unit, as in Figure 5–2a.

NETWORK INTERWORKING SCENARIOS

Figure 5–3 shows the structure and layers for interworking Frame Relay and ATM with what is known as scenario 1: the connection of two Frame Relay networks/CPE using B-ISDN. The interworking unit

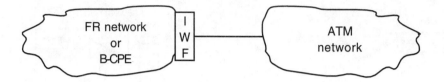

(a) Possible access configuration A2 or A3

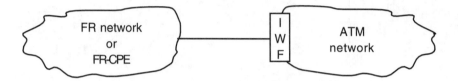

(b) Possible access configuration A1 or A2

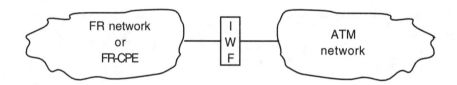

(c) Possible access configuration A1 or A2

where:
    CPE   Customer premise equipment
    FR   Frame Relay
    IWF   Interworking function

Figure 5–2   Configuration possibilities.

processes frames at the Frame Relay UNI with the user device using the Frame Relay Q.922 core procedures.

Scenario 1 supports the following reference configurations: A1–B1, A1–B2, A2–B2. Scenario 1 is also known as "Frame Relay Transport over ATM."

The IWF assumes the job of mapping functions between the Frame Relay network and the ATM network. The use of the B-ISDN network by the two Frame Relay networks/CPE is not visible to the end users. Therefore, the IWF must provide all mapping and encapsulation func-

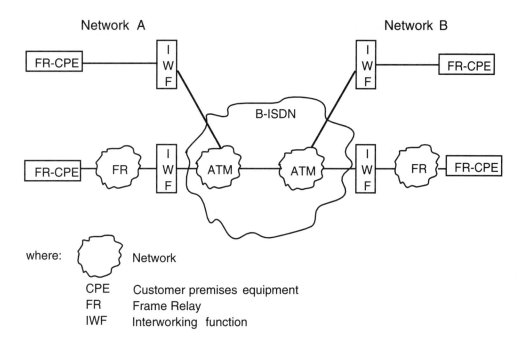

(a) Reference configuration

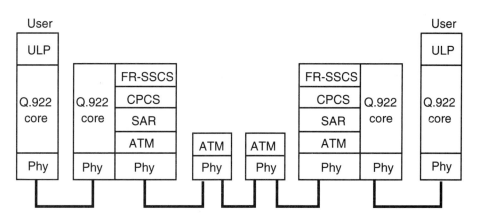

(b) Protocol stacks

where:
CPCS   Common part convergence sublayer
FR-SSCS   Frame Relay service specific convergence sublayer

Figure 5–3   Network interworking scenario 1.

tions to ensure that the ATM presence does not change the end-to-end Frame Relay service.

The FR-SSCS (Frame Relay-service specific convergence sublayer) FR-SSCS supports variable length frames at the FR UNI over preestablished connections (PVCs). Each FR-SSCS connection is identified with a Frame Relay data link connection identifier (DLCI: equivalent to the ATM VPI/VCI). Multiple FR-SSCS connections can be associated with one Common Part CS (CPCS).

The principal job of FR-SSCS is to emulate the FR UNI. In so doing, it supports Frame Relay forward and backward congestion notification (FECN, BECN), as well as the discard eligibility (DE) bit.

The CPCS is responsible for the following operations:

- Support of message mode (fixed-length blocks) or streaming mode (variable-length blocks) operations.
- Nonassured operations: CPCS is not responsible for traffic integrity.

For scenario 1, the use of the B-ISDN network is not visible to the end users, which means the end user protocols are not impacted. The IWF is responsible for encapsulation and mapping the end users' traffic in a transparent manner.

Scenario 1 supports the following network internetworking configurations: (1) A1 to B1, (2) A1 to B2, and (3) A2 to B2.

The second scenario for network internetworking is scenario 2, which requires the B-ISDN CPE to support the Frame Relay service specific convergence sublayer (FR-SSCS) (see Figure 5–4). In this scenario, the use of ATM and B-ISDN must not be visible to the Frame Relay end user.

The reference configurations that must be supported by scenario 2 are A1 to B3 and A2 to B3. For this scenario, the reference configuration of A3 to B3 is not discussed in the ITU-T I.555.

NETWORK INTERWORKING FUNCTIONS

The Frame Relay/ATM network interworking specification defines six network interworking functions that are based on the ATM Forum B-ICI (Broadband Intercarrier Interface) specification. These functions are as follows (and each is explained in the following material):

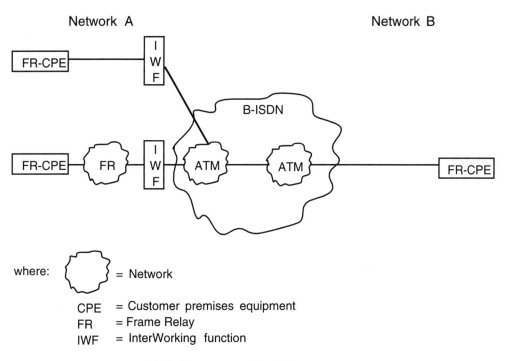

(a) **Reference configuration**

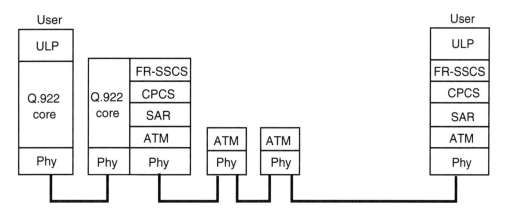

(b) **Protocol stacks**

where:
CPCS   Common part convergence sublayer
FR-SSCS   Frame Relay service specific convergence sublayer

Figure 5–4   Network interworking scenario 2.

- Variable length PDU formatting and delimiting
- Error detection
- Connection multiplexing
- Discard eligibility and cell Loss priority mapping
- Congestion indication (forward and backward)
- PVC status management

Variable Length PDU Formatting and Delimiting

The network interworking function supports variable length PDUs. The convention is to accept a PDU format that is identical to the Frame Relay Q.922 core PDU less the flags, the FCS field, and the zero bit insertion operation. This is the type of PDU that is expected by FR-SSCS. The FR/ATM IWF must use the FR-SSCS in accordance with ITU-T I.365.1 and the PDU formats shown as shown in Figure 5–5. The FR/ATM IWF must also use the AAL5 CPCS and SAR in accordance with ITU-T I.363.

As shown in Figure 5–5, the system must support the 2-octet format, whereas the 3-octet format is for further study and the 4-octet format is optional. Notice that the address extension bit (EA) is set to 0 to indicate that the header is extended one more octet.

Error Detection

Figure 5–6 shows the relationship of the FR-SSCS PDU to the CP-AAL5 and the ATM layers. AAL5 performs its conventional segmentation and reassembly functions by delineating the traffic into 48-byte data units with the addition of an 8-byte trailer as part of the last data unit.

The error detection operation is provided by the AAL5 CRC-32 calculation over the FR-SSCS PDU.

Connection Multiplexing

It may be desirable to map multiple Frame Relay connections to a single ATM connection. For the networking interworking specification, the FR-SSCS must support connection multiplexing on either a one-to-one basis (a single FR connection is mapped to a single ATM connection) or many-to-one basis (multiple FR connections are mapped to a single ATM connection). In both cases, a correlation must be made between the Frame Relay data link connection identifier (DLCI) and the ATM virtual path identifier/virtual channel identifier (VPI/VCI). These operations are

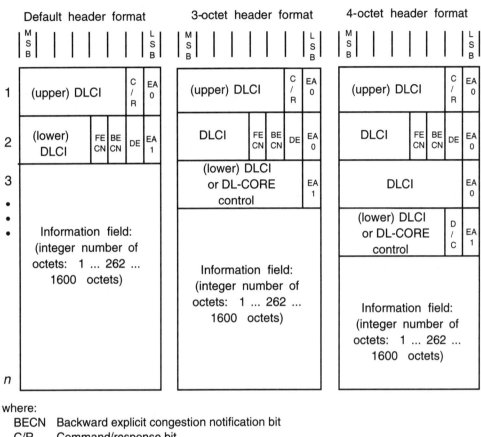

where:
BECN   Backward explicit congestion notification bit
C/R   Command/response bit
D/C   DLCI or DL-CORE control indicator
DE   Discard eligibility bit
DLCI   Data link connection identifier
EA   Address extension bit
FECN   Forward explicit congestion notification bit

Figure 5–5 Variable length PDU formatting and delimiting.

also described in ITU-T I.555. Let us now examine the two modes of connection multiplexing (see Figures 5–7 and 5–8).

One-to-One Multiplexing. For the case of one-to-one multiplexing, the multiplexing is performed at the ATM layer using ATM VPIs/VCIs. The Frame Relay DLCIs can range from 16 to 991 and the values must be agreed upon between the ATM end systems (that is to say, IWFs or ATM end users). Otherwise, a default value of 1022 will be used for the operation. These rules apply for 2-octet Frame Relay header. If 3- or

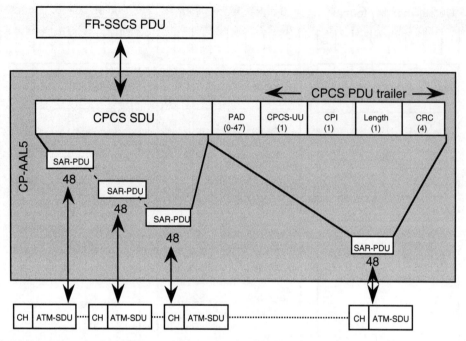

Note: Error detection is provided over the complete FR-SSCS PDU for the AAL5 CRC operation
where:

ATM	Asynchronous transfer mode
CH	Cell header
CP-AAL5	Common part ATM adaptation layer type 5
CPCS SDU	Common part convergence sublayer service data unit
CPCS-UU	CPCS user to user
CPI	Common part indicator
CRC	Cyclic redundancy check
FR-SSCS	Frame Relay service specific convergence sublayer
SAR PDU	Segmentation and reassembly protocol data unit

Figure 5–6   FR-CPCS operations (including error detection).

4-octet headers are used, the DLCI value must be agreed upon between
the two ATM end systems and the standards do not specify a default
value.

Many-to-One Multiplexing.   For the case of the many-to-one multiplexing, the Frame Relay connections are multiplexed into a single ATM
virtual channel connection (VCC) and identification of the Frame Relay
traffic is achieved by using multiple DLCIs. The many-to-one operation

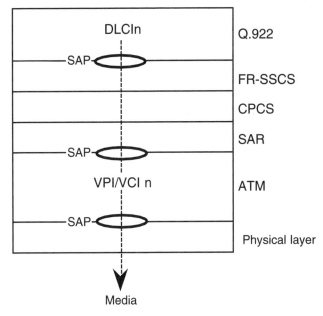

where:

ATM	Asynchronous transfer mode
CPCS	Common part convergence sublayer
DLCI	Data link connection identifier
FR-SSCS	Frame Relay service specific convergence sublayer
SAP	Service access point
SAR	Segmentation and reassembly
VCI	Virtual channel identifier
VPI	Virtual path identifier

Figure 5–7   Connection multiplexing (one-to-one).

is restricted to Frame Relay connections that terminate on the same ATM-based system.

The specification has no rules on the DLCI values that are to be used. Therefore, they must be agreed upon between the two ATM end systems.

Discard Eligibility and Cell Loss Mapping

The IWF equipment must support two modes of operation for discard eligibility and cell loss priority bit mapping (see Table 5–1). Be aware that these modes operate in the Frame Relay to B-ISDN direction.

For mode 1, the discard eligibility (DE) bit in the Frame Relay frame header must be copied without alteration into the DE bit that is coded in

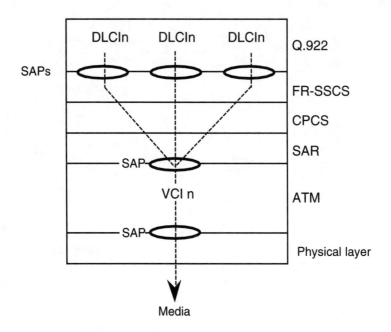

where:
  ATM   Asynchronous transfer mode
  CPCS   Common part convergence sublayer
  DLCI   Data link connection identifier
  FR-SSCS   Frame Relay service specific convergence sublayer
  SAP   Service access point
  SAR   Segmentation and reassembly
  VCI   Virtual channel identifier
  VPI   Virtual path identifier

Figure 5–8   Connection multiplexing (many-to-one).

**Table 5–1   Discard Eligibility and Cell Loss Mapping
(Frame Relay to B-ISDN Direction)**

Mode 1:

- Discard eligibility bit (DE) if Frame Relay frame header copied into DE bit of FR-SSCS header

- Then, copied into cell loss priority bit (CLP) of each ATM cell header created in the segmentation process

Mode 2:

- Discard eligibility bit (DE) if Frame Relay frame header copied into DE bit of FR-SSCS header

- Then ATM CLP bit is set to a constant value of 0 or 1

- This constant value is determined at setup time, and must remain unchanged

---

the FR-SSCS header. Next, this bit must be mapped into the cell loss priority (CLP) bit in the header of each ATM cell that is generated as a result of segmenting each specific Frame Relay frame.

For mode 2, the DE bit in the Frame Relay frame header must be copied without alteration into the DE bit in the FR-SSCS header and the ATM CLP bit shall be set to a constant value of 0 or 1. This value is decided when the connection is set up and must be used for all cells generated from the segmentation process for every frame. It must remain unchanged until such time that a ATM connection has its characteristics changed.

To support discard eligibility (DE) and cell loss priority (CLP) mapping in the B-ISDN to Frame Relay mapping, the network provider can choose between two modes of operations. For mode 1, if one or more ATM cells pertaining to a segmented frame has its CLP bit set to 1, or if the DE bit of the FR-SSCS PDU is set to 1, then the IWF must set the DE bit to 1 of the Frame Relay frame. For mode 2, the FR-SSCS PDU DE bit is copied without alteration into the Q.922 DE bit. This operation is independent of any cell loss priority indications received by the ATM layer. Figure 5–9 summarizes these modes of operation with four tables.

FR-to-ATM (Mode 1)				FR-to-ATM (Mode 2)				ATM-to-FR (Mode 1)				ATM-to-FR (Mode 2)		
fromQ.922 Core	mapped toFR-SSCS	mapped to ATM layer		fromQ.922 Core	mapped toFR-SSCS	mapped toATM layer		fromATM layer	fromFR-SSCS	toQ.922 Core		fromATM layer	fromFR-SSCS	toQ.922 Core
DE	DE	CLP		DE	DE	CLP		CLP	DE	DE		CLP	DE	DE
0	0	0		0	0	Y		0	0	0		X	0	0
1	1	1		1	1	Y		1	X	1		X	1	1
								X	1	1				
Note 1				Note 2				Note 3						

Note 1: For all cells generated from the segmentation process of that frame.
Note 2: Y can be 0 or 1.
Note 3: For one-or-more cells of the frame, X indicates that the value does not matter (0 or 1).

Figure 5–9　Discard eligibility and cell loss mapping (B-ISDN to Frame Relay direction).

Congestion Indication

The congestion indication function is organized as follows:

Congestion indication (forward):
   Frame Relay-to-B-ISDN direction
   B-ISDN-to-Frame Relay direction

Congestion indication (backward):
   Frame Relay-to-B-ISDN direction
   B-ISDN-to-Frame Relay direction

The forward congestion indication is supported with the Frame Relay FECN bit and the ATM forward congestion indication bit. For the Frame Relay to B-ISDN direction, the FECN bit in the frame header must be copied unchanged into the FECN field of the FR-SSCS PDU. The ATM forward congestion indication bit must always be set to congestion not experienced.

For the B-ISDN-to-Frame Relay direction, the forward congestion indication bit in the last ATM cell of the segmented frame received must be set to congestion experienced. However, if the FECN bit of the received FR-SSCS PDU is set to congestion experienced, then the IWF must set the FECN bit in the Frame Relay frame header.

The rules for the use of the congestion indication (forward) operations are summarized in Figure 5–10.

FR-to-ATM

Q.922F ECN	SSCSFE CN	ATMEF CI
0	0	0
1	1	0

ATM-to-FR

ATMEF CI	SSCSFE CN	Q.922F ECN
0	0	0
X	1	1
1	X	1

Note: 0 indicates congestion is not experienced
       1 indicates congestion is experienced
       x indicates that the value does not matter (0 or 1)

where:
   0 indicates congestion is not experienced
   1 indicates congestion is experienced
   X indicates that the value does not matter (0 or 1)

Figure 5–10   Congestion indication (forward).

As a general rule, the backward congestion indication operation is supported only by the Frame Relay BECN bit.

For the B-ISDN-to-Frame Relay direction, the BECN bit in the FR-SSCS PDU must be copied unchanged into the BECN bit of the Frame Relay frame header.

For the Frame Relay-to-B-ISDN direction, two conditions must be met if the BECN bit in the FR-SSCS PDU is set to congestion experienced by the IWF. These conditions are:

- The BECN bit is set in the frame header relayed in the Frame Relay- to-B-ISDN direction or
- The ATM forward congestion indication bits were set to congestion experienced in the last ATM cell of the last segmented frame that was received in the B-ISDN-to-Frame Relay direction.

The Frame Relay Forum document specification number FRF.5 and the B-ICI provide a state diagram to describe the operations to exit the congestion state depending on the activity of the ATM virtual channel. In

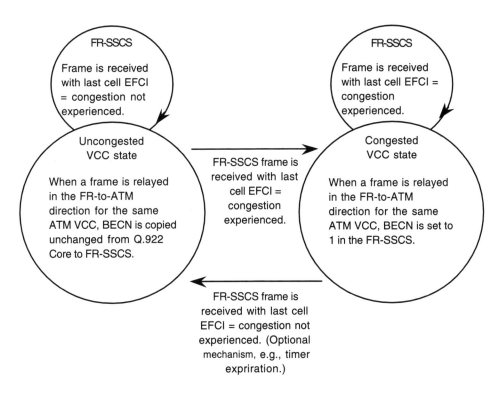

Figure 5–11   Congestion state diagram.

essence, Figure 5–11 shows that a timer can be used to reset a congestion state if no new congestion information is received in the B-ISDN-to-Frame Relay direction. The state diagram establishes that the congestion state must be cleared if the ATM forward congestion indication bits of the last cell in the next frame received is not set. If this event does not occur, the timer is restarted.

PVC Status Management

The network interworking for PVC management is based on the ATM Forum B-ICI specification. The basic idea is to allow the PVC ATM layer and the Frame Relay PVC status management of the FR-SSCS layer to operate independently of each other, as shown in Figure 5–12. This approach recognizes the difficulty of correlating management functions between two different protocols.

In essence, the individual management of Frame Relay PVCs at the Frame Relay UNI and Frame Relay NNI does not change. This operation only covers the management of the Frame Relay PVCs carried through the ATM network, which is stipulated in ITU-T Q.933 Annex A. These operations can consist of all six reference configurations described earlier in this chapter (A1–A3, B1–B3).

In addition, PVC management must adhere to ITU-T Q.933 Annex A, but with four changes: (1) the N391 counter default value is 1, (2) the T391 timer default value is 180 seconds, (3) the T392 timer default value is 200 seconds, and (4) the Frame Relay asynchronous message usage is recommended.

Rules for Multiprotocol Encapsulation. User protocols (upper layer protocols or ULPs) can be encapsulated into the Frame Relay information field based on the Frame Relay Forum Multiprotocol Encapsulation specification (FRF.3). This specification is based on the Internet RFC 1490 and ANSI T1.617a Annex F. This operation is centered around ISO/IEC TR49577, more commonly known as the network layer protocol id (NLPID). Chapter 2 provides information on the encapsulation operations and RFC 1490.

SUMMARY

Network interworking provides two scenarios, 1 and 2. With scenario 1, two Frame Relay networks/CPE are connected using B-ISDN. The interworking unit processes frames at the Frame Relay UNI with

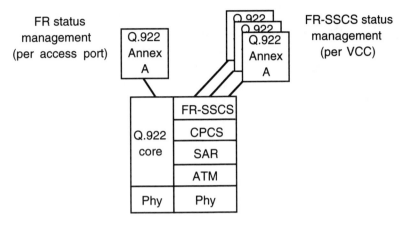

(a) At the IWF

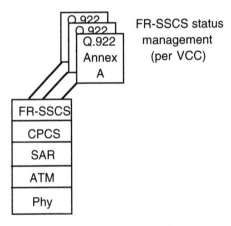

(b) At the B-ISDN CPE

where:
ATM   Asynchronous transfer mode
CPCS   Common part convergence sublayer
DLCI   Data link connection identifier
FR-SSCS   Frame Relay service specific convergence sublayer
SAP   Service access point
SAR   Segmentation and reassembly
VCC   Virtual channel connection

Figure 5–12   Permanent virtual circuit (PVC) status management.

the user device using the Frame Relay Q.922 core procedures. Scenario 1 supports the following reference configurations: A1–B1, A1–B2, A2–B2. Scenario 1 is also known as "Frame Relay Transport over ATM."

Scenario 2 requires the B-ISDN CPE to support the Frame Relay service specific convergence sublayer (FR-SSCS). In this scenario, the use of ATM and B-ISDN must not be visible to the Frame Relay end user.

6

Service Interworking

This chapter describes the ATM Forum's Service Interworking specification, published as Document FRF.8. The emphasis is on how an ATM network is used to support transmission of traffic between Frame Relay and ATM systems. The network-interworking combinations are explained as well as the configuration options. The correlation of the Frame Relay quality of service features and those of ATM are also explored.

DEFINITIONS OF SERVICE INTERWORKING

As introduced in Chapter 1, service interworking is similar to network interworking, but the ATM service user has no knowledge of the remote Frame Relay system. The Frame Relay service user performs no ATM services and the ATM service user performs no Frame Relay services. All interworking operations between the user are performed by the IWF.

Figure 6–1 shows the structure of service interworking and the protocol stacks. The location of the IWF is not dictated by any standard and can be placed in a single node or multiple nodes, depending upon the specific topology of an interworking environment.

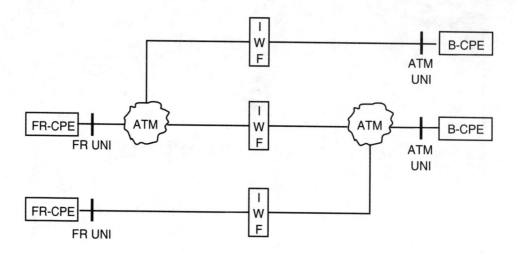

(a) Configuration

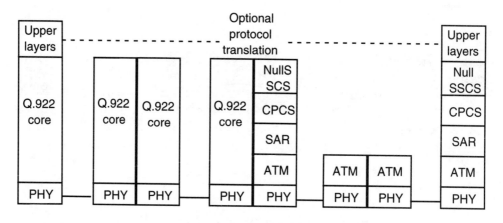

(b) Protocol stacks

where:

ATM	Asynchronous transfer mode
B-CPE	Broadband customer premise equipment (ATM-based)
CPCS SDU	Common part convergence sublayer service data unit
CPCS-UU	CPCS user to user
IWU	Interworking unit
PHY	Physical layer
SAR	Segmentation and reassembly
SSCS	Service specific convergence sublayer
UNI	User network interface

Figure 6–1   Service Interworking.

The B-ISDN service user (labeled the B-CPE in the figure) uses B-ISDN class C AAL5 operations with message mode, and unassured operations. AAL5 SAR is used, as well as AAL5 CPCS, and a null SSCS.

FR-ATM INTERWORKING SERVICE

As shown in Figure 6–2, the FR-ATM interworking service is provided through a combination of the FR-ATM IWF at the ATM network edge and a series of ATM interfaces (hops) to the remote ATM network edge. The service characteristics of the FR-ATM connection are a combination of the service characteristics of the FR-ATM IWF and the FR UNI. The FR-ATM IWF (through the FR UNI functionality) is connected to either a third-party Frame Relay network or CPE (both of which are external to the ATM network).

Frames are identified at the Frame Relay interface through the 10-bit data link connection identifier (DLCI), which is an identifier with local significance only. The DLCI permits multiple logical connections to

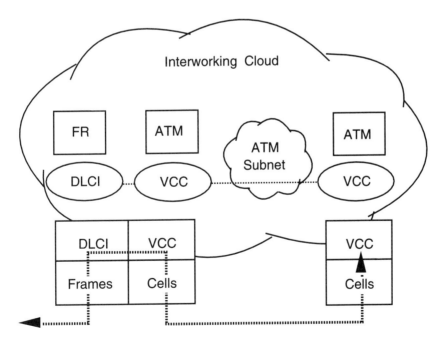

Figure 6–2 Frame Relay-ATM interworking cloud.

many destinations over a single access channel. Frames belonging to each logical connection are identified by distinct DLCI values and are correlated with an ATM VCC.

SERVICE INTERWORKING FUNCTIONS

The FR-ATM IWF operation must support a bearer service that is order-preserving, reliable, and operating with best-effort delivery of frames from the network edge of the FR UNI to the network edge of the ATM connection point.

For each connection in the user data transfer protocol stack (U-plane), the bearer service has the following operating characteristics:

- Provides bidirectional transfer of frames
- Preserves the frame order as given at the UNI upon delivery to the ATM network or end-point
- Detects transmission, format, and operational errors
- Provides transparent transport for each frame's user data contents; only the administrative (including the address and the frame check sequence [FCS]) fields are modified
- Does not acknowledge frames
- Does not retransmit frames

The FR-ATM interworking service supports ANSI T1.606 Addendum1:

- Compliance with the standard implementation of committed information rate (CIR), committed burst (Bc), excess burst (Be), and discard eligibility (DE)
- Forward explicit congestion notification (FECN) and backward explicit congestion notification (BECN) congestion signaling
- Frame discard preference under congestion

Table 6–1 lists the Frame Relay service I.233.1 Core Functions and correlates these functions to the B-ISDN Class, Message Mode, unassured operations. For this mode, the table lists the ATM functions and the AAL5 SAR and CPCS functions.

Table 6-1 Comparison of Functions in FR-ATM Service Interworking

Frame Relay Service		B-ISDN Class C, Message Mode, Unassured	
I.233.1 Core Functions	*ATM Functions*		*SAR and CPCS Function (AAL5)*
Frame delimiting, alignment, and transparency			Preservation of CPCS-SDU
Frame muxing/demuxing using the DLCI field	Muxing/demuxing using VPI/VCI		
Inspection of the frame to ensure that it is neither too long or too short			
Detection of (but not recovery from) transmission errors			Detection of (but not recovery from) transmission errors
Congestion control forward	Congestion control forward		
Congestion control backward			
Command/response			CPCS-UU
Congestion control discard eligibility	Cell loss priority		

The B-ISDN service is sparse. This intent is to provide few services in order to improve efficiency. Of course, since the SSCS in null in this stack, there are not a lot of operations that the AAL5 can execute.

The Frame Relay/ATM service interworking specification defines four network interworking functions that are based on the ATM Forum B-ICI (Broadband Intercarrier Interface) specification. These functions are as follows:

- Frame formatting and delimiting
- Discard eligibility and cell loss priority mapping
- Congestion indication
- Mapping the DLCI

This section of the chapter provides a summary of these four operations and Table 6-2 provides a summary of this discussion.

Table 6–2 Service Interworking Functions

- Frame formatting and delimiting
  FR-to-ATM: FR fame mapped to AAL5 PDU, with flags, stuffed bits, and FCS
    removed. Some of the Q.922 fields are mapped to ATM header
  ATM-FR: The opposite operations occur
- Discard eligibility and cell loss priority mapping
  FR-to-ATM:
    Mode 1: Discard eligibility bit (DE) in the Frame Relay frame header mapped to
      ATM CLP bit of every cell of the SAR operation
    Mode 2: ATM CLP bits are set to a constant value of 0 or 1
  ATM-to-FR:
    Mode 1: If one or more cells has CLP bit set, DE bit is also set
    Mode 2: DE bit must be a constant value configured at set up time
- Congestion indication forward
  FR-to-ATM:
    Mode 1: FECN bit mapped to the ATM explicit forward congestion indication
      (EFCI) field of every cell generated from the SAR operation
    Mode 2: FECN field is not mapped to the ATM EFCI field, but set to a constant
      value of "congestion not experienced"
  ATM-to-FR:
    ATM EFCI field (congestion or not congestion) is set to the FECN bit of the Frame
      Relay frame header
    Congestion indication backward
  FR-to-ATM:
    BECN bit is ignored
  ATM-to-FR:
    BECN bit is always set to 0
- Mapping the DLCI
    A one to one mapping is always made between DLCIs and VPI/VCIs

Frame Formatting and Delimiting

Frame formatting and delimiting differs depending on the direction
of the traffic flow. For the Frame Relay to ATM direction, the frame is
mapped into an AAL5 PDU. During this operation, the frame flags and
FCS field are stripped away and any bit stuffing operations are reversed.
Additionally, the Frame Relay header is removed with some of its fields
mapped into the ATM cell header fields.

For the ATM-to-Frame Relay direction, AAL5's message delineation
capability is used to align frame boundaries for the bit stuffing operations to occur. In addition, flags and the FCS field are inserted and the
encapsulation fields are translated into the protocol fields of the frame.

Discard Eligibility and Cell Loss Priority Mapping

The operations described for discard eligibility and cell loss priority mapping are organized in the Frame Relay-to-ATM direction and the ATM-to-Frame Relay direction. In both directions, two modes of operation are supported.

For the Frame Relay-to-ATM direction, mode 1 must be supported with mode 2 provisioned as an option. If both modes are supported in the IWF equipment, they must be configurable on a specific virtual connection basis.

In the mode 1 operation, the Frame Relay DE bit is mapped to the ATM CLP bit in every cell generated by the segmentation process. In the mode 2 operation, the DE bit of the frame header is set to a constant value. The value is configured on a PVC basis at subscription time.

For the ATM-to-Frame Relay direction, two modes of operations also are permitted with mode 1 required and mode 2 optional. Once again, if both modes are available, each must be configurable per virtual connection.

In the mode 1 operation, if at least one cell belonging to a frame has its CLP bit set, the IWF must set the DE bit of the resulting Frame Relay frame. In the mode 2 operation, the DE bit of the frame is set to a constant value. The value is configured on a PVC basis at subscription time.

Congestion Indication

Congestion Indication Forward.   In the Frame Relay to ATM direction, two modes of operation can be selected for mapping forward congestion indication. In mode 1, the FECN bit in the Frame Relay frame header is mapped to the ATM explicit forward congestion indication (EFCI) field of every cell generated from the SAR operation. In mode 2, the FECN field of the Frame Relay frame header is not mapped to the ATM EFCI field. The EFCI field is set to a constant value of "congestion not experienced."

In the ATM to Frame Relay direction, the ATM EFCI field (congestion or not congestion) is set to the FECN bit of the Frame Relay frame header.

Congestion Indication Backward (BECN has no equivalent function in AAL5 or ATM).   In the Frame Relay-to-ATM direction, the BECN bit is ignored. In the ATM-to-Frame Relay direction, the BECN bit is always set to 0.

Mapping the DLCI

Finally, a one-to-one mapping between Frame Relay DLCIs and ATM VPI/VCIs always occurs in service interworking.

PVC MANAGEMENT PROCEDURES

UTU-T Recommendation Q.933, Annex A defines the PVC management procedures. For service interworking, these procedures must be bidirectional, with the support of asynchronous operations optional.

The ATM Forum UNI and B-ICI specifications establish the procedures for PVC management on the ATM side of the IWF. The IWF is tasked with mapping the alarms from Frame Relay to ATM and from ATM to Frame Relay.

Figure 6–3 shows the configurations for PVC management operations and lists the PVC management procedures. Volume 1 of this series provides information on these operations.

FORMATTING AND IDENTIFICATION PROCEDURES

Figure 6–4 shows the formatting and identification conventions for the interworking of Frame Relay frames with the AAL5 CPCS PDUs. The frame and the PDU use the ongoing standards (RFC 1483, Chapter 2) for these operations. They are:

Control: The control field, as established in High Level Data Link Control (HDLC) standards

NLPID: The network level protocol id, as established in the ISO/IEC TR 9577 standard

OUI: The organization unique id, as established in RFCs 826, 1042, and several others

LLC: The logical link protocol, as established in the IEEE 802.x standards

Bridged PDUs

Figure 6–5 shows the conventions for header translation of the local area network (LAN) 802.3, 802.4, 802.5, and FDDI protocol data units

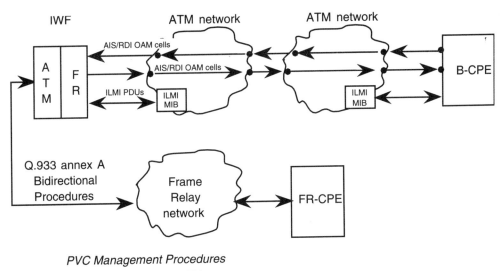

PVC Management Procedures

Frame Relay   *ATM*
Link integrity verification
New/Deleted PVCs   Added/Deleted PVCs
Active/Inactive PVCs   Active/Inactive PVCs
AIS/RDI   AIS/RDI

where:
  ILMI Interim local management interface
  AIS   Alarm indication signal
  RDI   Remote defect indication
  MIB   Management information base
  OAM Operations, administration, and maintenance

Figure 6–3   PVC management operations.

(PDUs). The NLPID header is set to 0x80, which indicates a SNAP header follows.

These PDUs are called bridged PDUs, because they are encapsulated using the SNAP OUI field of 0x00-80-C2, which is a reserved value for this type of encapsulation (OUI = 0x00-80-C2 is reserved for IEEE 802.1 encapsulation).

The PID part of the SNAP header identifies the type of LAN traffic that is encapsulated. These values indicate the presence of 802.3, 802.4, 802.5, or FDDI traffic as follows:

Preserved FCS	FCS not preserved	LAN type
0x00-01	0x00-07	802.3/Ethernet*
0x00-02	0x00-08	802.4
0x00-03	0x00-09	802.5
0x00-04	0x00-0A	FDDI
0x00-05	0x00-0B	802.6

* Ethernet cited in RFC 1294

The AAL5 CPCS-PDU header contains the logical link control (LLC) header of destination service access point (DSAP), which is set to 0xAA (170_{10}); source SAP (SSAP), which is also set to 0xAA (170_{10}); and the conventional HDLC control field, which is set to 0x03. The coding of 0xAA-AA is reserved in LLC to indicate that a SNAP header is present.

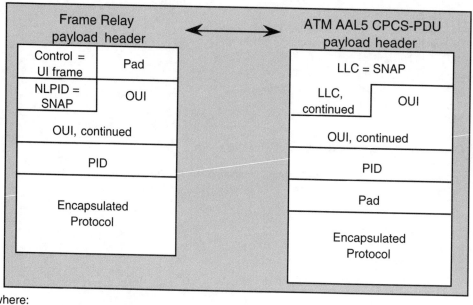

where:
LLC	Logical link control
NLPID	Network level protocol id
OUI	Organization unique id
Pad	Align to a 2-octet boundary (optional)
PID	Protocol id
SNAP	Subnetwork access protocol
UI	Unnumbered acknowledgment frame

Figure 6–4 Formatting and identification conventions.

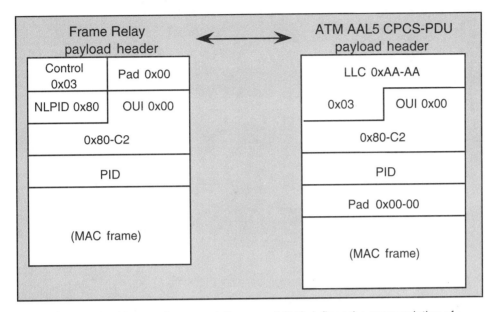

Note: RFC 1483 (multiprotocol encapsulation over AAL5) defines the encapsulation of Ethernet with an OUI of 0x00-00-00, followed by the Ethertype field.

where:

Term		Meaning of hex values coded above
LLC	Logical link control	Presence of SNAP header
NLPID	Network level protocol id	Presence of SNAP header
SNAP	Subnetwork access protocol	The OUI and PID fields
OUI	Organization unique id	Bridged PDUs (0x00-80-C2)
PID	Protocol id	Type of traffic and FCS use—see text

Figure 6–5   Header translation for bridged PDUs (IEEE 802.3, 802.4, 802.5, 802.6, FDDI).

Bridges and Source-Routed PDUs. The conventions cited above are quite similar to those used to encapsulate Bridge PDUs (BPDUs) and source-routed BPDUs. For the former, the PID is 0x00-0E. For the latter, the PID is 0x00-0F.

Routed IP PDUs. For the encapsulation of IP datagrams, the NLPID in the Frame Relay payload header of 0xCC (the reserved NLPID value for IP) is mapped to/from the PID value of 0x08-00 (the reserved PID value for IP) (see Figure 6–6).

In the AAL5 CPCS-PDU payload header, the OUI is set to 0x00-00-00.

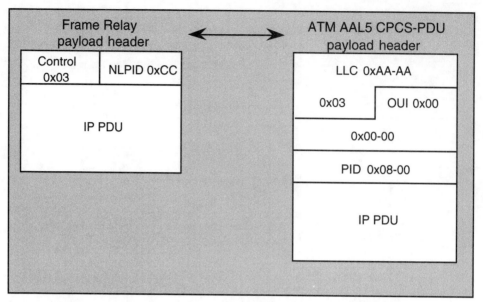

Note: Mapping is performed between the Frame Relay payload header of 0xCC (the reserved NLPID value for IP) and the PID value of 0x08-00 (the reserved PDI value for IP).

Figure 6–6 Frame Relay /ATM payload header for routed IP PDUs.

Routed OSI PDUs

The operations of encapsulation should be understood by now. The next few examples are based on the previous discussions and use some reserved NLPIDs and LLC SAPs to identify other types of traffic. Figure 6–7 shows the conventions for header translation of routed OSI PDUs.

Other Encapsulations

Figure 6–8 shows the procedure for encapsulation of X.25/ISO 8202 packets.

As a final example, Figure 6–9 shows the relationship of the Frame Relay and AAL5 header translations for the signaling procedures (switched virtual calls, or connections on demand).

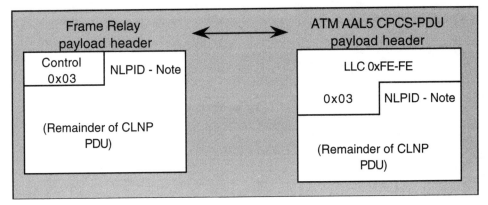

Note: Allowed NLPID values are 0x81, 0x82, and 0x83.
where:
0x81 identifies connectionless network protocol (CLNP) traffic
0x82 identifies end-system to intermediate system (ES-IS) traffic
0x83 identifies intermediate system to intermediate system (IS-IS) traffic

Figure 6–7 Frame Relay /ATM payload header for routed OSI PDUs.

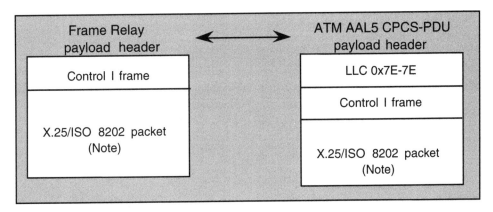

Note: The first octet identifies the NLPID.

Figure 6–8 Frame Relay /ATM payload header for X.25/ISO 8208 packets.

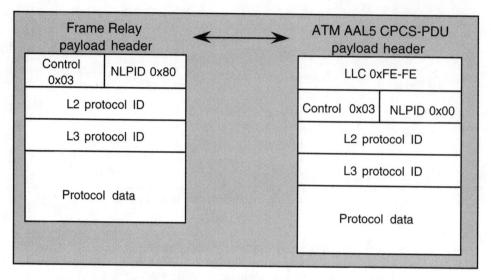

Figure 6–9   Frame Relay /ATM payload translation for Q.931, Q.933, or Q.2931 protocols.

ARP PROCEDURES

Chapter 2 introduced the Address Resolution Protocol (ARP). It is published as RFC 826, and Inverse ARP is published as RFC 1293. Frame Relay uses RFC 1490 and ATM uses RFC 1577 for ARP-type operations.

FRF.8 provides the specific configuration for ARP operations, and defines the responsibility of the IWF to support ARP mapping (see Figure 6–10). The IWF uses a mapping table to correlate the Frame Relay and ATM virtual circuit labels. The table contains the following information:

- Frame Relay port number on IWF interface P1
- Frame Relay DLCI value on this port (notation ee in the figure)
- ATM port number on IWF interface P2
- ATM VPI/VCI values on this port (notation aaa/bbb in the figure)

It is the responsibility of the Frame Relay network to correlate a Q.933 Frame Relay address (E.164) to a DLCI at dd in the figure. Likewise, it the responsibility of the ATM network to correlate a Q.2931 ATM address to a VPI/VCI at yyy/zzz in the figure.

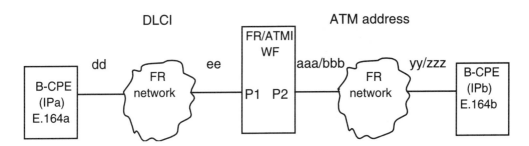

Figure 6–10   Configuration for address resolution.

ARP Message Formats

For Frame Relay-ATM interworking, ARP is modified as shown in Figure 6–11 with the notes depicted in Table 6–3.

The ATM Forum defines three structures for the combined use of number and subaddress:

	ATM Number	ATM Subaddress
Structure 1	ATM Forum NSAPA	null
Structure 2	E.164	null
Structure 3	E.164	ATM Forum NSAPA

TRAFFIC MANAGEMENT

The traffic management operations for Frame Relay-ATM service interworking are established in Q.933 Annex A, T1.617 Annex D and vendor-specific operations. This section focuses on the service interworking operations implemented by Nortel in its Passport and Magellan products.[1]

Traffic management across the FR-ATM IWF focuses on two areas:

1. QOS class mapping between Frame Relay and ATM, to determine emission priority and discard priority
2. Traffic management

---

[1]I thank Nortel for their information on this aspect of ATM internetworking. Further information is available in Nortel's various user and programming guides on Nortel's Magellan ATM family.

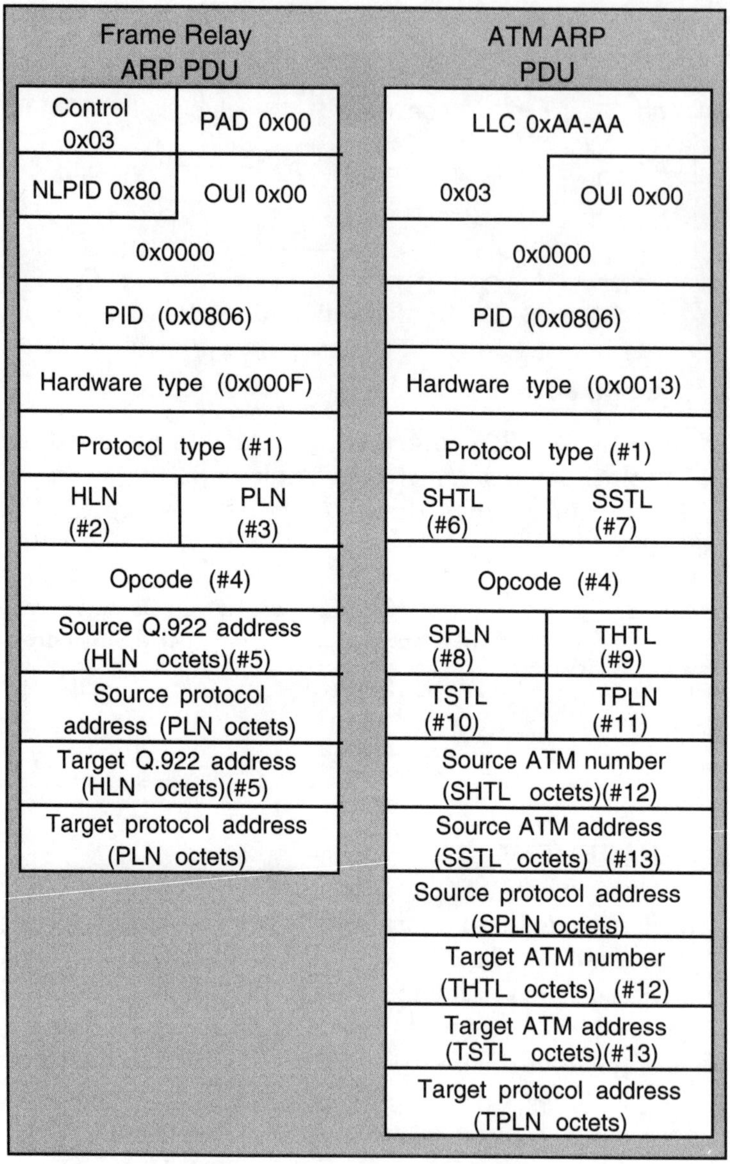

Frame Relay ARP PDU		ATM ARP PDU	
Control 0x03	PAD 0x00	LLC 0xAA-AA	
NLPID 0x80	OUI 0x00	0x03	OUI 0x00
0x0000		0x0000	
PID (0x0806)		PID (0x0806)	
Hardware type (0x000F)		Hardware type (0x0013)	
Protocol type (#1)		Protocol type (#1)	
HLN (#2)	PLN (#3)	SHTL (#6)	SSTL (#7)
Opcode (#4)		Opcode (#4)	
Source Q.922 address (HLN octets)(#5)		SPLN (#8)	THTL (#9)
Source protocol address (PLN octets)		TSTL (#10)	TPLN (#11)
Target Q.922 address (HLN octets)(#5)		Source ATM number (SHTL octets)(#12)	
Target protocol address (PLN octets)		Source ATM address (SSTL octets) (#13)	
		Source protocol address (SPLN octets)	
		Target ATM number (THTL octets) (#12)	
		Target ATM address (TSTL octets)(#13)	
		Target protocol address (TPLN octets)	

See Table 6–3 for note references #1 through #14.

Figure 6–11   ARP message PDU formats.

Table 6–3 Notes to Figure 6–11

#1: Ethertype; IP is 0x08-00

#2: HLN: Hardware address length: 2 or 4 for Frame Relay

#3: PLN: Protocol address length: 4 for IP

#4: ARP request is 1, ARP reply is 2; reverse ARP request is 3, reverse ARP reply is 4; inverse ARP request is 8, inverse ARP reply is 9; ARP NAK (ATM only) is 10

#5: C/R, FECN, BECN, and DE bits are set to zero

#6: SHTL: Type and length of source ATM number (#14)

#7: SSTL: Type and length of source ATM subaddress (#14)

#8: SPLN: Length of source protocol address: 4 for IP

#9: THTL: Type and length of target ATM number (#14)

#10: TSTL: Type and length of target ATM subaddress (#14)

#11: TPLN: Length of target protocol address: 4 for IP

#12: ATM number (E.164 or ATM Forum NSAPA)

#13: ATM subaddress (ATM Forum NSAPA)

#14: The encoding of the 8-bit type and length value for SHTL, SSTL, THTL, and TSTL is shown in Box 6–1

Box 6–1 8-Bit TLV Encoding

MSB	8	7	6	5	4	3	2	1	LSB
	0	1/0	Octet length of address						

where:
bit 8   (reserved)   = 0 (for future use)
bit 7   (type)   = 0 ATM Forum NSAPA format
            = 1 E.164 format
bit 6-1   (length)   = 6-bit unsigned octet length of address (MSB = bit 6, LSB = bit 1)

Table 6–4   Emission and Discard Priorities

FR Emission Priority	Traffic Type
Class 0	Multimedia (e.g., voice) with high emission priority
Class 1	Data with medium-high emission priority
Class 2	Data with medium emission priority
Class 3	Data with normal emission priority

FR Discard Priority	Traffic Type
Class 0[1]	Control traffic (not used by Frame Relay)
Class 1	High importance
Class 2	Medium importance
Class 3[3]	Low importance

Notes
1. Not provisionable
2. Not provisionable; automatically assigned for DE = 1 traffic

Frame Relay Quality of Service

Provisioning the QOS class for a FR-ATM connection is identical to that for a FR UNI or FR NNI connection. The emission priorities and discard priorities of the connection are separately provisioned to provide the QOS desired. These priorities are summarized in Table 6–4.

ATM Quality of Service

For ATM connections, there is no change in the provisioning of a QOS class. The QOS classes are specified directly based on the traffic type, as shown in Table 6–5. The emission and discard priorities are then automatically assigned. This table is only applicable for CLP=0 traffic; CLP=1 cells are treated as having a Class 3 discard priority.

FR-ATM Quality of Service

To provide maximum versatility, and recognizing that the selection of the mapping between the Frame Relay and ATM classes of service is dependent on network traffic types and engineering considerations, no

Table 6–5   ATM QOS Classes

ATM QOS Class	QOS Class Name and Usage	Emission Priority	Discard Priority
Class 1	Constant bit rate (CBR)—ATM Forum Class A. Intended for circuit emulation and CBR video	Class 0	Class 1
Class 2	Variable bit rate (VBR) Real Time—ATM Forum Class B. Intended for packetized audio and VBR video	Class 1	Class 1
Class 3	Connection oriented (CO)—ATM Forum Class C. Intended for connection-oriented protocols	Class 2	Class 2
Class 4	Connectionless (CNLS)—ATM Forum Class D. Intended for connectionless protocols	Class 2	Class 2
Class 0	Unspecified bit rate (UBR)	Class 2	Class 3

restrictions are imposed on the selection of the available QOS classes. The network provider can tailor this mapping to best match network capacity.

Table 6–6 shows a typical mapping between the Frame Relay and ATM QOS classes. Voice applications are assigned to the highest Frame Relay emission priority and the ATM VBR class. This table also differentiates between three types of data. This differentiation allows the best match of application demands to network performance.

The discard priority of the connection is also dependent on the settings of the Frame Relay DE and ATM CLP bits. Based on the assump-

Table 6–6   FR-ATM Typical Mapping between FR and ATM QOS Classes

Traffic Type	FR Emission Priority	FR Discard Priority	ATM QOS Class	ATM QOS Name
Packetized Voice	Class 0	Class 1	Class 2	VBR
Data	Class 1	Class 2	Class 2/3	VBR/CO
Data	Class 2	Class 2	Class 3	CO/CNLS
Data	Class 3	Class 3	Class 0	UBR

Note: Frame Relay discard priority Class 3 is not directly provisionable. Traffic can be forced to DE = 1 by provisioning CIR = 0.

Table 6–7   Discard Priority Mapping

ATM CLP	Provisioned Frame Relay Discard Priority	Resulting FR Discard Priority	Frame Relay DE
0	Class 1	Class 1	0
0	Class 2	Class 2	0
1	Don't care	Class 3	1

Frame Relay DE	ATM Discard Priority (see Note)	Resulting ATM Discard Priority	ATM CLP
0	Class 1	Class 1	0
0	Class 2	Class 2	0
0	Class 3	Class 3	1
1	Don't care	Class 3	1

Note: Provisioned by selecting ATM QOS.

tion that the DE-CLP mapping option is enabled, Table 6–7 shows the effect that these bits have on the connection discard priority that results from applying FR-ATM IWF for each direction.

Connection Policing and Traffic Shaping

A typical strategy is to perform policing at the receiving interface on the network and traffic shaping at the ATM transmit interface (if connected to an external ATM network). This strategy protects the network from excessive traffic on particular connections and offers some buffering to smooth out the inherent bursts that results from frame-to-cell conversion.

Standard Frame Relay rate enforcement of committed information rate (CIR) and excess information rate (EIR) with tagging applies. Applicable provisionable parameters at the Frame Relay ingress are CIR, Bc, and Be. The typical ATM traffic parameters are PCR_{0+1}, SCR_0, and the MBS. These parameters are specified at every ATM hop as well as at the ATM endpoint where shaping is enabled.

The mapping between these traffic parameters is subject to engineering considerations, and is largely dependent on the balance between acceptable loss probabilities and network costs.

SUMMARY

Chapter 6 has explained how service interworking relieves the ATM user from the need to know about the remote Frame Relay system and vice versa. Note that the Frame Relay and ATM user perform no mapping services because the IWF is responsible for the mapping services, and that service interworking defines a wide variety of encapsulation and header mapping functions.

7

Introduction to LAN Emulation

This chapter introduces ATM LAN Emulation (LANE). A review is made of the major operations of LANs in relation to ATM, and the rationale for the use of LANE is examined. A description is provided of the major LANE components, which consists of a variety of clients and servers.

Once again, we examine the Address Resolution Protocol (ARP) and learn how the LANE version of ARP is used to resolve MAC and ATM addresses. The chapter introduces LANE virtual channel connections (VCCs) and compares control and data virtual channels. The chapter also describes the LANE interfaces (SAPs and service definitions) between the layers of the LANE model.[1]

The chapter concludes with a description of the role of Q.2931 in the setting up of VCCs.

COMPARING LANS AND ATM

Much of the traffic sent between user equipment emanates and terminates over local area networks (LANs), the most prominent being Ethernet/IEEE 802.3, and IEEE 802.5 networks.

---

[1]The terms service specifications and service definitions are used interchangeably in this book.

As discussed in Chapter 1, LAN traffic is considerably different from ATM traffic because LAN traffic is connectionless and ATM traffic is connection-oriented. Moreover, since LANs use a shared medium, it is an easy matter to provide multicast and broadcast operations. Certainly, multicast and broadcast features can be provided in an ATM network, but these services require more operations on the part of the ATM switch than in a simpler LAN configuration. The ATM switch must use a routing table to determine which output port the traffic is to be sent to.

LAN addresses, which identify a LAN user workstation, are based on the well-known MAC address. This address is a serial number of the manufacturer of the LAN card and another number chosen by the LAN manufacturer. These flat, non-hierarchical addresses have nothing to do with the identification of the network and are therefore independent of a network topology. ATM addresses are based on the OSI addressing conventions and can identify networks, subnetworks, hosts, and other entities.

Purpose of LAN Emulation (LANE)

If an enterprise wishes to migrate to ATM technology, it is faced with the fact that ATM and LAN technologies are quite different. It is best not to change any components on an end user station during the migration to and installation of ATM networks. LAN emulation is designed to provide transparency to the end user application and permits the applications to interact with each other as if ATM did not exist. Table 7–1 provides a summary of these concepts.

The LAN emulation specification published by the ATM Forum is based on emulating the LAN MAC service. It does not explore operations at the network layer, which is left to other specifications, covered in Chapters 10 and 11 of this book.

Table 7–1   LAN Emulation (LANE)

- ATM and LAN technologies are different.
- User equipment should not be changed during migration to ATM networks.
- LAN emulation is designed to provide transparency to the end user application.
- LAN emulation permits users to interact with each other as if ATM did not exist.
- The LAN emulation specification (published by the ATM Forum) is based on emulating the LAN MAC service.
- LAN emulation does not explore the emulation of the network layer, which is left to other specifications.

SUPPORT OF KEY LAN OPERATIONS

The ATM Forum LAN emulation specification is designed to support several key LAN operations. First, connectionless operations are emulated. This operation means that the LAN stations can function as usual and need not be concerned with setting up connections before sending traffic. Even though the traffic traverses across ATM connections, end users are not aware of the connection-oriented part of the transfer process. LAN emulation supports MAC broadcast or multicast operations. LAN emulation supports MAC driver interfaces in ATM stations. This concept allows existing applications to access an ATM network through traditional protocol stacks such as IP, IPX, APPN, and AppleTalk. In today's environment, these protocol stacks operate directly over the MAC layer with a MAC driver. Therefore, LAN emulation must offer the same MAC driver service primitives to the upper layers so that they do not have to change their interface to the MAC layer.

Several "standardized" interfaces are available for MAC device drivers. The Network Driver Device Specification (NDIS) is available from 3COM/Microsoft under the *LAN Manager: Network Driver Interface Specification*, October 8, 1990. The Open Data Link Interface (ODI) is available from Novell, Inc. under the *Open Data Link Interface Developers Guide,* March 20, 1992. The Data Link Provider Interface (DLPI) is available from UNIX, International under *Data Link Provider Interface (DLPI) Specification,* Revision 2.0.0, OSI Workgroup, August 1991.

LAN EMULATION COMPONENTS

Thus far in the development of LANE, each emulated LAN is either an Ethernet/IEEE 802.3 or IEEE 802.5 network. Regardless of the specific LAN, each emulated LAN must consist of the following entities (see Figure 7–1):

- A set of LAN emulation clients (LE clients or LECs)
- A single LAN emulation service (LE service)
  The LE service consists of the following:
  - An LE configuration server (LECS)
  - An LE server (LES)
  - A broadcast and unknown server (BUS)

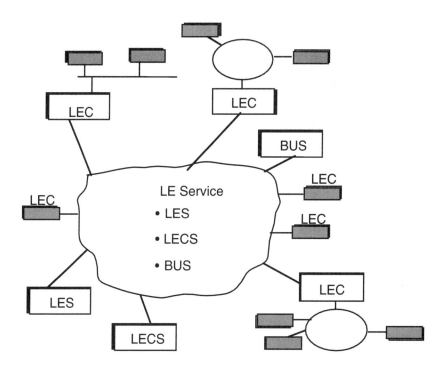

where:
BUS   Broadcast and Unknown Server
LEC   AN Emulation Client
LECS LAN Emulation Configuration Server
LES   LAN Emulation Server

Figure 7–1 LAN Emulation components.

The LE client is housed within an ATM end station. The LE client represents a set of users, which are identified by their MAC addresses. In contrast, the LE service may be part of an end station or may be housed in a switch. Moreover, it may be centralized into one station or distributed over multiple stations.

The major functions and attributes of these entities are as follows:

1. LEC
   • Entity in end system that sends data and performs address resolution
   • Bridges LAN frames between LANs (using MAC addresses)[2]

---

[2]A component that connects these conventional (legacy) LANs and an ATM network is also called an edge device. This component is examined in more detail in Chapter 11.

- Contains ATM interfaces for emulated LAN
- Identified by an ATM address
- Associated with MAC stations (MAC addresses), reachable through its ATM address

2. **LES**
   - Used to register MAC addresses, resolve MAC/ATM addresses (802.5 route descriptors)
   - Responds to LEC address resolution requests
   - Identified by an ATM address
   - Configured as one LES per emulated LAN

3. **BUS**
   - Acts as a multicast server by handling data sent by LEC with MAC addresses of "all 1s"
   - Each LEC is associated with one BUS
   - Handles unknown destination traffic (before a target ATM address has been resolved)
   - May be multiple BUSs per ELAN
   - Identified by an ATM address

4. **LECS**
   - Assigns LE clients to emulated LANs
   - . . . does so by giving the LEC the ATM address of the LES and a number of operating parameters (discussed later)
   - One LECS serves all ELANs, if multiple ELANs exist within a system

The location of these entities is not defined. For efficiency of operations, they should be housed in routers or ATM switches.

REGISTRATIONS

Figure 7–2 shows how a LAN emulation client makes known its ATM address and the MAC addresses for which it is responsible. Using the registration procedure, LEC A provides the LES its ATM addresses and the MAC addresses of the workstation (WS) on its attached LANs.[3] Thereafter, when other entities need to know about these address bindings, they can send queries to the LES.

---

[3]The specific configuration might have the LEC operating in a bridge. Alternately, a bridge could be located behind a separate node that houses the LEC.

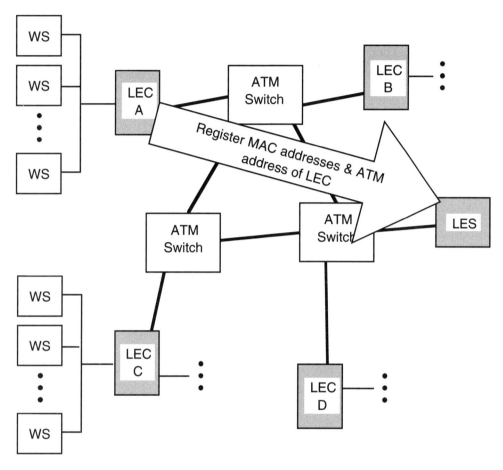

where: WS = Workstation

Figure 7–2 The registration operation.

ARP OPERATIONS

In Figure 7–3, LEC C receives a LAN frame with the MAC destination address of A in the frame header. Since LEC C does not know the ATM address associated with MAC address A, it sends a query to its LES. This query takes the form of an ARP request message.

Because LEC A had previously registered MAC address A and ATM address 123 with the LES that is servicing LEC C, it is an easy matter for the LES to inform LEC C about the queried address binding. This operation is performed with the ARP response message (see Figure 7–4).

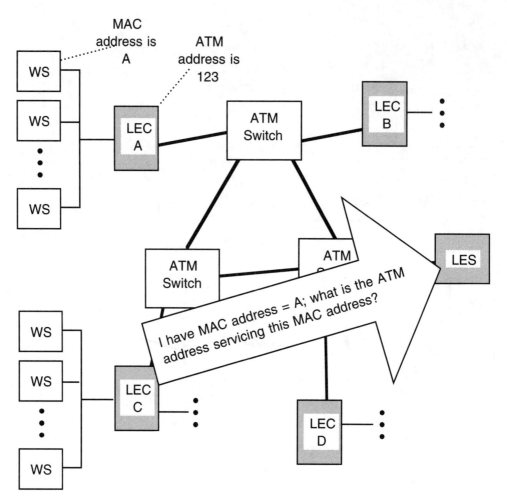

Figure 7–3   The ARP request operation.

CONNECTION SETUP

Now that LEC C knows where to reach MAC address A, it can set up an ATM connection to the LEC responsible for this MAC address. As shown in Figure 7–5, this process entails a setup operation with a switched virtual call (SVC). Later discussions will explain this call setup operation in more detail.

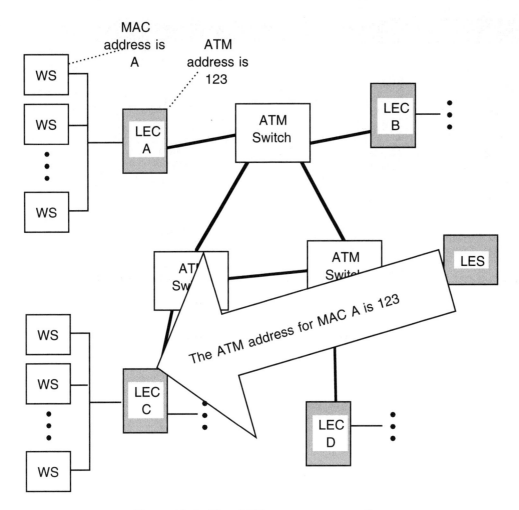

Figure 7–4   The ARP response operation.

VIRTUAL CHANNELS

As shown in Figure 7–6, communication among LE clients and between LE clients and the LE service occurs through ATM virtual channel connections (VCCs). Control and data VCCs are established for LAN emulation and each LE client must communicate with the LE service over these VCCs. The technology supports switched virtual circuits (SVCs), or permanent virtual circuits (PVCs).

As shown in Figure 7–6b, LAN emulation consists of a user-to-network interface (UNI), which is called LAN Emulation UNI, or LUNI.

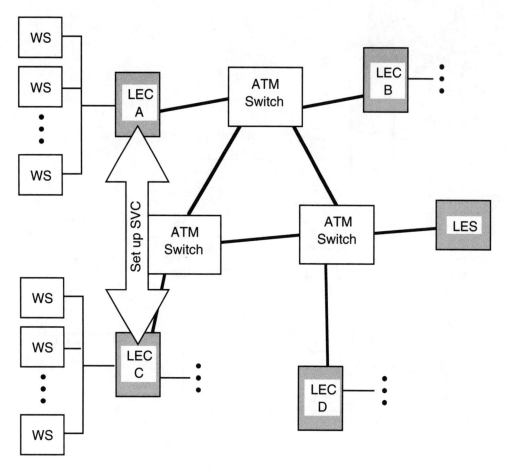

Figure 7–5   Set up the connection.

The LUNI specifies the protocol interactions between an LE client and the LE service over the ATM network.

LANE USE OF PRIMITIVES (SERVICE DEFINITIONS)

It is worthwhile to review the concepts of service primitives (also called service definitions and introduced in Chapter 2) as they pertain to layer interactions and their relationship to the protocols that flow across the UNI. The primitive is used by the layer to invoke the service entities and create any headers that will be used by the peer layer in the remote station. This point is quite important. The primitives are received by ad-

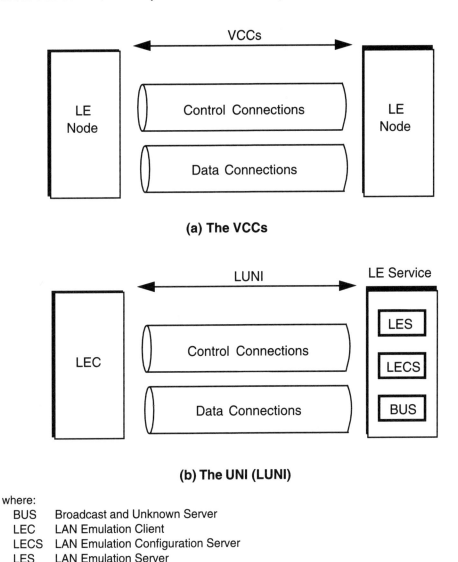

(a) The VCCs

(b) The UNI (LUNI)

where:
  BUS   Broadcast and Unknown Server
  LEC   LAN Emulation Client
  LECS   LAN Emulation Configuration Server
  LES   LAN Emulation Server

Figure 7–6   Virtual channel connections (VCCs) and the UNI.

jacent layers in the local site and are used to create the headers used by peer layers at the remote site.

At the receiving site, the primitive is used to convey the data to the next and adjacent upper layer and to inform this layer about the actions of the lower layer. These concepts are shown in a general way in Figure 7–7. For LAN emulation, primitives are defined between the LAN emulation entity (layer) and upper layer protocols (ULPs, also called the ser-

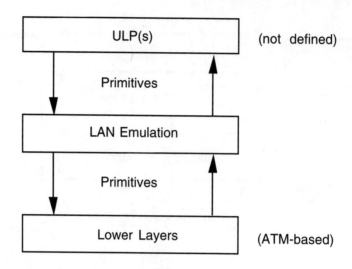

Figure 7–7   Primitives.

vice user). These upper layers are not defined in the LAN emulation specifications. Primitives are also defined between LAN emulation and lower layers, which we shall see are ATM-based layers. Chapter 8 provides a detailed description of these operations.

THE LANE PROTOCOL MODEL

Figure 7–8 shows the LAN Emulation layered model. As the reader can see, the LAN Emulation entity (layer) makes use of ATM layers and sublayers.

The layer interactions occur through four sets of service definitions labeled 1 through 4 in Figure 7–8. The service definitions are examined later in Chapter 8, but for our initial discussions, a brief summary is provided of each of the service definition interfaces:

- *Interface 1:* This interface defines the interactions with service definitions between the LAN emulation layer and upper layers, principally for the transmitting and receiving of user traffic. Since the on-going user layers are not to be affected with the ELAN operations. This interface is where the NDIS and ODI interfaces come into play.

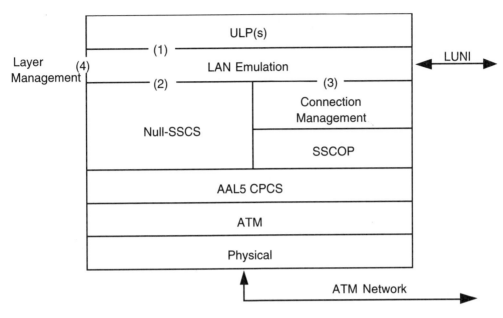

where:
  AAL   ATM adaptation layer
  ATM   Asynchronous transfer mode
  CPCS   Common part convergence sublayer
  LAN   Local area network
  SSCOP Service specific connection-oriented protocol
  SSCS   Service specific convergence sublayer
  ULP   Upper layer protocol(s)

Figure 7–8   LANE layered model.

- *Interface 2:* This interface defines the interactions with service definitions between the LAN emulation layer and the ATM adaptation layer (AAL), principally for the sending and receiving of AAL5 protocol data units (PDUs). Keep in mind (from previous chapters) that AAL5 accesses lower layers, including the ATM and physical layers. The interface service access points (SAPs) are identified by SAP-IDs. These SAP-IDs have a one-to-one mapping to VCCs.

- *Interface 3:* This interface defines the interactions with service definitions between the LAN emulation layer and the connection management entity. These service definitions are used to set up and release VCCs. Remember that this entity must handle both SVCs and PVCs.

- *Interface 4:* This interface defines the interactions with service definitions between the LAN emulation layer and the layer management entity. Its purpose is to initialize and control the LAN emulation entity and to receive status information about the ongoing LAN emulation operations.

PRINCIPAL LUNI FUNCTIONS

Figure 7–9 provides a functional view of the LAN emulation user-to-network interface (LUNI). Notice that the interface defines the operations between the LAN emulation clients (LECS, which are housed in an ATM end system) and the LAN emulation service. The requirements for the LUNI pertain to (1) initialization, (2) registration, (3) address resolution, and (4) data transfer.

The initialization operation entails obtaining the ATM addresses of the LE service, joining or leaving an emulated LAN (which is specified by the ATM address of the LE service), and declaring if a particular LE client wishes to receive address resolution requests for any traffic with unregistered destinations.

The registration operation entails the furnishing of a list of individual MAC addresses (and/or a list of Token Ring source-route descriptors) that the LE client represents. These source-routed descriptors consist of 802.5 segment/bridge pairs that are used for source-route bridging.

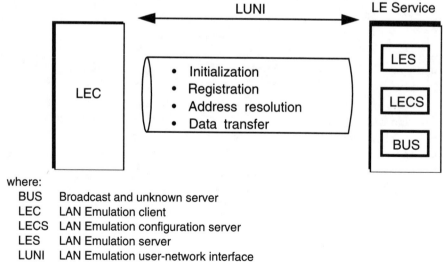

where:
   BUS   Broadcast and unknown server
   LEC   LAN Emulation client
   LECS   LAN Emulation configuration server
   LES   LAN Emulation server
   LUNI   LAN Emulation user-network interface

Figure 7–9   LUNI functions.

The address resolution operation is used to obtain the ATM address(es) (that represents the LE client) with a particular MAC address. This MAC address may take the form of a unicast address, a broadcast address, or a segment pair.

The data transfer operation moves traffic from the source to destination by encapsulating the LE service data unit (LE-SDU) into an AAL5 PDU for transmission by the LE client. It also entails the forwarding of the AAL5 PDU by the LE service, and the receiving and decapsulating of the AAL5 frame by the LE client.

CONTROL AND DATA CHANNEL CONNECTION

Control Channel Connections

We have learned that LAN emulation operations take place over virtual channel connections (VCCs). The connections are organized around control connections and data connections. The control connections are used for control traffic such as address resolution requests and responses. The data VCCs are used to transmit encapsulated LAN frames. Each VCC carries traffic for one emulated LAN, and the VCCs are provisioned to support a mesh of connections between the LAN emulation entities.

Let us examine the control connections first. The control VCC links the following entities: LEC to LECS and LEC to LES. They are never allowed to carry user traffic and they are set up as part of the LEC initialization phase, which is discussed later in this chapter.

Currently, three control connections are defined in the specification (see Figure 7–10): (1) configuration direct VCC, (2) control direct VCC, and (3) control distribute VCC.

The configuration direct VCC is used to obtain configuration information and may be setup by the LEC (as an option) as part of the LECS connect operation. The entity is allowed to maintain the configuration direct VCC while participating in the emulated LAN. That is to say, it can keep this connection open for further queries to the LE configuration service while participating in the overall emulated LAN operations. This channel can also be used to inquire about other LE clients (by other, I mean other than the one to which the channel is attached). As we shall see later, this connection uses broadband low layer information (B-LLI) to indicate that it is carrying LE control traffic.

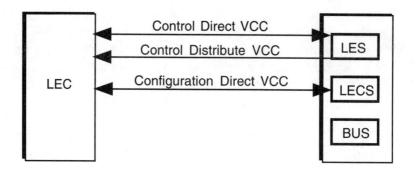

where:
  BUS   Broadcast and unknown server
  LEC   LAN Emulation client
  LECS   LAN Emulation configuration server
  LES   LAN Emulation server

Figure 7-10   Control channel.

The second control connection is the control direct VCC. It operates between the LEC and the LES in a bidirectional manner for sending ongoing control traffic. It is set up by the LEC during the initialization phase and, since it is bidirectional, it implies that the LEC must accept control traffic from this connection. This connection must be maintained by the LEC and the LES while these entities participate in the emulated LAN.

The last control connection is the control distribute VCC. This VCC is typically set up by the LES during the initialization phase. The use of this connection is optional and, if implemented, is set up in unidirectional point-to-point or point-to-multipoint arrangement. It is used by the LEC to distribute control traffic to the LEC or LECS. If this channel is established, the LEC is required to accept the traffic on the channel. And finally, both the LEC and LES must keep this connection up while participating in the emulated LAN.

Data Channel Connections

The data connections are used to send traffic between the LECs, which as we learned earlier are Ethernet/IEEE 802.3 or IEEE 802.5 frames. The data connections can also support flush messages, which are explained in more detail later. The flush message is a control message, but this is the only control traffic the data VCCs can support.

Currently, three data connections are defined in the specification (see Figure 7-11): (1) data direct VCC, (2) multicast send VCC, and (3) multicast forward VCC.

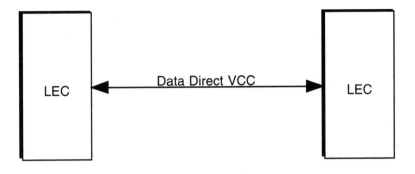

(a) Data direct VCC

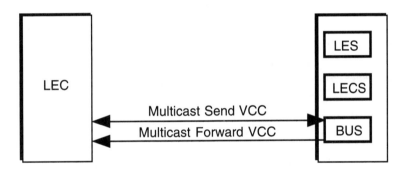

(b) Multicast send VCC and multicast forward VCC

where:
   BUS   Broadcast and unknown server
   LEC   LAN Emulation client
   LECS   LAN Emulation configuration server
   LES   LAN Emulation server

Figure 7–11   Data channel connections

The data direct VCC is used to transmit unicast traffic between LECS. Let us assume an LE client has traffic to send but it does not know the relevant ATM address for the destination node. The LE client generates an address resolution request to learn about the ATM address for the destination. The address resolution request, based on ARP, is called the LE_ARP message. Upon receiving a reply to the LE_ARP request, it can then establish a data direct VCC. Thereafter, all traffic can be sent to the destination LAN. The LEC that initiates the LE_ARP operations is responsible for establishing the data direct VCC with the responding client that was identified in the LE_ARP response. If the data direct VCC cannot be established (for example, due to bandwidth limitations), the LEC is not allowed to send traffic to the BUS. Its only option is to disconnect an existing data direct VCC in order to free up resources.

The second type of data connections is the multicast send VCC. This channel is setup with the BUS. It uses the same procedures that we discussed for data direct VCCs (using LE_ARP). The multicast send VCC allows the LEC to send multicast traffic to the BUS and to send initial unicast traffic to the BUS. In turn, the BUS uses the VCC return path to send traffic to the LEC. And, once again, this VCC must be maintained by the LEC while it participates in the emulated LAN.

The last data connection is the multicast forward VCC. It is utilized after the LEC has established the multicast send VCC. This VCC is used by the BUS to send traffic to the LEC. The multicast forward VCC can be either point-to-multipoint or unidirectional point-to-point. An important rule associated with this channel is that it must be established from the BUS to the LEC before the LEC can participate in the emulated LAN and, as in the other channels, the LEC should maintain this VCC while participating in the emulated LAN.

Another rule should be stated at this point. The BUS is allowed to forward traffic to the LEC on the multicast send VCC or the multicast forward VCC. However, the BUS is not allowed to send duplicate traffic on these two channels. But the LEC must accept traffic from each of them.

THE INITIALIZATION FUNCTION

The functions of the LAN emulation service are organized around (1) initialization, (2) registration, (3) address resolution, (4) connection management, and (5) data transfer.

This section will explain the initialization function with reference to Figure 7–12. As the figure illustrates, the initialization function proceeds from an initial state to an operational state through five phases.

In the initial state, the LE server and LE clients have parameters stored dealing with addresses, operational characteristics, and so on, which are discussed later. This information is about themselves that they will eventually share with other entities.

The first phase in the initialization function is called the LECS connect phase and entails the LE client finding and establishing a configura-

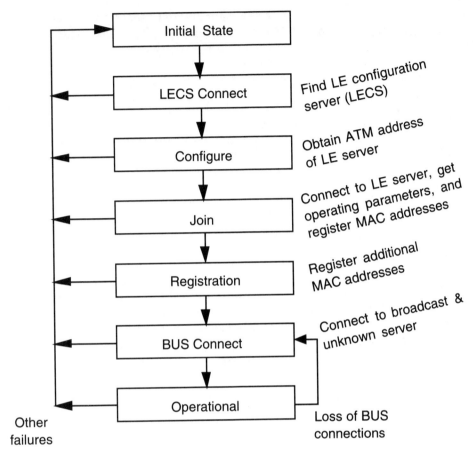

Figure 7–12   The initialization function.

tion direct VCC to the LE configuration server. The LECS is located
through a predetermined procedure: (a) an ILMI (Interim Local Management Interface) operation or (b) an established PVC (permanent virtual
circuit) to the LECS.

The next phase is the configuration phase in which the LE client
discovers the LE service, which entails obtaining the ATM address of the
clients' LE server. Also, during this phase, the LECs will downline load
several operating parameters to the client. During this phase, the characteristics of the emulated LAN are given by the LEC to the LECS (type
of LAN, maximum frame size).

Next, in the join phase, the LE client sets up a control direct VCC to
the LE server. Upon completion of the join phase, the LE client will be

identified with a unique LE client identifier (LECID). In addition, the LES now knows the emulated LAN's type (i.e., Ethernet), and the emulated LAN's maximum frame size, and the LEC has registered its MAC and ATM addresses with the LES.

The next phase is called registration. This operation allows the LE client to register one or more than one MAC addresses, and/or route descriptors with the LE server.

The final phase is the bus connect phase, which requires that the LE client send LE_ARPs for the all 1s broadcast MAC address. Once this is received by the BUS, it can then set up the multicast forward VCC to the LE client.

ADDRESS RESOLUTION OPERATIONS

As just explained, the registration procedure is used for a client to provide address information to the LAN emulation server. Consequently, this LE server can respond to address resolution requests if the LECs have previously registered their LAN addresses.

Assuming registration operations have been performed properly, the address resolution procedure allows a LAN destination address to be associated with an ATM address of another client or the BUS itself. The purpose of the address resolution procedure is to provide a mechanism for setting up the proper data connect VCCs to carry the traffic.

Upon receiving a frame in which the destination MAC address is unknown to the LEC, this LEC issues an LE_ARP request frame to the LES on its control direct VCC (see Figure 7–13). Upon receiving this request, the LES can issue an LE_ARP reply on behalf of a client that has previously registered the requested MAC destination address with the LES, which is shown in the bottom part of Figure 7–13. Otherwise, the LES forwards this LE_ARP frame to an appropriate client or clients on the control distribute VCC or 1-to-n control direct VCCs. Assuming that a client responds to the LE_ARP request with an LE_ARP reply, the LES will relay this reply over the control distribute VCC, which is shown in the top part of Figure 7–13.

Like conventional ARP operations, an LE_ARP client maintains an LE_ARP cache that stores the information contained in the LE_ARP replies. The cache is managed through timers that "age" the cache entries. I will provide more information about LE_ARP cache later in this book.

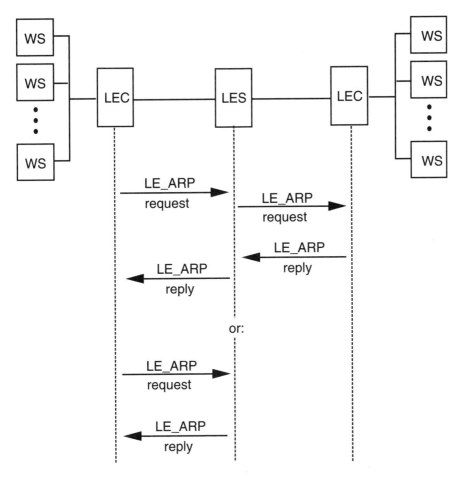

Figure 7–13   Address resolution.

CONNECTION ESTABLISHMENT PROCEDURES

In order to use the data direct VCC, a version of Q.2931 is implemented to support a call establishment. This is shown in a Figure 7–14, which deals with the protocol stack in Figure 7–8, titled "Connection Management."

Figure 7–14 shows the use of the Q.2931 SETUP, CONNECT, and CONNECT ACK messages. These messages are explained briefly in this chapter and they are covered in detail in Volume II of this series. The READY_IND and READY_QUERY are defined in the LAN emulation specification.

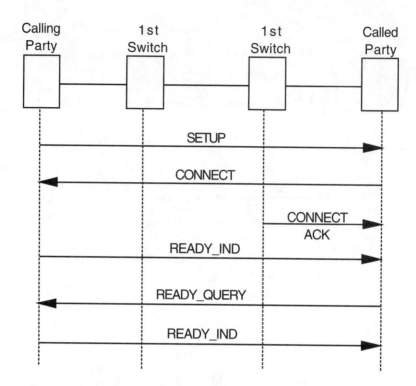

Figure 7–14   Establishment procedures.

A few rules should be clarified at this time pertaining to call establishment operations. First, the called party should not send a CONNECT message until it is ready to receive frames on the new VCC. This obviously means that the calling party assumes the VCC is available when it receives the CONNECT message. Since the CONNECT ACK message has local significance only on the called party side, the called party does not know that its initial data will be received by the calling party until it receives some end-to-end indication from the far end. This situation is endemic to the way that Q.2931 operates. In turn, upon receiving a CONNECT message, the calling party knows the allocation of the VPI/VCI values. The CONNECT message also allows the calling party to enable itself to receive traffic.

The READY_IND message is sent by the calling party after it has performed its housekeeping chores and is ready to receive frames on the VCC. It may also begin to send traffic immediately on the VCC. Upon receiving the CONNECT ACK message, the called party starts a timer. The use of this timer overcomes the problem with the local nature of the CONNECT ACK message. Upon expiration of the timer, if the called party has not received the READY_IND message, it can send a READY_QUERY message to the calling party on the VCC. In effect, this "ping" assures that both parties are aware of the connection. As Figure 7–14 shows, the calling party must respond to the READY_QUERY message with a READY_IND message.

The SETUP Message

Figure 7–15 shows the information elements associated with the SETUP message. A brief description of these information elements follow.

The AAL parameters information element contains five fields.

1. AAL type: Coded as 5 to stipulate the use of AAL5.
2. Forward maximum CPCS-SDU size: Coded to indicate the number of octets for this field; value depends on type of LAN being used.
3. Backward maximum CPCS-SDU size: Coded to indicate the number of octets for this field; value depends on the type of LAN being used.

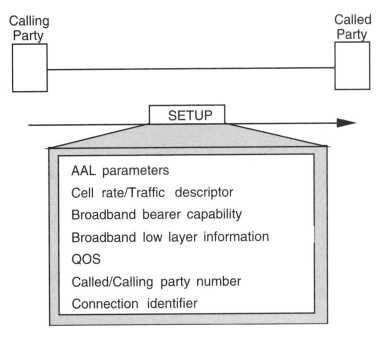

Figure 7–15   Contents of the SETUP message.

4. Mode: Coded as 1 to indicate message mode.

5. SSCS type: Coded as 0 to indicate null SSCS.

The ATM user cell rate/ATM traffic descriptor information element contains three fields.

1. Forward peak cell rate: Coded to indicate line rate in cells per second.

2. Backward peak cell rate: Coded to indicate line rate in cells per second.

3. Best effort indicator: Coded as 0xBE.

The broadband bearer capability information element contains five fields.

4. Bearer class: Coded as 16 to indicate BCOB-x.

5. Traffic type: Coded as 0 to indicate no indication.

6. Timing requirements: Coded as 0 to indicate no indication.

7. Susceptible to clipping: Coded as 0 to indicate not susceptible to clipping.

8. User plane connection configuration: Coded as 0 for point-to-point and 1 for point-to-multipoint.

The broadband low layer information element contains five fields.

- User information layer 3 protocol: Coded as 11 to identify the ISO/IEC TR9577 specification is to be used to identify an encapsulation header.

- ISO/TR 9577 Initial Protocol Identifier: Coded as 0x64 to identify a SNAP header.

- SNAP ID: Coded as 0x80 to indicate that the SNAP organization unit identifier (OUI) and the protocol identifier follow.

- SNAP organization unit identifier (OUI): Coded as 0x00-A0-3E to identify the ATM Forum OUI.

- PID: Coded with several values to indicate the type of VCC that is being setup, the rules for this field are described in Chapter 2.

The QOS information element contains two fields.

1. QOS class forward: Coded as 0 to indicate class 0.

2. QOS class backward: Coded as 0 to indicate class 0.

The called party number and calling party number information elements contain the fields pertaining to the ATM address format (discussed in Appendix B).

The last information element is the connection identifier which contains the VPI/VCI values that are assigned by the network for the connection. The called party uses these parameters to identify the VCC being established.

RULES FOR SENDING USER TRAFFIC

LAN emulation defines two types of paths for the transfer of user traffic (data frames). The first path is used between individual LAN emulation clients and is the data direct VCC described earlier. The other type of transfer uses the multicast send VCC and multicast forward VCC for the LEC-to-BUS communications process.

Assuming that the LAN emulation client knows the relationship of the MAC destination address to the ATM address, then it can simply send the traffic across the data direct VCC. However, if the client does not know which data direct VCC to use for the destination MAC address or if the data direct VCC has not been established, it is allowed to send this traffic over the multicast VCC to the broadcast and unknown server (BUS). It is then the responsibility of the BUS to forward the traffic to the destination client. If the MAC address is not registered, then the frame must be forwarded to all known clients.

Multicast operations are implemented in a slightly different manner than unicast operations. The rule is simple: for a multicast MAC address the LE client sends these frames to the BUS and not to the client. This means that during address resolution for multicast and broadcast traffic, the ATM address of the BUS is provided and not the end clients. In turn, if an LE client wishes to receive multicast traffic, it need only be connected to the BUS.

SPANNING TREE OPERATIONS

To prevent the looping of traffic, the ELAN runs the IEEE 802.1 spanning tree protocol. If a loop is detected, a node must block one of ports that is involved in the loop. Because ARP table entries may exist after a node is no longer present, a LE_TOPOLOGY_REQUEST message is used by the LEC upon encountering a bridge configuration update message. The LE_TOPOLOGY_REQUEST message is sent to the LES, which informs other LECs. This approach allows the ARP cache entry to be aged-out sooner.

SUMMARY

LAN emulation is designed to provide transparency to the end user application when interworking LANs with ATM machines. LAN emulation permits Ethernet and Token Ring users to interact with each other as if ATM did not exist.

The LAN emulation specification (published by the ATM Forum) is based on emulating the LAN MAC service. Upper layer protocol "emulation" (e.g., L_3) is not covered in LANE. MAC and ATM Forum addresses must be used in LAN Emulation.

8

Service Specifications[1]
and Protocol Data Units (PDUs)

T his chapter examines the four sets of service specifications that were introduced in the previous chapter. The chapter also describes the protocol data units (PDUs) employed in LANE.

As a brief review, service specifications are useful to designers because they provide guidance on programming the interfaces to drivers. Recall also that LAN emulation stipulates four service specifications: (1) LAN emulation-ULP, (2) LAN emulation-AAL, (3) LAN emulation-connection management, and (4) LAN emulation-layer management.

BASIC CONCEPTS

Service specifications are implemented with primitives. For the programmer, a primitive is better known as a system or function call. The primitive defines the "transaction" between the layers.

The OSI Model makes use of illustrations that show how the layers interact with each other (see Figure 8–1): The OSI Model refers to layers with the terms N, N+1, and N-1. The particular layer that is the focus of

---

[1]As a reminder, the OSI service definitions are called service specifications in LANE.

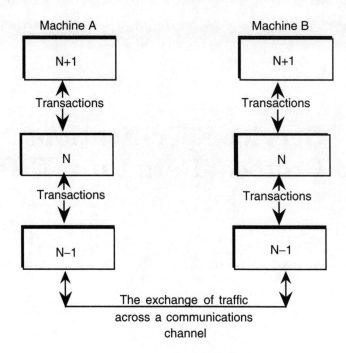

Figure 8–1   Documenting layer interactions.

attention is designated as layer N. Thereafter, the adjacent upper layer to layer N is designated as layer N+1 and the adjacent lower layer to layer N is designated as layer N–1.

In this manner, designers can use generic terms in describing the OSI layers. Moreover, the transactions between the layers can be developed in a more generic sense as well.

The services invoked at a layer are dictated by the upper layer passing primitives (transactions) to the lower layer. In Figure 8–2, users A and B communicate with each other through a lower layer.

Services are provided from the lower layer to the upper layer through a service access point (SAP). The SAP is an identifier that identifies the entity in N+1 that is performing the service(s) for layer N.

An entity in machine A can invoke some services in machine B through the use of SAPs. For example, a user that sends traffic can identify itself with a source SAP id (SSAP). It identifies the recipient of the traffic with a destination SAP value (DSAP).

It is the responsibility of the receiving lower layer N (in concert, of course, with the operating system in the receiving machine) to pass the traffic to the proper destination SAP in layer N+1. If multiple entities

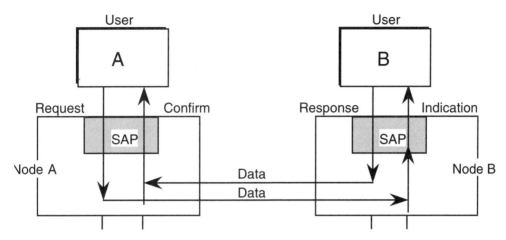

Note: The lower layers follow identical procedures
where:
  SAP Service access point

Figure 8–2   Communications between adjacent layers.

(e.g., processes) exist in the machine, the DSAP serves to properly identify the process.

The primitive is used by the layer to invoke the service entities and create any headers that will be used by the peer layer in the remote station. This point is quite important. The primitives are received by adjacent layers in the local site and are used to create the headers used by peer layers at the remote site. At the receiving site, the primitive is used to convey the data to the next and adjacent upper layer, and to inform this layer about the actions of the lower layer.

The OSI Model uses four types of primitives, summarized in Table 8–1, to perform the actions between the layers. The manner in which they are invoked varies. Not all four primitives must be invoked with each operation. For example, if the remote machine has no need to respond to the local machine, it need not return a response primitive. In this situation, a request primitive would be invoked at the local site to get the operation started. At the remote site, the indication primitive would be invoked to complete the process.

Of course, if the remote station were to send traffic back, it would invoke the operation with a response primitive, which would be mapped to the confirm primitive at the local machine.

Table 8–1   The Functions of the Service Definitions

At user A:

• *Request*. A primitive initiated by a service user to invoke a function.

• *Confirm*. A primitive response by a service provider to complete a function previously invoked by a request primitive. It may or may not follow the response primitive.

At user B:

• *Indication*. A primitive issued by a service provider to (a) invoke a function, or (b) indicate a function has been invoked.

• *Response*. A primitive response by a service user to complete a function previously invoked by an indication primitive.

LE-ULP SERVICE SPECIFICATIONS

The LE-ULP service specifications are based on the IEEE and Ethernet service specifications (see Figure 8–3). Two primitives are implemented for these service specifications. The LE_UNITDATA.request is

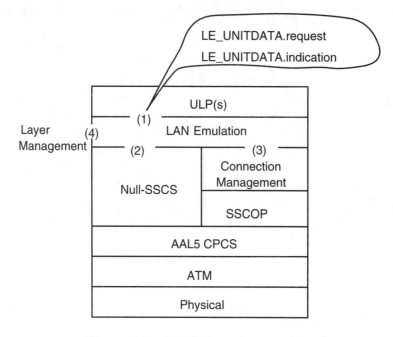

Figure 8–3   LE-ULP service specifications.

used to transfer traffic from a local entity to a remote entity and the LE_UNITDATA.indication transfers the traffic from the LAN emulation entity to the upper layer.

The parameters in the two primitives are almost identical. The only difference is that the LE_UNIDATA.indication primitive contains the service class parameter.

Each primitive contains: (1) destination address, (2) source address, (3) routing information (if applicable, for source routing on a token ring network), (4) frame type (if applicable), (5) data, and (6) priority (if applicable, for priority scheduling on a token ring network).

LE-AAL SERVICE SPECIFICATIONS

This LE-AAL service specifications defines the interface between the LAN emulation entity and AAL. As Figure 8–4 shows, the specification assumes a null SSCS. The AAL service interfaces are identified by a SAP-ID (service access point identifier) and these services apply only to the LE clients and the LE service.

Each LE client includes three types of SAPs: (1) control SAPs for initialization, registration, and address resolution; (2) data forwarding SAPs for the transfer of traffic; and (3) control SAPs that can handle configuration.

Two primitives are defined at this interface. The AAL_UNITDATA. request is used to transfer traffic from one LAN emulation layer to another. The AAL_UNITDATA.indication transfers traffic from AAL5 to the emulation layer.

Both primitives contain a SAP_ID parameter and payload parameter. The SAP_ID parameter in the request primitive is associated with the point-to-point or point-to-multipoint VCC and the payload parameter identifies the traffic that is to be transmitted. For the indication primitive, the SAP_ID is associated with the VCC on which data was received and the payload parameter identifies the received traffic.

LE-CONNECTION MANAGEMENT SERVICE SPECIFICATIONS

The LE-connection management service specifications must support permanent virtual circuits (PVCs) and switched virtual circuits (SVCs) (see Figure 8–5). The overall system must provide a mapping from a

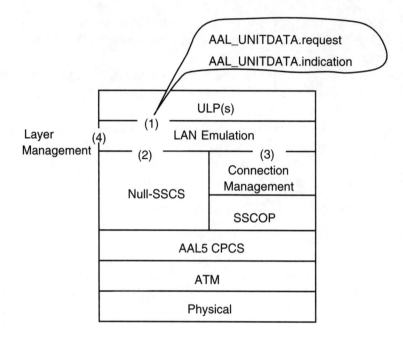

(a) The specifications

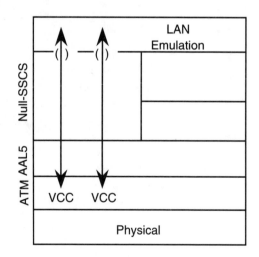

(b) SAPs and VCCs

Figure 8–4   LE-AAL service specifications.

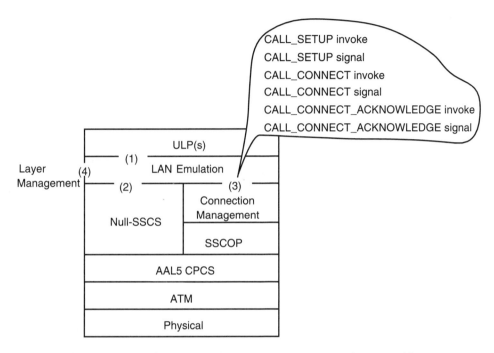

Figure 8–5 LE-connection management service specifications.

near-end ATM address, far-end ATM address, or broadband low layer information (B-LLI) to a VPI/VCI.

Since PVCs are preprovisioned, connection management is responsible for selecting an available connection that is associated with a near-end ATM address, far-end ATM address, and the B-LLI value. How these operations take place is an implementation specific matter, but the LE client must know which VPCs it is allowed to use, which PVC clients are associated with the PVCs, and which ATM addresses and B-LLI values are associated with the PVCs.

The switched virtual circuits are provided with the ATM Forum version of Q.9231. The reader may refer to Volume II of this series for more information on Q.9231. Our goal here is to explain Q.9231 in relation to LAN emulation.

First, the setup procedure is used to initiate a connection. It consists of six service specifications listed as follows:

CALL_SETUP invoke
CALL_SETUP signal
CALL_CONNECT invoke

CALL_CONNECT signal

CALL_CONNECT_ACKNOWLEDGE invoke

CALL_CONNECT_ACKNOWLEDGE signal

Parameters for the Connection Service

Table 8–2 lists the parameters that are required for a switched virtual circuit operation with LAN emulation. Once again, these parameters are defined in other standards and references. I will describe them in the context of LAN emulation. The AAL parameters defines AAL type 5 for use. The forward and backward maximum CPCS_SDU size is 1516 octets for all control VCCs and one of several options for data VCCs, as shown in Table 8–2.

Tables 8–3 and 8–4 provide more information on the LANE Q.2931 message parameters. In addition, the mode setting must equal message mode and the SSCS type must equal null SSCS.

The cell rate descriptor parameter must be coded to define both forward and backward peak cell rate in cells/second and the best effort indicator must be coded as 0xBE.

The broadband bearer capability parameter indicates what type of connection is required. The LAN emulation specification recommends using service type X or service type C as an alternative. In addition, the bearer class is set to 16, traffic type is set to 0 (no indication), timing requirements is set to 0 (no indication), susceptibility to clipping is set to 0 (not susceptive to clipping), and user plane connection configuration is set to 0 for point-to-point and 1 for point-to-multipoint.

The QOS parameter must be coded as class 0 for both forward and backward parts of the connection, which indicates a best effort requested connection.

Table 8–2   Parameters for Switched Virtual Circuit

AAL-5 SDU Max Octets	AAL-5 PDU Max Octets	Basis for SDU Size
1516	1536 (32 cells)	IEEE 802.3/Ethernet
4544	4560 (95 cells)	IEEE 802.5 Token ring 4 Mbit/s
9234	9264 (193 cells)	RFC 1628
18190	18240 (380 cells)	IEEE 802/5 token ring 16 Mbit/s

Table 8–3   Q.2931 Message Parameters Required by LAN Emulation

- AAL parameters
- ATM user cell rate/traffic descriptor
- Broadband bearer capabilities
- Broadband low layer information
- QOS parameter
- Called party number
- Calling party number
- Connection identifier

The called and calling party numbers are coded in accordance with ATM Forum address rules and must use the ATM Forum private UNI address format of 20 octets.

Finally, the connection identifier is coded to indicate what VPI, VCI values have been assigned by the network for the connection. This information is placed in the SETUP message by the network and conveyed to the called party. In turn, the VPI, VCI values are placed in this parameter in the CONNECT message and are used by the called party.

Table 8–4   The Broadband Low Layer Information Codes

Field	Value
User information layer 3 protocol	11 (ISO/IEC TR 9577)
ISO/IEC TR 9577 Initial Protocol Identifier	65 (SNAP Identifier-0x80, spread over 2 octets, left justified)
Continued from previous octet	Continued (Ext bit is set to 1)
SNAP ID	0x80 (indicates SNAP and PID follow)
SNAP Organization Unit Identifier	0x-00-A0-3E (ATM Forum OUI)
PID	0001 for LE configuration direct VCC, Control Direct VCC and Control Distribute VCC
	0002 for Ethernet/IEEE 802.3 LE Data Direct VCC
	0003 for IEEE 802.5 LE Data Direct VCC
	0004 for Ethernet/IEEE 802.3 LE Multicast Send VCC and Multicast Forward VCC
	0005 for IEEE 802.5 Multicast Send VCC and Multicast Forward VCC

Next, the release procedure is used to release a connection. It consists of four service specifications listed as follows:

CALL_RELEASE invoke
CALL_RELEASE signal
CALL_RELEASE_COMPLETE invoke
CALL_RELEASE_COMPLETE signal

ADD AND DROP PARTY PROCEDURE

The add party/drop party procedure is used to add or drop a party to an existing connection. It consists of ten service specifications listed as follows (see Figure 8–6). These operations are covered in Volume II of this series:

CALL_ADD_PARTY invoke
CALL_ADD_PARTY signal
CALL_ADD_PARTY_ACKNOWLEDGE invoke
CALL_ADD_PARTY_ACKNOWLEDGE signal
CALL_ADD_PARTY_REJECT invoke
CALL_ADD_PARTY_REJECT signal
CALL_DROP_PARTY invoke
CALL_DROP_PARTY signal
CALL_DROP_PARTY_ACKNOWLEDGE invoke
CALL_DROP_PARTY_ACKNOWLEDGE signal

LE-LAYER MANAGEMENT SERVICE SPECIFICATIONS

The LE-layer management service specifications define seven primitives at this interface. The primitives are listed in Figure 8–7 and in this section we will learn about their operations. The LM_LEC_INITIALIZE. request configures the LE client and enables it to join the emulated LAN. It is generated by the local management entity and, when received by the LE client, the client must release all VCCs, start all over again (in essence) by entering the initial state described in the previous chapter. The primitive is coded as follows:

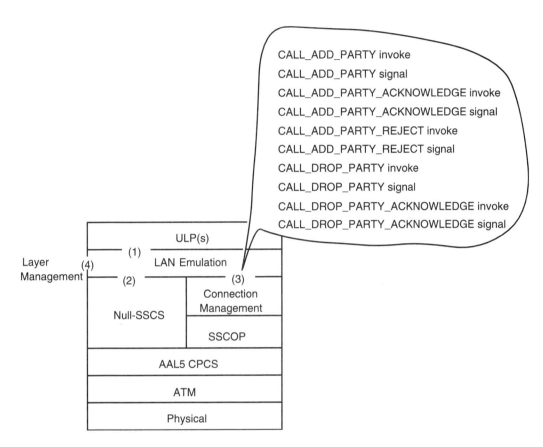

Figure 8–6   Add party/drop party service specifications.

LM_LEC_INITIALIZE.request(LEC_ATM_address, Server_ATM_address, MAC Address, Configure_mode, LEC_proxy_class, Requested_LAN_type, Requested_max_frame_size, Requested_ELAN_name, Joint_time-out)

The ATM address of the LE client is specified in LEC_ATM_address parameter. The ATM address of the LE configuration server or the LE server is contained in the Server_ATM_address parameter. The contents of this parameter depend on how the Configure_mode is coded. It may be coded as autoconfigure or manual. It specifies if the LEC will autoconfigure (which means the LEC attaches to an LECS to discover the LES ATM address). For manual configuration, this parameter specifies the ATM address of the LES. This parameter is left blank if the Configure_mode is set to autoconfigure. The MAC address is optional.

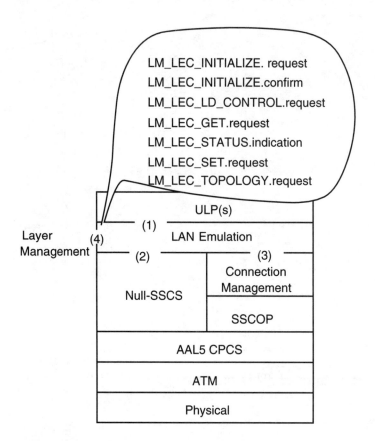

Figure 8–7   LE-layer management service specifications.

The LEC_proxy_class is coded as proxy or nonproxy. The Requested_LAN_type specifies the type of LAN that will be used for the operation. The Requested_max_frame_size can be set to 1516, 4544, 9234, or 18190 octets. The Request_ELAN_name parameter may be unspecified or contain the name of the emulated LAN the client wishes to join. Finally, the Join_time-out parameter contains a minimum time that the client should wait for a response to its join request or its configuration request.

The LM_LEC_INITIALIZE.confirm primitive confirms the request primitive and also indicates if the LECs interface is functional. It contains only one parameter, the Join_status. This parameter indicates if the initialization was a success or failure. If the Join_status indicates success, the LEC service user can begin sending and receiving traffic.

The LE client maintains a database of MAC addresses and route designators. The route designators contain the addresses that the LEC represents and, therefore, identifies the addresses for which it should receive frames. The LM_LEC_LD_CONTROL.request primitive is used to maintain this database. It allows entries to be added, deleted, or updated to the database. This primitive is coded as follows: LM_LEC_LD_CONTROL.request (LD_action, LD_type, LD_proxy_class, LAN_destination_address).

The LD_action parameter indicates if the address is to be deleted or added or if all entries are to be cleared. This later operation will clear all entries that match the specified LD_type and LD_proxy_class.

The LD_type parameter specifies multicast, unicast, or route designator.

The LD_proxy_class parameter specifies either proxy or local.

The LAN_destination_address parameter for a unicast or multicast LD_type is the conventional 48–bit MAC address. If the LD_type is a route designator, then the LAN_destination_address is a conventional 16-bit route designator that consists of the 12-bit segment ID and 4-bit bridge number.

The LE client contains a Management Information Base (MIB). The LM_LEC_GET.request is invoked by layer management to obtain information from the MIB. This primitive contains only one parameter, which is called the Attribute_id. This parameter can identify object identifiers in the MIB. The actual contents of this parameter are implementation specific.

In response to the previous primitive, the LE client sends the LM_LEC_STATUS.indication primitive with the status_report parameter. This parameter contains the information requested in the request primitive. Additionally, this primitive can be used by the LE client to provide layer management with alarms, statistics, error reports, and other functions.

The LM_LEC_SET.request primitive is used by layer management to control the behavior of the LE client. It actually operates on the LE client's MIB, which in turn will affect the operations of the LE client. The primitive contains the Attribute_id parameter discussed earlier and the Attribute_value parameter, which specifies the new value that is to be written into the MIB.

Finally, the LM_LEC_TOPOLOGY.request primitive is used to inform other LE clients about the change of a LAN topology. Its actual implementation varies but is used for example in transfer and bridge operations when a bridge sends out a configuration bridge protocol data unit (PDU). The primitive contains one parameter, the Topology_change_status, which is coded to indicate topology change or no topology change.

The receipt of this primitive from layer management requires the LE client to send a topology request frame to the LES.

DATA FRAMES

The two data frames used in LAN emulation are shown in Figure 8–8. The top frame shows the IEEE 802.3/Ethernet frame and the lower frame shows the IEEE 802.5 frame.[2]

For the top frame, the minimum AAL5 SDU length is 62 octets. The LAN emulation header (LE header) is 2 octets in length and contains either the LEC id of the sending LEC or is set to all 0s. The next fields con-

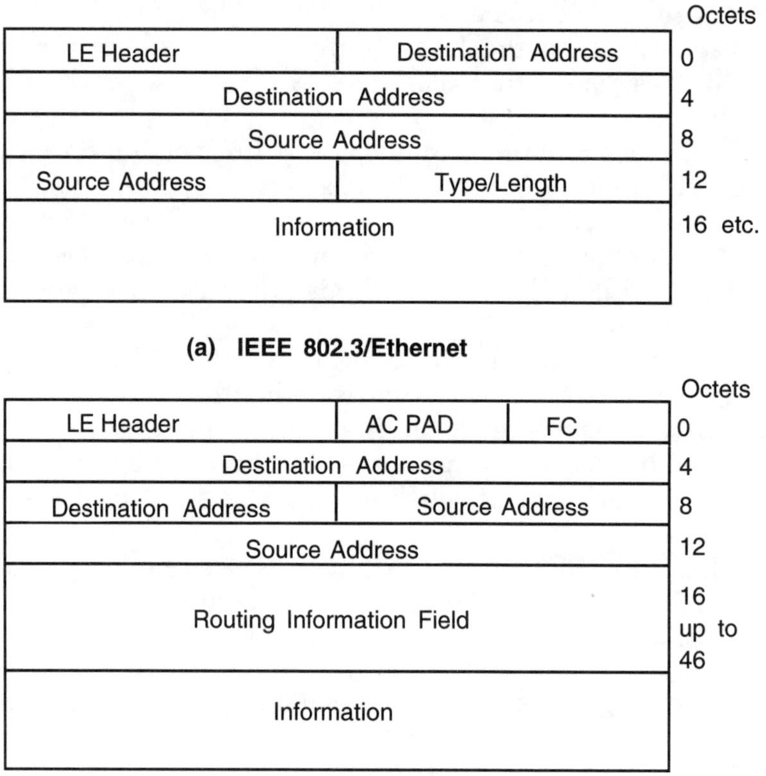

```
                                                        Octets
 ┌──────────────────┬──────────────────────────┐
 │    LE Header     │   Destination  Address    │  0
 ├──────────────────┴──────────────────────────┤
 │          Destination  Address                │  4
 ├──────────────────────────────────────────────┤
 │              Source Address                   │  8
 ├──────────────────┬──────────────────────────┤
 │  Source Address  │       Type/Length         │  12
 ├──────────────────┴──────────────────────────┤
 │                                              │  16  etc.
 │              Information                      │
 │                                              │
 └──────────────────────────────────────────────┘
```

(a) IEEE 802.3/Ethernet

```
                                                        Octets
 ┌──────────────────┬───────────┬──────────────┐
 │    LE Header     │  AC PAD   │     FC       │  0
 ├──────────────────┴───────────┴──────────────┤
 │          Destination  Address                │  4
 ├──────────────────────┬───────────────────────┤
 │ Destination  Address │    Source Address     │  8
 ├──────────────────────┴───────────────────────┤
 │              Source Address                   │  12
 ├──────────────────────────────────────────────┤
 │                                              │  16
 │         Routing Information Field            │  up to
 │                                              │  46
 ├──────────────────────────────────────────────┤
 │                                              │
 │              Information                      │
 │                                              │
 └──────────────────────────────────────────────┘
```

(b) IEEE 802.5

Figure 8–8   Data frame format.

***

[2]Part of the LANE specification uses the notations X"——" or X——   to depict hex values.

tain the destination and source MAC addresses followed by the type/length fields.

LAN emulation must support both LLC frames and Ethernet frames.

The second format in the lower frame of Figure 8–8 is intended for token ring LANs. For this frame, the minimum AAL5 SDU length is 16 octets. The AC pad octet is not used in this specification. Furthermore, with 802.5 networks, only LLC frames are supported. Consequently, the FC octet must adhere to the IEEE 802.5 1992 specification.

Figure 8–9 and Table 8–5 show the syntax and format for LAN emulation control frames. All frames use the structure shown in this figure, with the exception of the READY_IND and READY_QUERY frames, which use a format described later.

Type/Length (TL) Operations[3]

Since LAN emulation supports IEEE 802.2 (LLC) and Ethertype encapsulations, a convention is established on how the TL information is used. The rules can be summarized as follows:[4]

			Octets
Marker = X"FF00"	Protocol =X"01"	Version = "01"	0
Op-Code	Status		4
Transaction-ID			8
Requester-LECID	Flags		12
Source LAN Destination			16
Target LAN Destination (see Table 8–6)			24
Source ATM Address			32
LAN-Type / Maximum-Frame-Size / Number-TLVS / ELAN-Name-Size			52
Target-ATM-Address			56
ELAN-Name			76
TLVs Begin			108

Figure 8–9   Control frame format.

---

[3]Some of the specifications in this book use the term type, length, value (TLV) in place of type, length.

[4]These rules also apply to MPOA; see Chapter 11.

Table 8–5   Table for Figure 8-9

Marker	Control frame = X"FF00"	2
Protocol	ATM LAN Emulation protocol = X"01"	1
Version	ATM LAN Emulation protocol version = X"01"	1
OP-Code	Control frame type	2
Status	Always X"0000" in requests	2
Transaction ID	Arbitrary value supplied by the requester and returned by the responder to allow the receiver to discriminate between different responses.	4
Requester-LECID	LECID of LE Client sending the request (X"0000" if unknown).	2
Flags	Bit flags:	2
	X"0001" = Remote Address (LE_ARP_RESPONSE) X"0080" = Proxy Flag (LE_JOIN_REQUEST) X"0100" = Topology Change (LE_TOPOLOGY_REQUEST)	
	Meaning of remainder of fields depends on OP-Code.	92

- For Ethernet traffic, the Ethertype field is placed in the TL field
- For LLC traffic:
  - Frames less than 1536 octets (including the LLC field and data but not including padding and FCS) must have this length placed in the TL field, followed by the LLC data.
  - Longer frames must have a 0 in the TL field, followed by the LLC data.

Table 8–7 shows the coding rules for the status field that resides in the header shown earlier. This field is not used in a request frame, it is used in a response frame to provide the status of an ongoing operation. As Table 8–7 shows, most of the status information deals with identify-

Table 8–6   Rules for Coding the LAN Destination Fields

Name	Function	Octets
TAG	X"0000" = not present X"0001" = MAC address X"0002" = Route Descriptor	2
MAC address	6-octet MAC address if MAC address specified	6
RESERVED	0, if Route Descriptor specified	4
Route Descriptor	If Route Descriptor specified	2

Table 8–7 Control Frame Status Field

(dec)	Name	Meaning	Responses
0	Success	Successful response.	All responses
1	Version not supported	VERSION field of request contains a value higher than that supported by the responder.	All responses
2	Invalid request parameters	The parameters given are incompatible with the ELAN.	All responses
4	Duplicate LAN Destination registration	SOURCE-LAN-DESTINATION duplicates a previously registered LAN address.	Join or Register
5	Duplicate ATM address	SOURCE-ATM-ADDRESS duplicates a previously registered ATM address.	Join or Register
6	Insufficient resources to grant request	Responder is unable to grant request for reasons such as insufficient table space or ability to establish VCCs.	Configure, Join or Register
7	Access denied	Request denied for security reasons.	Configure or Join
8	Invalid REQUESTOR-ID	LECID field is not zero (Configure or Join) or is not LE Client's LECID (others).	Configure, Join, Register, Unregister, ARP
9	Invalid LAN destination	LAN destination is a multicast address or on an Ethernet/802.3 ELAN, a Route Descriptor.	Configure, Join, Register, ARP, Flush
10	Invalid ATM address	Source or target ATM address not in a recognizable format.	Configure, Join, Register, ARP, Flush
20	No configuration	LE client is not recognized.	Configure
21	LE_CONFIGURE Error	Parameters supplied give conflicting answers. May also be used to refuse service without giving a specific reason.	Configure
22	Insufficient information	LE client has not provided sufficient information to allow the LECS to assign it to a specific ELAN.	Configure

Table 8–8   Rules for Coding the OP-CODE Field

Value	Function
X"0001"	LE_CONFIGURE_REQUEST
X"0101"	LE_CONFIGURE_RESPONSE
X"0002"	LE_JOIN_REQUEST
X"0102"	LE_JOIN_RESPONSE
X"0003"	READY_QUERY
X"0103"	READY_IND
X"0004"	LE_REGISTER_REQUEST
X"0104"	LE_REGISTER_RESPONSE
X"0005"	LE_UNREGISTER_REQUEST
X"0105"	LE_UNREGISTER_RESPONSE
X"0006"	LE_ARP_REQUEST
X"0106"	LE_ARP_RESPONSE
X"0007"	LE_FLUSH_REQUEST
X"0107"	LE_FLUSH_RESPONSE
X"0008"	LE_NARP_REQUEST
X"0108"	Undefined
X"0009"	LE_TOPOLOGY_REQUEST
X"0109"	Undefined

ing problems that occurred during the exchange of control frames. Table 8–7 shows the name of each status value, a brief description of its meaning, and which response frames carries this field.

The OP-CODE field in the control frame header is coded to identify the type frame. The field is coded in accordance with the convention shown in Table 8–8.

SUMMARY

The LAN emulation service specifications define operations between the layers in a node while OSI-based SAPs and primitives are used.

LANE defines four sets of primitives: (1) LAN emulation—ULP service specifications, (2) LAN emulation—AAL service specifications, (3) LAN emulation—AAL service specifications, and (4) LAN emulation—layer management service specifications. In addition, LANE specifies the formats, syntaxes and contents of the PDUs.

9

Configuration, Registration, and ARP Procedures and LNNI

T his chapter discusses the major housekeeping operations employed in a LANE. The focus is on (1) how the LANE is initially configured, (2) how the clients and servers register themselves and their respective addresses, and (3) how the LANE ARP is employed for address resolution.

This chapter delves into these three operations with several examples that are amplified with an analysis of the various PDU formats (LANE uses the term frame to describe basic MAC frames as well as LANE PDUs).

The concluding part of the chapter introduces the LAN Emulation Network-Network Interface (LNNI). The explanation of LNNI is brief because it uses many of the LNNI concepts.

THE CONFIGURE OPERATION

The configure operation was introduced in Chapter 7. Recall that it is used for the LE client to discover the LE service. Upon completion of the configuration phase, the LE client will be identified with a unique LE client identifier (LECID) and a ELAN name. In addition, the LE client now knows the emulated LAN's type (i.e., Ethernet), and the emulated LAN's maximum frame size.

Figure 9–1 shows some of the key information in the configure request and response messages that are exchanged by the LEC and LES. It will be helpful to consult Table 9–1 during this discussion. The MAC ad-

Table 9–1   A Configuration Frame Format

Name	Function	Size
Marker	Control Frame = X"FF00"	2
Protocol	ATM LAN Emulation protocol = X"01"	1
Version	ATM LAN Emulation protocol version = X"01"	1
OP-Code	Type of request: X"0001" LE_CONFIGURE_REQUEST X"0101" LE_CONFIGURE_RESPONSE	2
Status	Always X"0000" in requests. See Status field for a list of values.	2
Transaction ID	Arbitrary value supplied by the requester and returned by the responder.	4
Requester-LECID	Always X"0000" in requests, ignored on response.	2
Flags	Always X"0000" when sent, ignored on receipt	2
Source-LAN-Destination	MAC address or Route Descriptor of prospective LE Client. May be encoded as "not present."	8
Target-LAN-Destination	Always X"0000" when sent, ignored on receipt.	8
Source-ATM-Address	Primary ATM address of prospective LE Client for which information is requested	20
LAN-Type	X"00" unspecified, X"01" Ethernet/IEEE 802.3, X"02" IEEE 802.5	1
Maximum-Frame-Size	X"00" unspecified, X"01" 1516, X"02" 4544, X"03" 9234, X"04" 18190	1
Number-TLVS	Number of Type/Length/Value elements encoded in Request/Response.	1
ELAN-Name-Size	Number of octets in ELAN-Name (may be 0).	1
Target-ATM-Address	ATM Address of the LE Server to be used for the LE Client described in the request if Configure Response and Status = "Success," else X'00'	20
ELAN-Name	Name of emulated LAN.	32
ITEM_1-Type	Three octets of OUI, one octet identifier	4
ITEM_1-Length	Length in octets of Value field. Minimum = 0.	1
ITEM_-Value Etc.	See Table 9–2	Var.

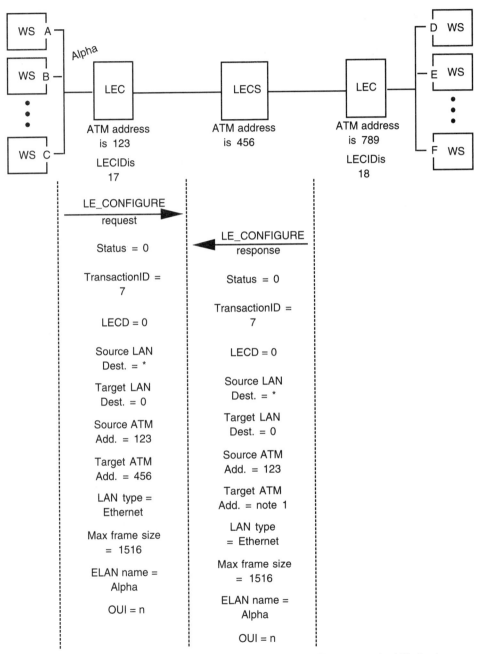

Note 1: This field in the response can optionally identify the LE server or the LE client

Figure 9–1   A configure operation.

dresses are not pertinent for this operation, since it entails only the registration of ATM addresses. The * notation in the Source-LAN-Destination field means this field can be coded as "not present." Also, the LANE specification uses a prefix X to connote hex values; other systems described in this book use 0x.

The LEC wishes to register its ATM address (123) with the LECS. It also registers the name of an ELAN (alpha) and the characteristics of the LAN itself (LAN type = Ethernet; maximum frame size = 1516 octets). The target ATM address (456) identifies the LECS through which this configuration is to occur.

The status field is always x0000 in the request message. Its contents in the response depend upon the outcome of the configuration operations (see Table 8–7 of Chapter 8). The transaction ID (7) is selected by the requestor and used again in the response to correlate the request and response messages.

After this exchange, the LECS knows about the ELAN alpha and its associated ATM addresses at the LEC. As noted in note 1 of Figure 9–1, the LECS also informs the LEC of its LES.

Table 9–1 shows the content and syntax for the configuration frame format. As the OP code indicates, it can carry a request or response frame. Other fields in the frame are used to identify the type of LAN, the maximum frame sized to be used, and the ATM address of the LE server that the LE client considers appropriate. This address (if appropriate) is acknowledged by the LE server in its response to the LE client. Notice also that the name of the emulated LAN is included as well as the organization unique ID (OUI, explained in Chapter 2).

Table 9–2 provides more information of the contents of the configuration response frame. It deals with numerous operations that will go into effect on this connection. The description of each of these fields are summarized in the left column. The type/length/value fields are coded to convey this information to the LE client.

THE JOIN OPERATION

Figure 9–2 provides an example of the join operations, which is used by the LE client to establish a connection with the LE server to store the operating parameters of the emulated LAN. The join operation also permits the LE client to register one MAC address with the LE server. In this example, the source LAN destination address A is being registered and bound to the source ATM address of 123.

Table 9–2   Configuration Response Frame (see Appendix C for the Cn parameters)

Item	Type	Length	Reference/Value/Units
Control Time-out	00-A0-3E-01	2	C7/in seconds
Maximum Unknown Frame Count	00-A0-3E-02	2	C10
Maximum Unknown Frame Time	00-A0-3E-03	2	C11/in seconds
VCC Time-out Period	00-A0-3E-04	4	C12/in seconds
Maximum Retry Count	00-A0-3E-05	2	C13
Aging Time	00-A0-3E-06	4	C17/in seconds
Forward Delay Time	00-A0-3E-07	2	C18/in seconds
Expected LE_ARP Response Time	00-A0-3E-08	2	C20/in seconds
Flush Time-out	00-A0-3E-09	2	C21/in seconds
Path Switching Delay	00-A0-3E-0A	2	C22/in seconds
Local Segment ID	00-A0-3E-0B	2	C23
Mcast Send VCC Type	00-A0-3E-0C	2	C24:
			X0000 Best Effort: LE Client should set the BE flag. Peak Cell Rates should be line rate.
			X0001 Variable: LE Client should provide a Sustained Cell Rate.[1]
			X0002 Constant: LE Client should provide a Peak and a Sustained Cell Rate.[1]
Mcast Send VCC AvgRate	00-A0-3E-0D	4	C25/in cells per second
Mcast Send VCC PeakRate	00-A0-3E-0E	4	C26/in cells per second
Connection Completion Timer	00-A0-3E-0F	2	C28/in seconds

[1]Where: 00-A0-3E is the ATM forum OUI.

The LE server returns the response to the LE client, which is coded in the status field to acknowledge or deny the join request.

It is evident that the LANE messages are similar for configurations, joins (and others). Therefore and hereafter, I will not describe each field in these messages, but refer you to a table that describes the fields.

Figure 9–2 shows the principal fields that are coded in the messages. Other fields reside in this messages and are explained in Table 9–3.

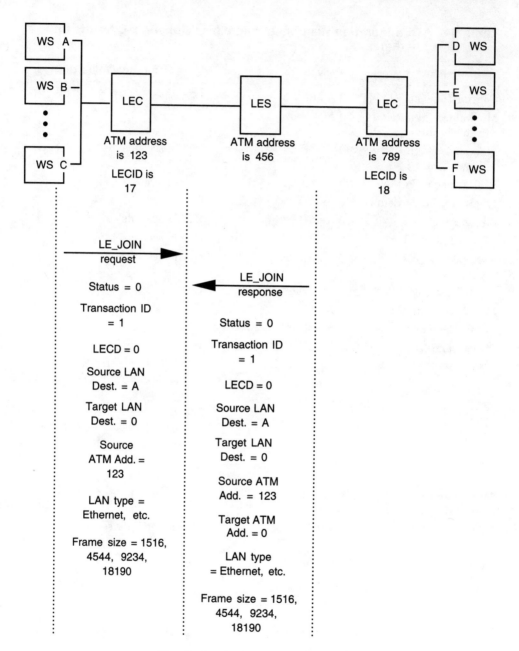

Figure 9–2   The join operation.

Table 9–3 Join Frame Format

Name	Function	Size
Marker	Control Frame = X"FF00"	2
Protocol	ATM LAN Emulation protocol = X"01"	1
Version	ATM LAN Emulation protocol version = X"01"	1
OP-Code	Type of request: X"0002" LE_JOIN_REQUEST X"0102" LE_JOIN_RESPONSE	2
Status	Always X"0000" in requests. See Status table for a list of values.	2
Transaction ID	Arbitrary value supplied by the requester and returned by the responder.	4
Requester-LECID	Assigned LECID of joining client if join response and STATUS = "Success", else X"0000".	2
Flags	Each bit of the FLAGS field has a separate meaning if set.	2
	X"0080" is the Proxy Flag: LE Client serves non-registered MAC addresses and therefore wishes to receive LE_ARP requests for non-registered LAN destinations.	
Source-LAN-Destination	Optional MAC address to register as a pair with the SOURCE_ATM_ADDRESS.	8
Target-LAN-Destination	Always X"00" when sent, ignored on receipt.	8
Source-ATM-Address	Primary ATM address of LE Client issuing join request.	20
LAN-Type	X"00" unspecified, X"01" Ethernet/IEEE 802.3, X"02" IEEE 802.5	1
Maximum-Frame-Size	X"00" unspecified, X"01" 1516, X"02" 4544, X"03" 9234, X"04" 18190	1
Number-TLVS	Always X"00" when sent, ignored on receipt.	1
ELAN-Name-Size	Number of octets in ELAN-Name. X"00" indicates empty ELAN-Name.	1
Target-ATM-Address	Always X"00" when sent, ignored on receipt.	20
ELAN-Name	Name of emulated LAN.	32
	Expresses LE Client's preference in LE_JOIN_REQUEST, specifies name of LAN joined in successful LE_JOIN_RESPONSE, else not used. Format is SNMPv2 DisplayString.	

THE REGISTRATION OPERATION

Figure 9–3 provides an example of registration operation. This procedure is used by the LE client to provide the LE server with LAN destination/ATM address pairs that have not yet been registered. The join procedure may have these addresses established. However, as new workstations are added to a LAN, the registration procedure becomes a useful tool for bringing all entities up to date about the new workstations.

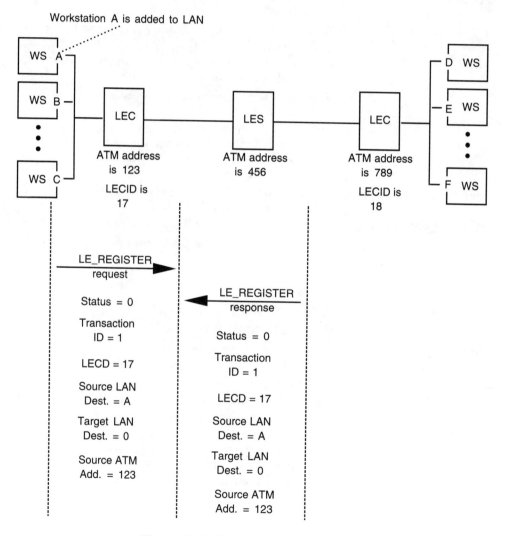

Figure 9–3   Registration example.

As with the join operation, this example shows that the registration is binding MAC address A to ATM address 123 and is confirmed by the LES returning a register response frame to the LEC.

An LE client may also request the LE server remove an address pair with an unregister request frame (which is not shown in Figure 9–3). In turn, the LE server will respond with an unregister response that will confirm or deny the unregistration request.

Registration Frame Format

Table 9–4 shows the content and syntax of the registration and unregistration frames. As the OP code indicates, this frame can be coded as a request or a response. The Source-LAN-Destination and Source-ATM-Address fields provide the values for the address pairs.

Table 9–4   Registration Frame Format

Name	Function	Size
Marker	Control Frame = X"FF00"	2
Protocol	ATM LAN Emulation protocol = X"01"	1
Version	ATM LAN Emulation protocol version = X"01"	1
OP-Code	Type of request: X"0004" LE_REGISTER_REQUEST X"0104" LE_REGISTER_RESPONSE X"0005" LE_UNREGISTER_REQUEST X"0105" LE_UNREGISTER_RESPONSE	2
Status	Always X"0000" in requests. In Responses: See Table 8–7 in Chapter 8 for a list of values.	2
Transaction ID	Arbitrary value supplied by the requester and returned by the responder.	4
Requester-LECID	LECID of LE client issuing the register or unregister request and returned by the responder.	2
Flags	Always X"00" when sent, ignored on receipt.	2
Source-LAN-Destination	Unicast MAC address or Route Descriptor LE client is attempting to register.	8
Target-LAN-Destination	Always X"00" when sent, ignored on receipt.	8
Source-ATM-Address	An ATM address of LE Client issuing the register or unregister request.	20
Reserved	Always X"00" when sent, ignored on receipt.	56

THE LANE ADDRESS RESOLUTION PROTOCOL

Previous chapters in this book have described the operations of ARP. In Chapter 2, we introduced the use of ARP in ATM and Frame Relay operations. This chapter picks up on earlier discussions and focuses in more detail on the LAN emulation ARP.

THE ARP FRAMES

Four frames are employed for address resolution. The LE_ARP_RE-QUEST frame is used to associate the ATM address with a MAC address or a route descriptor. This frame is sent by an LE client.

In turn, the LE_ARP_RESPONSE frame is sent by either an LE client or an LE server in response the to LE_ARP_REQUEST frame.

The LE_NARP_REQUEST frame is sent by an LE client when changes occur in the addresses associated with the LE client.

The LE_TOPOLOGY_REQUEST frame is sent by either an LE server or an LE client whenever changes to network topologies occur.

LE CLIENT USE OF ARP

All ARP requests and responses emanating from the LE client must be sent over the control direct VCC (see Figure 9–4). In turn, receiving requests or responses may arrive either on the control direct VCC or the control distribute VCC.

To prevent uncontrolled operations in the emulated LAN, an LE client may not participate in ARP operations until it has joined the emulated LAN.

Upon receiving an LE_ARP_REQUEST frame, the LE client examines the requested addresses in the frame and checks these addresses against its local addressees. If it finds a match in (a) local unicast MAC address, (b) route descriptors, or (c) remote unicast MAC addresses, it must respond with an LE_ARP_RESPONSE frame. It is not allowed to respond to any other addresses.

The LE client can obtain the address of the broadcast and unknown server by sending an LE_ARP_REQUEST for the broadcast group address.

In an SVC environment, when the LE client receives a response that resolves an unresolved cache entry and there is no existing data direct VCC, a setup operation must be initiated by this client.

Another rule is important regarding the frequency that the LE client can transmit ARP requests, The rule is that these requests cannot be sent to the same destination more than once every second.

Many ARP implementations allow a node to listen passively to the ARP responses going across a communications channel. Thereby, learning about address mappings. Some systems call this system gleaning. This specification calls it eavesdropping and the LE client is permitted to update its cache by eavesdropping the responses.

LE SERVER USE OF ARP

The LE server must adhere to a set of rules also. First, it can only process request and response frames that are received on a control direct VCC. It is not permitted to process these frames if they are received on any other VCC. In turn, it sends requests and responses to an LE client on a control direct VCC or on a control distribute VCC.

The LE server is not allowed to service requests for an unregistered LAN destination—only registered MAC addresses are supported. Furthermore, the LE server is not allowed to flood requests further to LE clients if it responds to the request. In contrast, if it does not respond to the request, it must forward that request to LE clients.

As I just mentioned, an unfulfilled request can be sent to other clients and is also forwarded back to the requesting LE client.

The LE server also processes topology request frames. Upon receiving a topology request frame from any client, it must forward this frame to all LE clients. This operation supports the concept of flooding topology information throughout the emulated LAN. The LE server also issues topology requests and need not rely on the LE client to initiate this action.

EXAMPLE OF ARP OPERATIONS

Figure 9–4 shows how the ARP operation is invoked to obtain an ATM address pertaining to a destination MAC address. Workstation A transmits a frame with destination address D. Upon arriving at the LEC, it is discovered that address D and its associated ATM address is not known. Therefore, this LEC forms an ARP request message and transmits this message to its LES. Since a previous join or registration operation had resulted in MAC address D and its associated registration address of 789 being registered with the LES, this LES can satisfy the ARP

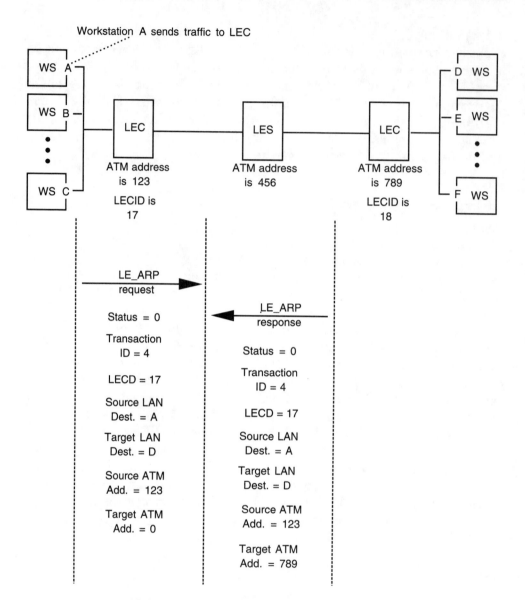

Figure 9–4   Example of the ARP operations.

request with the ARP response, which informs the requesting LEC that ATM address 789 is associated with the destination MAC address.

ARP Frame Format

Table 9–5 describes the format and contents of the LE_ARP frame. As a reminder from previous discussions, these frames are coded in one of two formats.

The first format is coded as the LE_ARP_REQUEST frame, which is sent by the LE client and is used to determine the ATM address associated with a MAC address or a route descriptor.

Table 9–5 The LE_ARP Frame Format

Name	Function	Size
Marker	Control Frame = X"FF00"	2
Protocol	ATM LAN Emulation protocol = X"01"	1
Version	ATM LAN Emulation protocol version = X"01"	1
OP-Code	Type of request: X"0006" LE_ARP_REQUEST X"0106" LE_ARP_RESPONSE	2
Status	Always X"0000" in requests. See STATUS values in the control frame for a list of values.	2
Transaction ID	Arbitrary value supplied by the requester.	4
Requester-LECID	LECID of LE client issuing the LE_ARP request	2
Flags	Each bit of the FLAGS field has a separate meaning if set: X"0001" Remote address. The TARGET-LAN-DESTINATION is not registered with the LE server.	2
Source-LAN-Destination	Source MAC address from data frame that triggered this LE_ARP sequence. May be encoded with "not present" LAN destination tag.	8
Target-LAN-Destination	Destination unicast MAC address or next Route Descriptor for which an ATM address is being sought.	8
Source-ATM-Address	ATM address of originator of LE_ARP request.	20
Reserved	Always X"00" when sent, ignored on receipt.	4
Target-ATM-Address	X"00" in LE_ARP request. ATM address of LE client responsible for target LAN destination in LE_ARP response.	20
Reserved	Always X"00" when sent, ignored on receipt.	32

The second format is coded as the LE_ARP_RESPONSE frame, which is sent by the LE server or LE client to provide the information that was requested in the LE_ARP_REQUEST.

LE_NARP Frame Format

Table 9–6 shows the format for the LE_NARP frame. This frame is generated by an LE client to inform other clients that a remote LAN-ATM address binding has changed. The binding that is changed in coded in the Target-LAN-Destination field, and the Target-ATM-Address field. The address of the LE client that sends this frame is contained in the Source-ATM-Address field.

In addition to changing the binding, this frame also informs its recipients that the client at the Source-ATM-Address is now representing the LAN destination (that is, the address in the Target-LAN-Destination field).

Table 9–6   LE_NARP Frame Format

Name	Function	Size
Marker	Control Frame = X"FF00"	2
Protocol	ATM LAN Emulation protocol = X"01"	1
Version	ATM LAN Emulation protocol version = X"01"	1
OP-Code	Type of request: X"0008" LE_NARP_REQUEST	2
Status	Always X"0000".	2
Transaction ID	Arbitrary value supplied by the requester.	4
Requester-LECID	LECID of LE client issuing the LE_NARP request.	2
Flags	Always X"00".	2
Source-LAN-Destination	Not used. Encoded as X'00'.	8
Target-LAN-Destination	Destination unicast MAC address or next Route Descriptor for which the target ATM address no longer applies.	8
Source-ATM-Address	ATM address of originator of LE_NARP request.	20
Reserved	Always X"00" when sent, ignored on receipt.	4
Target-ATM-Address	ATM address of LE client which was previously representing the target LAN destination.	20
Reserved	Always X"00" when sent, ignored on receipt.	32

LE_Topology_Request Frame Format

The format for the LE_Topology_Request frame is shown in Table 9–7. This frame is sent only on a network that is using the IEEE 802.1D transparent bridge operations. The LE_client that is acting as the transparent bridge must sent one LE_Topology_Request frame to its LE server for every configuration BPDU it sends to the BUS.

LAN EMULATION NETWORK-NETWORK INTERFACE (LNNI)

The ELAN defines a single point of service for the LEC and LECS, which can result in bottlenecks and outage (from a single point of failure).

To address these problems, the ATM Forum has published the LAN Emulation Network-Network Interface (LNNI). It is quite similar to LANE and LUNI, but has the following additional capabilities:

- Multiple LECs are permitted and can be located in geographically dispersed locations. These LECs appear as one service (a virtual ELAN)
- Thus, LNNI is scaleable, and permits many MAC nodes, LANS, and ELAN servers to interact
- The server cache synchronization protocol (SCSP) is used to keep all LNNI servers and clients updated with consistent and correct information.

Table 9–7   The Topology Request Frame Format

Name	Function	Size
Marker	Control Frame = X"FF00"	2
Protocol	ATM LAN Emulation protocol = X"01"	1
Version	ATM LAN Emulation protocol version = X"01"	1
OP-Code	Type of request: X"0009" LE_TOPOLOGY_REQUEST	2
Status	Always X"0000".	2
Transaction ID	Arbitrary value supplied by the requester.	4
Requester-LECID	LECID of LE client issuing the Topology Change request	2
Flags	Each bit of the FLAGS field has a separate meaning if set: X"0100" Topology Change Flag. A network topology change is in progress.	2
Reserved	Always X"00" when sent, ignored on receipt.	92

LNNI uses the VCCs and 802.1 spanning tree operations that are used in LUNI. Most of the LUNI messages (registration, etc.) are also used

Some of the deficiencies of LNNI are:

- Unknown unicast traffic is broadcasted throughout the LNNI spanning tree, which may create excessive traffic (broadcast storms) and overload servers
- LNNI is still an overlay network, treating ATM as a simple layer 2 service, and thus does not avail itself of the full features of ATM

Nonetheless, LNNI is a positive and welcome addition to the ATM internetworking family and a substantial enhancement to LUNI.

SUMMARY

In Chapter 9, three operations have been addressed: the configuration operation, the join operation, and the registration operation.

We learned that the configuration operation allows the LE client to obtain an ATM address of the LE server. The join operation supports the connection to the LE server, the exchange of operating parameters, and the registration of MAC addresses; and the registration operation allows for additional MAC addresses to be registered.

We have also covered three major facets of ARP. First, the ARP messages are used to bind a MAC address to an ATM address. Second, prior registration procedures may reduce the amount of ARP traffic that must be exchanged; and third, ARP messages are also used to update MAC address/ATM address bindings.

10

Next Hop Resolution Protocol (NHRP)

This chapter discusses the Non-Broadcast Multi-Access (NBMA) Next Hop Resolution Protocol (NHRP). The term NBMA refers to a nonbroadcast subnetwork. This type of network does not operate with broadcasting operations because it is inherently non-broadcast (i.e., an X.25 network) or because it is a broadcast network but broadcasting is not feasible because of the size of the network. Hereafter, I refer to the term NRHP without the term NBMA in front of it.

The information contained in this chapter provides a summary of the NHRP specification (NHRPv8). This specification is still a draft but is probably the last one before going to RFC status. Be aware that the final RFC will likely have changes, but the summary of NHRP in this chapter should closely resemble the final specification.

PURPOSE OF NHRP

The purpose of NHRP is to discover and correlate a layer 3 (the internetwork layer address) and the NBMA subnetwork address of the NBMA *next hop* to a destination station. The term NBMA subnetwork address refers to the underlying layer beneath the internetworking layer. Examples of NBMA subnetwork addresses are X.25 addresses, ATM addresses, and SMDS addresses.[1] Examples of internetwork layer addresses are the IP address, the Connectionless Network Layer Protocol (CLNP) address, and the IPX address.

If the L_3 destination address is connected to the NBMA subnetwork, then the next hop is directly to the destination station. If the destination is not connected to the NBMA subnetwork, then the next hop must be to an egress router that can reach the destination station. Ideally, this router is the best path to the destination, but NHRP is not designed to resolve address mappings or path analysis beyond the NBMA subnetwork. Of course, for a system to function properly, conventional route discovery protocols should be employed between NBMA subnetworks to find these paths. Notwithstanding, NHRP can find an egress router by its own operations and does not have to rely on other discovery protocols, even though ARP can co-exist with NHRP.

NHRP is also designed to reduce or eliminate extra router hops that are part of the conventional LIS model. Recall that classical IP over ATM does not permit bypassing intermediate routers on different logical IP subnetworks (LISs) (that are connected even to the same ATM network). NHRP eliminates this restriction.

In effect, NHRP is based on the classical IP model but:

- uses the concept of a NBMA in place of the LIS
- uses the concept of an NHRP server (NHS) in place of a conventional ARP server

MODELING THE NBMA NETWORK

NBMA establishes two methods to model the NBMA network. The first method is quite similar to the model in RFC 1577, Classical IP and ARP over ATM, which is described in Chapter 2. This method uses logically independent IP subnets (LISs) with the following attributes:

---

[1]Strictly speaking, this definition of an NBMA subnetwork addresses is not correct, although it is used throughout the NHRP specifications. X.25 is a internetwork layer operation but the idea behind the NHRP is to define the conventional internetworking layer (layer 3) to operate over the NBMA subnetwork. So, for X.25 we could have two layer 3 protocols involved in the process with, say, IP running on top of X.25.

- LIS members have the same IP address and address mask.
- LIS members are all connected to the same NBMA subnetwork.
- All stations outside the LIS must be accessed through a router.

With RFC 1577, address resolution is resolved only when the next hop address of the destination station is a member of the same LIS as the source station. If this situation does not exist, the source station forwards traffic to a router that may belong to multiple LISs. In such a case, the hop-by-hop address resolution may result in multiple hops through the NBMA subnetwork.

The second method to model the NBMA is to use the concept of local address groups (LAGs).[2] The LAG concept moves away from routing based on addressing toward routing based on quality of service features (such as delay, throughput, etc.). This concept represents the overall thrust of advanced networks: implementing sophisticated routing and route discovery mechanisms that are responsive to end user applications' requirements.

NHRP Operations

Some of the concepts of NHRP are closely related to LANE (discussed earlier in this book in regards to the use of clients and servers) (see Figure 10–1). In this technology, the server is called the next hop server (NHS). Its responsibility is to perform the next hop resolution protocol within the NBMA subnetwork. The term client refers to the next hop client (NHC). The client initiates NHRP requests to the next hop server in order to obtain correlations between layer 3 addresses and NBMA subnetwork addresses.

In Figure 10–1, three NBMA networks are connected through an ATM backbone. The routers supporting these networks are configured with next hop client (NHC) capabilities. The next hop server (NHS) is also connected to the ATM backbone.

In general, NHRP operates as follows:

- The NHC sends a request to its NHS to resolve an IP address to an ATM address in order to setup an ATM connection
- The NHS responds with the mapping information. If it does not know the IP/ATM address relationship, it sends the query toward

---

[2]Further information on the concept of local address groups can be found in a Pending RFCxxxx, titled: "Local/Remote Forwarding Decision and Switched Data Link Subnetworks," authored by Yakov Rekhter and Dilip Kandlur.

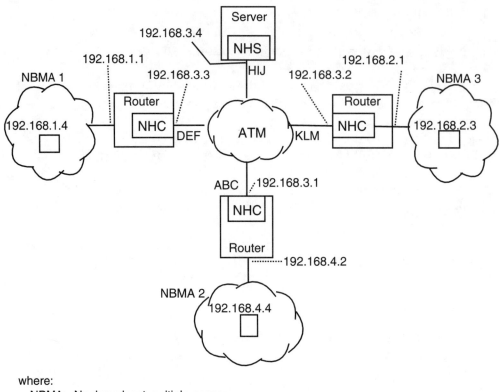

where:
NBMA   Nonbroadcast multiple access
NHC   Next hop client
NHS   Next hop server

Figure 10–1   The NBMA configuration.

the destination address based on routes discovered by conventional route discovery mechanisms (for example, OSPF).

- As the query proceeds along its way, any intermediate (transit) NHS may service the query if the NHS has the information in its cache (from previous NHRP messages).

- Otherwise, the query will arrive at the NHS just before the destination NHC and this NHS responds to the query (this NHS is called the serving NHS).

- The response is sent back on the same path as the query, which allows the transit NHSs to update their cache.

- Upon receiving the response the NHC has enough information to send an ATM Q.2931 setup message to the ATM network to setup an SVC.

The NHSs must be capable of answering next hop resolution requests that find the ATM node that services a L_3 address. These NHSs are configured to serve a set of destination hosts, which may be connected directly to the NBMA subnetwork (but need not be). In addition to running NHRP within their respective subnetworks, the NHSs may also participate beyond their subnetworks to disseminate routing information beyond the NBMA boundaries through conventional route discovery protocols. The NHS can also support conventional ARP services.

In order to resolve address mapping requests, the NHS maintains a cache known as next hop resolution cache. The cache is a table of address mappings that correlate internetwork layer addresses to NBMA subnetwork layer addresses. Like most ARP-type operations, the table is built from the replies to next hop resolution requests or from eavesdropping registration packets that establish these correlations.

Like LANE, registration operations are evoked when a node decides to be part of NHRP. The registering station sends an NHRP registration message to an NHS, which contains the NBMA information about that station. Thereafter, the NHS is responsible for making this information known to other NHSs or NHCs.

One more point: A host or router can be configured as an NHS. If it is not so configured, it must be able to identify the NHS that is configured to serve it.

EXAMPLES OF NBMA OPERATIONS

For this example (using Figure 10–1), let us assume that a station residing in NBMA 1 receives traffic that requires the resolution of an NBMA address to get the traffic to its destination (192.168.4.4) in NBMA 2. In this context, a station can be a router or a host computer that has an NHRP capability. Upon receiving a datagram from host 192.168.1.4, a next hop client (NHC, which is typically a router with HNC capabilities) determines the next hop to the final destination station through normal routing operations. If the next hop is reachable through the NHC's NBMA interface, the NHC constructs a Next Hop Resolution Request packet that contains (1) the internetwork layer target address (192.168.4.4), (2) the internetwork layer source address (192.168.3.3, which is called the next hop resolution request initiator), and (3) the NHC's ATM address (DEF in this example).

The NHC in NBMA 1 sends a Next Hop Resolution Request message to its NHS, using the source NBMA address of DEF. This message arrives at the NHS, which is identified with an ATM address of HIJ.

The NHS with address HIJ checks to determine if it serves station 192.168.4.4 (the subnet 192.168.4). By "serve," it is meant that station HIJ has a next hop entry in its next hop resolution table for subnet 192.168.4. If HIJ does not serve the destination subnet, it forwards the next hop resolution request message to another NHS.

Since NHS HIJ serves subnet 192.168.4, it constructs a positive next hop resolution reply message that contains either the next hop internetwork layer address of a directly attached station, or the internetwork layer address of the egress router through which traffic can be forwarded. For this example, the second option is executed, since the destination address in on another NBMA network. Therefore, the NHRP reply informs NHC 192.168.3.3/DEF that the next hop is node 192.168.3.1/ABC.

In summary, the request message contains:

1. Source NBMA address   = DEF
2. Source protocol address   = 192.168.3.3
3. Destination protocol address   = 192.168.4.4

The reply message contains:

1. Source NBMA address   = DEF
2. Source protocol address   = 192.168.3.3
3. Destination protocol address   = 192.168.4.4
4. Next hop NBMA address   = ABC
5. Next hop protocol address   = 192.168.3.1

Authoritative and Nonauthoritative Replies

NHRP replies are either authoritative or nonauthoritative. If an NHS serves the node associated with the destination address, its reply is authoritative. Otherwise, the reply is nonauthoritative in this regard: An intermediate NHS that receives a next hop resolution reply may cache this information. Upon receiving a subsequent next hop resolution request, it may respond with the cached reply, but it must be identified as nonauthoritative.

Restrictions on the Messages

NHRP request and replies are not allowed to cross the borders of a logical NBMA subnetwork. All L_3 traffic into and out of the NBMA subnetwork must pass through a L_3 router at the NBMA border.

Station Configurations

An NHRP station must be configured with the NBMA address of its NHS. The NHS(s) may also be the station's default router. It is possible for a station to be attached to more than one subnetwork; if so, the station must be configured to receive routing information from all NHSs in order to determine which L_3 addresses are reachable through which subnetworks.

A MORE DETAILED EXAMPLE

The next example, in Figure 10–2, provides more detailed information on the contents of the NHRP Next Hop Resolution Request and Reply messages. We assume the NHC with addresses DEF/192.168.3.3 receives a datagram destined for station 192.168.2.3 that is located in NBMA 2. NHC DEF sends an NHRP request message to the NHS whose address is HIJ/192.168.3.4. Notice that the request message has the destination protocol address coded as the target protocol address of 192.168.2.3.

The NHS NHRP tables reveal that subnet 192.168.2 is reachable through NHC KLM/192.168.3.2. Therefore, the NHS sends back the NHRP response message with the next hop fields coded to identify the egress router to NBMA 2. This router is identified with addresses KLM/192.168.3.2. This NHRP response provides sufficient information for NHC DEF to setup an ATM SVC to NHC KLM, or use an existing PVC, if appropriate.

THE NHRP MESSAGES

This section examines the format and contents of the NHRP messages. Each message consists of a fixed part, a mandatory part, and an extensions part. The fixed part is the same for all messages; the mandatory part is also common to all messages, but its content varies, depend-

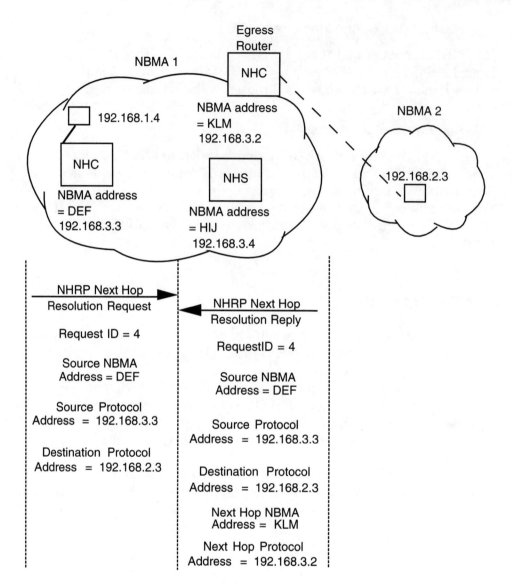

Figure 10–2   The request and reply messages.

ing on the type of message. The extensions part may not be present, and also varies with the message type.

The fixed part of the message is shown in Table 10–1. The function column describes the function of each field.

The mandatory part is shown in Table 10–4. As before, the function column describes the function of each field.

Table 10-1   Fixed Part of the NHRP Message

Name	Function	Size
ar$afn	Defines link layer address being used, based on the Internet address family number published in RFC 1700.	2
ar$pro.type	Protocol type, see Table 10-2 for more information.	2
ar$pro.snap	Used as a SNAP extension when ar$pro.type = 0x0080. SNAP used to code the protocol type.	5
ar$hopcnt	Maximum hop count for an NHRP packet, which represents maximum number of NHSs that can be traversed before the message is discarded.	1
ar$pktsz	Total length of packet, including link layer encapsulation.	2
ar$chksum	IP-type checksum over entire NHRP packet.	2
ar$extoff	Existence and location of NRHP extensions.	2
ar$op.version	Set to 0x01 for use by NHRP.	1
ar$op.type	Type of NHRP packet, see Table 10-3 for more information.	1
ar$shtl	Type and length of NBMA address indicated in ar$afn; example: ar$afn = 8, an E.164 address is coded here.	1
ar$sstl	Same as previous field, except for NBMA subaddress. NBMA may not use a subaddress, in which case, no storage is allocated.	1

Table 10-5 shows the format for the NHRP resolution request message. The request message follows the routed path from the source protocol address to the destination protocol address. The mandatory part of the message was explained earlier, and this table shows the rules for coding the mandatory part for the request message. The Function column of the table explains the functions of each field in the message. The request message may have additional fields called the client information entries (CIEs), which is beyond the scope of this chapter and not needed for this

Table 10-2   Coding for Protocol Type Field

Contents	Meaning
0x0000–0x00FF	Protocols defined by equivalent NLPIDs
0x0100–0x03FF	Reserved for use by the IETF
0x0400–0x04FF	Used by ATM Forum
0x0500–0x05FF	Experimental or local use
0x0600–0xFFFF	Protocol defined by equivalent Ethertypes

**Table 10–3   Coding for NHRP
Packet Type**

Contents	Meaning
1	Next hop resolution request
2	Next hop resolution reply
3	Registration request
4	Registration reply
5	Purge request
6	Purge reply
7	Error indication

discussion. The reader can refer to Section 5.2.0.1 of the NHRP specification if more information is needed.

Table 10–6 shows the format for the NHRP resolution reply message.

PROS AND CONS OF NHRP

The advantage that NHRP has over the conventional methods of IP/ATM internetworking is the ability to by-pass intermediate routers. It also has some deficiencies:

Table 10–4   Format for Mandatory Part (Common Header)

Name	Function	Size
Src Proto Len	Length of source protocol address	1
Dst Proto Len	Length of destination protocol address	1
Flags	Depends on message	2
Request ID	Used to correlate request and reply messages (and any subsequent purge)	4
Source NMBA address	NBMA address of the sender of request message	v
Source NMBA subaddress	NBMA Subaddress of the sender of request message	v
Source protocol address	Address of station sending request message	v
Destination protocol address	Address of station for which the NBMA next hop is requested (the "target" address)	v

Table 10–5   Format for NHRP Next Hop Resolution Request Message

Name	Function	Size
Src Proto Len	Length of source protocol address	1
Dst Proto Len	Length of destination protocol address	1
Q/A/D/U/S bits	Q: 1=sender is a router, 0=sender is a host	2
	A: 1=reply should be an authoritative answer	
	D: Not used	
	U: 1=Used for managing duplicate entries in NHS cache.	
	S: 1=The binding between the source protocol address and the source NBMA information is stable	
Request ID	Used to correlate request and reply messages (and any subsequent purge)	4
MTU	Maximum transmission unit for target station	2
Holding time	Time that client information is considered valid (used for cache management)	2
Source NMBA address	NBMA address of the sender of request message	v
Source NMBA subaddress	NBMA subaddress of the sender of request message	v
Source protocol address	Address of station sending request message	v
Destination protocol address	Address of station for which the NBMA next hop is requested (the "target" address)	v

- Routing information may not be sent across the same path as data. This situation is a result of cut-through routing which can result in a stable routing loop. To handle this problem, the NHS that responded to an NHRP request message must be aware of any topological change could affect the current (cached) topology data. If a problem is detected, the NHS must send to all nodes a message directing them to purge the invalid information.

- It is permissible for an ingress router to receive a datagram and send a resolution request message, but forward the datagram before an NHRP path is established. Each router along the path might do the same thing. This situation is called the domino effect, and scenarios are being developed to handle the problem (but are not completely spelled-out in the specification).

Table 10–6   Format for NHRP Next Hop Resolution Reply Message

Name	Function	Size
Src Proto Len	Length of source protocol address	1
Dst Proto Len	Length of destination protocol address	1
Q/A/B bits	Q: 1=sender is a router, 0=sender is a host (copied from request message A: 1=reply is an authoritative answer D: 1=association between destination and next hop information is stable (route is reliable) U: 1= used for managing duplicate entries in NHS cache. S: Copied from request message	2
NAK code	0=reply is positive, information on binding of internetwork layer and NBMA address has been found	1
Request ID	Used to correlate request and reply messages (and any subsequent purge)	4
MTU	Maximum transmission unit for target station	2
Holding time	Time that client information is considered valid (used for cache management)	2
NH addr T/L	Type and length of next hop NBMA address	1
NH Saddr T/L	Type and length of next hop NBMA subaddress	1
NH Proto len	Length of next hop protocol address	1
Preference	Preference of next hop entry	1
Source NMBA address	NBMA address of the sender of request message	v
Source NMBA subaddress	NBMA subaddress of the sender of request message	v
Source protocol address	Address of station sending request message	v
Destination protocol address	Address of station for which the NBMA next hop is requested (the "target" address)	v
Next hop NBMA address	NBMA address of station in the next hop for traffic bound for the internetwork address specified	v
Next hop NBMA subaddress	NBMA subaddress of station in the next hop for traffic bound for the internetwork address specified	v
Next hop protocol address	Internetwork address of the next hop, which is the destination host if it is directly attached to NBMA subnetwork, otherwise it is the address of the egress router to the destination	v

OTHER NHRP OPERATIONS

This chapter describes the basic NHRP functions. The specification provides more information on:

- PDU forwarding options
- Deployment ideas
- More information on configuration
- Purge operations
- Transit NHSs

SUMMARY

The next hop resolution protocol (NHRP) is responsible for providing a internetwork layer address and its corresponding NBMA subnetwork address for the next hop to a destination station. NHRP is also responsible for finding the egress router from the local NBMA if the destination device is not attached locally to the NBMA network. A number of the NHRP concepts pertain to LANE operations and NHRP employs the client/server model in a manner similar to LANE. The principal difference between LANE and NHRP is that LANE resolves MAC and ATM addresses while NHRP resolves layer 3 and ATM addresses (as well as performing next hop discovery operations).

11

Multiprotocol over
ATM (MPOA)

This chapter explains the operations of Multi-protocol over ATM (MPOA). The discussion revolves around version 1.0 published by the ATM Forum. MPOA has not reached the final ballot. It was approved on a letter ballot, May 29, 1997. This chapter provides the reader with the latest information on MPOA, but be aware that it may change (slightly) as the specification goes through its final balloting.

PURPOSE OF MPOA

In previous chapters, we learned that LAN emulation (LANE) emulates the services of Ethernet, 802.3, and Token Ring LANs through an ATM network. We also learned that LANE allows a subnetwork to be bridged across an ATM/LAN boundary. LANE provides a means for bridging intra-subnet data across an ATM network, but it does not define the operations for inter-subnet traffic that is forwarded through routers, since it uses MAC addresses and not L_3 internetwork addresses.

Advantages of L_3 Operations

L_3 operations provide several advantages over L_2 operations. L_3-based systems are capable of routing datagrams and do not need the broadcast mechanisms of L_2-systems. One reason for this improvement is the fact that L_2 addresses (MAC addresses) are flat addresses and have no hierarchical structure, whereas L_3 addresses (specifically IP and OSI addresses) are structured with a hierarchical syntax. This hierarchical structure is more efficient for route table lookups, since the upper hierarchy values can be examined (for example, network address) without regard to the lower hierarchy structures (for example, a node address) until the datagram reaches the network node (router) to which the end station is attached. Then, the lower-hierarchy address can be examined to determine the final destination end-node.

In addition, L_3 protocols contain a field in the L_3 header called either the type of service (TOS) or quality of service (QOS). This field can be used by the network to tailor the service to the user, a capability that is becoming increasingly important in multiserve environments.

INTRA-SUBNET AND INTER-SUBNET OPERATIONS

With these ideas in mind, let us return to the concepts of intra-subnet operations and inter-subnet operations shown in Figures 11–1 and 11–2. In Figure 11–1, an emulated LAN (ELAN) is connected through bridges or edge devices by ATM LANE. The network and subnetwork address for the bridges and hosts is 192.168.1. All units in this ELAN are identified by the same IP subnet address (class C addresses in

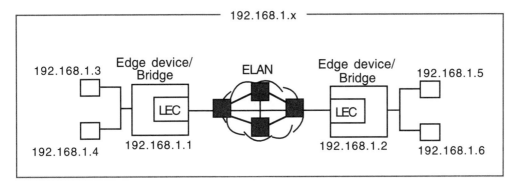

where:

■ = ATM switch

Figure 11–1   Bridging intra-subnet traffic across an ATM network.

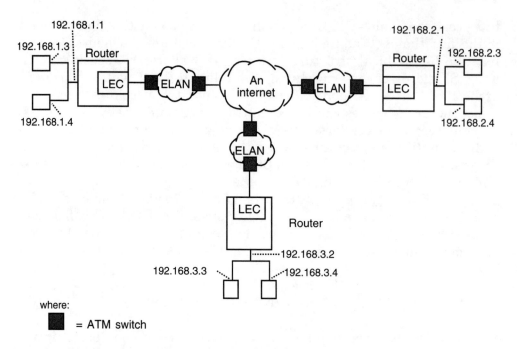

Figure 11–2   Routing inter-subnetwork traffic across ATM and Internet networks.

this example). Thus, each host number is based on this subnet address and intra-subnet operations are bridged across the ATM/LAN boundary. Indeed, the only reason that the bridges might be given an IP address is for purposes of management, but a bridge does not need a L_3 address for its ongoing bridging operations.

Figure 11–2 shows an example of inter-subnetwork operations. In this scenario, we have three subnetworks, identified as 192.168.1, 192.168.2, and 192.168.3, that are connected through ELANs into an internet. Conventional LANE operations will not work in this environment, because L_3 addresses are needed to route the traffic beyond the LANs.

Recall from Chapter 10 that the Next Hop Resolution Protocol (NHRP) allows intermediate routers to be bypassed, and in Figure 11–2, the routers in the internet may be bypassed if a shortcut (a VCC) exists between two of these subnetworks. However, NHRP does not define how to discover addresses beyond its NBMA and relies on an egress router in the NBMA to find the address through conventional route discovery protocols. Furthermore, NHRP assumes the routers involved in its operations perform internetwork layer route calculations.

MPOA goes several steps further than LANE and NHRP. First, it incorporates the operations of LANE and NHRP, thus retaining the advantages of bridging, but it also supports the use of internetwork layer communications (L_3 routing). It continues to use ATM VCCs for the transfer of traffic and has schemes for bypassing routers. At the same time, inter-subnet operations are supported (for unicast traffic). Furthermore, MPOA defines operations that enable an edge device to perform internetwork layer datagram *forwarding* operations without having to perform *route calculations*. This feature reduces the complexity and expense of these machines.

As a result of this extension, MPOA devices define shortcut interfaces for shortcut VCCs, as shown in Figure 11–3. Traffic coming from a bridge connected to an ELAN can be sent to another ELAN through a LEC service interface or to a shortcut VCC through a shortcut interface. Traffic coming from a shortcut VCC can be relayed to a local ELAN, or to another shortcut VCC.

Figure 11–4 illustrates the MPOA approach. Additional components are added to the system, and one is called the MPOA client (MPC). The MPC, say the MPC at subnet 192.168.1, is able to determine that a better path exists between subnets 192.168.1 and 192.168.3. The path is an ATM VCC and is used to provide the shortcut between the two systems.

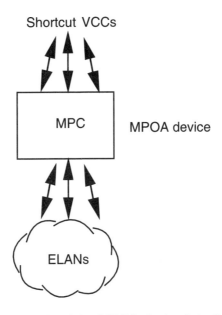

Figure 11–3   Example of the MPOA device interfaces.

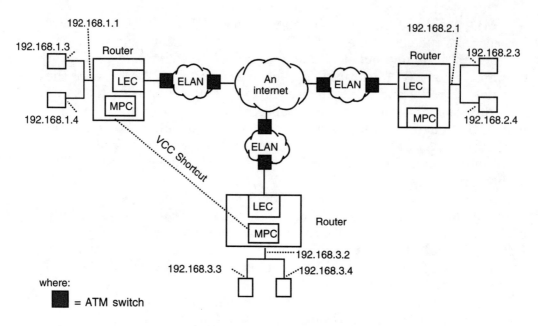

Figure 11–4   The VCC shortcut.

The MPOA resolution request protocol is used to obtain the information about the shortcut and is discussed shortly.

In summary, the principal objective of MPOA is to support the transfer of inter-subnet unicast traffic in a LANE environment. MPOA allows the inter-subnetwork traffic based on layer 3 protocol communications to occur over ATM virtual channel connections (VCCs) without requiring routers in the data path. The goal of MPOA is to combine bridging and routing with ATM in a situation where diverse protocols and network topologies exist.

The job of MPOA is to provide this operation to allow the overlaying of layer 3 protocols (also called internetwork layer protocols) on ATM. MPOA is designed to use both routing and bridging information to locate the optimal route through the ATM backbone.

Virtual Routing

MPOA supports the concept of virtual routing, which is the separation of internetwork layer route calculation and forwarding. The idea behind virtual routing is to enhance the manageability of internetworking by decreasing the number of devices that are configured to perform route calculation. In so doing, virtual routing increases scalability by reducing the number of devices that participate in the inter-network layer route calculations. The edge device cited above is one such example.

MPOA REQUIREMENTS

MPOA is based on the implementation of the ATM Forum's signaling protocol that supports Releases UNI 3.0, UNI 3.1, or UNI 4.0. It requires the use of LANE Version 2.0. It also requires the use of NHRP.

MPOA CACHE

Ingress Cache

The overall operations of MPOA are managed by cache entries. If an incoming datagram's protocol is "enabled"—this means it is eligible for shortcut routing. The MPC examines its ingress cache for a match of the datagram's internetwork destination address and a like entry in the ingress cache. The ingress cache contents are:

- *Key:* MPS control ATM address
- *Key:* Internetwork layer destination address
- *Contents:*
  - Destination ATM address or a VCC
  - Encapsulation information
  - Other (timers, flow counts, etc.)

Therefore, the ingress cache contains the necessary information to resolve the L_3 destination address to an ATM address of VCC.

In summary, ingress cache deals with traffic entering the MPOA system and is used to detect flows that can use a shortcut and an appropriate shortcut VCC.

Egress Cache

Egress cache is used to determine how L_3 datagrams coming from a shortcut are to be encapsulated and forwarded.

For the traffic coming on a shortcut, the egress MPC is searched for a hit on a source/destination ATM address pair and the internetwork layer destination address. The egress cache contents are:

- *Key:* Internetwork layer destination address
- *Key:* ATM source/destination address
- *Key:* Optional tag
- *Contents:*
  - LEC identifier
  - DLC header
  - Other (holding time, etc.)

Therefore, the egress cache contains the necessary information to resolve the ATM and L_3 addresses to an LEC.

MPOA CLIENTS AND SERVERS

Like many protocols in the ATM internetworking families, MPOA uses the client-server architecture. The client is called the MPOA client (MPC) and the server is called the MPOA server (MPS). These clients and servers are connected through an ELAN. The relationship of MPC and MPS are shown in Figure 11–5. MPOA also describes the edge device cited earlier, which supports connections to legacy LANs. The edge devices support L_3 forwarding but do not have to perform L_3 route discovery (OSPF, RIP, etc.).

In this section, a description is provided of the egress/ingress MPSs and MPCs. It will be helpful to refer to Figure 11–6 during this discussion.

The datagram is received by an ingress MPC. A default path entails the bridging of the traffic through a LANE to a router (through MPC 1). Eventually, it leaves the system via MPC 2's LEC interface.

However, if the datagram is associated with a shortcut flow, the ingress MPC removes the DLL encapsulation and sends the datagram

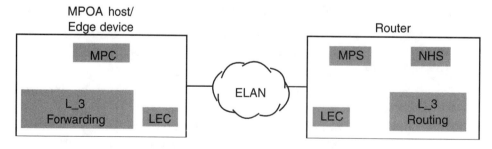

Figure 11–5   MPOA components.

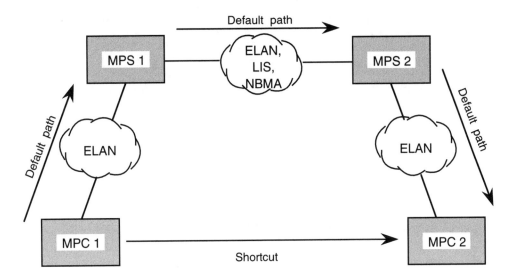

Figure 11–6   Shortcuts and default paths.

onto the ATM shortcut (perhaps adding tagging information, discussed later).

If there is no shortcut flow detected, each datagram is counted (a count is accumulated relative to a destination L_3 address). When the count reaches a threshold, the ingress MPC1 must send an MPOA resolution request message to MPS1. The purpose of this message is to obtain the downstream ATM address for the shortcut—in this example, MPC2. This process is illustrated on the left side of Figure 11–6. Now, we can move forward to an analysis of the roles of the MPCs and MPSs and also examine the other aspects of Figure 11–6.

The MPC

The principal function of the MPC is to perform internetwork layer forwarding of traffic. But it is not required to run the internetwork layer routing protocols. The MPC acts as a source and sink for the internetwork shortcuts. The MPC must support one or more L_3 addresses and an ATM address in this fashion:

- L_3 address of MPC (and an associated ATM address) represents the address of the node having the MPC
- L_3 addresses (and an associated ATM address) that are reachable through the node (when the node is an edge device or a router). The L_3 addresses are typically IP subnet addresses.

The MPC performs different functions in its ingress role (recall that ingress is the point where inbound data flow enters the MPOA system) and its egress role (also recall that egress is the point where outbound data flow exits the MPOA system).

For the ingress operation, the MPC must detect traffic that is being forwarded over an ELAN to a router that contains an MPS. Its job is to recognize a flow that could benefit from a shortcut that bypasses the on-going routed path. To support this operation, it sends an MPOA resolution request to the ingress MPS to establish a shortcut to the desired destination. Upon obtaining this information, the MPC stores this information, sets up the shortcut VCC, and forwards the traffic over the shortcut to the destination.

As the traffic flows into the MPC, the frames are checked to determine if the destination MAC address is for an MPS. If so, and detection is enabled for the protocol (it is subject to a shortcut), the MPC then examines the internetwork destination address in the datagram header and looks up the corresponding entry in the ingress cache. The key values in the ingress cache are <MPS ATM address, Internetwork layer address>. If this is a hit, and a valid shortcut is defined in the ingress cache for this traffic, the traffic is sent to the ingress shortcut service interface. If it is not a valid shortcut, it is sent onto an outbound LEC service interface.

For the egress operation, the MPC is tasked with forwarding traffic to its local users. It performs this operation by receiving traffic from other MPCs. Upon receiving frames received over a shortcut, the MPC must add the appropriate data link layer (DLL) encapsulation operations and forward this traffic to the higher layers. These higher layers may be an upper-layer internal protocol family stack or it may be a bridge port. The DLL encapsulation must be provided to the egress MPC by its egress MPS. This information must be stored at MPC (in the call MPC egress cache). The egress MPC may also send the traffic onto one of its ELAN interfaces.

The egress MPC is also responsible for responding to cache imposition request messages sent by an egress MPS. The message is sent to the egress MPC to determine if this node has the required resources to support a new VCC and to maintain the cache entry. The message also provides encapsulation information that will be needed by the egress MPC when it encapsulates outbound traffic.

The role of the ingress MPOA server (MPS) to answer MPOA queries from local MPCs (NHS may be co-located in the router that houses the MPS). It also is responsible for providing DLL encapsulation information to egress MPCs. The MPS also provides DLL encapsulation information to egress MPCs. It is also responsible for converting between MPOA requests and replies as well as NHRP requests and replies.

If the ingress MPS cannot answer to the MPOA resolution request (from the local MPC) because the target address is not local, then it simply resends ("re-originates" is the term used in the specification) the message through the routed path to the local NHRP next hop server (NHA). This message is changed slightly: The L_3 source protocol address field is filled in with the reoriginating ingress MPS so that a reply is returned to it and not the actual originator. However, the MPC's ATM address remains as the source NBMA address; otherwise, a correlation cannot be made to the actual originator. When the ingress MPS receives a reply to its reoriginated message, it returns an MPOA resolution reply to the ingress MPC.

The egress MPS receives NHRP resolution requests targeted for a local MPC (in this example, the egress MPS is the NHRP authoritative server for that MPC). Based on the contents in the NHRP resolution request message, this egress MPS constructs an MPOA cache imposition request and sends this message to the egress MPC. The function of this message was described in the description of the role of the egress MPC.

THE USE OF TAGS

The egress cache may contain a tag. A tag is used to encapsulate data that is sent over a shortcut. An egress cache is used to find an appropriate shortcut (if one exists). When outbound packets are received, the egress MPC looks for a hit on ATM address and destination internetwork layer address. Optionally, a tag can be stored for the cache entry, and the hit can be made on the tag. This concept is called by various names in the industry—a common descriptor is tag switching. The goal of tag switching is to avoid the slow lookups with conventional L_3 routing tables.

MPOA INFORMATION FLOWS

MPOA operations entail several information flows that are categorized as MPOA control flows and MPOA data flows. All control and data flows operate over ATM VCs using LLC/SNAP encapsulation, in accordance with RFC 1483. The control flows are further defined as (1) configuration flows, (2) MPC/MPS control flows, (3) MPS/MPS control flows, and (4) MPC-MPC control flows. The configuration flows use the conventional LANE formats, and the LANE LECS. The MPOA data flows are categorized as MPC-MPC data flows and MPC-NHC data flows. Examples of these flows are provided in Figure 11–7.

Configuration flows are used by MPSs and MPCs to communicate with the LAN emulation configuration server (LECS) to receive configuration information in accordance with the LANE specification.

MPC/MPS control flows are used between an edge device or MPOA host and a router for MPC cache management. It also allows the ingress MPC to obtain shortcut information. In addition, the MPS can take the

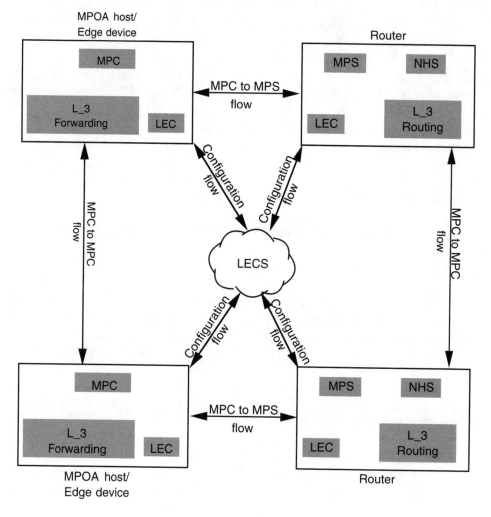

Figure 11–7   MPOA flows.

action by sending a trigger message to the MPC. Also the egress MPS gives the egress MPC egress cache information with a cache imposition reply message. These messages are discussed later.

The MPS-MPS control flows are exchanged between two routers in accordance with ongoing routing protocols and NHRP.

The MPC-MPC control flows are used by an egress MPC to send a purge to an ingress MPC if it received misdirected packets from that MPC.

Finally, the MPOA data flows (MPC-MPC and MPC-NHC) are used for the transfer of traffic between MPCs and between an MPC and an NHC. MPC-MPC data flows are used for shortcut VCCs, and MPC-NHC data flows are used to send unicast data to an MPC.

MAJOR MPOA OPERATIONS

MPOA is responsible for five major operations:

1. *Configuration:* This operation obtains configuration information from the ELAN LECS.
2. *Discovery:* MPCs and MPSs dynamically learn of each other's existence. MPCs and MPSs discover each other by using minor additions to the LANE LE_ARP protocol. These messages carry the MPOA device type (MPC or MPS) and its ATM Address
3. *Target Resolution:* This operation uses a modified NHRP Resolution Request message MPCs to resolve the ATM Address for the end points of a shortcut. Also, the mapping of a target to an egress ATM address is provided, as well as an optional tag (discussed later) and a set of parameters used to set up a shortcut VCC to forward traffic across subnet boundaries.
4. *Connection Management:* This operation controls the ongoing management of VCCs transfer control information and data.
5. *Data Transfer:* This operation is responsible forwarding of internetwork layer traffic across a shortcut.

EXAMPLES OF MPOA OPERATIONS

This section provides three examples of MPOA operations with the goal of piecing together the concepts covered thus far in this chapter. The focus in the examples will be how the MPC in a machine discovers a data

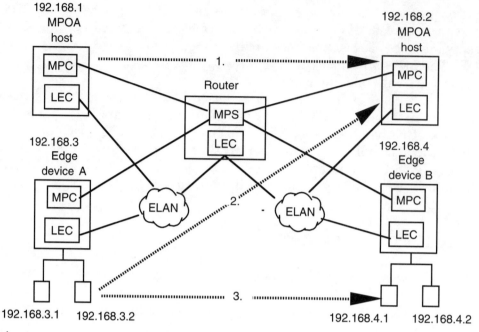

where:
    Shortcut 1: MPOA host-to-MPOA host.
    Shortcut 2: Edge device-to-MPOA host.
    Shortcut 3: Edge device-to-Edge device.

Figure 11–8   Three shortcut examples.

flow that can benefit from a shortcut and how the shortcut is used. The
three examples are listed here and depicted in Figure 11–8 with the
dashed lines. This figure will also be used for each of our examples:

- Shortcut 1: MPOA host-to-MPOA host
- Shortcut 2: Edge device-to-MPOA host
- Shortcut 3: Edge device-to-edge device

MPOA Host-to-MPOA Host

Figure 11–9 shows how a shortcut is established between two
MPOA hosts. One host resides on subnet 192.168.1 and the other host resides on subnet 192.168.2. Before the shortcut is established, MPOA host
192.168.1 forwards its traffic in a LANE frame to a router through a
LANE data direct VCC. This operation is shown in Figure 11–9a with
the notation ELAN above the arrow (the direction of the arrow symbol-

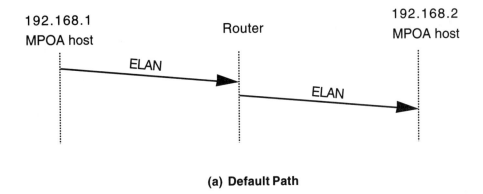

(a) Default Path

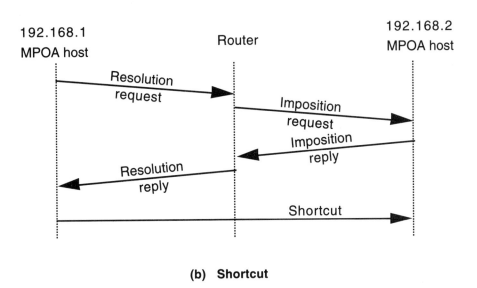

(b) Shortcut

Figure 11–9   Shortcut example 1: MPOA host—MPOA host.

izes the flow of the traffic). The router receives the traffic but must use a different data direct VCC to forward the LANE frame to MPOA host 192.168.2.

The sending MPOA host has been examining the headers in this flow, and it is able to detect the internetwork layer address of the receiving MPOA host. Based on this detection, it sends an MPOA resolution request message to the MPS to obtain an ATM address. This message is sent to the router. In effect, the router uses the information in the MPOA resolution request message to construct and send an MPOA cache imposition request message to MPOA host 192.168.2. This message will ask host 192.168.2 to provide an egress cache entry.

This host then creates an MPOA cache imposition reply that indicates that it will accept the shortcut. As shown in Figure 11–9b, this reply is sent back to the router, which translates this message into an MPOA resolution reply. It then sends this reply to the originating host. The reply contains the ATM address of MPOA host of 192.168.2. Upon receiving the MPOA resolution reply message, the MPOA host 192.168.1 updates its ingress cache and establishes the shortcut to the other MPOA host.

Now that these important housekeeping functions have been completed, MPOA host 192.168.1 sends its internetwork layer traffic (typically IP datagrams) using the appropriate encapsulation procedures defined for the shortcut. The identification of the appropriate VCC for this shortcut is contained in the ingress cache entry.

H2 Edge Device-to-MPOA host

Figure 11–10 shows the operations for the development of a shortcut between an edge device and an MPOA host. For this example, traffic emanates from host 192.168.3.2 and is to be forwarded to the MPOA host 192.168.2. The operations in this example are the same as in the previous example. The only addition is the depiction of traffic flowing from host 192.168.3.2 to its edge device (labeled edge device A). Just as in the previous example, MPOA resolution operations occur between the edge device and the router and cache imposition operations occur between the router and the MPOA host. The end result is still the same, the agreement on a shortcut with its appropriate VCC and the subsequent use of that shortcut.

Edge Device-to-Edge Device

Finally, Figure 11–11 shows the use of a shortcut to deliver traffic between two edge devices (edge device A and edge device B) and the subsequent traffic to the hosts attached the devices. The ongoing operations entailing MPOA resolution and cache imposition messages are identical to the previous examples.

ROLES OF MPS AND MPC IN MORE DETAIL

This section provides a more detailed look at the roles of the MPS and MPC. I have included in Figure 11–12 the MPC data path processing logical block diagram, which is derived from the MPOA ATM Forum BTD-MPOA-MPOA-01.16 specification.

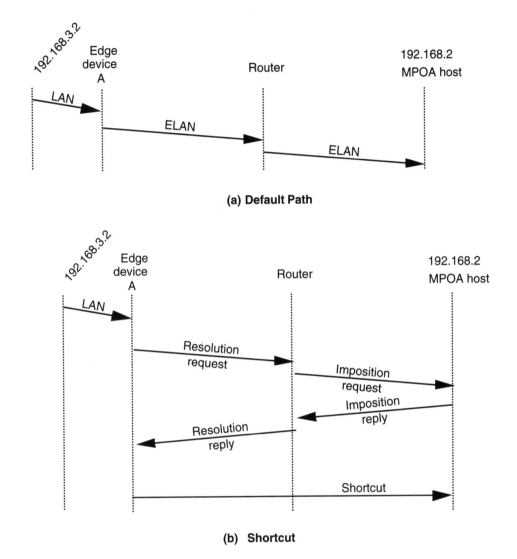

(a) Default Path

(b) Shortcut

Figure 11–10   Shortcut example 2: Edge device—MPOA host.

An ingress MPC discovers the MAC addresses of MPSs attached to its ELANs from the device type type-length-values (TLVs) in LANE LE_ARP responses. The MPC performs flow detection, based on the L_3 destination address, on packets destined for the MAC addresses.

Default forwarding takes place through routers, and this route will remain unless a shortcut is discovered. When the MPC becomes cognizant of a traffic flow that might benefit from a shortcut, the ingress MPC must determine the ATM address associated with the egress device. To obtain the ATM address for a shortcut, the ingress MPC sends

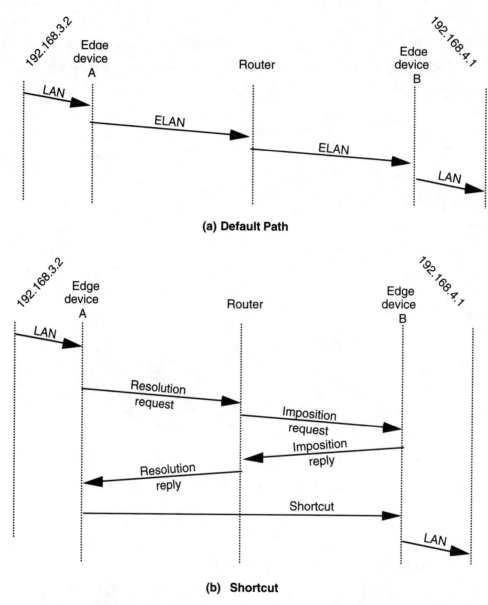

(a) Default Path

(b) Shortcut

Figure 11–11   Shortcut example 3: Edge device—Edge device.

an MPOA resolution request packet to the appropriate ingress MPS. When this MPS is able to resolve the MPOA resolution request, a reply is returned to the ingress MPC.

The ingress MPS processes MPOA resolution requests sent by local MPCs. The ingress MPS is allowed to respond to the request if the destination is local. If the address in non-local, the MPS sends (reoriginates) the

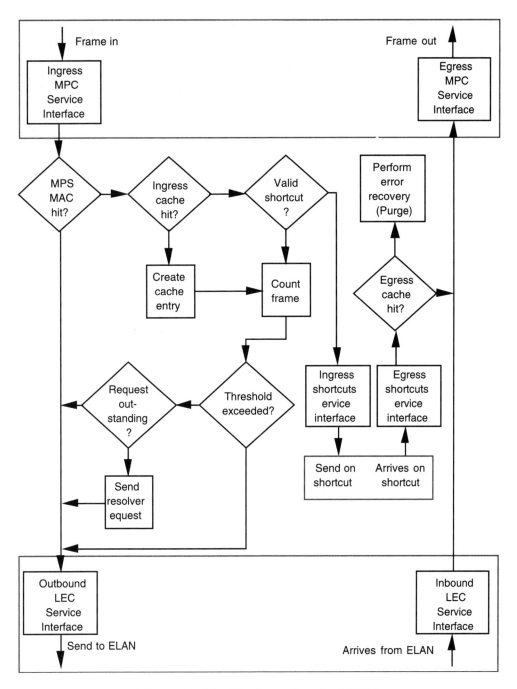

Figure 11–12   The logic flow for MPOA.

request through the routed path. The ingress MPS uses its internetwork layer address as the source protocol address in this request. This operation provides assurance that the reply is returned to the originating MPS.

The MPS copies all other fields from the resolution request packet. The MPC's data ATM address is used as the source NBMA. The MPS generates a new Request ID for the reoriginated request. On receiving a reply to this reoriginated request, the ingress MPS sets the Request ID field and source protocol address to the original values and returns an MPOA resolution reply to the ingress MPC.

When an resolution request packet targeted for a local MPC arrives at the egress MPS serving that MPC, the egress MPS constructs an MPOA Cache Imposition Request, which is sent to the egress MPC.

The Cache Imposition Request provides encapsulation and state maintenance information needed by the egress MPC, and the MPOA Cache Imposition Reply provides status, address, and ingress tagging information used by the egress MPS to formulate the NHRP resolution reply packet.

After receiving the Cache Imposition Reply packet from the egress MPC, the egress MPS sends an resolution reply packet toward the request originator.

The egress MPC must send an Cache Imposition Reply packet for every Cache Imposition request. To formulate the reply, the MPC decides if it has the resources needed to maintain the cache entry and support a new VCC. If the Cache Imposition is an update of an existing egress cache entry, the resources should be available. If the MPC cannot accept either the cache entry or the potential VCC, it sets the appropriate error status and returns the MPOA Cache Imposition Reply to the MPS. Otherwise, the MPC inserts an ATM address and sends the Cache Imposition Reply to the egress MPS.

The main incentive for including a tag is to solve the egress cache conflict. But, tags can also be used to improve the egress cache lookup. This improvement can be achieved by providing an index into the egress cache as the tag. When the tag is an index into the cache, the cache search is reduced to a direct cache lookup.

THE MPOA PROTOCOL DATA UNITS (PDUs) FORMATS

Figure 11–13 shows the encapsulation formats for LLC and tagged traffic. There is little information to add here; these formats have been covered extensively in Chapters 2 and 6.

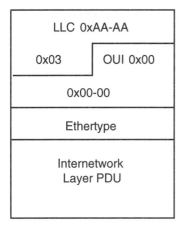

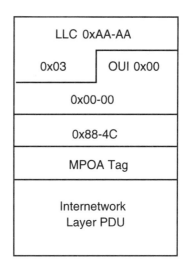

(a) RFC 1483 LLC Encapsulation   **(b) Tagged Encapsulation**

Figure 11–13   Encapsulation conventions.

FORMAT AND SYNTAX FOR THE MPOA MESSAGES

Most of the rules for coding the MPOA messages are derived from NHRP. Tables 11–1, 11–2, and 11–3 explain the fixed part and the resolution request and response messages.

Table 11–1   Fixed Part of the MPOA Message

Name	Function	Size
ar$afn	Defines link layer address being used	2
ar$pro.type	Protocol type, see Table 10-2 for more information	2
ar$pro.snap	Used as a SNAP extension when ar$pro.type=0x0080	5
ar$hopcnt	Maximum hop count for an NHRP packet	1
ar$pktsz	Total length of packet, including link layer encapsulation	2
ar$chksum	IP-type checksum over entire NHRP packet	2
ar$extoff	Existence and location of NRHP extensions	2
ar$op.version	Set to 0x01 for version 1	1
ar$op.type	Type of MPOA message (e.g., 134=MPOA Resolution Request, 135=MPOA Resolution Reply)	
ar$shtl	Type and length of ATM address indicated in ar$afn; example: ar$afn=8, an E.164 address is coded here	1
ar$sstl	Same as previous field, except for ATM subaddress	1

Table 11–2   Format for MPOA Resolution Request Message

Name	Function	Size
Flags (NRHP)	Not used	2
Source NMBA address	ATM address of the ingress MPC from which interwork layer datagrams will be sent	v
Source NMBA subaddress	ATM subaddress of the ingress MPC from which interwork layer datagrams will be sent	v
Source protocol address	Address of MPC sending request message (optional)	v
Destination protocol address	Address of the final destination to which datagrams will be sent	v

Note: The header preceding these fields is based on the NHRP fixed header.

Several other messages are used, of course, such as the imposition requests and replies. The reader should refer to the details of the specifications, if more information is needed.

OTHER MPOA OPERATIONS

We have learned about the basic architecture and operations of MPOA. But, we have only touched the surface. The complete specification is 101 pages in length (excluding Annex C, NBMA). The interested reader might wish to obtain the specification to learn about these other MPOA features:

Table 11–3   Format for MPOA Resolution Reply Message

Name	Function	Size
Flags (NRHP)	Not used	2
Source NMBA address	ATM address of the ingress MPC from which interwork layer datagrams will be sent	v
Source NMBA subaddress	ATM subaddress of the ingress MPC from which interwork layer datagrams will be sent	v
Source protocol address	Copied from corresponding MPOA request message	v
Destination protocol address	Address of the final destination to which datagrams will be sent	v

Note: The header preceding these fields is based on the NHRP fixed header.

- Configuration operations
- Registration operations
- Cache management in more detail
- Connection management and the use of UNI signaling
- Design considerations

SUMMARY

We have learned that MPOA builds on the services offered by LANE and NHRP. Its additional services allow for inter-subnet operations and retains the advantages of both L_2 bridging and L_3 routing. In addition, MPOA provides a means to: (1) bypass intermediate routers by employing a bypass ATM virtual circuit, (2) employ the use of tags to enhance cache lookup, and (3) provide a means for devices to perform internetwork layer forwarding operations without incurring the overhead of performing route calculations for this traffic.

Appendix **A**

Basics of Internetworking

This Appendix provides an introduction to internetworking. The topics covered are (1) how internetworking came about; (2) route discovery operations (3) connection-oriented and connectionless networks, and (4) bridges, routers, and gateways.

INTERNETWORKING CONFIGURATION

Figure A–1 shows the relationship of subnetworks and routers (internetworking units) to layered protocols. In this figure, it is assumed that the user application in host A sends traffic to an application layer protocol in host B, such as a file. The file transfer software performs a variety of functions and appends a file transfer header to the user data. In many systems, the operations at host B are known as *server* operations and the operations at host A are known as *client* operations.

As indicated with the arrows going down in the protocol stack at host A, this data is passed to the transport layer protocol (the data is called a protocol data unit [PDU]). This layer, often implemented with the Transmission Control Protocol (TCP), performs a variety of operations and adds a header to the PDU passed to it. The unit of data is now

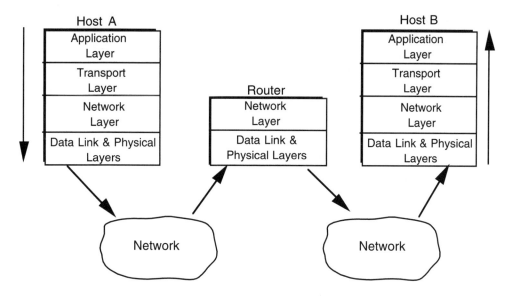

Figure A–1 Layers in an internetworking system.

called a *segment*. The PDU from the upper layers is considered to be data to the transport layer.

Next, the transport layer passes the segment to the network layer, also called the Internet Protocol (IP) layer, which again performs specific services and appends a header. This unit (now called a datagram in Internet terms) is passed down to the lower layers. Here, the data link layer adds its header as well as a trailer, and the data unit (now called a *frame*) is launched into the network by the physical layer. Of course, if host B sends data to host A, the process is reversed and the direction of the arrows is changed.

The host computers are unaware of what goes on inside the network. The network manager is free to manipulate and manage the PDU in any manner necessary.

The router receives the traffic and makes routing decisions based on the addresses provided by the host computer.

The destination (host B) eventually receives the traffic at its lower layers and reverses the process that transpired at host A. That is to say, it decapsulates the headers by stripping them off in the appropriate layer. The header is used by the layer to determine the actions it is to take; the header governs the layer's operations.

EVOLUTION TO INTERNETWORKING

In the early days of internetworking, and especially during the pioneering days of the development of the Internet and packet switching, designers were wrestling with the problem of interfacing different types of host computers (IBM, UNIVAC, Telex terminals) into one network (which was dubbed a backbone network, since it connected these machines together).

The problem was twofold: how to connect the computers with the network nodes (the packet switches) and how to connect the computers to each other, through the network.

For the first problem (we discuss the second problem later), it was decided to build an interface at these network switches that would allow the hosts to connect to the network and send their data to the intended destination. So, the switches would act as a "gateway" into and out of the network (see Figure A–2).

These switches also had to communicate with each other and inform each other about their readiness to accept traffic (or not accept traffic) from each other. That is, they needed a protocol to govern their operations with each other. This protocol became known as a "gateway protocol" in some circles. As the term proliferated, it became associated with the procedures that entailed the exchange of routing information between the switches, as well as between the switches and the hosts.

CONNECTING NETWORKS TOGETHER (INTERNETWORKING)

Due to the many sites in an enterprise (company, government agency, etc.) that needed to communicate with each other, it became necessary to connect existing networks together. As these connections grew, so did the problems associated with a larger (and more complex) system (see Figure A–3).

One of the problems was being able to determine how hosts could be reached through their respective regional networks. Another problem has being able to determine if a switch was capable of relaying traffic to the host; that is, if the switch was "up." In most systems, it was determined that the evolving data network should be able to find a host, find its respective network, and if necessary, divert traffic around a faulty switch or network to reach the host.

In other words, a mechanism should exist that allowed the discovery of a route to the host through switches and networks that were capable of

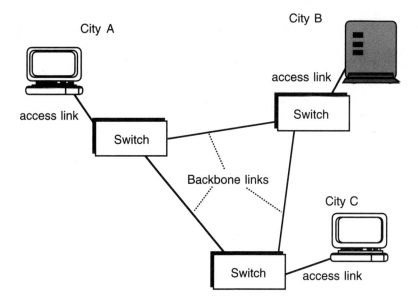

(a) In the early stages of internetworking

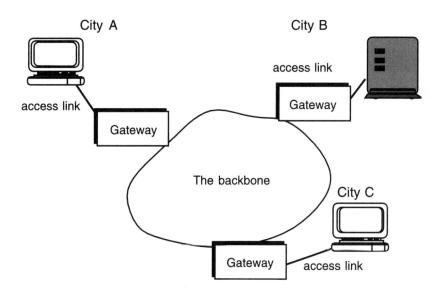

(b) As things evolved . . .

Figure A–2 Evolution of some internetworking terms.

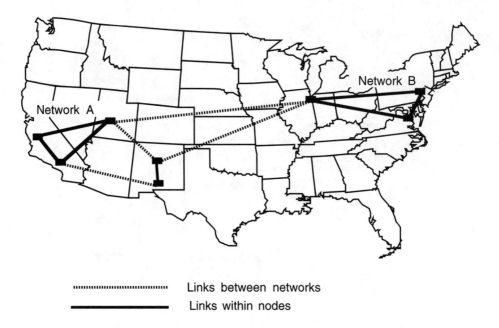

============================== Links between networks
———————————————— Links within nodes

Figure A–3   Connecting the networks.

supporting the route. This process entailed the exchange of information among the switches and hosts to keep each other aware of their existence and readiness to accept traffic.

As stated earlier, for lack of a better term, the industry called this overall process a "gateway protocol." Other terms are used today, such as route discovery or routing exchange, but the term gateway protocol is still used.

ROUTE DISCOVERY

The industry has developed several tools for route discovery. They can be classified as a distance, vector (more commonly called minimum hop) or link state metric protocol (see Figure A–4). The distance, vector protocol is based on the idea that it makes the best sense to transmit the traffic through the fewest number of networks and switches (hops). In the past, network designers held that this approach led to the most efficient route through an internet, and perhaps more to the point, it was easy to implement. The fewest hops approach could be debated, but we will confine ourselves to how the approach works, rather than its relative merits. The term distance = a hop count (also called the path length, ob-

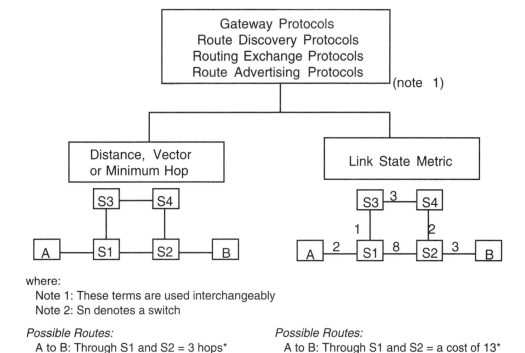

where:
  Note 1: These terms are used interchangeably
  Note 2: Sn denotes a switch

Possible Routes:
  A to B: Through S1 and S2 = 3 hops*
  A to B: Through S1, S3, S4, then S2 = 5 hops*

Possible Routes:
  A to B: Through S1 and S2 = a cost of 13*
  A to B: Through S1, S3, S4, then S2 = a
                 cost of 11*

* known also as path length

Figure A–4   Typical ways of finding and maintaining a route.

viously a misnomer, since the chosen path has nothing to do with the length of the path); the term vector = a destination address.

The link state metric protocol is based on a number of criteria called type of service factors (TOS). The OSI Model uses the term quality of service factors (QOS). These factors are defined by the network administrators and users and may include criteria such as delay, throughput, and security needs. Each link is assigned a value (metric), which could represent delay, throughput, or any factor that is important to the network administration. A smaller value represents a better service. The chosen path from the source to the destination is the individual link values that sum to the smallest total.

The path through an internet is chosen based on the ability of the switches and networks to meet a required service. This technique is also called *link state routing*, because the TOS values are applied to each communication link in the internet. It is also called shortest path first (SPF), once again the term "shortest" does not mean the shortest distance, but the smallest total of the link state metrics.

Figure A–4 shows examples of the two techniques and some possible routes for traffic sent from host A to host B. For the minimum hop protocol, the best path is from host A→S1→S2→host B, because it goes through the fewest number of hops. For the link state metric protocol, the best path is from host A→S1→S3→S4→S2→host B. The link between S1 and S2 precludes using this link because of the high cost (8). This cost could be a result of a low-speed link, or a link that is experiencing degraded throughput.

CONNECTIONLESS AND CONNECTION-ORIENTED PROTOCOLS

The concept of connectionless and connection-oriented operations is fundamental to any communications protocol. See Tables A–1 and A–2. It is essential that the reader has a clear understanding of their features.

The connection-oriented service requires a three-way agreement between the two end users and the service provider (for instance, the network). It also allows the communicating parties to negotiate certain options and quality of service (QOS) functions. During the connection establishment, all three parties store information about each other, such as addresses and QOS features, in tables. Once data transfer begins, the PDUs need not carry much overhead protocol control information (PCI). All that is needed is an abbreviated identifier to allow the parties to access the tables to determine the route and its associated QOS. Since the session can be negotiated, the communicating parties need not have prior knowledge of all the characteristics of each other. If a requested service cannot be provided, any of the parties can negotiate the service to a lower level or reject the connection request.

The connection-oriented service may or may not provide for the acknowledgment of all data units. Also, this approach entails fixed routing within the network since the PDUs do not contain sufficient address information to permit dynamic (on-the-spot) routing decisions. This route is also called a virtual connection (VC).

Table A–1   Connection-Oriented Networks

- Connection mapped through network
- Abbreviated addressing (a virtual circuit ID)
- Usually fixed routing between/within network(s)
- Accountability of traffic may or may not be provided

Table A–2   Connectionless Service

- Limited or no end-to-end mapping of connection
- Full addressing in each protocol data unit (PDU)
- Can use alternate routing
- Accountability of traffic may or may not be provided

Connectionless protocols do not create a connection or virtual circuit. Since no information is kept about the users of this approach, each PDU must have complete addressing information, which can result in large headers for *each* PDU. On the other hand, full addressing permits dynamic routing, since the switches do not have any "preconceived" rules for the route (no virtual circuit mapping tables). Finally, most connectionless protocols do not offer acknowledgment or sequencing services.

Figure A–5 illustrates the concepts of connection-oriented and connectionless systems. As just stated, in order for machines to communicate through a connection-oriented network, they must go through a handshake, also called a connection establishment. During this process, the switches may negotiate the services that are to be used during the session. Once the connection is established, data are exchanged in consonance with the negotiations that occurred during the connection-establishment phase.

The connection-oriented network provides a substantial amount of care for the signaling PDUs that set up the connection. The procedure requires an acknowledgment from the network and responding user that the connection is established; otherwise, the requesting machine must be informed as to why the connection request was not successful. The network must also maintain an awareness of the connection. Flow control (i.e., making certain that all the data arrives correctly, in order, and does not saturate the user computers in the various parts of the network) is also required of most connection oriented networks.

As we just learned, the connectionless (also called *datagram*) network goes directly to the data transfer mode, followed later by the idle condition. The major difference between this network and the connection-oriented network is the absence of the connection establishment and release phases. Moreover, a connectionless network has no end-to-end acknowledgments, flow control, or error recovery.

It should be noted that a network may use a mixture of connection-oriented and connectionless techniques. Indeed, some organizations (that must transfer data between networks) use X.25 or Frame Relay as the connection-oriented, user-to-network interface and then implement a connectionless protocol within the network.

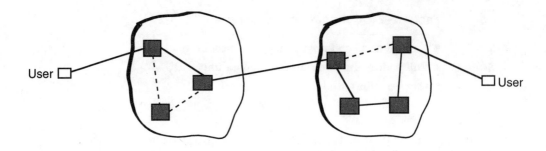

- - - - - Dashed line means switch/router did not
participate in the call connection procedure

Switch/router with solid lines map source & destination
addresses to a virtual circuit number

(a) Connection-Oriented Procedure

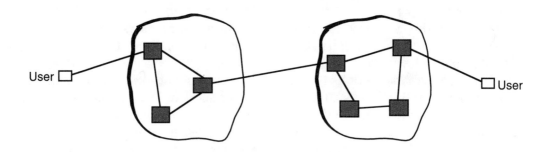

Switch/router performs no setup & relies on actual
addresses for identifying traffic

(b) Connectionless Procedure

Figure A–5   Connection-oriented and connectionless networks.

INTERFACES

Network services are typically provided at three interfaces: (1) the
interface between the user and the network; (2) the interface between
networks; and less frequently, (3) the interface within a network. These
interfaces are shown in Figure A–6, as well as the common terms associated with the interfaces. They are:

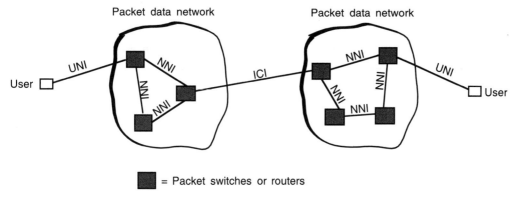

Note 1: The initial NNI is also used as: (a) network-network interface, (b) network-node interface, and may also identify the interface between networks (the ICI in this figure).

where:
    UNI = User-network interface
    NNI = Node-node interface
    ICI = Intercarrier interface

Figure A–6   Where network services are provided.

- The user-network interface (UNI)
- The node-node interface (NNI) (see note 1 for Figure A–6)
- The intercarrier interface (ICI) (see note 1 for Figure A–6)

The initial thrust of network services was on the interface between the user and the network (the UNI). However, the intercarrier interface is also quite important, because many organizations that need to communicate with each other are connected through different networks. Historically, the operations within a network have been proprietary and specific to a vendor's implementation. This situation is changing, although most internal operations still remain proprietary and are not standardized.

GATEWAYS, BRIDGES, AND ROUTERS

Networks were originally conceived to be fairly small systems consisting of a relatively few machines. As the need for data communications services has grown, it has become necessary to connect networks together for the sharing of resources and distribution of functions and for administrative control. In addition, some LANs, by virtue of their restricted distance, often need to be connected together through other de-

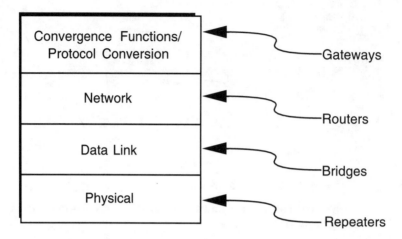

Figure A–7   Placement of internetworking units.

vices. These devices are called a number of names in the industry; in this section we will explain and define each of these machines.

Figure A–7 shows the relationships of these devices vis-à-vis a layered model. A *repeater* is used to connect the media on a LAN, typically called media segments. The repeater has no upper layer functions, its principal job is to terminate the signal on one LAN segment and regenerate it on another LAN segment. The repeater is not an internetworking unit (IWU).

The term *bridge* is usually associated with an IWU. It operates at the data link layer. Typically, it uses a 48-bit media access control (MAC) address to perform its relaying functions. As a general rule, it is a fairly low-function device and connects networks that are homogeneous (for example, IEEE-based local area networks [LANs]).

A *router* operates at the network layer because it uses network layer addresses (for example, IP, X.121, E.164 addresses). It usually contains more capabilities than a bridge and may offer flow control mechanisms as well as source routing or nonsource routing features.

The term *gateway* is used to describe an entity (a machine or software module) that not only performs routing capabilities but may act as a protocol conversion or mapping facility (also called a convergence function). For example, such a gateway could relay traffic and also provide conversion between two different types of mail transfer applications.

Yet another term that has entered the market is the term *brouter,* which is used to describe a machine that combines the features of a router and a bridge. This somewhat artificial term is falling into disuse in the industry.

To avoid any confusion about these terms, some people use the term *internetworking unit (IWU)*. An IWU is a generic term to describe a router, a gateway, a bridge, or anything else that performs relaying functions between networks. Several standards groups use the term interworking unit in place of internetworking unit.

Bridges are designed to interconnect LANs; therefore, it is convenient for them to use a MAC address in determining how to relay the traffic between LANs. Additionally, a bridge "pushes" the conventional network layer responsibilities of route discovery and relaying operations into the data link layer. In effect, a bridge has no conventional network layer.

By virtue of the design of a bridge (no technical reason exists why a bridge could not exhibit more functionality), it has relatively limited capabilities. On the other hand, bridges are fast and they are easy to implement. Indeed, most bridges are self-configuring. This feature relieves network managers of many onerous tasks, such as constant management of a number of naming and network reconfiguration parameters.

Routers can use the same type of route discovery and relay operations as a bridge. Indeed, many routers and bridges use the same type of operation to determine how to route traffic to the next network. As examples, minimum hop operations and link state routing can be used at either the data link or the network layer.

Therefore, other than addressing, what is the difference between a router and a bridge and why should there be options to use one or the other? A bridge is designed for fewer functions than a conventional router. A router typically allows multiple network protocols to run on the machine. As examples, AppleTalk, DECnet IV, IP, and IPX are commonly supported in routers. In contrast, since a bridge does not use the network layer, it does not have these components. Multiprotocol traffic can certainly pass through the bridge, but the bridge is unaware of these operations; its job is to examine the MAC address in the frame and relay the frame to the next node (bridge or user device). Finally, LAN bridges use broadcasting in many of their operations; that is, the traffic is sent to *all* stations on a network (or networks).

Additionally, bridges have been designed to support the internetworking of LANs only. Consequently, the use of a MAC layer and the MAC relay entity is consistent with LAN architecture. The MAC relay entity can be implemented in hardware, which makes bridge operations efficient and fast.

In contrast, routers are usually implemented with software and provide more extensive value-added features than bridges. Their software orientation makes them more flexible that bridges. Additionally, routers use a layer three address, such as IP, which is designed to support hierarchical routing and is more efficient than the MAC address, which is a flat (nonhierarchical) address. Routers can also route based on TOS/QOS. For example, a field in the PDU may stipulate a certain priority for the traffic and the router can treat the PDU accordingly. This feature will become increasingly important as routers integrate ATM into their architectures, which is the subject of much of this book.

Appendix B

Addressing Conventions

INTRODUCTION

This appendix provides a review of addressing conventions, and concentrates on the addresses used by the technologies covered in this book: (a) IEEE 802 MAC addresses, (b) IP addresses and (c) ATM addresses.

THE MAC ADDRESS

The IEEE assigns universal LAN physical addresses and universal protocol identifiers. Previously this work was performed by the Xerox Corporation by administering what were known as block identifiers (Block IDs) for Ethernet addresses. Previously, the Xerox Ethernet Administration Office assigned these values, which were three octets (24 bits) in length. The organization that received this address was free to use the remaining 24 bits of the Ethernet address in any way it chose.

Due to the progress made in the IEEE 802 project, it was decided that the IEEE would assume the task of assigning these universal identifiers for all LANs, not just CSMA/CD types of networks. However, the IEEE continues to honor the assignments made by the Ethernet administration office although it now calls the block ID an *organization unique identifier (OUI)*.

The format for the OUI is shown in Figure B–1. The least significant bit of the address space corresponds to the individual/group (I/G) address bit. The I/G address bit, if set to a zero, means that the address field identifies an individual address. If the value is set to a one, the address field identifies a group address which is used to identify more than one station connected to the LAN. If the entire OUI is set to all ones, it signifies a broadcast address which identifies all stations on the network.

The second bit of the address space is the local or universal bit (U/L). When this bit is set to a zero, it has universal assignment significance–for example, from the IEEE. If it is set to a one it is an address that is locally assigned. Bit position number two must always be set to a zero if it is administered by the IEEE.

The OUI is extended to include a 48 bit universal LAN address (which is designated as the *media access control [MAC]* address). The 24 bits of the address space is the same as the OUI assigned by the IEEE. The one exception is that the I/G bit may be set to a one or a zero to identify group or individual addresses. The second part of the address space consisting of the remaining 24 bits is locally administered and can be set to any values an organization chooses.

Is the 48 bit address space sufficient for the future? 48 bits provide for a 2^{48} value, which can identify about 281.475 trillion unique addresses, so it should be sufficient for a while.

Each OUI gives an organization the 24-bit address space (which is quite large), although the true address space is 22 bits because the first

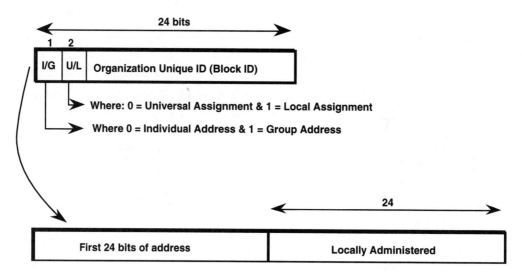

Figure B–1   The MAC address.

two bits are used for control, and administrative purposes. This means that the address space is 2^{22}.

The second part of the address space consisting of the remaining 24 bits is locally administered and can be set to any values an organization chooses. This part of the address is shown in the figure as "Locally Administered".

THE IP ADDRESS

Internet networks use a 32-bit address to identify a host computer and the network to which the host is attached. The structure of the IP address is depicted in Figure B–2. Its format is:

IP Address = Network Address + Host Address

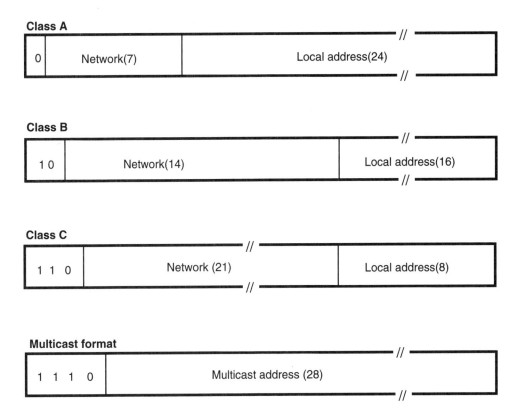

Figure B–2 The IP address format.

IP addresses are classified by their formats. Four formats are permitted: class A, class B, class C, or class D formats. The first bits of the address specify the format of the remainder of the address field in relation to the network and host subfields. The host address is also called the local address.

The *class A* addresses provide for networks that have a large number of hosts. The host ID field is 24 bits. Therefore, 2^{24} hosts can be identified. Seven bits are devoted to the network ID, which supports an identification scheme for as many as 127 networks (bit values of 1 to 127).

Class B addresses are used for networks of intermediate size. Fourteen bits are assigned for the network ID, and 16 bits are assigned for the host ID. *Class C* networks contain fewer than 256 hosts (2^8). Twenty-one bits are assigned to the network ID. Finally, *class D* addresses are reserved for multicasting, which is a form of broadcasting but within a limited area.

For ease in reading, the IP address is depicted in a decimal form of X.X.X.X, where each X represents an eight-bit byte. For example, an IP address can appear as 172.16.17.88.

THE OSI ADDRESS FORMAT

ISO 7498 3 and X.213 (Annex A) describe a hierarchical structure for the network service access point (NSAP) address, and ISO 8348/DAD 2 (Draft Addendum 2) specifies the structure for the NSAP address. It consists of four parts, shown in Figure B–3:

- *Initial Domain Part* (IDP): Contains the authority format identifier (AFI) and the initial domain identifier (IDI).
- *Authority Format Identifier* (AFI): Contains a two-digit value between 0 and 99. It is used to identify (a) the IDI format, the authority responsible for the IDI values, and (b) the syntax of the domain specific part (DSP).
- *Initial Domain Identifier* (IDI): Specifies the addressing domain and the network addressing authority for the DSP values. It is interpreted according to the AFI.
- *Domain Specific Part* (DSP): Contains the address determined by the network authority. It is an address below the second level of the addressing hierarchy. It can contain addresses of user end systems on an individual subnetwork.

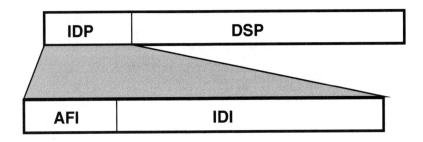

where:

IDP   Initial domain part
AFI   Authority format identifier
IDI   Initial domain identifier
DSP   Domain specific Part

And Where for AFI

00-99   Reserved-will not be allocated
10-35   Reserved for future allocation
36-59   Allocated by ITU-T and ISO
60-69   For new IDI formats, assigned by ISO
70-79   For new IDI formats, assigned by ITU-T
80-99   Reserved for future allocation

Figure B–3   The OSI address.

ATM ADDRESS FORMAT

Figure B–4 shows an example of the OSI addressing scheme, as used by the Asynchronous Transfer Mode (ATM). The ATM address is modeled on the OSI network service access point (NSAP), and is coded as follows:

1. The Initial *Domain Part* (IDP): Contains the authority format identifier (AFI) and the initial domain identifier (IDI), described earlier.

2. The *Authority Format Identifier* (AFI): Identifies the specific part (DSP). For ATM, AFI field is coded as:

   39 = DCC ATM format
   47 = ICD ATM format
   45 = E.164 format

3. *Initial Domain Identifier* (IDI): It is interpreted according to the AFI (where AFI = 39, 47, or 45). For ATM, the IDI is coded as (a)

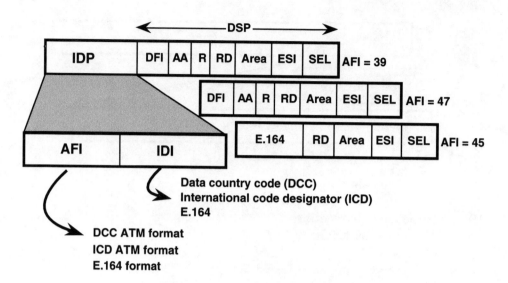

Figure B–4   The ATM address format.

a data country code (DCC), in accordance with ISO 3166, (b) an international code designator (ICD), which identifies an international organization, and is maintained by the British Standards Institute, or (c) an E.164 address, which is a telephone number.

4. The *Domain Specific Part* (DSP): For ATM, the contents vary, depending on value of the AFI. The domain specific part identifier (DFI), specifies the syntax and other aspects of the remainder of the DSP. The administrative authority (AA) is an organization assigned by the ISO that is responsible for the allocation of values in certain fields in the DSP. The R field is a reserved field.

The routing domain identifier (RD) specifies a domain that must be unique within either: (a) for AFI = 39, DCC/DFI/AA; (b) for AFI = 47, ICD/DFI/AA, and (c) for AFI = 45, E.164. The area identifies a unique area within a routing domain, and the end system identifier (ESI) identifies an end system (such as a computer) within the area.

The selector (SEL) is not used by an ATM network. It usually identifies the protocol entities in the upper layers of the user machine that are to receive the traffic. Therefore, the SEL could contain upper layer SAPs.

ATM public networks must support the E.164 address and private networks must support all formats.

Appendix C

LANE Parameters

The following parameters are part of the LANE specifications, and are cited in the LANE chapters.

C1 **LE Client's ATM Addresses.** The LE Client's own ATM Addresses.

C2 **LAN Type.** The type of LAN of which that the LE Client is, Ethernet/IEEE 802.3, IEEE 802.5, or Unspecified.

C3 **Maximum Data Frame Size.** The maximum AAL-5 SDU size of a data frame that the LE Client wishes to send on the Multicast Send VCC or to receive on the Multicast Send VCC or Multicast Forward VCC.

C4 **Proxy.** Indicates whether the LE Client may have remote unicast MAC addresses in C27.

C5 **ELAN Name.** The identity of the emulated LAN the LE Client.

C6 **Local Unicast MAC Address(es).** Each LE Client has zero or more local unicast MAC addresses.

C7 **Control Time-out.** Used for timing out most request/response control frame interactions.
Value: Minimum = 10 seconds, Default = 120 seconds, Maximum = 300 seconds.

C8 **Route Descriptor(s).** Used for source-routed IEEE 802.5 LE Clients that are Source-Route Bridges.

C9   **LE Server ATM Address.** The ATM address of the LAN Emulation Server is used to establish the Control Direct VCC.

C10   **Maximum Unknown Frame Count.**
Value: Minimum = 1, Default = 1, Maximum = 10. (See parameter C11.)

C11   **Maximum Unknown Frame Time.** Within the period of time defined by the Maximum Unknown Frame Time, an LE Client will send no more than Maximum Unknown Frame Count frames to the BUS for a given unicast LAN Destination.
Value: Minimum = 1 second, Default = 1 second, Maximum = 60 seconds.

C12   **VCC Time-out Period.** To release any Data Direct VCC that LEC has not been used to transmit or receive any data frames for the length of the VCC Time-out Period.
Value: Minimum = None specified, Default = 20 minutes, Maximum = Unlimited.

C13   **Maximum Retry Count.** An LE Client MUST not retry an LE_ARP_REQUEST for a given frame's LAN destination more than Maximum Retry Count times, after the first LE_ARP_REQUEST for that same frame's LAN destination.
Value: Minimum = 0, Default = 1, Maximum = 2.

C14   **LE Client Identifier.** Each LE Client has an LE Client Identifier (LECID) assigned by the LE Server during the Join phase.

C15   **LE Client Multicast MAC Address(es).** A list of multicast MAC addresses which the LEC wishes to receive and pass up to the higher layers.

C16   **LE_ARP Cache.** A table of entries, each of which establishes a relationship between a LAN Destination external to the LE Client and the ATM address to which data frames for the LAN Destination will be sent.

C17   **Aging Time.** The maximum time that an LE Client will maintain an entry in its LE_ARP cache in the absence of a verification of that relationship.
Value: Minimum = 10 seconds, Default = 300 seconds, Maximum = 300 seconds.

C18   **Forward Delay Time.** The maximum time that an LE Client will maintain an entry for a non-local MAC address in its LE_ARP cache in the absence of a verification of that relationship, as long as the Topology Change flag C19 is true.

Value[16]: Minimum = 4 seconds, Default = 15 seconds, Maximum = 30 seconds.

C19   **Topology Change.** Indication that the LE Client is using the Forward Delay Time C18, instead of the Aging Time C17, to age non-local entries in its LE_ARP cache C16.

C20   **Expected LE_ARP Response Time.** The maximum time that the LEC expects an LE_ARP_REQUEST/LE_ARP_RESPONSE cycle to take.

Value: Minimum = 1 second, Default = 1 second, Maximum = 30 seconds.

C21   **Flush Time-out.** Time limit to wait to receive an LE_FLUSH_RESPONSE after the LE_FLUSH_REQUEST has been sent before taking recovery action.

Value: Minimum = 1 second, Default = 4 seconds, Maximum = 4 seconds.

C22   **Path Switching Delay.** The time since sending a frame to the BUS after which the LE Client may assume that the frame has been either discarded or delivered to the recipient.

Value: Minimum = 1 second, Default = 6 seconds, Maximum = 8 seconds.

C23   **Local Segment ID.** The segment ID of the emulated LAN.

C24   **Multicast Send VCC Type.** Signaling parameter used by the LE Client when establishing the Multicast Send VCC.

C25   **Multicast Send VCC AvgRate.** Signaling parameter used by the LE Client when establishing the Multicast Send VCC.

C26   **Multicast Send VCC PeakRate.** Signaling parameter used by the LE Client when establishing the Multicast Send VCC.

C27   **Remote Unicast MAC Address(es).** The MAC addresses for which this LE Client will answer LE_ARP_REQUESTs, but which are not registered with the LE Server.

C28   **Connection Completion Timer.** In Connection Establishment this is the time period in which data or a READY_IND message is expected from a Calling Party.

Value: Minimum = 1 second, Default = 4 seconds, Maximum = 10 seconds.

REVIEW 1

X.25 and Related Protocols

1. Summarize the main functions of X.25.

2. Answer true or false.
   a. X.25 is a packet-switching protocol.   T   F
   b. X.25 defines the network interface with the user.   T   F
   c. X.25 defines the internal network operations.   T   F
   d. X.25 is a connectionless protocol.   T   F
3. Contrast connectionless and connection-oriented protocols.

4. Can a network exhibit both connectionless and connection-oriented characteristics? Explain why or why not.

5. What are the differences between logical channels and virtual circuits?

6. Briefly describe the functions of the X.25 layers.

Abbreviations

AAL CP: AAL common part
AAL5: ATM adaptation layer, type 5
ACL: Automatic congestion level
AESA: ATM end system address
ARP: Address Resolution Protocol
AA: Administrative authority
AAL: ATM adaptation layer
ACCS: Automated calling card service
ACM: Address complete message
AE: Application entity
AEI: Application entity invocation
AFI: Authority format identifier
AIS: Alarm indication signal
AP: Applications process
ASE: Application service element
ATM: Asynchronous Transfer Mode
B-ISDN: Broadband-ISDN
B-ISUP: Broadband-ISDN user part
BC: Bearer capability
BCC: Bearer connection control
BER: Basic encoding rules
BGAK: Begin acknowledge
BGN: Begin
BGRE: Begin reject
BOM: Beginning of message
BR: Buffer release
BRI: Basic rate interface

BSS: Broadband Switching System
C: Cell loss priority
CAC: Connection admission control
CBR: Constant bit rate
CC: Call control
CC: Country code
CCIS: Common channel interoffice signaling
CCRI: Consistency check result information
CCITT: International Telecommunications Union-Telecommunication Standardization Sector (see also ITU-T)
CCS: Common channel signaling
CCS I/F: CCS interface
CMIP: Common management information protocol
COM: Continuation of message
CPCS: Common part convergence sublayer
CPCS: Common part CS
CPCS-UU: Common part convergence sublayer-user-to-user
CPE: Customer premises equipment
CPI: Common part id
CPI: Common part indicator
CRC: Cyclic redundancy check
CS: Convergence sublayer

CUG: Closed user group
DCC: Data country code
DN: Destination network
DPC: Destination point code
DSAP: Destination SAP
DSID: Destination signaling identifier
DSP: Domain specific part
DSS: Digital subscriber signaling system
ENDAK: End acknowledge
E800: Enhanced 800
EOM: End of message
ER: Error recovery
ERAK: Error recovery acknowledge
ESI: End system identifier
FEC: Forward error correction
FERF: Far End Receive Failure
FOT: Forward transfer message
GFC: Generic flow control
GSM: Global systems for mobile communi-
    cations
GT: Global title
HEC: Header error check
HEC: Header error control
HO DSP: High order domain specific part
IAA: IAM acknowledgment
IAM: Initial address
IC: Interchange carrier
ICD: International code designator
ICI: Intercarrier interface
ID: Interface data
id: Identification
IDI: Initial domain identifier
IDP: Initial domain part
IE: Information elements
IP: Internet Protocol
IPI: Initial protocol identifier
ISDN: Integrated Services Digital Network
ISUP: ISDN user part
IT: Information type
ITU-T: International Telecommunications
    Union-Telecommunication Standardiza-
    tion Sector (ITU-T, formerly, the CCITT)
IXC: Interchange carrier
LCN: Logical channel number
LE: List element
LEC: Local exchange carrier
LI: Length indicator
LLC: Logical link control

LLC: Low layer compatibility
LM: Layer management
LMI: Local management interface
MC: Maintenance control
MCI: Message compatibility information
MD: Management data
MID: Message id
MTP 3: Message transfer part 3
MTP: Message transfer part
MU: Message unit
MUSN: MU sequence number
N-BC: Narrowband bearer capability
N-HLC: Narrowband high layer capability
N-ISDN: Narrowband Integrated Services
    Digital Network
NLPID: Network level PID
N-LLC: Narrowband low layer compatibility
NDC: National destination code
NNI: Network-node interface
NNI: Network-to-network interface
NSAP: Network service access point
N(S)N: National (significant) number
OSI Model: Open Systems Interconnection
    Model
OAM: Operations, administration, and
    maintenance
OUI: Organization unique ID
OPC: Originating point code
OSID: Origination signaling identifier
PAD: Padding
PBX: Private branch exchange
PC: Point code
PCI: Protocol control information
PCM: Pulse code modulation
PCR: Peak cell rate
PCS: Personal communications services
PDU: Protocol data unit
PHY: Physical layer
PID: Protocol id
PL: Physical layer
PM: Physical medium sublayer
PRI: Primary rate interface
PTI: Payload type identifier
PTO: Public telecommunications operators
PVC: Permanent virtual circuit
QOS: Quality of service
REL: Release
RES: Resume

RJE: Remote job entry
RLC: Release complete
ROSE: Remote operations service element
SAAL: Signaling ATM adaptation layer
SACF: Single association control function
SAO: Single association object
SAP: Service access point
SAR: Segmentation and reassembly
SCCP: Signaling connection control point
SCP: Service control point
SD: Sequenced data
SDU: Service data unit
SE: Status enquiry
SEL: Selector
SID: Signaling identifier
SIO: Service information octet
SLS: Signaling link selection code
SN: Sequence number
SN: Subscriber's number
SNAP: Subnetwork access protocol
SNMP: Simple Network Management Protocol
SNP: Sequence number protection
SONET: Synchronous Optical Network
SP: Signaling point
SPF: Shortest path first
SS7: Signaling System Number 7
SSAP: Source service access point
SSCF: Service-specific coordination function
SSCOP: Service-specific connection-oriented protocol
SSCOP-UU: SSCOP user-to-user
SSCS LM: Service specific convergence sublayer layer management

SSCS: Service specific convergence sublayer
SSM: Single segment message
SSN: Subsystem number
SSP: Service switching point
STAT: Solicited status response
STP: Signaling transfer point
SUS: Suspend message
SVC: Switched virtual call or channel
TA: Terminal adapter
TCAP: Transaction capabilities application part
TC: Transmission convergence sublayer
TC: Trunk code
TCP/IP: Transmission central protocol/Internet protocol
TDM: Time division multiplexing
TUP: Telephone user part
UD: Unnumbered data
UI: Unrecognized information
ULP: Upper layer protocol
UNI: User-network interface
USTAT: Unsolicited status
VBR: Variable bit rate
VC: Virtual channel
VCC: Virtual channel connection
VCI: Virtual channel identifier
VCI: Virtual circuit identifier
VPC: Virtual path connection
VPCI: Virtual path connection identifier
VPI: Virtual path identifier
VPN: Virtual private network

Other References

In addition to the formal standards for the systems described in this book, these references should prove useful to the reader. Many of them were used for the development of this material.

[AHMA93] Amhad, R., and Halsall, F. (1993). Interconnecting high-speed LANs and backbones, *IEEE Network*, September.

[AMOS79] Amos, J.E., Jr. (1979). Circuit switching: Unique architecture and applications. *IEEE Computer*, June.

[ARMT93] Armitage, G.J., and Adams, K.M.(1993). Packet reassembly during cell loss, *IEEE Network*, September.

[ATM92a] ATM Forum. (June 1, 1992). *ATM user-network interface specification, Version 2.0.*

[ATM93a] ATM Forum. (August 5, 1993). *ATM user-network interface specification, Version 3.0.*

[ATM94a] ATM Forum. (March, 1994). *Education and training work group*, ATM Forum Ambassador's Program.

[ATM94b] ATM Forum. (July 21, 1994). *ATM user-network interface specification, Version 3.1.*

[ATT89a] (January, 1989). Observations of error characteristics of fiber optic transmission systems, CCITT SGXVIII, San Diego, CA.

[BELL82] Bellamy, J. (1982). *Digital Telephony*, New York, NY: John Wiley and Sons.

[BELL90a] (May, 1993). Generic requirements for frame relay PVC exchange service, TR-TSV-001369, Issue 1.

[BELL89a]. (September, 1989). Synchronous optical network (SONET) transport systems: common generic criteria, TR-TSY-000253, Issue 1.

[BELL94] Bellman, R.B. (1994). Evolving traditional LANs to ATM, *Business Communications Review*, October.

[BLAC89] Black, U. (1989). *Data Networks, Concepts, Theory and Practice*, Prentice Hall.

[BLAC91] Black, U. (1991). *X.25 and related protocols*, IEEE Computer Society Press.

[BLAC93] Black, U. (1993). *Data link protocols*, Prentice Hall.

[BLAI88] Blair, C. (1988). SLIPs: Definitions, causes, and effects in T1 networks, *A Tautron Application Note, Issue 1*, September. (Note: my thanks to this author for a lucid explanation of slips.)

[BNR92a] Bell Northern Research. (1992). Global systems for mobile communications, *Telesis*, 92.

[BNR94a] Discussions held with Bell Northern Research (BNR) designers during 1993 and 1994.

[BROW94] Brown, P.D. (ed.). (1994). The price is right for ATM to become a serious competitor, *Broadband Networking News*, May.

[CCIT90a] (1990). Voice packetization-packetized voice protocols, CCITT Recommendation G.764, Geneva.

[CDPD93] (July 19, 1993). Cellular digital packet data system specification, *Release 1.0*.

[CHER92] Cherukuri, R. (August 26, 1992). Voice over frame relay networks, A technical paper issued as Frame Relay Forum, FRF 92.33.

[CHEU92] Cheung, N.K. (1992). The infrastructure of gigabit computer networks, *IEEE Communications Magazine*, April,.

[COMM94a] Korostoff, K. (April 18, 1994). Wide-area ATM undergoes trial by MAGIC, *Communications Week*.

[DAVI91] Davidson, R.P., and Muller, N.J. (1991). *The Guide to SONET*, Telecom Library, Inc.

[DELL92] Dell Computer, Intel, and University of Pennsylvania, A study compiled by Marty Baumann, *USA Today*, date not available.

[dePr91] dePrycker, M. (1991). *Asynchronous Transfer Mode*. Ellis Harwood Ltd.

[dePR92] de Prycker, M. (1992) ATM in Belgian Trial. *Communications International*, June.

[DUBO94] DuBois, D. Simnet Inc., Palo Alto, CA. A recommendation from a reviewer of *Emerging Communications Technologies*. (Thank you Mr. DuBois.)

[ECKB92] Eckberg, A.E. (1992). B-ISDN/ATM traffic and congestion control, *IEEE Network*, September.

[EMLI 63] Emling, J.W., and Mitchell, D. (1963). The effects of time delay and echoes on telephone conversations. *Bell Systems Technical Journal*, November.

[FORD93] Ford, P.S., Rekhter, Y., and Braun, H.-W. (1993). Improving the routing and addressing of IP. *IEEE Network*, May.

[FORU92] Frame Relay Forum Technical Committee. (May 7, 1992). "Frame relay network-to-network interface, phase 1 implementation agreement, Document Number FRF 92.08R1–Draft 1.4.

[GASM93] Gasman, L. (1993). ATM CPE—Who is providing what?, *Business Communications Review*, October.

[GOKE73] Goke, L.R., and Lipovski, G.J. (1973). Banyan networks for partitioning multiprocessor systems. First Annual Symposium on Computer Architecture.

[GRIL93] Grillo, D., MacNamee, R.J.G., and Rashidzadeh, B. (1993). Towards third generation mobile systems: A European possible transition path. *Computer Networks and ISDN Systems*, 25(8).

[GRON92] Gronert, E. (1992). MANS make their mark in Germany. *Data Communications International*, May.

[HAFN94] Hafner, K. (1994). Making sense of the internet. *Newsweek*, October 24.

[HALL92] Hall, M. (ed.). (1992). LAN-based ATM products ready to roll out. *LAN Technology*, September.

[HAND91] Handel, R., and Huber, M.N. (1991). *Integrated broadband networks: An introduction to ATM-based networks*. Addison-Wesley.

[HERM93] Herman, J., and Serjak C. (1993). ATM switches and hubs lead the way to a new era of switched internetworks. *Data Communications*, March.

[HEWL91] Hewlett Packard, Inc. (1991). Introduction to SONET, A tutorial.

[HEWL92] Hewlett Packard, Inc. (1992). Introduction to SONET networks and tests, An internal document.

[HEYW93] Heywood, P. (1993). PTTs gear up to offer high-speed services. *Data Communications*, August.

[HILL91] SONET, An overview. A paper prepared by Hill Associates, Inc., Winooski, VT, 05404.

[HUNT92] Hunter, P. (1992). What price progress?, *Communications International*, June.

[ITU93a] ITU-TS (1993). ITU-TS draft recommendation Q93.B "B-ISDN user-network interface layer 3 specification for basic call/bearer control. May.

[JAYA81] Jayant, N.S., and Christensen, S.W. (1981). Effects of packet losses on waveform-coded speech and improvements due to an odd-even interpolation procedure. *IEEE Transactions of Communications*, February.

[JOHN91] Johnson, J.T. (1991). Frame relay mux meets cell relay switch. *Data Communications*, October.

[JOHN92] Johnson, J.T. (1992). "Getting access to ATM. *Data Communications LAN Interconnect*, September 21.

[KING94] King, S.S. (1994). Switched virtual networks. *Data Communications*, September.

[KITA91] Kitawaki, N., and Itoh, K. (1991). Pure delay effects of speech quality in telecommunications. *IEEE Journal of Selected Areas in Communications*, May.

[LEE89] Lee, W.C.Y. (1989). *Mobile cellular telecommunications systems*. McGraw-Hill.

[LEE93] Lee, B.G., Kang, M., and Lee, J. (1993). *Broadband telecommunications technology*. Artech House.

[LISO91] Lisowski, B. (1991). Frame relay: what it is and how it works. *A Guide to Frame Relay, Supplement to Business Conmunications Review*, October.

[LIZZ94] Lizzio, J.R. (1994). Real-time RAID stokrage: the enabling technology for video-on-demand. *Telephony*, May 23.

[LYLE92] Lyles, J.B., and Swinehart, D.C. (1992). The emerging gigabit environment and the role of the local ATM. *IEEE Communications Magazine*, April.

[McCO94] McCoy, E. (1994). SONET, ATM and other broadband technologies. TRA Document # ATL72 16.9100, *Telecommunications Research Associates*, St. Marys, KS.

[MCQU91] McQuillan, J.M. (1991). Cell relay switching. *Data Communications*, September.

[MINO93] Minoli D. (1993). Proposed Cell Relay Bearer Service Stage 1 Description, T1S1.1/93-136 (Revision 1), ANSI Committee T1 (T1S1.1), June.

[MORE9] Moreney, J. (1994). ATM switch decision can wait, *Network World*, September 19.

[NOLL91] Nolle, T. (1991). Frame relay: Standards advance, *Business Communications Review*, October.

[NORT94] Northern Telecom. (1994). Consultant Bulletin 63020.16/02-94, Issue 1, February.

[[NYQU24] Nyquist, H. (1924). Certain factors affecting telegraph speed. *Transactions A.I.E.E.*

[PERL85] Perlman, R. (1985). An algorithm for distributed computation of spanning tree in an extended LAN. *Computer Communications Review, 15*(4) September.

[ROSE92] Rosenberry, W., Kenney D., and Fisher, G. (1992). *Understanding DCE.* O'Reilly & Associates.

[SALA92] Salamone, S. (1992). Sizing up the most critical issues. *Network World.*

[SAND94] Sandberg, J. (1994). Networking. *Wall Street Journal*, November 14.

[SHAN48] Shannon, C. (1948). Mathematical theory of communication, *Bell System Technical Journal, 27*, July and October.

[SRIR90a] Sriram, K. (1990a). Dynamic bandwidth allocation and congestion control schemes for voice and data integration in wideband packet technology, *Proc. IEEE. Supercomm/ICC '90, 3*, April.

[SRIR90b] Sriram, K. (1990b). Bandwidth allocation and congestion control scheme for an integrated voice and data network. *US Patent No. 4, 914650*, April 3.

[SRIR93a] Sriram, K. (1993). Methodologies for bandwidth allocation, transmission scheduling, and congestion avoidance in broadband ATM networks. *Computer Networks and ISDN Systems, 26*(1), September.

[SRIR93b] Sriram, K., and Lucantoni, D.M. (1993). Traffic smoothing effects of bit dropping in a packet voice multiplexer. *IEEE Transactions on Communications*, July.

[STEW92] Steward, S.P. (1992). The world report '92. *Cellular Business*, May.

[WADA89] Wada, M. (1989). Selective recovery of video packet loss using error concelment. *IEEE Journal of Selected Areas in Communications*, June.

[WALL91] Wallace, B. (1991). Citicorp goes SONET. *Network World*, November 18.

[WERK92] Wernik, M., Aboul-Magd, O., and Gilber, H. (1992). Traffic management for B-ISDN services. *IEEE Network*, September.

[WEST92] Westgate, J. (1992).*OSI Management*, NCC Blackwell.

[WILL92] Williamson, J. (1992). GSM bids for global recognition in a crowded cellular world. *Telephony*, April 6.

[WU93] Wu, T.-H. (1993). Cost-effective network evolution. *IEEE Communications Magazine*, September.

[YAP93] Yap, M.-T., and Hutchison (1993). An emulator for evaluating DQDB performance. *Computer Networks and ISDN Systems, 25*(11).

[YOKO93] Yokotani, T., Sato, H., and Nakatsuka, S. (1993). A study on a performance improvement algorithm in DQDB MAN. *Computer Networks and ISDN Systems, 25*(10).

Index